The Children of Aataentsic

VOLUME TWO

The Children of Aataentsic II

A History of the Huron People to 1660

BRUCE G. TRIGGER

MCGILL–QUEEN'S UNIVERSITY PRESS Montreal and London 1976

© McGill–Queen's University Press 1976
ISBN 0 7735 0239 4
Legal Deposit Second Quarter 1976
Bibliothèque nationale du Québec
Design by Richard Hendel
Printed in Canada by Richardson, Bond and Wright Ltd.

The preparation of the manuscript was aided by grants from
the Faculty of Graduate Studies and Research, McGill
University and the book has been published with the help
of a grant from the Social Science Research Council of
Canada using funds provided by the Canada Council.

Contents

Illustrations   vii

List of Maps   ix

CHAPTER 7   *The Interregnum and the*
            New Alliance   455

            New France in Eclipse   455
            The Huron and the English   459
            The Return of the Mohawk   463
            Quebec: A Jesuit Mission Colony   467
            Brûlé's Murder   473
            The New Alliance   476
            The Defeat of the Algonkin   485

CHAPTER 8   *The Deadly Harvest*   499

            The New Beginning   499
            The Black Years   526
            Interlude   559
            The New Order   572
            The Great Illness   588
            Conclusion   601

CHAPTER 9   *The Storm*   603

            The Huron and the French   603
            Trade and Warfare   617
            War on the St. Lawrence   634
            War in the Huron Country   658

CHAPTER 10   *The Storm Within*   665

The Jesuit Mission   665
Brébeuf and the Neutral   688
The Huron Church   699
Conclusion   724

CHAPTER 11   *The End of the Confederacy*   725

The Growing Power of the
Iroquois   725
The Defeat of the Traditionalists   744
The Destruction of the Huron
Confederacy   751
The Winter at Gahoendoe   767
The Move to Quebec   782

CHAPTER 12   *Betrayal and Salvation*   789

Temporary Havens   789
The Huron Refugees at Quebec   801
The Huron of the Upper Great
Lakes   820
The Huron among Their Enemies   826

CHAPTER 13   *Conclusions*   841

Notes Volume Two   851

References   857

Index   885

Illustrations

PLATE 32
Jones's reconstruction of the fortifications erected
under Jesuit guidance at Ossossané c. 1637.   514

PLATE 33
Corographie du Pays des Hurons.   579

PLATE 34
Chorographia Regionis Huronum, hodie desertae.   580

PLATE 35
Description du Pais des Hurons.   582

PLATE 36
Huronum Explicata Tabula.   583

PLATE 37
Part of the Novae Franciae Accurata Delineatio, *1657.*   584

PLATE 38
Le Canada, ou Nouvelle France, *published by*
N. Sanson d'Abbeville, 1656.   585

PLATE 39
François Du Creux's Tabula Novae Franciae, *1660.*   586

PLATE 40
Jury's plan of Sainte-Marie I.   670

PLATE 41
Kidd's plan of features revealed by the excavation of
the central part of Sainte-Marie I.   675

PLATE 42
Plan of a portion of Kidd's excavation, showing the
remains of wooden flooring.   676

PLATE 43
Plan of Kidd's excavations showing the arrangements
of post molds and soil markings.   678

PLATE 44
*View of the modern reconstruction of Sainte-Marie,
looking south.*   682

PLATE 45
*View of the modern reconstruction of Sainte-Marie
from the Wye River.*   683

PLATE 46
*Iron axes recovered in Jury's excavations at
Sainte-Marie I.*   686

PLATE 47
The martyrdom of Brébeuf and Lalemant from the
Novae Franciae Accurata Delineatio, *1657.*   765

PLATE 48
*Plan of the remains of Sainte-Marie II on
Christian Island.*   773

PLATE 49
Sketch of the ruins of Sainte-Marie II.   774

PLATE 50
Anonymous map of Lake Erie, c. 1680.   798

PLATE 51
Anonymous map of southeastern Ontario, c. 1680.   838

Maps

MAP 22. *Intertribal relations, 1634.* 487

MAP 23. *Dates at which certain Huron villages were first visited by the Jesuits after 1634.* 566

MAP 24. *Intertribal relations, 1641.* 636

MAP 25. *Intertribal relations, 1643.* 641

MAP 26. *Hypothetical placing of Mohawk settlements described by Van den Bogaert for 1634–35. The corresponding large settlements mentioned by Jogues for 1643 were Ossernenon, Gandagaron, and Tionontoguen. Megapolensis (1644) associated these settlements with the Tortoise, Bear, and Wolf clans respectively.* 646

MAP 27. *Intertribal relations following the peace of 1645.* 656

MAP 28. *Centres and boundaries (where known) of Jesuit missions to the Huron from 1639 to 1648.* 690

MAP 29. *Intertribal relations, 1648 to 1650.* 727

MAP 30. *Tionnontaté settlements, c. 1639 to 1650.* 741

MAP 31. *Reconstruction of the field pattern and natural setting of Teanaostaiaé c. 1648 (Lot 12, Conc. IV, Medonte Twp.; after C. E. Heidenreich).* 753

MAP 32. *Disintegration of the Huron confederacy, 1647 to 1650.* 768

MAP 33. *Intertribal relations, 1650 to 1657.* 793

MAP 34. *Intertribal relations, 1659 to 1663.* 796

MAP 35. *Locations and dates for Huron settlements in the vicinity of Quebec City.* 819

MAP 36. *Dispersal of Huron refugees after 1649.*   822

MAP 37. *Settlements of the four western Iroquois tribes, showing
           the location of Gandougarae.*   829

Chapter 7 The Interregnum and the New Alliance

New France in Eclipse

Relations between the Huron and the French were disrupted by the brief war that began between France and England in 1627. In the course of the war, Quebec was captured by the English, thus upsetting the precarious balance of relations that had existed in eastern Canada since 1615. The years 1628 to 1634 were a period of great uncertainty for the Huron, not only in their trading relations with Europeans, but also because of the intrigues of the Algonkin, who were anxious to exploit a confused situation to regain their former role as middlemen.

The war also wrecked important plans for the development of New France that the French Jesuits had played a major role in helping to formulate. In 1626 the Duc de Ventadour's confessor, Philibert Noyrot, returned to France after a brief sojourn in Quebec, in order to seek official support to have the monopoly of the Compagnie de Caën revoked and for the development of New France as a Roman Catholic colony. The plans that the Jesuits proposed were similar to those being advocated by Joseph Le Caron, but they pursued their objectives with much greater vigour and perspicacity. Soon after he returned to France Noyrot had an audience with Cardinal Richelieu, who was seeking to strengthen French naval power and to encourage commercial adventures abroad. Later, through the intervention of the Duc de Ventadour, he persuaded Richelieu that Protestants should be forbidden to settle in New France. It is also believed to have been on Noyrot's advice that the Duc de Ventadour resigned his vice-regal office and the Marquise de Guercheville gave up her rights in Acadia (Monet 1966a). These initiatives significantly aided Richelieu's efforts to improve the management of New France by founding a merchant company on the model of ones already being operated by the English and the Dutch. Ventadour's resignation allowed the cardinal to assume direct control of New France and to dissolve the Compagnie de Caën. The latter was replaced by a new company, called the Compagnie des Cent-Associés and later the Compagnie de la Nouvelle France. This company was granted a fifteen-year monopoly over all trade with North America and a perpetual monopoly of the fur trade. In return it had to agree to establish 4,000 settlers in New France by 1643, to subsidize mission work, and to provide adequate defences for the colony. To prevent these obligations from being ignored by profit-hungry traders, Richelieu arranged for courtiers and officials to be enrolled as shareholders; it was stipulated that noblemen and churchmen could engage in this trade without incurring a loss of status. It was also decreed that Indians who were baptized should enjoy the same rights of citizenship as did settlers from France (Lanctot 1963:131).

To honour its obligations, in spring 1628 the company set about establishing an unprecedented 400 settlers in New France at a cost of 400,000 livres. Although the French and English were already at war, these vessels sailed unescorted from Dieppe under the command of Claude Roquemont de Brison. Roquemont's vessels were accompanied by a Jesuit supply ship that had been chartered by Father Noyrot and by a number of fishing boats that sought the protection of the larger vessels for the Atlantic crossing.

With the outbreak of war, Gervase Kirke, an English merchant who had lived in France and who may have had business connections with Guillaume de Caën (Morton 1963:33), formed a company that secured a commission from Charles I authorizing it to seize Canada from the French. In 1628 his sons sailed up the St. Lawrence with Jacques Michel, who had formerly worked for Champlain as pilot. The Kirkes seized Tadoussac, where they were welcomed by the Montagnais as independent traders. The Montagnais concealed the arrival of the English from the French at Quebec and informed the English that the latter were on the point of starvation (Biggar 1922–36, 5:275, 307). The English pillaged the farm at Cape Tourmente (5:274–75) and demanded the surrender of Quebec. Champlain, however, was still expecting the arrival of Emery de Caën's ships and therefore refused this demand. David Kirke decided against attacking the settlement, but on the way home he intercepted and captured the fleet belonging to the Compagnie des Cent-Associés, near Gaspé. The loss of these ships was a financial disaster for the company and meant that in 1628 no supplies or trade goods got through to the already hard-pressed trading post at Quebec.

One of the passengers aboard the captured French vessels was Amantacha, who was returning home after his two years in France. When the Kirkes were told that he was the son of a native "king," they thought he might be useful to them; thus, when they returned to England they kept him in their custody, although the other prisoners were allowed to return to France. Amantacha appears to have spent the winter of 1628–29 in London, where he was treated as a person of some importance and presented with several new suits of clothing. By that time, American Indians were no strangers in England. The first had arrived as early as 1502 and since then a number, including Pocahontas, had become celebrities. Amantacha was, however, the first person born in Ontario to set foot in the British Isles. The failure of the French to return him to his father for the second consecutive year must have greatly troubled the Huron and may explain why no Huron youth was ever again permitted to travel to France.

Champlain continued to weaken his desperate position by his foolish and high-handed treatment of the Montagnais, who were already angry about the high prices that the traders at Quebec charged for their goods. He refused to release an Indian whom he had imprisoned because he suspected him of the murder of two Frenchmen in 1627. The Montagnais regarded this as an unwarranted form of punishment and, as the prisoner's health deteriorated as a result of his confinement, they became increasingly angry. Had he died while being held captive by the French, the Montagnais would surely have sought blood revenge. When the autumn fishing was over, the Montagnais agreed among themselves that until the prisoner was released, they would sell the French only a small number of eels at the exorbitant price of one beaver skin for every ten eels (5:298). In this way, the Montagnais forced the French to part with 120 skins, which the Indians no doubt intended to trade with the English the following summer. When Champlain still refused to release the prisoner, another council was held and it was decided to sell no food to the French until he was freed. Only the alcoholic and obsequious Chomina and his family broke this agreement.

When the spring came and once again no ships arrived from France, the inhabitants of Quebec were forced to go into the forests to dig for edible roots. To ensure the safety of his men, Champlain decided that he had best release the prisoner, who was now so ill he could not walk. Even so, he demanded that in return the Montagnais headmen should agree to supply him with food and to obey his orders. In spite of their apparent acceptance of these demands, Champlain rightly concluded that they had no intention of fulfilling the promise he had extracted from them. Champlain made matters worse by also demanding in return for the prisoner's freedom that a council of headmen be formed, which would henceforth regulate relations between the French and their Algonkian-speaking allies. The despised Chomina was to be recognized as the head of this council, while influential headmen, such as Erouachy from Tadoussac, Batiscan from Three Rivers, and Tessouat from the Ottawa Valley, were to be only subordinate members (6:7–22). Chomina and his equally alcoholic brother, Negabamat, were the only Indians who had rushed to Quebec to help defend the settlement the previous year and Champlain's aim in so conspicuously rewarding this loyalty was to encourage other Indians to emulate it.

All Champlain accomplished was to insult respected headmen who, while maintaining friendly relations with the French, put their own people's interests first. Matters were made worse by Champlain's refusal to return to their families two Montagnais girls whom he had obtained under duress early in 1628, and whom he was planning to take to France and enrol in a convent school. These personal abuses, combined with longstanding Montagnais resentment over the trading monopoly, led most of the Indians to wish for the expulsion of the French from Quebec. It was therefore not surprising that as the summer of 1629 began to pass and no French ships appeared, only Chomina and his relatives remained at Quebec. The rest of the Montagnais were at Tadoussac awaiting the return of the English.

Since the French had no trade goods and were expecting the return of the English, they did not go up the St. Lawrence to meet their Indian trading partners in 1629. Some Montagnais made the journey in the hope of obtaining some much-needed corn from the Huron. Having become dependent on agricultural produce, they were almost as near to starvation as the French traders were as a result of no ships having come from France. On 17 July some Huron arrived at Quebec, accompanied by all the French who had been living in the Huron country. Champlain reports there were twelve canoes (6:45); Sagard says there were twenty (Sagard 1866:847). Both figures seem low, since a minimum of twenty-one French had wintered among the Huron in 1628–29, and it is unlikely that more than one Frenchman would have travelled in each canoe. It is possible, however, that some Huron had been content to trade with the Montagnais and Algonkin on the upper St. Lawrence and a number of French had travelled the rest of the way to Quebec with the Montagnais. In any case, because they feared there might be no trade goods, fewer Huron seem to have come to the St. Lawrence than in normal years.

The amount of corn that the residents of Quebec were able to acquire was disappointingly small. Most of the French who returned from the Huron country preferred to transport furs for their own profit rather than corn to succour their hungry comrades. Some had 700 to 800 livres worth of furs with them, which, depending on whether the value cited was that of the furs in France or Quebec, could mean from seventy skins to many times that number (902). Brébeuf brought four or five sacks of corn meal, weighing fifty pounds each, for the use of the Jesuits (Biggar 1922–36, 6:47), and the Recollets managed to purchase two more sacks from the Huron (Sagard 1866:895). Olivier, an assistant agent at the trading post, secured another sack on behalf of Gravé Du Pont (Biggar 1922–36, 6:47; Sagard 1866:895). Champlain had hoped to obtain some corn for himself by giving Chomina knives to barter at Three Rivers, but Chomina brought nothing back (Biggar 1922–36, 6:42); whatever extra corn the Huron brought with them was sold to the Montagnais and Algonkin. Champlain complained bitterly about the unwillingness of the French who were living at Quebec to share what they had with one another and, in particular, about their lack of concern for him, although he was their commander (6:48). These complaints indicate not only Champlain's weakness, but the disarray resulting from the competing factions that had developed at Quebec during the previous two decades.

Two days after the Huron arrived at Quebec, the settlement surrendered to the English on the best terms that Champlain was able to negotiate. The relief ships he had counted on to save the colony were blown off course and when Emery de Caën finally arrived, he was defeated by the Kirkes. The latter refused to accept de Caën's word that the war had ended in April, since to have done so would have been to admit the illegality of their retaining possession of Quebec. Some of the priests thought of going to live with the Algonkin in order to pursue their mission work and to maintain French influence among them until Quebec was restored to the French (Sagard 1866:844). It was finally agreed, however, that they, along with Champlain and most of the French who lived at Quebec, should be repatriated. While the Recollets were treated with some courtesy by the English, the Jesuits were handled more roughly. David Kirke accused the Jesuits of seeking to control the fur trade that had formerly belonged to Guillaume de Caën and Jacques Michel said they were more interested in beavers than in saving souls (Biggar 1922–36, 6:137).

The Huron and the English

While most of the French returned home, some decided to remain and work for the English. A few men had entered the service of the Kirkes even before they set sail for Quebec. One of these was Jacques Michel, the French shipmaster who piloted the English fleet up the St. Lawrence in 1628 and 1629 (Biggar 1922–36, 6:81). Another was Le Baillif from Amiens who had formerly worked as a trading agent for de Caën (5:88). Many of the interpreters also entered the service of the English. These included Brûlé, the Huron interpreter, Marsolet, the Montagnais one, and an Algonkin interpreter nicknamed Gros-Jean, who was probably Jean Richer.[1] These men had been intermediaries for their respective tribes for so long that the company or nationality employing them was probably of little importance. Whatever they thought of the English, they must have welcomed the chance to throw off the yoke that the Jesuits had fastened onto them. It was probably, in part, on the basis of their complaints that the English accused the Jesuits of having meddled in the fur trade. Either by accident or by design, Jean Nicollet, the Nipissing interpreter, continued to live with his people, probably spending the winters with them in the Huron country. He seems to have made no public profession of loyalty to the English and later it was claimed that he had tried to discourage the Nipissing from trading with the English (Hamelin 1966*b*:517); however, Nicollet became a friend of the Jesuits who may be representing his behaviour at this time in as favourable a light as possible. Thomas Godefroy was another interpreter who lived among the Indians between 1629 and 1632 (Vachon 1966). The Couillard family, who inhabited the Hébert farm, also chose to remain at Quebec. The English let them trade their surplus produce for furs and agreed to pay them four livres for every beaver skin. Under French rule, trade of this sort had been forbidden to settlers (Biggar 1922–36, 6:70–71).

The man most pleased by the arrival of the English must have been Soranhes. He had travelled to Quebec for a third summer only to find that the French had not brought back his son. When the English arrived, Amantacha appeared dressed in an expensive suit of English clothes. Sagard recounted with some glee that when Thomas Kirke learned that Amantacha's father was not a king, but a "hungry, naked Indian," he wanted to take back all the clothing that the English had given Amantacha. He was persuaded, however, perhaps by Brûlé, that it was unwise to anger the Huron by doing this. Amantacha was, therefore, allowed to keep the clothes he was wearing and was told that if he led many Huron to trade the following year, he would be allowed to take away all the clothes that the English had given him (Sagard 1866:835–37). Amantacha returned to the Huron country with Brûlé and his father, and there had a chance to describe in detail what he had seen in France and England (Biggar 1922–36, 6:101–102).

Because of his natural abilities, and also because he was old enough to have mastered the basic skills needed to operate in his own culture, Amantacha was not fatally damaged by his stay in France, as the young Montagnais child Pastedechouan had been. The Recollets had taken Pastedechouan to France in 1620 and had kept him there for six years, teaching him to read and write both French and Latin. Pastedechouan never had an opportunity to learn how to hunt or get along in the forest; hence when he returned to Canada he found himself reduced to a parasitic existence, which led him to be dependent on, and ultimately to loathe, both his own people and the French. As a result of his inability to adapt to either culture, he became increasingly addicted to alcohol and in 1636 he starved to death in the forest (Grassmann 1966*a*).

By contrast, Amantacha seems to have resumed life among his people where he had left off, and soon was an active hunter and young warrior. Because of his long sojourn in Europe and his ability to speak and write French, he was able to inform his people about his experiences with greater accuracy and understanding than Savignon had done. He was also a successful intermediary between the Huron and the Europeans. In 1629, the French observed that he had already accommodated himself to the "freer ways" of the English (Biggar 1922–36, 6:101), and later Jesuit accounts written in the Huron country were to note that there he was living after the fashion of his own people and "not as he ought to be" (Thwaites 1896–1901, 8:149). In spite of this, when he visited the Jesuits at Quebec, he always managed to convince them of the sincerity of his Roman Catholicism. While his efforts to insinuate himself with both the French and the English might suggest that he, like many of the interpreters, had developed the psychological characteristics of a "marginal man" who is deeply committed to neither of the cultures with which he has dealings, Amantacha's behaviour amongst his own people makes it clear that he was first and foremost a Huron.

Although Quebec had been seized in peacetime, Charles I was reluctant to restore it to France until the French court agreed to pay the remaining portion of his wife's dowry. Negotiations over the dowry and the ownership of the furs that the Kirkes had seized at Quebec proceeded slowly. Meanwhile, the Company of Adventurers continued to use Quebec as a trading post until the treaty of Saint-Germain-en-Laye was signed in 1632. During these three years Thomas Kirke was in charge at Quebec, with ninety men under his command during the winter months (Biggar 1922–36, 6:183). These were more men than had ever been there during the French period. Altogether, over 200 men were maintained in Canada by the Company of Adventurers (Moir 1966:405). Although the land that had been cleared by the Recollets and Jesuits was cultivated by company employees, because of the uncertain future, the Kirkes did not proceed with their plans to expand the fur trade and to exploit more of the colony's natural resources (Biggar 1922–36, 6:103–04). A major accomplishment of this period was that large ships were taken up-river to Quebec for the first time in the seventeenth century (6:182). Hitherto, the channel above Tadoussac had been judged too dangerous for regular navigation. This development would ultimately terminate Tadoussac's importance as the head of trans-Atlantic navigation.

The trade carried on at Quebec in 1630 appears to have been a record up to that time; perhaps 30,000 skins were purchased from the Indians (6:183).[2] Many Huron must have come down-river that year, bringing with them the furs they had collected but had been unable to barter with the French over the two previous years. The Huron must have been running short of European goods and were therefore anxious to benefit from the arrival of the English in order to replenish their supplies. Their confidence in the English was strengthened by the return of Amantacha and the favourable reports that he and Brûlé provided.

In spite of this, it seems that the Huron encountered problems in their dealings with the English. These problems may have resulted from the sale of alcohol by the English (Thwaites 1896–1901, 5:49). Wine and liquors had been made freely available to the Indians by the independent traders who had long been operating along the lower St. Lawrence (6:251); hence they were well known to the Montagnais. The latter viewed these beverages as magical substances that enabled a person to become possessed by powerful supernatural forces. Champlain, however, had vigorously opposed the sale of alcohol to the Indians in areas under his control (6:253); thus the Huron may have been unfamiliar with and terrified by the riotous conduct that resulted from excessive drinking. Such an experience could have persuaded many Huron not to return to Quebec the following year and made the rest more susceptible to the rumour-mongering of the Algonkin, who were always looking for ways to discourage Huron journeys to the St. Lawrence in order to regain their former role as middlemen.

Whatever the reason, trade plummeted in 1631. Guillaume de Caën secured a license to operate in New France that year and the English agreed to share the trade with him. When, however, the English saw how few Indians were coming to Quebec, they forbade his cousin, Emery de Caën, to have any dealings with the Indians. De Caën was only permitted to unload his goods and leave a clerk at Quebec with permission to barter with the Montagnais over the winter (Biggar 1922–36, 6:214–16). That the Huron did not have an exceptionally large number of furs to trade in 1632 suggests that they may have traded some of their 1631 supply to the Algonkin in return for European goods.

The Return of the Mohawk

As the position of the French at Quebec grew more untenable, the established pattern of relationships on which trade in eastern Canada had depended for over a decade began to be disrupted by a resurgence of Iroquois militancy in the St. Lawrence Valley. To understand what was happening, it is necessary to examine briefly what occurred among the Mohawk after they made peace with the French and the Algonkin in 1624 and had begun to wage war on the Mahican. The ensuing conflict was not an easy one and for a time it appears to have gone against the Mohawk, whose easternmost settlement was destroyed about 1626 (Jameson 1909: 157). The Dutch traders at Fort Orange knew that the Mohawk wished to gain control of the territory around their settlement to prevent the Dutch from developing trading relations with the Algonkin and Montagnais. It is therefore not surprising that as the war began to turn against the Mahican, these traders abandoned their official policy of neutrality and commissioned the commandant at Fort Orange, Daniel Van Krieckenbeeck, and a small party of musketeers to help these Indians. This expedition was soundly defeated and some of its members were consigned to the flames by the victorious Mohawk. When the Dutch traders realized the danger in which they had placed themselves, they hastened to dispatch an itinerant trader, Pieter Barentsen, to visit the Mohawk and re-establish good relations with them (ibid. 84–85).

This defeat did not, however, prevent Isaack de Rasiere, the provincial secretary of New Netherland, from revealing his own wishes and those of the traders at Fort Orange when he wrote later in 1626 that if the Mohawk were unwilling to grant the northern Algonkians a perpetual right-of way to visit the Hudson Valley, the Dutch should go to war to compel them to do so (Van Laer 1924:212–15). American historians have erroneously assumed that because the Amsterdam directors opposed this policy, de Rasiere's proposal was only an idle threat. It is clear from Champlain's writings that this was not so. By the following year, the Dutch had distributed presents among the northern Algonkians who visited Fort Orange to persuade them to break their truce with the Mohawk (Biggar 1922–36, 5:214–15). The men who did this were probably associates of the late Van Krieckenbeeck, the man whom Kiliaen Van Rensselaer, a settler and therefore no friend of the company traders at Fort Orange, was later to accuse of having led the Mahican into the war in the first place (Van Laer 1908:306). Van Krieckenbeeck did not arrive at Fort Orange, however, until after the war had begun; hence, in making this accusation, Van Rensselaer must have been thinking of Van Krieckenbeeck's efforts to expand trade northwards. These efforts were part of a general policy that had angered the Mohawk.

The Algonkian-speaking headmen who accepted presents at Fort Orange returned to the St. Lawrence Valley and began to urge their followers to join the Dutch and Mahican in an attack on the Mohawk villages (Biggar 1922–36, 5:215). When Champlain learned about this, he was very angry and threatened to aid the Iroquois if war broke out (5:217). Many of the Algonkian headmen were also opposed to a renewal of warfare at this time, and they and the French were well on their way to preserving the peace, when a party of young warriors treacherously captured two Mohawk who had gone fishing and began to torture them. Even then, Champlain persuaded the Algonkians to release these prisoners and to try to renew their treaty with the Mohawk. A party that included a Frenchman, Pierre Magnan, and the Montagnais headman, Cherououny, set out to escort the prisoners home. These men were slain when they reached the first Mohawk village, allegedly because a Kichesipirini, who disliked Cherououny, had informed the Mohawk that his main reason for coming was to spy on them (5:308–12).[3] There was, however, a more important reason for these killings: Mohawk anger and resentment had been fanned by news of the negotiations going on between the northern Algonkians and the Dutch. It is quite likely that either the Dutch or the Mahican informed the Mohawk about these negotiations, hoping thereby that the peace between the Mohawk and the northern Algonkians would collapse.

Early in 1628, the Mahican suffered a decisive defeat. Those living near Fort Orange who were not taken prisoner were forced to abandon their band territories and flee eastward to the Connecticut Valley, where they settled down and began to cultivate the land (Jameson 1909:89, 131). While the Mahican sold the legal title to their abandoned land to Van Rensselaer in 1630 and 1631 (Van Laer 1908:166–69, 181–83, 306), the victory of 1628 gave the Mohawk control to the very doorstep of the Dutch trading post. This made it possible for them to enforce their policy of not permitting the Algonkians, or any other northern people, to trade with the Dutch. If more furs were to be obtained from the north in the near future, it would have to be with the Mohawk as intermediaries. While Dutch traders and officials were anxious to circumvent this boycott, their military weakness, combined with rising trade figures, reconciled them to the new political situation, at least until more settlers should arrive and the Dutch were strong enough to control the Mohawk (ibid. 248). The French traders benefited from the Mohawk victory, because it temporarily eliminated the possibility of northern Algonkians being able to play French and Dutch traders off against one another to lower the value of European trade goods. This more than offset their loss of trade with the Iroquois and the disruption of hunting patterns that renewed warfare brought about among the Algonkian bands with whom the French traded.

Those who emerged most disadvantaged by these events were the northern Algonkians. They were again at war with the Mohawk, who no longer had the Mahican to deal with and whose supplies of European goods were more secure than ever. There is, however, no evidence that the Mohawk sought to press their advantage immediately after their defeat of the Mahican. Both the Algonkin and the Mohawk sent raiding parties against each other, but some of the prisoners taken on both sides were released to explore the possibility of a renewed peace (Biggar 1922–36, 6:3). The Montagnais similarly expressed an interest in ending hostilities. The northern Algonkians wanted peace because they dreaded the Iroquois and were afraid that the French would no longer be able to protect them. The Mohawk wanted to maintain good relations with the French so that they could continue driving down the price of European goods by playing French and Dutch traders off against one another. The main problems were that the French could not agree to a treaty from which their Indian allies were excluded, while neither they nor the Mohawk could afford a peace that would allow these same allies to trade with the Dutch. To get around the first of these difficulties, the Mohawk were evidently seeking peace with the northern Algonkians in order to trade with the French. In so doing, however, they left unresolved the long-term problem of how to prevent these Algonkians from trading with the Dutch once a general peace had been arranged. The French traders, no less than the Mohawk, seem to have clung to the hope of profiting from a series of short-term solutions to this problem.

Champlain, however, had made up his mind that no further accommodation with the Iroquois was possible. Even if they showed signs of wishing to be friendly, to him they were allies of a colonial power that threatened the existence of New France, as well as an impediment to exploration and the development of trade routes in the upper part of the St. Lawrence Valley. After 1627 Champlain consistently advocated that the Iroquois should either be exterminated or have French laws and customs imposed on them. In the winter of 1628–29 he fancied that if no help arrived from France the following spring, he and his men might seize an Iroquois village and live there on the corn they had captured until they were relieved

(5:304–05). Likewise, when he returned to Quebec in 1633, he had plans to form an army of 120 French soldiers and several thousand Indians, equip it with explosives, and use this army to conquer the Iroquois (Bishop 1948:330–31). The ineffectiveness of such expeditions, even when New France was far more populous than it was in 1633, shows that although Champlain's analysis of the basic problem may have been accurate, his proposed solution was unrealistic.

During 1628 and 1629 mutual hopes for peace helped to keep warfare between the Mohawk and Algonkians at a low key. The collapse of French power on the St. Lawrence meant, however, the disappearance of the major factor that for many years had maintained a balance of power in the region. Blood feuds slowly began to spiral into a major war, once the Iroquois realized that they could again attack the upper St. Lawrence Valley with impunity. Sometime after the summer of 1629, Iroquois raids led to the abandonment of a settlement that the Montagnais and Algonkin had built at Three Rivers prior to 1623 (Sagard 1866:846; Thwaites 1896–1901, 6:151). Le Jeune reports that this village, which he saw after it had been "burned by the Iroquois," had been surrounded by a strong palisade and by several acres of corn fields (Thwaites 1896–1901, 8:27–29).

Not all of the victories were on one side. In October 1632 a number of Algonkians were defeated in battle by the Iroquois (5:93); on the other hand, not long before, the Montagnais had returned from a foray with nine male Iroquois captives, six of whom were claimed by the Montagnais from Quebec and three by the Montagnais from Tadoussac (5:27–29; 45–49). While the Montagnais spoke of using these prisoners to negotiate for peace, all but one of them were killed during a bout of general drunkenness. The remaining youth was spared only after Emery de Caën had offered the Montagnais valuable presents not to kill him. He remained a prisoner among the Montagnais and apparently died a few years later (7:171). In spite of such successes, the Montagnais were so terrified of the Iroquois that once again they feared to disperse for their winter hunts and ran to the Europeans for protection whenever they thought that the Iroquois were near Quebec (5:107). Thus, by the early 1630s the political situation in the St. Lawrence Valley resembled that of 1608, when Champlain arrived at Quebec.

One of the reasons for the return of political chaos to the St. Lawrence Valley was the refusal of the English to police the river, or to provide military aid to their Algonkian-speaking trading partners. When the Indian headmen pressed them for support, they were told that it was necessary to keep all of the English at Quebec to guard it against recapture by the French (5:195). The English were willing to sell muskets to the Indians, and a few Montagnais learned to use these weapons proficiently (6:309). Yet, these few guns did not provide the crucial psychological advantage over the Iroquois that an English presence on the upper St. Lawrence would have done. Because of this, it is likely that all the tribes who formerly had alliances with the French came to mistrust what seemed like cowardice and neutrality on the part of the English. War and mistrust as well as Huron grievances account for the falling-off of trade at Quebec in 1631.

Quebec: A Jesuit Mission Colony

When Quebec was restored to France in 1632, Guillaume de Caën was granted permission to trade there for one more year to compensate him for the termination of his monopoly by the charter given to the Compagnie des Cent-Associés. Emery de Caën was named commandant for the year, with Charles Du Plessis-Bochart, the head clerk of the Compagnie des Cent-Associés, as his lieutenant. At the same time, the Jesuits pressed for exclusive missionary rights in Canada so that they might work without interference from other orders. Richelieu's adviser, the Capuchin Father Joseph, disliked the Recollets and persuaded the Cardinal to assign the mission field to his own order. The Jesuits mounted an intensive, though discreet, opposition to this appointment and their supporter, Jean de Lauson, director of the Cent-Associés, finally persuaded the Capuchins to work in Acadia and to help him convince Richelieu to grant the rest of New France to the Jesuits. In 1632 Richelieu issued letters patent ordering the Jesuits to resume their duties at Quebec. For the next three years, Lauson countered, by fair and foul means, all of the Recollets' efforts to return to Quebec (Lanctot 1963:148–49). The Recollets were angered by this and accused the Jesuits of having intrigued to get rid of them. Thus began a series of polemics and a struggle for the religious control of New France that was to outlast the century.

Whatever intrigues were involved in gaining control of the Canadian mission, the Jesuits' success in defending this monopoly for several decades must be attributed to the nature of their mission program, as it then began to unfold. Although they returned to Quebec with far greater powers than any missionaries had possessed previously, the Jesuits were anxious to avoid the antagonisms that had formerly pitted Recollets and traders against one another. The Jesuits clearly recognized that trading alliances with the Indians made their mission work possible, and that much of the money for the support and expansion of missions was derived from the profits of this trade (Du Creux 1951–52:92). Thus, while the Jesuits strove to control the manner in which the fur trade was conducted, they agreed that the prosperity of New France and of their missions depended on the successful operation of this trade. They were therefore prepared to consider the needs of the company and to fashion policies that were in harmony with these needs, in a way that the more narrow-sighted Recollets had never been willing to do.[4]

Jesuit policy was diametrically opposed to that of the Recollets in a number of ways. Whereas the Recollets believed it necessary to settle a large number of French families among the Huron in order to convert them, the Jesuits preferred to isolate them as much as possible from Europeans. Far from believing, as the Recollets did, that these settlers would provide a model of Christian life that the Huron might emulate, the Jesuits feared that they would acquaint the Huron with the vices of France which were no less repellent to these missionaries than was a non-Christian religion. As an extension of the policy, the Jesuits rejected the Recollets' idea that to be Christian the Indians had to become French in language and culture. On the contrary, the Jesuits had to master the language and beliefs of the Huron so that they could use this knowledge to persuade the Huron to become Christians. The Jesuits' aim was to eliminate, or replace, only those customs that did not accord with Christian teachings and morality. At first, they did not anticipate any need for a major refashioning of Huron life.

The Jesuits applied the same policy of keeping the Indians separate from the French and teaching them in their own language to the Montagnais, abandoning it only very unwillingly and temporarily when forced to do so by the French government in the 1660s (Lanctot 1964:63). A similar policy was applied successfully by Spanish-speaking Jesuits among the Guarani Indians of South America (Métraux 1948; Mörner 1953) and the reports of this work were well known to the Jesuits when they renewed their Canadian mission (Thwaites 1896–1901, 5:33). This approach was therefore not adopted as a matter of convenience, but reflected the attitude of the order to the whole question of conversion.

Another aim of the Canadian Jesuits that differed from those of the Recollets was to convert whole communities as quickly as possible. If the Huron were to become practising Christians, a framework of social sanctions was required that only a Christian community could provide. Whereas the Recollets tried to persuade Huron converts to move to Quebec, the Jesuits hoped to use these converts to start a chain reaction that would lead to a whole village becoming Christian. That community would then become the framework within which they could expand and refine their converts' understanding of Christianity. Le Jeune, writing in 1633, was of the opinion that the conversion of the Indians would be a simple matter since being "removed from all luxury, they are not given to many sins" (5:35). Earlier, however, the more realistic Charles Lalemant had expressed the opinion that six to twelve years would be required before there were many converts (4:223).

All of the Jesuits who came to the Huron country had received an education that was rigorous and exacting by the standards of the age. Part of their training involved the inculcation of new standards of observation and experimentation. The result is evident in their reports, in which they were careful to distinguish between their conclusions and the evidence on which these were based, and to record and evaluate their sources of information (Tooker 1964:7). Their linguistic studies were methodologically far in advance of those of the Recollets (Hanzeli 1969), while their geographical training enabled them to produce the first tolerably accurate maps of the interior of eastern Canada and to use eclipses to investigate the longitude of French and Huron settlements (Crouse 1924).

The intellectual approach of these seventeenth-century Jesuits to the task of conversion and their careful reporting of strange customs strikes a sympathetic chord in modern scholars who, for this reason, are tempted to regard the Jesuits as entertaining more modern views than, in fact, they held. Sharing experiences that their missionaries had gained working in India, China, Japan, South America, and elsewhere had made the Jesuits keenly aware of the diversity of human behaviour and the degree to which customs and values varied from one culture to another. Le Jeune summarized this view in 1633: "Oh, how weak are the judgments of men! Some see beauty where others see nothing but ugliness. In France, the most beautiful teeth are the whitest; in the Maldive Islands white teeth are considered a deformity, so they paint them red to be beautiful, and in Cochin China, if I remember correctly, they paint them black. Who is right?" (Thwaites 1896–1901, 5:107).

This statement, and others like it, have led certain scholars to conclude that by the seventeenth century the Jesuits had adopted a concept of cultural relativism similar to that held by most anthropologists (Kennedy 1950; Duignan 1958). This would mean that the Jesuits had abandoned any universal criteria for judging human behaviour and were attempting to evaluate all beliefs and practices in terms of the meaning assigned to them within each particular culture. The belief that the Jesuits in this or any other way transcended their own time to anticipate modern secular concepts is totally unwarranted. While the Jesuits may have been able to treat cultural variations in what they regarded as relatively trivial or morally neutral matters with equanimity or even intellectual curiosity, they were wholly unprepared to extend the same toleration to the sphere of religious beliefs or morality. Like the vast majority of Europeans, they were convinced that their own beliefs about such matters were correct and that all other beliefs were wrong. It was therefore their ambition, whenever possible and by whatever means, to win converts to Roman Catholicism and to stamp out other religions.

We have already noted that in 1625 the Jesuits had taken action to curb what they regarded as the immoral behaviour of the French interpreters who were living among the Indians by gaining control over them. As the Jesuits developed their plans for renewing their mission work, they decided that their plan to convert the Huron would succeed only if there were no Europeans living among the Indians who by word or deed might work at cross purposes to them. This made it necessary to broaden their earlier campaign against the interpreters and seek to prevent all independent traders from living among the Indians. The Jesuits had sufficient influence to gain their way in this matter, and men such as Jean Nicollet, Thomas Godefroy, and Nicolas Marsolet were compelled to settle down in new jobs at Quebec or Three Rivers. No new interpreters were sent to replace these men among the Algonkin and Nipissing even though no Jesuits went to live with these groups. Presumably this was because the Jesuits feared that such interpreters might spend the winters in the Huron country. In return the Jesuits agreed to have a number of laymen attached to the Huron mission, who could discharge the most vital functions that the traders and interpreters had performed hitherto. These included encouraging the Indians to trade and travelling with them to and from the St. Lawrence each year to protect them against Iroquois attacks and Algonkin intimidation.

Thus, the *coureurs de bois* of former days were replaced by men who were employed by the Jesuits and controlled by them. The Jesuits were reimbursed by the trading company for the wages and maintenance of these men, whom Le Jeune stated explicitly "we keep with us so they may not become debauched among the Indians and offer a bad example, as did those who were here formerly" (Thwaites 1896–1901, 6:83). In the early days of the renewed Huron mission, these tasks were carried out by hired men, who also performed domestic chores for the Jesuits. Seculars were preferred to lay brothers, as the latter were forbidden to carry guns, which were essential for hunting and to reassure the Huron that the French desired to protect them (21:293).

The Jesuits' obvious involvement in the Huron fur trade added apparent substance to widespread charges that the order as a whole was profiting from this trade. These rumours were sufficiently damaging that the Jesuits found it necessary to deny them publicly in the *Relation* of 1642–43. They also appended to that relation a letter from the directors and associates of the Compagnie des Cent-Associés stating that they were in no way involved in the administration of the company or in the trafficking that was carried on by it (25:75–79). There is no evidence that the Jesuits were exporting furs from New France or making money at the expense of the company. Instead, they were unobtrusively selling their furs to the trading company, either directly or indirectly, at the fixed price that was set for the purchase of all furs.

There is, however, no doubt that within Canada the Jesuits, like other colonists, derived some profit from trading in furs, which were the principal medium of exchange. The concern that the Jesuits expressed in 1645 about a declaration to the effect that henceforth no one was to be allowed to trade for furs with the Indians (27:99) suggests that this internal trade was of considerable financial importance to them (Jaenen 1970). Some of the furs the Jesuits sold to the company were given to them as gifts by converts. Others were purchased from the Indians at lower rates than the company would have paid; yet, if such sales saved the Indians the trouble of carrying these furs to the St. Lawrence, they probably did not view them as a bad bargain. It is known that the Jesuits shipped wampum beads, elk skins, and other items to the Huron country in order to exchange them for things they needed (Thwaites 1896–1901, 9:175). This trade may have been extended to include the purchase of beaver pelts.

The Jesuits pointed out that they were compelled to give the Indians considerable quantities of trade goods as presents and in return for favours, while the profits that they made no more than compensated them for the twenty-five percent markup on goods imported from France (9:173). Whatever profits they made, even when combined with the subsidies they received from the trading company, were insufficient to support the Jesuit missions in Canada without substantial donations from well-wishers in France. In 1672 Frontenac was to repeat Jacques Michel's accusation that the Jesuits were more interested in beavers than saving souls, and through him this remark has passed into history (Delanglez 1939). More recently the Jesuits have been described as clerks of the fur trade and agents of French imperialism, thereby implying that such activities were their primary aims (Hunt 1940:70–71). Francis Parkman (1927:466) was undoubtedly much closer to the truth when he concluded that "to impute mercenary motives [to the Canadian Jesuits] is manifestly idle." The Jesuits undoubtedly managed their finances in a resourceful way and saw the success of their mission as related to the general prosperity of New France, but economic and political considerations remained for them means to ends rather than ends in themselves. The driving ambition of the Jesuits during the first half of the seventeenth century was to use rational and worldly means to achieve other-worldly ends. The behaviour of the Jesuits in New France makes sense only if viewed in terms of counter-reformationary zeal.

Three Jesuits were sent to Quebec in 1632 to lay the foundations for future work in the colony. Their leader was Father Paul Le Jeune, who was to remain the Jesuit superior at Quebec until 1639. A youthful convert to Roman Catholicism, Le Jeune was one of many young Jesuits who had been exposed to Father Massé's enthusiasm for the Canadian missions while studying at the Jesuit college at La Flèche. In addition to formulating clear policies for the Jesuit mission in New France, Le Jeune's first report, dispatched to the French Provincial of the Society of Jesus in August 1632, became the prototype for the annual *Jesuit Relations*, which continued to be published until 1673, and upon which so much of our knowledge of the history of this period is based. The aim of these duodecimal volumes was to disseminate knowledge of Jesuit mission work in Canada among well-to-do Frenchmen and to encourage temporal and spiritual aid for this work. While this influenced the selection of material that appeared in the *Jesuit Relations*, it does not prevent them from being used as reliable, though partial, sources of information about this period. Le Jeune was accompanied by Father de Noüe, who was to serve at Quebec and Three Rivers until his death in 1646, and by lay brother Gilbert Burel, who had first come to Canada in 1625.

The Huron, who probably had learned the previous year that the French were likely to return to Canada in 1632, came to Quebec that year in fifty canoes (Thwaites 1896–1901, 5:71). Le Jeune's statement that they made a fine sight upon the river suggests that unlike their usual custom, these Huron travelled together. They probably did this to defend themselves against the Mohawk and so they might better confront unexpected developments at Quebec. Although the Huron do not appear to have brought an unusual number of furs with them, they were no doubt anxious to obtain

trade goods to make up for the small trade the year before. While Amantacha travelled with the Huron and impressed the Jesuits with his intelli-
gence and knowledge of Roman Catholicism, no mention is made of Brûlé.
No doubt, as a self-proclaimed traitor whom Champlain had already
threatened with exemplary punishment, he was afraid to put in an
appearance. There is no mention of any formal ceremony to reaffirm the
French-Huron alliance and it appears that the Huron were more anxious
to sound out the French than to conclude new treaties with them. Referring
to their negotiations, Le Jeune said that it was impossible to describe "how
cunning this nation is" (5:73).

Brûlé's Murder

In the spring of 1633 Brûlé was murdered at Toanché. Sagard, writing in
France, stated that he was condemned to death and eaten by the Huron
(Sagard 1866:431). This has given rise to much lurid speculation about how
and why a man who had known the Huron for twenty-three years suddenly
should have been killed by them. The most popular suggestion is that he
was tortured to death because of some sexual indiscretion;[5] though, given
the nature of Huron attitudes towards sex, it is difficult to imagine a less
likely reason. Moreover, the fact that Brûlé was given a proper burial
indicates that he was not tortured or eaten, as Sagard imagined. While the
burial of his body in the earth and away from the regular cemetery may
have been done in imitation of the burial the Huron had seen the French
give Guillaume Chaudron a decade earlier (Thwaites 1896–1901, 10:305),
interment was the traditional form of burial for anyone who had died a
violent death. Brébeuf spoke of Brûlé being barbarously and treacherously
murdered (8:93), but not as having been eaten by the Huron.

The reason for Brûlé's murder was not made clear until 1641. When
Fathers Brébeuf and Chaumonot visited the Neutral confederacy, the
Huron grew concerned about their trading monopoly and a rumour began
to spread that the missionaries had gone south to make an alliance with
the Seneca in order to harm the Huron. The Jesuits report that "some
[Huron] warned us privately to beware of this undertaking as there had
been no other cause for the murder of one of our Frenchmen that occurred
here some years ago, than just such journeys which made the country
uneasy and fearful of a transference of trade" (21:211). Since Brûlé was
the only Frenchman whom the Huron had killed, it seems certain that this

account refers to him (Talbot 1956:227), and this, in turn, makes it clear that his murder was not a crime of passion or a senseless butchery, but a political assassination. Brûlé was killed because certain Huron knew or believed him to be dealing with the Seneca, or some other tribe whose rivalry the Huron feared. In 1616 he had lived among the Seneca for several months and, on leaving, had promised that he would make peace between them, the Huron, and the French. Thus the Huron's fears may have been far from groundless.

What is less certain is what Brûlé was planning to do. He may have been trying to persuade the Seneca to trade with the French, hoping that if he succeeded, Champlain would pardon him for his dealings with the English. This policy would almost certainly have earned him the undying hatred of the Huron headmen, who did not want their worst enemies to become rival trading partners with the French. The Huron would have been as determined to prevent the conclusion of an alliance between the Seneca and the French as the Mohawk had been to prevent one between the Dutch and the northern Algonkians. Alternatively, Brûlé may have surmised that Champlain was implacable and, knowing that the Jesuits were determined to get rid of him, he may have decided to defect to the Iroquois and work for the Dutch. Such a switch in political allegiance was not unknown among the *coureurs de bois* of later decades.

The individual who was believed to be chiefly responsible for Brûlé's murder was an important northern Attignawantan headman who bore the hereditary name Aenons. Unfortunately, a certain amount of mystery surrounds the identity of this man. At the time of Brûlé's death, Aenons appears to have been living in Toanché; later he resided in Wenrio, one of the two villages into which Toanché divided. His influence, however, extended beyond Toanché. In 1636 he presided over the torture of an Iroquois prisoner at Arenté (Thwaites 1896–1901, 13:61). The same year he played a leading role in the preparations for the Feast of the Dead that the Attignawantan were about to celebrate (10:305) and in the negotiations for reuniting certain northern Attignawantan villages (10:235–43). He claimed that it was he who had brought Etienne Brûlé to the country (10:309). Even if this only means that it was he who arranged that Brûlé should live among the Attignawantan rather than the Arendarhonon, it suggests that Aenons was connected with the fur trade at an early period.

Aenons's position as a council chief among the northern Attignawantan and his connections with the fur trade help to account for the leading role he appears to have played in Brûlé's murder. Indeed, given the grave implications of an assassination of this sort, it appears unlikely that any northern Attignawantan would have dared to do it if he had not been sanctioned by a leading headman who was credited with a special understanding of Huron relations with the French. All of this suggests that Aenons was the principal headman of the northern Attignawantan, which would make him the same person as, or the successor of, Auoindaon, who was the principal headman of this grouping at the time of Sagard's visit. Although the two names seem quite different, it is significant that there is no mention of Auoindaon after 1630, while Aenons is not mentioned before that time.

This identification is, however, beset by problems. Throughout his long sojourn among the Attignawantan, Brûlé was associated with the village of Toanché, where Aenons was living at the time of Brûlé's murder. If Aenons had brought Brûlé to the Attignawantan country after 1615, it seems likely that he would have taken him to his own village. On the other hand, in 1623 Auoindaon was living, not in Toanché, but in Quieunonascaran (Wrong 1939:174). As we have seen, however, sometime after 1623 Quieunonascaran split apart and became three hamlets, although these were still located near to one another (Thwaites 1896–1901, 13:125). It is significant that when the Jesuits were planning to return to the Huron country in 1633, Toanché and Ossossané were rivals to receive them, while Quieunonascaran, although it had been the first Huron village to have a resident priest, made no such effort. This suggests that Quieunonascaran not only had split apart but had declined in political importance. It may be that as Quieunonascaran declined, Aenons and his clan segment moved to Toanché, which, in any case, was more favourably located for trading with the French than was Quieunonascaran.[6]

Another problem is Aouandoïé, who in 1634 was living in Ihonatiria, the other of the two villages into which Toanché had split (8:93–97). He is described as having been one of the wealthiest Huron. Although he does not appear to have been a headman of any significance, it has been suggested that he, rather than Aenons, was the descendant or namesake of Auoindaon (E. Jury 1966e). While one would still have to account for why he moved from Quieunonascaran to Toanché, it is possible that sometime between 1623 and 1633 the leadership of the northern Attignawantan shifted from one leader to another. If Aenons was not Auoindaon's legitimate successor, he had managed to supplant him as the leader of the northern Attignawantan. By 1633 Aenons was clearly recognized by all the Huron as the spokesman for this group.

Not all of the Huron, or even all of the people of Toanché, approved of Brûlé's murder. We are informed that the dissensions it aroused led to the abandonment of Toanché and the founding of Wenrio and Ihonatiria (Thwaites 1896–1901, 5:255). This split was probably between clan segments that supported the murder and those that were anxious to disclaim responsibility for it. It is unlikely, however, that a headman of Aenons's standing would have permitted Brûlé to be slain unless he had been certain that the French were unlikely to demand satisfaction for his death. No doubt, one of the things that Amantacha and the other Huron who visited Quebec in 1632 sought to determine was whether Brûlé was still regarded as a traitor. From what they were told, Aenons may have concluded that Brûlé was no longer protected by the French-Huron alliance and thus felt free to kill him because of his dealings with the Iroquois. Other Huron may not have felt so certain and, in spite of repeated French assertions that Brûlé's death meant nothing to them, these latter continued to express anxiety about it for a long time to come. In spite of the murder, a very large number of Huron decided to travel to Quebec in 1633, where their headmen could conclude a new alliance with Champlain, who was expected to return from France that year. Their aim was to repeat the formal initiation of an alliance as this had been done on Montreal Island in 1611. The one headman who absented himself from this journey, on the plea that he had business elsewhere, was Aenons (10:237–39). Even he saw no point in taking chances.

The New Alliance

The Compagnie des Cent-Associés never recovered from the many losses it suffered, beginning with the disaster of 1628. To reduce their obligations, in 1632 the associates agreed to lease their trading rights for the next five years to a private association that had Jean de Lauson as its director. Thus, once again, merchants were in control of the company and its obligations to settle New France were to go unfulfilled (Lanctot 1963:151). The Jesuits were less concerned about this than the Recollets would have been, since colonization was not of such direct importance to their missionary program as it had been to that of the Recollets. While the Jesuits did what they could to establish schools, hospitals, and even an Indian reserve at Quebec, their program assisted, rather than sought to undermine, that of the company. In 1633 three English vessels continued to trade at Tadoussac, suggesting to the Montagnais that free trade had been restored on the St. Lawrence. This was, however, the last year that such vessels would visit

New France. On 22 May 1633 Champlain returned to Quebec having been appointed not Governor, as he had wished, but Commander of New France in the absence of Cardinal Richelieu.

After Ventadour became Viceroy of New France, Champlain had gradually shifted his allegiance from the Recollets to the Jesuits, though he must have found the latter's mission program far less congenial to his own aspirations. In 1626 he invited Charles Lalemant to become his confessor (Thwaites 1896–1901, 4:227), and it has been suggested that he allowed the last edition of his *Voyages* to be revised and put through the press by a Jesuit editor.[7] Great prominence is given in this publication to the Jesuits, while there is no longer such lavish praise for the early missionary work done by the Recollets. After his return to New France Champlain attempted to run the habitation along quasi-religious lines, having the lives of the saints read at supper, presiding over public self-examination and prayers each evening, and ordering the angelus to be sounded according to church custom (6:103). On his deathbed in 1635, he was to forget his wife and make the Virgin Mary his heiress.

Yet, in spite of the control that the Jesuits exercised over him in the last years of his life, they do not seem to have regarded him as an indispensable ally. Champlain was to die not knowing that Charles Huault de Montmagny had already been appointed Governor of New France, and was to arrive in Quebec the following spring with orders to relieve him of his command. Montmagny was a knight of the Order of Malta, had been educated by the Jesuits, and was very well disposed towards them. From the Jesuits' point of view, no better appointment could have been made. Under Montmagny's administration, the closest possible coordination of Jesuit policy and that of the vice-regal administration was to be achieved.

Two days after he had returned to Quebec in 1633, Champlain met a group of Montagnais from Three Rivers, who were accompanying their headman, Capitanal, down-river to Tadoussac (8:55). Champlain pleased these Montagnais by promising to defend them against the Iroquois and telling them that the French planned to establish a settlement at Three Rivers which would protect the Indians in that area. The Montagnais' enthusiasm cooled, however, when Champlain let them know that he would be very displeased if any of them were to attempt to trade with the English at Tadoussac. Capitanal replied that he would tell his people that they should not go there, but that it was difficult to restrain young men and there was no guarantee that he would be obeyed (5:209). While stressing his friendship for the French, Capitanal warned Champlain that if the French attempted to re-introduce their trading monopoly, this would anger the Indians and might lead to acts of violence, as it had done on two previous occasions (5:211).

In the following weeks, the French were heartened to see that in spite of the danger of Iroquois attacks, Algonkians, among them a group of Nipissing accompanied by Jean Nicollet, were coming down the St. Lawrence River to trade. Not long before, the French had experienced the Iroquois menace on the upper St. Lawrence firsthand. A party travelling up the St. Lawrence to meet Indian traders had been ambushed by thirty to forty Iroquois who scalped two Frenchmen and discharged a hail of arrows at the rest. The Iroquois were only prevented from boarding the shallop that the dead men had been towing when they were fired on and when they saw that a larger vessel was closing in on them (5:213–15). This attack demonstrated that the Mohawk were once again active in the St. Lawrence Valley and that their fear of Europeans had diminished. Greater familiarity with firearms, as well as their victory over Van Krieckenbeeck, may have contributed to this confidence.

The determination of the French to reinforce their trading monopoly soon had its familiar consequences. The Montagnais at Tadoussac were displeased by the resurgent power of the French traders (7:61) and on 2 July a Frenchman who was washing his clothes at Quebec was attacked and killed by a Weskarini Algonkin. The assailant had allegedly been planning to kill a certain Iroquois when he went to war, but, being in a drunken condition, he had attacked and killed a Frenchman instead (5:223–25). The Indians claimed that this was an unfortunate accident for which the alcohol of the French was responsible. The fact, however, that it followed so closely a warning that violence might occur if the French attempted to interfere with free trade, indicated that the resentment and hostility that had been felt towards the French monopolists prior to 1629 were still very strong. Even allowing for the drunken condition of the Indian, it is unlikely that this murder would have occurred had the Algonkians been generally well disposed towards the French. To make matters worse, two Montagnais informed the French who the murderer was and Champlain had the accused arrested and imprisoned him in the fort. Champlain's refusal to accept a reparations payment as a settlement for the killing or to release the man greatly angered the Algonkin, as similar action had done among the Montagnais in 1628–29.

The same day this murder was committed Amantacha arrived at Quebec. Although he was accompanied only by a few Huron (5:225), his arrival pleased the French who feared that the threat of Iroquois attacks might have dissuaded the Huron from travelling down-river that year (5:191–93,

219). In the course of his stay, Amantacha carefully sounded out the French before telling them that Brûlé had been murdered and that a great number of Huron had come down-river but that they were reluctant to appear at Quebec unless they knew that Champlain would not punish them for Brûlé's murder. Champlain informed him that Brûlé was no longer regarded as French because he had gone over to the service of the English (5:241). He asked Amantacha to return to the other traders, who were in the Ottawa Valley, and persuade them to continue their journey to Quebec.

When Amantacha reached these traders they already knew about the murder that had been committed at Quebec. The Algonkin were warning them that if they attempted to trade with the French, Champlain would condemn one or more of them to death to avenge Brûlé, just as he was planning to kill the Weskarini he had arrested (5:239–41). The Huron leaders knew that the Algonkin were anxious to purchase Huron furs at a low rate of exchange so that they themselves could carry them to the French and English (5:241). They were therefore not inclined to believe the Algonkin; nevertheless they wanted assurance that it was safe for them to go to Quebec. Amantacha's reassurances were such that all but a few Huron who had lost their furs gambling decided to continue on their journey (5:241). In spite of the crisis that had arisen, the Algonkin were unable to regain their role as middlemen. Soon groups of seven to twelve Huron canoes began to arrive at Quebec and, finally, on 28 July an immense fleet of 140 canoes appeared, carrying an estimated 500 to 700 Huron (5:239). While the reports of these figures may be inflated, they suggest that this was the largest number of Huron ever to travel to the St. Lawrence in a single year. The reason was not only the danger of Mohawk attack but also because sixty or more headmen and elders accompanied this expedition. The safety of so many leading men must have been of exceptional concern to the Huron; hence they were accompanied by many warriors.

Four more Jesuits arrived at Quebec in 1633. These were Fathers Brébeuf and Massé, who sailed from Dieppe with Champlain, and Antoine Daniel and Ambroise Davost, who had spent the previous winter on Cape Breton Island. The wish of the Jesuits was that Brébeuf, Daniel, and Davost should proceed to the Huron country as soon as possible, accompanied by three hired labourers. Antoine Daniel had been born in 1601 and had studied law before he entered the Jesuit novitiate at Rouen in 1621. Between 1623 and 1627, he had taught junior classes at Rouen and it is possible that Amantacha was one of his pupils. Thereafter he studied theology at Clermont, and taught and was minister in the College at Eu before leaving for the New World. Ambroise Davost had been born in 1586, became a Jesuit in 1611, and had studied principally at Bourges.

Brébeuf and Le Jeune asked Amantacha to help them gain approval from the Huron to renew their mission work among his people. Being a young man, Amantacha lacked the authority to discuss such matters, but he assured the Jesuits that many Huron were anxious for Brébeuf to return and promised to transport one of them in his own canoe. He also asked for an illustrated religious book to show to his countrymen and wrote letters of respect to the Jesuit provincial in France and to various other Frenchmen (5:245). The training that he had received in France was not yet lost on him.

The day after the Huron arrived in strength at Quebec, their headmen and elders held a general council with the French. Those from each tribe and village sat near one another on the ground (5:247), while the younger men, who did not have a voice in the proceedings, stood about looking on. Champlain attended as the chief representative of the French and the Jesuits were accorded a prominent place in the assembly. The meeting began with the chief spokesman for the Huron announcing that his people regarded the French as their friends and brothers and that the purpose of the assembly was to strengthen the alliance between them. As proof of his sincerity, he presented Champlain with several packages of beaver skins amidst general expressions of approval (5:249). While the Huron sought to renew their alliance, they expressed no regret about the killing of Brûlé, nor did they offer any condolences or reparations presents. No doubt, they accepted Champlain's denunciation of Brûlé as a traitor as indicating that the French did not claim the right to expect such observances.

Through an interpreter Champlain reassured the Huron that he had always loved them and that his king had ordered him to do all he could to protect them. This was the reason he had sent the vessels up the St. Lawrence River that had been attacked by the Iroquois. He also admonished the Huron not to listen to rumours that were being spread by tribes who were trying to make them fear the French and break off trading with them. Champlain described to the Huron in what high esteem the Jesuits were held by the French and how their aim, in wanting to live with the Huron, was not to promote trade with other tribes but to instruct them, as Amantacha could verify. Champlain stated that if the Huron loved the French, they would allow the Jesuits to live with them. He thereby implied that the Huron's acceptance of the Jesuits, and their continued good treatment of them, were necessary conditions for the renewal of the French-Huron alliance.

The Huron had always been pleased to have Frenchmen living in their country to protect their villages and vouch for the good treatment of Huron who went to the St. Lawrence to trade. This, however, was the first time that the French had implied that the acceptance of specific individuals was a necessary condition of this alliance. The Huron did not reply specifically to this proposal, the novelty of which made it something that would have to be discussed by the confederacy council before a formal reply could be given. Instead, two headmen reaffirmed their respect for Champlain and their goodwill towards the Jesuits. The council ended with Brébeuf delivering a speech in the Huron language, in which he stated that the Jesuits wanted to spend the rest of their lives in the Huron country and become a part of the Huron people. He assured the Huron that the Jesuits were equally well disposed towards all of them, but pointed out that because the missionaries were still few in number, they could not live everywhere. He promised that the time was not far off when one priest would be stationed in each village (5:253). This promise, which was meant to prevent undue envy among the Huron villages, was met with general approval.

Even if the Huron were not particularly anxious to have the missionaries return with them at this time, once it became clear that Champlain was insisting that they be embarked, competition arose concerning where they would settle. The Huron from Toanché offered to provide transport for the Jesuits if they would agree to live with them. They pointed out that this would demonstrate that the French had truly forgiven these people for the death of Brûlé and might put an end to the schism that had led to the establishment of two separate villages. The traders asked if the Jesuits wished to live with the Indians or in a separate house and, when they were informed that the Jesuits preferred the latter, they promised to erect such a house for them, around which they might reassemble their village (5:255).

Anenkhiondic, the headman of Ossossané, talked with Father Brébeuf in private and tried to persuade him to settle in that town. He pointed out the importance of Ossossané, which was the principal town of the Attignawantan, who, in turn, were the largest and most important tribe in the Huron confederacy (5:259). He also offered to transport as many French to the Huron country as Brébeuf wished to send there. Brébeuf discussed this offer with Le Jeune and they concluded that since Ossossané was the place where most meetings of the confederacy council took place, mission work should begin there (5:261).

In order not to offend other communities, Brébeuf persuaded Champlain to announce that it was his desire that all the French going to the Huron country should settle in Ossossané under Brébeuf's direction and control. This proclamation satisfied everybody except the people of Toanché, whose headman protested vigorously. In an attempt to soothe his feelings, Brébeuf asked the leading Huron to gather once more in council. The men from Toanché refused to attend and reproached Anenkhiondic with having been the cause of the French not agreeing to go to their village. As a result of this attack, Anenkhiondic withdrew his offer to furnish passage to any of the Jesuits, giving as an excuse that his canoe was manned only by inexperienced young men. It was decided that as a compromise, canoes from other villages should help to carry the Jesuits and their secular assistants up-river. Since the French gave presents to Huron who provided passage in their canoes, this arrangement meant that these presents would be distributed more evenly among the tribes and villages that made up the confederacy (5:259–63).

After several days were spent trading, Champlain provided a great feast for the Huron on 3 August. Corn soup flavoured with peas, bread crumbs, and prunes was served to the guests, who showed their appreciation with much singing and dancing (5:267). The following day, which was the one before the Huron were to leave for home, another council was held at which Champlain distributed presents corresponding in trade value to the furs that the Huron had given him a week earlier (6:7). At this council Champlain attempted to settle the final details concerning the departure of the Jesuits for the Huron country. The Huron asked that as a favour to them, the Algonkin prisoner should be released. Champlain explained that according to French law, this was not a proper thing to do. When it became apparent that he would not change his mind, the Huron did not press the matter. They spoke of their alliance with the French and said that if having the Jesuits come to live in their country would strengthen the alliance, they would be happy to take them. Those who were to embark the Jesuits were given their presents in advance and the baggage that was to accompany the Jesuits was entrusted to them (6:7).

Prior to this council, a meeting had been held at which the Algonkin and Montagnais headmen had asked the Huron to secure the release of the Algonkin whom Champlain was holding prisoner. Although the Huron were reluctant to become involved in this affair, had they refused this request they would have endangered seriously their relations with their eastern neighbours. They therefore asked the French for his release, though they made the request in a rather half-hearted manner. The night after this request had been rejected, Tessouat visited the Huron camp and warned them not to embark any Frenchmen in their canoes because the relatives of the prisoner were watching along the Ottawa River and planned to kill any French they could in retaliation for what Champlain had done (6:7–9). This resulted in feverish consultation between the Huron and their Indian allies.

The next morning, the Huron delayed their departure and Champlain met all the Indians who were at Quebec. Tessouat pointed out that if any Huron were killed while attempting to defend the French who were travelling with them, it would lead to a blood feud between the Huron on the one hand and the Weskarini and their Algonkin allies on the other. This implied that either Champlain had to release his prisoner or the Huron must not be allowed to take any Frenchmen home with them. If the French had agreed to the first option, the Algonkin, under Tessouat's leadership, would have won a significant victory; if they did not the French-Huron alliance, at least in Algonkin eyes, would have been that much weaker. The Huron, for their part, said they would be pleased to have the Jesuits in their country, but the Ottawa River did not belong to them and the feelings of the Algonkin had to be respected if they were to travel safely through their territory (6:11). Champlain threatened that he would punish the Algonkin if they did not behave better, but he was mockingly reminded that under French law the Indians who were at Quebec could not be held responsible for the behaviour of the prisoner's kinsmen.

In a final effort to persuade the Algonkin to relent, Le Jeune publicly requested that Champlain pardon the prisoner. This was done, however, by pre-arrangement. Champlain replied that he could not do this, but agreed to suspend the execution of the sentence until he could learn the king's pleasure in this matter. Le Jeune then addressed the Huron and Algonkin, pointing out that the Jesuits did not desire the man's death and, for this reason, his kinsmen should let them travel up the Ottawa River. Tessouat was in no way deceived by these amateur dramatics and informed the Jesuits that they could not travel to the Huron country until the prisoner was released. Champlain became furious and said he would not give in to blackmail of this sort; until the Algonkin learned to behave "properly," he gave his men permission to fire on any of them seen bearing arms (6:15). This outburst effectively put an end to any hope that the Jesuits would reach the Huron country in 1633. Champlain and Le Jeune agreed that nothing should be done that might lead to further conflict between the Huron and Algonkin, since such conflict would seriously damage the fur trade and the prosperity of New France (6:17). The Jesuits and the Huron parted on good terms, with both sides expressing the hope that the Jesuits would be able to travel to the Huron country the following year.

It is impossible to unravel the full web of intrigue that lies behind these events. No doubt, the Algonkin would have liked to put an end to all direct trade between the French and the Huron, provided that they did not consequently expose themselves to attack by the Iroquois. The simplest way of halting this trade would have been for the Algonkin to have provoked a war with the Huron. Such a war was impossible, however, for two reasons. Firstly, the Huron greatly outnumbered the Algonkin and they probably could have counted on the French for support. Secondly, if the Algonkin were at war with the Huron, they could not have profited from being middlemen between the Huron and the French.

It is reasonable to conclude that a wily politician like Tessouat did not aim to cut off all trade between the French and the Huron. He probably hoped, however, that by preventing the French from travelling to and from the Huron country, he could exact higher tolls from the Huron and prevent the re-establishment of the close relationship that had formerly existed between these trading partners. This would make it easier to sow distrust and anxiety among Huron traders and to dissuade some of them from travelling to the St. Lawrence, thus allowing the Algonkin to regain control of at least part of the fur trade that was currently in the hands of the Huron.

The intentions of the Huron headmen are more difficult to fathom. Did they prefer to have French seculars living with them, but decide that if Champlain insisted that they take priests they would do so? Or did they fear that if they had Frenchmen living with them and a young Huron were to injure these guests, they would be compelled either to surrender this man to the French (which, by their own laws and customs, they could not do) or to break off relations with them? Some may have feared that Brûlé's murder had set a precedent that irresponsible persons might be tempted to imitate. Or was it that the Huron did not want the priests and found the crisis that had developed a good excuse for not having them?

Brébeuf seems to have been popular with the people of Toanché and they may have been pleased that he wished to return to their country. On the other hand, the clear preference that the Huron had for men who could bear arms had not diminished (7:217). Moreover, for all the respect the Huron had for the priests' shamanistic powers, many probably still suspected them of being sorcerers and were annoyed by their persistent refusal to live with Huron families. Le Jeune believed that the desire expressed by the Huron to have the Jesuits in their country was largely feigned because Champlain insisted that the renewal of the alliance required the Huron to allow the Jesuits to live among them (6:19–21). The Huron may have hoped that by the following year Champlain would have reconsidered the matter, and men more to their liking would be sent to them.

It is unreasonable to assume that all of the Huron headmen shared the same opinions. Given the unsettled conditions that followed Brûlé's murder, the Huron may have found the turmoil at Quebec a convenient excuse for delay and for avoiding still more argument and division concerning with whom the Jesuits should live. Whatever they thought of the Jesuits, most Huron probably felt that such an exchange was premature until the new alliance had been ratified by the confederacy council and confirmed by another round of visits.

The Defeat of the Algonkin

The resumption of French patrols on the St. Lawrence combined with other factors to produce a reorientation of Mohawk foreign policy that was decidedly to the advantage of the French. For some time the Mohawk and Oneida had been annoyed by the high prices that the Dutch were charging for trade goods. Their anger reached the boiling point, however, when Hans Jorissen Hontom was appointed the new commissary at Fort Orange. Hontom was a trader who appears to have kidnapped a Mohawk council chief and murdered him by castration (Trelease 1960:51; Grassmann 1969:44). In October 1633 the Mohawk attacked the Dutch settlement, burned the trading company's yacht, and killed most of the cattle at Rensselaerswyck. The Dutch realized the weakness of their position and immediately acted to improve their relations with the Iroquois tribes (Van Laer 1908:302–4, 330). In spite of this, the eastern tribes remained fearful of Dutch reprisals and, being determined to reduce the price of trade goods through competition, were anxious to re-establish an alternative trading relationship with the French. The first step in doing this was for the Mohawk and Oneida to make peace with the Algonkin and Montagnais.

By a curious conjunction of circumstances, the turmoil at Quebec provided the Algonkin with pressing reasons for wanting to diversify their trading relations at this time. Tessouat, in particular, believed that a treaty which made it possible for his people to secure European goods either from the Mohawk or the Dutch would greatly strengthen his position when it came to bargaining with Champlain. A formal treaty was concluded with the Mohawk in the autumn of 1634, after the Montagnais released an Iroquois prisoner they had captured recently (8:23–25; map 22). News of this treaty caused great anxiety among the French as well as the Dutch. Both began to distrust the loyalty of their Indian trading partners, and feared what the other stood to gain from it. The Dutch knew that the Mohawk were making peace with the Algonkin in hopes of being able to trade with the French (Jameson 1909:139), and, while Le Jeune attributed the desire of the Algonkin for peace to weariness of war (Thwaites 1896–1901, 8:25), the French traders feared that the Algonkin were once again being seduced by the wampum traders at Fort Orange. Any arrangement that made it possible for the Algonkin to obtain trade goods from the Hudson Valley, whether from the Dutch or from the Iroquois, was seen as making the Algonkin that much more difficult to control.

It is clear, however, that this treaty, unlike the one negotiated in 1624, involved neither the French nor the Dutch and therefore gave neither Indian group the right to trade with the other's European partner. No doubt the Algonkin and Mohawk hoped that this peace would eventually permit them to trade with the Dutch and the French respectively, but, while both sides wanted this privilege for themselves, neither was willing to see it extended to the other. The main advantage of this treaty was that, given the difficulties that the Algonkin and Mohawk were having with their respective trading partners, it allowed them to obtain European goods from each other. Unsatisfactory as this arrangement might have been in the long run, for the moment it lessened both groups' dependence on their European trading partners and gave them additional bargaining power in their dealings with them.

The Mohawk, however, enjoyed one advantage that the Algonkin did not. The Dutch accepted that in their present state they were not strong enough to risk a confrontation with the Mohawk. Therefore, however much they wished to develop trade with the Algonkian-speaking peoples to the north, they knew that this was impossible so long as the Mohawk were opposed to it (Van Laer 1908:248). The French traders, on the other hand, were seeking not only to regain but also to expand their former trading network. One manifestation of this was the dispatch of Jean Nicollet on his famous voyage to the shores of Green Bay, Wisconsin in July 1634. Historians have speculated that the purpose of this trip was to prevent a trading alliance between the Winnebago and the Dutch, to find a route to China (since he took with him a robe of Chinese damask), or to take possession of copper mines around the upper Great Lakes.[8] None of these

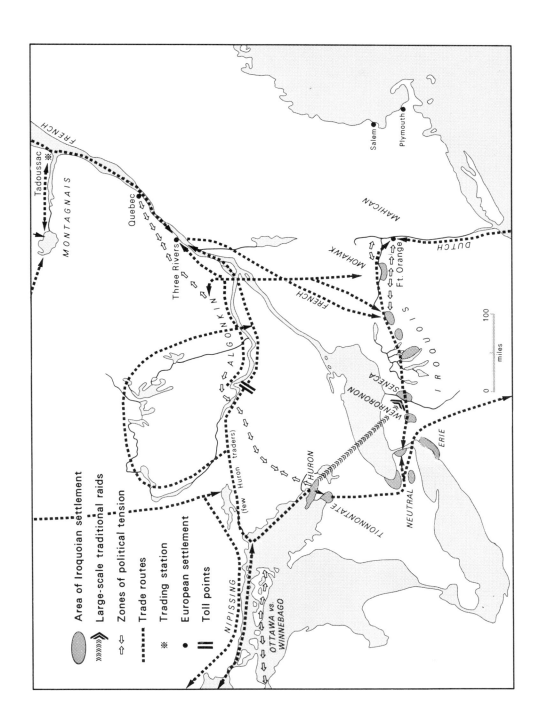

MAP 22. *Intertribal relations, 1634.*

explanations is at all convincing, however. The stated aim of his journey was to negotiate peace between the Winnebago and the Ottawa,[9] no doubt so the latter could resume trading in this region. It is uncertain whether this particular conflict was only with the Winnebago or extended to other tribes; however, in 1632 Le Jeune reports having baptized at Quebec an "Assistaronon" child whose parents had been captured in war and tortured to death by the Algonkin (Thwaites 1896–1901, 5:73). Even if the term Assistaronon were here being applied to the Winnebago, this passage suggests that the conflict had wider ramifications than are commonly attributed to it. It appears that the truce Nicollet arranged came to an end sometime before June 1636. It was then that the headman of the Amiskou, or Beaver band of the Ottawa, requested the French to provide protection for his people; two of whom had been eaten by the Winnebago (10:83).

In the summer of 1634 six French traders visited the Oneida and possibly the Onondaga and offered them high prices for their furs (Jameson 1909:148–54). It is not known whether these traders reached the Oneida by travelling overland or up the St. Lawrence River to Lake Ontario and then inland by way of the Oswego River to Lake Oneida (Crouse 1924:16). Interestingly enough, this remarkable journey is nowhere reported in the French sources and it took place only a year after Champlain had been formulating plans to subjugate or destroy the Mohawk. This suggests that the traders at Quebec were pursuing policies that ran counter to those of Champlain and that, for strategic reasons, they deemed it best to keep secret. Brûlé could have been involved in plans to extend these trading links to the Seneca.

When the Dutch learned about the activities of these French traders, they became alarmed and dispatched a surgeon named Harmen Meyndertsen van den Bogaert to investigate the situation. He visited the Mohawk and Oneida and found that both of these groups wanted higher prices for their furs, similar to those they said were being received by the Indians who traded with the French (Jameson 1909:139). He also discovered that they wanted peace so they could hunt safely in the Adirondacks. The Oneida praised the generosity of the French, but informed the Dutch that if they gave them better value for their furs and promised that the types of goods the Iroquois wanted would be on hand when they came to Fort Orange, they would be willing to trade exclusively with them (ibid. 151). Some Onondaga who were visiting the Oneida also promised that if the Dutch were willing to pay more, they would bring many skins to Fort Orange. They likewise promised to show the Dutch where the French came to trade each year on the St. Lawrence (ibid. 154), which suggests that at least some of them had visited this area along with the Oneida and the Mohawk. The Iroquois might have made these expressions of goodwill toward the Dutch simply as a matter of diplomacy. More likely, however, they regarded the truce with the Algonkin as temporary and were anxious to derive what benefits they could from it before the Dutch were once again their only trading partners.

In the spring of 1634 over 500 Huron went to attack a Seneca village, apparently in the style of their raid against the "Entouhonoron" in 1615. It is possible that this raid was undertaken to retaliate for the dealings that the Seneca had, or were suspected of having, with Brûlé. Unfortunately for the Huron, the Seneca learned of their plans and assembled a large force of warriors, which surprised the Huron as they were travelling south. In the ensuing conflict, over 200 Huron were killed and another hundred taken prisoner. Amantacha was among the latter, while Soranhes fled the battle and, although crippled by illness, eventually made his way home by way of the Neutral country. Amantacha managed to free himself, but only after the Iroquois had cut off one of his fingers (Thwaites 1896–1901, 7:213–15; 8:69, 139, 149, 151).

Rather than following up their victory by an attack on the Huron, the Seneca decided to entreat for peace. They spared the lives of their most important prisoners, and dispatched some of their headmen to discuss a treaty with the Huron (7:215). The Huron accepted their proposals and, in 1635, an embassy was sent to the Seneca to confirm the peace. The four other tribes of the Iroquois confederacy also expressed an interest in making peace with the Huron (8:115–17). This suggests that in spite of their remarkable victory, the Seneca did not feel free to treat the Huron with contempt. Conceivably, Seneca and other Iroquois had been taken prisoner by the Huron in recent years and their relatives hoped to recover them by means of a truce. In spite of this isolated defeat of the Huron, the peace that followed is evidence that a balance of power continued to exist between the Huron and the Iroquois.

After his return to Quebec, Champlain set about fortifying the colony and extending French control farther up the St. Lawrence River. A fort was built on Sainte Croix Island to guard the Richelieu Rapids and, in 1634, a settlement was established at Three Rivers, which hereafter was the main trading post for Indians who came from the interior. The same year, six more Jesuits arrived in New France, including Father Charles Lalemant. It was decided to try again to send Brébeuf, Daniel, and Davost to the Huron country. They were to be accompanied by four hired men, François Petit-Pré, Simon Baron, Robert Le Coq, and Dominique, and by two youths, Pierre and Martin. The latter were no doubt sent to learn the Huron language so that they might serve as interpreters and trading agents under Jesuit supervision.[10]

Unfortunately, because of the defeat they had suffered and their fear of further attacks by the Seneca, few Huron came to trade with the French in 1634 (7:215). Those who did ventured down-river in small parties after they had learned about the truce between the Iroquois and the Algonkin. While these traders had no doubt been given permission to come to Quebec by the headmen who controlled these routes, they do not seem to have included many influential Huron, or any men who were empowered to negotiate with the French or to make treaties with them. By 5 July only a small number of canoes had arrived at Three Rivers, some manned by Attigneenongnahac, others by Arendarhonon. These were insufficient to transport both the men the Jesuits wanted to send to the Huron country and the European goods that the Huron had come to purchase (8:71). In spite of this, the Jesuits persevered with their efforts to get to the Huron country. Father Brébeuf spoke to the Huron in private and persuaded them to take at least some Frenchmen home with them. When, however, an influential Kichesipirini called the Partridge heard about these promises, he publicly warned the Huron not to embark any Frenchmen. The clear implication was that the Weskarini were still prepared to kill any French-men they found passing through their territory.

This threat frightened the Huron into withdrawing their offer. Du Plessis-Bochart, the chief clerk of the company and the general of its fleet, held a meeting with the Algonkin and tried to persuade them to drop their opposition to letting the Jesuits travel with the Huron. In spite of strong objections from the Partridge, the Algonkin eventually seemed won over by the presents that were offered to them (7:215–17; 8:71). The next morning, however, when the plan was discussed jointly by all the parties concerned, the Huron traders continued to demur, apparently because although the Algonkin now appeared to be well-disposed towards the French, they were secretly continuing to intimidate the Huron traders. Thus, while the Huron might have been willing to take armed Frenchmen with them, they were frightened to embark unarmed priests who might be killed on route, and whose deaths could involve the Huron in a blood feud with both the French and the Algonkin (7:217). Because of this, the Huron were unwilling to agree publicly to embark any Frenchmen for a journey into the interior.

After the meeting was over, however, one of the Attigneenongnahac invited Brébeuf to his cabin and announced that he was willing to risk taking three Frenchmen up-river, if the French would agree to trade his load of tobacco at a more favourable rate than usual (7:217). When Du Plessis-Bochart agreed to do this, the Arendarhonon became enthusiastic for a similar arrangement, and they too agreed to take three French (8:71). Presents were lavished on these Huron by the French and a feast was provided for them. Before they left, however, several Indians became ill and fear of sickness was used as an argument to reduce the number of French from six to three. The Huron's insistence that these should be two hired men and one priest shows that they were still frightened of the Algonkin and were having second thoughts about the offer they had made. Under great pressure from the French, the Huron were persuaded to take two priests and one hired man, although the priests had to promise to help paddle the canoes in which they were travelling. Thus, on 7 July Fathers Brébeuf and Daniel and the hired man Baron embarked for the Huron country, leaving behind instructions that if the others could make their way there, they should all gather at Ihonatiria, one of the successors of Toanché, the town Brébeuf knew best (7:219; 8:75, 99).

Additional small groups of Huron traders came to Three Rivers after the first ones had departed. Among these were one or more groups of Attignawantan, including Aenons, who was now willing to trust his life to the French. He is reported to have been well treated and returned home convinced that the part he had played in Brûlé's death was not held against him. He is the only headman of note who is mentioned as visiting the St. Lawrence in 1634, and it may be that his visit was an exception prompted by his failure to come the year before. The other Attignawantan who is mentioned by name as being among those who visited Three Rivers was Oukhahitoüa from the village of Onnentisati (8:139). When these latecomers learned about the presents that had been lavished on the Attigneenongnahac and the Arendarhonon for agreeing to take Frenchmen home with them, they were anxious to emulate their example. On 15 July Father Davost and two others embarked in three Huron canoes and eight days later the rest were able to leave Three Rivers with yet another party (7:221; 8:75).

The transportation to the Huron country that the Jesuits had secured by bribery, rather than with the approval of the confederacy council or in most cases even of individual headmen, turned out to be far from satisfactory. Because many of the Huron became ill, the Jesuits had to help paddle the canoes (7:225–27). Brébeuf, who was an experienced traveller, had a fairly uneventful passage; however, his Attigneenongnahac travelling companions complained about the weight of the equipment that he carried with him in order to celebrate the mass. He was also told that, at one point, the owner of his canoe had spoken of abandoning him, although he was treated with such affection that he doubted the truth of this story (8:83–85).

The other Frenchmen, who were unknown to the Huron and did not speak their language, had a much harder time. Father Daniel's companions decided to visit a settlement that was located away from the Ottawa River and, failing to find it, they were all on the verge of starvation (7:227). Later, his companions, many of whom were ill, proposed to leave him among the Kichesipirini, and were persuaded only with great difficulty to take him any farther. Finally, he encountered Anenkhiondic travelling in a canoe paddled by six men. This powerful headman rescued Daniel and took him to Ossossané (8:85).

Father Davost was well treated during the early stages of his journey (7:227), but later was robbed by his companions and left among the Kichesipirini. He was also compelled to throw away a little steel mill, many of the books, and most of the paper and linen he was carrying with him (8:81). The young men, Pierre and Martin, were abandoned on route, although the latter was left among the Nipissing, who travelled to the Huron country in September (8:81). The Huron also talked about abandoning Baron among the Kichesipirini (8:85) and, on the day that they arrived in the Huron country, his companions were prevented only by force of arms from robbing him of everything he had with him (8:81). In general, those who suffered least were the four hired men who were armed and thus were able to command the respect, if not the affection, of their travelling companions.

These difficulties must be viewed in a broader context. The year before, many Huron headmen had travelled to the St. Lawrence to renew their alliance with the French, but had decided that the situation was not propitious for the Jesuits to visit their country. The next year, only a few traders came down-river and although they had no sanction from their headmen to bring the Jesuits and their staff home with them, they were bribed by the French to accept them as passengers. Given the additional burden of widespread illness, it is not surprising that these Huron fulfilled their promises badly. The abandonment or threatened abandonment of individual Frenchmen among different Algonkin groups, particularly among the Kichesipirini, must have stemmed from their lack of confidence in dealing with these formidable people, who were both allies and competitors of the Huron. This weakness was compounded by the Huron traders' realization that they were not committed in advance to answer for the safety of the French to their own people. This attitude inadvertently had been encouraged by Du Plessis-Bochart's statement that he would not hold the Algonkin responsible for what happened to the Jesuits while they were living among the Huron (7:215–17). From this the Huron traders inferred that if they abandoned the Jesuits among the Algonkin, the latter, rather than themselves, would be held accountable for them by the French.

The French were unwise to commit themselves to Huron who lacked an understanding of intertribal relations or sufficient authority to assure the safety of the French who were travelling with them. It was also unwise for newly arrived Jesuits to travel with members of Huron tribes who knew that the Jesuits had no intention of coming to live with them. In this respect, it was significant that Anenkhiondic, who was the principal head-man of the Attignawantan, took Father Daniel into his canoe with such a warm display of friendship. If the last group of Frenchmen to travel up-river did so under Aenons's protection, this may explain why no particular difficulties are reported for at least three Frenchmen. In the final analysis, it appears that the difficulties that were experienced by the Jesuits at this time resulted from their impatience to reach the Huron country and their consequent circumvention of the alliance that assured their safety and good treatment.

Brébeuf arrived in the Huron country on 5 August and was left alone at the embarkation place for the village of Toanché, while his companions headed south to their homes in Attigneenongnahac territory. Finding the landing place deserted, and knowing that the people of Toanché had moved, Brébeuf had asked these Huron either to accompany him to the new village or to sleep on the beach and guard his belongings until he had made his presence known. Instead, they left Brébeuf with the assurance that someone was certain to find him (8:89–91). Brébeuf hid his packages in the woods and, taking with him what was most valuable, set out to find the people of Toanché. He passed the former village which, except for one longhouse, was in ruins and following a well-beaten trail he came to the new village of Ihonatiria.[11] There he was welcomed by many old friends and a band of young people helped him to fetch his baggage (8:93). That evening and the whole of the next day were spent receiving greetings, visits, and salutations from the people of the village (8:97).

On the following days, old acquaintances came to greet Brébeuf and to each of them he gave a small present as an expression of goodwill. These visitors complained of bad harvests during Brébeuf's absence and expressed the hope that his shamanistic powers would once again produce better ones. The traders of Ihonatiria interpreted Brébeuf's arrival as evidence that the

French bore them no ill will. They told him that the Algonkin and the inhabitants of other Huron villages had been telling them that if they went to trade with the French, the French would kill them in order to avenge Brûlé, but now that Brébeuf had returned, they would be able to trade without fear (8:99).

While waiting for all of the Frenchmen to arrive in the Huron country, Brebeuf decided to live in the house of Aouandoïé, who was one of the richest and most hospitable men in the village. Twice, when Toanché had caught fire, Aouandoïé's longhouse had been saved. In order to avoid any suspicion of witchcraft, he had distributed over 100 bushels of corn among his fellow villagers (8:95). Brébeuf was on good terms with this man and judged that his household would be the least inconvenienced by visitors who required food and shelter until they had their own cabin (8:93).

Brébeuf spent two weeks visiting other villages and assembling the French, who were arriving in different parts of the Huron country (8:99). These travels took Brébeuf at least as far as Ossossané, where Father Daniel had arrived on 9 August. Davost did not appear until 24 August and was in such a state of fatigue and dejection that it was feared he would not recover. For over a month and a half Brébeuf, the two other priests, and another Frenchman continued to live with Aouandoïé, while the rest were billeted with another household (8:97).

Once all the French had arrived in the Huron country, Brébeuf decided to make Ihonatiria their headquarters, at least for the near future. Although Ossossané had been the Jesuits' choice the year before, that community was planning to relocate the following spring; hence any decision to settle there immediately would have involved extra work for both the French and the Huron (8:101). Brébeuf was convinced that other advantages were to be gained by remaining in Ihonatiria. Its inhabitants were accustomed to priests, while those of Ossossané were not. Moreover, the close ties that Brébeuf had with them would make it easier for the French to work in Ihonatiria and gradually acquire a knowledge of the Huron language. Brébeuf feared that in Ossossané the young people would harass the newcomers and thus make it more difficult for them to become accustomed to working among the Huron (8:103). He also hoped that since the people of Ihonatiria had been exposed to Christian teachings longer than other Huron, more conversions might be expected there (8:101). Finally, if the Jesuits left Ihonatiria, this would be interpreted as evidence of French ill will and might frighten the villagers into abandoning their trade with the French (8:103).

Although it was the wrong time of year for building bark houses, presents were offered to the councils of Ihonatiria and Wenrio to encourage them to work together to erect on the outskirts of Ihonatiria a Huron-style longhouse in which the Jesuits and their workmen could live. The workers from Wenrio proceeded very slowly, since their headmen still hoped to persuade the Jesuits to live in their village. Their bad example discouraged the volunteers from Ihonatiria so greatly that the cabin was not finished until October. Its interior, which was about thirty-six feet long and eighteen to twenty feet wide, was divided into three compartments by the French. The first served as a storeroom, while the second was a general living room, work room, and bedroom. In the latter, the Jesuits set up a carpentry shop and their mill for grinding flour, though they soon discovered that they preferred maize that had been pounded, Huron-style, in a wooden mortar (8:111). The third room was a chapel. The carpentry of this house, and the furnishings that the Jesuits brought with them, greatly interested the Huron. In particular, they were impressed by the European-style doors that were placed at the entrance to the cabin and between the first and second rooms, by the mill, and by the clock (8:109). Visitors took turns working the mill and believed that because the clock made a noise, it was alive. For this reason, they called it the Headman of the Day and enquired about the kind of food it ate and what it was saying. The Jesuits found that by telling the Huron that when it sounded four times it was telling them to leave, they could assure themselves of being left alone after four o'clock (8:113).

While these novelties had been brought to the Huron country for their utilitarian value, the Jesuits had transported other items hither especially to interest the Huron. These included a lodestone, a glass that reflected a single object eleven times, and a phial in which a flea looked as big as a beetle. All of these things enhanced the reputation of the Jesuits as possessors of supernatural power, so that they came to be called ondaki. While the Jesuits were pleased to think that this increased the respect that the Huron had for their Christian teachings (8:109), such a reputation was two-edged, because the Huron believed that these powers could be used for evil purposes no less than for good ones.

By the autumn of 1634, it was clear that even if the Jesuits had not come to the Huron country with the consent of the Huron headmen, their arrival was welcomed as a pledge of French goodwill. The Jesuits' role as guests of the Huron was officially confirmed on 22 July 1635 at a council that was held between the Huron and the French at Quebec. The Huron travelled down-river rather than trading at Three Rivers, thereby showing that they attached much the same importance to this meeting as they had to the bigger one in 1633. Champlain again stressed the love that the French had for the Jesuits and other Frenchmen who were living among the Huron, and made it clear that if the Huron wished to maintain their trading alliance, they had to treat these men with respect. At Le Jeune's request, Champlain also told the Huron that in order to preserve and strengthen their friendship with the French, they must agree to become Christians and, the following year, they must bring many little boys to Quebec, whom the Jesuits would care for and instruct in a residential school they were planning to establish there. Champlain assured the Huron that if they became Christians, God would make them victorious over their enemies. He also promised that many French men would come to live in their country who would marry their daughters and teach the Huron how to make iron hatchets, knives, and other useful items (8:49).

Because the Huron believed Christianity to be only one more ritual society, the advantages they might derive from such an arrangement must have seemed very enticing. Moreover, the French traders assured the Huron that it was not necessary for them to become Christians at once; it was enough if they did so in four years (17:171). Thus by postponing the least comprehensible aspect of Champlain's proposal, these traders softened the demands that the Jesuits had persuaded them to make. Champlain asked the Huron to call a general council when they returned home at which Brébeuf could read a message that Champlain was addressing to their headmen. At this council Brébeuf would also present a goodwill present that the Jesuits in Quebec were sending to the council chiefs of the Huron confederacy. The Huron traders agreed to convey this message, but complained that while all the Huron cherished their friendship with the French, the Jesuits had decided to settle in only one village (8:49–51). They also agreed to take two more Jesuits, François-Joseph Le Mercier and Pierre Pijart, home with them. Although many Huron volunteered to take these priests, they travelled with individuals whom Brébeuf had designated in a letter as being particularly reliable.

The Algonkin did not cease their efforts to prevent the renewal of a close relationship between the French and the Huron. To undermine confidence in the Huron, the Kichesipirini began to accuse them of Father Viel's murder. This story was reported by Le Jeune as early as August 1634 (7:233) and may have been told to the French at Three Rivers when the Partridge was trying to dissuade the Jesuits from embarking for the Huron country. As Brébeuf was travelling to the Huron country, the Algonkin told him that the Huron would kill the Jesuits as they had killed Brûlé. They urged the Jesuits to break off the journey and remain with them, promising them that if they did they would be well treated (8:83). When Tessouat visited the Huron country in the spring of 1636, he again urged the Jesuits to leave the Huron, or at least to stop living with the Attignawantan, whom he regarded as his worst enemies. He charged that the Attignawantan had murdered Viel and Brûlé, as they had murdered eight of his own people. Tessouat argued that it was foolish for a man of Brébeuf's importance to risk his life among the Attignawantan; as soon as he perfected his knowledge of the Huron language, he should return to Quebec and conduct his business with the Huron from there (10:79). At the same time, Tessouat was telling the Huron that Champlain did not wish to have the Jesuits remain in their country and that he was determined to avenge the death of Brûlé by cutting off four Huron heads (8:103). By playing on the fears of the Huron and the French, Tessouat was hoping to undermine their good relations.

To terrify the Huron traders a Kichesipirini headman, who bore the hereditary name Oumasasikweie and was known to the French as La Grenouille (The Frog), spread a rumour that the Iroquois were inciting the Algonkin of the Ottawa Valley to wage war on the Huron (8:59). The French believed that this story was true and that the Dutch had instigated the Iroquois to do this in order to prevent the Huron from coming to trade on the St. Lawrence (8:61). The Algonkin were clearly anxious to eliminate trade between the Huron and the French, but, as we have already stated, it was not in their own interest to attack the Huron. Therefore, it is reasonable to conclude that unless the Mohawk had miscalculated, it was the Algonkin who invented this rumour. No doubt they hoped that the Huron would become even more uncertain and circumspect in their annual trips to the St. Lawrence if they believed that the Iroquois might be urging the Algonkin to attack them.

In 1635 the Kichesipirini overreached themselves. Once a peace had been arranged with the Mohawk, their next hope was to be able to trade with the Dutch as well as with the French. This not only would have permitted them to bargain for better prices, but would have compelled the French, who tended to slight the Kichesipirini in favour of the Huron, to pay more attention to them. When Oumasasikweie, who had played a leading role in arranging the peace treaty with the Mohawk, tried to slip through the Mohawk country on his way to Fort Orange, he and twenty-two of his companions were slain by the Mohawk (9:95–97). Desrosiers (1947a: 149) suggested that the Dutch had encouraged Oumasasikweie's mission, because they knew that it would force the Mohawk to slay these allies of the French and thus would put an end to friendly relations between the

French and the Mohawk. The Kichesipirini accused two Montagnais of receiving presents from the Iroquois and of having played a role in persuading them to kill Oumasasikweie. These accusations brought the Algonkin and the Montagnais to the brink of war, which was averted only when Du Plessis-Bochart convinced the Kichesipirini of the Montagnais' innocence (Thwaites 1896–1901, 9:245). It seems evident that given the interests of both the Mohawk and the Kichesipirini, external intrigues need not be invoked in order to explain what happened. While it was in the interest of every group of Indians to trade with more than one group of Europeans, no group was sufficiently self-confident that it was prepared to allow enemies, or even potential enemies, to trade with the same European power with which it had an alliance.

Oumasasikweie's death brought an end to the truce between the Mohawk and the Algonkin. In August 1635 it was reported that the Iroquois had attacked the Weskarini (8:59), and in March 1636 the Kichesipirini tried to enlist the support of the Algonkin, Nipissing, and Huron for a war of revenge against the Iroquois. The Nipissing refused to participate, however, because of the extortion that had been practised against them by the Kichesipirini. Help was also not forthcoming from the Huron, in part because the Kichesipirini refused to have dealings with the Attignawantan, whom they accused of having killed some of their men. Mainly, however, the Huron seem to have been angry with the Kichesipirini because of their interference with trade.

Tessouat threatened that he would permit neither the Huron nor the Nipissing to visit the French trading places in future. He further boasted that he was the master of the French and could make them recross the sea, if he so wished (10:75–77). The Huron were not intimidated by these threats and, faced with renewed hostility by the Iroquois, the Kichesipirini and their Algonkin allies eventually were forced to mend their diplomatic fences with the French and the Huron. Though the Huron feared they would not be allowed to use the Ottawa River in 1636, an advance party found that the Algonkin made no attempt to stop them. Thus, after a period of considerable disruption, the patterns of trade and warfare in eastern Canada began to re-acquire the same general pattern they had prior to 1629. The schemes of the Kichesipirini had been decisively crushed and a good working relationship had been restored between the French and the Huron. Except for the influence that the Jesuits now exercised over the government of New France, everything was moving forward as if the British interregnum had never happened.

Chapter 8 The Deadly Harvest

The New Beginning

By an unlucky coincidence, the return of the Jesuits to the Huron country coincided with the beginning of a series of virulent epidemics that were to reduce the Huron population by approximately fifty percent within six years. These same diseases infected all the tribes who had dealings with the French and penetrated along the trade routes into areas no European had yet visited.

Prior to the arrival of the Europeans, the American Indians had never been exposed to many infectious diseases common in the Old World and had little natural immunity against them; hence when these diseases were transmitted to the Indians, they died in great numbers. The most dangerous killer was smallpox although various respiratory illnesses accounted for many deaths. Even childhood diseases that had a low mortality rate in Europe, such as measles, chickenpox, and whooping cough, killed many people of all ages when they broke out in Indian communities. As these diseases gradually spread westward across North America, aboriginal populations were cut drastically. Entire peoples lost their identity through depopulation (Dobyns 1966:410–12; Stearn and Stearn 1945).

Epidemics of this sort may explain the marked decline that took place in the population of the southeastern United States and in the level of cultural development in that area in the sixteenth century (Sauer 1971: 302–3). It has also been suggested though without evidence that epidemics played an important role in the dispersal of the St. Lawrence Iroquoians (Fenton 1940:175). In the summer of 1611 numerous Algonkin died of a fever (Biggar 1922–36, 2:207) and in the winter of 1623–24 many Weskarini perished of disease and hunger in the Ottawa Valley (Wrong 1939:263). It is impossible because of inadequate reports to determine whether or not these were epidemics of European diseases. Although there were such epidemics along the east coast of the United States prior to 1620, there is no evidence of a major epidemic in eastern Canada prior to 1634. Nor is there evidence that the Huron had been affected by European diseases prior to that time. The reason for the swift succession of epidemics beginning in 1634 is unknown, but it may be connected with the rapid increase of European settlement along the eastern seaboard of North America.

While the Indians of eastern Canada died by the thousands between 1634 and 1640, the French rarely became ill and, when they did, they almost always recovered. When the Indians failed to arrest these epidemics with their inadequate pharmacopoeia and rituals that were meant to appease malevolent spirits, they became convinced that they were victims of a powerful witchcraft. Since the French had the power to remain well, or to cure themselves, it seemed inexplicable that they did not use this power to assist the Indians unless they wished to see them die. A remorseless logic, innocent of any knowledge of the varying susceptibility of different populations to the same infection, led the Indians to conclude that the French were using witchcraft to destroy them. Many reasons were suggested why the French should do this and the Indians disagreed whether the French should be appeased or slain as sorcerers. The most fatalistic were the Montagnais around Quebec City, whose hunting territories were becoming depleted and who were increasingly poverty stricken and dependent on the French (Thwaites 1896–1901, 16:93). They were convinced that the French had determined to exterminate them so they could take possession of their land.

THE EPIDEMIC OF 1634

In the summer of 1634 an epidemic, possibly introduced by the ships that had arrived from France in June, began to sweep the St. Lawrence Valley. The oft-repeated claim that the disease was influenza (Talbot 1956:131) is only a layman's guess. Le Jeune described it as "a sort of measles and an oppression of the stomach" (Thwaites 1896–1901, 7:221). Brébeuf stated that among the Indians the disease began with a high fever, followed by a rash and, in some cases, by blindness or impaired vision that lasted for several days and was terminated by diarrhoea. The rash was described as "a sort of measles or smallpox, but different from that common in France" (8:89). The ailment was not smallpox which was recognized immediately when it broke out among the Indians in 1639. Some French became ill, but the symptoms were much milder than among the Indians and all recovered after a few days (7:221). Brébeuf was not even certain that the French and the Indians had suffered from the same disease.

When the Huron arrived at Three Rivers in July 1634, the Montagnais and Algonkin were dying there in large numbers (6:61; 8:87). Before they started for home the disease had spread up the Ottawa Valley, infecting many more Algonkin (7:221). At Three Rivers many of the Huron became ill, which in part explains their reluctance to embark Frenchmen as passengers in their canoes (7:217). Few of the Huron who returned home from Quebec escaped being ill and the epidemic spread through all the Huron villages during the late summer and autumn. So many were sick that fishing and harvesting of crops were seriously impaired and much food was left rotting in the fields. Many who had been ill remained debilitated throughout the winter (8:87–89).

There can be no doubt that many Huron were stricken by this epidemic. Brébeuf stated that he personally did not know anyone who had escaped it and that a large number had died (8:87–89). In spite of this the Jesuits baptized only a few people who they judged were about to die, and the Huron do not seem to have regarded the epidemic as being of unprecedented severity.[1] It is unclear whether the French also overestimated the death rate among the Algonkin and Montagnais or whether, because of their nomadic existence, the latter were physically less fit to withstand this particular epidemic. What does seem certain is that this was the least lethal of the epidemics that were to afflict the Huron in the course of the next six years.

JESUIT POLICY AMONG THE HURON

Brébeuf was a man of courage and physical endurance who combined a humble sense of duty with a mystical temperament and a burning zeal to convert the Indians. Although able to learn languages easily and to express himself well, Brébeuf's most valued qualities were not intellectual ones but those of the heart and will (Latourelle 1966:126). He was neither a politician interested in promoting the welfare of his mission among the powerful in France nor a theoretician anxious to devise the intellectually perfect strategy to convert the Huron. His approach was empirical and based on a belief that sincere effort and personal sacrifice, accompanied by divine favour, would suffice to accomplish the task. On numerous occasions, his reliance on such favour, combined with overzealousness, led him to do tactless things and to expose himself and his co-workers to great danger in their efforts to save souls. Brébeuf's natural conservatism and his former association with Father Daillon probably explain why the Jesuits who went to the Huron country in 1634 carried on their day-to-day work of conversion much as the Recollets had done, in spite of the fundamental differences between the general philosophy of missionary work of the two orders. The implementation of the distinctive features of a Jesuit approach remained to be worked out in the critical years that followed.

Like the Recollets, the Jesuits under Brébeuf's leadership were anxious to usurp the role of shamans by using masses and prayers to stop droughts or otherwise protect crops. They also believed that the best way to convert the Huron was to establish their influence among the young; hence much of their early mission work was concerned with the instruction of children. Like the Recollets, they were convinced that it was necessary for them to live apart from the Huron, although Brébeuf knew that doing so increased the danger of being accused of witchcraft and made it necessary for the Jesuits to buy food and other necessities from the Huron, which otherwise would have been supplied free of charge. While Brébeuf echoed Le Caron's arguments that for missionaries to live permanently with particular households would incite the jealousy of others, he was also aware that a better understanding could flow from this close association with the Huron. Some Jesuits were appalled by the physical discomfort of living with a traditional Huron family, but the discipline of the order was such that these discomforts alone would not have deterred them from such a life if they had believed it necessary to achieve their goals.

What made a prolonged stay in a traditional Huron longhouse an intolerable proposition was not its physical discomfort, but its psychological dangers. On the way to the Huron country, the Huron noted with surprise that the Jesuits were too ashamed to undress in order to wash although only men were present. Nor could the Jesuits endure to see Huron men do so (Thwaites 1896–1901, 13:51). The naked children, the scantily clad women, the bustle of domestic life, and the religious rituals of the Huron were all abhorrent to the priests, who feared their influence and needed a cloister to which they could retire for work and meditation. Even before their departure for the Huron country, Charles Lalemant had ruled out living with Huron families on the simple ground that "religious eyes could not endure the sight of so much lewdness" (4:197).

The Jesuits' own austere life also involved many voluntary forms of self-mortification which would have been difficult to explain to the Huron, even though Huron men were used to vigils, fasting, and testing their courage by means of various ordeals. In spite of such customs, the wearing of belts equipped with iron points next to the skin or self-flagellation once or more a day using a whip with iron points (39:261; 40:23) would have seemed monstrous to them. These were activities that the Jesuits realized it was prudent to perform in seclusion.

In spite of their intellectual accomplishments, the Jesuits believed themselves to be serving a god who could intervene in human affairs at any moment. War, disease, and drought were among the means he employed to advance or hinder human designs. Moreover, while the Jesuits did not believe in magic in the strict sense of thinking that Roman Catholic rituals gave them the power to control nature automatically, they were convinced that their god would answer prayers for rain or good harvests, if this would convince the Indians of his glory and help the priests to undermine the Indians' respect for their own shamans. In their fasts, vigils, and the course of their daily activities God and the saints appeared to these missionaries in visions of compelling realism to offer them advice and encouragement.

In addition to believing in the power of their god, the Jesuits ardently believed in the power of Satan and his attendant devils. The latter were identified with the deities the Huron worshipped and the work of converting the Indians was conceived of as a valiant struggle to liberate them from thraldom to these supernatural enemies. Some Jesuits, including Brébeuf and Jérôme Lalemant, believed that these devils personally opposed their work among the Huron. Sometimes they became incarnate before the eyes of the priests, only to vanish before the sign of the cross. Other Jesuits were more sceptical and tended to explain most of the Huron's behaviour in terms of their "foolishness" or "ignorance of the truth" (33:197). None of them, however, doubted the existence of Satan or the importance of the spiritual war that they were waging against him.

The climacteric event in this struggle was the ritual of baptism. All of the Jesuits who worked among the Huron were convinced that any human being who remained unbaptized was doomed after death to suffer in the fires of hell. Curiously enough, this folk belief had never been affirmed by the church as dogma, and Thomas Aquinas had taught that the unbaptized might put themselves in a state of grace, either by personally choosing good rather than evil or by a sincere act of charity (Robinson, in Du Creux 1951–52:199 n. 2; Thomas Aquinas 1852–73; 13:107, 752). The wretched fate that they believed was facing the unbaptized embued the disciples of Ignatius Loyola with a special sense of militancy as they marched into battle against the devil. An infant who died after being baptized was assured a place in heaven, while for an adult convert there was every hope of salvation, so long as he did not lapse into heretical belief or sinful conduct (Thwaites 1896–1901, 8:169). Thus to baptize the Huron and lead them to heaven was an act of charity for which the Jesuits were willing to court martyrdom (8:175). Martyrdom was viewed as a sacrifice that supernaturally would further their efforts to convert the Huron and might well be vital to achieve that end.

In terms of their beliefs about the supernatural forces that were at work in the world, Jesuit and Huron shared considerably more in common with each other than either does with twentieth-century man, whose values have been moulded in a tradition of rationalism and evolutionary thought. It is precisely because we can now view this clash between the religious ideas of the Huron and the Jesuits dispassionately, that its real nature has become apparent (LeBlanc 1968).

FIRST FRUITS

The Jesuit priests spent the autumn and winter of 1634–35 in Ihonatiria. Although the Huron knew that the epidemics that raged in the autumn had come from Quebec, the Jesuits encountered no hostility, nor did the Huron attempt to avoid contact with them. Much of the time was spent learning the Huron language. Brébeuf could already speak Huron and, prior to leaving Quebec, Davost and Daniel had studied the manuscript material that was available there (Thwaites 1896–1901, 6:37). Throughout the winter of 1634–35, the two newcomers compiled lists of Huron words and, under Brébeuf's direction, practised putting them together to form sentences. The grammatical complexities of Huron and its unfamiliar structure were formidable obstacles to learning the language, but by the spring Brébeuf reported that Davost and Daniel knew as many words as he did, although they could only put a limited number of sentences together in a halting manner (8:131–33).

In October 1634 Brébeuf briefly visited the Tionnontaté, passing through Ossossané and other Huron villages along the way. Likely he accompanied some of the Jesuits' hired men who were also working for the trading company. The aim of their visit was to renew relations between French and Tionnontaté traders and to encourage the latter to come to the Huron country. In the course of his journey, Brébeuf baptized three small dying children (8:135). In mid-January Brébeuf set out from Ihonatiria to visit Amantacha and his father, who had returned to Teanaostaiaé from their disastrous expedition against the Seneca. He was welcomed by Soranhes and Amantacha, but was disappointed to learn that, among his own people, Amantacha was not living according to the Christian principles that he professed whenever he came to Quebec (8:149). As Brébeuf was passing through Onnentisati, he found that Oukhahitoüa, who had brought one of the Jesuits' party to the Huron country the previous summer, was very ill and managed to baptize him shortly before he died (8:139).

In the autumn and winter of 1634–35 the Jesuits baptized ten more Huron. Nine baptisms were in Ihonatiria, the other was in nearby Wenrio. None of the Indians who permitted themselves or their children to be baptized understood the Christian significance of this rite. The Jesuits continued to observe the regulation that only Indians who were obviously dying should be baptized without prolonged instruction and trial of their faith, but the epidemic led the Jesuits to try to save as many souls as possible during it. To elicit the goodwill of the people of Ihonatiria and nearby villages, they distributed their supply of prunes and raisins to the sick and sent their hired men hunting so that they could carry portions of game to the sick (8:149). The good health of the French and the reputation that the priests had already acquired as shamans convinced many Huron that they possessed the power to cure the current illness. Baptism was thus interpreted as a healing rite, similar in nature to those performed by the Atirenda or Awataerohi, and becoming a Christian was viewed as analogous to a sick person joining one of these societies. The only clue that it was different lay in the fact that the Jesuits gave each person they baptized a Christian name. While they did this strictly in accordance with their own beliefs, it was an action that the Huron might have been expected to interpret as symbolizing the assumption of new duties and a new role in society.

The first four people who were baptized lived in the same longhouse as did the child Brébeuf had baptized prior to his departure from the Huron country in 1629. This child had been expected to die, but after being baptized had recovered and was still alive in 1635 (8:135–37). His recovery must have suggested to his relatives that baptism was an effective curing ritual. It is, therefore, not surprising that soon after their return to the Huron country the Jesuits were able to baptize two very young sick girls who were members of this family. Both died soon after, but since shamans were not always successful with their cures this did not seriously impair the Jesuits' reputation (8:133). On 26 October they baptized another resident of the same longhouse, Oquiaendis, who was a grandmother of one of the girls and the mother of Sangwati (10:11), the headman of the village (8:133–35). She recovered soon afterwards, which her family attributed to the shamanistic skills of the Jesuits. After 20 October Joutaya, the father of the boy Brébeuf baptized in 1629, also was baptized. Although near death, he lingered for a considerable time and the prolongation of his life was seen as yet another manifestation of the Jesuits' life-giving powers

(8:135). These results led many other Huron, including ones who were only slightly ill, to clamour for baptism (8:141–43).

On 21 October the Jesuits baptized Sondaarouhané, a man forty to fifty years old, who survived for about a month, and Tsindacaiendoua, who was said to be about eighty and who died the next day (8:137). Another old man, Tsicok, was baptized 27 November and died in mid-December (8:139). Following this, either because the epidemic had run its course in Ihonatiria or because the Huron had lost faith in the efficacy of the ritual, there were no more baptisms until late March when Oatij, a young man who had been ill since the autumn, was baptized. He died a few weeks later (8:139). This was followed by the baptism of Tsindacaiendoua's daughter who was living in Wenrio (8:141) and of his grandnephew in Ihonatiria (8:155). The latter recovered, to the joy of the missionaries, who hoped that this would refute the growing opinion that no one could hope to recover from an illness after being baptized.

The latter opinion was encouraged by the emphasis that the Jesuits placed on the after-life in the instructions that preceded baptism. This suggested to the Huron that baptism might not be a curing ritual but one designed to send the soul of the sick person to the realms of the dead. The degree to which one or the other interpretation was believed depended largely on the experiences of friends and relatives, but the Jesuit policy of baptizing only those who were gravely ill seemed to support the more sinister interpretation.

The Huron were also troubled when the Jesuits told them that the souls of the baptized would go to heaven rather than to the traditional Huron villages of the dead. The idea of alternative destinations for human souls was not unfamiliar to the Huron, who believed that some souls, such as those of the very young, the very old, and of people who had died violent deaths, lived apart from the majority of the Huron dead. Such differences had no ethical significance, however, and the Huron no doubt interpreted the notion of Christians' souls going to heaven in this ethically neutral sense also. It is significant in this regard that while most Huron did not question the Jesuits' claims about heaven, few appear to have taken seriously their claim that non-Christian Huron would go, not to the villages of the dead, but to a fiery hell.[2] The Jesuits further emphasized the dichotomy between the after-lives of traditional Huron and Christians when they gained permission to bury Tsindacaiendoua and Joutaya with Christian rites and in a place removed from the village cemetery of Ihonatiria.

The emphasis that the Jesuits placed on the separation of Christians and non-Christians after death influenced individual Huron in opposed ways. Many were loath to be baptized if they believed that this would cut them off from friends and relatives who had already died without being baptized; for example, after Joutaya had been baptized, he dreamt that one of his dead brothers was reproaching him for having chosen not to live with him after death (8:137–39). On the other hand, once baptized Huron had died, some relatives were motivated to seek baptism so as not to be separated from them after death. The desire of Tsindacaiendoua's daughter to follow him played an important role in her "conversion" (8:141) and similar considerations may have influenced his family to allow the Jesuits to baptize his grandnephew.

Thus differing opinions as to whether baptism was a curative ritual or showed people the way to heaven and the desire to join particular kinsmen after death led some Huron to seek baptism and others to oppose it. These opinions tended to run in families and to reflect their particular experiences. Only a small number of Huron were compelled to make such decisions and, as the winter wore on, most sick people seem to have avoided contact with the Jesuits until they could ascertain better what was going on. There is no evidence of personal animosity being expressed, either individually or collectively, towards the Jesuits at this time. Not enough Huron were yet involved nor had the epidemic been serious enough to make this a vital public issue.

A PUBLIC WITNESS

In early December, after the people of Ihonatiria had settled down for the winter, Brébeuf began preaching to them. Periodically, men, women, and children were invited to the Jesuits' cabin, either by a public announcement or by the ringing of a hand-bell. Male attendance was encouraged in traditional Huron fashion by the liberal dispensation of tobacco (Thwaites 1896–1901, 13:141, 219), which, moreover, was a scarce commodity at that time (10:301). When an audience had gathered, the Jesuits chanted the Lord's Prayer in Huron and the children were invited to participate in a catechism at which a good performance was rewarded with highly valued glass and wampum beads. The Huron were happy to see their children win such prizes and encouraged them to learn the correct answers; indeed, some adults learned the answers themselves so they could teach them to their children (10:25). To set an example for the Huron, the two French boys who had been sent to learn the Huron language were made to participate in these catechisms. The principal message that the Jesuits sought to convey at this time was the choice that each person had of going to heaven or hell after death. By speaking so much about death, the Jesuits manifested a preoccupation with a topic that adult Huron found worrisome and repugnant (8:143–45).

The Jesuits concluded their sessions by soliciting the reactions of the headmen and old men of the village. They were exasperated by the way in which these men would approve of their teachings, and sometimes even ask for more instruction, but then refuse to renounce their old ways (10:17–19, 25). Some Huron attempted to harmonize their traditional beliefs with the teachings of Christianity, such as a man who stated that he had learned in a dream that all the Huron souls had left the villages of the dead and gone to heaven (8:147). The older men, who were most knowledgeable about Huron beliefs, explained them to the Jesuits, and must have been offended when Brébeuf repeatedly used such occasions to censure and ridicule what they were saying. The Huron reminded the Jesuits that they had different customs and should respect each other's beliefs (8:147). Every Huron, when pressed by the Jesuits to explain why he believed something, replied that it was the custom of his country and soon the Huron began to complain that the Jesuits were seeking to overturn the Huron way of life (10:27). The Jesuits did not realize that the Huron approved of what they said from a sense of politeness which they expected the French to reciprocate. Instead, they concluded that the Huron were so attached to their old ways that they were content to recognize the truthfulness of the Christian religion without embracing it.

As the Jesuits acquired more linguistic skills they began to visit the houses in Ihonatiria daily to instruct the women and children. They attempted to teach the children to cross themselves and to recite a few simple prayers, which were no doubt memorized because they were believed to be shamanistic spells. Religious services were held for the children every Sunday morning and in the afternoon they were taught the Ledesma catechism. Many children attended these sessions, obviously drawn there by material rewards and by their curiosity to observe the behaviour of the strange newcomers (10:19–25).

The Jesuits attempted to provide separate instruction for older men, whom they were anxious to convert since they managed the public affairs of the village (10:15). At first these men listened to them more attentively than the women and children did; but, as the winter progressed, they became so engrossed in their own councils and in the traditional round of feasts, dances, and games that it became increasingly difficult to draw them together to discuss religion. Moreover, while these men continued to listen politely to what the Jesuits had to say, it was impossible to persuade them to become Christians (10:15–19).

The open hostility of the Jesuits towards Huron religious beliefs eventually began to create serious difficulties with the people of Ihonatiria. In January 1636 a man named Ihongwaha became psychologically disturbed after he public-spiritedly had broken a fast designed to make him a master shaman in order to perform an Awataerohi curing ceremony for a sick person in the village. When three or four public curing ceremonies failed to alleviate Ihongwaha's difficulties, many Huron said that the Jesuits were to blame because they had condemned these rituals and thereby rendered them ineffective (10:199–201). The wrongdoing that the Huron were objecting to was not religious intolerance, which had no meaning for them, but rather opposition to helping a member of one's own community regain his health. To the Huron, such behaviour was little different from witchcraft.

In the spring of 1635 the Jesuits offered presents to the headmen of Ihonatiria and Wenrio urging them to settle their differences and re-establish a single village (8:105). Aenons, in particular, wished the two villages to unite and the Jesuits approved the scheme because it would permit them to minister to a larger number of people more easily and eliminate the rivalry between the headmen of these villages as to where the Jesuits should live. Moreover, Brûlé's murder had been the cause of Toanché splitting apart and the Jesuits wanted the Huron to forget that this event had ever happened. Yet, while the reunification of these villages was discussed at intervals over the next several years, nothing came of it. Having just erected new houses and cleared new land, few Huron were prepared to relocate until a longer interval had passed.

About this time, Brébeuf was invited to join a delegation made up of representatives of all the Huron tribes that was on its way to the Seneca country to reaffirm the recent peace treaty between them (8:117). Since the French were allied with the Huron it was appropriate that Brébeuf should have been invited to participate in this mission. Brébeuf refused to go, however, to avoid giving the Huron cause to suspect the Jesuits of being other than missionaries. No doubt remembering Daillon's difficulties, Brébeuf was anxious not to suggest that he might wish to have dealings with the Seneca.

The winter of 1634–35 was short and mild (8:155) and was followed by scarcely any rain from the end of March until the middle of June (10:35). According to Heidenreich (et al. 1969:121), this was the worst drought on record in the first half of the seventeenth century. Because of the extreme dryness, houses caught fire easily. Two Huron villages were totally consumed by flames within ten days and the large town of Teanaostaiaé was partly destroyed (Thwaites 1896–1901, 8:105). The Jesuits' own cabin caught on fire, although the blaze was quickly put out.

Because of the drought, crops were failing and the whole Huron confederacy feared a famine over the coming winter. Villages and tribes sought help from reputable shamans. Brébeuf's former rival, Tehorenhaegnon, promised to produce rain if he were given a present worth ten iron axes and the appropriate ceremonies were performed. As in 1628, these ceremonies failed to produce rain and Tehorenhaegnon blamed his failure on the cross that the Jesuits had erected in front of their cabin. He also accused the Jesuits of being sorcerers whose sole purpose in coming to the Huron country was to make the Huron die. This charge was also pressed by Huron not living in Ihonatiria, who reported that the Algonkin were attributing the epidemic of the previous autumn to a spell that the French had cast on the Huron. Certain Huron told the Jesuits that they should take down their cross and threatened that if the crops did not mature they would be slain as sorcerers. There were also rumours that certain Huron planned to tear down the cross themselves (10:35–39).

Within Ihonatiria, however, there was considerable support for the Jesuits and the people of the village asked the Jesuits to make rain for them, as Brébeuf had done in the past. Brébeuf told them that if they resolved to abandon their traditional behaviour and to serve God as he would instruct them, the Jesuits would offer a novena of masses and organize a procession to implore divine assistance. Nine days later, as the procession was making its way through the village, rain began to fall and showers continued for about a month. There was a further drought in the latter half of July, but after another novena was begun this drought was also broken and there was a plentiful harvest (10:39–43). These apparently successful ventures in rainmaking silenced the rumours that had been circulating against the Jesuits and greatly enhanced their reputation as shamans. They also belittled the power of the native arendiwane who had failed to produce rain.

THE SUMMER PROGRAM

Efforts to proselytize the Huron were suspended temporarily in the summer of 1635, when the Huron men left the villages to trade and wage war and the women went with their children to tend their fields. As they were to do each year thereafter, the Jesuits withdrew to their cabin to perform their spiritual exercises and consolidate their knowledge of the Huron language. The latter involved drafting dictionaries and grammars, based on what each Jesuit had learned from the Huron (Thwaites 1896–1901, 10:55), rather than on the manuscript studies of the Recollets, which were now judged to be inadequate. These works served as a record of what had been accomplished and made it easier for newcomers to learn the language. Nor were the latter long in arriving. In August 1635 Fathers François-Joseph Le Mercier and Pierre Pijart joined the mission. Responsible headmen had taken charge of these men at Three Rivers and consequently they were well-treated on their journey to the Huron country (10:57). They too began to study the Huron language. The Jesuits viewed the ability to express themselves as an essential weapon in their battle against Satan. Language learning was therefore an endeavour in which individual priests expected and claimed to experience supernatural aid (19:129).

Throughout the year the Jesuits spent much time listening to native conversations in the hope of catching new words and phrases. Often they had to interrupt such conversations to ask for explanations. They did this with such enthusiasm that in 1637 Brébeuf had to warn missionaries travelling to the Huron country not to trouble their Indian travelling companions by asking them too many questions (12:119). Like modern linguists, the Jesuits also worked with selected native informants, recording and analysing their answers to questions and reading material back to them. Whole narratives were taken down from these informants so that the style of the language, as well as formal points of grammar, might be investigated (21:225). In later years, these informants were often converts.

The study and preparation of manuscript grammars and dictionaries continued to be an essential first step for each Jesuit in learning the Huron language. This was followed by the translation into Huron of liturgical texts, songs, prayers, and catechisms, and later by the translation of important Biblical passages, homilies, and rites. In order to produce accurate translations, these works were read to native informants before being used and were revised by a succession of priests, each of whom attempted to improve the work of his predecessor (Hanzeli 1969:53).

In the course of translating Roman Catholic dogma into the Huron language, numerous problems were encountered. For example, the obligatory use of person markers in Huron made impossible a literal translation of the expression "Father, Son, and Holy Spirit." After a painstaking review of church teaching, the Jesuits suggested that the phrase might be translated "our Father, his Son, and their Holy Spirit" (10:119); however, the implementation of this proposal required approval from ecclesiastical officials in Europe. Huron linguistic etiquette also had to be learned and respected. This included not referring to God as Father in the presence of a Huron whose own father was dead, since under this circumstance even inadvertent references to a father constituted a serious affront (10:121).

Individual Jesuits had varying linguistic ability. Brébeuf, Chaumonot, and Daniel displayed outstanding talent, while Chabanel and de Noüe had exceptional difficulties. Even a man endowed with linguistic skills, such as Daniel, required more than six months to acquire a rudimentary working knowledge of Huron, while, after living among the Huron for three and a half years, Brébeuf's knowledge was far from perfect. In 1723 Father Sébastien Rasles was to express the opinion that even with the initial aid of a good grammar, a missionary was fortunate if he could speak eloquently after ten years of study (67:147).

During the summer, the Jesuits also had a chance to review their impressions of Huron life and to decide what changes were necessary if the Huron were to become Christians. Although the Jesuits totally disapproved of Huron religious beliefs, as yet they had no awareness of the degree to which these beliefs penetrated every sphere of Huron life. Instead, they confined themselves to approving, or seeing the need to abolish, specific customs. They were pleased to find that the Huron practised monogamy and avoided marrying blood relatives in direct or collateral lines (8:119). They also believed that the Huron's sexual modesty, their stoicism, and their generosity to one another and to strangers offered hope of producing Christians whose behaviour was in certain respects superior to that of Europeans (8:127–31). On the other hand, the Jesuits disapproved of what they felt was laziness and a lack of respect for private property (8:127) and were determined that divorce (8:119–21), blood feuds, and torture (10:227) be abolished. While some of the changes that the Jesuits believed were necessary, such as the abolition of divorce, might have been effected solely through religious conversion and a change in values, others, such as the abolition of blood feud, would have required a far-reaching remodelling of Huron society along European lines. Thus, while the Jesuits laid far less emphasis on the assimilation of French culture than the Recollets had, their tacit identification of European and Christian values often led them to view Europeanizing (or "civilizing") the Indians as part of their general work of conversion (10:27). Even at this early period, the Jesuits' concept of conversion was implicitly committing them to a far more extensive program of trying to alter Huron life than they themselves foresaw.

BEING USEFUL

Although the Huron now had a truce with the Seneca, who were tradition-ally their principal enemies, peace did not materialize with the other four Iroquois tribes. There was fear of raids even in Ihonatiria, although it lay far from the frontier of the Huron country. One alarm lasted through June 1635 and seems to have been caused by a few Iroquois raiders. Another alarm, the following winter, turned out to be without foundation (Thwaites 1896–1901, 10:49–53). The inhabitants of Ihonatiria were, on both occasions, ready to disperse in the forest or to take refuge in the nearest fortified village. These threats were regarded as sufficiently serious that in February 1636 the young men of Ihonatiria were expected to help construct a palisade around Angoutenc (10:203). This village, located not far from Ossossané (Heidenreich 1966:121), appears to have supplanted Quieunonascaran and Toanché as the principal village of the northern Attignawantan.

The Jesuits won the approval of the Attignawantan by supplying them with iron arrowheads and promising that if the Iroquois attacked, their hired men would defend the threatened village with their muskets (Thwaites 1896–1901, 10:53). In this way the Jesuits not only honoured Champlain's promises to help the Huron, but appropriated the credit for doing so. Their ability to command armed men gave substance to the stories that French traders told about the power of the priests to defeat the Huron's enemies.

Brébeuf also urged the Huron to erect square palisades around their towns. In this way, a few Frenchmen armed with muskets could defend even a large settlement from towers erected at the four corners. The Huron are reported to have applied this advice when Ossossané was relocated about a quarter of a league north of its previous position in the spring of 1635 (10:53; 8:101; Heidenreich, personal communication 1972). The fortifications of the new Ossossané were apparently under construction in 1637, when Charles Garnier wrote that two towers, made of about thirty poles each, were being built at the corners of the ramparts, so that each would command two sides of the enclosure (Jones 1908:306; plate 32). While this was a modification of Brébeuf's original plan, it was a strategi-cally sound one that would have permitted two or more gunmen to defend the perimeter of the town. We are also informed that the palisade around the new Ossossané was of stakes ten or twelve feet high and about six inches thick. The use of larger posts appears to be yet another change

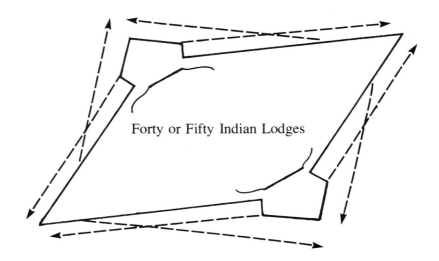

Forty or Fifty Indian Lodges

PLATE 32. *A. E. Jones's reconstruction of the fortifications erected under Jesuit guidance at Ossossané c. 1637. Jones bases this reconstruction on letters by Charles Garnier. From* Wendake Ehen, *p. 306. Courtesy Archives of Ontario.*

brought about by European technology. It is unclear how widespread quadrilateral palisade construction became, but it seems likely that other communities would have copied what was done at Ossossané, in the hope that the French would protect them too. Jury (and Jury 1954:28; 1955) claims to see evidence of French influence in the fortifications and layout of houses at the site he has identified as the small village of St. Louis, burned in 1649. At the same period, Taenhatentaron was regarded as impregnable because of the defences the French had constructed there (Thwaites 1896–1901, 39:247). This suggests, although it does not prove, that the Jesuits may have initiated considerable changes in military architecture throughout the Huron country after 1635.

The Huron particularly appreciated the renewed French protection of their villages because of some small defeats they had suffered in the spring of 1636. Twelve warriors who were members of a group that was on its way to attack the Iroquois were killed in the night on the southern borders of the Huron country (10:83). After Easter, Amantacha and his uncle joined a raid against the Iroquois, in the course of which Amantacha was again taken prisoner (10:81). While some of his relatives maintained that he had been killed, others believed that he was still alive and had been adopted by a Mohawk family (14:45–47). No more was heard of him, and it may be assumed that he was killed by torture. His death was a serious loss for the Attigneenongnahac and for the Huron as a whole, since it meant that their council chiefs and traders no longer had the advice of a man who, although young, had a far more detailed knowledge of European ways than any other Huron was to acquire prior to their dispersal.

The Jesuits deeply regretted Amantacha's death. In the autumn of 1635 he had expressed the desire to lead a more Christian life and, to prove his sincerity, he said that he wished to spend the winter living with the Jesuits at Quebec. He apparently did this because his father was anxious to forge closer ties with the French to allow him to ask for more European goods in return for his furs. Although Amantacha found an excuse not to go to Quebec, he spent part of the winter living with the Jesuits at Ihonatiria (10:31). There he assisted them by translating some catechisms into Huron and by acting as their interpreter (14:11). He also began to pray, confess, and attend mass regularly. Finally, he spent Holy Week with the Jesuits, prior to setting out for the Iroquois country (10:81). Such behaviour convinced the Jesuits that he was once more a sincere Christian and that his death represented the loss of considerable support for their mission.

Huron fear of the Iroquois was intensified in August 1636, when an eclipse of the moon that appeared in the southeast was interpreted as the omen of a grievous defeat for them (10:59). The shaman Tehorenhaegnon organized a great feast in an effort to turn aside the unluckiness of the eclipse.

RELIGION AND POLITICS

Although Brébeuf visited Teanaostaiaé and Scanonaenrat in the autumn of 1635 (Thwaites 1896–1901, 10:11), the Jesuits spent their second year in the Huron country, as they had their first, in Ihonatiria. At first they continued to baptize a few children and adults who appeared to be dying. Among those who did die was Sangwati, the headman of Ihonatiria (10:11–13).

In spite of the occasional baptism, the Jesuits feared that their mission work would be jeopardized when they realized that most of the people of Ihonatiria and Wenrio had become convinced that baptism would shorten their lives. To counteract this fear, the Jesuits decided to baptize some young children who either were ill but seemed likely to recover or had shown a special interest in their catechisms. The recovery of a pregnant woman who was extremely ill, after she had agreed to be baptized, marked another turning point in the northern Attignawantan's attitude towards baptism (10:67). On 8 December 1635, three young girls were baptized, and, before the end of the month, twenty-seven more people had been (10:69). Of the eighty-six Huron who were baptized between the summers of 1635 and 1636, ten or fewer died, four being adults. This makes it possible that as many as eighty baptisms were of children (10:11).

The Huron began to believe that baptism was a ritual that protected children against sickness and misfortune (10:13, 73) and children were brought to the Jesuits from distant parts of the country. While the Jesuits knew that the parents interpreted baptism as a physical healing ritual, they saw in their work the saving of many souls, particularly if the children should die young. They also hoped that by reminding the Huron, at a later date, that the souls of baptized children would be separated forever from those of non-Christians, they might persuade the parents of these children to want to become Christians (10:31). In order to increase the respect that the Huron had for baptism, the Jesuits made it a rule to baptize healthy children only at solemn ceremonies in their own chapel (10:83). Because of this new policy and a healthy winter, the Jesuits soon found themselves cleared of all former suspicions and their rituals again popular as good shamanistic practices.

As a result of their growing popularity, in the spring of 1636 the Jesuits received numerous invitations to live elsewhere than in Ihonatiria. These came from the Arendarhonon and from important towns such as Teanaostaiaé and Ossossané (10:235); however, the most persistent invitation was from Aenons who won the Jesuits' support for a plan to have the five small villages in the northern part of the Penetanguishene Peninsula, including Wenrio and Ihonatiria, join together to form a single town that could be fortified against the Iroquois (8:105; 10:245). Aenons hoped that if he could persuade the Jesuits to move to Wenrio that village would become the nucleus of the new town and his claim to be its principal headman would be assured. He pointed out that since Sangwati's death, there was no experienced headman in Ihonatiria who could protect the Jesuits and ensure they were treated properly; on the other hand, in the new town, Aenons promised to see that they were provided with all the food they needed and with transportation to and from Quebec (10:241–43).

To convert the Huron, Brébeuf was prepared to follow the example of early Christian missionaries and, where it seemed appropriate, to treat the matter as a political issue. He announced that the Jesuits did not look with disfavour on the plan to found a new village, but they were unwilling to commit themselves to live in that community unless the headmen of the five villages would pledge that they and their "subjects" would become Christians (10:245). Brébeuf still misunderstood the nature of Huron society and believed that headmen had the power to treat clansmen as subjects and commit them to a predetermined course of action. The Jesuits were not present at the council that met to discuss the move, but later were informed that the headmen had agreed to their proposal and were coming to transport the Jesuits to the site of the new town (10:245–47). Yet in spite of this conference, the planned merger of the villages did not take place and soon Aenons was asking the Jesuits to move to Wenrio and settle in his longhouse (10:247). Most of the people the Jesuits had baptized were living in Ihonatiria and the various disputes that were troubling the northern Attignawantan made any move a delicate matter. The Jesuits therefore decided to remain at Ihonatiria for another year (10:247). This pleased the inhabitants of the village so much that they enlarged and repaired the Jesuits' now dilapidated cabin, while accepting only a portion of the presents that the Jesuits offered them. All the men of the village, young and old, joined in this work and completed it within three days (10:247–49).

The transferring of Ossossané to a new location in the spring of 1635 was the occasion for the celebration of a Feast of the Dead among the Attignawantan. During the winter, meetings were held to make arrangements for this feast and at one of them Aenons was commissioned to ask the Jesuits if the bodies of Guillaume Chaudron and Etienne Brûlé might be disinterred and reburied with the Attignawantan. Among the Huron, the burial of their dead in a common grave constituted the most solemn expression of friendship between two groups of people. If the Jesuits would agree, the Attignawantan and the French would be united by the most sacred of alliances (10:305).

To their surprise, Brébeuf did not accept this proposal. He explained to Aenons that church regulations forbade that Christians and non-Christians be buried together and that it was not a Christian custom to raise the bodies of the dead (10:305). Seeming to meet the Huron halfway, Brébeuf offered to rebury Chaudron and Brûlé near the Ossossané ossuary, but only provided that all the Huron who had died after being baptized could be buried in the same separate grave with them. Brébeuf hoped that in future such a precedent would make it easier to persuade converts to have their bodies interred separately from those of non-Christians and in cemeteries specifically consecrated for that purpose. He also believed that by reburying these bodies within the context of the Feast of the Dead, he could claim official sanction for the public performance of other Roman Catholic rituals and that by erecting a cross over the grave, the Huron would be compelled to honour it publicly. In this way, the Huron might be dissuaded from abusing or desecrating other crosses that the Jesuits might erect (10:305–7). What Brébeuf did not reveal to Aenons was that he had serious moral reservations about moving Brûlé's body, since this would require giving the renegade a Christian burial (10:309–11). Aenons and the other Attignawantan headmen agreed to Brébeuf's proposal. Nevertheless, since the Huron regarded the mingling of bodies as a symbol of unity and friendship, it is highly unlikely that Brébeuf's emphasis on the ritual separation of Christians and non-Christians either pleased or reassured them.

Towards spring a quarrel broke out between the headmen of the five northernmost Attignawantan villages and those of the rest of the tribe. According to Brébeuf, the northern headmen complained that they were being excluded from secret councils and were not receiving a fair share of the reparations payments and other gifts that were made to the tribe as a whole (10:281). Because of this quarrel, the five northern villages decided to hold their own Feast of the Dead (10:307). It is not certain, however, that the Feast of the Dead was necessarily a tribal ritual and the celebration of separate feasts by the major Attignawantan villages may have been more common than Brébeuf surmised. The proposal that Brébeuf mentions for a single feast embracing all the Attignawantan villages may have been an innovation reflecting a growing sense of tribal unity as a result of the fur trade. Alternatively, it is possible that the argument between Aenons and Anenkhiondic, who were apparently the headmen in charge of the Feast of the Dead in their respective areas, was never about whether there should be two feasts or one, but about the role that each division of the Attignawantan should play in the other's feast. Aenons seems to have nurtured a personal grievance about the southern Attignawantan spoiling an earlier feast he had arranged.

In April, Brébeuf was invited to be present when the principal Attignawantan met to discuss the Feast of the Dead one more time. Brébeuf took advantage of this opportunity to draw attention to Champlain's exhortations of 1635 that all Huron should become Christians if they wished to seal their alliance with the French, and that they should send some Huron children to Quebec the following summer to be instructed by the Jesuits. After preaching a sermon, Brébeuf presented the council with a collar [3] of 1200 wampum beads that he said was to smooth the way to heaven for the Huron (10:27–29). Although one headman replied that no Huron was enough of a coward to fear torture in the Jesuits' hell (10:29–30), the acceptance of this collar, and the nominal approval of what Brébeuf had said, convinced the Jesuits that these headmen had no strong objections to Brébeuf's teachings or to his proposals. Presumably the Huron respected the right of their French trading partners to ask for Huron children in return for the Jesuits; however, aside from their desire to preserve and strengthen their alliance with the French and to be polite, these headmen manifested no positive enthusiasm for Brébeuf's proposals.

At this same meeting, Brébeuf was asked about a matter that had evidently become a subject of controversy among Attignawantan: did the French wish to rebury their dead at Ossossané or at the Feast of the Dead that the five northern villages were planning to celebrate? Brébeuf tactfully left the solution of this problem to the Attignawantan headmen, who eventually decided that Chaudron's body should be buried at Ossossané where he had died, while Brûlé should remain in the north. In the course of the discussion, one of the southern Attignawantan was heard to remark that it was appropriate that Aenons should honour Brûlé's bones since it was he who had murdered him. Although the meeting proceeded in an orderly fashion, once it was over a bitter quarrel broke out between Aenons and Anenkhiondic. In his anxiety not to reopen the dispute about who had killed Brûlé, Aenons ceased to lay claim to his body. Anenkhiondic and the Jesuits jointly decided that under the circumstances, neither Brûlé nor Chaudron ought to be buried at Ossossané, and the whole question of a separate Christian burial was dropped (10:307–9).

Brébeuf states that the five northern Attignawantan villages celebrated their own Feast of the Dead in 1636. Yet he does not describe the northern ceremony and it is uncertain that the French attended it. After the quarrel between Aenons and Anenkhiondic, Brébeuf and Anenkhiondic were on good terms (10:309), but some Huron were furious that no Frenchmen were reinterred, since this prevented them from claiming to be kinsmen of the French and foreign tribes would say that there was no real friendship between the Huron and the French (10:311). These sound like the sentiments of Aenons and his people, who remained in disrepute about the murder of Brûlé. Still, the Jesuits mention attending only one Feast of the Dead in the fifteen years they lived in the Huron country; hence their failure to mention attending this northern Attignawantan one may be simply an oversight.

They did attend, and describe in detail, the ceremony at Ossossané (10:279–305). That bodies were taken from Ihonatiria to Ossossané for burial does not contradict the assertion that Ihonatiria and neighbouring villages had their own ossuary; the bodies were probably of people who had been born in the eight or nine southern villages, but had gone to live in the north after marriage. Although given temporary burials in the cemeteries of the villages in which they died, most people were probably interred in the ossuary of the community into which they had been born. Having failed to secure a separate ossuary for the Huron they had baptized, the Jesuits were to witness fifteen or twenty such bodies buried without Christian rites in the Ossossané pit.

During the ceremony, Anenkhiondic offered the Jesuits a beaver robe in return for the collar Brébeuf had given to the Attignawantan; however, Brébeuf refused the gift and told Anenkhiondic that the only thing the Jesuits wished in return was for the Huron to become Christians. Even if Christianity were perceived by the Huron merely as a healing ritual or as the expression of an alliance with the French, the Jesuits had already made their intentions plain enough that such a remark could only be interpreted as further evidence of their desire to undermine Huron traditions.

Early in the summer of 1636 there was so much talk of war with the Iroquois as well as concern about Algonkin hostility that the Jesuits feared the Huron might not go to trade with the French that year (13:7). Yet, as noted in chapter 7, Aenons succeeded in restoring a working relationship with the Kichesipirini, and he and six other Huron continued on to Three Rivers. Aenons and a Huron named Kionché agreed to transport Fathers Pierre Chastellain and Charles Garnier to the Huron country (9:251). Like Pijart and Le Mercier the year before, these missionaries were well-treated on the journey. They were allowed to wear shoes, although the Huron usually made Frenchmen travel bare-footed, so as not to injure their canoes (9:277). As a matter of course, the French now provided each canoe in which a priest was travelling with a sheet that could be used as a sail. This was done to compensate for the priests not paddling.

While Aenons and his companions headed down the Ottawa River from Morrison Island, two Huron returned to Georgian Bay to inform the other traders that the Ottawa River was open again (9:247). By late July, many Huron and a large quantity of furs were ready to depart for the St. Lawrence. Fathers Daniel and Davost and several hired men accompanied the crews as they set out in small groups (9:273–75; 13:9). On route, they were joined by some Nipissing traders. When the first Huron reached Morrison Island, they learned that Tessouat had died and the Kichesipirini once again were not allowing the inland tribes to use the river. These Huron remained where they were until Father Daniel arrived; he negotiated with the Kichesipirini and secured the latter's agreement that they might continue down-river, presumably without having to present the immoderate condolence presents that the Kichesipirini were demanding (9:275–77). In a letter that he wrote while supervising the passage of the Huron past Morrison Island, Father Daniel noted that the role the French played in this sort of difficulty helped to convince the Huron that it was important for the Jesuits to remain in their country (9:273). Father Daniel and the vanguard of the Huron traders arrived at Three Rivers on 19 August.

In spite of this, Huron traders continued to straggle down-river until well into September. Since a permanent French settlement had been established at Three Rivers, they knew that they would be able to trade there no matter how late in the year they arrived. Father Davost did not reach Three Rivers until late August and it is possible that he had become involved in the rituals for installing the new Tessouat (12:125). Although none of the Huron visited Quebec on official business that year, their headmen began their councils with the French at Three Rivers by presenting gifts to Du Plessis–Bochart to condole the French for the death of Champlain and to renew the friendship they had made with him many

years before (9:281–83). The new governor, Charles Huault de Montmagny, was not at Three Rivers, but it may have been on this occasion that
he was given the name Onontio or "Great Mountain," a literal translation
of Montmagny (20:221). The name is not attested, however, before 1640.
One wonders if it was because of Jesuit influence that his name, rather than
Champlain's, was the one that the Huron, and later the Iroquois, were to
apply to all the governors of New France.

When the commercial trading was over, a second set of councils was
convened, at which it was the custom for the French to present their
counter-gifts and discuss their business with the Huron. The usual presents
were given to encourage the good treatment of the Jesuit missionaries and
to ensure that the Huron would return to Three Rivers the following
summer. As usual, the traders from Ossossané demanded to know why no
Frenchmen had come to live with them. To try to satisfy them, they were
given the lucrative task of transporting Father Isaac Jogues to the Huron
country.

THE JESUITS AS SCHOOLMASTERS

Since at least 1635, one of the Jesuits' main goals had been to gain custody
of a number of Huron children whom they could instruct for one or more
years. The Jesuits already knew that the Huron respected old people more
than young ones and that all important matters of public concern were
regulated by mature males (Thwaites 1896–1901, 10:15). Brébeuf had also
learned from experience that it was easier to discuss theological questions
with men than with women and children (10:19). In spite of this, the
Jesuits clung to the Recollets' belief that the long-term hope for converting
the Huron lay in influencing the children, who were as yet uncorrupted by
traditional beliefs (10:21). In spite of their equivocal experience with
Amantacha, they were determined to secure more Huron children to train
as a corps of missionary assistants (8:181).

To ensure necessary isolation from their families, Le Jeune argued that
Montagnais children should be sent to France for two years of training
(6:85–89), while Huron should be brought to Quebec (6:153–55). The
resulting separation from their families would give the Jesuits a free hand
to instruct these children in the French language and customs, since their
relatives would be unable to carry them off whenever they wished. Le
Jeune feared that the Indians would object to their children being scolded
and physically punished, which he regarded as essential to their education.

He also argued that the children would experience fewer distractions if they were removed from their own people and that the Huron children would serve as hostages to ensure that the Jesuits and their assistants were well-treated. No doubt, the Jesuits wished to send some Huron children to France for additional training, but after the delays in returning Amantacha to his family, such a request would likely have been turned down by the Huron.

In 1635 Etienne Binet, the French Provincial of the Society of Jesus, authorized Le Jeune to open a school for Indian children at Quebec, since donations were now available to support such an enterprise.[4] The Jesuits judged this project to be of such great importance that it was decided that Fathers Daniel and Davost should return to Quebec to instruct these children, although they were the missionaries who, next to Brébeuf, had been in the Huron country the longest and who best knew the Huron language (13:9). The Jesuits began to give special instruction to twelve young boys from Ihonatiria whom they wished to take with them (9:283; 12:39). No girls were chosen, because there were as yet no nuns at Quebec. The Huron were also probably unwilling to allow girls to be taken to Quebec, since this involved exposing them to a dangerous canoe voyage and to life among a strange, and therefore potentially hostile, people. Dangers of this sort were appropriate adventures for young men, but not for young women.

Only one youth seemed anxious to go with the Jesuits. This was Satouta, the grandson of the council chief Tsondechaouanouan, who was entrusted with all matters pertaining to foreign peoples whom the Huron visited by water, and in whose name the Huron sent formal messages to other tribes and confederacies (12:53–55). Satouta was nearly an adult and was in line to inherit his grandfather's office, which would require him to have many dealings with the French. It is therefore not surprising that in his desire to secure the Jesuits' goodwill, he said he was willing even to go to France, if they should wish it (12:41).

When the time came to depart, the women of the households that these twelve boys came from raised so many objections that only three of the twelve boys were permitted to embark with their fathers or uncles (9:283; 12:41). The departure of these boys was a matter of vital concern to their extended families, and in family matters Huron women had a strong voice. The key role ascribed to the grandmothers, or head women, of these households, clearly indicates that matrilineal and matrilocal principles remained important among the Huron. When the trading at Three Rivers was over, Satouta was the only boy whose male relatives were willing to let him stay with the French. To honour Satouta and encourage other Huron to leave their children with them, the French, in defiance of Huron custom, gave him seating precedence ahead of Huron headmen at formal meetings. In spite of this, the relatives of the two other children made excuses for taking them home with them (9:285). Du Plessis-Bochart rebuked such behaviour for showing a lack of trust in the French. He promised that if the Huron allowed up to twenty children to come to Quebec, he would send an equal number of armed Frenchmen to defend the Huron villages (9:287). Since only three children were present, it is difficult to know whether or not this promise was made in good faith.

Father Daniel warned the Huron headmen that by refusing to leave these children with the French, they were breaking pledges they had made to the Jesuits both individually and in council. To maintain the alliance the Huron must send some of their own people to live with the French, in return for the French who were sent to live with them. This appeal to Huron traditions, accompanied by much individual persuasion, finally resulted in the two other youths being left with the Jesuits. News of this decision encouraged a spirit of emulation among the Huron and a group of traders who came to Three Rivers later left three more children with the French. These too were taken to Quebec. It is unclear whether these included some of the twelve children that the Jesuits had selected in the Huron country. Not all were, however, since at least one boy had never heard Christian teaching prior to coming to Quebec and some were not Attignawantan. Still more youths were offered by traders who arrived early in September, but these could not be accepted because all the Huron interpreters, who were necessary for holding a formal council, had returned to Quebec. Before returning home, Endahiaconc came to Quebec to see how his nephew was faring and was persuaded to take home with him one of the Huron boys (not his nephew) who could not get along with the others (12:45–47; 13:125). Endahiaconc was also accompanied up the Ottawa River by Simon Baron.

Who were the five youths who remained at Quebec and why had their male kinsmen given in to French demands, in spite of the opposition of their female relatives? Satouta, as we have seen already, was the grandson and heir of an important Attignawantan headman who had relatives in both Ihonatiria and Ossossané (9:273; 13:119–23). Tsiko was a nephew of Endahiaconc, the principal headman of the Attigneenongnahac,[5] and Tewatirhon was the nephew of a council chief named Taratouan who seems to have lived near Teanaostaiaé (12:97) and of an unnamed war chief (12:95). After his return to the Huron country, and possibly after he had married, Tewatirhon lived in Taenhatentaron, which may have been his home village (21:173). About the other two boys, Andehoua (Ariethoua) and Aiandace (Aiacidace), we know only that the former came from Scanonaenrat.[6] All of these boys appear to have been matrilineal kinsmen (nephews or grandsons) of important headmen who profited from controlling their clan segments' trade with the French. These men were therefore the Huron who had most reason for wanting to establish close ties with the French. The exchange of children or adults traditionally constituted a bond of friendship between trading partners. Thus Taratouan and other headmen could now boast that they were kinsmen of the French and, in that capacity, lay claim to be counted among the "masters of the St. Lawrence River" (13:125).

The Huron boys experienced various difficulties adjusting to life among the French. They had to accustom themselves to wearing French clothes and eating French food. Their habit of caressing people as a sign of friendship was also wrongly interpreted. Satouta and Tsiko both became ill and died not long after they had fights with Frenchmen. Although they appear to have succumbed to infectious diseases, the Jesuits attributed their illnesses to overeating, resulting from their unfamiliarity with the solid nature of French food. To prevent a recurrence of this tragedy the surviving boys were fed partly, after the Huron fashion, on corn soup (12:53). The deaths of Satouta and Tsiko were witnessed by an Algonkin who knew Satouta's family and the Jesuits feared that he might report they had died from fighting or witchcraft, for which the French would be held accountable (12:51). If their relatives believed such charges, it was feared they might retaliate by trying to kill some of the Jesuits in the Huron country.

The surviving boys followed a well-defined daily routine at Quebec: following prayers, attendance at mass, and breakfast, they were taught reading, writing, and catechism. After the noonday meal, there were more prayers, followed by instruction and a free period during which the older boys often made weapons and hunted and fished near the Jesuit house. After supper, there was an examination of conscience, prayers, and early bed (12:63–65). In their free-time activities the younger boys followed the example of the older ones (12:67). During the winter, the latter cleared a patch of ground which, since there were no women present, they themselves sowed with corn in the spring. They also built a cabin near the field, in which the harvest could be stored (12:77). They urged the Jesuits to baptize them (12:67–69), so they might conclude a closer alliance with the French, and announced that if they could obtain their families' permission, they would persuade some Huron girls to marry them and return to found a Huron colony at Quebec (12:79). No doubt, they were attracted in part by the food, clothing, and tools that the French were giving them (12:79), but they also may have believed that such a colony would benefit Huron traders.

During their first two years in the Huron country, the Jesuits had made progress in learning to use the Huron language and had begun preaching to the Attignawantan. They had also established themselves as the sole representatives of French officials and fur traders among the Huron and had persuaded the Huron to send some young people to Quebec to be indoctrinated and to serve as hostages for the safety of the missionaries. These successes were based on the Huron accepting the Jesuits in their country as a necessary condition of their trading alliance with the French. Instead of tactfully working to transform this relationship into an even more solid one based on personal trust and confidence, Brébeuf proceeded to exploit the French–Huron alliance and to offend cherished Huron beliefs in the hope of bringing about mass conversions. By so doing, he accomplished little that was positive and did many things that were to harm the Jesuits in the critical years ahead. Already, his behaviour had created widespread resentment, which was still fairly well controlled on the political level, but was giving rise to many rumours that the Jesuits were practising witchcraft.

The Black Years

THE EPIDEMICS OF 1636 AND 1637

The autumn of 1636 saw the beginning of a far more prolonged and deadly series of epidemics than had afflicted the Huron in 1634. A disease that appears to have been influenza began to spread from the St. Lawrence Valley in mid-August and reached the Huron country before mid-September. It also diffused through northern Ontario and during the winter it caused many deaths, both directly and from subsequent starvation, among the hunting peoples of that area (Thwaites 1896–1901, 11:197). The northward spread of the epidemic was attributed to trade goods that the Nipissing had carried there (11:199), thus indicating that the Indians had pinpointed the source of the epidemic. Of the six priests and four hired men at Ihonatiria, only Brébeuf and Petit-Pré escaped the infection. For about two weeks, the French were confined to their beds with cramps and fever. For a time, one of the domestics was believed to be dying (11:13; 13:87–111). Nevertheless, although not all of the Jesuits and their assistants were out of danger until 15 October, all of them did recover.

The Huron were less fortunate. Already in early September, some people were ill at Ossossané, Ihonatiria, and elsewhere, but the disease grew more common as the Huron settled into their villages for the winter. In Ihonatiria, it began to spread rapidly after 29 September (13:115). By mid-October, thirteen or fourteen out of a population that could not have exceeded 300 were ill at one time (13:131) and the epidemic did not reach its peak there until after 10 November (13:145). About a week later, the number of people who were falling ill declined sharply and those who survived began to recover (13:149); however, it was not until spring that the malady ceased completely (13:165; 14:85).

In other villages the epidemic followed a similar course, although the timing was different. There were few, if any, sick in Onnentisati prior to mid-October, but many inhabitants were stricken afterwards (13:131–33). At Ossossané, the epidemic did not reach its peak before December (13:165), but the outbreak was especially severe there and remained critical into January (13:235). Fifty were sick by 4 December (13:165) and, shortly after, Simon Baron bled over 200 who were ill (13:181). The winter of 1636–37 was a particularly long one (13:249) and the cold weather seems to have dampened the spread of the disease. In the early spring, however, it flared up again, particularly in such villages as Andiataé and Onnentisati (14:7–15). Probably because food was running low, the disease had a higher incidence of fatality at this season than it had earlier (14:53).

It is clear that many, if not all, of the Attignawantan settlements were visited by this epidemic. Unfortunately, we have no information concerning the three other tribes of the Huron confederacy, although it seems unlikely that they could have escaped it. Nevertheless, Le Mercier's comment that the disease assailed only some villages (15:13), and a statement that the Attigneenongnahac village of Ekhiondastsaan escaped the epidemic (14:29), suggest that the eastern parts of the Huron country may not have been as badly affected as Ossossané and the Penetanguishene Peninsula. In the description of Brébeuf's visit to Teanaostaiaé and Scanonaenrat in the spring of 1637, for instance, there is no mention of these places having suffered a high mortality (14:25–29).

The number of Huron who died in this epidemic is especially difficult to estimate. The statement that many were ill in Onnentisati, "several (plusieurs) of whom died" (13:133) does not suggest a high mortality. It is clear, however, that many people died in other Attignawantan villages. Ihonatiria was devastated by the epidemic (13:165), with numerous deaths reported in most longhouses (13:163). By January, over fifty people had died in Ossossané (13:213). The Nipissing, who were wintering in the Huron country, carried away seventy bodies when they left for the north the following spring (14:37). Since Champlain had estimated the entire Nipissing population to be between 700 and 800 (Biggar 1922–36, 3:40), this suggests a mortality rate of about ten per cent. If a similar ratio were applied only to the Attignawantan, it would indicate that nearly 1000 Huron died. Yet, allowing for the better diet and housing of the Huron, this may be too high an estimate. Doubling the partial estimate for Ossossané suggests about 500 deaths among the Attignawantan. What is imponderable, however, is how many died among the other tribes.

Soon after the Huron had departed to trade at Three Rivers in the summer of 1637, there was a new outbreak of disease that affected the entire Huron confederacy (Thwaites 1896–1901, 15:13). Unlike the previous epidemic, many who became ill died within two days (15:69). The Huron who went to Three Rivers to trade were also stricken, either on their way down the Ottawa River or while they were trading, and many died on route (12:231). Unlike the previous year no Frenchmen became ill, either at Three Rivers or in the Huron country (12:261; 14:229). Thus, while it is possible that this epidemic was yet another outbreak of the former one, it is more likely to have been a European childhood ailment against which most Frenchmen had already acquired immunity. Although the epidemic reached the Huron country before the beginning of the trading season, this does not rule out the possibility that it was carried inland from the St. Lawrence. Alternatively, and in my opinion more likely, the epidemic spread northward from the Susquehannock, who in February 1637 suffered from an unidentified malady (14:9). The new ailment, which seems to have killed many more people than did the last one, persisted into the autumn of 1637.

Except for Guillaume Chaudron in 1623, the Huron had probably not seen a Frenchman seriously ill before the autumn of 1636. The people from Ihonatiria flocked to visit the ailing French and offer them advice. They were surprised by Brébeuf's efforts to keep his cabin quiet and to prevent those who were sick from being disturbed (13:99–101). The Huron regarded this treatment, which was so different from their own, as further evidence of the deviant, hence sinister, practices of the Jesuits. Much as he would have liked to, Brébeuf found himself unable to prevent these visits.

Tsiouendaentaha, who prided himself on his friendship for the Jesuits, requested that they allow a famous shaman to visit them. This was Tonneraouanont, a small hunchback from Onnentisati who claimed to be the incarnation of a powerful spirit that had penetrated into a woman's womb (13:105–7). No doubt, in making this claim, Tonneraouanont was trading on his deformity, since the Huron visualized a number of important mythological figures as dwarfs. Tonneraouanont offered to heal the French in return for a payment of ten glass beads and an extra bead for each patient (13:103). Since this shaman valued his services highly, his fee indicates how highly such trade goods were still valued and esteemed. When the Jesuits refused to have anything to do with his healing rites, Tonneraouanont pointed out several roots that he believed were helpful for alleviating fevers and instructed the Jesuits how to use them; yet the missionaries ignored even this advice in order to scorn all assistance from someone they believed to be in league with the devil (13:105). This incident demonstrates the considerable extent to which the later hostility between priests and shamans was of the Jesuits' own making.

When the Jesuits recovered from their own illnesses, they began extending practical help to the Huron. Meat and broth were given to those who were ill and prunes, raisins, sugar, lemon peel, senna, and similar items were distributed for whatever medicinal value they had (13:113–15, 147). At the same time, Simon Baron was kept busy bleeding those who were ill (13:115). Although well aware of the limitations of their pharmacopoeia, the Jesuits hoped that by doing the work of physicians, they might be able to undermine or discredit the shamans (15:69). Such work also brought them into contact with the dying, thus increasing their chances of being able to baptize them.

As the original epidemic of 1636 grew worse, the Huron turned to their shamans and curing societies in hope of finding an individual or group who possessed the knowledge to control the disease. It was regarded as a moral duty for anyone who had such skills to put them at the service of their community. When the Jesuits began to recover from their own bouts of influenza, and thereby demonstrated their power over it, the people of Ihonatiria turned to them for help. The Jesuits were anxious to use the epidemic as a means of advancing their mission work and for this purpose were willing to rely on their own idea of supernatural aid. Brébeuf informed the Huron that the only certain way to overcome the epidemic was to believe in the Christian deity and vow to keep his commandments. He recommended that the people of Ihonatiria should make a public vow that if it would please God to end the contagion, they would agree to serve him and in the following spring would erect a cabin in his honour. On 29 November, the headmen of Ihonatiria visited the Jesuits and promised to do whatever they said was necessary to combat the disease. The Jesuits were annoyed, however, that various men, including Taretandé, the new headman of the village (13:215), left before any Christian ceremony began (13:161).

The next day, while still professing to be Christians and saying they were ready to be baptized, Ihonatirians who were members of healing societies donned their masks and performed traditional rituals (13:175). At the same time, they enquired when they should assemble to pray. This led the Jesuits to denounce their hypocrisy. What the Jesuits did not understand was that the Huron regarded Christianity as another curing society and membership in one society did not rule out membership in another. Far from the Huron being hypocrites, the Jesuits had failed to convey to them their own understanding of baptism.

Early in December 1636, the headmen of Wenrio invited Brébeuf to attend a village council in order to discuss what curing rituals the Jesuits might perform for the village. Disappointed about what had happened at Ihonatiria, Brébeuf stated that the people of Wenrio would have to agree that marriages would be binding for life and that they would give up their belief in dreams. They would also have to stop eating human flesh, attending eat-all feasts, and participating in andacwander and Awataerohi rituals. Aenons and Onaconchiaronk, who were the principal headmen present, said that it was impossible to accept Brébeuf's proposals, as to do so would destroy the Huron way of life. They asked Brébeuf to recognize that French ways were not suited to the Huron and to respect that they served different gods. Brébeuf openly rejected this suggestion and the council broke up with no more being said (13:169–75). The epidemic had grown so serious, however, that the next day it was decided that it was better to agree to Brébeuf's conditions than to go on dying. The men of Wenrio therefore agreed to accept Brébeuf's proposals and promised to build a chapel in the spring if the epidemic was brought to an end. As at Ihonatiria, however, villagers soon turned to other cures when those offered by the Jesuits proved ineffective (13:175). On 12 December the council of Ossossané agreed to the same terms that Wenrio had and Okhiarenta, an important shaman, was sent through the town stating what must be done if the Jesuits were to stop the epidemic (13:187). The epidemic continued, however, and, as happened elsewhere, the people of Ossossané soon looked elsewhere for an effective cure.

As illness increased, the Jesuits regarded it as their duty to try to baptize as many of the dying as possible. Throughout the fall and early winter, and again in the spring of 1637, small parties of Jesuits visited most of the Attignawantan villages searching for children to baptize and dying adults whom they might attempt to instruct. Although Ihonatiria remained the base for their operations, many visits were to Ossossané, the largest and most important of the Attignawantan settlements. Other communities they visited were Wenrio, Anonatea, Onnentisati, Arenté, Andiataé, the three hamlets of Khinonascarant (Quieunonascaran), and Iahenhouton. Their renewed emphasis on baptizing the sick reopened the question of whether baptism healed or killed the sick. In Ossossané, where the Jesuits had arrived fairly recently, many people seem to have still regarded it as a healing rite, but in and around Ihonatiria, where Jesuit teachings were better known, increasing numbers of people rejected this explanation. The Jesuits described baptism as showing the way to heaven, a claim that linked baptism with death in the minds of these Huron. The Jesuits reinforced this interpretation by stressing to potential converts that baptism was a medicine not for the body but for the soul (13:189).

In spite of such beliefs, a certain number of Huron still wanted baptism, either for themselves or for their children. Some were people who no longer believed that it restored health, but who were anxious, after death, to join relatives who had already been baptized (13:29, 127–29, 149). To counteract this, the Jesuits began to refuse baptism to those who did not explicitly acknowledge some other reason for requesting it. Others, who had seen relatives recover after being baptized or who knew of people who had, still seem to have been convinced that baptism was a healing rite, in spite of what the Jesuits said about it. Some people apparently agreed to be baptized in order to be left in peace or so as not to offend the Jesuits. Their state of mind is made credible by a Huron named Joachim Annieouton who, around 1671, confessed that although he had been considered a good Christian for more than twenty-five years, he had been one in appearance only. He had given this impression in order to gratify the Jesuits and so they would stop trying to convert him. He explained that while he had originally said "Yes, I will be converted," the Huron had two ways of saying the word *aaao*; a clipped form meaning "yes" and a more drawn-out one that they used when they wished only to appear to yield to a request (55:297). The latter was the form that Annieouton had used. That this could be found out in 1670 is some indication of the gap in understanding that must have separated the Jesuits from those they baptized in 1636. Huron who recovered after baptism ignored the admonitions of the Jesuits and continued to live as before (13:133). Such behaviour does not indicate perversity or ingratitude but simply that on an individual as well as a collective level, the Huron were unaware of the significance that the French attached to baptism.

In general, however, resistance to baptism stiffened during 1636, especially in and around Ihonatiria. Even at Ossossané, baptisms plummeted as the death rate soared. Many households refused to permit further baptisms after the deaths of baptized members (13:183). Individuals refused baptism because they did not want their souls to be separated from close relatives and friends who had died without it (13:135, 151). When Arakhié, who was one of the boys the Jesuits wished to take to Quebec, fell ill, his family partitioned off the section of the cabin in which he lay and kept watch so that the Jesuits could not get near to baptize him (13:117–25). They did this because a kinsman named Akhioca had died without baptism at Ossossané only a short time before (13:123). Some people expressed the fear that heaven would be full of Frenchmen, who would be unwilling to share their food with Indians (13:127). Others gave more idiosyncratic reasons, such as a woman who refused to promise that she would never divorce her husband since this was an unacceptable constraint on her liberty (13:141). Still others began to manifest open contempt for the teachings of the Jesuits and to ridicule them (13:141–43); however, an old man named Anerraté requested baptism when his daughter Khiongnona died after she had refused it (13:133–41).

The growing reluctance of Huron to permit their children to be baptized led the Jesuits to attempt to baptize ailing children without their families' knowledge. This was done by the pretext of giving the children raisins or sugar water (13:167; 14:41), by pretending to feel their pulse or wipe their brow (14:67–69), or straightforwardly when no one else was looking (14:7–9). In each instance, a handkerchief dipped in water was used. The Huron were no doubt aware of these baptisms and the clandestine behaviour of the Jesuits must have aroused additional fears.

Between the summers of 1636 and 1637, the Jesuits baptized about 250 people (14:107). Most were in the autumn of 1636 and the early part of the following winter; about fifty were in the spring of 1637 (cf. 13:35; 14:53, 107). These baptisms were performed in various Attignawantan villages, but many were in Ossossané. Both children and adults were baptized and almost all were believed to be in danger of dying (13:35). The following year, few people were baptized, except in Ossossané, where the figure reached 100 (15:69). At least forty-four of these died, including twenty-two children still on cradleboards. In addition, there were eleven baptisms in Ihonatiria (15:129).

The spread of illness also encouraged a general upsurge in Huron healing practices. The curing societies performed their rituals in every village, and shamans sought to enhance their reputations by divining the cause of the epidemics and recommending effective cures. Tsondacouané, who was in much repute around his home town of Onnentisati, entered into communion with various spirits who inhabited features of the landscape and on their recommendation prescribed the Awataerohi and the erection of straw masks above the doors of houses and human figures on the roofs (13:227–33). Later, he advised that the dead should be buried in the ground for a time before being placed in bark tombs in the village cemetery (13:259). Another cure was revealed to Tehorenhaegnon after a twelve-day fast on the shores of Nottawasaga Bay. In January 1637 he shared his new power with three other shamans, Saossarinon, Khioutenstia, and Iandatassa (13:241), who were deputized to practise his cure. At the climax of this ritual those who were sick were sprinkled from a kettle filled with a mysterious water, while the shamans followed the kettle fanning them with a turkey wing that had been supplied by Tehorenhaegnon (13:237–43).

The sprinkling of the sick may have been imitated from the ritual of baptism. Alternatively, the claim that the ritual was revealed by a lake suggests a possible resemblance to those performed by the Iroquois Otter Society, who also sprinkle the sick with water (Tooker 1964:103 n. 96). It is possible that an indigenous pattern for this ritual already existed in Huron culture. It is also possible that Tehorenhaegnon's rite was a syncretistic one, at least in terms of its symbolism. Its popularity may have been derived from the fact that it equated the powerful magic of the Jesuits with practices that were familiar to the Huron and were recognized by them as being unambiguously beneficent. The novel features of this ritual may explain why Tehorenhaegnon and his assistants showed a professional interest in measuring its efficacy (13:243). While the Jesuits condemned the ritual as a failure and claimed that its practitioners were soon discredited, the same rite was performed at Ossossané in 1639 (19:243) and a similar one, in which those who were ill drank from a kettle, was performed the same year among the Arendarhonon (20:29). If this rite originated in 1636, it appears to have enjoyed approval and diffused rapidly among the Huron tribes.

Harold Blau (1966:577–79; Thwaites 1896–1901, 13:243, 263) has also suggested that a ceremony first reported in February 1637, in which the participants appeared as hunchbacks, wore masks, and carried sticks, was an invention of this period and was first performed in honour of Tonneraouanont who had died two weeks earlier, after he was injured in an accident. Blau suggests that the purpose of this ceremony organized by Tsondacouané was to gain the power credited to Tonneraouanont or to trick the disease-causing spirits into believing he was still alive. Yet, the placing of masks at the entrances to the houses, which took place at the end of this ceremony, resembles the ritual performed some time before Tonneraouanont's death, also on the orders of Tsondacouané. Inasmuch as dwarfs or hunchbacks seem to have had considerable religious significance among the Huron (10:183), both Tonneraouanont's claims of power and these rituals may be traced to a common theme in Huron culture, rather than being historically related to each other in the way Blau has proposed.

THE SEARCH FOR A CAUSE

Measured by any standards familiar to the Huron, the epidemics of 1636 and 1637 were extraordinarily severe. To stop these illnesses, the Huron attempted to determine their cause. They believed that uncontrollable illnesses were likely to be brought about by especially powerful witchcraft. The problem thus was to find and counteract those who were practising it. The Nipissing blamed the epidemics on the Kichesipirini and claimed that the latter had afflicted surrounding nations with pestilence because these groups had refused to help the Kichesipirini wage war against the Iroquois (Thwaites 1896–1901, 13:211); however, almost all of the Huron who believed that witchcraft was the cause of the epidemics blamed them on the French, and more specifically on the Jesuits. The Jesuits recognized that the most intelligent Huron were driven to this conclusion by their inability to understand why the Jesuits wanted to live in their country and why the French traders insisted that the Huron let them do so (17:125). Traders and warriors had legitimate reasons for visiting remote tribes and men and women might intermarry with foreign groups, but what reason could these bizarre, celibate shamans have for wishing to dwell among them? The Huron saw the Jesuits as protecting themselves and other Frenchmen from disease and, like other Indians, they concluded that the Jesuits were not ordinary men, but possessed of powerful spirits (13:165).

Questions that were not so easily answered were why the Jesuits did not use their power to help their Indian allies; and what the significance of baptism was. The Jesuits' behaviour suggested extremely sinister motives. Death was a source of great anxiety for the Huron, who did not think it right that the Jesuits should ask a sick man if he wished to go to heaven or to hell; instead, they should wish for his recovery (13:127). The Huron perceived a seemingly ungenerous spirit (which was the hallmark of witchcraft) in other aspects of Jesuit behaviour. The frequently closed door of their cabin and their refusal to admit Huron visitors except at specified times of the day strongly suggested that sorcery was being practised within (15:33). Likewise, their adamant refusal to give presents to satisfy the desires of people's souls was proof that they wished to see individual Huron suffer and die (15:179–81). The same lack of desire to help was also apparent in the Jesuits' condemnation of curing rituals, such as the Ononharoia and the andacwander (17:171–89). It even appeared to manifest itself in the stinginess that the Huron believed led the Jesuits to skim the grease from the broth they gave to the sick. This led the Huron to accuse them of making the broth merely to accumulate grease for their own use (13:147).

The Huron also saw evidence of witchcraft in the Jesuits' public utterances. It was claimed that when Brébeuf had returned in 1634, he had said he would remain with the Huron for only five years. This was interpreted as evidence that the Jesuits believed they could annihilate the Huron within that space of time (15:59). The wampum collar that Brébeuf had presented to the Attignawantan in 1636 in order to show them the way to heaven was an even clearer statement that he intended to kill them (13:209). It was reported that in 1636 Father Daniel had warned a Huron youth who was planning to return to the Huron country that he should remain at Quebec, since pestilence was about to devastate his country (15:25). It was over a year before the Huron headmen were to proclaim Daniel innocent of this charge (15:139). Among those who were most active in spreading these rumours was the shaman Tonneraouanont, whose skill and goodwill the Jesuits had scorned and rejected (13:213). When Tonneraouanont was injured and dying, he refused a Jesuit offer of ointments to treat himself, just as they had refused his cures (13:225).

As the Huron became convinced that the Jesuits were responsible for their illnesses, supernatural evidence began to accumulate against them. It was claimed, for example, that a Tionnontaté who was stricken by the epidemic had vomited up a lead pellet, which proved that the French had bewitched him (15:21). It was also widely rumoured that an Arendarhonon had returned from the dead to report that in the other world he had met two women who came from England. These women said that the Jesuits were evil men who would not return home until they had killed all the Huron (15:51). Another story that was current in the autumn of 1637 was that four English pinnaces had ascended the St. Lawrence River as far as

the Rivière des Prairies and that their commanders had said that the
Jesuits were the cause of all the sickness (15:31). It is uncertain whether or
not this story incorporates knowledge of anti-Jesuit propaganda that was
current at Quebec after 1629. Both stories, however, seem to reflect a
romantic memory of the English as trading partners who did not foist
their shamans on the Indians.

The Huron believed that until the Jesuits' methods were known, they
would be unable to combat their witchcraft. Most speculation saw the
Jesuits acting, not on their own initiative, but as agents of the French
officials at Quebec. Much credence was given to an Algonkin report that
shortly before his death Champlain had told a Montagnais headman that if
he died, he would carry off the Huron with him. This story, which was
undoubtedly spread by the Algonkin to undermine the Huron's confidence
in the French, was believable because Indian headmen who thought themselves bewitched sometimes requested that if they died, their relatives
should exact blood revenge from those whom they held to be responsible
for their condition (12:85–87; 13:147).

This story was similar to the still more popular one that the Jesuits had
been sent to the Huron country to avenge the murder of Etienne Brûlé
(12:87). Many Huron suspected that the disowning of Brûlé by the French
was a ruse to cover their intended revenge. Rumours, fashioned in the
idiom of a matrilineal society, claimed that either Brûlé's sister (14:53) or
his uncle (14:17) was seeking to annihilate the Huron. One Algonkin
reported seeing a French woman infecting the whole country with her
breath (14:53), although this supernatural agent by no means absolved
the Jesuits of responsibility for what was happening. When the epidemic
afflicted a group whom Le Mercier identifies as Cheveux Relevés, but who
were probably the Nipissing,[7] they concluded that it was because some of
them had once robbed Brûlé of a collar containing 2400 wampum beads.
They therefore offered to return a like number of beads to the Jesuits if
they would withdraw their scourge. The Jesuits refused to accept these
beads because they feared that if they did, the Huron would assume that
they were concluding some agreement with the Nipissing that was detri-
mental to the Huron (14:101–3).

Even more varied were the means by which the Huron imagined that
the Jesuits were practising their witchcraft. The sugar that the Jesuits gave
to the sick was an obvious means of injecting charms into victims; therefore Tsondacouané and other shamans warned the Huron not to allow
themselves to be fed this "French snow" (14:51). Such warnings were
extended to all the food and drugs that the Jesuits distributed in their

efforts to counteract the influence of the shamans. Because the Huron practised cannibalism, the Jesuits tried to keep their belief that the communion wafers were the body of Christ secret from all except those whose faith in Christianity had been well tested. In 1637 a rumour began to spread that the Jesuits had brought a corpse from France which they kept in the tabernacle in their chapel and that it was this corpse that was causing the Huron to die (12:237–39; 15:33). It was also said that the Jesuits had caused a great many children to die by taking a child, or a picture of a child, into the forest and stabbing it with a large needle (15:33; 12:237). The Huron regarded as spirits the anthropomorphic beings that were portrayed in the colourful paintings of religious themes that the Jesuits were importing as objects of instruction. Rumours circulated about the dangerous influences that emanated from the images that the Jesuits kept in their chapel and which reputedly penetrated into the bodies of Indians who looked at them (14:53, 97). When life-sized paintings of Christ and the Virgin Mary were exhibited in the chapel at Ossossané in 1637, these were said to cause illness. Illustrations of hell were interpreted as representations of the fevers and other torments that afflicted the Huron (14:103; 15:35). During the epidemic of 1637–38, certain Tionnontaté who had seen the Jesuits' chapel offered them a beaver robe if they would prevent illness from issuing therefrom (15:57). Finally, there was a rumour that the French had bewitched a cloak and buried it near Three Rivers, but in such a way that the Huron were bound to steal it (12:87; 13:147). This, or a cloth that the Jesuits kept hidden in their cabin, was said to cause the epidemic (15:45). It is possible that clothing stolen at Three Rivers was in fact one of the means by which European illnesses were communicated to the Huron.

Disasters always gave rise to charges of witchcraft among the Huron themselves and the epidemics of the 1630s were no exception. In November 1636, a man named Oaca accused a Huron living in Ihonatiria of causing his illness. Others took up the charge and it was said that the accused had been seen roaming about at night casting flames out of his mouth (13:155–57). Although he was only threatened with death, in the hope that this would make him stop practising witchcraft, within a year two other suspected witches were slain among the Attignawantan (15:53). These may or may not have included a woman who was tortured in order to force her to name her accomplices before being killed in Ossossané in April 1637 (14:37–39). All of these killings were sanctioned by headmen or war chiefs in the hope that such action would frighten other witches. For any Huron who had many enemies or whose behaviour was regarded as deviant, it was a dangerous time.

As the circumstantial evidence against the Jesuits increased daily, there was talk of either killing them or forcing them to go back to Quebec (11:15); however, during the autumn of 1636 and the following winter, such talk was confined principally to Ihonatiria and the four other villages that were at odds with the rest of the Attignawantan. As the headmen of these villages pondered what the Jesuits had said and done since their return, their distaste for the Jesuits' teachings grew. They began to argue that mankind could not have come from the Garden of Eden, as the Jesuits claimed, since the Indians could not have crossed the ocean in their frail canoes; moreover, if they had done so, they would have known how to make the same things that the French did (13:219). Some expressed the opinion that nothing the French said was true. By clearly defining their own beliefs in opposition to those of the Jesuits, these headmen began to dissipate some of the aura of mystery that had formerly surrounded the Jesuits' teachings.

In December Taretandé, the new headman of Ihonatiria (probably the brother of the dead Sangwati), and his brother Sononkhiaconc met the headmen of neighbouring villages in order to discuss what should be done with the Jesuits. Taretandé said that if anyone in his family died, he would murder the first Frenchman he encountered, while Achioantaeté, who otherwise claimed to be a friend of the Jesuits, said that if he were the principal headman of the Attignawantan, he would order the Jesuits to be killed. The council seems to have decided that the most prudent policy for dealing with the Jesuits was the normal one of accusing them of witchcraft, in the hope that this would frighten them into desisting from the practice. Taretandé visited the Jesuits and denounced them as sorcerers. He said that the best they could hope for was to be sent back to Quebec in the spring (13:215–17). The children of Ihonatiria teased the Jesuits that they would soon have their heads split; and the Jesuits began to fear from these taunts that the headmen had already given orders for this to be done (11:15). From December onwards, the Jesuits found it necessary to stop visiting Ihonatiria to preach and instruct the children. Any mention of death aroused the instant hostility of the villagers (13:221).

THE MOVE TO OSSOSSANÉ

By late spring 1637 the epidemics had come to an end in most places and with it the hostility to the Jesuits had ceased. Ihonatiria, however, had suffered many deaths and was a ruined village (Thwaites 1896–1901,

13:165). Already in the spring of 1636, when evidence was uncovered that seemed to indicate that witchcraft was being practised in the village, one of its wealthiest inhabitants, possibly Aouandoïé, moved with his household to Arenté (10:285).[8] In January 1637 Taretandé, Sononkhiaconc, their mother, and other members of the village headman's family died (13:217–23). The mother was Oquiaendis, who had been baptized in 1634, but was now as opposed to the Jesuits as her sons were. These losses, together with a generally high rate of mortality, made it likely that in the near future those who were still alive in Ihonatiria would transfer to other villages. Under these circumstances, the Jesuits began to consider moving to a larger and friendlier community.

On 17 March Brébeuf and Le Mercier met with the headmen of the five northernmost Attignawantan villages. At this meeting they posed two questions: Were the northern Attignawantan now prepared to believe what the Jesuits taught? Would it be possible for some of the Jesuits' hired men to marry Huron women (14:15–17)? In the Jesuits' minds, these two questions were closely linked. Champlain had been anxious to see French men and Huron women intermarry to produce a single people and Brébeuf believed that under the right circumstances such marriages could help to promote the spread of Christianity. It would appear, however, that the main reason that the Jesuits wanted to see their hired men married was to prevent a resurgence of the promiscuous relationships with Huron women that had existed prior to 1629.

The Attignawantan were not inclined to show much enthusiasm for the Jesuits' teachings, even though they stressed that they no longer bore them any personal ill-will. The headmen stated that Frenchmen were free to marry Huron women and noted that, in the past, they had done so without asking the permission of headmen. This reference to Brûlé and his companions led Brébeuf to explain that whereas those Frenchmen had been content to live like Indians, his desire was to turn the Huron into Christians. Therefore, any further marriages would have to follow French custom and be indissoluble. A few days later, the head of the council came to enquire into certain practical aspects of the proposal: the kind of betrothal presents a man would give his wife; whether or not a husband would take his wife to France with him if he left the Huron country; and if there were a divorce, what property a woman would have the right to keep (14:19–21). The inability of the headmen to view the problem of marriage as a religious issue convinced the Jesuits that it was best to drop the subject. This left unsolved the problem of controlling their hired help.

Since any relocation of their mission would entail fewer difficulties if the

Attignawantan were again on good terms, Brébeuf was anxious to smooth over as many difficulties within the tribe as possible. He therefore enquired on 17 March if the northern villages wished to be reconciled with the rest of the Attignawantan. Being informed that they did, he made several journeys to and fro in the hope of persuading the Attignawantan to convene a general council for this purpose. He also offered to present 1200 wampum beads to the two parties to help forge a new bond between them. The head-men of Ossossané and the other southern villages agreed to meet at Andiataé to effect a reconciliation but because of Aenons's reluctance to attend, the meeting had to be called off (14:15–23). These negotiations nevertheless provided the Jesuits with an opportunity to establish still closer relations with the headmen of Ossossané (14:33).

On 29 March the Jesuits met with the leaders of Ihonatiria to learn whether they would remain where they were for another winter or were planning to unite with the people of Wenrio. They replied that they intended to remain in the village for one more year, but might rejoin the people of Wenrio the following spring. Pressed to state whether they believed what the Jesuits taught, the men of Ihonatiria replied that some believed but the rest could not be answered for (14:23–25).

In the spring, it was once again safe to travel and Father Garnier accompanied Brébeuf on a visit to Teanaostaiaé, where Brébeuf offered condolence presents to Amantacha's family. Both Scanonaenrat and Ekhiondastsaan were visited in the course of this journey. Brébeuf hoped that in the near future the Jesuits would be able to establish a residence at Teanaostaiaé (11:17). Later, Father Garnier accompanied the Jesuits' hired men on a trading expedition to the Tionnontaté. The Jesuits had heard that many people were sick there, although the peak of the epidemic was past before Garnier arrived. He managed to baptize only ten children and two old women (14:35).

After further inconclusive negotiations designed to reunite Ihonatiria and Wenrio and to promote goodwill among the Attignawantan, on 17 May the Jesuits informed Anenkhiondic of their desire to establish a residence at Ossossané. This was approved by the Ossossané council who agreed to provide a cabin twelve yards long for the Jesuits to live in. The people of Ossossané were so anxious to have the Jesuits living in their village that when the council was over, each member took his hatchet and they and a large crowd began to prepare the building site (14:57). On 21 May Father Pijart and two French workmen left for Ossossané to supervise the building of the cabin, which was finished by 7 June (14:75). On 9 June forty or fifty men and women came from Ossossané to Ihonatiria in order to carry the Jesuits' corn and furniture to their new home. Headmen supervised this operation and the people of Ossossané worked without asking for presents in return (14:105). All of the large towns along the southern border of the Huron country expressed pleasure that the Jesuits were moving nearer to them. Brébeuf, Le Mercier, and Garnier were to spend the following winter at Ossossané with Father Paul Ragueneau who had arrived in the Huron country in the summer of 1637 while, for the time being, Pijart, Chastellain, and Jogues remained at Ihonatiria.

HURON HOSTILITY BECOMES GENERAL

When the second epidemic broke out in all the Huron villages in the summer of 1637, the fear and hatred of the Jesuits that formerly had been confined to the northern villages of the Penetanguishene Peninsula became general throughout the Huron confederacy. The previous autumn, Frenchmen as well as Huron had been ill and this had tended to alleviate the hostility that was felt towards the French (Thwaites 1896–1901, 13: 111). This time, however, the Jesuits remained in good health and fears that formerly had been confined to the north began to spread. Within a few days it was generally agreed that the Jesuits were responsible for what was happening. Only the Jesuits' new hosts in Ossossané remained more favourably disposed towards them.

In Angoutenc, where the epidemic was particularly severe, people were reluctant to speak to the Jesuits and would not let them enter their houses, fearing they would fall victims to their witchcraft. Several visits were made there to minister to the dying, but without effect (15:23). When one war chief saw some Jesuits about to enter his longhouse, he threatened to split their heads if they advanced any farther. As the epidemic grew worse the war chiefs, who were responsible for the elimination of witches, began to clamour for action against the Jesuits and to challenge the power of the more conservative headmen.

Early in June Ondesson, one of the most celebrated Huron war chiefs, and another headman invited the Jesuits in Ossossané to attend a council in Angoutenc to clear themselves of the accusations that were being made against them. At the same time one of the Ossossané headmen warned the French that the people of Onnentisati were convinced that the Jesuits were sorcerers (15:25–27). It was clear that the Jesuits were being summoned to Angoutenc to stand trial for witchcraft. In spite of the danger to which they were exposing themselves, the Jesuits decided to go to Angoutenc.

The village headmen received them courteously and invited them to explain to the people of the village what had brought them to the Huron country. The Jesuits explained that they had come out of goodwill. They consoled the Huron for their dead and stated that it was their aim to live and die themselves among the Huron. Two headmen recapitulated what the Jesuits said and warned the young men of the village not to strike a blow that the whole country would regret (15:29). This and accompanying expressions of goodwill convinced the Jesuits that they had been found innocent. Notwithstanding, the Jesuits continued to be treated with so much hostility that they decided to discontinue their visits to Angoutenc (15:31). Later, rumours had it that after the Jesuits had left, the council had reassembled and resolved to kill the first Frenchman who fell into their hands (15:25–31), thereby terminating the French–Huron alliance.

Throughout the summer the public clamour against the Jesuits increased, even in Ossossané. On 4 August the headmen of the Huron confederacy met in Ossossané to coordinate their foreign policy and to deal with the Jesuits. The majority of those who were present were council chiefs; however, some war chiefs attended in place of council chiefs who had died in the epidemic but whose successors had not yet been named (15:43). The presence of these war chiefs was another indication of their growing influence during this episode of crisis.

At the first session of this council, which discussed peace and war, the Jesuits presented several hundred wampum beads as evidence of their concern for the general welfare of the Huron. The second meeting was held on the evening of the same day. It was presided over by Ontitarac, an elderly, blind man, who lived in Ossossané but whose name is otherwise not recorded (15:39). He admonished those who were present not to conceal anything they knew about the cause of the epidemic or how it might be halted. Anenkhiondic more pointedly suggested that the Jesuits were among those who had knowledge of what was happening. Ostensibly so that he might follow the proceedings more easily but, in fact, in order to sway the council more easily, Brébeuf asked for and was granted permission to sit among the principal headmen in the centre of the longhouse. The headmen who were present then lamented the suffering of the country and each enumerated the sick and dead among his own clansmen. They blamed the Jesuits for what was happening and demanded that they be punished. No one defended the Jesuits and as the meeting progressed the headmen began to urge Brébeuf to produce a piece of bewitched cloth that was said to be the source of the illness. The Jesuits were promised that their lives would be spared if only they would admit that they had caused the epidemic and would reveal how they had done it. The Huron believed that such a confession automatically would strip the Jesuits of the power to do evil.

When Brébeuf found the headmen unwilling to believe his denials, he offered to let them search the Jesuits' cabin and to destroy all the cloth they found there. Ontitarac replied that this was the way sorcerers and guilty people always talked (15:45). Brébeuf then attempted to deliver a sermon explaining the nature of the Christian God and the rewards and punishments he inflicted on mankind. Contrary to normal Huron practice, this speech was interrupted repeatedly, especially by Ontitarac. Even Anenkhiondic, who had so far remained silent, accused the Jesuits of always repeating the same thing and only talking about the oki or spirit they worshipped (15:49). Many headmen walked out in the middle of Brébeuf's speech and one announced that if someone were to kill the Jesuits, the Huron leaders would have no objection. Many Huron expected that the confederacy council would order the Jesuits to be slain and the fact that the council was taking the charges against them seriously greatly enhanced fears and mistrust of them among the general population (15:53). The headmen decided to postpone any final decision about what would be done with the Jesuits until the traders had returned from Three Rivers, so that if they were killed, as many Huron as possible would be safe from French reprisals (15:47).

In the following weeks, the Jesuits were told that the headmen were losing control over the young men, who were anxious to purge the country of sorcerers (15:53). An uncle of Amantacha suggested that the priests should help several stricken headmen to recover, since the war chiefs would be without restraint if they died. The Jesuits were warned that their cabin at Ossossané would be burned when they least expected it and when a fire broke out on 3 October, they believed this to be an attempt on their lives (15:53).

Soon after the traders had returned from Three Rivers in mid-October, the headmen of Teanaostaiaé are said to have exhorted the young men of their village to kill the Jesuits while the people of Ossossané were away fishing (17:59). When the Jesuits learned of this, their hired men prepared to die fighting and Le Mercier went to summon Brébeuf from Ihonatiria (15:57–59). Soon the Jesuits learned that their would-be assailants had been persuaded not to take unilateral action, but that a meeting was being held in Ossossané at which new plans were being formulated to kill them. It was reported that when the Jesuits entered this meeting, it had already been decided that if their faces betrayed any sign of fear or guilt, they were to be slain on the spot. The only headman who remained well disposed towards them had been persuaded to leave town so that any decision to massacre the Jesuits might be unanimous. When Brébeuf arrived that evening and went to greet the principal headmen, they bowed their heads, indicating that the Jesuits were condemned men. Faced with the likelihood of death, Brébeuf drew up a spiritual testament that he entrusted to one of the few Huron who were still well inclined towards the French. He also gave orders that the French who survived any massacre should shelter among Huron who were their personal friends and that special efforts be made to convey the manuscript of their principal Huron dictionary to Quebec (15:61–65).

At the same time, in order to show that he did not fear death as a sorcerer might, Brébeuf gave an athataion, or death feast, to which he invited the people of Ossossané. He addressed them, as he had a right to do on such an occasion, concerning the interest that the Jesuits had in the welfare of the Huron and explained to them the nature of Christian beliefs about life after death. Many Huron attended this feast and listened to Brébeuf without interrupting him. Several days passed and, to the astonishment of both the Jesuits and the people of Ossossané, the headmen ceased to threaten the missionaries (15:67). By 6 November the epidemic had run its course and the missionaries were left in peace.

THE JESUITS' PROTECTION

How did it happen that when native sorcerers were being slain and the Jesuits were almost universally believed to be responsible for the epidemics, they too did not perish? In their *Relations*, the Jesuits expressed wonder at this and piously ascribed their survival to God's providence (Thwaites 1896–1901, 20:75); however, the Jesuits' real protection was the fur trade. Since the French officials emphasized that the continuation of this trade required the Huron to accept the Jesuits in their country and treat them well, the Huron believed that any action that endangered the Jesuits also endangered trade. That the Jesuits were not slain or even asked to return to Quebec at this time, despite the extreme hostility that many families must have felt towards them, is evidence of the degree to which the Huron now felt themselves to be dependent on French trade goods.

As might be expected, the most vocal supporters of the Jesuits were the headmen most deeply involved in trading with the French. One of these was Aenons. When during the winter of 1636–37 the headmen from the

Ihonatiria region debated whether the Jesuits ought to be killed or at least deported, Aenons argued that such action would be very dangerous and might lead to the destruction of the country. He said that if the Huron were unable to trade with the French for only two successive years, they would be reduced to such extremities that they would consider themselves lucky if they could beg assistance from the Algonkin (13:215–17). He persuaded the other headmen to come with him to ask the Jesuits not to send reports of their ill treatment to Quebec, lest the French retaliate against Huron traders who went to the St. Lawrence (12:89; 13:233). Later that same winter, Aenons was one of the principal exponents of the theory that the Mohawk had transmitted the current illness from the Susquehannock to the St. Lawrence (14:9). He was seeking to protect the Jesuits by shifting responsibility from them to the Huron's chief enemies. Another outspoken defender of the Jesuits was the headman Taratouan, whose nephew was living in the school at Quebec and who therefore claimed to be a relative of the French. He offered his fellow headmen a rich present of wampum beads in return for a promise not to harm the Jesuits (12:89).

Although the major epidemic in 1637 broke out prior to the trading season, the trade that year was not interrupted. While some Huron feared that everything that came from France was bewitched and therefore capable of transmitting disease, only one village (not identified by name) decided to abandon the use of European goods and break off all relations with the French (15:21). When it was most feared that the Huron might kill the Jesuits, Huron who were on good terms with them asked for written testimonials so that they might visit Three Rivers and Quebec safely, to trade as well as carry news of what had happened (15:13–15).

When the Huron gathered at Three Rivers to trade in September 1637, Achille de Bréhaut Delisle, who was Montmagny's lieutenant, formally denied that Champlain had ever wished to harm the Huron people and he rebuked Oumasasikweie, the namesake and successor of the Kichesipirini headman who had been killed by the Iroquois in 1635, for spreading this rumour. No Huron could be found who would substantiate the other accusations that were being levelled against the Jesuits; instead traders from one village said they had first heard them from another (12:245–47). Bréhaut Delisle praised the steadfast friendship that bound the French and Huron together and repeated some of the same religious sentiments that Brébeuf had expressed in the Huron country. He gave the Huron traders hatchets, iron arrowheads, and a large quantity of dried peas to wish them a safe journey home. He also presented a fine kettle and still more hatchets and arrowheads to the inhabitants of Ossossané for having accepted the Jesuits and built a cabin for them (12:257). He reminded the Huron of the love that the French felt towards the Jesuits and warned them that they must continue to treat the Jesuits well if they wished to remain on good terms with the French (12:259). Le Jeune commented that it was generous of the French officials to ascribe to religious motives what in any case had to be given to the Indians in order to retain their friendship (12:257).

Bréhaut Delisle's speeches and presents and the friendly treatment that the Huron traders had received at Three Rivers caused them to return home in a good mood. Since they had observed nothing that was sinister or suspicious at Three Rivers, they no longer believed that the Jesuits were the cause of the epidemic (15:55). While this did not prevent a final outburst of hostility against the Jesuits in late October, the Jesuits attributed their survival during this dangerous period to the goodwill of the traders (15:55–57).

It is ironic to note, however, that while the safety of the Jesuits depended almost entirely on the Huron's reluctance to break the terms of their trading alliance with the French, the French officials at Quebec were worried about having committed themselves too firmly to a policy of stopping trade if the French who were living in the Huron country were mistreated. It seems to have been agreed that if the Jesuits were killed as a result of a general conspiracy, the only course of action would be to stop trading with the Huron. If, however, their murder was the work of individuals, the French were anxious to assure those Huron who were innocent of their continued friendship (14:245). Had the Huron known or guessed that the fur trade was as important to the French as it was to them, the fate of the Jesuits might have been very different.

BECOMING FRENCH

The vast majority of adult Huron who were baptized in the early years of the Jesuit mission viewed it as a curing ritual or a means of joining friends and relatives who had died and were believed to be living in heaven. Almost all of those who recovered from their illnesses showed no further interest in Christianity and were regarded by the Jesuits as apostates. Such experiences made the Jesuits unwilling to baptize healthy adults (13:121). In spite of this, a small number of able-bodied Huron actively sought baptism. These were traders who saw baptism as a means of becoming kinsmen of the French, just as headmen sending their sons or nephews to live with the French was another. The first traders who actively sought baptism were not headmen and it may be that ordinary traders saw baptism as a more expedient means of establishing a personal alliance with the French. Such men were willing to risk the dangers that seemed inherent in baptism in order to enjoy the advantages that accrued from a ritual kinship with their trading partners.

This attitude was encouraged by the trading company, which offered substantial benefits to Indian traders who were Christians that they did not extend to those who were not. Since Christian Indians were theoretically French citizens, they had the right to receive the same set prices for their furs that Frenchmen did, which were considerably higher than were those paid to Indians. Moreover, money was set aside so that additional presents could be given to Christian Indians who came to trade, as evidence of the love that the French had for those who shared their religion (16:33; 12:257). It was also general policy to give converts places of honour in all the councils that were held at Three Rivers and Quebec (9:287; 12:243).

The Jesuits knew why these traders sought baptism. Yet, they were convinced that if they held out the hope of eventual baptism, this would be an effective way of motivating these men to acquire greater knowledge of Christianity, and that eventually they would believe in it. The Jesuits were especially anxious to convert older and more influential men. Thus a contest developed between Huron traders, who wished to convince the Jesuits of their sincerity, and the Jesuits, who wished to exploit the traders' desire for baptism as a means of genuinely converting them.

The first trader to request baptism was Amantacha's father, Soranhes. He attributed his escape from the Iroquois to the intervention of the Jesuits' god and, the following winter, declared that he and his entire household were anxious to be baptized and to see Teanaostaiaé become Christian. Brébeuf regarded both him and Amantacha as "crafty spirits" and refused to grant his wish (8:149–51). In September 1635, Soranhes again requested that his family be baptized and about the same time Amantacha began to express a renewed interest in Christianity. In November, Brébeuf and Pijart returned to Teanaostaiaé and, with Amantacha as their interpreter, they instructed his family in basic Christian beliefs. These teachings were received with apparent interest and approval. Soranhes stated that he would encounter little trouble in learning the necessary prayers, but had difficulty learning to cross himself. While the Jesuits were present, the family also observed Friday and Saturday as fast days, as was the custom in Catholic Europe at that time (10:61–67; 13:23–25). Soranhes came to stay with the Jesuits from time to time during the following winter, but, although he repeatedly asked to be baptized, the

Jesuits detected his continuing attachment to worldly interests. They were confirmed in these doubts by Amantacha's report that his father was expecting to benefit from baptism in his trading relations with the French. To ingratiate himself with the Jesuits, Amantacha explained that he had offered his father all of his wampum necklaces if he would desist from such thoughts of worldly profit (9:281).

In the spring of 1636 Soranhes revealed these interests even more clearly when he asked for letters of recommendation to take with him when he went to trade. He also said that he wished to be baptized when the ships arrived at Quebec. Brébeuf informed him that the place of his baptism was of no importance, but invited him to stay with the Jesuits for a few days before he left for Quebec, in order to consider whether or not he was ready to be baptized. Soranhes promised to do this but sensing that Brébeuf was unwilling to permit his baptism, he left to trade immediately afterwards (13:25–27). On his return from Three Rivers, he travelled as far as the Nipissing country with one of the Jesuit priests, but there he changed into another canoe and returned directly to Teanaostaiaé (13:27). He died unbaptized in August of that year. Although his relatives would not confirm the report, Soranhes was said to have committed suicide over the loss of his son (13:23, 27).

The first adult Huron to be baptized in good health was Tsiouendaentaha (14:77–95).[9] A resident of Ihonatiria, he was about fifty years old and although apparently not a headman the Jesuits described him as an influential person with good connections. Like Soranhes, he had expressed a wish to be baptized, but the Jesuits had put him off, fearing the Huron tendency to dissemble and believing that he was motivated by self-interest and a desire for presents. Moreover, while he made a point of listening to the Jesuits and approving of what they said, when he fell ill he had traditional Huron rituals performed for his recovery. In spite of this, his attachment for the Jesuits increased, particularly when his family came through the epidemic of 1636 without loss. As spring approached, he became more anxious for baptism and during Lent he came to receive instruction almost every day. He also won the confidence of the Jesuits by praising their teachings to other Huron. Moreover, Tsiouendaentaha no longer pressed for baptism; on the contrary, he argued that he had not been able to remember enough of what he had been taught to qualify for it. This persuaded the Jesuits of his sincerity.

Finally, the Jesuits began to press Tsiouendaentaha to be baptized. When he promised to give up all Huron customs that were incompatible with Christianity, it was agreed that he should be baptized prior to his departure for Three Rivers. With the Jesuits' approval, Tsiouendaentaha celebrated this event by providing a great feast for the people of Ihonatiria. The Jesuits hoped that if he made a public declaration of what he intended to do, his own people would give him more liberty to live as the French did. In reciprocity, the Jesuits gave their own feast to express their rejoicing at his conversion; however, when Tsiouendaentaha began to speculate about what kind of presents he would be given when he went to Three Rivers, the Jesuits had to console themselves with the hope that someday he would understand Christianity better (14:91).

Tsiouendaentaha's conversion did not go unrewarded at Three Rivers. Bréhaut Delisle took him aside and gave him a fine present as evidence of the affection that the French now felt for him (12:257) and he was publicly entrusted to carry to the Huron country the picture of Christ that was to hang in the chapel at Ossossané (12:251). These honours encouraged Tsiouendaentaha to remain a Christian although his wife and a niece died in the summer of 1637 and, shortly after he returned from trading, one of his daughters and a brother-in-law were carried off by disease (15:19). Many Huron pointed out that his family had not been stricken until after he had become a Christian.

A different attitude towards baptism was exhibited by the headman Aenons. To win and retain the goodwill of the French, he consistently urged his people not to harm the Jesuits, listened to the priests, and approved of what they said. Nevertheless, he declined to express any wish to be baptized in the near future, saying that he doubted he could live as the Jesuits wished him to (11:135). He became ill on his way to Quebec in 1637 and arrived there in a weakened condition in early August. Knowing he was about to die, he offered a present to the French governor and urged him to treat well the Huron who were coming to trade. Likewise, he told his own people that he did not hold the French at Three Rivers responsible for his death and that they should not attempt to avenge him by doing any harm to the French who were living in the Huron country (12:199; 11:135). Asked whether he wished to become a Christian, he stated that since he had been invited to visit the French, it was well that he should die firmly allied to them (12:199). He was baptized on 6 August and died soon after. Because he had become a Frenchman, his Huron companions permitted him to be buried in the French cemetery at Three Rivers, rather than burning his body and taking his bones home with them. No doubt the French gave him a fine funeral procession as they had another Huron who had been baptized when already almost unconscious on 18 July. This procession had greatly pleased the Huron (11:127–31) and news of it may have stimulated Aenons to covet a similar honour for himself. Aenons's baptism led to those of two more traders, Tsondaké and Arachiokouan, who also were stricken with illness when they arrived at Three Rivers (11:135).

CHIHWATENHA'S CONVERSION

A different kind of conversion was that of Chihwatenha, an inhabitant of Ossossané. He was about thirty-five years old and although not a wealthy or prominent man, was a nephew of Anenkhiondic. While occasionally he may have visited Three Rivers prior to his conversion, he had trading partners among the Tionnontaté and his main trading activities seem to have been in that direction. The *Jesuit Relations* report that he had married only once and never in his life had smoked, gambled, given curing feasts, or relied on charms (Thwaites 1896–1901, 15:79). These claims are hagiographic and almost certainly exaggerated. If only partly true, however, they suggest that his personality was an abnormal one by Huron standards. As soon as the Jesuits began to visit Ossossané, Chihwatenha showed himself anxious to please them and after they settled there he spent much time talking with them and helping to baptize young children (15:81). In the summer of 1637, he was stricken by the epidemic then raging in Ossossané and immediately went to the Jesuits in hopes of being cured. Although the Jesuits believed that he accepted their offer of baptism in the spirit of a true Christian, more likely he sought it as a curing ritual. He attributed his recovery to his baptism and at a feast of rejoicing that he gave to celebrate his cure he publicly announced his desire to live as a Christian (15:81–85).

Unlike most baptized Huron, Chihwatenha continued to manifest friendship for the Jesuits and a desire to live according to the rules they prescribed. At first, he may have been motivated to do this by gratitude for his recovery and by the belief that he could become a member of the Jesuits' curing society, thereby continuing to protect his own health. Gradually, however, he also seems to have been attracted by the prestige, or at least the notoriety, that accrued from being the Jesuits' favoured disciple and closest Huron associate. Eventually he was to boast that in this capacity he would be remembered forever among the Huron (19:155).

As an expression of his adherence to the Jesuits, Chihwatenha spent considerable amounts of time praying and receiving instruction. He refused to participate in Huron rituals, was assiduous about confession, and took pleasure in repeating the Jesuits' teachings to fellow Huron (15:95–97).

When his own longhouse was stricken by the epidemic less than a month after he had recovered, he refused to let any shaman enter it. His son, sister-in-law, a nephew, and three nieces were all baptized, although the son and one niece died soon after (15:89–91). Many of the people of Ossossané, including his relatives, rebuked him for preventing those who were sick from seeking traditional forms of aid and, in derision, the people of his longhouse were called "the family of Christians" (15:89, 99). Chihwatenha's wife, Aonetta, was for some time unwilling to give up her traditional beliefs, but soon after the death of her son she agreed to be baptized.

To celebrate his wife's baptism, Chihwatenha provided a great feast for his relatives and friends, who included some of the most important men in Ossossané. A large crowd flocked to the Jesuits' cabin where the rite was performed. Following Aonetta's baptism, she and Chihwatenha were re-married according to the rites of the Roman Catholic Church and, after the crowd had dispersed, they and their nephew were allowed to participate in a mass. The other members of the family, who had been baptized in illness but had not yet proved themselves as Christians, were not allowed to receive this sacrament (15:101–5; 16:59). While this was going on, Chihwatenha's sister-in-law fell ill and died. She had already been baptized and her sudden death led bolder Huron to ask the Jesuits' hired men what reparations the Jesuits planned to give Chihwatenha's family for having murdered her (15:105). Chihwatenha and his family continued to follow the precepts of the Jesuits although for about ten months they were the only Christian family in Ossossané (17:41). The Jesuits hoped that their example would demonstrate to other Huron that it was possible for Indians to live as Christians.

During the winter of 1637–38 Chihwatenha asked the Jesuits to teach him to write. They accepted the task and he was able to compose letters by the spring. It was, however, much harder for him to learn to read. His professed aim in learning how to write was to record not only religious matters but also the affairs of the country. This, no doubt, would have been a great source of prestige for him. In return, he helped the Jesuits to analyse Huron grammar and compose religious homilies (15:111–13).

A DEFEAT ON THE ST. LAWRENCE

The truce that the Huron had arranged with the Seneca appears to have been observed by both sides until 1638. Blood feuds continued with the four other Iroquois tribes and thus the Huron country was never completely free from the threat of raiders. In September 1637 a band made up of Attignawantan, Attigneenongnahac, and Arendarhonon warriors surprised twenty-five or thirty Iroquois who were fishing along the shore of Lake Ontario. Eight Iroquois were taken prisoner; one was killed on the spot and the seven others were brought home to be tortured (Thwaites 1896–1901, 13:37). One of these was a Seneca about fifty years of age. He had refused to accept the peace treaty that his tribesmen had concluded with the Huron and had married among the Onondaga so that he might continue fighting (13:45). In April 1637 an Indian who had recently come from the Seneca country was said to have warned the Huron that the other Iroquois tribes were planning to attack either the Huron traders on their way to the St. Lawrence or the Huron country while these traders were away. The Jesuits doubted the truth of this story, since similar ones were circulated by the Huron headmen every year in order to make sure that enough armed men remained at home to protect their villages (14:39). Prior to April, however, the Huron had been discussing plans to wage war on the Iroquois to ensure that their fields were safe for the women to work in the following summer (13:265).

The main clash between the Huron and the Iroquois during the summer of 1637 occurred, not in Ontario, but along the St. Lawrence. After the murder of Oumasasikweie, both the Algonkin and the Montagnais were again at war with the Mohawk and they therefore decided to forget the differences that for a time had divided them (9:245). In 1636 it was reported that as many as 300 Iroquois warriors had penetrated the Richelieu Valley. Some stragglers belonging to this group were slain and later a Montagnais war party lay in ambush near one of the Mohawk villages, where they killed twenty-eight of the enemy and took five prisoners (9:251–55). In contrast, a joint force of Montagnais and Algonkin that attempted to invade the Mohawk country in the spring of 1637 was soundly defeated. Both of their leaders were killed and those who escaped returned home in disarray (12:153–61). In June, a group of Onontchataronon warriors defeated their Iroquois opponents in a battle fought on a lake or river and captured thirteen prisoners, one of whom was sent to Three Rivers to be slain. This victory was attributed to the birchbark canoes of the Onontchataronon, which were lighter and swifter than the elm bark ones used by the Iroquois (12:181).

During this period the Algonkin and Montagnais were unsuccessful in securing support from either the French or the Huron. The French refused to accompany their war parties because they regarded Algonkin warriors as undependable and feared their lack of discipline. They also claimed that the refusal of these Indians to offer their children to the Jesuits for instruction relieved the French of any obligation to fight alongside them (9:219). The Huron had been angered by the Kichesipirini's efforts to sever their trade with the French and thus saw little reason to help the Algonkin. Moreover, up to and including 1636 their traders had not seriously been attacked by the Iroquois while they were on their way to or from the St. Lawrence.

In August 1637 a force of Iroquois estimated at 500 men established a camp on the north shore of the St. Lawrence at the head of Lake St. Peter. Their aim was to watch the river and intercept Indians as they came down-river to trade with the French (12:207). The French first learned about the presence of the Iroquois when the latter attacked some Huron who were returning up-river. One of the two canoes that were attacked escaped and its crew returned to Three Rivers (12:199–201). The seriousness of the Iroquois menace was only fully realized, however, when an Iroquois canoe appeared at Three Rivers and challenged the French and their allies to come out and fight (12:201). A pinnace that was sent to drive away this canoe, reported that Lake St. Peter was thick with Iroquois, both on the water and along the shore. Later that day, a single Huron canoe arrived at Three Rivers and reported that nine other canoes making up the party of the Huron headman, Taratouan, had been attacked on their way to Three Rivers. The attack had taken place in the narrow north channel of the St. Lawrence River at the west end of Lake St. Peter (12:99–105; 207–09). Twenty-nine Huron, including Taratouan, had been captured, and one prisoner had been killed immediately. Taratouan was seen being tortured by the Mohawk, but presumably he was kept alive until they returned to their villages (12:215). On 11 August two armed pinnaces made their way up-river, only to find that the Iroquois had withdrawn the day before. This retreat permitted the main body of about 150 Huron traders to arrive at Three Rivers without mishap in late August (12:235).

The need to avenge Taratouan and his companions was the final factor compelling the Huron to reactivate their military alliance with the Algonkin. The general council of the Huron confederacy that met to discuss a question of war on 4 August 1637 was convened too early to be a response to this incident, especially since the issues being debated had already been discussed by each village council. Nevertheless, rumours of an impending Iroquois attack on the St. Lawrence had been circulating since the spring and these may have prompted the Huron headmen to consider possible courses of action. If this was the reason for this council,

the Huron were well prepared for the decisive response they were to make
the following spring.

THE JESUIT SCHOOL CLOSES

In the spring of 1637 Father Pierre Pijart attempted to recruit more Huron
children for the school at Quebec. It was feared that this would be more
difficult than the year before since meanwhile accusations of sorcery had
been levelled against the Jesuits (Thwaites 1896–1901, 12:91) and a
rumour had been current among the Huron since the winter that two of
the boys who had gone to Quebec the previous summer were dead. In spite
of this, various families expressed an apparent willingness to send their sons
to live with the French (14:45). These offers came from Ossossané,
Teanaostaiaé, Ekhiondastsaan, and five or six other villages, and were more
numerous than the French were able to accept (12:113–15). Although the
Jesuits feared that Tsiko's and Satouta's relatives would be angered by
their deaths and might seek blood revenge, neither family appeared to
blame the French when the news was confirmed. Both agreed that the boys
had been well looked after and stated that since so many people had died in
the Huron country, their deaths were not unexpected (12:93). It is impossible to know whether this attitude reflected greater trust in the French
among Huron leaders or it was the politic dissimulation of traders who did
not wish to undermine their relationship with the French.

At the beginning of the summer the three boys who had survived the
winter at Quebec were sent to Three Rivers to await their relatives. On his
way down to Three Rivers Tewatirhon's uncle, who was a war chief, heard
what under the circumstances was a highly plausible rumour: that two
Frenchmen had been killed in the Huron country. Fearing that when the
French heard this rumour they would exact blood revenge, Tewatirhon's
uncle asked to take the boy home with him. When the French learned why
he wanted to remove his nephew they attempted to detain the uncle and
finally arrested him when he tried to steal away secretly with Tewatirhon
and another boy (12:95). Even after the rumour was revealed to be false,
Tewatirhon said that he wished to return home to visit his relatives, especially his mother. This was agreed to, and Tewatirhon and Father Paul
Ragueneau left for the Huron country in the same canoe. As they were
travelling up the Ottawa River they met Tewatirhon's other uncle, Taratouan, who was on his way to Three Rivers. Taratouan chided Tewatirhon

for leaving the French when they had treated him so well, and made him return to Three Rivers with him (12:97). Tewatirhon was thus with his uncle when the latter was captured by the Iroquois. During the attack, Tewatirhon made his way to shore and after hiding for a day managed to steal an Iroquois canoe and reach Three Rivers (12:101–3, 211). Tewatirhon returned to Quebec where, in obedience to Taratouan's wishes, he remained over the following winter. In the spring of 1638 he wished to join the Montagnais in a raid against the Iroquois, but the Jesuits would not give him permission to do so (12:105). Andehoua, the second of the Huron scholars, had apparently become accustomed to the relative ease and luxury of Quebec and he and his relatives were willing for him to stay with the Jesuits until 1638 (12:105–9). By contrast, the youngest of the boys wished to go home for a year and he embarked with Father Pijart (12:109). It appears that he died the next year, after becoming ill on his way back to Quebec (15:137).

Two of the youths from Teanaostaiaé who were supposed to remain at Quebec were captured by the Iroquois, but a third escaped and agreed to spend the winter with Tewatirhon (12:109–13). Two other boys offered to stay with the Jesuits, but when Tewatirhon informed the Jesuits that one of them suffered from melancholy, that boy was sent home. Of the many youths who had been promised by the Huron, four were accepted by the Jesuits, although one of these was soon enticed away by his relatives (14:231). The new students are reported to have given themselves up to gluttony, gambling, idleness, and other irregularities. They responded in a hostile manner to the Jesuits' efforts to discipline them and mocked Tewatirhon and Andehoua for obeying the priests. Finally, they stole enough provisions for the trip home and set off one night, carrying with them as many other things as they could manage (14:233). Thus the youths returned home with what they had stolen, while their families kept the presents that they had been given for them.

The two boys who remained showed the same favourable disposition as they had the year before. Both were baptized during the winter and Andehoua was persuaded to mortify his body by holding his hands in ice water and standing up to his waist in it (14:235). Although self-testing was part of the Huron cultural pattern, under Jesuit tutelage Andehoua developed an aversion to sexuality that was alien to traditional Huron behaviour (14:237). When Andehoua was travelling home the following year, he risked his life to save a portable mass kit that he was transporting in his canoe (14:245–47). Tewatirhon, who was older, showed less enthusiasm for Jesuit teachings and was therefore judged to be the duller of the two, as Savignon had once been judged duller than Amantacha (14:239).

One disappointment for the Jesuits was their failure to promote the idea of a Huron colony at Quebec (12:255). When 150 Huron traders arrived at Three Rivers in September 1637, Bréhaut Delisle exhorted them to bring some families to live near the French. He assured them that these settlers would be given food and helped to clear land and build houses. In reply the Huron said that their women would not undertake so long a journey or go to live among foreigners (12:255). The central role played by Huron women as guardians of village life was clearly manifested.

Throughout the winter of 1637–38 the reports that were received in Quebec led officials to fear that there might be a general massacre of the Jesuits and their assistants in the Huron country (14:243). In the spring, Montmagny was anxious to send some Frenchmen to the Huron country to learn what was happening there. Tewatirhon and Andehoua argued that these Frenchmen might be murdered if the Huron had already declared war and that it would be safer if they performed this task (14:243). They may have hoped by doing this to extricate themselves from possible French reprisals. Their offer was accepted and they, together with Father Daniel and a young French workman, were dispatched with some Algonkin in June 1638 (12:243–45). Daniel's orders were to return to Quebec immediately if the Jesuits had been killed on the orders of the Huron confederacy council, but if the murders turned out to be the work of individuals, he should remain and assure the rest of the Huron of the continued friendship of the French (14:245). Thus a fine line was drawn between business-as-usual and protecting the Jesuits who went to work among the Huron.

When Daniel reached Morrison Island, he encountered some of Andehoua's relatives and learned that the Jesuits had not been in any danger since the previous autumn. In spite of this, he decided to continue inland with a group of Huron who were on their way home. Two days later they met some friends of Tewatirhon who were going to trade; deeming it advisable that Tewatirhon should pass one more winter at Quebec in order to strengthen him in the Christian faith, Daniel persuaded him to return to Three Rivers. When they reached the Huron country, Daniel joined the Ossossané mission while Andehoua returned to his natal village to become a native preacher (14:251–53). He was obviously proud of his connections with the French and the zealousness with which he discharged his job of preaching led the Jesuits to request that Tewatirhon be sent home as soon as possible to assist him (14:255). They also requested that the Jesuits at Three Rivers should attempt to enrol as many Huron youths as possible in their school; after the troubles of the preceding year, it was impossible for the Jesuits in the Huron country to persuade parents to send their children to Quebec. Yet, likewise, Huron who came to Quebec were reluctant to leave any young men behind. They feared that more trouble might arise with the Jesuits in the Huron country and were therefore reluctant to leave any of their people as hostages at Quebec.

The difficulties of keeping Huron boys at Quebec had already become evident there in the autumn of 1637, but at that time the troubles had been compensated for by the devotion of Andehoua and Tewatirhon. After the latter were back in the Huron country for a while, the problems involved in using young men as native preachers began to reveal themselves. Andehoua settled in Scanonaenrat and was later described as living a morally pure life and professing to be a Christian. In 1641 he accompanied a war party on a raid against the Iroquois and his prayers were credited with saving their canoes from shipwreck when they were caught in a storm on Lake Ontario (23:173–77). There is, however, no evidence of him serving as a preacher after 1638. No doubt because of his youth, the Huron paid little attention to what he had to say (16:171).

Tewatirhon quickly returned to traditional ways, particularly in his sexual behaviour. He continued, however, to profess a belief in the Jesuits' teachings and after he had been badly burned in a fire about 1641, the Jesuits were convinced that he died a good Christian (21:173–75). A member of Atironta's family who had spent a winter at Quebec appears to have hated the time he spent there and after he returned home he persistently mocked the Jesuits and their teachings. He too, however, asked the Jesuits to pardon and baptize him shortly before he died about 1641 (21:171–73).

By 1639 experience had convinced the Jesuits who were working in the Huron country that their original plan of trying to convert the Huron by first instructing their children was in error. It was very difficult to instruct most of the children or to make them behave contrary to their will. Moreover, even if one did succeed in instructing a young man, this had no effect upon his elders since the latter did not take young people seriously. This attitude would, in turn, discourage Huron youths from trying to proselytize. It was also agreed that if young men returning from school did not marry quickly, most would be drawn into promiscuous behaviour and, thereby, into resuming their old ways generally (16:251). Yet Christian marriages were impossible until girls were available who understood and accepted the Christian faith and there had been no suitable converts (15:125). If a Christian man were to marry a non-Christian woman and she were to leave him, by Roman Catholic law remarriage was impossible for him. Such considerations threw strong impediments in the way of any plans to instruct large numbers of young men.

This led the Jesuits to reject completely the policy that they and the Recollets had followed since their arrival in the Huron country. The Jesuits concluded that far from being able to convert the Huron by instructing their children, the instruction of children was impossible without the prior conversion of their parents (16:251). It was decided that the primary aim of the Jesuits should be to convert older men and especially the heads of stable families (17:33). Their experience with Chihwatenha suggested that when the male head of a household had been converted, other members tended to follow his example (15:109). Henceforth, only the children of Christians and adults who wished to receive more intensive instruction were to be allowed to live with the Jesuits at Quebec.

We do not know how many Huron boys spent the winter of 1638–39 at Quebec under Father Pijart's direction. None of them had been there before and the decision taken the following year to stop having Huron youths stay at Quebec (24:103) suggests that these ones must have been as difficult and unpromising as those of the previous year. The most curious scholar that winter was an elderly Huron named Ateiachias who had resolved to spend the winter at Quebec after Tewatirhon told him how well he had been treated (16:169–79). The Jesuits could not dissuade him and probably agreed with his argument that it was more profitable to instruct an old man than a young one. They decided, therefore, to let him stay. Like Andehoua, he showed great enthusiasm to learn whatever the Jesuits wished and to imitate their behaviour. Possibly he hoped that by so doing he would acquire their shamanistic powers.

Some fifteen or sixteen Huron who had come with Ateiachias to Quebec and found themselves stranded there over the winter lived for a time near the Jesuits' residence. These men censured Ateiachias for deserting the ways of his own people and no longer wanting to be a Huron (16:175). Ateiachias paid no attention to them, however, and by the spring he was ready to be baptized. When he was preparing to return home in order to select new recruits for the school, his canoe overturned and, wearing bulky and absorbent French clothes, he drowned (16:177–79). Following this accident, Father Pijart returned to the Huron country and for several years no attempt was made to recruit new students for the school.

Interlude

AVENGING TARATOUAN

In the spring of 1638 the Huron went to war against the eastern tribes of the Iroquois confederacy to avenge the killing of Taratouan and his companions. As in the raid of 1615 they were accompanied by Algonkin allies and altogether made up a force of about 300 men (Thwaites 1896–1901, 17:71). It is not known whether the expedition set out from the Huron country and travelled down the Trent Valley or moved south from the Ottawa Valley. Nor is it known where the Huron had their principal encounter with the enemy. Eventually, however, they made contact with about 100 Iroquois, who in Du Creux's (1951–52:257) words had come to rob rather than to fight. This suggests that the Iroquois were on their way to the Ottawa or St. Lawrence Valleys to plunder Indians who were bringing their furs to Three Rivers. The Iroquois were first discovered by a Huron scouting party. One Huron was captured and told the Iroquois that the Huron were few in number and could easily be overpowered. Because of this, the Iroquois decided not to withdraw with their prisoner, but to build a fort and await the enemy. They were therefore taken by surprise when 300 Huron and Algonkin surrounded their fort. In retaliation for his deception, the Huron captive was immediately torn to pieces (Thwaites 1896–1901, 17:71–73).

Seeing that they were surrounded, the majority of Iroquois were in favour of making a run for their lives. This was opposed by the headman, Ononkwaia. He argued that such cowardice was possible only if it were night-time or if the sky were overcast, but that since the spirit of the sun could see what was happening, it was necessary for each man to fight as bravely as he could. In the ensuing combat, seventeen or eighteen Iroquois were killed and only four or five managed to escape. About eighty prisoners were shared by the victors. Most of them were taken back to the Huron country, where they were distributed among different villages and finally tortured to death (17:73). Over twenty more Iroquois were taken prisoner in other engagements that year, bringing the total number of prisoners to well over a hundred (17:63).

It is certain that Ononkwaia was an Oneida (17:65) and that at least one Mohawk was captured. The latter individual had gone to visit another (unidentified) tribe, intending to trade wampum for beaver skins, but when he lost his wampum gambling he decided to join this expedition rather than return home (17:77). This story makes it likely that the Iroquois war party was made up largely of Oneida. If so, this battle may account for the particular hatred that the Oneida felt towards the Huron a few years later, as well as their claim that the Huron and Algonkin had slain most of the men of their tribe in a battle. Because of their losses, the Oneida women are said to have been compelled to ask for Mohawk men to marry so that their tribe might not become extinct (27:297; 28:281). In later decades, the Oneida are estimated to have had about 140 men capable of bearing arms (49:257). If this figure applies even approximately to the 1630s, the Oneida may indeed have lost the majority of their warriors at this time.

The prompt action that the French had taken against the Mohawk in 1637 and this disastrous defeat of the Oneida less than a year later seem temporarily to have restored the St. Lawrence Valley as a peaceful artery of trade. This may explain why in the summer of 1638 the Huron felt safe to travel to Three Rivers in small, straggling groups (14:255). Nevertheless, there is evidence of at least some Iroquois marauding that year (16:213). Chaumonot noted in 1640 that each year a number of Huron were killed on the way to or from Three Rivers (18:33). These killings probably took place along the Ottawa River, where French control had always been least effective.

This great victory over the Oneida also seems to have encouraged certain Huron youths to murder a member of the Seneca tribe. Following this, the Huron decided to resume war with the Seneca rather than pay reparations to preserve the peace (17:111). Although some headmen probably opposed the resumption of war, most Huron were sufficiently confident that they were willing to encourage the young men of their tribes to win more honours by fighting the enemy on a broader front. The reason generally given for attacking the Seneca was that some Huron families could no longer control their desire to avenge losses that the Seneca had inflicted on them prior to 1634. By the spring of 1639 the first raid had been launched against the Seneca, and by the end of May twelve prisoners had been brought back to the Huron country (17:111).

THE JESUITS BECOME RESPECTABLE

As soon as the epidemic of 1637 was over, the Huron ceased to live in dread of the Jesuits and the latter were no longer in danger of losing their lives. While many Huron continued to regard the Jesuits as potentially dangerous they began to elicit their goodwill either in hopes of receiving better

treatment when trading with the French or because they hoped that the
Jesuits could be persuaded to use their magical powers to confer long life
and other benefits on them. The summer of 1638 was another dry one,
although less so in the Huron country than farther south where many
Neutral had to enter into special trading relationships with other tribes in
order to avoid starvation (Thwaites 1896–1901, 15:157). As the fields of
Ossossané became parched, the Jesuits were asked to produce rain, and,
once again, were greatly admired when three days of it followed the first
mass that was said for this purpose (17:135–37). This exhibition of concern
for the Huron's welfare led many of them to apologize for their former
animosity towards the Jesuits (17:115).

As early as December 1637 the Jesuits were free to renew their mission
work at Ossossané. They began by inviting about 150 headmen and heads
of households to a feast at which they announced their intention to resume
public instruction. In return, Anenkhiondic invited the Jesuits to a feast in
Ossossané on 9 January. At this assembly, Brébeuf was given an opportunity
to reiterate the reasons why the Jesuits had come to the Huron country and
to answer those who still asked why no Frenchmen had died during the
epidemics (15:113–17). Once again the Jesuits were being listened to with
respect by men who were anxious to live up to the terms of the French-
Huron alliance (17:117–19). After this meeting, several weeks were
devoted to performing an Ononharoia ceremony for one of the wealthiest
men in Ossossané.

When it was over, Brébeuf persuaded an influential man to sponsor yet
another feast so that he could address the Huron on the subject of hell.
This feast was held on 1 February and was attended by more people than
the first two. When it was over, the headmen who were present announced
that henceforth they would recognize Brébeuf as a fellow headman. This
gave him the right to announce and hold public meetings in his cabin any
time he chose. It was also the first time that the Jesuits had been accepted
as a fully enfranchised segment of a Huron community (15:117–19). Thus,
with the official sanction of their headmen, many of the people of Ossossané began to satisfy their curiosity to see the Jesuits' images and hear their
songs by attending prayers on Sundays and Feast Days. The prayers were
followed by a catechism and a discussion period in the fashion of the early
services at Ihonatiria. At Ossossané, however, Chihwatenha played an
important role, explaining the Jesuits' ideas to fellow Huron and engaging
in debate with men who were older and of higher status than himself
(15:121–23).

In 1638 the Jesuits undertook to erect the first European-style building in the Huron country. This was a timber chapel thirty feet long, sixteen feet wide, and twenty-four feet high (15:139, 175). Like the missionary cabin, it appears to have stood on the outskirts of Ossossané. The chapel was built by the Jesuits' hired men, who were now twelve in number (15:157–59), and was described as a handsome edifice. It was meant to serve as yet another indication to the Huron of the technological superiority of the French.

During the summer of 1638 the Jesuits were also kept busy by the arrival of several hundred refugees. These were a portion of the Wenroronon tribe who, when they found themselves constrained to abandon their homeland in western New York State, decided to join the Huron. Accordingly, they sent some of their headmen to ask the Huron to accept them. The proposal was debated in each Huron village and was approved by the confederacy. A considerable number of Huron then set out to defend the Wenroronon refugees and to help them carry their possessions northward. In spite of this help, the hardships of the journey were such that a large number of Wenroronon became ill, either along the way or soon after they arrived in the Huron country, and many who became ill died (17:25–27). Chihwatenha was among those who journeyed the entire way with the Wenroronon, following which he suffered from a fever for forty days (17:49–51).

Ossossané was the first Huron settlement that the Wenroronon reached and although some eventually went to live in other Huron villages, the majority were to remain there.[10] They were given temporary lodgings with Huron families and in spite of the fear of a bad harvest, chests of corn were put at their disposal. The Jesuits bled those who were ill and provided them with other forms of medical assistance. They also risked their reputations by trying to baptize all those who were in danger of dying. For two months, the Jesuits at Ossossané were so busy attending to the Wenroronon that they had to abandon their routine mission work in the village (17:25–31; 15:159–61). According to Bressani, the Wenroronon had been in contact with Protestant traders along the east coast of the United States prior to their arrival in the Huron country and soon after their arrival they repeated many harmful stories about the Jesuits that they had heard from these traders (39:141).

When the Jesuits returned to their regular routine in November 1638, they discovered that a number of Huron individuals, and even whole families, were anxious to follow Chihwatenha's advice and become Christians (17:31). During the winter, twelve families and a total of fifty persons were solemnly baptized (15:169–85, 189; 17:33). Husbands and wives celebrated Roman Catholic remarriages and were presented with wedding rings by the Jesuits (15:173–75). Unfortunately, we know little about these early converts except that the Jesuits tended to delay the baptism of young men and to favour the baptism of older men and the heads of families (15:125, 193). Among those who were baptized in good health were a few visitors to the Huron country, possibly Susquehannock, who were about to return home (17:37). Many of the sixty people who professed to be Christians in Ossossané in the summer of 1639 were Wenroronon who had been baptized in ill health. During the previous year, the Jesuits had baptized over 120 sick people in Ossossané, perhaps including Iroquois captives who were about to be slain (15:189). Fifty-two of those who were ill were children and of these twenty-seven died, while seventy-four were adults, of whom twenty-two died (17:25). Many baptized in the extremity of their illness showed no further interest in Christianity after they had recovered (17:37).

THE MISSIONS EXPAND

The Jesuits remained in Ihonatiria until the summer of 1638, baptizing eleven more people there and in neighbouring villages. Atsan, a leading war chief from Arenté (Thwaites 1896–1901, 13:57–59), expressed an interest in being baptized (15:131). By the spring of 1638, however, Ihonatiria was generally abandoned, the survivors of its epidemics having moved away to join more flourishing communities. The Jesuits interpreted the disappearance of the village as divine punishment for the contempt that its inhabitants had shown for Christianity (17:11). Many Huron feared that the destruction of the village presaged what would happen to any Huron settlement in which the Jesuits were allowed to establish themselves (17:115).

The Jesuits decided to transfer their oldest mission from Ihonatiria to Teanaostaiaé. Even if the latter community had been extremely hostile to them in 1637, the Jesuits probably had more personal contacts there than elsewhere. Moreover, with its eighty houses and an estimated 2000 inhabitants it was now the largest Huron settlement and, therefore, of considerable importance to Jesuit strategy. Brébeuf visited Teanaostaiaé and spoke with the village council. The latter, no doubt with an eye on French trade, agreed to accept missionaries and to provide them with an empty cabin that probably had been abandoned as a result of the epidemic. By 25 June the Jesuits were established in the principal town of the Attigneenongnahac (17:61).

Events in Teanaostaiaé followed much the same course as at Ossossané. During the following year, forty-nine sick children were baptized and forty-four adults who may include twelve or thirteen Iroquois prisoners (17:63); of these, eighteen children and twenty-six adults died (17:61). The first convert in good health was not baptized until December 1638. This was Aochiati, a man about seventy years old and the master of the Dance of the Naked Ones (17:79–81). In order to be baptized he had to agree to give up his membership in the curing society. Two of his grand-daughters were baptized with him and, soon after, eleven other people. As the inhabitants of Teanaostaiaé came to believe that baptism did not automatically cause people to die, more presented themselves as candidates. Of the fifty people who either in sickness or in health received reasonable instruction before being baptized (15:189), about thirty continued to call themselves Christians (17:83). As elsewhere, many who sought healing through baptism had no further interest in the Jesuits' teachings once they recovered.

The Jesuits' success in Teanaostaiaé encouraged them to visit other Huron settlements to lay the foundations for the eventual establishment of still more residences. Their immediate objective was to establish themselves in Scanonaenrat, which was located between their two existing missions. The inhabitants of this town were famous for their shamanism and healing rites (17:89). It was also a town that Brébeuf had visited a number of times on his way to Teanaostaiaé and the home of Jean-Armand Andehoua. The first mission to Scanonaenrat began in November 1638 and lasted over the winter (15:169). The two priests assigned to this mission found lodging in a cabin that was occupied by a single family. They then met with the ten or twelve headmen who made up the village council and informed them that they had come to preach to the people of Scanonaenrat, as they had done at Teanaostaiaé. Here too, with an eye to establishing closer trading relations with the French, the priests were made welcome (17:91–93).

By this time, experience had taught the Jesuits that it was best to commence their missionary activities with a number of general meetings to which all the villagers were invited. The relative novelty of the Jesuits ensured that these first meetings were well attended and they could be used to determine those who were inclined to be friendly towards them (17:93). After that, the Jesuits encouraged the headmen and elders of the village to attend more select gatherings with generous distributions of tobacco. Chihwatenha addressed some of these meetings and the Jesuits were also helped to some extent by their former pupils (17:95; 15:171). After a month of hard work in Scanonaenrat, four heads of families were baptized. These included the Jesuits' host and two headmen. Their wives and children were not baptized, however, since in this community, unlike in Ossossané and Teanaostaiaé, the fear that baptism caused death was still too great. In all, only twenty people in good health and a few who were ill were baptized that year (15:171; 17:97). It is noteworthy that in this community where the Jesuits as yet had few personal contacts, it was men, and especially prominent men, who sought baptism, while the women feared it. This is an indication of the degree to which the Huron still viewed Christianity as a ritual of alliance with the French and of the important role that trade must have played in encouraging requests for baptism. The manpower required in Ossossané, Teanaostaiaé, and Scanonaenrat prevented the Jesuits from establishing other missions. They did, however, make a brief visit to Taenhatentaron in November 1638 (17:99), and the following spring two groups of priests were sent out to visit all the Huron villages (15:185; 17:103–5). These tours provided an opportunity to baptize the dying but mainly were intended to accustom all Huron to receiving visits from the Jesuits in the hope that this would make the establishment of future missions easier (17:105). This was the first time that the Jesuits visited the eastern villages of the Huron confederacy (map 23).

MODUS VIVENDI

Even though less than a year earlier, the vast majority of Huron had regarded the Jesuits as malevolent sorcerers, by the summer of 1639 the Jesuits counted almost 100 professing Christians among them (Thwaites 1896–1901, 17:53) and another 200 people had been baptized (15:187). The Jesuits tended to regard their success as an intellectual triumph. According to them, the Huron were greatly impressed not only by the logic and authority with which they expounded Christian doctrines, but also by the strict conformity of these doctrines as they were explained both at Three Rivers and in the Huron country (10:19; 15:121). The Jesuits also attributed their success to the confidence that the Huron had learned to place in written messages as opposed to oral traditions, and to the impact that the courage of the Jesuits, as well as their generosity and moral self-control, had upon the Huron (15:121).

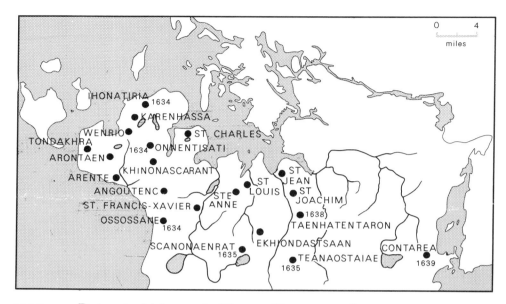

MAP 23. *Dates at which certain Huron villages were first visited by the Jesuits after 1634.*

There can be no doubt that the Huron regarded the Jesuits as shamans or sorcerers who controlled immense power and, therefore, had to be treated with great circumspection. Evidence of this power was perceived in their ability to transmit messages on pieces of paper, to control the weather, and to avoid or easily recover from illnesses that proved fatal to the Indians. The Jesuits further enhanced their reputation by predicting the lunar eclipses of 1637 (15:139) and 1638 (15:175), which made many Huron believe they had caused these events to happen (17:119). The Jesuits also acquired prestige as the representatives of a people of recognized technological superiority. This allowed them to argue that if the Huron regarded French tools as superior to their own, they should regard the Jesuits' teachings in the same manner. Whether or not the Jesuits suggested the idea to him, Chihwatenha was to argue publicly that if the Huron valued French kettles and axes more than they did their own, it was wrong for them to deny that the Jesuits' teachings were superior to their traditional religion (17:49).

To the majority of Huron, such an argument was unconvincing. In the past they had tended to regard the French as intellectually inferior to themselves and to attribute European technology to the possession of magical powers that essentially were no different from their own. Moreover, if the Jesuits were sorcerers, all of their teachings might be lies that would lead the Huron to destruction. There was nothing in the Huron cultural tradition that would incline them to be interested in theological disputations for their own sake. Most of their religious beliefs were part of a tradition that no one ever questioned, and new rites, charms, and songs were judged empirically by their effectiveness. In their dealings with the Jesuits, the aim of the Huron was to determine the kind of powers the priests possessed and to put themselves into a position where these powers could be acquired and benefited from if the Jesuits were willing, or neutralized if the Jesuits proved hostile. Beyond this, the Jesuits' teachings were only of passing interest. When the Huron visited Three Rivers, it was reported that all talk of religion had to precede the distribution of presents to the Indians, since otherwise most of the Indians would leave as soon as the priests began to speak (12:249).

Father Jérôme Lalemant observed that in 1638 and 1639 the Huron's principal aims in seeking baptism were to secure long life and prosperity for themselves and for their children (17:133; 18:19). This does not mean that all converts believed that the Jesuits were not responsible for the epidemics; on the contrary, many of them probably hoped that by gaining the Jesuits' goodwill they would be spared in any future epidemic. The majority of these so-called converts probably wished to continue practising their traditional beliefs and were only prevented from doing so by their fear that if the Jesuits found out about it, they would inflict supernatural punishments on them. A few Huron, like Ateiachias and Chihwatenha, seem to have believed that by identifying themselves with the Jesuits they could acquire their magical powers, and to accomplish this they were willing to incur the enmity of their own people.

Additional problems were posed for Huron who traded with the French. The Jesuits had been accepted as guests as one of the conditions that the French had laid down for renewing the French-Huron alliance. The French extended special privileges to Christian traders and furthermore had stated that the realization of a perfect alliance would require all Huron to become Christians. Under these circumstances, traders must have felt impelled not only to avoid the anger of the Jesuits but also to realize the practical advantages of a closer alliance with the French by being baptized. Many temporized, however, by being friendly with the Jesuits and holding out the promise that eventually they would become Christians.

Still other Huron resented the efforts of the French to intimidate them and began to realize the threat that Jesuit activities posed for their traditional way of life. These people accused the Jesuits of wanting to ruin the Huron country and to destroy the Huron way of life through the prohibition of many Huron customs (17:115). Many, whose relatives had died after being baptized, continued to hold the Jesuits responsible for these deaths and to nourish resentment against them. The Jesuits were also accused of harming individual Huron by their refusal to satisfy the desires of their souls. According to Huron thinking, this made the Jesuits responsible for the prolonged sickness and eventual death of individuals whose relatives were entitled to reparations or blood revenge (15:181; 17:173). Still more Huron were offended by the Jesuits' mockery of their customs (17:173, 201).

This resentment resulted not only in individual criticism of the Jesuits but in headmen denouncing them in general meetings. The most hostile headmen warned people not to attend Jesuit meetings, as their purpose was to harm the Huron; instead ways should be found of getting rid of them (17:117). Other leaders attended Jesuit meetings in order to oppose what they had to say (17:117). The opposition of such men encouraged children and ordinary people to harass the Jesuits by breaking down the doors of their cabins and throwing snowballs, sticks, and other rubbish over their heads or into their dwellings (15:165; 17:117). The most gruesome event of this sort occurred in December 1638. After the Jesuits had baptized an Iroquois captive whom the Huron were torturing, the Huron burned holes through his hands and feet with a red hot iron in mockery of the crucifixion, and after they had killed him they threw one of his hands into the Jesuits' cabin, as if giving them their share of the feast (17:73–77). Baptized Huron were mocked and were told that by having dealings with the Jesuits, they were bound, sooner or later, to bring misfortune and death upon themselves (17:85, 129). These rumours were reinforced when some Susquehannock visited the Huron in 1638. They reported that their English trading partners had informed them that the Jesuits wanted to destroy the whole world and that whenever the English discovered a Jesuit they promptly put him to death (17:121–23). In spite of this, a Susquehannock named Arenhouta was baptized. Eight years later, he was reported to be living in his own country and still calling himself a Roman Catholic (30:85–87).

Despite this hostility, none of the French who were living in the Huron country were killed, nor were any of them attacked except a young boy whom some Huron were said to have tried to strangle in the spring of 1638 (15:51). There were rumours that some hot-headed young men planned to harm the Jesuits, but none of their threats materialized. Such people were restrained by public opinion and this, in turn, was influenced by headmen and elders who believed that the best interests of the confederacy made it essential that the Jesuits not be harmed, since the Huron's trading alliance with the French depended on it. This argument had been strong enough to protect the Jesuits during the epidemic of 1637, so it is not surprising that it was effective in better times. Some of these same men also tried to persuade the Jesuits that being so critical of Huron ways only made enemies for themselves (17:171). Rarely has well-meaning advice fallen on deafer ears. The headmen were most effective in restraining their clansmen during the trading season. When, however, the traders returned and the Jesuits renewed their "batteries of sermons and instructions," many Huron could no longer be restrained from harassing them, even if everyone agreed that no serious harm should befall them (17:115).

In their eagerness to be successful, the Jesuits acted overhastily and planted the seeds of future difficulties for themselves. It formerly had been their policy not to baptize healthy adults before they had made prolonged trial of their sincerity and understanding. Now, in their eagerness to see the beginnings of a Christian church, the Jesuits relaxed these standards. Although Easter and Pentecost were the traditional dates for baptizing converts it was felt that this was too long to make many of them wait (17:31). Baptism was extended to all who requested it and had received sufficient instruction, leaving the "perfecting" of these converts until later. To make life easier for converts, certain observances were also relaxed. For example, the Jesuits did not insist on converts kneeling, since this was an unfamiliar and painful position for a Huron. Moreover, since spring was one of the few times of the year when deer meat was relatively plentiful, converts were not obliged to abstain from eating it during Lent (15:183). Some did, however, give up eating meat in order to imitate the Jesuits.

By contrast, the Jesuits were very inflexible when it came to liturgical matters for which they themselves were reponsible. Wheat and wine for celebrating the mass were imported from Quebec until the Huron mission began to grow its own grain and to press wild grapes, probably in 1637 (15:137–39, 159). They would have regarded Lescarbot's (1907–14, 1:187–88) suggestion that communion be celebrated using the standard bread and drink of each country as utterly impious. If they ate beaver, muskrat, and otter on fast days, this was only because these aquatic animals had long been regarded as fish by the clergy, and therefore were appropriate for such occasions (Denys 1908:361).

The Jesuits also insisted that their converts had to abandon all the traditional rituals that had been proscribed in the vows they had administered at Wenrio and Ossossané in 1636. They also began a minute examination of Huron beliefs and practices in order to provide converts with more precise spiritual guidance (Thwaites 1896–1901, 17:145). These prohibitions proved far more trying than the Jesuits had anticipated. Because converts were forbidden to attend any feasts, they were deprived of the best food that was available and of the main source of entertainment during the winter (17:129, 163). Their inability to participate in these feasts resulted in a breakdown in reciprocity and of good relations with their neighbours (17:163–65). At the same time, the converts' sense of security was undermined by demands that they abandon the charms and rituals they relied on to preserve their health and to bring them luck in war and hunting (17:121, 129–31).

To some degree, Christian medals and prayers replaced traditional charms and rituals, but on the whole they seem to have been regarded as less effective, perhaps because the Jesuits did not explicitly attempt a one-to-one replacement. Members of curing societies had to leave them and Christian headmen were forbidden to perform many of the traditional functions of their office. It is, therefore, not surprising that those who persevered as practising Christians usually did not hold the highest positions in Huron society. The latter either refused to become Christians or quickly abandoned their affiliation. Others claimed to be Christian but continued to discharge their traditional duties; if the Jesuits learned about such behaviour, they expelled such individuals from any further meetings of Christians (17:139). When Ondihorrea, one of the principal headmen, became ill and found that the usual Huron ceremonies did not cure him, he asked to be instructed and baptized. As he had done more than anyone else to make it possible for the Jesuits to settle in Teanaostaiaé, they were happy to grant his wish. After he recovered, however, he attended mass only once. When he learned that he would have to give up many of his chiefly duties and his membership in a curing society, he was no longer interested in remaining a Christian (17:137–39).

BAPTIZING THE IROQUOIS

One of the most extraordinary aspects of mission work during this period was the large number of Iroquois prisoners that the Jesuits managed to instruct and baptize before and while these prisoners were being tortured to death. The Jesuits regarded it as their duty to try to save the souls of these men and when they were successful they consoled themselves with the thought that God had caused these Iroquois to be captured and slain so that he might confer the gift of eternal life upon them (Thwaites 1896–

1901, 13:81–83). The first such prisoner was baptized in Arenté in the autumn of 1636 (13:37–83). In 1638 the Jesuits baptized twenty-one of the many prisoners that were captured that year (15:173). Three were baptized at Scanonaenrat and thirteen or fourteen at or near Teanaostaiaé (17:63). One of the latter was the Oneida headman Ononkwaia, who defied his Huron tormentors to his last breath (17:65–71). Still another prisoner was baptized at Taenhatentaron (17:101–3). All the prisoners who were assigned that year to settlements where the Jesuits had missions or to villages in their vicinity appear to have been baptized (17:63–65). The Jesuits baptized eleven Seneca prisoners tortured to death in May 1639 (15:185; 17:105); the twelfth refused baptism. These prisoners seem to have been brought first to Ossossané, where they underwent preliminary torture and where nine of them were killed. When the other three were taken elsewhere, they were accompanied by Jesuits who managed to baptize two of them (15:185–89).

It is uncertain why these prisoners agreed to be baptized. They were probably aware that the Jesuits were French; in any case, it was clear to them that the Jesuits were friendly with the Huron. The Jesuits believed that the Iroquois were moved by their kindness and disinterested compassion (13:43), but one cannot be sure that the Iroquois were able to distinguish such sentiments from the mock kindness with which they were treated by the Huron. Jesuit offers to save them from the fires of hell may have led these prisoners to hope for rescue from torture if they were baptized, although this does not explain why many of them continued to repeat phrases that they had been taught by the Jesuits throughout their torture. Nor is such constancy likely if their acceptance of baptism was a mock response to what they conceived of as a taunting offer. Probably they too viewed the Jesuits as sorcerers and saw in baptism a charm that would give them more courage to face their final hours. The repetition of phrases such as *Jesus taïtenr* ("Jesus, have pity on me") may have been regarded as analogous to a death song. Others set Jesuit teaching into song and used these songs to brave their tormentors (17:65).

The Huron did not understand why the Jesuits wished to baptize Iroquois prisoners. Many Huron drew an analogy between Jesuit descriptions of hell and their own ritual torture and were angry that the Jesuits were seeking to save the souls of their enemies from eternal torment (13:73). In 1636 a young Huron was willing to assist the Jesuits by acting as an interpreter for them on such an occasion (13:43–45). Later, when the people of Ihonatiria wished to decline further Jesuit exhortations to become Christians, they said that it was a pity that the Jesuits had baptized an Iroquois prisoner since his soul would try to drive them away from heaven if any of them wished to go there (13:177–79). The Huron also suggested that the Jesuits had shown kindness to this prisoner out of fear, hoping that if they were captured by the Iroquois they would be treated better for it. They warned the Jesuits that this was a vain hope and gently berated their cowardice (13:73).

Some Huron related the Jesuits' general objections to Huron torture to their efforts to baptize prisoners and this led them to suspect that the Jesuits were seeking to be friends with the Iroquois. In an effort to find out if this were the case, the Jesuits were asked if the French did not kill anyone. They replied that men indeed were executed, but not with such cruelty. Then, perhaps guided by stories that Savignon or Amantacha had told them about France, the Huron asked if the French never burned anyone. To this the Jesuits replied that the French did, but only for enormous crimes, and that those who were condemned often were strangled first (13:75). In fact, the habits of seventeenth-century Europeans were not so far removed from those of the Huron in this respect as the Jesuits wished to imply. Later, exceptional fortitude was shown by some of the Iroquois who had been baptized. Since failure to make a prisoner scream and plead for mercy was believed to bring misfortune on his executioners, the Huron blamed the Jesuits for this, and many resolved to let no more Iroquois be baptized (17:65). Thus, in the spring of 1639 the Jesuits found themselves having to struggle hard to gain access to prisoners and to obtain permission from their adoptive kinsmen for their baptism (17:105).

The New Order

JÉRÔME LALEMANT

In August 1638 Brébeuf was replaced as superior of the Huron mission by Father Jérôme Lalemant who had arrived in Canada for that purpose the same summer. Jérôme was a younger brother of Charles Lalemant who returned to Paris the same year to become the first procurator of the mission of New France. The new superior of the Huron mission was highly esteemed for his administrative abilities, which he had demonstrated at Clermont College and as rector of the Jesuit College in Blois. Two other priests arrived in the Huron country in 1638: François Du Peron and

Simon Le Moyne. There were now twelve hired men working for the Jesuits in the Huron country (Thwaites 1896–1901, 15:157)—a doubling of both clerical and lay staff since 1634. This increase, combined with a growing conviction that the success of the Huron mission was vital for the long-term security of New France, had convinced Jesuit officials in France that it was necessary to have a trained administrator take charge of this mission. Lalemant knew nothing about the Huron language and was inexperienced as a missionary, but these officials did not regard this as an impediment to his appointment. The missionaries who were already working among the Huron regretted that the new superior lacked local experience and remained critical of him throughout his four-year tenure of office (30:149; 32:61–63).

In spite of the doubts of his co-workers, Lalemant's arrival in the Huron country marked the continuation of a successful career both in Canada and in France. In 1644 he returned to Quebec to become the superior of all the Jesuits in New France, a post which he held until 1650 and again after 1659 when he played a leading role in revitalizing mission work in Canada. In the intervening years he served for a time as rector of the *Collège royal de La Flèche* in northern France. Not the least of Lalemant's talents was his sense of discretion, which allowed him to retain the confidence of the rival factions whose quarrels dominated the administration of New France in his later years.

Yet, in spite of his undoubted administrative talent, Jérôme Lalemant now seems a curious choice to be superior of the Huron mission. He was deeply interested in complicated problems of international diplomacy as these affected the Jesuit missions in New France, but was unable to convince even his own brother of the wisdom of what he advocated.[11] By contrast, his entries in the *Journal des Jésuites*, which he kept from 1645 to 1650, reveal a preoccupation with trivial details of rubrics as they were observed or not observed in the churches at Quebec, and with recording petty animosities among the local religious orders. These entries seem to be those of a parish priest rather than of a trained administrator. This aspect of his character was evident to Marie de l'Incarnation, who wrote approvingly that "he seems to have been brought up in all the ceremonies, which is not usual for a Jesuit" (Pouliot 1966:414). Moreover, even measured by the standards of the time, the literal manner in which he perceived himself doing battle against the devil suggests considerable naïveté.

It is evident, in retrospect, that the positions that Jérôme Lalemant held in the Jesuit colleges of France were not the best preparation for running the Huron mission. Lalemant was determined to enforce punctiliousness and careful observance of routine and was unwilling to adapt these routines to the habits of the Huron or of his fellow missionaries, who had already gained considerable experience working among them.[12] Throughout his stay in the Huron country the Huron's houses appeared to his fastidious mind to be "a miniature picture of hell" filled with "fire and smoke, on every side naked bodies ... mingling pellmell, with dogs sharing the beds, plates, and food of their masters." In his opinion, merely to visit a longhouse was to befoul oneself with soot, filth, and dirt (17:13–15), while to have to live and work amongst the Huron was to be a martyr without being killed (17:13). He was also appalled that at the time of his arrival the food and lodging of the missionaries differed hardly at all from those of the Indians. Lalemant's aversion to Indian life had been strengthened during his journey up the Ottawa River, when he was attacked by a Kichesipirini whose child had died after being bled by a Frenchman a few days before (15:151).

DISCIPLINE

Lalemant's ideas about how the Huron mission should be run were to alter drastically the relationship between the Huron and the Jesuits. This is ironic, since the common motive for all of his innovations was the desire to ensure greater discipline and punctiliousness among the Jesuits and their workmen. His reforms were directed against the relatively informal spirit of cooperation that had hitherto prevailed among the Jesuits. Either through lack of familiarity with the situation or because of the ingrained habits of a schoolmaster, Lalemant was willing to sacrifice the close relations that the missionaries had been building up with the Huron in order to achieve this goal. Yet, while some of his ideas proved wrong and ultimately had to be abandoned, his policies were valuable in one respect; the administrative machinery that he constructed ensured that the vastly expanded mission that was soon to develop under his leadership would function adequately.

Lalemant was determined that in spite of their mission work, the Jesuits' routine would be as well ordered as it was in the colleges of France. Periods were assigned in the morning and afternoon when the priests might visit the Indians and special days of the week were set aside for teaching children, the leading people of the village, and converts only (Thwaites 1896–1901, 16:241–49; 15:165–67). Lalemant required the doors of the missionaries' cabins to be closed by four in the afternoon and that no one was to go out after that hour. To preserve the quiet of these residences, he also decreed that, henceforth, only Indians who came on proper business might be admitted. Lalemant soon discovered, however, that it was not a simple matter to refuse to admit the Indians (17:15), especially since the latter were used to visiting the Jesuits whenever they pleased (16:241). Ossossané and Teanaostaiaé were divided into as many districts as there were priests who spoke enough Huron to make daily rounds. Unfortunately, we do not know to what degree this primordial parish system corresponded with the divisions of these towns into clan districts (16:243; 17:29–31).

DONNÉS

The second problem that Lalemant tackled was ensuring discipline among the lay workmen attached to the Jesuit mission. By 1639 there were fourteen of them. The previous year Le Mercier had praised, perhaps too hopefully, the chastity and good behaviour of these men (Thwaites 1896–1901, 15:137). In 1637, however, the Jesuits had been anxious to guard against sexual laxity by arranging Christian marriages between some of their hired men and Huron women. This plan had not worked out and Montmagny and the trading company were charged by the Jesuits with ensuring the irreproachable conduct of these men (17:47). This suggests that the labourers were threatened with disciplinary action, should the Jesuits report they were not behaving properly. Yet, control based on negative sanctions had obvious drawbacks as far as the missionaries were concerned.

Even before he arrived in Canada, Lalemant planned to introduce to the Huron mission a new category of lay assistant known as a donné. The use of such men had been experimented with in the province of Champagne and been approved by the French provincial, Father Binet (Côte 1956–57; 1961–62). The Canadian donné was to bind himself by civil contract to abjure all personal possessions, to work for the Jesuits without pay, to obey the Jesuit superior, and to be chaste. The Jesuits, for their part, guaranteed to provide the donné with clothes, food, lodging, and other necessities, and to care for him in sickness and old age. This plan won the whole-hearted approval of Brébeuf and Le Jeune, who were convinced that devout laymen would do more for the mission than ordinary hired men could do. The Canadian Jesuits pressed for the maximum incorporation of these men into the order, including taking of vows and wearing a religious costume. The latter proposals were disapproved of by the Jesuit provincial in France and by the general of the order, Mutius Vitelleschi, and were therefore abandoned by Lalemant in 1643 (Rochemonteix 1895–96, 1: 390). The French provincial also disapproved of the agreements to care for the donnés being made binding on the whole order, rather than on the Huron mission. As a compromise, it was agreed that the Jesuit mission to New France, rather than the Huron mission, would guarantee these obligations (Thwaites 1896–1901, 21:297).

In spite of the restrictions, the donnés soon became an important part of the Huron mission (21:293–301). The first to enrol was the hired man Robert Le Coq, who signed his contract 23 December 1639 (21:305). Since his arrival in 1634 he appears to have served as the *negotiator*, or business manager, of the mission and in this capacity he travelled between the Huron country and Quebec each year (Jones 1908:302). The three other men who had been working for the Jesuits since 1634, Petit-Pré, Dominique, and Baron, ceased to do so about this time. Since hired men as well as donnés later joined the mission, it is possible that they were dismissed by the Jesuits. By the summer of 1640, Lalemant had recruited six donnés, some of whom may have been present among the fourteen seculars who were working for the Jesuits in the autumn of 1639. Nine years later, more than twenty donnés were working for the Huron mission, as compared with eleven hired men and six boys (ibid. 384–85).

A NEW MISSION SYSTEM

The most significant change that Lalemant proposed to carry out was to abandon the individual residences that the Jesuits had sought to establish in each of the major Huron towns and to construct in their place a single mission headquarters that would be independent of any particular Huron settlement. Lalemant argued that by doing this the missionaries would not have to move their residences every decade when the Huron relocated their villages (Thwaites 1896–1901, 19:133); hence they could erect French-style buildings of stone and timber in which they could live much as they did in a Jesuit residence in France. Such a headquarters would also eliminate a duplication of services in different Huron villages and permit the Jesuits, who were increasing in numbers, to grow their own food, rather than having to buy corn from the Indians. This, it was reasoned, would reduce the long-term cost of the mission. Although Lalemant did not explicitly state so in his public writings, his arguments imply that the

European-style chapel that Brébeuf had erected at Ossossané was a waste of effort, since the settlement would soon be abandoned. Lalemant planned for all the Huron settlements to be served by itinerant priests, who, rather than having permanent accommodation in each town and being supported there by a staff of domestics, would return to headquarters at regular intervals for prolonged periods of study and devotion. The implementation of Lalemant's plan was a setback for Brébeuf's efforts to have individual priests become identified with particular communities and develop a prolonged and intimate relationship with their inhabitants. Instead, his plan stressed the role of the Jesuits as representatives of a foreign although allied people living among but apart from the Huron (Talbot 1956:209).

In proposing to found a mission centre, Lalemant was specifically influenced by the reports of Jesuit mission work in Paraguay. The missions to the Guarani had begun in 1587, and in 1609 the Jesuits had founded the first of their reductions or mission centres in which the Indians were encouraged to settle down as Christians. In return the Jesuits offered them protection against enslavement. By 1631 the Jesuits were compelled to resettle farther down the Alto Paraná River, where a new series of reductions was founded. These flourished until the Jesuits were expelled in 1767. Under Jesuit supervision over 100,000 Indians observed Christian discipline and were taught to produce large surpluses of cotton and linen cloth, tobacco, wood products, hides, and maté for export to Europe. Some were also trained as armourers, silversmiths, painters, musicians, and printers. The ideal Paraguayan reduction was located on slightly elevated land, along the bank of a river, and was surrounded by fields cut out of the forest. In the centre of the village were a church, a priests' house, a school, a hospital, and a cemetery, while the houses of the Indians were arranged in rows along a series of shaded streets (Rochemonteix 1895–96, 1:385–86).

The idea of the Paraguayan reduction had already helped to inspire the Indian settlement founded at Sillery, near Quebec, in 1638 (Thwaites 1896–1901, 12:221). The beaver in that area had been overhunted and, as the Indians grew poorer, they became a charge on the trading company. To alleviate this situation, the Jesuits proposed to found a settlement in which the Montagnais would be encouraged to settle down and become farmers (8:57–59). As an inducement, houses, food, and clothing were provided for these Indians from funds the Jesuits collected. Only Indians who agreed to become Christians were allowed to enjoy these benefits and they had to submit to close supervision by the Jesuits who ran the settlement. Because it was now a practical economic proposition, this first

Indian reserve in Canada received the enthusiastic support of the French traders, although only a few years before these same traders had violently opposed the Recollets' plans to settle the Montagnais.

The apparent success of the Sillery scheme must have encouraged Lalemant to hope that individual Huron converts might be persuaded to leave their villages and settle around a Jesuit headquarters on the Paraguayan model. Eventually, this headquarters, or a number of them, would become a new Christian society, replacing the traditional Huron settlements. This scheme was radically different from the earlier Jesuit plan to convert one entire Huron village, and then more, until all the Huron had become Christians. Lalemant, like the Recollets, assumed that the best course of action was to convert individuals and families, and use these to build new Christian communities.

In the spring of 1639, Lalemant sent out the Jesuit missionaries in groups of two to visit all the Huron settlements (17:103–5). This was followed by another round of visits the following summer, when a saint's name was given to every Huron village (19:125). It was probably at this time that Lalemant began his "census" of the houses and families in each Huron and Tionnontaté village (19:125–27), the purpose of which was to allow him to organize mission work more systematically. Although the detailed findings of this survey have not been preserved, the figures in the *Jesuit Relations* suggest that it was neither as thorough nor as detailed as Lalemant implies. The reconnaissance of the villages was apparently not completed before the winter of 1639–40. The unnaturally low average of three persons per family and the fact that the combined population of 12,000 for the Huron and the Tionnontaté continued to be accepted as accurate for the next decade suggest that the published figures were adjusted to take account of the substantial loss of population that occurred in the autumn of 1639 and over the following winter.

Another result of Lalemant's surveys seems to have been the preparation of a map of the Huron country. This was almost certainly the prototype of the large-scale *Corographie du Pays des Hurons* (plate 33), a manuscript map showing the location of Huron villages between 1642 and 1648. Heidenreich (1966:111–13) has studied this map and on the basis of the handwriting has tentatively suggested that the surviving copy may have been drawn by Jérôme Lalemant. There is also no doubt that a map of this type was the basis of the detailed representation of the Huron country that Du Creux published in 1664 in his *Historiae Canadensis* (plate 34). These maps represent what might be called the official Jesuit cartography of the Huron country.

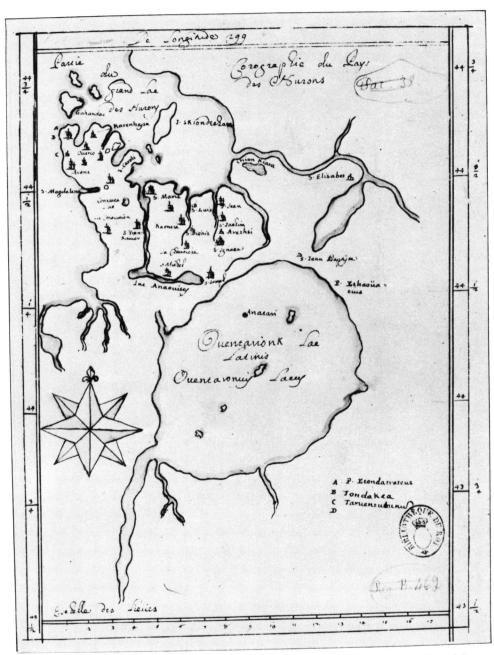

PLATE 33. Corographie du Pays des Hurons. *Heidenreich describes this manuscript map as the best large-scale one of the Huron country. It shows the area between 1639 and 1648 and may have been drawn by Jérôme Lalemant. Courtesy Public Archives of Canada.*

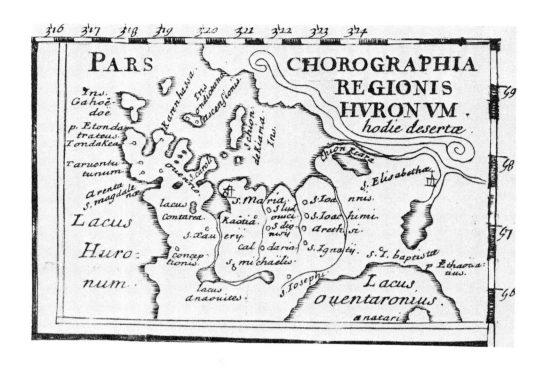

PLATE 34. Chorographia Regionis Huronum, hodie desertae. *This large-scale inset map is taken from the* Tabula Novae Franciae, *published in François Du Creux's* Historiae Canadensis. *Long believed to be the only large-scale map showing the Huron country in the middle of the seventeenth century, it now appears to be based on the* Corographie du Pays des Hurons, *with minor differences resulting from faulty copying.* Courtesy Public Archives of Canada.

An alternative tradition is represented by a manuscript map titled *Description du Pais des Hurons* (plate 35), bearing the date 1631, later amended to 1651, and by the engraved inset entitled *Huronum Explicata Tabula* (plate 36), which is part of a map of New France published in 1657 (plate 37) and probably drawn by Father Bressani. Although the place names on these two maps differ, the outlines are very similar; therefore Heidenreich (1966:115) suggests that Bressani copied the outlines of the older map and placed on it the distribution of Huron villages as he remembered them. Heidenreich (ibid. 114) also suggests that the earlier map may be the work of Father Brébeuf. It depicts the locations of settlements between 1639 and 1648, except for an *x* which marks the site of Sainte-Marie II built in 1649. Thus, despite its date, it is essentially contemporary with the *Corographie*. While more of Georgian Bay appears on this map than on the *Corographie*, the delineation of the Huron country is of inferior quality. It is possible that this map was found among Brébeuf's papers in 1649 and that he may have begun to work on it soon after he returned to France in 1629.

Around 1639 the Jesuits also prepared a general map of the lower Great Lakes region, noting on it the Huron names of many of the sedentary peoples of Ontario, New York State, Ohio, and Michigan. Although this map has been lost, the names Father Vimont copied from a duplicate that Father Ragueneau sent him, indicate that it served as the prototype for the Sanson map of 1656 (plate 38) and others (plate 39). It is uncertain how the Jesuits collected so much accurate information about the outlines of lakes and rivers, but much of it must have come from Indian informants. Other data may have been collected by the Jesuits' assistants, in the course of trading voyages. Detailed knowledge of the area is reflected in the *Novae Franciae Accurata Delineatio* which, as we have already noted, was probably the work of Father Bressani who lived in the Huron country from 1645 to 1649. The accuracy and scale of this map are better than on any other maps of the lower Great Lakes prior to Dollier and Gallinée's map of 1670 (ibid. 105–9).

On the basis of his preliminary survey, Lalemant was able to select the ideal location for his headquarters and planned reduction. The site was along the east bank of the Wye River, midway between Mud Lake and Georgian Bay. There, a low rise of well-drained land provided space to erect buildings and plant crops, while the river on one side and the marsh on the other offered the settlement a considerable degree of protection. From this location it was possible to travel down the Wye River to Georgian Bay, less than a mile away. The site also stood equidistant between the

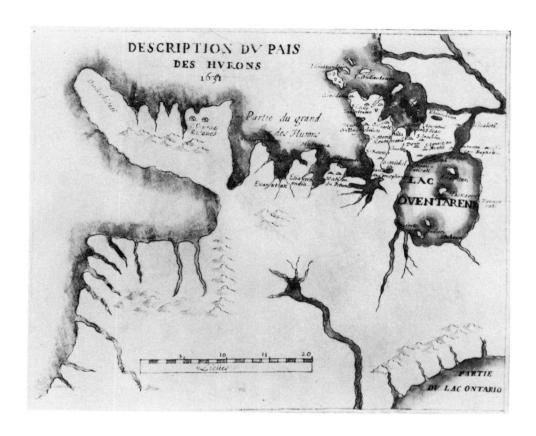

PLATE 35. Description du Pais des Hurons. *This manuscript map is dated 1631 but was changed to 1651, probably when an x was added to indicate the location of Sainte-Marie II on Gahoendoe. Heidenreich suggests that the map may have been drawn by Jean de Brébeuf. Courtesy Public Archives of Canada.*

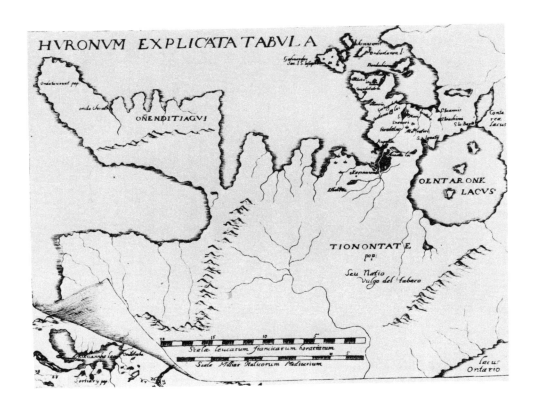

PLATE 36. Huronum Explicata Tabula. *This inset map is from the* Novae Franciae Accurata Delineatio, *1657. The map was engraved by Giovanni Federico Pesca and was probably the work of François-Joseph Bressani. St. Ignace and St. Xavier are both misplaced and St. Jean and St. Joachim are along the wrong river. Courtesy Public Archives of Canada.*

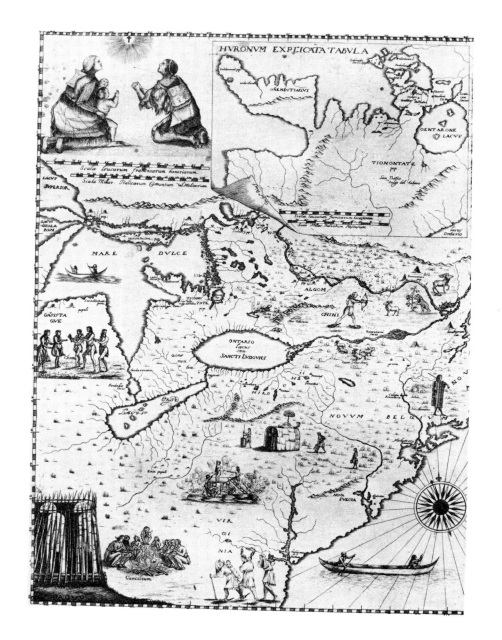

PLATE 37. *Part of the* Novae Franciae Accurata Delineatio, *1657. This map was probably drawn by Bressani, who had access to Jesuit maps already in existence by 1640. Heidenreich describes it as the most accurate map made of the Great Lakes prior to Dollier and Gallinée's map of 1670 and as one of the most beautiful maps of eastern Canada ever drawn. Courtesy Public Archives of Canada.*

PLATE 38. Le Canada, ou Nouvelle France, *published by N. Sanson*
d'Abbeville, 1656. Already in 1650, Sanson had published his map
Amérique septentrionale *on which the whole of the Great Lakes system*
except the west end of Lake Superior and the south end of Lake Michigan
is accurately portrayed. The 1656 map is more detailed and is
ethnographically interesting for the many tribal names that it bears.
It is not known from where Sanson obtained his information but presumably
he had access to manuscript maps made by the Jesuits in the preceding
decade. While Bressani had access to one or both of Sanson's maps, he also
had access to additional information when he produced his Novae Franciae.
Courtesy Public Archives of Canada.

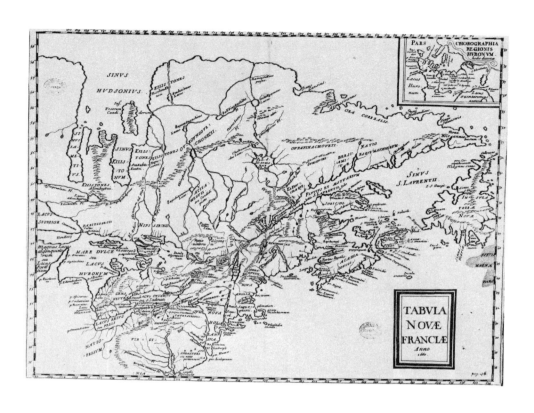

PLATE 39. *François Du Creux's* Tabula Novae Franciae, *1660. This map was published in 1664 in Du Creux's* Historiae Canadensis. *It is not a simple copy of Sanson's maps, although both appear to be derived from similar sources. Courtesy Public Archives of Canada.*

most easterly and westerly of the Huron villages. The location was well suited for communicating with Quebec and for carrying out mission work.

The land that Lalemant wanted belonged to the Ataronchronon and their permission was required before the Jesuits could begin to build there. Lalemant had reason to fear that they might not agree to his proposal and he later commented that if the affair had been delayed for even two hours, the Jesuits might not have succeeded in getting what they wanted (Thwaites 1896–1901, 19:135). It may be that some of the Ataronchronon feared to have the Jesuits living nearby, although such feelings had not prevented other communities from welcoming the Jesuits. More likely, if the people of Ossossané or Teanaostaiaé had learned that the Jesuits were planning to withdraw from their midst, they would have exerted pressure to make sure that neither the Ataronchronon nor anyone else allowed them to build elsewhere.

In the summer of 1639, Lalemant had his lay assistants begin work on the new residence of Sainte-Marie. The first year, only a single building seems to have been erected, without an adjoining palisade. Wilfrid Jury has identified this building with the remains of a Huron-style house, some forty feet long and twenty feet wide that he found beneath later French constructions at the site (Jury and Jury 1954:21–23). He claims that this house differs from Huron ones in having uniform-sized post molds and walls that ran in straight lines, while inside the house he noted traces of a partition. Finally, he states that there was evidence that the building had been chopped down to make way for a later Jesuit construction that covered its southern end. Jury's claim gains support from Father Chaumonot's statement that when he arrived in the Huron country in 1639, the Jesuits were living in three residences constructed of bark, like the houses of the Indians (Thwaites 1896–1901, 18:17).

Unfortunately, it is extremely difficult to evaluate Jury's claims since no detailed report of his findings at Sainte-Marie has so far been published. While it is true that Lalemant complained about the lack of tools and workmen at this time, a European-style chapel had already been erected at Ossossané, with no more tools and even fewer French labourers. Moreover, when describing a vision that he had in February 1640, Brébeuf mentions a gable on the house at Sainte-Marie (Ragueneau 1925:73), which suggests that the original building was not precisely like a Huron longhouse. It is possible that Jury uncovered some hybrid structure that was soon demolished; however, until more evidence is published, it is also possible that he found a small Huron longhouse that predated the arrival of the Jesuits.

In the autumn of 1639 the Jesuits abandoned their residence at Ossossané, leaving the town with no resident priests. The chapel was placed in the care of Joseph Chihwatenha. The residence at Teanaostaiaé was not abandoned, possibly because it was feared that it would offend the inhabitants of the village to do so so soon after settling there. Lalemant divided the Huron country into four mission areas, assigning to each a central community from which the priests could make their rounds during the winter. Four villages, now named Ste Anne, St. Louis, St. Denys, and St. Jean were served from the new Jesuit headquarters. This mission was called Sainte-Marie to the Ataronchronon. The mission of St. Joseph to the Attigneenongnahac operated out of Teanaostaiaé (which the Jesuits called St. Joseph) and embraced Scanonaenrat, Taenhatentaron, and other nearby villages; while La Conception to the Attignawantan had its headquarters in Ossossané and served twelve other Attignawantan villages. The mission of St. Jean-Baptiste to the Arendarhonon was to Contarea, St. Joachim, and an Algonkin encampment called Ste Elizabeth. A fifth mission was to the Tionnontaté. While these missions roughly corresponded with tribal divisions, they did not do so precisely. The mission to the Attigneenongnahac also served the Tahontaenrat, while the one to the Arendarhonon served at least one Algonkin winter camp (Thwaites 1896–1901, 19:125). The return of Father Pierre Pijart in 1639, following the closing of the Huron school at Quebec, and the arrival of Fathers Joseph-Antoine Poncet de La Rivière and Pierre-Joseph-Marie Chaumonot brought the total number of priests in the Huron country to thirteen. The new mission system came into operation 1 November 1639.

The Great Illness

SMALLPOX

In the summer of 1639 smallpox spread through the St. Lawrence Valley, killing many Indians who came to trade at Quebec and Three Rivers (Thwaites 1896–1901, 15:237; 16:53). This epidemic appears to have started in New England and was carried to the St. Lawrence by a group of Kichesipirini returning from a visit to the Abenaki (16:101). Soon the Algonkin were dying in such numbers that the living were unable to bury the dead, whose bodies were eaten by hungry dogs (16:155, 217–19). The epidemic reached the Huron country when the Huron traders returned from Quebec. The first Huron who suffered from smallpox landed near Sainte-Marie and was carried to his home in the Ataronchronon village of Ste Anne (19:89). The epidemic lingered throughout the winter (21:131), striking an extraordinarily large number of Huron. The Jesuits baptized more than 1000 people who were in danger of death; of these, 360 children under the age of seven died, as well as 100 more children under the age of seven who had been baptized in previous years. In addition, many older children and adults died (19:77–79, 123). These figures suggest a total mortality of several thousand. By the time the epidemic had run its course, the Huron population was reduced to about 9000 people, or only about one-half of what it was before 1634. Of the three cycles of epidemics that had attacked the Huron since that date, the smallpox epidemic accounted for by far the greatest loss of life.

RENEWED FEARS

This new illness coming from the St. Lawrence resulted in fresh outbursts of hostility against the Jesuits. When Robert Le Coq was returning from Quebec, he became ill and was so covered with pustules that his Huron travelling companions judged him as good as dead and abandoned him on the shores of Georgian Bay. When these Huron returned home, the story began to circulate that before he died, Le Coq had told these men that the Jesuits caused disease by nourishing in their cabin an *angont*, or supernatural serpent used to perform witchcraft. Others reported him saying that the disease was caused by a spirit that the Jesuits concealed in the barrel of a gun, which they fired off to send it anywhere in the country. Soon, every Huron man, woman, and child had heard these stories which were widely believed because they were said to have come from the mouth of a dying man who wished to help the Huron (Thwaites 1896–1901, 19:95–97).

For a long time Le Coq lay on the shores of Georgian Bay. He was avoided by many Huron who were too frightened of his illness to help him, although one group did not scruple to rob him. He was finally rescued by a Huron whom he had helped the year before. This man and a companion transported Le Coq back to Sainte-Marie, where he was nursed to health by the Jesuits (19:97–113). Le Coq's public denial that he had ever made any accusations against the Jesuits made little impression on the Huron. A new rumour began to circulate that his illness was a ruse to deceive the Huron, and his recovery was interpreted as evidence of the control that the Jesuits exercised over the epidemic (19:115).

If the Jesuits were seen kneeling by a fire to recite their office, this constituted evidence of witchcraft. So was asking people's names so they might record them in their register of baptisms (19:129). It was widely believed that the Jesuits later tore these names out of their books in order to cause the death of the persons concerned. Their efforts to reach the dying by visiting as many villages and houses as possible were viewed as further evidence of witchcraft, particularly since none of the French except Le Coq became ill (19:93). The suspicions of the Huron were exacerbated by the special efforts that the Jesuits made to baptize dying children even against opposition from their families (19:93).

By moving about as much as they did, the Jesuits may unwittingly have helped to spread the epidemic. Thus there may have been a factual basis to the Huron claim that the most people died in places where the Jesuits were the most welcome and where they had baptized the largest number of people (19:93). Within a short time the majority of the Jesuits' converts had publicly renounced Christianity and taken up the old healing cults (19:81). They did this either because deaths in their families convinced them of the inability or unwillingness of the Jesuits to cure them in spite of their being Christians (19:233), or because they feared that if they remained Christians they would be included in any general massacre of the Jesuits and their supporters.

The missions that began in November were the most difficult and dangerous that the Jesuits were ever to undertake in the Huron country. The single-minded zeal with which they pursued their objective of instructing and baptizing those who were ill testifies to the sincerity of these missionaries. As soon as it became clear to the inhabitants of Ste Anne that baptism did not restore health, the Jesuits were accused of sorcery and many longhouses were closed to them (19:167). As the smallpox spread, the other villages of the Ataronchronon mission became similarly hostile. For at least part of the winter, the Jesuits were forbidden to visit one or more of these villages (19:169). When Le Mercier encountered Oscouenrout, a principal headman of the Attignawantan, in St. Louis, the latter fell into a frenzy and told the priest that he would never leave the village alive, since its inhabitants had resolved to burn him to death as a sorcerer (19:175). While this threat was not carried out, it undoubtedly reflected the continuing debate that went on within most Huron villages concerning how the Jesuits ought to be dealt with.

The Ataronchronon's hatred of the Jesuits appears to have been less intense than was encountered among the missions to the Attignawantan and Attigneenongnahac, where the Jesuits had been active for a longer period. In Ossossané only a few converts remained faithful. These included Chihwatenha and his family and a man named Tsondihwané, who was the head of one of the most important families in the community. Yet, Tsondihwané's family, especially his wife, were violently opposed to his behaviour and, after many had died in his longhouse, they persuaded him to have a curing ceremony performed for his daughter when she fell ill (19:239–45). An old woman who bore the Christian name Anne refused to renounce Christianity, even when the death of two daughters and a niece left her with three ailing children to care for (19:233–39).

These were exceptions, however. The Attignawantan knew more about the Jesuits' teachings than other Huron did and they became more vociferously hostile than any of the other tribes as the mortality rate soared. The Jesuits accused them of circulating the worst rumours about them and of calling the most loudly for their deaths. The Jesuits believed that the Attignawantan hoped that someone from one of the other tribes would kill them. In this way, the Attignawantan would be rid of the Jesuits without being directly responsible for their murder (19:209–11). The Huron groups adopted this strategy on other occasions and since many would have been happy to be rid of the Jesuits, there is no reason to doubt that the Attignawantan were encouraging others to murder the Jesuits. They were doubtlessly not the only Huron tribe to do this.

The widespread mortality among baptized families led many of them to abandon Christianity and to refuse to let the Jesuits enter their longhouses. This happened not only in Ossossané but in all the Attignawantan villages (19:213). If the Jesuits entered a house without permission, the Huron refused to listen to them and either drove them out or left themselves. When Father Ragueneau tried to enter the village of Ste Térèse, a young man seized him by the throat and was about to strike him with a hatchet. A woman stopped him from doing this and the young man finally contented himself with carrying off Ragueneau's crucifix. When Ragueneau asked the village council to restore the crucifix, the young man agreed to do so, but only if the Jesuits promised that smallpox would no longer ravage the village (19:213–15). One Huron, said to be among the most intelligent men in Ossossané, stated that he did not believe the Jesuits were practising witchcraft; rather their god was punishing the Huron for having listened to the Jesuits without following their teachings. To the Jesuits' surprise, he suggested that the solution was for the Huron to stop listening to them (19:217).

In Teanaostaiaé, the Jesuits were staying with a headman named Tsondakwa (23:241). A few Huron who lived in this community asked for baptism apparently during the early stages of the epidemic. One of these was Torichés, a headman who had fallen ill and was hoping for a cure (19:191). Another was a man who had formerly listened to the Jesuits but who had become terrified when he thought that a picture of Christ looked at him in such a way as to threaten him with death (19:203–7). Yet another was a young man who wished to go to heaven because the word the Jesuits used to translate heaven was part of his name (19:191). On the whole, however, the inhabitants of Teanaostaiaé were more violently opposed to the Jesuits than were those of Ossossané. As public resentment grew, most Christians, including Saouenhati, who was the head of a notable family, abjured their conversions in order to avoid rising public anger (23:139). Leading headmen talked of having the Jesuits killed. Young people harassed the Jesuits by throwing sticks at them, hitting them, knocking down their crosses, and threatening to set fire to their cabin.

Brébeuf was singled out as the most dangerous sorcerer (19:195; 34:185–87). A young man whom Brébeuf had told that he was taking the path to hell dreamt that his life could be saved only if he killed the missionary. He became so violent that the more responsible headmen warned the French not to venture outside their houses. To appease the man's dream, the village council presented him with the recently taken head of an enemy, thus satisfying his soul wish and diverting his anger from the Jesuits.

Finally a riot broke out. Brébeuf and Chaumonot were attacked and beaten, their domestic, Pierre Boucher, was wounded in the arm, and their house seems to have been set on fire. After this, the Jesuits were ordered to leave Teanaostaiaé and return to Sainte-Marie (18:25; 19:195; 34:185–87). The councils of Scanonaenrat and Taenhatentaron also forbade the Jesuits to visit these towns. The reason that the headmen of these towns gave was their desire to protect the Jesuits against plans that some young men had made on their lives. In fact, they were trying to prevent the Jesuits from visiting these towns to stop them from practising their witchcraft in them. The Jesuits were unable to work in these settlements until the epidemic was almost over (19:207).

Although the Arendarhonon were the oldest Huron allies of the French, 1639 was the first year that the French attempted any serious mission work among them. Arendarhonon territory extended as far west as the Sturgeon River, but their prinicipal town, which at this period was called Contarea, was located near the Narrows of Lake Couchiching, considerably to the east of its predecessor, Cahiagué (Heidenreich 1966:114, 123–24). The very isolation of this eastern "bulwark" of the Huron country probably helped to delay the arrival of the smallpox, which became generally prevalent only after Fathers Daniel and Le Moyne had come there. The Jesuits' arrival in Contarea was greeted with great joy, as their arrivals in Ossossané and Teanaostaiaé had been. After the priests took up residence in the longhouse of Atironta and had erected a small chapel there (Thwaites 1896–1901, 20:25), the village council granted them permission to address the community, individual households invited the Jesuits to visit them, and everyone spoke of becoming a Christian.

Rumours about the dangers of baptism that were common among the three western tribes do not seem to have penetrated this far east, or if they had the Arendarhonon had paid little attention to them. Baptism was sought for both young and old who were ill (20:23) and the Jesuits' raisins and sugar were in demand for their presumed curative powers (20:21). The Jesuits' reputation as healers was enhanced when a number of Arendarhonon recovered after receiving their aid. Ononrouten, a young man noted for his ability as a hunter and warrior, had been stricken with smallpox in September but survived after he was baptized. When Daniel and Le Moyne arrived in Contarea in November they found him blinded by an inflammation, but when they applied holy water to his eyes he recovered his vision (20:23–25). A young girl was likewise cured of a dangerous ulcer and a woman named Atatasé recovered from colic after she was shown a picture of Christ and had been baptized (20:25–27). As smallpox became more prevalent and people who were baptized began to die, most of the people of Contarea grew hostile towards the Jesuits. They began to repeat the same accusations against them that the rest of the Huron were making and the Jesuits were forced to remain inside Atironta's longhouse. Even there, however, everyone except Atironta began to harass them in an effort to drive them away. The leader of this persecution was the eldest female in the house (20:31–33).

The Arendarhonon's dislike of the Jesuits was reinforced by dreams that people in Contarea reported having. In one, the Jesuits were seen outside the village palisade or on the shore of a lake, unfolding books from which sparks of fire spread everywhere, carrying the smallpox with them (20:31–33). Another man reported that when he was fishing, Iouskeha appeared to him in a vision and informed him that he was the spirit that the Jesuits called Jesus, but about whom the French knew very little. Iouskeha stated that it was the Jesuits travelling in pairs throughout the Huron country who were causing disease and that they would not stop until all the Huron were dead. Iouskeha advised that if the people of Contarea wished to save themselves, they should drive away the Jesuits and perform a ritual that

Iouskeha proceeded to describe in detail. The man reported his vision to the village council, which gave orders that the ritual should be performed. It began in Atironta's longhouse and, in addition to dream-guessing, involved carrying a great kettle of ritually treated water through the village, from which the sick were encouraged to drink (20:27–31). This vision is of special interest because it is the first recorded attempt by a Huron group to reassert traditional beliefs and to denigrate those being advocated by the Jesuits. The vision marks the beginning of a series of minor nativistic movements in which Huron visionaries attempted to organize some sort of ideological resistance to Christianity by reinforcing the basic tenets of the Huron oral tradition. As a result of the upsurge in native ritualism in Contarea and growing doubts about the efficacy of baptism, the Arendarhonon whom the Jesuits had baptized soon rejected their teachings.

In spite of this, Atironta, as the successor of the first Arendarhonon headman who had concluded an alliance with the French, continued to take seriously his role as protector of the Jesuits. It was he who called a meeting at which the Jesuits were invited to defend their innocence. Chihwatenha addressed this meeting for over two hours, explaining the Jesuits' teachings. No one expressed any desire to be baptized, but the persecution of the Jesuits soon ceased and once again they were able to visit the majority of households. Thus they baptized more than 140 people, most of whom died soon after (20:37). A war chief refused to be baptized, saying that he had no fear of death or hell and even in Atironta's household the Jesuits were not allowed to baptize at least one child (20:37–39). The Jesuits also visited neighbouring Arendarhonon and Algonkin settlements but their mission work made no significant progress there.

By far the most dangerous mission was the one to the Tionnontaté. No Huron would accompany Fathers Garnier and Jogues on their journey there. As they travelled from one Tionnontaté village to another, children cried out that disease and death were coming and women fled and hid their infants. In most villages it was impossible to find a house in which to sleep and nowhere were the Jesuits allowed to say mass. At Ehwae the principal headman at first protected the Jesuits and allowed them to stay in his longhouse; however, when he saw them praying, he accused them of sorcery and drove them out (20:43–51). The Huron who came to trade with the Tionnontaté accused the Jesuits of even worse crimes, no doubt hoping that they might persuade the Tionnontaté to kill the missionaries. Soon the Jesuits were warned that if they set foot in certain villages they would be slain (20:51–53). During this period the Jesuits were joined by

Chihwatenha who attempted to use his influence with his trading partners ("relatives") to secure better treatment for the missionaries. While he succeeded in winning a single night's lodging for the priests in several villages, as soon as they were discovered trying to baptize the dying, they were forced to leave and Chihwatenha was denounced for associating with sorcerers. When the Jesuits returned to Ehwae, they found that community more hostile than before and were forced to leave before nightfall. The principal headman of the village gave a feast at which he exhorted some young men to slay the Jesuits, but they were unable to overtake them before they reached the next village. The next day this same headman visited the Jesuits and apologized. He was denounced by Chihwatenha for abandoning the hospitality and good manners that were customary among the Huron and Tionnontaté (20:55–65). It is unclear how much longer the Jesuits remained among the Tionnontaté or how many of the dying they managed to baptize. Some of the latter were Neutral Indians who had been forced to seek refuge among the Tionnontaté, apparently by a second consecutive year of famine in their own country (20:49–51).

LIVES IN THE BALANCE

Since the Huron and Tionnontaté both agreed that the Jesuits were using sorcery to cause yet another epidemic, it is surprising that the Jesuits managed to survive the winter. Most Huron, including many council chiefs appear to have wished and called for their death and specific plans were formulated to accomplish this. None of these plans came to anything, however, and when individual Jesuits were attacked, other Huron came to their aid. To a large degree, the Jesuits were protected by the segmentary nature of Huron society, which made not the confederacy but the tribes, villages, clan segments, and even individual lineages responsible for the actions of their members. Each group wanted closer trading relations with the French and was convinced that if it took the initiative in killing or even harming the Jesuits, other groups would profit at its expense. The internal quarrels that had arisen following Brûlé's assassination were too flagrant an example of the disintegrative effects of such behaviour to encourage any group to take responsibility for murdering the Jesuits. Huron headmen spent their time trying to persuade other Huron and non-Huron to kill the Jesuits while refusing to be persuaded themselves. Even the Tionnontaté, who did not trade directly with the French and therefore had less to lose, understood what was going on and refused to become cat's-paws for their

Attignawantan neighbours. The Huron discussed refusing to sell the Jesuits any more corn in an effort to force them to stop practising witchcraft, but even this relatively innocuous plan foundered on the self-interest of the groups involved (Thwaites 1896–1901, 17:229). None of them was willing to forego the supplies of European goods that were received in payment for the corn.

In March 1640 a general council met at St. Louis to discuss what the Huron confederacy as a whole should do about the Jesuits. An entire night was spent debating this issue and the majority of headmen who were present said they were in favour of killing them as soon as possible. One tribe, however, opposed this action arguing that it would ruin the country (19:177). It is not stated which tribe this was, although it may have been the Arendarhonon, playing their traditional role as allies of the French. This led to further argument about which tribe would bear responsibility if the Jesuits were killed, and finally the project was abandoned. It was decided that since it was likely that native sorcerers were also at work, these should be hunted down and slain before further action was taken against the Jesuits (19:179). There is no evidence that the Huron attempted to revive the old plan of compelling the Jesuits to return to Quebec the following spring.

The fundamental reason that the Jesuits survived was that the Huron dared not kill them or force them to leave the country. When they were angry, Huron might prevent the Jesuits from preaching, or they might insult or even strike a priest. In spite of this the Huron believed that the French governor gave the Jesuit mission his complete backing. Because of this, they were convinced that the survival of the French-Huron alliance depended on the Jesuits remaining in their midst and being well treated by them. That this knowledge could be converted into sufficient psychological pressure to protect the Jesuits' lives, in spite of the hostility that their behaviour generated, is a measure of the degree to which the Huron were now dependent on the French.

In the beginning, French trade goods had appealed to the Huron as novelties, but over the years these goods had become increasingly vital to the Huron economy. At first the Huron could reduce or suspend trade for a year or more if it was in their own interest to do so; however, by 1636 Aenons said that the Attignawantan (and presumably the rest of the confederacy) could not afford to let more than two years go by without trading with the French. Yet, so long as the Huron did not perceive themselves as dependent on the French, they were able to deal with the latter as equals. The relatively small amount of political or cultural pressure that the French exerted on the Huron prior to 1629 did not challenge this feeling of independence.

In 1634 the Huron headmen found their trading and military alliance with the French transformed into a mechanism for compelling them to allow missionaries to live in their midst whose behaviour was incomprehensible to them and who wished to overturn the traditional Huron way of life. The Huron headmen were convinced that these priests had the backing of the French traders and officials and could only be expelled at the cost of giving up the French alliance. To make things worse, there was no alternative to trading with the French. European goods could no longer be done without and the Iroquois, who were the principal enemies of the Huron, lay between them and the Dutch. The Huron could therefore perceive no opportunity in the foreseeable future of switching their trade from the St. Lawrence to the Hudson Valley. Knowledge that there was no alternative and that they were dependent on the French inculcated a sense of frustration and resignation among a number of Huron headmen. Yet, while a realization of the need for good relations with French traders seems to have been widespread enough to ensure the protection of the Jesuits, its more crippling effects were not generally realized until some time later. The period between 1634 and 1640 was not the time when most Huron first became aware of their loss of independence.

Lalemant records that when the Huron went to trade in 1640, Montmagny punished them for the acts of violence they had committed against the Jesuits during the previous winter (21:143). Nothing is recorded concerning the precise nature of this punishment, although it was probably directed against the traders who had been most active in opposing the Jesuits rather than against the Huron as a whole. Punishments meted out to the Montagnais suggest that some traders may have been seized, imprisoned for a few days, and made to pay fines. Alternatively, they may have been denied the right to trade until they promised to behave differently in future. Montmagny warned the Huron of severe penalties that he would inflict on any Huron who in future attempted to harm the Jesuits.

However much the Huron resented such coercion, they were intimidated by Montmagny's threats and did not attempt to defend their honour by making any sort of counter-threats against the French. When the traders returned home, several Huron tribes offered reparations to the Jesuits to atone for the behaviour of those who had sought to injure them. From this time on, however hostile certain individuals may have felt towards the

Jesuits, the Huron headmen treated them with circumspection. Lalemant rejoiced at the success of Montmagny's action, which he described as a pious employment of secular power.

This event, though inadequately reported, was clearly a turning point in French-Huron relations. Not long before, the French had feared the loss of the fur trade and were making contingency plans to try to come to terms with the Huron even if the Jesuits were slain. Now that half of the Huron population had died, the French became convinced that the Huron were economically and politically dependent on them, and this encouraged Montmagny to assert his power. As the Jesuits in the Huron country observed the success of this new policy, Montmagny was encouraged to press home his advantage.

SULLEN AFTERMATH

By the spring of 1640 the smallpox epidemic had come to an end. With its termination, Huron hostility towards the Jesuits subsided. Once again, it became possible for them to visit all of the Huron settlements. Of Christian converts of former years, only three or four heads of families and a few old women continued to profess their adherence (Thwaites 1896–1901, 17: 229). The rest had publicly renounced Christianity or their faith had been swept away in the upsurge of healing cults that had taken place during the winter. Bitter feelings against the Jesuits persisted and reflected themselves in a number of different ways. In May 1640 a shaman in St. Jean predicted the death of Brébeuf, who was once again working in Teanao-staiaé. The same day Brébeuf suffered from a high fever and pains in the stomach, which lasted for more than twenty-four hours. The Huron regarded Brébeuf as the leader of the Jesuits, and the Jesuits suspected that one or more shamans had attempted to poison him (19:179–81).

A more certain victim of Huron resentment was Joseph Chihwatenha, who was killed on 2 August while he was cutting down some trees in a field near Ossossané. His death was not witnessed by anyone, but the Huron headmen who investigated the slaying reported that it had been committed by two Seneca who had rushed at Chihwatenha from the woods, wounded him with a spear, finished him off with two hatchet blows, and carried off his scalp as a trophy. His body was not discovered until evening when his failure to return home caused others to look for him (20:79). While the Jesuits accepted the claim that he had been slain by the Seneca (20:95; 21:161–63, 211), there are strong reasons for believing that he was murdered by his own people and that the headmen in Ossossané had either ordered his murder or at least approved of it in advance.[13] Killings of this sort were among the ways that Huron headmen dealt with those who were believed guilty of sorcery and treason. The killing occurred only a few days before Chihwatenha was planning to leave for the St. Lawrence (20:79).

In the summer of 1639 Chihwatenha had visited Quebec, where he met Marie Guyart and two Ursuline nuns, who had arrived from France that year planning to found a nunnery and a school for French and Indian girls (19:161). Following this visit, and at considerable inconvenience to himself, he had transported some relics and other religious equipment from Quebec to the Huron country (19:251). Far from faltering in his support for the Jesuits during the smallpox epidemic, Chihwatenha went to great lengths to aid them and identify himself with them, not only in Ossossané, but throughout the Huron country and among the Tionnontaté (19:259). These activities strengthened Huron suspicions that he was in league with the Jesuits to kill his own people. On several occasions Chihwatenha replied to these accusations by stating that he was willing to be slain as a sorcerer rather than cease helping the Jesuits (19:247–49). In 1640 Chihwatenha was persuaded to spend eight days performing spiritual exercises at Sainte-Marie to help him cope with the stresses of the period (19:137). In the course of these exercises Chihwatenha persuaded one of a group of Huron, who had come to Sainte-Marie to denounce the Jesuits, to be baptized. This convert, named Louis, was described as one of the noblest spirits in the country (19:151).

After these exercises Chihwatenha visited a village near Sainte-Marie, where he attempted to persuade a brother, or maternal cousin, to become a Christian. He informed this relative that, because he intended to do more to help the Jesuits in the future than he had done in the past, he anticipated that the charges of sorcery that were being levelled against him would increase. Chihwatenha told this kinsman not to be surprised if he heard that he was condemned and slain as a sorcerer (19:153). Chihwatenha denied being a sorcerer. He also told his kinsman that he would continue to regard him as a brother only if he became a Christian (19:159). The relative confirmed to Chihwatenha that there was talk of killing both him and the French and warned him that his death might be imminent (19:157). When Chihwatenha attempted to convert other people in the village, he was told that this was a matter for the headmen to decide which implied that it was an affair in which a young and unimportant individual like himself should not be meddling (19:163).

The idea that Chihwatenha was in league with the Jesuits to destroy his own people had been entertained at Ossossané as early as 1637 (15:99). With his increasing involvement in mission work, this opinion became more widely accepted. It is indicative, however, of the manner in which the Huron dealt with matters related to the French, that they waited until most of the traders had left for Quebec before they took steps to eliminate him.

Chihwatenha appears to have had some knowledge of the immediate danger he was in on 2 August. Around noon, he ordered his three nieces who had accompanied him to the fields to gather some squashes and return home as quickly as possible (20:81). Had he suspected that the Iroquois were lurking nearby, he would have accompanied his nieces to safety and raised a war party to track the enemy. His actions are logical, however, if he knew that his own people were determined to kill him and make it look like the work of Iroquois raiders; by sending his nieces home, he prevented them from being killed as witnesses. It appears that his whole family knew why and by whom he had been killed, but in the face of general hostility they dared not complain or question the findings of the village council. When one of Chihwatenha's nieces heard that he had been slain, her only comment was that even if "they" massacred the whole family, she would never cease to believe in the Christian god (23:195). This statement suggests that she believed that her uncle was killed by his own people.

Such knowledge may also explain the decision that Chihwatenha's elder brother Teondechoren made, only three days after the killing, to become a Christian and carry on his brother's work (21:149–51). For many years Teondechoren had been a prominent member of the Awataerohi society and although he and Chihwatenha lived in the same village and probably in the same longhouse, he had rejected all of Chihwatenha's proposals that he should become a Christian. Teondechoren's sudden change of mind may be interpreted as a tacit protest against the killing of his brother. He remained a faithful convert and, as an outward symbol of his desire to continue his brother's work, the Jesuits followed Huron custom and allowed him to "revive" his brother's Christian name.

Enough information is presented in the *Jesuit Relations* to permit present-day scholars (including Jesuit ones) to infer that Chihwatenha was killed by his own people (Talbot 1956:221–22). It therefore seems highly unlikely that the Jesuits working in the Huron country also did not suspect this. Why then did they remain silent, preventing Chihwatenha from being recognized as the first martyr of the Huron mission? It may be that they lacked proof and therefore felt obliged to accept the Huron's explanation of what happened. Or they may have felt, as they did after Father Chabanel's murder, that it was more prudent "to let suspicions sleep which might have been a ground for animosities and nothing more" (Du Creux 1951–52:553). This would have been an even more honourable policy had the Jesuits known that Chihwatenha was slain for political reasons such as helping the Jesuits among the Tionnontaté, rather than because his affirmation of Christianity had convinced the Huron that he was a sorcerer. It must be noted, however, that as a result of the Jesuits' missionary work among the Huron, Le Caron's opinion that it was impossible to be a martyr among the Indians was no longer valid (Le Clercq 1691:283). The Jesuits had built up an image of Chihwatenha as a model convert in successive instalments of their *Relations*; they may therefore have feared that if they publicly attributed his death to the Huron, they would lose the sympathy of their readers for the continuation of the Huron mission. What is more surprising is that scarcely any references are made to Chihwatenha in later volumes of the *Jesuit Relations*.

Conclusion

If the great political and psychological development of the period 1634–40 was the Huron's gradual realization of the degree to which their reliance on French trade goods was curtailing their freedom of action, an equally serious tragedy was the loss of approximately half their population. A large number of those who died were children and old people. The loss of the former must have meant that towards the end of the following decade, when the attacks of the Iroquois increased sharply, the Huron had fewer young men to defend their villages than their total numbers would suggest. The high mortality rate among older people was even more serious because of their key role among the Huron. They included many of the most skilful artisans, both male and female, as well as headmen and village elders who were knowledgeable about local and foreign affairs and had the most experience in dealing with the Jesuits. Traditional religious lore was also largely a prerogative of the elderly (Thwaites 1896–1901, 8:145–47). In the epidemics many must have died before they could transmit this knowledge to their heirs. The loss of such a broad spectrum of experience made the Huron economically still more dependent on the French and less equipped to resist the theological inroads of the Jesuits. The Jesuits, of course, could not resist seeing the hand of God at work in the death of the native religious specialists. This was interpreted as evidence that the Almighty was intervening to win the Huron to Roman Catholicism.

The remnants of the Huron found themselves living in villages that were too large for them. Many longhouses were empty or almost empty, since up to half of their inhabitants were dead. In the summer of 1640 this resulted in a decision to relocate the town of Ossossané, although the existing settlement was only five years old (21:159). The extra labour involved in founding a new, albeit smaller, town so soon after the last move must have been a heavy burden to the people of Ossossané. It may be assumed that similar, premature moves were made in other parts of the Huron country.

It has often been assumed that this decimation of the Huron people put them numerically at a disadvantage by comparison with other tribes and, in particular, with the Iroquois. This conclusion is based on the erroneous assumption that the Huron were decimated while other Iroquoian peoples were not. When Bogaert visited the Mohawk in the winter of 1634–35 the principal headman of Onekagoncka, their most easterly fortified village, was living about a quarter of a mile away because so many people had died of smallpox (Jameson 1909:141). The Susquehannock were stricken by an epidemic in 1636 or early 1637 (Thwaites 1896–1901, 14:9) and the Wenroronon's decision to move to the Huron country in 1638 is said to have been made, in part, as a result of large numbers having perished from disease (15:159). The Neutral suffered to an unusual degree from wars, famine, and disease prior to 1641. Even if Neutral villages were smaller than Huron ones, the estimate of only 300 people per village in 1641 hints at population losses that may have been of a similar magnitude to those experienced by the Huron. Finally, in the winter of 1640–41 a serious epidemic, probably smallpox, was reported to be raging among the Seneca (21:211). During the following decade, particularly in 1646 and 1647, the Iroquois were afflicted with contagious diseases that do not appear to have reached the Huron (30:229, 273; 31:121). These random reports, combined with what we know about the ravages of disease among the Indians of the St. Lawrence and Ottawa Valleys, complete a picture of general population decline throughout the region. It therefore seems reasonable to conclude that the Huron and Iroquois had been roughly equal in numbers before the epidemics began and that both had lost approximately one half of their population by 1640. In strictly demographic terms this gave neither side an advantage over the other.

Chapter 9   The Storm

The Huron and the French

GROWING DEPENDENCE ON TRADE

By 1640 not only the Huron but most of the Indians in eastern Canada and adjacent parts of the United States had become dependent on the fur trade. Novel economic pressures were transforming their lives and inter-relationships at an accelerating rate. In particular, increasing demands for European goods began to generate new kinds of conflicts as tribes were driven to compete for the limited supplies of beaver skins that were available. Exacerbated by the competitiveness of rival European traders, these conflicts were to shatter the established tribal patterns of this area within scarcely more than a decade. Unlike some earlier conflicts, the new ones were not over access to European traders or trade goods, but over obtaining the furs with which European goods could be purchased.

Serious readjustments in the economic life of the entire region were necessitated by the sharp drop in human population between 1636 and 1640. Since both the Huron and the northern hunting peoples probably declined by about half, it would be reasonable to expect a proportional decrease in the number of furs that were traded after this time. Yet the figures for the decade between 1640 and 1650 suggest that the annual volume of furs supplied to the French did not drop. In 1645 an estimated 30,000 pounds of beaver skins were exported from New France (Thwaites 1896–1901, 27:85). The following year the figure was 32,000 pounds (28:235), and in 1648 it was 22,400 pounds (32:103). While a beaver pelt weighs approximately one and a half British pounds, Jérôme Lalemant's statement that furs were selling in France for ten livres per pound in-conclusively suggests that at this period a pound generally signified an individual skin (28:235). This would make possible a direct comparison with earlier documents in which statistics are given in terms of skins rather than weights. Yet even if the pounds referred to are actual weights, these figures indicate an increase in the annual volume of trade over the average 12,000 to 15,000 skins that were exported before 1627 (4:207). It thus appears that after 1635 the number of skins obtained by the French rose as the Indian population declined. In part, this may be explained by an increase in the extent of French trading networks along the St. Lawrence. Closer relations with the Abenaki, who lived in Maine and adjacent parts of New England, brought some furs to Quebec. Yet this increase could not have offset losses proportional to the probable decline in the Indian population of Ontario and Quebec.

It may also be argued that these high figures are for the few years in the 1640s when trade was successful and include furs that the Huron and other tribes had accumulated over several preceding years, when they were unable to trade with the French. There are, however, major rebuttals to such an argument. In most years when the Huron and other tribes failed to trade with the French in large numbers, they made an effort to do so, often losing most of their furs to the Iroquois. The years when the Iroquois were most active were also those when it was least possible for the Algonkin and Montagnais to hunt or trade with other tribes, hence the returns carried forward to the following year were unlikely to be of considerable volume. For both of these reasons, it is reasonable to accept the figures for such peaceful years as 1645 and 1646 as indicating the volume of furs that the Indians who were allied to the French were capable of supplying them in any single year.

There are no direct figures concerning the number of furs that the Huron supplied in any one year, but there is information about the number of Huron who came to trade with the French. Like the data for earlier times, these figures mainly take account of traders who arrived in sizable groups; hence they probably fall short of the totals for most years. We know, for example, that in June 1643 a single group of about 120 Huron came to Quebec to trade and were attacked by the Iroquois on their way home a few weeks later (24:121; 26:235–37). We also know that at least two bands of Huron were attacked that year on their way to or from Quebec (28:45), so the total number of traders must have considerably exceeded 120. The following year, sixty Huron came to Three Rivers, proclaiming that their aim was to fight the Iroquois rather than to trade. They returned home, however, laden with presents and no doubt with trade goods, and were accompanied by an escort of French soldiers (26:53–73). The same year three other bands of Huron traders were attacked by the Iroquois (28:45). Even if these were bands of no more than forty men each, the minimum number of Huron attempting to trade on the St. Lawrence that year would have been 180.

In 1645 no Huron came to the St. Lawrence before September, when sixty canoes arrived at Three Rivers (27:89, 277). Although approximately thirty Frenchmen were travelling with them, it is reasonable to assume that there were about 200 Huron in this group. At least some of them visited Quebec and their safe return home filled the Huron country with joy, since they brought with them an abundant supply of French goods which had become scarce during the previous five or six years as a result of Iroquois attacks on traders travelling to and from the St. Lawrence (29:247). In late August of the following year, over eighty Huron canoes came in a single group to trade (28:141, 231). These canoes carried about 300 Indians (29:233), in addition to some thirty warriors who had come down-river earlier (29:229). At least two canoeloads of Huron were still at Quebec a month later (28:235). So many skins were brought down-river that year that the Huron had to take twelve bundles home with them for lack of French merchandise (28:231). In 1648, 250 Huron came to trade in about sixty canoes (32:179, 185). While none of these figures is as high as the 140 to 150 canoes that were reported to have come down-river in 1633, the annual totals are as large, or larger, than the average of sixty canoes and 200 traders per year that has been estimated for the period 1615 to 1629. The figures for 1646 are also the second highest on record. This suggests that not only the total amount of trade with the French, but also the number of Huron who were participating in it, were no less after the epidemics than they had been prior to 1629. As before, the Huron probably provided close to half of the total number of furs exported from Quebec each year, which probably meant 12,000 to 16,000 skins.[1] Lalemant reports that the twenty-two French soldiers who were sent to the Huron country in 1644 returned the following year with 3000 to 4000 furs (27:89). The dispute that arose concerning who had the right to purchase these skins clearly indicates that they were ones these soldiers had obtained by barter, rather than the total Huron consignment for that year.

Even though the mortality of 1639 to 1640 had fallen most heavily on the young and old, the number of Huron and Algonkians who died in the prime of life must have been very great. For a population that had been halved to maintain its former level of trade with the French required very considerable changes in organization. These changes must have represented an even more severe drain on manpower because of the large numbers of traders who were killed or taken prisoner by the Iroquois, particularly between 1641 and 1644. Unfortunately, we have no clear evidence to explain how the Huron managed to maintain the volume of their trade at its former level. It is theoretically possible that they extended their trading networks geographically, although the only evidence that there is of this (which I will discuss later) is of the Huron taking over markets that were abandoned by their trading partners. There is no evidence that the Huron tapped new sources of furs to the north or west, which alone would have augmented the numbers of furs reaching Quebec by way of the Huron country. More intensive exploitation of the fringes of the existing Huron trading network may have netted more furs than before, without requiring greater effort on the part of individual Algonkian hunters, but this is unlikely to have maintained the intake of beaver pelts at its former level. The conclusion therefore seems inescapable that throughout much of this trading area, individual Algonkians were encouraged to trap considerably more beaver than they had done previously.

While the deaths of many hunters may have allowed those who survived to increase the number of beaver that they caught with less than a proportional increase in effort, it is unlikely that the numbers of animals being trapped could have been doubled without considerably more time being devoted to this task. This was probably accomplished as it had been among the hunting peoples of the Maritimes, by using time that tradition-ally had been spent fishing and hunting larger game animals. The resulting weakening of the subsistence base was compensated for by relying more heavily on corn and beans, which the northern Algonkians obtained from their Huron trading partners. It is possible that the Algonkians were more than happy to do this, since this arrangement seemed to offer them more security against starvation during the winter than did their traditional subsistence pattern. All that may have been needed to stimulate more trapping at the expense of hunting and fishing was an increase in the volume of corn that the Huron made available to their northern trading partners. It is also likely that as a result of the epidemics, the Algonkians, like the Huron, had lost many of their most skilful artisans and were more anxious for European goods than they had been previously. Thus, growing dependence on both the Huron and the French drew the Algonkians more deeply into a network of interrelationships that made them increasingly dependent on what was happening among their southern neighbours.

If an equal proportion of the Huron and their northern trading partners died between 1634 and 1640 and the economic relations between them had not changed, the surviving Huron would have had to spend no more or no less time producing corn than they had done previously. Growing reliance on Huron foodstuffs by the Algonkians must, however, have increased the amount of time that Huron women had to spend tending their crops and that Huron men had to spend clearing new fields. Moreover, in relationship to the population, approximately twice as many Huron men must have been involved in trading with the Algonkians and the French as had been before. This increase is well documented in terms of the number of Huron who came to the St. Lawrence to trade each year, which remained roughly constant in spite of the dramatic decline in population. It is also likely that because of increasing production and consumption, as many men as before were required to transport corn and skins between the Huron country and the north in spite of the decreased population.

The greater input of labour into the fur trade meant that less time was available for other activities. In particular, the amount of time available for traditional warfare, which, like trading, was a warm weather activity, must have been sharply reduced. Whenever French trade goods could be substituted for traditional Huron products that took long to manufacture, the increasing time taken up by the fur trade must have encouraged the Huron to substitute these items for their own. Thus, the demand for French goods, which had already been intensified by depopulation and the loss of old skills, was further increased as a result of the fur trade. It is also possible that the need to grind more corn and manufacture more nets for the northern trade may have reduced the time that was available during the winter for traditional ritual activities. A decline in such activities would have left the Huron more vulnerable to the ideological assaults of the missionaries.

With their growing dependence on the fur trade, the geographical position of the Huron rendered them far more vulnerable to attack than were the Iroquois. The Mohawk had to travel only forty to fifty miles down the Mohawk Valley to trade at Fort Orange; hence individuals and small groups were able to move easily and at any time of the year between their own villages and the Dutch settlements. While the western Iroquois tribes had to walk overland for much longer distances, their route was through territory belonging to the other tribes of the Iroquois confederacy. Huron or Susquehannock raiders might ambush these traders, but at this period such ambushes seem to have been uncommon. Finally, for all of the Iroquois tribes, protecting their tribal territory and their trade routes were one and the same operation, while for the Huron, they were not. The Huron had to defend their villages and tribal territory against Iroquois raiders, who mostly came from the western part of the Iroquois confederacy. In addition, whenever Huron traders travelled along the Ottawa and St. Lawrence rivers, they were in danger of being attacked by Mohawk and Oneida. Since small bands of Iroquois were able to hide along the banks of these rivers and wait the best opportunity to fall upon their victims, these attacks were much easier for the Iroquois to launch than for the Huron to guard against. One response was for the Huron to travel in large groups, which they began to do as early as 1643. Prior to 1648, however, these bands had a tendency to split up if no danger appeared to be threatening and this resulted in unexpected attacks. Huron also came to the Ottawa and St. Lawrence valleys to fight the Iroquois, but as attacks on the Huron homeland grew more severe a strong element of risk was involved in diverting large numbers of men to fight there.

Thus, as the Huron grew more dependent on European goods and their manpower was increasingly tied up in trading activities, their inland location that had formerly sheltered them from so many of the disrupting effects of European contact became a liability. Because of this, the balance of power that had formerly existed between the Huron and the Iroquois began to tip in the latter's favour. The Huron found themselves not only economically, but also militarily, more dependent on the French than they had been before. To many, the goodwill of the French must have seemed essential to their survival. The desire that most Huron seem to have had for closer relations with the French encouraged Montmagny and his Jesuit advisers to design new strategies to promote at least an external acceptance of Christianity.

TAKING OVER ALGONKIAN TRADE ROUTES

During and after the epidemics, the Huron enjoyed a number of advantages which made it easier for them to collect furs to trade with the French. As I have already noted, when the Jesuits returned to New France in 1632, they made certain that no employees of the trading company were allowed to live among the Nipissing or Algonkin. Nicollet, who had resided for a long time among the Nipissing, settled as a clerk of the Compagnie des Cent-Associés at Three Rivers in 1633 and, thereafter, since the Jesuits did not establish a mission among the Nipissing, there were no Frenchmen living with them. It is therefore not difficult to understand why, when the Nipissing incurred Tessouat's wrath in 1636 for refusing to help him wage war on the Iroquois, they no longer dared to travel down the Ottawa River to trade with the French. It was not until the summer of 1640 that they ventured to send a few canoes to Three Rivers (Thwaites 1896–1901, 21:241). To encourage the Nipissing to trade, the Jesuits decided to establish a mission amongst them and Fathers Claude Pijart and Charles Raymbaut were sent to the Huron country for this purpose. In the winter of 1640–41 these missionaries made contact with 250 survivors of the tribe who were wintering in the Wye Valley, and in the spring of 1641 they travelled with the Nipissing to their tribal territory (21:239–49). In 1642 the Jesuits again travelled north with the Nipissing and participated in an Algonkian version of the Feast of the Dead that was held along the eastern shore of Georgian Bay. This ceremony was attended by all the trading partners of the Nipissing, who were given presents at two separate assemblies: one held for the Huron and the other for the Algonkian-speaking tribes. At this gathering, the Jesuits had a chance to meet the various bands who lived along the eastern and northern shores of Lake Huron.

At this Feast of the Dead, the Baouichtigouian or Ojibwa Indians from Sault Sainte Marie, who had already entertained Brûlé and other Frenchmen, invited the Jesuits to visit their country. Thus, in September Fathers Raymbaut and Jogues accompanied a party of Huron to Sault Sainte Marie, but returned to the Huron country in the late autumn (23:225–27). This marked the beginning of a series of Algonkian-speaking missions to the Indians at the Sault, to the Ottawa bands living west of the Tionnontaté and along the northern and eastern shores of Georgian Bay, and to the Algonkin who came to winter or find refuge among the Arendarhonon. The most important of these missions was that of St. Esprit to the Nipissing. It is uncertain to what degree the Huron-based missionaries were able to encourage the Nipissing to resume their trade with the French. No priests were available to travel with them to Three Rivers and, while there are occasional references to the Nipissing coming to Three Rivers to trade, there is nothing to indicate that this trade was carried on even to the limited degree that it had been before 1636. The chief beneficiaries of this Nipissing reluctance to trade must have been the Huron who until 1640 and probably afterwards obtained more furs from the Nipissing than they had done for many years previously.

The Huron may also have gained direct access to more furs as a result of growing disorder among the Algonkin. Starting apparently in the late 1630s, the Iroquois began to supplement their summer attacks on fur shipments along the Ottawa and St. Lawrence River with winter raiding parties. The aim of these raids was to penetrate Algonkin and Montagnais hunting grounds and to rob these Indians of their catch while they were dispersed in small family groups and therefore unable to come together to defend themselves (27:37). The Iroquois also hunted in these territories. Because of these raids, many Algonkin and Montagnais were too frightened to hunt and began to seek the protection of the French at Sillery, Three Rivers, Fort Richelieu, and the new French settlement at Montreal. Still others sought temporary refuge in the upper part of the Ottawa Valley (14:225) or in the Huron country (24:267).

When Tessouat wintered along the St. Lawrence in 1640–41, he was still self-confident enough to persuade the Montagnais at Sillery to defy the Jesuits by resuming traditional religious practices. In the winter of 1642–43, however, even the Kichesipirini were refugees from the Iroquois and the following spring both Tessouat and Oumasasikweie embraced Christianity and expressed a desire to settle under French protection at Montreal (24:237–45). That the headmen of the Kichesipirini, who prided themselves on their independence of the French both before and after this period, should have become so submissive can be accounted for only by their fear of the Iroquois. The same year, the Onontchataronon, who traditionally wintered among the Arendarhonon, were joined there by Algonkin from all parts of the Ottawa Valley, who were seeking refuge from the Iroquois (24:267–69; 27:37). These refugees were reported to be hoping that once the Montreal area became more secure, they could establish a permanent village there under French protection, no doubt much like the Indian village at Three Rivers.[2] Although the Algonkin had long discussed the advantages of having a refuge on Montreal Island, the fact that large numbers of them were now willing to abandon their tribal territories is an indication of the danger that existed at this time. For the Kichesipirini to consider having their summer headquarters there was a particularly desperate move, since it meant foregoing the lucrative tolls they collected on Morrison Island.

Many Algonkin, particularly from bands in the lower part of the Ottawa Valley, began to frequent the French settlement of Ville Marie and to plant crops there (29:145–47), while the Onontchataronon asserted traditional claims to Montreal Island as being their ancestral home (Pendergast and Trigger 1972:77–80). Henceforth, the majority of Algonkin hedged their bets by maintaining their connections with the major centres of French population, whatever the political situation was like and wherever they spent most of their time. It is not surprising, however, that as soon as a shaky peace was arranged with the Mohawk, Tessouat and his people returned to Morrison Island (Thwaites 1896–1901, 29:149).

HURON TRADE IN CENTRAL QUEBEC

The general disruption of Algonkin life at this time may have stimulated the Huron to intensify their trade with the Indians of central Quebec.

We know from Sagard that the Huron were trading into that area by the 1620s, while archaeological evidence hints that even in prehistoric times some of them may have travelled as far east as Lake St. John. In the 1640s, however, the references to Huron trade in central Quebec become more abundant. The Huron were reported to come each year to "Maouatchihitonnam" to trade with the Kakouchakhi and other hunting groups of central Quebec (Thwaites 1896–1901, 24:155). It is tempting to identify this trading place as Matabachouwan on Lake St. John, which may have been the eastern terminus of the prehistoric copper route leading from Ontario. Such a location was ideal for trade with the bands of the upper Saguenay and was probably where the Attikamegue, or White Fish people, who lived in the upper part of the St. Maurice Valley, came to trade with the Huron. In 1647 when the Huron were unable to come down the St. Lawrence, the Jesuits at Three Rivers asked the Attikamegue to carry letters destined for the Huron country to Huron with whom they traded in the interior of Quebec. They not only delivered these letters, but returned bearing others that the Jesuits in the Huron country had asked the Huron to send to Quebec by way of the Attikamegue (31:219). From these letters we know that some fifty Huron traders came to Maouatchihitonnam, bringing with them corn, corn meal, nets, and other small wares (probably including tobacco), which they exchanged for animal skins (31:209, 219).

The goods that the Huron brought with them also demonstrate that they came directly from the Huron country. Moreover, the fact that none of these Huron is described as coming to Three Rivers or Tadoussac and, more specifically, their failure to deliver the letters from the Huron country to the French in person suggest that after their trading they returned to the Huron country or at least to the Ottawa Valley, where they exchanged their furs with Huron who were authorized to trade with the French (32:289).[3] It is uncertain by what route they made their way eastward and westward across the network of lakes and rivers of central Quebec. Those who went by way of Lake Timiskaming may have travelled as far north as Lake Matagami before turning southeastward to Lake St. John. This route would have taken them through Nekouba which, when it was first visited by the French a few years later, was described as the location of an annual market, similar to Maouatchihitonnam (46:275). Indeed, Father Ragueneau may have been referring to Nekouba when he mentioned a group of Huron who in the summer of 1641 left their country on a trading expedition to Ondoutawaka (22:75). Two years later, Jérôme Lalemant explained that the Huron went every year to trade with the Andatouha people who lived "about a hundred leagues above the Saguenay towards the north" (27:27). These people were reported to have acquired a smattering of Christian knowledge on their visits to Tadoussac and Three Rivers.

There clearly were opportunities for the Huron to expand trade in this region and, as the fur trade became more important to them, they must have taken advantage of such opportunities, particularly as the Algonkin's control of the trade of this region became less effective. Yet these references to Huron activity in central Quebec do not prove that their trade in this area was a new thing; they may simply reflect a growing awareness on the part of the French of what was going on north of the St. Lawrence. Huron traders had been active in Quebec for at least two decades and possibly longer. Whatever expansion of Huron trade took place in the 1640s was based on established patterns.

HURON VISITORS TO THE ST. LAWRENCE

Another feature of this period was the growing number of Huron men who wintered in the St. Lawrence Valley, either among the French or in the Indian settlements at Sillery and Three Rivers. It has been suggested that they may have initiated the Huron trade in the Lake St. John region (Heidenreich 1971:259, 261, 264). I have not, however, been able to discover any satisfactory evidence that these men engaged in trade with the north and, as we have already seen, the logistics of this trade necessitated that it be a separate operation conducted from the Huron country. In the 1620s a few Huron had wintered at Quebec, apparently mainly from bravado or curiosity, and such motives should not be under-rated even in the 1640s; however, five additional motives explain why individual Huron wintered in the St. Lawrence Valley in the 1640s. Three reflect the growing menace of the Mohawk in the Ottawa and St. Lawrence valleys, while the other two indicate a growing sense of dependence on the French.

Some Huron came to avenge Mohawk attacks on Huron traders. By wintering in the St. Lawrence Valley, they could join the Montagnais in their spring raids. In April 1647 a number of Huron who had wintered at Sillery and Three Rivers set out on such a raid, although Montmagny tried to persuade them not to, in the hope that a short-lived peace with the Mohawk still might be preserved. One of the leaders of this band was Andehoua, the most loyal of the Jesuits' former pupils (Thwaites 1896–1901, 30:165–67).

Other Huron who wintered in the St. Lawrence Valley had been captured by the Mohawk and escaped from them, but were too late or too ill to return home before winter. Montreal, in particular, gained a reputation for being the nearest refuge for these escaped prisoners. Thirdly, because of their fear of the Iroquois, still other Huron delayed their return home past the season when travel was possible and these too took advantage of French or Montagnais hospitality to pass the winter. The extension of such hospitality was an accepted part of intertribal trading relations, but the Huron appear to have made more use of this privilege as Iroquois attacks increasingly disrupted their trading schedules.

The Compagnie des Cent-Associés had for some time supplied European goods to Christian Indians more cheaply than they supplied them to non-Christians. After 1640 discrimination in favour of Christians was intensified to put more pressure on traders to convert. At the same time, however, the Jesuits became more insistent on subjecting potential converts to a strict probation before baptizing them. This led to enterprising attempts by young men to convince the Jesuits of their religious sincerity.

When Brébeuf returned to Quebec in 1641, it was decided that it would be useful to re-open the Huron school, but this time to use it to instruct adults and confirm them in the Christian faith. An attempt was made to persuade a few Huron to stay at Quebec, but no suitable volunteers could be found. Soon after, two Huron from Scanonaenrat, Atondo and Okhukwandoron (Aotiokwandoron, 26:295), returned to Quebec stating that they preferred hunting with the Montagnais to facing the dangers involved in travelling home at the beginning of winter. They were brought to Sillery, where Brébeuf took charge of them and found them receptive to instruction. This seemed surprising since prior to 1640 Atondo, who was a headman of some importance, had shown considerable aversion to the Jesuits.

Atondo and Okhukwandoron remained at Sillery for the winter. They listened attentively to Brébeuf, prayed often, and observed fast days. They were well cared for by the French and the Christian Montagnais and received much special attention both from Montmagny and from the Ursuline and Hospital nuns who were now established at Quebec. Finally, the two men asked to be baptized. This was done with Paul de Chomedey de Maisonneuve and Jeanne Mance as godparents. The latter were spending the winter at Quebec before proceeding to found a colony on Montreal Island. When spring came and Atondo and Okhukwandoron prepared to leave for home, the Montagnais presented them with two parcels of smoked moose meat to feed them on the journey. The Huron promised that when they got home they would host a feast at which they would make a public profession of their new faith and that, hereafter, they would urge their relatives and tribesmen to become Christians (22:135–53).

The success of this new effort to instruct Huron in Christian beliefs led the Jesuits to repeat the experiment under Brébeuf's direction the following winter. Andehoua, who had received the baptismal name of Jean-Armand, and who was now known among his own people as Andeouarahen (23:175), retained the belief in, or fear of, Christianity that he had acquired when he had been a pupil at the first school the Jesuits had established at Quebec. In 1642 he was caught in a dangerous storm on Lake Ontario and vowed that if he escaped, he would again live as the Jesuits had directed. When he returned to the Huron country, he told the Jesuits of his vow and accepted their advice that he and another young Huron named Saouaretchi who had expressed the desire to become a Christian should spend the following winter at Sillery. Other Huron who came to Quebec no doubt had heard from Atondo and his companion how well they had been treated by the Jesuits during the previous winter; therefore a number of other young men volunteered to spend the winter there. The Jesuits were unable to support them, however, since they lacked room and board. The others were persuaded either to return home or to join the Kichesipirini at Fort Richelieu, in order to hunt and go to war with them.

In the middle of January one of these men, who was nephew of a headman from Arenté, came to Sillery and asked to be instructed in the faith. He was fed and lodged by the Hospital nuns. About a month later, room was found for two other men from Arenté, Atarohiat and Atokouchi-ouani, who were allowed to live with the Jesuits' workmen. These young men all behaved to Brébeuf's satisfaction and were baptized during the winter. In mid-June, they left Sillery to join the Huron who had come to trade at Three Rivers and to return to the Huron country with them. Brébeuf was now convinced that by having a number of young men spend a single winter each living amongst the French and the Indians of Sillery, the Jesuits would be able to instruct a corps of Christians who could assist them to convert their own people, as Chihwatenha had done. These men would be especially effective if they came from chiefly lineages and were in line to inherit important offices. Such men were anxious to establish a close relationship with the French for political and economic reasons (24:103–21).

Some Huron men stayed at Sillery during the winter of 1643–44 and received lessons from the Ursuline nuns, who, in turn, were attempting to learn their language (25:243). Brébeuf spent this winter at Three Rivers where, as procurator, he was concerned with the pressing problems of forwarding supplies to the Huron mission. There, a new school was opened in the Jesuit residence and six Huron received instruction. Four had come from the Huron country specifically for this purpose, while the other two were young men who had escaped from the Mohawk. Within two months of their arrival, all six had been baptized. Although they were troubled by dreams throughout the winter, they claimed not to obey these dreams and scrupulously observed Roman Catholic rituals. In late April these Huron set out for home in three canoes, taking with them Father François-Joseph Bressani, an Italian Jesuit who had arrived in New France in 1642 and had spent the following winter helping to instruct these Huron. They were also accompanied by a French boy twelve or thirteen years old. Although some of the Huron carried guns, they were depending mainly on the early date of their departure to save them from Iroquois attack. Seven or eight miles from Fort Richelieu, their canoes were attacked by a Mohawk war party, which included some of their Mahican allies and six former Huron who had been taken prisoner and were now naturalized Iroquois (26:37). In the ensuing conflict, one of the Huron, Sotrioskon, was killed and later eaten by the Iroquois. Seeing that escape was impossible, Bressani ordered the men in his canoe to surrender and finally all of the other Huron were captured by the Iroquois. None of the prisoners was subjected to preliminary torture except Henry Stontrats and Michel Atiokwendoron (not to be confused with Jean Baptiste Okhukwandoron), each of whom had one finger cut off (26:37). They were all carried off to the Mohawk country except Stontrats, who escaped and made his way back to the St. Lawrence (26:19–35).

The fate of the other Huron prisoners is unclear. One appears to have escaped torture by proclaiming his enmity towards the French (39:67, 73), but at least two others were killed (39:95). Bressani was taken from one Mohawk village to another and cruelly tortured for over a month before he was adopted by a Mohawk woman whose grandfather had been killed by the Huron (39:55–97). Rather than ordering his death, she gave the Mohawk presents not to kill him and then sold him to the Dutch for about 200 livres worth of trade goods (39:266 n. 8). After he was ransomed, Bressani returned to France, but by July 1645 he was back in Canada.

Although there is no explicit mention of Huron being instructed at Three Rivers or Quebec after Brébeuf's return to the Huron country in 1644, a Huron named Arenhouton was baptized at Quebec in May 1646 (28:191), perhaps after receiving instruction over the preceding winter. He may have been one of several Huron who spent the winter at Sillery and who were accused of stealing salt pork from Pierre Godois and beating him in retaliation for his having stolen some furs from them (27:91). While it would be unwarranted to deny these Huron some element of religious belief, most of them appear to have viewed a winter living with the Jesuits at Quebec or Three Rivers as an efficacious way to conclude a firm alliance with the French and to secure substantial material benefits from them. As such, it was a role that was especially popular among potential headmen and men who were anxious to trade on the St. Lawrence.

This period also saw a Huron girl brought to Quebec to be educated by the Ursulines. This was Chihwatenha's eleven or twelve-year-old niece Oionhaton.[4] Chihwatenha had met Marie de l'Incarnation and the Ursuline nuns at Quebec in 1639 and when he returned home had expressed the wish that his niece should go to live with the Ursulines for a time. In 1640, Teondechoren carried out his dead brother's wishes and took Oionhaton to Quebec, where she remained until 1642. During this period, she learned to read and write and attempted to follow the religious practices of the nuns. Like other precocious Iroquoian children, she loved to display her newly acquired knowledge by lecturing visiting Huron on the subtleties of Christian doctrine (22:191–97). When Oionhaton was travelling home in 1642 with her uncle and a number of other famous warriors, they were attacked by the Mohawk and she was taken prisoner (22:197).

Another manifestation of the desire to achieve a closer relationship with the French was Atironta's decision to bring his wife to Three Rivers with him when he attended the peace conference in 1645, and to remain with her, his small son,[5] and another Huron, named Acharo, at Quebec over the following winter. Atironta wished to be on hand to await news of the treaty that Huron envoys had gone to conclude with the Mohawk; traditionally he was also the principal Huron ally of the French and in addition he was now a Christian. No doubt, he regarded it as fitting that on a visit to the French, he and his relatives should spend some time with them. The French, however, who had to provide them with flour and eels, complained that the accommodation they occupied in the hospital at Sillery could better have been used for sick people (27:91–93, 103). During the winter Atironta's wife and son were baptized and were allowed to sit in the governor's pew in church (27:113). Stopping at Montreal on his way home, Atironta was said to have been so impressed with the corn that he saw growing there that he proposed to come with his own and another household and settle on the island (29:181). While the Jesuits hoped that he might persuade other Huron to settle near Ville Marie and that these might form the nucleus of a settlement of Christian Huron, nothing came of this suggestion. That it was made at all is a reflection of Atironta's conviction in his role as an ally of the French and therefore as having the right to consider himself one of them.

Trade and Warfare

THE IROQUOIS'S NEED FOR FURS

The 1630s witnessed a gradual resurgence of Mohawk attacks on the St. Lawrence Valley. These were encouraged at the beginning of the decade by the political instability at Quebec and were discouraged by the decisive steps that the French took to police the river in 1633 and 1637. In spite of this, increasing harassment of both Algonkin and Huron traders in the Ottawa Valley seems to indicate that the Mohawk and Oneida were more than taking advantage of an easy situation. Their attacks became more serious in the 1640s, while the western tribes of the Iroquois confederacy were becoming more aggressive towards their neighbours to the north and west. Many explanations have been offered for this increasing bellicosity, but none of them has gained general acceptance. It is therefore necessary to examine closely what was happening among the Iroquois at this time.

Unfortunately, the only Iroquois tribes for whom there is significant historical documentation prior to the 1650s are the Mohawk and Oneida. Most information concerns the Mohawk, who had the most intimate trading relations with the Dutch. The evidence suggests that their closer proximity to Europeans had resulted in their acquiring a wider range of European goods than is reported for the Huron. As early as 1634–35 Harmen van den Bogaert noted doors of hewn boards with iron hinges inside some Mohawk houses (Jameson 1909:141). Such doors would have had to be purchased ready-made or stolen from the Dutch and carried from the Hudson Valley inland to the Mohawk villages. Bogaert also reported seeing iron chains, harrows, hoops, and nails in their villages. By 1644 guns, swords, axes, and mallets were in common use among the Mohawk (ibid. 176), while, about the same time, Jogues and Bressani spoke of them possessing numerous iron rods and chains (Thwaites 1896–1901, 28:125; 39:71). By 1634–35 the mother of an Oneida headman had cloth to repair items of dress (Jameson 1909:153–54). It is perhaps significant that the Mohawk called the Dutch not only iron-workers (*charistooni*: a term analogous to the Huron's "men of iron"), but also cloth makers (*assirioni*) (ibid. 178). All of this suggests a dependence on European goods that much exceeded that of the Huron. The archaeological evidence indicates that by the 1630s even the Seneca had access to a considerable volume of European goods. Allowing for the difficulties of dating archaeological sites to within a few decades, glass beads, brass kettles, and iron goods appear to have been at least as abundant among the Seneca as they were among the Huron by this period (Wray and Schoff 1953:56–58). In the epidemics of the 1630s and 1640s the Iroquois must have lost many skilled craftsmen and like the Huron become more dependent on European goods.

The Dutch records indicate that prior to 1640 the number of beaver skins that were traded by the Iroquois was considerably less than the number traded by the Huron. In 1624 a total of 4700 beaver and otter skins reached the Netherlands, although this number rose to 7685 by 1628 and to 16,304 by 1635 (Trelease 1960:43). Only a portion of these skins came, however, from the upper part of the Hudson Valley and not all of the latter came from the Iroquois. Kiliaen van Rensselaer estimated that between 1625 and 1640, 5000 to 6000 skins were traded each year at Fort Orange (Van Laer 1908:483–84), and even in 1635 only 8000 furs came through that trading post.[6] These figures compare unfavourably with the 12,000 to 15,000 skins that the Huron appear to have supplied to the French each year. If, however, most of their furs were trapped by the Iroquois themselves rather than obtained from other tribes as the Huron's were, the profits that accrued to the Iroquois for each fur would have been considerably greater than those realized by the Huron. As long as the Iroquois were able to trap about 8000 beaver and otter per year, it is likely they could supply their wants at the level to which these had developed by the 1630s.

THE BEAVER SUPPLY

It is clear that beaver were still prevalent in the Iroquois country as late as 1635. Bogaert saw 120 beaver skins in a single Mohawk house and was shown streams where many beaver and otter were being trapped (Jameson 1909:142–47). Yet he found the Oneida anxious for peace with the Algonkin so they could hunt in safety in the Adirondacks and in the north generally (ibid. 150). This desire to expand hunting into the northern no man's land suggests either that the beaver supply in the Iroquois heartland was proving inadequate to meet the Iroquois's growing demand for trade goods or that it was diminishing as a result of beavers being over-hunted. The depletion of beaver was not an unusual phenomenon in eastern North America at this time. In the early 1640s, fear of their extinction in the St. Lawrence Valley led Le Jeune to advocate assigning specific hunting territories to each Montagnais family in order to encourage conservation (Thwaites 1896–1901, 8:57–59).

Unlike the Huron, the Iroquois were surrounded on all sides except the extreme northeast by peoples who, like themselves, were horticulturalists. For the most part, these groups traded with the French, the Dutch, or the Swedes. They were, therefore, competitors in the fur trade rather than potential suppliers of furs. The Seneca could trade European goods for furs with the landlocked Neutral, but even in this trade they had to compete with the Huron. It may be hypothesized that the increasing aggressiveness of the Iroquois was a response to a growing demand for furs that could not be satisfied either within their own heartland or by exploiting the no man's land that lay between them and their northern neighbours.

A proper evaluation of this proposal requires answers to two more specific questions: why did the Iroquois need to secure more furs? How was their warfare intended to achieve this end? In *The Wars of the Iroquois*, Hunt (1940:33–35) has offered what he believes are definitive answers to both of these questions. In his opinion, the Iroquois were driven to seek supplies of furs outside their tribal territories because by 1640 their local supply of beaver had been exhausted. He agreed with McIlwain (1915:xlii–xlv) that the aim of the Iroquois was to force the northern and western tribes, including the Huron, to trade with them rather than the French, thus establishing themselves as middlemen in a vast network of trade between the northern tribes and the Dutch.

Unfortunately, the evidence concerning the depletion of furs within traditional Iroquois hunting territories is highly unsatisfactory. There is no doubt that the Iroquois placed a high value on furs throughout the 1640s, as the Huron and Algonkin recognized when they exchanged furs for wampum at peace conferences (Thwaites 1896–1901, 27:295);[7] however, this does not prove that beavers were extinct in upper New York State. That the Mohawk were anxious to prevent the Dutch from developing trading relations with the northern Algonkians could be interpreted as evidence that they sought for themselves a middleman position in such trade. Alternatively, and in my opinion more probably, such behaviour can be interpreted as evidence that the Mohawk were still determined that their enemies, who had access to more and better furs than they did, should not have an opportunity to conclude treaties with the Dutch which in turn might be used to undermine the Mohawk's own security. The best evidence that Hunt could raise in support of his argument that beaver were exhausted by 1640 is a statement contained in a narrative of Governor de Courcelle's voyage to Lake Ontario (for 1671) that the Iroquois, and especially the four western tribes, had long ago exhausted the beaver on the south side of Lake Ontario and could now find scarcely a single one there (O'Callaghan 1856–87, 9:80). Hunt (1940:34–35) also construed a comment by Kiliaen van Rensselaer to the effect that the falling off in trade at Fort Orange in 1640 did not occur because the independent traders at Rensselaerswyck had siphoned off the available furs to mean that the Iroquois no longer had access even to the limited supplies of beaver skins that had been available to them in former years.

Hunt omitted, however, to consider a section of Van Rensselaer's letter which stated explicitly that the Mohawk did not lack furs. Van Rensselaer went on to suggest that the failure of the Dutch to obtain these furs resulted from a lack of trade goods, from the high prices they charged, and, most importantly, because the English in the Connecticut Valley were contacting the Mohawk and offering them more trade goods for each pelt in order to draw off their furs. Van Rensselaer suggests that the Mahican, who were now allies of the Mohawk, had played an important role in bringing the English and the Mohawk together (Van Laer 1908:483–84). This totally vitiates the arguments that Hunt based on this passage. Arent van Curler was to note a similar dearth of skins at the Fort Orange trading post in 1643, although "so great a trade was never driven" as that year. In 1643, however, the culprits were not the English, but the Dutch settlers, to whom freedom of trade had been granted in 1639 (Trelease 1960:118 n. 12).

Francis Jennings (1968:24) has attempted to demonstrate that beaver were not extinct in the Iroquois country using Adriaen van der Donck's (1841:209–10) statement that about 80,000 beaver a year had been killed in New Netherland and adjacent territories in the nine years since 1642. The figure he cites seems, however, to be the total number of skins traded in the French, English, Dutch, and Swedish colonies and cannot be cited as necessarily having a bearing on the condition of the fauna of upper New York State at this time.

There are strong reasons for believing that prior to 1640 the Iroquois were hunting beaver more intensively in their own territories in an effort to satisfy their growing demand for European goods. It is quite possible that this might have led to the exhaustion of beaver in that area, although there is no proof that this happened as early as 1640.[8] What is clear is that the Iroquois's demand for trade goods was increasing rapidly and that eventually, to satisfy these demands, it was necessary to obtain furs from beyond their tribal territories. A depletion of beaver may have intensified this trend, but in the long run it can account for only a small part of it. By the late 1630s a growing desire for trade goods seems to have pressed the annual fur budget of the Iroquois to the point where not only the Mohawk, but all of the Iroquois tribes, were looking for new sources of furs beyond their tribal territories.

STRATEGIES FOR OBTAINING FURS

In the late 1630s, three methods of obtaining furs were feasible for the Iroquois: they could attempt to bring about a realignment of trading patterns by persuading or compelling fur-rich peoples like the Huron to trade with them; they could expand their hunting territories by expelling or asserting their authority over adjacent peoples; or they could steal furs or trade goods from their neighbours. The first of these solutions, which is the one that McIlwain and Hunt suggest they attempted to put into practice, was probably the most effective long-term solution for their problems. Moreover, so long as the Mohawk were able to prevent the Dutch from concluding separate alliances with the Huron and the northern Algonkians (and now that the defeated Mahican were the Mohawk's allies, the chances of the Dutch doing this seemed more remote than ever), this solution must have seemed an attractive one to the Dutch traders since it would permanently have diverted the northern fur trade away from the St. Lawrence and destroyed the economic basis of New France. It is probable that the Dutch were urging their Mohawk partners to establish trading links with the north both in the hope of getting furs and that the Dutch might later establish direct trading links with these tribes in spite of Mohawk objections. Van Rensselaer may have had such plans in mind when he wrote in 1641 that he hoped within a few years to be able to divert much of the French trade to the Hudson Valley (Van Laer 1908:553).

It is certain, however, that formidable difficulties lay in the way of such an arrangement. Under normal circumstances the Huron would have been unwilling to abandon their alliance with the French or to become dependent for trade goods upon traditional enemies, with whom no peace treaty had ever proved to be more than a short-lived truce. Only if trade between the

Huron and the French had been made impossible, might the Huron have been bullied into accepting such an arrangement. If the Huron would not make peace, an alternative strategy was for the Iroquois to destroy them and to attempt to trade directly with the Huron's northern trading partners. Evidence of an attempt to coerce the Huron into a trading alliance has been read into the diplomatic activities of the Mohawk prior to 1646; however, the Mohawk's refusal to consider an offer to trade that the Huron made to the Iroquois the following year can hardly be attributed solely to their jealousy of the Onondaga or to pique over the failure of earlier efforts. Furthermore, the Iroquois's failure even to try to establish any kind of peaceful trading relations with the northern hunting peoples for several decades after the dispersal of the Huron suggests that they lacked either the skill or inclination to engage in such activities.

It is at this juncture that the major cultural difference between the Huron and the Iroquois noted in chapter 3 becomes important. The Iroquois traded with neighbouring tribes for flint, wampum, and other luxury goods, but had not acquired the subtlety and expertise that characterized the far more vital and extensive trade that the Huron had long been carrying on with the northern Algonkians. Even in their dealings with the Dutch, the Mohawk revealed a quarrelsomeness that was only offset by the willingness of the Dutch to tolerate robbery, personal abuse, and the destruction of their property in the interests of trade. To the Dutch, the Iroquois were a source of prosperity; therefore their other characteristics had to be endured (Trelease 1960:115). As late as 1664, Pierre Boucher (1664:101) observed that the Iroquois had shown no skill as traders. According to him, they did not trade with other Indians because they were hated by them; while, by contrast, the Huron traded everywhere. This difference was noted by Parkman and other nineteenth-century writers, although it was explained by them in terms of ethnic stereotypes and was forgotten when explanations of this genre became discredited.

I have already suggested that historical and geographical reasons explain this difference. The Huron lived in an area where a symbiotic trade in vital goods had grown up with hunting peoples long prior to European contact. The Iroquois, on the other hand, were surrounded by peoples who had economies similar to their own and who were competing for the same resources. Because of this, waging war and building political alliances were the main skills that the Iroquois had acquired for dealing with their neighbours, while trade was of relatively little importance. Given this background, the Iroquois were unpromising candidates to replace the Huron as large-scale middlemen.

TERRITORIAL EXPANSION

There is, however, ample evidence that the Mohawk were anxious, and able, to exploit more hunting territory. After the peace of 1645 they hunted throughout the no man's land between themselves and the Algonkin, exploiting areas that both sides had avoided for many years for fear of each other (Thwaites 1896–1901, 28:279). They are reported to have killed many animals in this area, although the Jesuits do not refer specifically to beaver, but to some 2000 deer that the Mohawk slaughtered during a single winter (28:287). It also appears that the Iroquois who invaded Algonkin and Montagnais territory each winter were active as hunters as well as warriors. Nevertheless, these examples do not provide evidence of the permanent annexation of such hunting territories, in a manner comparable to what had been going on for some time among the Indians of the Maritime provinces.

There is, however, some evidence that has been interpreted as an indirect indication that such annexation was going on. Marian White (1971a:32–36) has suggested that the Wenroronon were expelled from their tribal territories in western New York State by the Seneca, who were in need of more furs and hence anxious to expand their hunting territories at the expense of their neighbours. Other factors that may have contributed to the Wenronon's inability to defend themselves were epidemics (which may have been critical for a small population) and the severing by their former allies, the Neutral, of an alliance that had existed between them (Thwaites 1896–1901, 17:25–27). Under these circumstances, the Wenroronon decided in 1638 to abandon their tribal territory, some seeking refuge among the Huron and others among the Neutral (21:231–33).

White's explanation of the dispersal of the Wenroronon makes sense in terms of the strategy of the fur trade. It is possible that in order to preserve their neutrality between their Huron and Seneca trading partners, the Neutral were willing to sacrifice an ally in the face of Seneca determination to expand their hunting territories. If the Wenroronon had closer trading connections with the Susquehannock than with the Iroquois (39:141), the Seneca would have had good reason to decimate them, rather than attempt to secure their furs through trade.

Unfortunately, the evidence in support of this interpretation is far from satisfactory. Only once is it definitely stated that the Wenroronon decided to disperse because of Iroquois attacks (15:159) while references to a disagreement between the Wenroronon and the Neutral might be construed as evidence that the latter were the cause of their dispersal (17:27). Although the Jesuits stated that the Wenroronon who were living in the Neutral village of Khioetoa were refugees (21:231–33), it is not impossible that they came there as captives. The Wenroronon may also have been attracted to Khioetoa by the hope of being reunited with relatives who had been captured by the Neutral. A final possibility that cannot be dismissed out-of-hand is that the Wenroronon were forced to disperse by the same enigmatic enemies "from the west" who compelled the Erie to move inland about the same time (33:63).[9]

Another possible example of the Seneca's efforts to expand their hunting territories is their destruction in 1647 of the principal town of the Aondironnon, who are described as the Neutral living nearest to the Huron.[10] The reason given for this attack was that a Seneca warrior, who had been raiding in the north the previous winter, had been pursued and slain by the Huron at the gates of this village. To punish the Neutral for their failure to provide this man with sanctuary, Seneca warriors visited the village under the guise of friendship and fell upon their hosts while they were being feasted (33:81–83). Hunt (1940:90–91) has interpreted this attack as part of an attempt to disrupt contact between the Huron and their Susquehannock allies. It is possible, however, that its real aim was to gain access to Neutral beaver grounds.

The Neutral provide the clearest example of a people who were waging expansive wars at this time. Early in the 1640s, the Neutral won a series of spectacular victories over the Assistaronon, which again was probably a generic term for all the Algonkian-speaking tribes living in southeastern Michigan.[11] In 1640 the Neutral are reported to have captured over 100 Assistaronon prisoners and an army of 2000 took 170 more the following year (Thwaites 1896–1901, 21:195). In 1643 an army of equal size laid siege to an Assistaronon village for ten days and brought back some 800 prisoners. They also tortured seventy of the best Assistaronon warriors to death before their return, and blinded and girdled the mouths of all the old men before abandoning them to die in the forest (27:25–27). Even allowing for gross exaggeration, these accounts suggest that the Neutral were taking advantage of easier access to iron weapons to inflict serious injuries on their traditional enemies. Their aim may have been to secure undisputed possession of the rich beaver hunting grounds around Lake

St. Clair. It is even possible that the Neutral sought to extend their hunting territories into southeastern Michigan and that by so doing it was they, rather than the Iroquois, who were responsible for the retreat to the north and west of some of the tribes who lived in this area. The central Algonkians probably did not distinguish between the Neutral and the Iroquois, but called them both Naudoway, meaning snakes or enemies; hence their later assertions that they had been driven from their original homeland by the Iroquois (55:183) may be interpreted as a memory of the wars that the Neutral had waged against them at this time (Hunt 1940:116 n. 28).

By 1642 some of the Potawatomi had abandoned their territory and sought refuge among the Ojibwa at Sault Sainte Marie (Thwaites 1896–1901, 23:225). The same wars may account for the retreat of the more southerly Michigan tribes, including the Sauk and Fox, into Wisconsin prior to 1650 (H. Wilson 1956). These tribes lived in river valleys in a parkland environment, where they raised corn and hunted deer, while at certain times of the year they moved west into the grasslands to hunt buffalo. This cycle of activities may have rendered them more vulnerable to attack and hastened their decision to retreat west of Lake Michigan, where the power of the Winnebago had already been broken by a series of wars and epidemics. Eventually the Wisconsin area was to become the overcrowded refuge not only for these people but for other tribes from Ontario and Michigan who were fleeing the Iroquois. The major dispersals of tribes in the lower Great Lakes area do not seem to have begun with the militancy of the Iroquois, but as a result of the Neutral exploiting the advantages that accrued to them from their geographical position in relationship to contemporary trading networks.

It is clear that the Mohawk combined hunting with raiding in their excursions against the Algonkians. What is uncertain is whether any of the Iroquois tribes consciously pursued a policy of seizing the hunting territories of other tribes as a means of obtaining more furs prior to the 1650s. The evidence that they did is, at best, equivocal. Moreover, as an explanation of the eventual expulsion of the Huron from southwestern Ontario (Trelease 1960:120), this proposition has serious shortcomings. If the Huron had exhausted the beaver in their own hunting grounds by 1630, the Iroquois would have been unable to obtain any extra furs by annexing this territory. They may have known that if an area is not hunted for a decade or more, its beaver population will revive, but to suggest that they sought to annex this area in the hope that it would eventually regenerate is to attribute to the Iroquois long-range objectives that bore no relationship to their immediate requirements for furs. In 1701, when the Iroquois placed their beaver grounds in southern Ontario under the protection of the King of England they stated explicitly that they had conquered the region in order to hunt there (O'Callaghan 1857–87, 4:908). There is no doubt that as early as the 1670s the Iroquois and their allies were trapping large numbers of beaver in that region.[12] It is therefore understandable that by 1701 they had come to believe that the use they were then making of southern Ontario was their reason for attacking its original inhabitants half a century before. This was, however, an anachronism and there is no sound reason to believe that the Iroquois regarded the Huron hunting grounds as worth fighting for in the 1640s.

FUR PIRATES

The third way of obtaining European goods was by piracy. At least among the Mohawk, the robbing of such goods from other tribes dates as early as the latter half of the sixteenth century. The amount of goods that could be acquired in this way must not be underrated and the continuation into the 1640s of attacks upon Huron and Algonkin leaving Three Rivers with European goods indicates that the Iroquois still had not abandoned this technique. Gradually, however, stealing European goods appears to have declined in favour of stealing furs, which were more portable and allowed the Iroquois to purchase what they wanted from the Dutch. Piracy seems to have been an important aspect of Iroquois warfare from the late 1630s at least through the 1650s. Winter as well as summer raids into Algonkin territory, summertime attacks on Huron and Algonkin traders on their way to and from French settlements, and increasingly violent attacks on the Huron and their neighbours all seem to reflect the efforts of the Mohawk, and later of the western tribes of the Iroquois confederacy, to satisfy a growing demand for European goods and for the furs needed to barter for such goods. These attacks became so violent that in some areas they resulted in the destruction or dispersal of the very people whom the Iroquois were robbing and thus reduced the base on which the Iroquois were able to prey in later years. Such behaviour is no evidence of irrational behaviour on the part of the Iroquois, but indicates how hard pressed they were to obtain furs. Hunt erred in assuming that the Iroquois necessarily followed the course of action that represented their best long-term interests; on the contrary, confronted by a pressing need for European goods, their behaviour became geared to very short-term objectives. Like most European traders, they were interested in doing what on an annual basis would bring in the most satisfactory returns with the least losses and trouble.

The Iroquois were clearly capable of profiting from alternative strategies, such as establishing trading relations with the French or the Algonkin when the opportunity for such relationships arose. Yet, not only was robbery the Iroquois's established means of acquiring furs and trade goods, but also, because of their geographical location and historical background, it required less reorienting of their lives than an effort to emulate the Huron as traders would have done. Finally, the number of economic stratagems that were open to the Iroquois was limited by political considerations. The Mohawk had learned from bitter experience that it was necessary, at all cost, to avoid situations in which their European trading partners were tempted to sacrifice the interests of the Iroquois in order to establish trading links with the Indians who lived in the rich fur-bearing regions to the north. So long as robbery satisfied their needs on a yearly basis and not too many Iroquois warriors were being killed, the majority of Iroquois probably paid little heed to the long-term negative features of such a policy.

The Iroquois had a further motive for waging war on their neighbours that was not primarily economic. Unlike the Huron, they were surrounded by potential enemies and on this account must have been particularly distressed by loss of population in the epidemics of the 1630s and 1640s. This led them to try to recoup their numbers by incorporating prisoners and conquered peoples into their society. The Iroquois had faith in their ability to use a combination of rewards and punishments to integrate large numbers of former enemies and were anxious to capture as many enemies as possible. As warfare escalated, the mortality rate increased and warfare became a means of trying to compensate for its own losses. Yet, in spite of the large numbers of prisoners and refugees that the Iroquois managed to incorporate into their tribal structures, they succeeded only in maintaining their population at about half of its aboriginal level in the face of continuing attrition resulting from disease and warfare.

GUN POWER

The Iroquois's motivation to acquire the furs they needed by violence does not explain their marked success in achieving this goal, especially after 1640. Before that time the Huron and Iroquois appear to have been about equally powerful and, with the help of the French, the Huron and the northern Algonkians could control the St. Lawrence River. In 1633 and again in 1637 the French had been able to stop Iroquois raids there by merely showing the flag. The Mohawk's success after 1640 did not result from any deterioration of French power along the St. Lawrence, which was considerably strengthened during the following decade, though not fast enough to match the growing power of the Iroquois.

The French realized that as long as the Mohawk were powerful enough to prevent the Dutch from concluding trading alliances with the northern tribes, it was in the interest of the Dutch traders to encourage the Mohawk to pirate furs from among these tribes. As early as 1633 Champlain had proposed to terminate this threat by conquering the Iroquois and then driving the Dutch and English settlers out of the territories adjacent to New France (Bishop 1948:331). Hating the Dutch came easily to the Jesuits, whose order had suffered serious setbacks from Calvinist opposition in India, Japan, and the East Indies (Robinson in Du Creux 1951–52:xviii). It was therefore not difficult for the Jesuits to believe that the Dutch were seeking to injure them in Canada as well. In a letter to Cardinal Richelieu in March 1640, Jérôme Lalemant accused the English and Dutch of inciting the Iroquois to attack the tribes allied to the French. Lalemant worded his letter to imply that the drop in Huron population, which he said was from 30,000 to 10,000 people in less than ten years, was entirely to be blamed on Iroquois raids (Thwaites 1896–1901, 17:223).

Lalemant's fear that Iroquois attacks might ultimately sever the commercial link between the Huron and the French was well founded, but his flagrant misrepresentation was obviously designed to make credible his request that action be taken to stop this trouble at its source by driving the Dutch out of North America. All of the Jesuits in Canada agreed that the Dutch should be expelled from the Hudson Valley and this was the plan that Father Le Jeune presented to Cardinal Richelieu in 1641 when he visited France to plead for help against the Iroquois (21:269–73). While his proposal was given some consideration, the French government was embroiled in the Thirty Years War and unwilling to risk a conflict with the Dutch by attempting to seize one of their colonies. Charles Lalemant, who was now the procurator of the Canadian Jesuits in France, understood the diplomatic subtleties that stood in the way of realizing Le Jeune's scheme. He recorded with apparent agreement the technical reasons which rendered it impractical as state policy (21:269–71).

Richelieu's niece, Marie de Vignerot, Duchesse d'Aiguillon nevertheless succeeded in obtaining the cardinal's promise to help defend New France

(21:269). Ten thousand écus were provided to send soldiers to the colony and to establish Fort Richelieu at the mouth of the Richelieu River. The purpose of this fort was to hinder the incursions of the Iroquois into the St. Lawrence Valley. The same year the colony of Ville Marie was founded at Montreal, thus providing the French with a post farther up-river. If strong enough, this colony could guard the entrance to the Ottawa River.

Charles Lalemant, who espoused the possible rather than the impossible, played a leading role in the planning of the colony. It was through his personal intervention that Montreal Island was ceded to the Société de Montréal and it was he who introduced Paul de Chomedey de Maisonneuve, the future governor of the colony, to Jérôme Le Royer de La Dauversière, the moving spirit in the founding of Ville Marie. He also did much to persuade Jeanne Mance and Louis d'Ailleboust de Coulonge and his wife to join the colony (Adair 1944). In spite of its contributions to the defence of the St. Lawrence Valley, this small settlement with its semi-autonomous status was to play a major role in undermining the control that the Jesuits had acquired over New France and which allowed them to treat the French settlements along the St. Lawrence almost exclusively as a base for their missionary work.

How then did the Mohawk overcome these efforts by the French to strengthen their control of the St. Lawrence Valley? The answer seems to be that they were able to obtain guns in greater numbers than were the Indians who were allied to the French. That the possession and use of guns conferred a military advantage on tribes has never been doubted. Yet the practical advantage of a cumbersome musket over a metal-tipped arrow is doubtful. The real power of the gun in Indian warfare appears to have been psychological; its noise and mysterious operation added to the terrors of foes and to the confidence of those who used them. For this reason, if no other, guns were a source of strength to the Indians, apparently largely in proportion to the numbers that any group possessed. The Mohawk soon learned to use their guns to intimidate other Indians and to meet the French on equal terms. Hunt (1940:9–10; 165–75) did a great disservice to the understanding of this period of Canadian history by denying that the Iroquois enjoyed superiority in the number of guns they possessed after 1640. The major errors in his argument have been exposed only recently (Tooker 1963:117–18).

The sequence by which the Indians of the St. Lawrence Valley and the lower Great Lakes area acquired firearms now seems reasonably clear. Both the French and Dutch trading companies opposed the sale of guns to the Indians, lest this would endanger the security of their ill-defended trading posts. As early as 1620, however, Champlain records that two illegal vessels from La Rochelle had traded a large supply of firearms, gunpowder, and shot to the Montagnais (Biggar 1922–36, 5:3). Fears were expressed that once the Montagnais were armed, their resentment of the trading monopoly might encourage them to attack Quebec. Throughout this period no guns were traded to the Huron or Algonkin, who both depended solely on the official trade that was carried on from Quebec. During the English occupation more firearms were sold to the Montagnais (Thwaites 1896–1901, 6:309), possibly after the English realized that they had no hope of retaining Quebec and hence had no interest in guarding the security of the colony. Le Jeune, writing in 1634, describes some of these Montagnais as good marksmen. Once the French returned to Quebec, the sale of guns appears to have been halted and only small quantities of powder and shot were bartered to Indians who already had them (6:309). There is no evidence that these guns gave the Montagnais any significant military advantage. We must therefore conclude that they had bought only a small number of guns and that since the Indians had no knowledge of how to repair them, most were soon out of commission.

It is clear that the Iroquois did not get guns as early as the Montagnais. None were in evidence when Van Krieckenbeeck and his men were killed in 1626, nor was anything but curiosity shown about them when Bogaert visited the Mohawk in 1634–35 (Trelease 1960:95). By 1639, however, the fur trade in New Netherland was no longer a company monopoly. Henceforth, settlers were free to import trade goods, to barter with the Indians for any number of furs, and to export these furs to Europe on their own account (ibid. 61, 112–13). The same year it was noted that individual traders were disobeying the standing orders of the West India Company by selling guns and ammunition to the Indians, and the death penalty was prescribed for those found guilty of this offence (Van Laer 1908:426). It is uncertain whether this particular ordinance was directed against the Dutch living around New Amsterdam or in the upper part of the Hudson Valley; but by 1641 such trade was specifically forbidden in Rensselaerswyck, under pain of a 100 guilder fine and deportation (ibid. 565).

The Rensselaerswyck ordinance was framed to curb a burgeoning trade in arms between the Dutch settlers and the Mohawk. So long as the fur trade had remained a company monopoly, considerations of security and the necessity of obeying orders seem to have kept guns out of the hands of the Iroquois. Once trade was made free, thoughts of security were thrown to the winds by traders who were anxious both to profit from selling guns and to arm the Mohawk, so that they could more easily pirate furs from the Indians who were allied to the French. The Mohawk must have found it necessary to obtain more furs to pay the high prices that were being demanded for weapons and ammunition.

Another factor also accounts for Dutch willingness to sell guns to the Mohawk at this time. The Mohawk are said to have got their first guns from the English (Jameson 1909:274); indeed, this seems to have been what was making them ignore the Dutch and carry their furs to the English traders from Windsor and Hartford who were operating along the Connecticut River in 1640 (Van Laer 1908:483–84). Thus commercial rivalry with the English as well as with the French convinced the traders at Rensselaerswyck of the soundness of their illegal enterprise. French figures provide some measure of the extensive trade in guns that went on between 1641 and 1643 and explain why the private traders at Rensselaerswyck were so prosperous by the latter date (Trelease 1960:118 n. 12). In 1641 a war party of 350 Mohawk had only thirty-six guns (Thwaites 1896–1901, 21:35–37), but by June 1643 the Mohawk had nearly 300 guns (24:271, 295). The passing of so many arms into the hands of the Iroquois must have had much to do with the first informal treaty that Arent van Curler negotiated between the Dutch and the Mohawk in 1643, and which was followed by another agreement in 1645 (O'Callaghan 1856–87, 14:15). These treaties appear to have legitimized the sale of arms to the Mohawk, thus fulfilling promises that the Dutch had first made in 1641 to assist the Mohawk against their enemies (Thwaites 1896–1901, 22:251). In 1644 a board of accounts in Holland reported that the Mohawk had enough guns and ammunition to supply 400 men, although trafficking arms with other Indians was still forbidden (F. Jennings 1968:24 n. 29). Thus, an illicit trade, carried on first by the English and then by the Dutch settlers, gradually persuaded Dutch officials to abandon their policy of caution in trading arms to the Mohawk. This policy was replaced by a new one that was designed to give the Mohawk the power to seize the furs that the Mohawk would not let the Dutch obtain from other Indians by means of trade.

The Dutch gun trade expanded through the 1640s, although French protests resulted in the re-enactment of the earlier ban against it in 1645 and Governor Peter Stuyvesant actually brought charges against two traders at Fort Orange in 1648. Fears that the Indians might become dangerous if they were officially denied arms led the Amsterdam directors to advise company officials to sell moderate quantities of arms to all the Indians, rather than having these supplied by private traders (O'Callaghan 1856–87, 14:83). In spite of official misgivings both in Holland and in

New Amsterdam, throughout the 1640s guns and ammunition became available not only to the Mohawk but also in smaller numbers to the other tribes of the Iroquois confederacy.

The arming of the Mohawk soon resulted in the French supplying guns to their allies as well. Yet, it was decided, no doubt under Jesuit influence, that guns should be made available only to Indians who had become Christians. It was hoped that this would provide a strong inducement for young men to become Christians and, when combined with the rigorous standards of conduct that the Jesuits required before they would baptize anyone, would serve as an anvil on which the Jesuits could remould the character of these men.

Guns appear to have been made available to the Montagnais and Algonkin in moderate numbers. In 1643 the Sieur de Maisonneuve gave Tessouat a high-quality musket and accessories as a baptismal present (Thwaites 1896–1901, 24:235–37), while Madame de La Peltrie gave a similar present to Oumasasikweie (24:233). By 1642 bands of Algonkin invariably had a few members who were armed with muskets (24:289–91), and by the middle of the decade the Algonkin living on Montreal Island had enough guns that they were able to fire a neat salute on festive occasions (29:181). In spite of this, it is generally agreed that fewer of the Algonkian-speaking allies of the French were able to obtain guns than was the case for the Mohawk. These guns were also of inferior quality, being shorter and lighter than those supplied by the Dutch (32:21).

Most authorities attribute the relatively small number of guns reaching the Algonkin to the tighter controls exercised by French officials and to their vigilance in denying guns to non-Christians. Hunt (1940:174) has concluded, however, that high French prices, held up by a monopoly and by an excessive desire for profits, were responsible for this situation, rather than political or religious considerations. This conclusion is feebly supported and ignores a fundamental difference between the French and Dutch colonists. The Dutch were prepared to take risks with their Indian trading partners and to arm them in the hope of greater commercial gain, even though this might later mean having to suffer from their insults and intimidations. Naroll (1969) has reminded us that the officials and priests who governed New France at this period did not share this bourgeois attitude. Accustomed to an older European tradition, they were sensitive of their honour and anxious, whenever possible, to have their Indian allies under control. While the French were willing to protect these allies if it were in their own interests to do so, they were unwilling to augment their fighting capacity without good reason since they feared that on some occasion the Indians might use this power against them. These attitudes, more than commercial reasons, seem to account for the smaller number of guns that the French were willing to make available to their Indian allies.

The French were even more reluctant to arm the Huron than to arm the Algonkin. They were afraid that guns might fall into the hands of non-Christians or apostates and be used against the Jesuits and their assistants. Moreover, it was recognized that by providing reliable converts with guns, the desire of the Huron men to become Christians would be strengthened and the power of these converts amongst their own people would be enhanced. The first Huron to possess a gun was Anenkhiondic's son, Charles Tsondatsaa (Thwaites 1896–1901, 20:215). It was given to him by Governor Montmagny, following his baptism at Quebec in June 1641. Montmagny said that he gave this gun so that Tsondatsaa could use it to protect himself against the Iroquois. Montmagny also promised that henceforth he would protect all Huron who were willing to declare themselves Christians, thereby implying that a similar protection was no longer being extended to non-Christians (20:219–21). At the same ceremony the Montagnais from Sillery presented Tsondatsaa with powder for his gun. Tsondatsaa replied that his having a gun would be a wonder to his countrymen and would demonstrate the goodwill that the French showed towards those who embraced their religion.

This policy allowed only a few guns to reach the Huron. Until the last three chaotic years of the Huron mission, relatively few Huron were accepted for baptism. Moreover, for a Christian to obtain a gun it was necessary for him to travel to Quebec or Three Rivers as a fur trader. Yet, as late as 1648 the number of Christian traders did not exceed 120 (32:179). Since only one gun was given or sold to each convert and care was taken that they were not passed from hand to hand, this figure may represent the maximum number of Huron who were eligible to obtain guns. The only statement that is contrary to this interpretation occurs in a letter said to have been written by François Gendron in 1644 or 1645. He expressed the opinion there that the military strength of the Huron had declined because they were trusting too much in the arms that the French sold to them at Quebec (Gendron 1868:17). This could be a reference either to the gun trade or to the older trade in iron axes and metal arrowheads. Gendron is a difficult source to use because of problems concerning the origin of part of his text and because other statements he makes contradict reliable contemporary sources.[13]

War on the St. Lawrence

NEW STRATEGIES

The acquisition of guns by the Iroquois altered their military tactics. Nevertheless, until the late 1640s the overall strategy was maintained of the Mohawk and Oneida directing their attacks against the Ottawa and St. Lawrence valleys, while the western tribes attacked the Huron in their own country. While there were changes in the nature and intensity of warfare in both theatres, the Mohawk's rapid acquisition of firearms and their close relationship with the Dutch initially produced far more dramatic changes in the east than in the west.

Prior to 1640 the Mohawk had slain a small number of Huron and Algonkin traders in their efforts to rob them of furs or European goods (Thwaites 1896–1901, 21:21). After their incursions along the St. Lawrence were checked by the French, they continued to raid the Ottawa Valley. By the late 1630s, however, these attacks were not securing enough furs and the Mohawk began to formulate a new policy. They sought to penetrate Algonkin and Montagnais territory in order to plunder furs and hunt there. Their first objective was probably the Rideau Lakes area, lying between the Ottawa and the St. Lawrence valleys. It was an especially productive hunting ground adjacent to Iroquois tribal territory (Heidenreich 1971:208). Prior to acquiring guns, the Mohawk had found it dangerous to penetrate Algonkin territory, particularly when the latter were on good terms with the Huron and the French. To overcome this opposition, the Mohawk resorted to their traditional strategy of trying to make peace with most of their enemies so they might wage war more effectively against one of them at a time. To secure their eastern frontier the Mohawk made peace with their former enemies, the Mahican, and with the Sokoki of the Connecticut Valley. Both tribes had formerly maintained alliances with the Algonkin, but were now willing to fight with the Mohawk against their former allies (Thwaites 1896–1901, 28:275). Prior to 1628 the Montagnais and Algonkin had regularly come south to trade for wampum with the Mahican and the Dutch; we must therefore assume that these good relations had come to an end after the Mohawk had disrupted this trade.

In 1645 the Mohawk reminded the Huron of peace talks that had taken place between them five years earlier (27:263). While nothing more is known about these talks, the Mohawk may have tried to persuade the Huron not to aid the Algonkin when the latter came under attack. What the Mohawk could have promised in return was to let Huron traders use the Ottawa and St. Lawrence rivers in safety. The Huron had probably been unwilling to abandon their renewed alliance with the Algonkin because they were convinced that the Mohawk could not resist the temptation to rob the rich Huron convoys. They therefore rejected the negotiations.

The Mohawk next sought to make peace with the French. In the autumn of 1640 ninety Iroquois made their way north of the St. Lawrence River to rob the Algonkin who they knew would be hunting between Montreal Island and Three Rivers (21:23). In February these warriors captured two Frenchmen, Thomas Godefroy and François Marguerie, who were hunting near Three Rivers, and carried them off to their villages. They were not tortured and, after some discussion, the Mohawk decided to return them to Three Rivers the following spring and to offer to make peace with the French, apparently on behalf of all the Iroquois tribes. Some Mohawk who had formerly been held prisoner at Quebec and Three Rivers and who had been well treated by the French had interceded for the lives of these two Frenchmen, as did Iroquois from some of the other tribes (21:23–41).

In April 1641 about 500 Iroquois set out for the St. Lawrence Valley. Some broke off to pillage the Huron and Algonkin, but 350 of them continued on to Three Rivers (map 24). In early June they built two forts, one on the south shore of the St. Lawrence from which they could negotiate with the French, and the other hidden away in the woods to which they could retire if they were attacked (21:63). Then, they released their prisoners and proposed to make peace with the French. As inducements they promised that following such an agreement, all the Iroquois tribes would come to trade at Three Rivers (21:47) and the French would be invited to erect another trading post near their country (21:39). In return, they asked the French to give them thirty muskets to add to the thirty-six that they had already purchased from the English and the Dutch (21:37).

François Marguerie made it clear that the Iroquois were only interested in making peace with the French and that they were determined to continue fighting with the Huron and Algonkin (21:37). Montmagny realized that it was impossible to make peace on these terms, since to do so would endanger the trade of New France even more than did the attacks that the Iroquois were making on the Indian allies of the French. He also feared that if the French concluded a separate peace with the Iroquois, the Algonkin and Montagnais might turn on them and cause them more trouble than did the Iroquois (21:55–57). Montmagny, therefore,

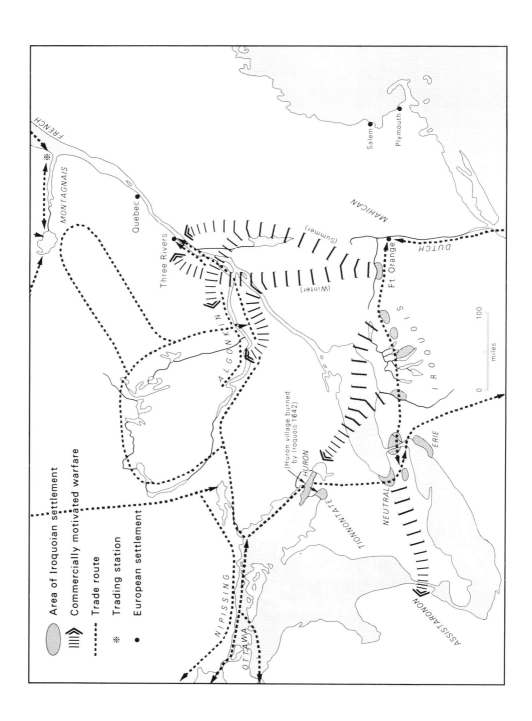

MAP 24. *Intertribal relations, 1641.*

informed the Mohawk that any peace would have to include the Huron and the Algonkians as well as the French. The Iroquois pretended to consider this request, but their attacks on isolated groups of Algonkin travelling to Three Rivers convinced the French that they were only trying to conclude a makeshift peace so they might attack the Huron and Algonkin without fear of immediate French reprisals (21:55). Matters came to a head when during the course of these negotiations, a French pinnace and longboats appeared and prevented the Iroquois from attacking seven Algonkin canoes loaded with beaver skins (21:59). The morning after this incident Montmagny approached the Iroquois fort to propose another meeting. The Iroquois jeered at him for not giving them guns and began shooting arrows and firing their guns at his boats. In retaliation the French opened fire on the Iroquois. Seeing that nothing further was to be gained at Three Rivers, the Iroquois stealthily retreated the next night (21:61–65).

While these events were taking place at Three Rivers, the remaining 150 Iroquois lurked along the banks of the St. Lawrence, hoping to plunder Huron and Algonkin traders on their way to the trading post. Father Brébeuf, who was travelling with four Frenchmen and six Huron, was spotted by the enemy, but reached Three Rivers unopposed on 20 June. A day or two later, five Huron canoes were attacked and plundered by the Iroquois. Some of the Huron escaped, but the rest were either killed or taken prisoner (21:65; 23:35). Some of those who escaped made their way to Three Rivers, while the rest went up the Ottawa River to warn other Huron of the danger. The St. Lawrence remained blockaded for some time, but eventually it was learned that the Iroquois had retired and the Huron traders were able to make their way down-river (21:75). No doubt on the basis of previous experience, the Iroquois were afraid that the French would send their gunboats up-river and had decided to retreat rather than to face them. As in former years, groups of traders were ambushed and robbed at various points along the Ottawa River (22:307).

The Mohawk were disappointed that they had failed to make peace with the French, and increased their attacks against the Algonkin. The following winter 200 Mohawk warriors came north and divided into two bands. One band roamed in the vicinity of Three Rivers hoping to capture some French, but withdrew when the death of one of their leaders was interpreted as a bad omen. Their arrival so terrified the Algonkin living at Three Rivers that most of them fled the area. Some went to Sillery, others joined the Kichesipirini in the upper part of the Ottawa Valley (22:93, 127, 249), a region that had hitherto been beyond the range of Iroquois attacks. Unfortunately, the rest of the Mohawk warriors were heading for precisely this area. They travelled over ice and snow as far as Morrison Island, where they surprised the few people living there (22:249). Following this, they spread out to attack Kichesipirini hunting parties dispersed in the forest and to seize their furs (22:253). Many Kichesipirini were killed and eaten on the spot, while others were carried off to the Mohawk villages. There the Mohawk avenged their failures of the previous year by torturing to death most of the men and older female captives. About thirty younger women were also tortured but their lives were spared so that they might be naturalized into Iroquois families. The following spring these women were used to carry provisions for the war parties that set out for the St. Lawrence (22:265–67).

Although the Mohawk talked of sending 700 men to raid the St. Lawrence Valley in 1642 (22:251), fewer raiders went north at any one time than the 500 who had set out the previous year. In the spring, 300 Mohawk attacked the Onontchataronon, killing some and carrying off a number of families (22:267–69). They next seem to have dispersed along the St. Lawrence to intercept traders on their way to Three Rivers. On 2 August two of these bands attacked twelve Huron canoes above Lake St. Peter. These Huron were returning home and had with them Father Isaac Jogues, Guillaume Couture, and René Goupil, a donné, who were carrying letters and supplies to the Huron mission. The Iroquois who launched this attack were well supplied with guns and the Huron became terrified and attempted to flee into the forest. All of the French and about twenty-five Huron were taken prisoner. The latter included Teondechoren, his brother or cousin Pierre Saoekbata, his niece Oionhaton, and Ahatsistari, a famous warrior from Teanaostaiaé. An old man named Ondouterraon was slain on the spot when he refused to try to keep up with the others (28:121; 39:183), but the rest of the prisoners were taken back to the Mohawk villages (22:269–71; 28:119–35). The French who were captured were not accorded the mild treatment that Godefroy and Marguerie had received. They and the Huron were tortured in the traditional manner immediately after they were captured and more severely in the Iroquois villages. Ahatsistari and his nephew Onnonhoaraton were killed in the villages of Tionontoguen and Ossernenon and a third Huron was slain at Gandagaron (26:195; 39:199; Grassmann 1969:610–37).

Although more Huron canoes were probably lost in this encounter than in any other, this was not the only serious loss that the Huron traders sustained that year. The same day that Jogues and his Huron companions were captured, a Huron trading party was attacked in the lower part of the Ottawa Valley and four Huron were taken prisoner. One of these was later tortured to death by the Mohawk (Thwaites 1896–1901, 26:195). It is unclear whether this was the same attack that the Mohawk made on a party of Huron traders who were hunting on an island in the Ottawa River, probably near the Chaudière Falls (26:35). There were eleven Huron canoes in this group, but the Iroquois only managed to carry off those individuals who had penetrated the island and were driving the game towards the water. Some of the survivors continued on to Three Rivers, while others returned up-river to warn other Huron of the danger (22:273).

In August 1642, 200 to 300 Mohawk set off for the St. Lawrence where they hoped to intercept the main Huron fur convoys going to Three Rivers (28:123). To their surprise, they found Montmagny and a party of work-men at the mouth of the Richelieu River, guarded by three pinnaces and engaged in constructing a fort there. Perceiving this threat to their easiest means of reaching the St. Lawrence Valley, the Mohawk abandoned their usual caution. They approached the fort from three sides and rushed upon the French in an effort to take them by surprise. The Mohawk fought bravely and some were able to fire into the fort through its gun holes. One Frenchman was killed and four wounded. Only after two Mohawk headmen and three ordinary warriors had been killed did the rest withdraw in good order. They first retired to a fort that they had constructed several miles up the Richelieu River and then set off for home. The repulse of this assault on Fort Richelieu prevented the Iroquois from carrying out their plan to harass the Huron and Algonkin who were on their way to Three Rivers (22:275–79).

Thus for two consecutive summers the Mohawk's efforts to lay siege to the St. Lawrence had ended unsatisfactorily for them. They had been able neither to secure the neutrality of the French nor to challenge their military superiority on the St. Lawrence. Moreover, with the building of Fort Richelieu and the new colony at Montreal, the French occupation of the St. Lawrence was more secure then ever before. While the Mohawk were soon to have 300 guns, these were more effective for intimidating the Algonkin and Huron than for winning any decisive victories over the French.

It became clear that the latter could be brought to terms only by depriving them of the furs on which they depended for their prosperity. The Mohawk therefore decided to abandon their large expeditions in favour of a new kind of warfare that would divert more of the furs destined for Three Rivers into their hands. Father Vimont noted that in former times the Iroquois had visited the St. Lawrence in large war parties for short periods in the summer. In 1643 the Iroquois separated into smaller bands that stationed themselves at points along the river and were organized so that when one band was ready to return home, another band replaced it (24:273) (map 25). The deployment of these war parties was probably the same in 1643 as it was the following year when there were said to be ten bands in action at any one time. Two of these were at the Chaudière Falls; one each at the foot of the Long Sault Rapids, above Montreal, on Montreal Island, and along the Rivière des Prairies; and three more between Montreal and Three Rivers. The tenth band went farther up the Ottawa Valley (26:35–37). The deployment of fighting men at so many strategic places from early spring until the following winter made it impossible for Huron or Algonkin traders to use the Ottawa or St. Lawrence rivers without being spotted. This cancelled out customary Huron efforts to avoid the Iroquois by coming to the St. Lawrence in the early spring or late autumn. Finally, the Iroquois avoided Fort Richelieu by blazing a trail across the narrow neck of land between the Richelieu and St. Lawrence rivers, about two leagues south of the fort (24:287–89).

This new strategy was to net a rich harvest of furs for the Mohawk. As early as 9 May Algonkin traders were attacked, and the robbing and killing of Algonkin persisted throughout the summer (24:275, 291). The Mohawk also continued to seek revenge for the five men who had been killed near Three Rivers the year before. Thirty Mohawk went marauding near Montreal; while twenty of them feigned an attack on the fort by firing over 100 gun shots, ten others managed to kill three Frenchmen who were working near the settlement and to carry off two others (24:277).

In August a considerable number of Iroquois were prowling in the vicinity of Fort Richelieu and indicating that they wished to discuss peace. A Huron who had travelled to Quebec in 1640 or 1641 and had been captured by the Iroquois was involved in this affair. This Huron, who had become an "Iroquois by affection," was deputized to carry a letter written by Father Jogues to the French and to discuss peace with them (24:291–93). The French suspected, however, that any talk of peace might be a ruse and believed that the Iroquois wished to ambush the fort.[14] Thus, when the Iroquois advanced towards the fort and refused to stop when ordered to do so, the French fired on them and drove them into the forest. A few days later under a similar pretext of wanting to discuss peace, about 100 Iroquois tried to lure some Onontchataronon into a trap, but although they fired on them, the latter escaped. This band of Mohawk came down to Fort Richelieu, but retreated when they perceived that the French were expecting them (24:293–95).

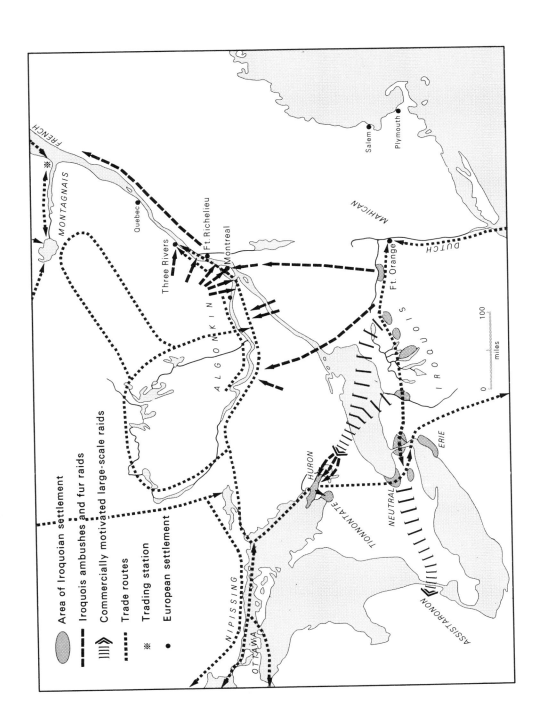

MAP 25. *Intertribal relations, 1643.*

It was the Huron, however, who suffered the most severely from the Mohawk's change in tactics. To avoid Iroquois ambushes the Huron had decided to descend to the St. Lawrence earlier than usual in 1643 with 120 traders travelling together in a single group (24:121). The size of this band seems to have intimidated the Mohawk and the Huron traders reached Three Rivers safely in early June. On 9 June, however, another band of sixty Huron on their way to Three Rivers in thirteen fur-laden canoes were attacked near Montreal by some forty Iroquois. One version states that the Huron were put to flight by gunfire. A variant account claims that they were attacked after the Iroquois had lured them into their fort under some friendly pretext. About twenty-three Huron were taken prisoner, while the rest escaped and made their way towards Montreal. Thirteen prisoners were beaten to death the next day and the rest were led off to the Mohawk country. So many furs were taken in this raid that the Mohawk were unable to carry all of them away with them (24:275-77).

Still greater misfortunes overtook the 120 Huron traders on their way home. They left Three Rivers in mid-June and somewhere near the Chaudière Falls about twenty of them were killed or taken prisoner. After they had passed this point, they continued up the Ottawa River and eventually believed themselves to be out of danger. The Mohawk, who had watched them come down, were unwilling to let them escape and, some-where in the upper part of the Ottawa Valley, they attacked the Huron while they were making a dangerous portage. The attack was so swift that those who were not killed or captured abandoned most of their trade goods and fled (26:235-37). Lalemant was exaggerating only slightly when he described these traders as returning to the Huron country "naked or pierced with musket balls after having escaped seven or eight times from the hands and cruelties of those barbarians" (27:63).

These two attacks resulted in serious economic loss to the Huron and further depleted their dwindling reserves of manpower (28:45). The latter loss was partially compensated by the escape of a number of Huron who had been taken prisoner by the Mohawk the year before and who were made to accompany the Iroquois on their raids. Three prisoners escaped from a band that was prowling along the north shore of Lake St. Peter; two were Teondechoren and his brother or cousin Saoekbata (24:279-81, 285). Huron who had been captured in former years also escaped from Iroquois bands that visited Lake St. Peter later in the summer (24:287) and another Huron escaped from the Mohawk after he had been captured at Montreal (26:21). Teondechoren wished to return home and to do so he joined the 120 Huron traders who were travelling up-river. On his way the

Iroquois shot him through the shoulder with a musket ball, so that he bled almost to death (26:237). Teondechoren managed to make his way home, filled with enough tales of adventure to satisfy a lifetime (26:233).

A TURNING POINT

During the winter of 1643–44 the Mohawk continued to attack Algonkin and Montagnais hunting parties. They increased their attacks until it was unsafe for these Indians to hunt south of the St. Lawrence even opposite Tadoussac. By depriving the Montagnais of important winter hunting grounds, the Mohawk reduced many of them to the point of starvation and forced them to seek charity from the Jesuits at Sillery (Thwaites 1896–1901, 25:107–9). The Iroquois exploited these hunting territories and greatly increased the number of beaver that they trapped that winter.

Even before spring had come, the Iroquois were laying siege to the St. Lawrence River in the same way that they had done in 1643. Among the first Huron to fall into their hands were the six converts who were taking Father Bressani to the Huron country. They had set out from Three Rivers on 27 April believing that because there was still ice on the river, there was little danger of Iroquois attack (26:29–31). In the course of the summer two other groups of Huron were attacked, one near Montreal, the other 150 miles up the Ottawa River (28:45).

Conversely, a group of sixty young men who came down-river with the intention of fighting any Iroquois they encountered reached Three Rivers without challenge. One of the leaders of this group was Charles Tsondatsaa, whose baptism Montmagny had sponsored in 1641. After they had arrived at Three Rivers, news was received that Iroquois canoes had been sighted on Lake St. Peter and the Huron, accompanied by a number of Algonkin, pursued the enemy as far as Fort Richelieu. During the night, two Huron canoes made their way past some thirty Iroquois who were posted as sentinels along the river, but discovering that the Iroquois force was larger than they were, these Huron beat a hasty retreat. They took with them two Huron who had managed to escape from the Iroquois. During this excursion, the Huron learned that ten Iroquois were hunting for Frenchmen in the vicinity of Fort Richelieu. The Huron and Algonkin surrounded these men and managed to capture three of them. The Huron retained two of the prisoners as their share of the booty and one was claimed by the Algonkin. Then they and the Algonkin returned to Three Rivers to celebrate their victory (26:53–57).

Hearing that three Mohawk had been captured, Montmagny hastened to Three Rivers, hoping to secure these prisoners so that he might use them to negotiate with the Iroquois. The Algonkin were persuaded to stop torturing their prisoner and to hand him over to the French in return for many presents. The Huron warriors refused to give up their prisoners, alleging that this was too important a decision for young men to make. They took their prisoners home with them, but offered to transmit Montmagny's presents to their headmen, which were to attest his desire that the prisoners be used to negotiate peace with the Iroquois. Montmagny agreed to this and the Huron promised him that the prisoners would be brought back to Three Rivers the following year (26:59–71).

As a result of Iroquois attacks, some Huron were saying that the cost of trade with the French was too dear and were suggesting that this trade might be broken off, at least on an annual basis (28:57). To strengthen the alliance with the Huron and to protect and encourage Huron traders, Montmagny decided to send twenty-two French soldiers to winter in the Huron country (26:71). These soldiers travelled up-river with the sixty Huron warriors and were accompanied by Brébeuf and by two other priests, Léonard Garreau and Noël Chabanel, who were on their way to join the Huron mission (26:71–73). The soldiers were newly arrived from France and the Jesuits had serious misgivings about dispersing them to various Huron villages (26:71; 28:47). The Jesuits appear to have solved the problem of controlling the morals of these soldiers by keeping them at Sainte-Marie. That it had not been intended the soldiers should live there may explain why Lalemant later complained that the company did not reimburse the Jesuits adequately for the cost of their maintenance. This involved providing them with food and lodging, as well as repairing their arms and nursing those who were ill. The soldiers were not, however, so cut off from the Huron that they could not use their trading privileges to barter for between 3000 and 4000 beaver skins, which they brought down-river with them in September 1645 (27:89).

The Mohawk continued to harass the St. Lawrence Valley throughout the summer of 1644. In late September ten or twelve Huron were killed or captured on an island near Fort Richelieu. Among those who escaped was a Christian named Aonkerati who had been attacked by the Iroquois twice before that year (27:223). The Iroquois continued to besiege Fort Richelieu until July 1645 (27:223–27).

Throughout this period of warfare the Mohawk continued to hope that they might break the alliance that united the French, Huron, and Algonkin and especially that they might persuade the French to play a more neutral role in their dealings with the Indians. The French, for their part, hoped that some kind of peace treaty might be arranged with the Mohawk. The least known of the diplomatic manoeuvres of this period were the persistent efforts of the Mohawk to negotiate with the Huron. There were fresh talks in the summer of 1643 and these made such progress that the Huron who spent the following winter in the school at Three Rivers believed that a peace treaty had already been concluded. This was one of the reasons why they had been willing to venture on to the St. Lawrence in April 1644 (26:31).

Jogues reports that he had been a prisoner of the Mohawk for only a short time when a dispute broke out whether or not he and the other French prisoners should be returned to their countrymen (28:127). Although this talk of repatriating the French may have been intended only to please the Dutchman Arent van Curler, who wished to ransom Jogues (39:201), it seems more likely that two factions were already in existence among the Mohawk, or at least were in the process of forming. One of these factions favoured making peace with the French and possibly with the Huron as well, no doubt in the hope of thereby being able to exploit Algonkin hunting territory; the other faction believed that peace with the French was impossible and favoured waging war against them and all their allies. These factions were soon to be identified with the two moieties into which the Mohawk were divided. The peace party was associated with the moiety made up of the Tortoise and Wolf clans, who were identified with the villages of Ossernenon and Tionontoguen respectively; while the war party was associated with the moiety of the Bear clan, whose main town was Gandagaron, located between the other two (8:300 n. 34; Jameson 1909:178–79). These three main Mohawk villages were located not far from one another, on three hilltops that flanked the Mohawk Valley (map 26).

This well-attested factionalism among the Mohawk makes it impossible to describe a single, clear-cut foreign policy for them, let alone to explain this policy purely in economic terms. The tribes of the Iroquois confederacy generally held differing opinions concerning matters of war and peace and there was no more unanimity within the other tribes than there was among the Mohawk. Bacqueville de La Potherie (1911–12, 2:44) observed that when it came to foreign policy, Iroquoian peoples generally divided into two factions, especially when they were afraid of the enemy. He also noted that instead of weakening them, these alternative positions made their foreign policy more flexible and helped them to fend off humiliating defeats.

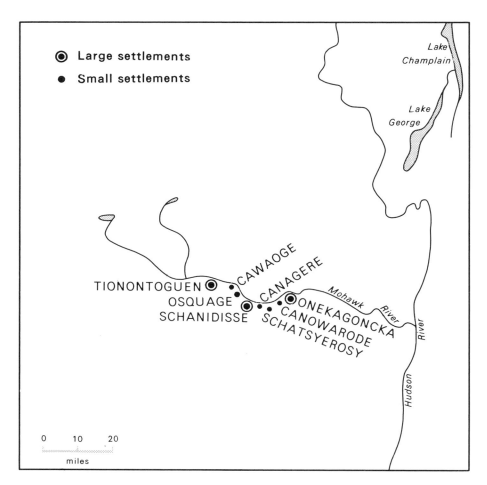

MAP 26. *Hypothetical placing of Mohawk settlements described by Van den Bogaert for 1634–35. The corresponding large settlements mentioned by Jogues for 1643 were Ossernenon, Gandagaron, and Tionontoguen. Megapolensis (1644) associated these settlements with the Tortoise, Bear, and Wolf clans respectively.*

After they had been tortured Jogues and his French companions were adopted into the Wolf clan. René Goupil was killed, not as a matter of public policy, but because an old man believed he was practising witchcraft when he saw him making the sign of the cross upon the body of a child (Thwaites 1896–1901, 28:133–35). At first, Jogues was treated badly by his adopters, but later he became the ward of a powerful old woman who protected him (39:213). In spite of this, he was again in serious danger when the Iroquois returned home to report that after they had delivered his letter to Fort Richelieu, they had been fired on by the French and five of their men had been killed (25:45–47). Even then, Jogues's adoptive relatives gave him permission to travel by himself. On the way back from their fishing camp he learned that the inhabitants of the town where he was living were planning to kill him, and accepted an offer from the Dutch to help him escape. Bressani was rescued from public torture and Guillaume Couture likewise had his life saved. While Mohawk families who had warriors slain by the French must have been anxious to see Frenchmen tortured to death in retaliation, the more moderate elements seem to have kept such passions in check to a remarkable degree.

THE PEACE OF 1645

The French were more anxious for peace than were the Mohawk. When in the autumn of 1642 a Sokoki who had been taken prisoner by the Algonkin was brought to Sillery, the French tended his wounds and persuaded their Indian allies to send him back to his own country (Thwaites 1896–1901, 24:183–85). Out of gratitude for being saved from his tormentors, this Sokoki arranged to have presents sent to the Iroquois allies requesting them to release at least one Frenchman. Jogues reports that contrary to normal practice the Iroquois kept the Sokoki presents but, for the time being, did not grant their request (25:53).

The opportunity that Montmagny had been waiting for came in the summer of 1644, when he obtained from the Algonkin at Three Rivers the Mohawk prisoner that they and the Huron had just captured. Although this man named Tokhrahenehiaron was half dead from torture, the French nursed him back to health. The next spring, a band of Algonkin armed with muskets defeated another group of Iroquois raiders and captured two more prisoners, whom they turned over to the French unharmed. One of these prisoners was Honatteniate, Jogues's adoptive cousin (27:265). Montmagny ordered Tokhrahenehiaron to be taken from Sillery to Three Rivers and there released to find his way home. He was instructed to tell his headmen that the French were willing to release the other two prisoners and that they wished to discuss a general peace with the Iroquois (27:229–45).

On 5 July Tokhrahenehiaron returned to Three Rivers, accompanied by two Mohawk headmen. Kiotsaeton, the leader of this deputation, arrived covered from head to foot with belts of wampum. He brought with him Guillaume Couture, whom the Iroquois released in exchange for

Tokhrahenehiaron. Montmagny hurried to Three Rivers and on 12 July a meeting was held between him and Kiotsaeton. This meeting took place in the courtyard of the French fort and was attended by Father Vimont, the superior of the Jesuit Mission, and by all the Indians who were at Three Rivers. Kiotsaeton presented five wampum belts to the French and two to the Huron at this meeting. Each belt was accompanied by an elaborate oration, which thanked the French for releasing Tokhrahene-hiaron, gave Couture his freedom, expressed a desire to bind the French, their allies, and the Iroquois together as allies, and invited the French to visit the Mohawk country. Kiotsaeton also affirmed that some of Mont-magny's presents had been forwarded to the other Iroquois tribes to invite them to join in a general peace with the French and he urged the Huron to conclude a treaty of their own with the Iroquois (27:251–65). Significantly, no presents were given directly to the Algonkin.

When the public ceremony was over, Kiotsaeton asked to speak with Montmagny privately and offered him a rich present if he would come to a secret understanding with the Mohawk. The arrangement that he proposed was that the Mohawk would stop attacking the French and their Huron trading partners if, in return, the French would cease to protect the Algonkin. Montmagny rejected this proposal and, for a time, it seemed that there would be no peace treaty. Finally, Fathers Vimont and Le Jeune persuaded Montmagny to promise secretly that if the Iroquois refrained from attacking Christian Algonkin, the French would regard other Algonkin as a separate issue (28:149–51; for trans. of the Latin see ibid. 315 n. 16).

Hunt (1940:78–79) is vehement in his denunciation of this understanding, which he interprets to mean that the Jesuits were prepared to forsake all Algonkin. How, he asks, was an Iroquois warrior to distinguish a Christian Algonkin from a non-Christian one? Such an argument may, however, be misleading. The intertribal warfare of this region was far less anonymous than our own and one may assume that the leaders of Mohawk war parties were often familiar with the people they were attacking and knew that certain of them were Christians. Cynical as the Jesuits' attitude appears to have been, they may have rationalized their actions by believing that this was yet another way to encourage more Algonkin to convert to Christianity. Moreover, their fears for the survival of the Huron mission, should trade be broken off as a result of continued hostilities along the St. Lawrence, may have convinced them that the dishonour involved in breaking a longstanding treaty with the non-Christian Algonkin was by comparison of far less consequence.

There are, however, good reasons to believe that this agreement was only a temporary manoeuvre designed to save the negotiations. On 14 July Montmagny gave the Mohawk envoys presents of his own and it was provisionally agreed that the Mohawk should commit no act of hostility against the French or any of their allies before bilateral treaties had been negotiated among all these groups. Afterwards the Algonkin, both Christian and non-Christian, were left in peace by the Mohawk. This seems to indicate that after the Jesuits had intervened to prevent the negotiations from breaking down, the French had been able to persuade the Mohawk not to wage war against the Algonkin. This may also explain why Jérôme Lalemant later recorded in his journal that the story of this secret agreement as rumoured by the Mohawk, was false, "at least for the most part" (Thwaites 1896–1901, 28:155).

At the time, the Algonkin do not appear to have suspected any duplicity in these negotiations on the part of either the French or the Mohawk. Only the Huron traders were uneasy about what was going on and one of them unsuccessfully attempted to undermine Kiotsaeton's confidence in the sincerity of the French (27:269). The Huron feared that friendly relations between the French and any of the Iroquois tribes might undermine the willingness of the French to give them military aid. It would also allow the French to play the Huron and Iroquois off against one another as commercial rivals. On 15 July Kiotsaeton left Three Rivers for home, accompanied by Guillaume Couture and another young Frenchman. The French helped Kiotsaeton to transport his presents, but were also sent as an indication of French confidence in the Mohawk (27:271). It was agreed that later in the year the Mohawk should return to ratify a formal truce with the French and to discuss peace with the latter's allies.

Word of what had happened was soon carried to all the Indians who traded with the French and their headmen were invited to assemble at Three Rivers in the autumn. The Montagnais reached Three Rivers in late August and the headmen of the various Algonkin bands arrived somewhat later. On 10 September sixty Huron canoes arrived, escorted by the twenty-two French soldiers who, we are told, after a winter under Jesuit tutelage returned better supplied with "virtue and a knowledge of Christian truths" than when they had gone to the Huron country (27:277). In these canoes were some of the principal headmen of the Huron confederacy, who had come on behalf of the confederacy council to discuss peace with the Mohawk. They also brought back with them one of the two prisoners who had been captured the year before. They alleged that the other, who was an Oneida, had escaped along the way (29:297).

Finally, on 17 September the four Mohawk envoys arrived. In all, more than 400 Indians had gathered at Three Rivers.

During the next few days speeches were made and many presents were exchanged. The Mohawk assured the French that they wished to be their friends and would welcome them in their villages, but added that if the peace were to continue, the Huron and Algonkin would have to bring their own presents to the Mohawk country and confirm a peace with the Mohawk headmen as the French had already done. They also added that if these negotiations were successful, the Mohawk were prepared to release all the French, Huron, and Algonkians who were prisoners in their country. The Huron freed the Mohawk prisoner they were holding and told the Mohawk to make ready to receive the envoys they would soon be sending to their country. They also invited the Mohawk to send to the Huron country envoys who would bring presents to secure the release of other Iroquois prisoners who were being held there. The Algonkin likewise said that they were ready to visit the Mohawk country to discuss peace. As a result of this conference, the peace treaty between the French and the Mohawk was confirmed, while the separate negotiations between the Mohawk and the Huron and the Mohawk and the Algonkin were carried forward. Montmagny celebrated these developments by providing a feast for all the Indians who had gathered at Three Rivers.

After this feast the Mohawk envoys returned to their own country accompanied by two Frenchmen, two Algonkin, and two Huron. Three Mohawk were left as hostages for the safety of the French, while the French who accompanied this expedition were meant, in part, to assure the safety of its Huron and Algonkin members (27:279–303). Both the Huron and Algonkin had further discussions with the Mohawk headmen in New York State (28:279) and it is likely that Mohawk envoys visited the Huron country. While the result of these negotiations was a short-lived peace between the Mohawk and all the allies of the French, we have no detailed information about the treaties that were concluded among these groups. This has given rise to much speculation about the general significance of the treaties of 1645. Unfortunately, such speculations are based almost entirely on the record of the Three Rivers meeting which, for the Huron and Algonkin, was only a preliminary step towards such agreements.

The most influential interpretation of the treaties of 1645 is that of Hunt (1940:81–82). He regards all of the events leading up to this peace as being narrowly concerned with trading rights. The sole aim of the Mohawk, according to Hunt, was to force the Huron and Algonkin to trade at least some of the furs they normally took to Three Rivers with them.

At first, they tried to accomplish this through negotiations, but when these failed they waged war on the Huron and Algonkin traders so successfully that the French had to sue for peace. The Mohawk hoped that as a result of this peace, the allies of the French would trade equally with the latter and with them. The French, however, were totally opposed to this happening and when the Huron and Algonkin continued to barter all of their furs to the French, the Mohawk were compelled to go to war again.

Hunt himself was uneasy that he could cite only two minor pieces of evidence in support of his interpretation. During the preliminary negotiations in July, Kiotsaeton presented the Huron with a wampum belt to encourage them not to be bashful but to pass by the Algonkin and the French and go to the Iroquois country (Thwaites 1896–1901, 27:263). During the September conference, the Mohawk presented the Algonkians with a belt urging them to hunt so that the Iroquois could benefit from their skill (27:291). Hunt claims that these exhortations constituted a plain demand that henceforth the Huron and Algonkians were to trade with the Iroquois, and he regards these as the principal terms of this treaty. All of the rest, he says, were nothing more than the "vague promises of amicability which are included in all treaties and which mean so little" (p. 78).[15]

It would be gratifying if matters were so simple. Unfortunately, there is no proof that these particular requests, made along with so many others in a preliminary discussion of the peace, were the key elements of such a treaty. When he told them to by-pass the French and the Algonkin, Kiotsaeton was almost certainly inviting the Huron to visit the Mohawk not to trade but to discuss peace. This is evident, since the request was made immediately after a present had been given to the Huron to remind them of the peace treaty they had been invited to make five years before (Thwaites 1896–1901, 27:263). Likewise, his invitation to the Algonkians to hunt was made in the context of a description of the common no man's land that both groups had been avoiding for many years. The Mohawk were obviously looking forward to being able to hunt in this region without fear of encountering enemies. The Mohawk "benefiting from the Algonkians' skill" is an allusion to both sides respecting the peace, if they met in this zone. The Iroquois were saying that since the Algonkians were renowned hunters, they expected to be entertained to a roasted animal whenever hunters from both sides met in this area.

On the basis of the existing evidence, we cannot rule out the possibility that one of the reasons the Mohawk agreed to make peace was because they hoped to secure furs from the north. They probably obtained a goodly number in the course of their formal negotiations with the Huron and Algonkin. Yet, to suggest as Hunt does that any interpretation but his own is meaningless is to fly in the face of much solid evidence. If the conclusion of fur trading alliances with the Huron and Algonkin were the Mohawk's primary goal, it would hardly have been in the long-term interests of the French to undermine their own trade by encouraging friendly contact between their trading partners and the Mohawk. Fear of diverting trade to the Dutch and of rendering their own allies more independent and more "insolent" almost certainly would have offset the anticipated benefits of peace. Moreover, to suggest that if trade of this sort had been the Mohawk's sole aim, they would have been so negligent or credulous as to agree to a treaty that gave their enemies freedom to use the St. Lawrence River with no specific promises in return, is seriously to discredit their political acumen.

The evidence suggests that Hunt erred seriously when he attempted to view the peace of 1645 as a European-style treaty and therefore as essentially different from the truces that the tribes of this region were accustomed to negotiate. The principal aim of these truces was to regain relatives or tribesmen who had been captured by the enemy, but were still alive. All Iroquoian-speaking peoples saw warfare as a means by which individual men acquired prestige and, hence, could not remain in a condition of total peace for any extended period. The Mohawk had also for several generations used this traditional warfare to steal European trade goods and, later, furs from their northern neighbours. The recent neutrality of the Dutch in quarrels between different groups of Indians must have made the Mohawk hope for a similar neutrality from the French. Moreover, French neutrality would have allowed the Mohawk to play two groups of Europeans off against one another in order to get the best prices for their furs. Under the right terms, peaceful relations with the French were highly desirable. When Montmagny proposed to release prisoners, the Mohawk were therefore willing to discuss peace. It is doubtful, however, in spite of their solemn rhetoric, that the Mohawk regarded their agreements with other Indian tribes as more than traditional truces which would last for only a few years. Mohawk families whose members were held prisoner by the French or their allies must have been especially anxious for such a truce.

The most crucial issue that the Mohawk had to face was whether such a truce was economically feasible. To get back all their prisoners, the Mohawk had, at least temporarily, to stop attacking Huron traders, and, under pressure from the French, they were persuaded to extend the truce to cover all the allies of the French. Hunt is correct that such an agreement would have cut off a major source of furs from the Mohawk, but he is wrong in suggesting that this loss could have been made up only if the Huron and Algonkin promised to trade with them. During previous years the Mohawk had penetrated Algonkin and Montagnais hunting territory and in the course of their negotiations with the French, they expressed keen interest in the hunting territories that lay in the no man's land between them. During the period of the truce, the Mohawk were free to trap as many furs as they wished in this area (27:289–91). It also may be that the ritual kinship acquired through the truce gave the Mohawk the right to hunt in Algonkin territory.[16] In addition, the Mohawk, along with the Mahican and Sokoki, seem to have begun their attacks on the Abenaki about this time (31:195). Peace with the French and their allies might have facilitated these attacks, which the Mohawk hoped would net them many furs with less danger than was incurred in their attacks along the St. Lawrence. Whatever the precise arrangements may have been, it seems likely that the Mohawk counted on either hunting in the north or waging war elsewhere to provide them with enough furs to compensate them, at least for a few years, for the furs lost through the cessation of their raids against the Huron and Algonkin. Although it lacks dramatic appeal, this explanation conforms better with what is known about Iroquoian behaviour than does Hunt's and accounts more completely for the manner in which the treaty was made and ultimately disintegrated.

WAR RESUMES

During the winter of 1645–46 the Algonkin became uneasy when rumours began to circulate concerning the secret talks that had taken place between the French and the Mohawk the previous summer. The source of these rumours was a Huron named Tandihetsi who seems to have been a member of the Huron negotiating party that visited the Mohawk after the September conference. Tandihetsi claimed that the Mohawk had revealed to him that in mid-February 300 of them would be coming north to attack the Algonkin (Thwaites 1896–1901, 28:149). When he heard this report Tessouat withdrew from Montreal to Three Rivers, and more Algonkin followed when the Mohawk informed them that the Oneida and Onondaga had decided not to make peace and that some of them might attack Montreal (29:147). A meeting was held at Three Rivers, which was attended by Atironta. At this meeting it appears to have been demonstrated that Tandihetsi's claim of an imminent attack by the Mohawk was false (28:155) and probably that the Mohawk had been persuaded to include all the Algonkin in their truce. The Mohawk were true to their word and did not attack the Algonkin that winter. During that period, some Mohawk visited Montreal Island to see the French. One of them was probably no more than stating the blunt truth when he sang in the presence of Algonkin that he wished to slay some of them but that Montmagny had arrested his anger (29:151). The only grave incident was the slaying of a number of Montagnais by the Sokoki, which at first was blamed on the Mohawk (28:277).

On 22 February Kiotsaeton and six other Mohawk envoys appeared at Montreal in the company of Couture and the two Huron who had visited their country in September. These Mohawk hunted in the vicinity of Montreal until 7 May when they met Montmagny at Three Rivers. There they renewed their treaty with the French and protested their innocence of the murders committed by the Sokoki. They warned the Huron that the other Iroquois tribes had refused to make peace, but stated that Mohawk envoys would soon be visiting the Huron country to discuss this problem in greater detail (28:301). Tessouat also offered presents to reinforce his own tenuous peace with the Mohawk (28:297–301).

At the conclusion of this meeting Montmagny decided to send Isaac Jogues and Jean Bourdon, an engineer and mapmaker, to reaffirm his peace with the Mohawk (28:303). They left 16 May, accompanied by four Mohawk and two Algonkin who were bearing gifts from Tessouat to the Mohawk. These envoys travelled south by way of Lake Champlain to Fort Orange and thence were led by the Mohawk to their villages. There Jogues attended a general council, where he attempted to negotiate the release of Oionhaton and a young Frenchman, whom the Mohawk still held prisoner. The Frenchman was released, but the Mohawk seemed unwilling to consider Oionhaton. They said she was now married and living among the Onondaga, and gave only a sibylline assurance that she would be restored to the French once she had been returned to the Mohawk (29:55).

In addition, Jogues urged the Mohawk to prevent the other Iroquois tribes from crossing their territory if their aim was to attack the French. The Mohawk genially promised to do what they could, knowing that they were not in a position to stop these tribes even if they wished to do so (29:59). Jogues annoyed the Mohawk when he gave 2000 wampum beads to visiting Onondaga headmen to announce the desire that the French had to visit their country. He added that the French and Onondaga might visit one another by way of the St. Lawrence River and Lake Ontario, or by travelling across Huron territory, as well as through the Mohawk country. The Mohawk expressed surprise at this proposal, which challenged their established role as intermediaries between the French and the other Iroquois tribes. Their main fear seemed to be that if the Onondaga established separate trading relations with the French, it would be difficult for the Mohawk to control these relations. The Mohawk informed Jogues that the other roads were too dangerous and that if the French wished to maintain friendly relations with them, they would be wise to conduct their dealings with the other Iroquois tribes through them. In spite of this, Jogues persevered with his efforts to establish a separate relationship between the French and the Onondaga (29:57). This episode is of special interest because it reveals for the first time a latent rivalry among the Iroquois tribes over relations with Europeans. Both French and Huron were later to try to exploit this rivalry.

During the summer of 1646 the peace between the Mohawk and the allies of the French permitted a record number of furs to be exported from New France (28:235; map 27). The calm of that summer was marred only by a few acts of violence. Tessouat and a group of Kichesipirini were attacked above the Long Sault Rapids of the Ottawa River by a band of Oneida, among whom were said to be two or three Mohawk. In this attack an Algonkin man was killed and a woman taken prisoner. The woman was rescued, however, when these same Oneida were defeated by the Onontchataronon (28:225). A Huron trader by the name of Ondiwaharea was also captured by the Iroquois when he tried to return to the Huron country by way of Lake Ontario (28:231). This is the only recorded instance of a Huron attempting to travel this dangerous route.

In September Father Jogues was commissioned to return to the Mohawk country, where he was to continue to promote peace with the other Iroquois tribes (29:181–83). He was accompanied by Jean de La Lande, a young donné, and by a number of Huron who were going to visit their captive relatives. Jogues and his companions were fearful about the outcome of this journey (31:111) and scarcely had got beyond Three Rivers when all but one of the Huron turned back. When Jogues and La Lande arrived in the Mohawk country they were both stripped and beaten, but not threatened with public torture. The day after he reached Ossernenon, Jogues was killed with a hatchet as he was entering a longhouse. La Lande was slain in a similar fashion early the next day and their bodies were both thrown into the river (31:117–19). The Huron who accompanied Jogues was not slain and he returned to Three Rivers in June 1647 and informed

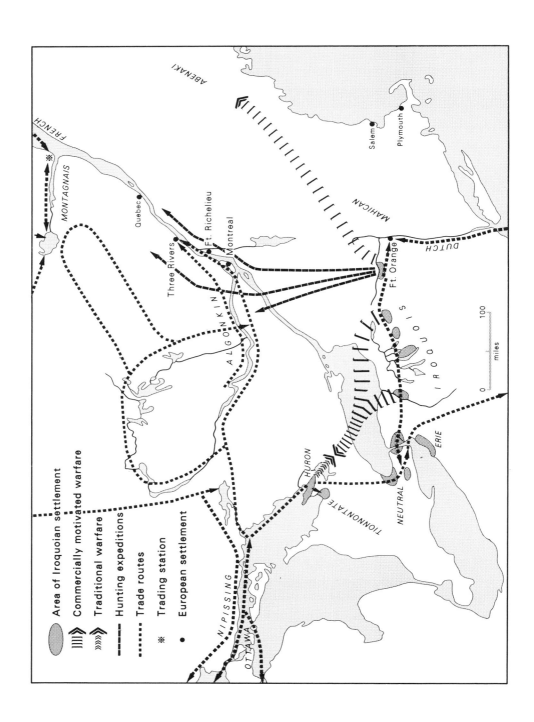

MAP 27. *Intertribal relations following the peace of 1645.*

the French what had happened. He is identified as the son of Ignace Otouolti [*sic*] (30:175–77).

Jogues was not slain with the general consent of all the people of Ossernenon, but by members of the Bear clan. The Tortoise and Wolf clans did what they could to save him and his adoptive relatives were particularly angered by his death. Moreover, the two other large Mohawk towns were not consulted before the deed was committed (31:117; 32:25–27). The previous summer had been a bad one for the Iroquois. An epidemic had caused many deaths, and after Jogues had departed in the spring worms had destroyed much of the Mohawk's corn crop (30:229, 273; 31:121). The Iroquois interpreted these disasters as evidence of sorcery and many people blamed them on a small chest of clothes that Jogues had left behind (30:229; 31:115). Hunt (1940:85–86) rejects this explanation on the grounds that if Jogues was really held to be guilty of sorcery, his death would have been more popular. Hunt argues that Jogues's death was a minor incident in the outbreak of a new war between the Iroquois and the French and their allies. According to Hunt, this war occurred because the French and Huron failed to live up to the terms of the commercial treaty they had made with the Mohawk in 1645; for two years, not a single Huron pelt had been traded to the Iroquois.

This explanation suffers from the general weaknesses of all Hunt's arguments. Had the Mohawk really believed themselves betrayed by the French, it is more likely that they would have been unanimous in their condemnation of Jogues and tortured him to death in the style they reserved for captive enemies. As it was, Jogues and La Lande were killed in the fashion prescribed for witches. It is reported that at this period Huron prisoners were telling the Mohawk that the Jesuits were demons whose aim was to destroy the Indians (Thwaites 1896–1901, 30:227). Among Iroquoians accusations of witchcraft tended to be controversial and easily led to just such differences of opinion as appear to have surrounded the slaying of these two Frenchmen. What happened to Jogues and La Lande is what might have happened repeatedly to Jesuits in the Huron country, had they not been protected by the trading alliance between the French and the Huron.

In any case, there is little reason to believe that the truce between the Mohawk and the northern Indian groups could have lasted long once it became evident that no more prisoners were to be released. It is also likely that hunting did not prove as prolific a source of furs as piracy, and that a growing need for furs played a major role in driving the Mohawk into battle once again. Even before Jogues's death, the Mohawk had sent presents to the other Iroquois tribes urging them to attack the French (30:227). Soon after, the Mohawk warriors spread out in order to attack as many French, Algonkin, and Huron as they could. It became dangerous to wander outside the fortifications of the French settlement at Montreal and Algonkin were being robbed and murdered in their winter hunting grounds (30:161, 229–51). While furs were preferred as booty, the Iroquois continued to steal whatever they could lay their hands on. In March 1647 they stripped two French houses near Three Rivers of all clothing, blankets, ammunition, and other valuables while their owners were attending mass. It was estimated that fifteen men were required to carry off everything that was taken (30:233). After two prosperous years, the economy both of New France and of the Huron country was once again being threatened by the attacks of the Mohawk.

War in the Huron Country

NEW GOALS

The attacks of the western Iroquois tribes on the Huron homeland grew increasingly severe through the 1640s. It is difficult to determine how important a role muskets played in all but the final years of this conflict, and evidence for Mohawk participation in these raids is equivocal (Thwaites 1896–1901, 26:35–37) except after 1647. It may be that the growing strength of the western Iroquois evident at this time resulted to a large degree from the Iroquois allocating more manpower to their attacks on the Huron than the Huron with their far-flung trading commitments were able to muster in their own defence. The nature of the attacks also changed as the western Iroquois sought to steal furs and trade goods from the Huron. The murder of a few individuals working in their fields or while moving between villages or the siege of a settlement with its attendant challenges to fight did not yield the amount of booty that the Iroquois now required. It therefore became necessary to penetrate Huron villages in order to seize the furs and trade goods that were stored inside them. The *Jesuit Relations* do not provide a systematic account of warfare between the Huron and the Iroquois from 1640 to 1647; nevertheless, from what is recorded, some understanding can be gleaned about what was happening at this time.

The most enigmatic event was the attack made on Ehwae, the main

Tionnontaté village, in the spring of 1640. Most of the houses of the village were reported to have been burned in this attack and many people were slain or taken prisoner (21:181). This attack is often attributed to the Iroquois, although on the basis of no direct evidence, since the attackers are not named.[17] It is unclear whether the Tionnontaté were traditional enemies of the Iroquois as the Huron were, or if they were too remote to have been drawn into conflict with them. The earliest explicit reference to an Iroquois raid on the Tionnontaté dates no earlier than the winter of 1646–47 (33:83). On the other hand, the Tionnontaté were close friends of the Ottawa who, in turn, were allies of the Neutral against the Assistaronon. It is therefore worth considering the alternative possibility that Ehwae was attacked by the Assistaronon (Jones 1908:224). This may have been one of the early events in the war between the Neutral and the Assistaronon that was to result in many Algonkian-speaking groups being expelled from southern Michigan. If we are correct in believing that prior to this time the Assistaronon controlled the eastern shore of Lake Huron south of the Bruce Peninsula, an attack on Ehwae is not impossible.

If the Iroquois were not responsible for the destruction of Ehwae, there is no evidence of a basic change in the pattern of Iroquois warfare in Ontario prior to 1642 except perhaps for the growing scale of conflict. A prominent figure in the engagements of this period was Ahatsistari, a man from Teanaostaiaé, who is said to have been regarded as the greatest Huron warrior of his time. In the summer of 1640 he and a band of Huron raiders were crossing Lake Ontario when they encountered several large Iroquois canoes on their way north. Although most of the Huron were in favour of using their lighter and swifter vessels to beat a retreat, Ahatsistari leapt into one of the Iroquois canoes and upset it. He then swam about killing the Iroquois before he returned to his own canoe. The Huron pursued the rest of the Iroquois who, in the meantime, had begun to flee. They captured a large number and brought them home as prisoners (Thwaites 1896–1901, 23:25–27).

The following summer, Ahatsistari led a band of fifty Huron which claimed to have scattered a force of 300 Iroquois and captured some of them (23:25). These prisoners were divided among the Huron tribes so that those whose relatives had recently been slain by the Iroquois might avenge their deaths (23:33). Raids into Iroquois territory continued as usual throughout the summer of 1641 and a band of warriors from Scanonaenrat almost perished when they were caught in a violent storm on Lake Ontario on their way home (23:173–75). It was at this time that the Jesuit scholar Andehoua decided to renew his commitment to Christianity. Not all Huron raids were successful, however. In particular, an Arendarhonon group was defeated by the Iroquois and among those who were taken prisoner and later slain was the tribal headman Atironta. His brother Aëotahon escaped from the battle and became the new Atironta. The Jesuits derived some short-term satisfaction from this defeat because the Arendarhonon had performed a "shameless" ceremony before setting out, in the hope that they would thereby assure themselves of victory over the Iroquois (23:159). This ceremony may have been the andacwander, which involved public fornication.

A NEW STYLE OF WARFARE

Already by 1640 Lalemant was alarmed by the extent of Iroquois penetration of the Huron country. Small bands of raiders appeared to be lurking in the forests everywhere and remained throughout most of the year. Women and children were not safe, even within sight of their own villages and sometimes, in traditional fashion, the Iroquois would steal into the villages at night and kill a few people, then try to escape unharmed (Thwaites 1896–1901, 22:305). These attacks appear to have been most severe among the Arendarhonon, whose geographical isolation from the rest of the confederacy made them a vulnerable target (23:33).

In the winter of 1641–42 a rumour spread that an Iroquois army was on the point of overwhelming Contarea, the principal village of the Arendarhonon. While this rumour was later found to be false, it was believed throughout the confederacy and created panic as far away as Ossossané (23:105–7; 57). There may have been a sound basis for Huron fears since, in June of the following year, a band of Iroquois attacked and burned a Huron village and was so successful that only a score of people are said not to have been killed or taken prisoner (26:175). One may imagine that, as happened with the destruction of other Huron villages, the strongest of these prisoners were kept alive and driven south, burdened with furs and other spoils that the victorious Iroquois were carrying off with them (34:135). Although the village that was destroyed is not identified by name, it was long believed to have been Contarea, since both were described as frontier villages and as hostile to Christianity (Jones 1908:331). This identification could only be sustained, however, so long as Contarea and St. Jean-Baptiste (which was still in existence until 1647) were believed to be different villages, whereas it now seems certain that they were the Huron and Jesuit names for the same community (Heidenreich 1966:123–24). The community that was destroyed in 1642 appears to have been a smaller Arendarhonon village, the name of which was not recorded. It was probably located near Contarea and it is not surprising that it followed the same course as the larger community in its reactions to the Jesuits.

The destruction of this village marks an important turning point in relations between the Huron and the western tribes of the Iroquois confederacy. Hitherto, warfare between these groups had been largely a matter of blood feud with ritualistic overtones, robbery being of only secondary importance. For the Huron with their easy access to furs, there was no need to change. Among the Onondaga, Cayuga, and Seneca, however, a growing need for European goods encouraged the development of an economically oriented warfare, analogous to that practised by the Mohawk and the Oneida for some time. Instead of robbing trading convoys and hunting parties, the western Iroquois concentrated on plundering the Huron in their own homeland. This not only led to more violent and intensive warfare but also encouraged the Iroquois to attack Huron houses and villages in order to seize the furs and trade goods that were stored inside them. Thus, the traditional siege of a Huron village aimed at challenging its defenders to come out and fight gave way to surprise attacks at dawn, followed by pillaging, burning, and long trains of captives carrying away booty. The year 1642 seems to mark the beginning of this pattern, although the 300 Iroquois who were defeated the year before may have made up a raiding party of this sort. Major attacks were supplemented by traditional assaults on individuals or small groups. Even in these cases, however, the stealing of valuables, including the skins that the victims wore as clothing, may have become a more important motive than was blood revenge.

In order to avenge their dead, the Huron continued to invade the Iroquois country. Tsondatsaa left on such an expedition not long before the attack on the Arendarhonon village in 1642 (Thwaites 1896–1901, 23:195–97). The following year a Huron raiding party of about 100 men suffered a stunning defeat. Before these men were able to disperse, they were surrounded by several hundred Iroquois and after a fight that lasted through an entire night all of them were either killed or taken prisoner (28:45, 89–91).

1643 was a year of devastating Iroquois attacks on the Huron country. Hundreds of Huron are reported to have been taken prisoner and many women were killed while working in their fields (27:65). Forty people who left Teanaostaiaé to gather hemp were attacked by the Iroquois in the night. Although there were only twenty assailants, they managed to kill or capture most of these Huron, only a few being able to escape (26:203–5). Bands of warriors who attempted to hunt down these raiders were themselves ambushed and individuals who had escaped from the Iroquois with bodies half burned and fingers mutilated were a common sight (27:65). The Huron also were afflicted by famine in 1643. It is unclear whether this was because women were unable to work in their fields or because of natural conditions, although the statement that famine prevailed for 100 leagues around suggests that drought may have been at least partly responsible. Hunger compelled the Huron to gather nuts and wild roots, which further exposed them to attacks by the enemy (27:65).

While there is very little information for the year 1644, Iroquois attacks appear to have been as bad or worse than they had been the year before. In the winter of 1644–45, the Huron feared the approach of an Iroquois army which was reported to be coming to ravage their settlements; however, the arrival of the French soldiers who accompanied Brébeuf to the Huron country that autumn was credited with making the Iroquois change their plan (28:47). Whether or not the Iroquois entertained such a plan, these rumours illustrate the insecurity of the Huron.

The truce that was arranged with the Mohawk in 1645 did not free the Huron from attack by the four other Iroquois tribes. Yet, according to Ragueneau, the Huron had somewhat more success in dealing with their enemies that year than they had formerly (29:247). Some of their raids were successful and resulted in the capture of prisoners who were brought home and tortured to death (29:251). At one point a band of Iroquois who were prowling in the vicinity of Teanaostaiaé managed to kill two Huron sentinels who had fallen asleep while guarding a village watchtower. To avenge this killing three Huron went to Sonnontouan where they entered a longhouse in the dead of night, killed three Seneca, and carried their scalps home (29:253–5).

Encouraging as these minor victories may have been, they did not check the incursions of the enemy or offset the growing drain on Huron manpower in which these raids were resulting. In spring of 1645 a band of Iroquois concealed themselves in a forest near Contarea and seized a group of women as they went out to work in the fields. The Iroquois carried these women off so quickly to their canoes, beached along the shores of Lake Simcoe, that 200 armed Huron were unable to rescue any of them (29:249).

Later in the summer a band of Huron discovered a group of Iroquois warriors hiding in the forest. They encircled their fortified camp and had almost seized them when the Iroquois asked to parley. They laid down their muskets and offered a number of large wampum belts to the Huron headmen and elders, then invited these men to confer with them in their camp. Tobacco was distributed to entertain the younger Huron warriors who remained outside. While this conference was going on, an Iroquois who some years before had been a prisoner of the Huron talked to the younger warriors and frightened them into withdrawing. Once most of them had gone, the Iroquois fell on the Huron headmen and killed or made prisoners of all who could not escape (29:249–51). The Iroquois were reported to have had designs on Teanaostaiaé during this period (29:251), and nearly destroyed at least one other Huron village (29:149).

Did these raids have any more long-term purpose than to secure furs and European goods by stealing them? Hunt (1940:91) has suggested that the original aim of this harassment was to bring pressure to bear on the Huron to compel them to trade their furs with the Iroquois as well as with the French. He argues that when the Iroquois saw this was impossible, they decided to drive the Huron from their tribal territory so that they could seize their trade for themselves. Alternatively, it has been suggested that the Iroquois wished to disperse the Huron so they could seize their land as hunting territory (Trelease 1960:120). Others have viewed the Iroquois as being motivated simply by a desire to settle old scores once their foes were no longer able to maintain the balance of power. All of these arguments have sought support in a letter that Jogues wrote from Ossernenon on 30 June 1643 in which he stated that the Iroquois' plan was to capture all the Huron, kill their leaders, and compel the rest to live as Iroquois (Thwaites 1896–1901, 24:297).

Those who stress the deviousness and cunning of the Mohawk interpret this letter as evidence that the future policies of the Iroquois were formulated almost a decade before they came to fruition. From this it must follow that all evidence that the Iroquois were behaving differently is only an indication of their duplicity. It is possible that certain Mohawk were considering plans for the destruction of the Huron confederacy. These might have been individuals who were especially intent on seeking blood revenge or who had been inspired to think along these lines by Dutch traders wishing to sabotage French commerce. Yet there is very little evidence that the Mohawk were participating in attacks on the Huron country prior to 1647, and it is difficult to see what gain there was in such a plan for Indians whose principal aim was to rob Huron and Algonkin fur convoys. Nor is there any evidence that Jogues's letter indicates that the Onondaga and Seneca were deliberately seeking to expel the Huron from their tribal territories. It is more likely that the plan he was describing was for dealing with the Huron traders whom the Mohawk were harassing each year on the St. Lawrence.

We have already ruled out the likelihood that the Iroquois were seeking new hunting territories at the expense of the Huron. It may have been that the Iroquois hoped to reduce the Huron to client status and force them to trade their furs with them, but, if so, this policy was badly executed. More likely, in their dealings with the Huron as in their dealings with the French, the Iroquois were not pursuing any long-term policy. Instead, they were following a number of short-term ones. The only constant requirement was to obtain enough furs or booty each year to supply their growing need for trade goods. If this was the case, desultory looting may have remained the principal objective of the western Iroquois as well as of the Mohawk until a more lucrative alternative presented itself or became necessary.

Chapter 10 The Storm Within

The Jesuit Mission

The changes that took place in Huron society between 1640 and 1647 had no less fatal consequences for the Huron than did the growing menace of the Iroquois. In these changes, the Jesuits played the leading role, which makes it necessary to understand their specific aims and organization at this period. The key to such an understanding is the headquarters of Sainte-Marie, which Jérôme Lalemant had established in the expectation that it would fulfil a dual role as a European-style Jesuit residence and the nucleus of a village of converts. While Sainte-Marie did not develop as Lalemant originally had planned, the growth of this headquarters significantly altered the Jesuits' role in relationship to the Huron.

PERSONNEL

Before 1640 the Jesuits and their lay assistants were few and were dependent on the Huron for food and protection. After this time, the number of Frenchmen in the Huron country slowly increased from thirteen priests to eighteen, and from fourteen lay assistants, of various categories, to a high of about forty-six, which was reached during the winter of 1648–49.[1] During this same period, Sainte-Marie grew from a single hut into a substantial, well-fortified French settlement, which at certain times of the year sheltered almost as many Europeans as Quebec had in 1629 (Kidd 1949a; Jury and Jury 1954; Desjardins 1966; Rochemonteix 1895–96, 1:385–88).

Lalemant intended that the farm that was attached to this settlement should feed all the French who were working in the Huron country. This would eliminate the cost of buying food and assure the Jesuits of a supply, should the Huron refuse to sell them what they needed. Lalemant also sought to make the settlement strong enough to withstand attack either by the Iroquois or by the Huron themselves and to ensure that it was able to provide enough services so that the Jesuits could continue to live as

Frenchmen in the Huron country, even if the Mohawk severed their contacts with Quebec. The hostility of the Huron in 1639 and the growing menace of the Iroquois thereafter were persuasive arguments for developing such independence. Moreover, pending the formal establishment of a *reduction* for Huron converts, the mission was able to provide various services for these converts. These included caring for the sick and providing a retreat where religious activities of both a personal and public nature could be carried on without distractions from non-Christians.

The core of the mission was a group of priests who had lived in the Huron country long enough to have learned the Huron language well and who had made the kind of personal contacts among the Huron that allowed them to sway particular individuals and whole communities. Fathers Brébeuf, Ragueneau, Daniel, and Poncet de La Rivière[2] were sent on business from the Huron mission to the French settlements in Quebec for periods of one to several years, but each of them eventually returned to the Huron country to resume his duties there. Three others, Ambroise Davost, Charles Raymbaut, and Pierre Pijart, were forced to return to Quebec by extreme ill-health; the first two died soon after they did so. Jérôme Lalemant left the Huron country for good in 1645 to become Jesuit superior for the whole of New France. His rigidity and preoccupation with rubrics had not won him the affection of his fellow missionaries, hence they were delighted when he was succeeded by Father Paul Ragueneau, who already had eight years of experience working among the Huron (Thwaites 1896–1901, 25:83; 30:149). Finally, Isaac Jogues did not return to the Huron mission after he was captured by the Iroquois in 1642. Yet, nineteen of the twenty-four priests who came to the Huron country, beginning in 1634, either died there or remained until the mission ended in 1650—a remarkable stability in personnel. Ten of these men worked among the Huron for ten or more years,[3] and seven saw from twelve to eighteen years of service. On the basis of such experience, the following priests made up the core of the Huron mission: Jean de Brébeuf, Antoine Daniel, François Le Mercier, Pierre Chastellain, Charles Garnier, François Du Peron, Simon Le Moyne, Pierre Chaumonot, and Paul Ragueneau. The latter's calm judgment and general good sense, which were conspicuously displayed at this period, combined the best qualities of his two predecessors as superior of the Huron mission.

The priests were assisted by a corps of workmen who erected buildings, grew crops, and provided many personal services for them. Some of these men were also responsible for encouraging as many Huron as possible to trade each year, a duty inherited from the long-banished company traders.

In the winter of 1644–45, and again in 1648–49 and 1649–50, soldiers were sent to protect Sainte-Marie and the Huron villages, but normally the Jesuits' assistants were lay brothers, donnés, hired men, and boys. The latter came to learn the Huron language and to assist the workmen. In the initial years of the Huron mission, lay brothers had not been wanted because regulations did not allow them to carry arms. After 1640 a more specialized division of labour developed and jobs were found for up to four of them at a time. Dominique Scot worked as a tailor until he was forced to return to France because of illness; Louis Gaubert was a blacksmith; Pierre Masson was first a gardener, but replaced Scot as tailor in 1645; Ambroise Brouet was a cook; and Nicolas Noircler arrived late and his occupation is unknown. None of these lay brothers did work that took him beyond the mission headquarters at Sainte-Marie.

The most valued assistants were the donnés, who grew from two in 1641 to twenty-three in 1648. Some had already signed on in this capacity before they came to the Huron country, others were hired men, or youths, who had been attached to the mission before they decided to dedicate their lives to supporting the work of the Jesuits. Spiritual motives or a desire for a more prestigeful role in the mission must have motivated such decisions, since becoming a donné required foregoing wages and giving up the right to trade for one's own profit (21:305).

The majority of the donnés are not listed as having particular trades and many were probably handymen who performed a wide variety of tasks.[4] Robert Le Coq, the first donné, was the business manager of the mission, a post which required him to travel to Three Rivers and back each summer. The surgeons who were recruited for the mission were also donnés. The first, René Goupil, was captured by the Iroquois before he reached the Huron country, but François Gendron, who in later life became a priest and king's counsellor, worked there from 1643 to 1650. He was assisted by another donné, Joseph Molère, who was pharmacist and laundryman. Charles Boivin was the master builder who supervised the erection of buildings for the Jesuits throughout the Huron country. An important part of his work was designing the scale models of proposed buildings that were the blueprints of the period (Jury and Jury 1954:49–50). While many of the donnés must have worked on Boivin's projects, Jean Guiet, who arrived in 1646, is the only one listed as a carpenter by profession. Jacob Levrier and Christophe Regnault were shoemakers.

Skilled trades were not restricted to donnés and lay brothers. Pierre Tourmente,[5] a professional stonemason, was employed by the Huron mission from 1646 to 1648, and again in 1649–50 (Thwaites 1896–1901,

34:59). In 1649 Pierre Oliveau, who was "a miller, or sent from France as such," was dispatched to the Huron country (32:101; 34:59), although probably not in his professional capacity.[6] Hired men not only received wages, but were granted certain rights to profit from trading for furs with the Indians (27:91). The latter privileges must have encouraged many ordinary labourers to learn to speak a little Huron or Algonkian and to acquire valuable experience in dealing with the Indians. Charles Le Moyne, who was an indentured servant of the Jesuits, was later to become a prosperous fur trader and the father of Pierre Le Moyne d'Iberville, the noted soldier and explorer. Médard Chouart Des Groseilliers worked in the Huron country before 1646, during which time he must have acquired experience valuable for his later travels of discovery in North America.

Donnés, as well as workmen, became proficient in dealing with the Huron and some of them later put these skills to public as well as private use. Pierre Boucher became governor of Three Rivers and author of a valuable description of New France, while Guillaume Couture, who was captured by the Iroquois in 1642, was later an important Indian diplomat and explorer. Eustache Lambert, who became a donné by 1646 (Jones 1908:356), eventually settled at Pointe-Lévy and carried on extensive trade with the Indians.

SAINTE-MARIE-AUX-HURONS

The Jesuits' *Relations* and surviving letters yield little information about the construction of Sainte-Marie. In May 1640 Lalemant wrote that the French were working to establish an abode that was suitable for their needs (Thwaites 1896–1901, 19:135), which suggests that a European-style dwelling was being constructed or enlarged. In 1641 the Jesuits had a Huron longhouse erected to shelter Indians who came to Sainte-Marie to perform their devotions (21:141; 23:21) in a chapel that had also been built by this time. The services in this chapel were said to be more elaborate than the Huron had previously beheld, while the chapel, although poor by French standards, was regarded by the Huron as one of the wonders of the world. This splendour was judged to be useful because it enhanced the Indians' respect for Christian rituals (23:23). It is possible that this building incorporated material from the French-style chapel built near the old site of Ossossané. No effort had been made to keep this building in use after Ossossané was relocated. A chapel to serve the new Ossossané had been constructed within a Huron longhouse (21:159).

Prior to the autumn of 1642 the Jesuits erected a hospital at Sainte-Marie (26:203). This hospital was built away from the priests' quarters so that women as well as men might be cared for in it. At the same time, a church was established for public worship, which was separate from the Jesuits' private chapel and seems to have been intended mainly for use by the Indians. A cemetery was consecrated near the church and, in addition to the cabin for Christian visitors, a separate facility was established where non-Christian Indians might be admitted by day, provided with hospitality, and hear the word of God (26:201–3). A woman from Ossossané had herself brought to Sainte-Marie so that she might die there. She was pregnant and, after she miscarried in the course of her illness, she and the infant were buried in the same grave (26:209). The second burial was of Christine Tsorihia, an elderly woman from Teanaostaiaé. She died in the winter of 1642–43 and her body was transported to Sainte-Marie for burial in spite of the bad weather (26:211, 289–91). In the spring of 1642 Cardinal Richelieu provided funds for the construction of a strong fort in the Huron country (Robinson, in Du Creux 1951–52:xxiv). Sainte-Marie appears to have been fortified from an early date, although the only explicit reference to the building of fortifications dates from the spring of 1649 (Thwaites 1896–1901, 33:253–55). Twice, however, in 1642 and again in 1649, Sainte-Marie was referred to as a French fort in the Huron country (23:205; 33:255).

Considerably more information has been obtained about the layout and architectural history of Sainte-Marie as a result of the archaeological work carried out there between 1941 and 1943 by Kenneth E. Kidd (1949a), and between 1947 and 1951 by Wilfrid Jury (and Jury 1954). From this work, a general impression can be gained of a complex structure almost 800 feet long and over 200 feet wide at the north end. The western edge of the settlement curved gently to follow the bank of the Wye River, while it grew narrower towards the south to avoid the swampy area that sheltered the site to the east. Jury (and Jury 1954:90–107) has named the southern half of the site the "Indian Compound." It was separated from the "European Compound" to the north by a projecting V-shaped wooden palisade which was inside a ditchworks that remained visible into the last century (ibid. 78; Kidd 1949a:17–20). The Indian Compound was subdivided into an inner and outer court which were both surrounded by palisades. Inside the inner court a large number of post molds were noted, which included the outline of a longhouse (plate 40).

The prevalence of Indian artifacts suggested that this was the area that had been cleared for the erection of a house for Huron visitors in 1641, and

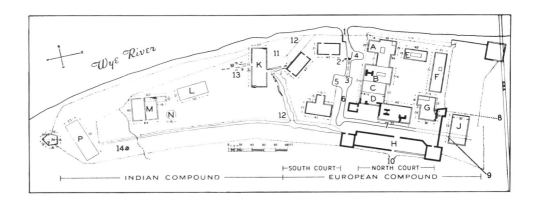

A—Dwelling

B—Chapel

C—Carpenter-shop

D—Blacksmith-shop

E—Cookhouse

F—Dwelling

G—Dwelling

H—Barracks

J—Barn

K—Indian Church

L—Huron longhouse

M—Hospital

N—Algonquin dwelling

P—Huron longhouse

1, 2, 3—Locks

4—Loading basin

5—Landing basin

6—East-West water channel

7—North-south water channel

8—Drinking-water aqueduct

9—Aqueduct

10—Gateway

11—Escape tunnel

12—Ditchworks for defence

13—Christian cemetery

14—Well

Timber construction _____   Stone construction _____   Palisade line - - - - - -

PLATE 40. *Wilfrid Jury's plan of Sainte-Marie I. Illustration by J. Griffith and P. Buchanan. Courtesy W. and E. Jury and Oxford University Press, Canadian Branch.*

which was subsequently used by the Christian Indians who came to visit the Jesuits. Traces of additional temporary Indian shelters were also noted in this area, as well as the plans of two large European buildings. The latter had walls constructed of two rows of horizontal two-inch planks, held in position by thick, upright posts and packed in between with clay and stones to provide insulation. This type of construction is known as *colombage pierroté* and was still common in France in the seventeenth century (Jury and Jury 1954:38–39). Jury has interpreted the more southerly of these buildings as the hospital, which the Jesuits said was kept separate from their own living quarters, while the other building is believed to be the church that was constructed for public worship. It was a structure seventy feet long and twenty-seven feet wide. Immediately to the south of this building was a cemetery, containing twenty Indian graves. Traces of coffins were found in these graves; of these, three were small and each may have held the remains of one or more children. The positions of the adult skeletons indicate that the bodies had been placed in their coffins either on their sides with the knees flexed or lying on their backs with their legs stretched out. Rosaries were buried with some bodies, but most graves contained more traditional offerings. One body was accompanied by a quantity of wampum beads, another by the teeth and jawbone of a dog.

A flexed male interment was accompanied, in the same coffin, by a native bundle burial. In the upper right-hand corner of this coffin was a small copper vessel, the bottom of which had been damaged. Alongside it was an iron knife-blade and a pewter pipe, fourteen inches long and beautifully decorated with a pattern that incorporated two fleurs-de-lis. This appears to have been the grave of an influential Huron whose wife had predeceased him and been buried in the traditional manner. Since non-Christians would not have been allowed to be buried in this cemetery, it must be assumed either that this woman had been baptized and given a traditional scaffold burial prior to her husband's death, or that she was a non-Christian whose bones were slipped into the coffin without the Jesuits knowing about it. Jury and Jury (1954:93) note that the grave offerings indicate that the Jesuits had not yet succeeded in suppressing the Huron custom of burying food and trinkets with the dead and they suggest that the pot may have been broken deliberately, to permit its spirit to escape. One of the Indians who was buried in this cemetery had died as the result of a gunshot wound in the head (ibid. 94).

The outer court was separated from the inner one by a palisade that was also flanked along the east side by a ditch. This outer court had a pentagonal blockhouse at the south end and, being itself surrounded by a palisade, it provided the inner court with a second line of defence. Post molds indicated that a seventy-foot longhouse had been erected in this court, which Jury has identified as the area to which non-Christians were admitted during the daytime only. The historical evidence suggests that this part of Sainte-Marie was completed by 1642, or 1643 at the latest.

In the layout of this section of the Jesuit settlement, we see various expressions of Lalemant's concern for authority and discipline. By forbidding entry into the inner court to non-Christians and not permitting the latter to sleep at Sainte-Marie, the privileged relationship that had already been accorded to Christian Indians was further emphasized. The building of the church also eliminated the need to admit Indians to the chapel that had been erected in what became the European section of the settlement. The public services that impressed Indian converts were transferred to the church, while the chapel was transformed into a setting for the Jesuits' own devotions. While privileged male converts may have been admitted to the Jesuits' living area, especially when they were performing retreats or spiritual devotions, the construction of the church made possible a total separation between the Jesuits' living area and the part of the settlement to which converts were admitted. The creation within the heart of this mission headquarters of an all-male, European section, completely separated from the world around it, gave physical embodiment to Lalemant's concern to maintain the detailed forms, as well as the spirit, of religious devotion among the Jesuit missionaries. In 1641 Brébeuf noted in a letter to Mutius Vitelleschi, the general of the Society of Jesus, that religious discipline was being enforced among the Jesuits in the Huron country exactly as in the great colleges of Europe and that the punctual observance of all the rules was being increased day by day (Thwaites 1896–1901, 20:103). Brébeuf's allusion to boarding schools was aimed at Lalemant and his comment may be construed as a veiled criticism of Lalemant's notorious emphasis on rituals and forms.

The northern half of Sainte-Marie, which Jury calls the "European Compound," contained many more buildings than did the Indian Compound and was more complicated in its layout. Immediately to the north of the Indian Compound was the "South Court," which was surrounded by a wooden palisade and separated from the living area to the north by a deep ditch. Inside the South Court were three European-style buildings. Two were built of earth-packed walls, while the third was of vertical cedar posts, flattened on the inside and plastered with mud both inside and out. None of these buildings had cellars, nor was anything noted inside them that would indicate that they had been used as living quarters or workshops. Jury and Jury (1954:78) have suggested that these buildings may have been storehouses. Supplies brought from Quebec could have been kept in this court, and, since it adjoins the Indian Compound, it is possible that it was from here that the Jesuits' assistants carried on their trade with the Huron. It was also in this area that Jury found traces of a three-foot-square set of timber molds that led to the riverbank. He has interpreted these as the remains of an escape tunnel (ibid. 78–81).

North of the main ditch, which bisects the site in an east-west direction, was a palisaded rectangle that appears to have been the main living area for Europeans. Jury has called this the "North Court" and interprets it as made up of an area facing east that was fortified with four stone bastions and which gave access to a large quadrangle flanked with wooden buildings, which extended almost to the bank of the river. Jury has interpreted these buildings, all of which had mud-packed walls, as serving a variety of functions: some as dwellings, others as a chapel, cookhouse, blacksmith shop, and carpentry shop. Two channels ran from north to south through this area. These carried water which flowed through underground wooden mains from springs located on the rising ground to the north. Both channels emptied into the main east-west ditch. At the extreme north end of the site was another quadrilateral courtyard, adjoining the North Court. It too was surrounded by a wooden palisade and in the northwestern corner was a large stone bastion. The remains of a large building that stood in this courtyard are interpreted as those of a barn and Jury and Jury have suggested that this area, as well as a row of what appear to have been stables along the west side of the North Court, constituted the farm buildings of the settlement.

CONTROVERSIES ABOUT SAINTE-MARIE

Unfortunately, there is still a good deal of uncertainty about the layout and history of the European Compound. Jury has not published a detailed account of his excavations at Sainte-Marie and the popular record of his work leaves many questions unanswered. In particular, difficulties arise when one tries to tie in Jury's findings with those made by Kenneth Kidd when he excavated the part of the North Court that lies inside the four stone bastions. Kidd's findings are described in detail in a report in which a very high standard of archaeological recording was achieved and which is one of the key publications of historic site archaeology in North America.

Jury's reconstruction of the layout of buildings in this area is based largely on grey-black soil stains, each about a foot wide, which indicate where earth-packed timber walls formerly stood. On the basis of these stains Jury delineated buildings which occupied three of the four sides of his proposed courtyard. The east side of the courtyard had, however, been excavated by Kidd. In this part of the site, and under and between the two eastern bastions, Kidd (1949a:87–88) recorded further soil stains of this kind, although the overall pattern was incomplete and what remained was highly confusing. What was clear was that throughout this part of the site these walls had been replaced by later ones constructed of stone or wood, although the floors and foundations of the wooden structures were preserved only where they had been charred (plate 41). Along what would have been the east side of Jury's quadrangle, Kidd (1949a:37–59) discovered the remains of two later buildings that had wooden floors and walls made of wooden stakes or upright timbers wedged into horizontal wooden sills. These sills were held in place and kept off the damp ground by iron clamps or wooden stakes. The buildings were better preserved on the west side than on the east, which suggests that they had burned when an east wind was blowing (plate 42). In his reconstruction of Sainte-Marie, Jury combined the smaller of the buildings that Kidd excavated with one of his own to make a single large building. In so doing, he seems not to have taken account that all four walls of Kidd's building were clearly defined, that his building was of earth-filled construction while Kidd's was of upright timbers, and, finally, that the more clearly defined of the two north-south trenches had run between these two structures.[7]

The condition of the stones in the fireplace of Kidd's (1949a:57–58) smaller building convinced him that this fireplace had been built late in the history of the settlement and was not used for long. The superimposition found throughout this part of the site suggests that extensive rebuilding went on in the later years of occupation. Older buildings, with walls filled with earth and stone, were replaced by new ones of timber construction. This rebuilding may have been limited to the eastern part of the North Court, where Kidd excavated. It is possible, however, that it was more extensive and that later structures were dug away without being noticed by Jury in the heavy deposits of ash, charcoal, and burned timbers that he says covered large areas of the site (Jury and Jury 1954:39). If there was a general replacement of earth-filled walls with wooden ones, this might indicate that the building nearest the river in the South Court was built somewhat later than its nearest neighbours (ibid. 77).

It is also likely that the stone bastions flanking the eastern entrance to Sainte-Marie were constructed late in the history of the settlement. The

A—Residence

B—Chapel

C—Storage pit

D—Southwest Bastion

E—Southeast Bastion

F—Northeast Bastion

G—Northwest Bastion

H—North Curtain

J—East Curtain

K—East Postern

L—Masonry Wall

M—Masonry Wall

N—Forge Flue Foundation

O—Masonry Foundation
   Wall

P—Double Hearth

Q—Refuse Pit

R—Central Hearth

S—Chapel Hearth

T—Well

V—Central Ditch

W—Main Moat

X—West Moat

Y—False Wall

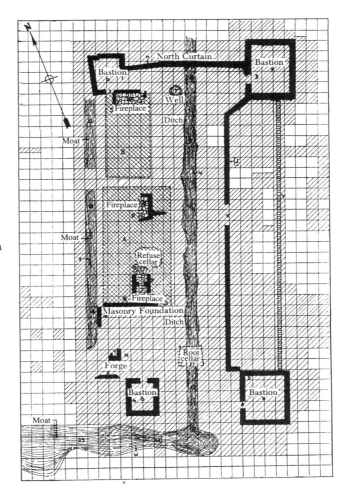

PLATE 41. *K. E. Kidd's plan of features revealed by the excavation of the central part of Sainte-Marie I. The arrangement of buildings should be compared with that proposed by Wilfrid Jury for the same part of the site. Courtesy K. E. Kidd and University of Toronto Press.*

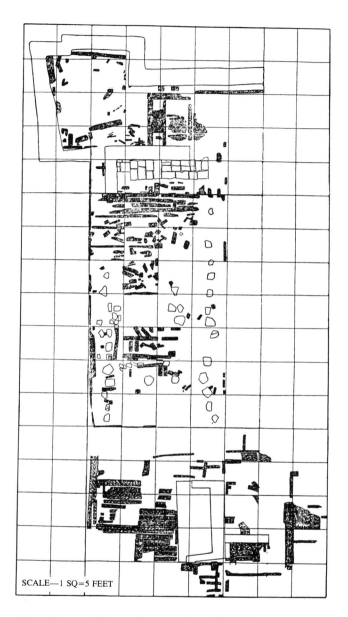

SCALE—1 SQ=5 FEET

PLATE 42. *Plan of a portion of Kidd's excavation, showing the remains of wooden flooring. This shows in its entirety the remains of the northernmost of the two buildings Kidd excavated within the area of the stone walls. The better preservation of the wood on the west side of the building results from greater charring and suggests that an east wind was blowing when the buildings were burned. Courtesy K. E. Kidd and University of Toronto Press.*

evidence for this is clearest for the northeast bastion, which covers the remains of a functionally similar structure built of *colombage pierroté* rather than stone (Kidd 1949*a*:55; plate 43). There also appear to be wooden prototypes for the stone walls joining these bastions. This indicates that stone fortifications replaced earlier wooden ones. There is some suggestion of haste in the later phases of the work and more than a little evidence that it was never finished. The northwest bastion is irregular in shape and far inferior in the quality of its construction to the others (Kidd 1949*a*:71). It may well have been altered in the course of its construction in order to hasten the progress of the work; however, the small south-west bastion seems to have been covered inside and out with a layer of hard white plaster (ibid. 65). Other bits of masonry have been interpreted as parts of a plan to join the four bastions with stone walls, in order to enclose a heavily fortified citadel within Sainte-Marie. If so, this work was abandoned before it was completed (ibid. 77–79).

Kidd and Jury also differ in their interpretation of the stone walls along the eastern perimeter of this part of the site. Jury (and Jury 1954:54) judges them to have been built of stone to a height of nine feet or more, whereas Kidd (1949*a*:36, 75) regards them as low curtain walls that were probably supplied with wooden superstructures. Jury (and Jury 1954:55) has used these walls to reconstruct a long, narrow building between the eastern bastions of Sainte-Marie, with the main entrance to the European Compound running through the centre of it and he has suggested that this building probably served as a barracks. Curiously, all but the northern portion of the east wall of this proposed building was of stone, while the latter, though an exposed outer wall, would have been built of timber (ibid. 55–56). Moreover, traces were found of a wooden palisade running between the north and south bastions, but farther east than either of these rows of stones. Kidd (1949*a*:77) has interpreted the east "wall" of this building as a mere line of stones that was intended to mark the line of a single stone wall that was later built twenty feet farther west. Since Kidd excavated this part of the site, his interpretation deserves more careful consideration than Jury and Jury have given it. It appears that much rebuilding was going on in this area about the time Sainte-Marie was abandoned. Half finished, half dismantled, and temporary constructions may be conflated in the archaeological record.

It is possible that the stone fortifications were begun in the spring of 1647, following the arrival of Pierre Tourmente late the previous year (Thwaites 1896–1901, 28:233). A growing concern with defence at this time is shown by the dispatch of a small cannon and a number of soldiers

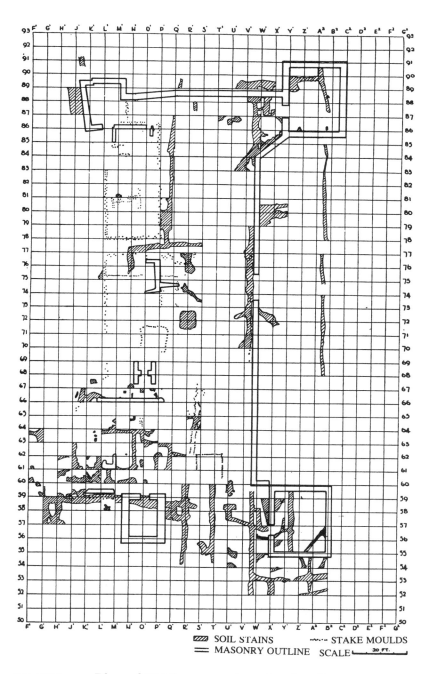

SOIL STAINS   ----- STAKE MOULDS

MASONRY OUTLINE   SCALE ⊢——— 20 FT. ——⊣

PLATE 43. *Plan of Kidd's excavations showing the arrangements of post molds and soil markings. The soil stains around the northeast stone bastion suggest that it replaced an earlier, similar structure of wood or* colombage pierroté. *Courtesy K. E. Kidd and University of Toronto Press.*

to the Huron country in August 1648 (32:99). The cannon is probably the same one that was later taken to Christian Island and was found there in the present century (Kidd 1949a:plate IIb). A considerable amount of energy must have been expended on the erection of these stone fortifications. Much of the rock that was used came from granite boulders that were collected nearby, about half of which were cut and trimmed before being used (ibid. 64). Flat limestone rocks, probably brought on a barge from Flat Rock Point near Port McNicoll, were used for corners or for chinking as well as for building fireplaces in some of the houses. It is uncertain whether the stone-laying operations came to an end with Tourmente's departure in 1648, or whether they continued under someone else's direction until 1649 (Jones 1908:378; Thwaites 1896–1901, 33:253). The speed with which the stone work was erected at Sainte-Marie II, under very trying circumstances, suggests that the work at Sainte-Marie I could have been finished in a relatively short period of time. It is possible that the north bastion, which was also of stone, was built about this time (Jury and Jury 1954:25). It is unclear whether this bastion was to afford increased protection to the route north, or if it was part of a plan for the more extensive rebuilding of Sainte-Marie in stone.

A final major problem in the reconstruction of Sainte-Marie is posed by the ditches associated with the North Court. The most prominent of these were the deep east-west ditch on the south side of the court and the two shallower north-south trenches that joined it. Originally it was assumed that these ditches had been built for defensive purposes. While most of the main ditch was above present river level, if in former times the level of the river had been higher, this section of the system might have been a moat used to unload canoes or barges laden with stone. Enlargements along the moat were interpreted as unloading basins; however, the discovery that the original pilings lining this ditch were burned off only about a foot above the present river level demonstrates that the Wye River stood at about the same height in 1649 as it does at the present time (Russell 1965:14). An alleged drop of four and a half feet in the level of the river since 1820 cannot be extrapolated back to the seventeenth century.

Wilfrid Jury uncovered the remains of wooden mains that brought spring water into the two north-south ditches. Jury and Jury (1954:60–61) pay scant attention to the more westerly and prominent of these ditches, but interpret the eastern one as part of a system of locks that permitted boats to be raised from the level of the Wye River into the heart of the settlement. They argue that this channel facilitated the building of the fort and the unloading of canoes (Jury and Jury 1954:61–75). Although

Jury's theory of locks has been incorporated into the Ontario government's reconstruction of Sainte-Marie, it has been viewed with misgivings by historians and archaeologists. Since no detailed account of what was found has been made available, it is impossible to evaluate the validity of the present reconstruction satisfactorily. In spite of this, serious objections can be raised against Jury's interpretation. Even allowing for a greater supply of water in the seventeenth century than at present, the operation of the locks would have been a slow process. One can scarcely credit that Frenchmen or Indians, who made over thirty-five portages on their way from the St. Lawrence, would have considered a series of locks at Sainte-Marie as worth the trouble that it took to build and operate them. The twisting nature of the waterway also makes it unsuitable for transportation and, as W. A. Russell (1965:14–15) has pointed out, the locks are too short to accommodate the normal-sized canoes that would have been used on Georgian Bay. At most, the canal might have been used to raise small barges loaded with stone, but this is an unlikely reason for such an elaborate construction. Recognition of these difficulties led Russell to suggest that the system might have been used to drive an undershot waterwheel, which turned a gristmill to produce the flour and meal required by the settlement; however, only circumstantial evidence can be advanced in support of this theory.

Moreover, still other problems require answers. The "upper lock" in the system was located along the eastern north-south channel, and was excavated and described in detail by Kenneth Kidd (1949a:61–64), who interpreted it as a storage pit that had been constructed by the French after they had ceased to use this water channel in favour of the one to the west. His detailed description of this feature appears to rule out any possibility of it having been a lock. On the other hand, the fact that the stone wall between the northeast and northwest bastions was built so as to pass over this channel and leave it open suggests that it may have been in operation late in the occupation of Sainte-Marie and this may indicate that the large quantities of seeds found in this pit were thrown in about the time the site was abandoned. The pit itself and the two other so-called locks discovered by Jury in the east-west ditch may have been chambers for storing water to make a reasonable supply available for fires and other emergencies.[8]

In all early seventeenth-century French settlements in Canada, much trouble was taken to ensure good drainage and this was required by the many cellars under the main buildings at Sainte-Marie. The system of ditches at Sainte-Marie may have been to provide such drainage and, at the same time, a controlled supply of drinking water for the settlement. Much of the system may have been cribbed with stakes and covered over for greater safety, cleanliness, and convenience.

In the reconstruction of Sainte-Marie, the western north-south channel has been totally ignored and several buildings, including the blacksmith's shop, have been erected where it stood. This has been done in spite of Kidd (1949a:86–87) having published clear evidence that this trench was open in 1649, when fragments of charred timber from an adjacent building collapsed into it. This trench appears to have been an open ditch, which probably passed between, rather than underneath, buildings before entering the main ditch.

I have not drawn attention to some of the problems involved in interpreting the archaeological evidence from Sainte-Marie in order to disparage the efforts that Jury has made to interpret these remains. It is important, however, to dispel the notion that his reconstruction of Sainte-Marie (plates 44, 45) is necessarily a duplicate of the original buildings. Not only do the interpretations of the archaeological evidence differ on many crucial points, but additions and rebuilding appear to have been going on up to the time the settlement was abandoned. No single reconstruction could hope to reconcile all of the alternative interpretations of the evidence or to reflect adequately the many transitions through which this site passed. Finally, we know of at least some projects that were never realized. In 1646 funds were provided to found a college in the Huron country, where young Indians would have been able to receive a Christian education without having to expose themselves to the dangers involved in travelling to Three Rivers or Quebec (Robinson, in Du Creux 1951–52:xiv). No doubt, this college would have been built at Sainte-Marie if time had been available or the state of the Huron country had allowed it. There is, however, no evidence that such an institution was founded prior to the collapse of the mission.

THE JESUIT ECONOMY AND MISSION PROGRAM

During the decade of its existence the missionaries endowed their settlement with a thriving subsistence economy. Already by 1636 they had brought a hen and a rooster from Quebec (Thwaites 1896–1901, 13:93, 101). The following year the Jesuits sowed a small plot of wheat at Ossossané so that wafers could be prepared for the Eucharist (15:137–39). With the founding of Sainte-Marie these first efforts at food production were

PLATE 44. *A general view of the modern reconstruction of Sainte-Marie, looking south. The European Compound is in the foreground. Courtesy Ontario Ministry of Natural Resources.*

PLATE 45. *A general view of the modern reconstruction of Sainte-Marie from the Wye River. Courtesy Ontario Ministry of Natural Resources.*

expanded greatly. The site was chosen with an eye to clearing fields and the first crops were harvested there in the autumn of 1640. By 1643 the Jesuits had sufficient reserves of corn that they could dispense it to their converts during the famine of that year (27:65–67), and in the final years of the mission they boasted of their settlement's self-sufficiency (32:61). Large crops of maize were harvested in order to provide food for both Indian visitors and the French themselves (19:135). At the same time, the Jesuits continued to buy corn from the Huron in good years in order to build up their reserves against an emergency.[9]

While there is no direct evidence that barley, wheat, or oats were planted, these crops were grown at Quebec[10] and they may have been grown at Sainte-Marie as well (Jury and Jury 1954:33). In 1641 Charles Garnier requested his brother to send the seeds of various medicinal herbs from France so that these might be planted by the missionaries (Thwaites 1896–1901, 20:101). It has been argued that every European seed or root crop grown at Quebec must eventually have made its way to Sainte-Marie in order to add greater variety to the diet there (Jury and Jury 1954:34). It has also been suggested that an apple orchard was planted near Sainte-Marie, from which 200 years later the military garrison at Penetanguishene were able to obtain their trees. It is, however, difficult to estimate how much credence should be given to claims that this and other pioneer orchards in the area were started from trees in the "old Jesuit orchards" (ibid.). From 1637 on, the Jesuits manufactured their own wine, but did so from wild grapes (Thwaites 1896–1901, 15:137–39; 35:135).

It is also not certain where the Jesuits' crops were planted. Some vegetables were probably grown within the walls of Sainte-Marie, where they were tended by Brother Masson. The ash swamp to the southeast of the settlement prevented agriculture in that area, but fields might have been planted either on the rising ground to the north and northeast of the site, or more likely, as Jury and Jury (1954:34) suggest, on the fertile flats on the opposite bank of the river. The Jesuits had a boat that was used to ferry French and Indian visitors across the Wye River (Thwaites 1896–1901, 33:247) and this would have made it easy for workmen to farm on the opposite shore. Production was limited, however, since neither horses nor oxen were available for ploughing. Because of this the Jesuits' farming, like that of the Indians, was horticultural rather than agricultural. As the Jesuits learned to use maize flour in European ways, they may have come to prefer maize as an easier crop to grow in this fashion than was wheat.

While the Jesuits may never have sought to make European cereals more than a source of variety in a vegetable diet based mainly on Indian corn, they worked hard to acquire a more familiar European diet by introducing European farm animals. The first pigs may have arrived at Sainte-Marie about 1644, since it is claimed that the jaw of a boar estimated to be about five years of age has been found there (Jury and Jury 1954:33); the first pigs would no doubt have been dispatched from Quebec soon after they had been weaned. The Jesuits' workmen are reported to have taken calves to the Huron country in May and August 1646 (Thwaites 1896–1901, 28:187, 229–31) and a heifer was sent there in August 1648 (32:99). Conveying such animals to Sainte-Marie must have been a formidable task, even when the animals were young, and small barges may have been built to accompany the canoes. These animals multiplied in the Huron country and by 1649 pork, beef, and milk products were providing the French with a diet similar to what they were used to at Quebec or in France (33:255). At an earlier period, the absence of milk products made it difficult to recruit workers for the mission (Desjardins 1966:39–40). Likewise, while most clothes and luxury items such as glassware continued to be imported from Quebec, many of the necessities of the mission eventually were manufactured on the spot. These included most goods made of wood, leather, and iron. The blacksmith manufactured not only the iron nails, fitments, and ornaments needed at Sainte-Marie, but also a considerable number of axes and other iron objects that the Jesuits traded with the Indians (Jury and Jury 1954:52; plate 46). He also appears to have repaired guns (Thwaites 1896–1901, 27:89).

Kidd (1949a:12) suggests that the Jesuits attempted to use Sainte-Marie to introduce new customs to the Huron. He thinks that it was meant in part as a model farm where the Huron would learn to tend domestic animals and to cultivate new species of fruits and vegetables. Perhaps too, the Jesuits wished to teach the Huron to manufacture pottery in the European style.[11] Insofar as Lalemant was taking the Paraguayan reductions for his model, he could have had such a plan in mind. What is lacking, however, for the Huron missions is evidence that even the slightest attempt was made to implement such a policy. The primary reason for transplanting French material culture to the Huron country seems to have been to make the lives of the Frenchmen who were living there easier and more secure. Eventually, Sainte-Marie might have been used for acculturative purposes, but these long-term aims do not explain what happened in the 1640s.

Lalemant's plan to persuade Christian families to leave their villages and settle around Sainte-Marie was soon abandoned. He was still hoping in the spring of 1641 that a reduction might be developed (Thwaites 1896–1901,

PLATE 46. *Iron axes recovered in the course of Wilfrid Jury's excavations at Sainte-Marie I. Courtesy Ontario Ministry of Natural Resources.*

21:141), but hereafter this plan is no longer mentioned. Lalemant had failed to reckon on the strength of village ties among the Huron. Even Christians remained too attached to their villages and clan segments to abandon them and settle near the French. Moreover, while the Jesuits had abandoned their residences at Ossossané and Teanaostaiaé in 1639 and 1640, these and other large villages continued to be the centres of their missionary activity; it was in them that the Jesuits spent most of their time and won by far the largest number of converts. It is, therefore, not surprising that in 1643, even before Lalemant was replaced as superior of the mission, the decision was taken to establish or re-establish Jesuit residences in these communities. This change made little difference to Jesuit routine as the priests already usually lived with Christian families when they made prolonged visits to the larger villages. Yet, the wheel had come full circle and the emphasis was once again being placed on encouraging the development of Christianity within Huron settlements, rather than on seeking to persuade individual converts to move elsewhere.

In the principal Huron communities chapels were enlarged, crosses erected, old kettles hung on poles to serve as bells, and Christian cemeteries consecrated and funerals solemnized in them (27:67). These communities served as headquarters for the Jesuits' work in neighbouring villages and became the foci of Christian religious life in each area. By 1646 the Jesuits had constructed chapels in these towns (29:259). Most appear to have consisted of ends of longhouses which the Jesuits' workmen partitioned off. Eventually, however, proper churches, probably resembling the chapel that had been erected by Brébeuf in Ossossané, were built in settlements that had large Christian congregations, such as Ossossané and Teanaostaiaé (33:259). The establishment of Christian cemeteries for each major community no doubt explains why so few graves were found at Sainte-Marie. Hereafter, only Christians who died at Sainte-Marie or who for special reasons requested it were buried at the Jesuits' headquarters. One such burial was of a child from Scanonaenrat in 1648–49 (34:111–15).

With the restoration of residences to the mission centres, the system that had existed prior to 1639 was in effect reconstituted, except that the Huron mission as a whole could now count on the support of a flourishing central headquarters. A considerable number of priests tended to the needs of this headquarters and all of the missionaries gathered there three times a year to confer about their work and encourage one another (29:257–59). Ideally, each mission was supplied with two priests who lived most of the year in the principal community of their mission.

As the years passed, the number of converts in the larger towns increased and they required the services of a resident clergy. To accommodate these needs more missions were established. A new mission was established at Scanonaenrat (St. Michel) in 1642, and another at Taenhatentaron (St. Ignace) in 1644. After the abandonment of Contarea in 1647, a separate mission was founded for the Attignawantan villages in the Penetanguishene Peninsula. This mission had its headquarters at Sainte-Magdelaine (33:143), which is identified as Arenté on the *Chorographia Regionis Huronum* (1660) and as Wenrio on the *Description du Pais des Hurons* (1651). For lack of missionaries Teanaostaiaé and Contarea were treated as a single mission in 1640–41 (21:169) and Scanonaenrat may have been attended from Taenhatentaron in 1646–47 (Jones 1908:360). The communities assigned to particular missions also varied from year to year. In 1641 the village of St. Jean, which was located in the northern part of the Sturgeon River Valley, was dropped from the Sainte-Marie mission, while the Attignawantan village of St. Francis-Xavier was added to it (Thwaites 1896–1901, 23:39). By 1648 twelve or thirteen unnamed villages were said to belong to this mission (33:143). In 1639–40 Scanonaenrat belonged to the mission of Teanaostaiaé, while in 1641–42 it was tended from Contarea (21:283). Likewise, Taenhatentaron was originally part of the Teanaostaiaé mission, but from 1640 until it became a separate mission it was serviced from Contarea (27:29; map 28). The manner in which individual villages were assigned first to one mission and then to another shows that the requirements of the mission and the growth of Christian congregations, rather than any concern for Huron tribal organization, were the principal factors determining the development of the mission system.

Brébeuf and the Neutral

In 1639 Jérôme Lalemant established a mission to the Tionnontaté in addition to the four that he set up for the Huron country. The following year the ambition of the Jesuits to work even farther afield led them to entrust the missions of Teanaostaiaé and Contarea to a single pair of priests and to establish new missions to the Neutral and Algonkians. The Jesuits had long desired to work among the Neutral, but had been prevented from doing so by a lack of manpower and by explicit orders that they should not attempt to do mission work among more distant peoples until they had scored substantial successes among the Huron (Thwaites

1896–1901, 21:187). Although the cutbacks that were involved seem to indicate that this effort to expand the scale of Jesuit operations was premature, Lalemant argued that he was justified in establishing a mission to the Neutral and looked forward to the time when a mission headquarters similar to Sainte-Marie would be built in their country. Because it was necessary to study the Neutral language Fathers Brébeuf and Chaumonot, who were both highly regarded for their linguistic skills, were chosen for this mission (21:187–89). It was decided that both of them should spend the winter in the Neutral country. In reaching this decision the Jesuits ignored longstanding Huron policy. Brébeuf had been living in the Huron country when Father Daillon's attempt to spend a winter among the Neutral and conclude a treaty with them had violently angered the Huron and confirmed their worst fears about the intentions of the Recollet priests. This was a precedent from which the Jesuits, and particularly Brébeuf, ought to have learned a lesson.

Brébeuf and Chaumonot left Sainte-Marie on 2 November with two servants, who were sent along so that the party might appear to be a regular group of French traders. Lalemant says that this was done so that the arrival of the priests would not alarm the Neutral, but it may also have been meant to deceive the Huron into believing that only a brief visit was intended and that the priests would return with the traders. The Huron were suspicious of the journey from the start. When the French arrived at Teanaostaiaé those who had promised to guide them to the Neutral country refused to do so, and the Jesuits had to be content with a young man they recruited on the spot (21:205). Leaving Teanaostaiaé, the Jesuits slept for four nights in the woods and on the fifth day arrived at the Neutral settlement of Kandoucho. From there they pressed on through a number of other villages until they came to Teotongniaton where Souharissen, the principal headman of the confederacy, was living. In Daillon's time this community, which the Jesuits describe as being in the middle of the country, had been called Ounontisastan.

The Jesuits' arrival spread fear in the villages they passed through, since their reputation as sorcerers had preceded them. These fears were largely calmed, however, by the Jesuits' pretext of having come to trade, and pursuing this role they were able to reach Souharissen's settlement in safety. There they were informed that Souharissen was at war and would not return until the following spring. The Jesuits presented a collar of 2000 beads to the town council and explained that they wished to form a special alliance with the Neutral by persuading them to become Christians. The council claimed that it lacked the authority to accept this present but

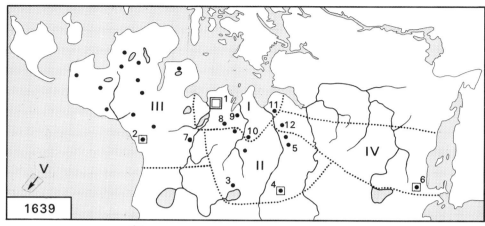

SAINTE-MARIE □

• Huron settlement   □ Mission centre   ..... Mission area, as far as known

NAMES OF VILLAGES

1. Sainte-Marie (Jesuit headquarters)
2. Ossossané
3. Scanonaenrat
4. Teanaostaiaé
5. Taenhatentaron
6. Contarea

7. St. Francis-Xavier
8. Ste Anne
9. St. Louis
10. St. Denis
11. St. Jean
12. St. Joachim

NAMES OF THE MISSIONS TO THE HURON
(numbered in order of foundation)

 I. Sainte-Marie to the Ataronchronon
 II. St. Joseph to the Attigneenong-
      nahac
III. La Conception to the Attignawan-
      tan

 IV. St. Jean-Baptiste to the Arendar-
      honon
VIII. St. Michel to the Tahontaenrat
  X. St. Ignace
 XI. Ste Magdelaine

MISSIONS TO OTHER TRIBES

 V. The Apostles to the Tionnontaté
     a. St. Jean at Etharita
     b. St. Mathias at Ekarenniondi
VI. The Angels to the Neutral
VII. The Holy Ghost to the Nipissing

 IX. Ste Elizabeth to the Onontchat-
      aronon
XII. St. Pierre (Manitoulin Island)
XIII. St. Charles (Algonkians)

N.B. Mission boundaries often unknown.

MAP 28. *Centres and boundaries (where known) of Jesuit missions to the Huron from 1639 to 1648.*

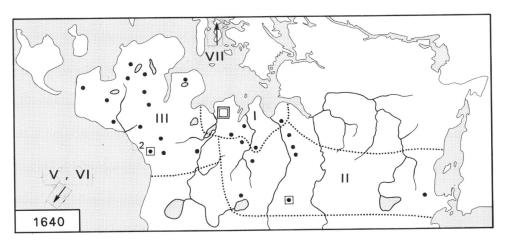

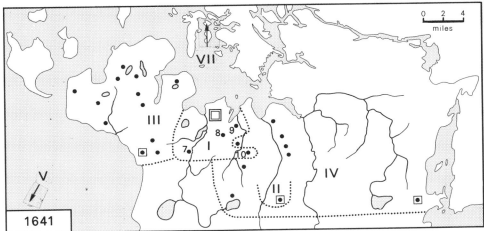

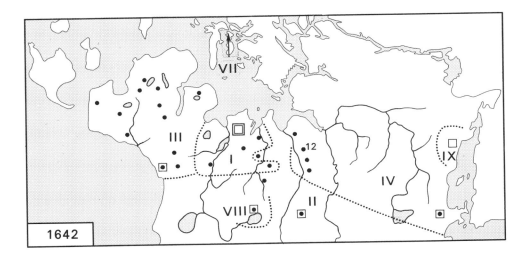

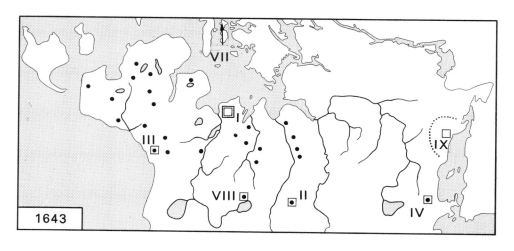

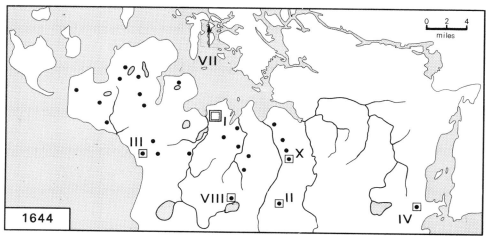

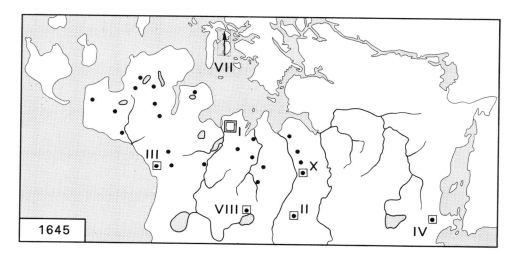

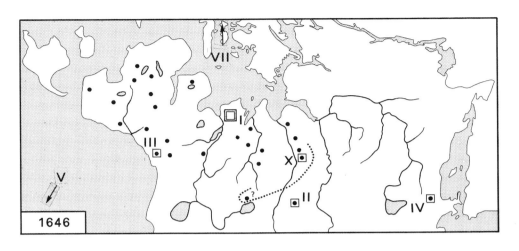

1646

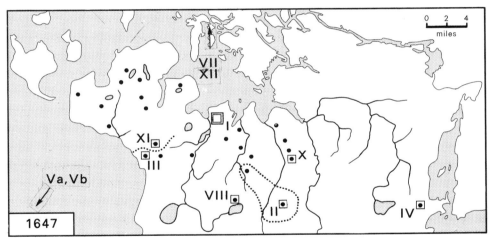

1647

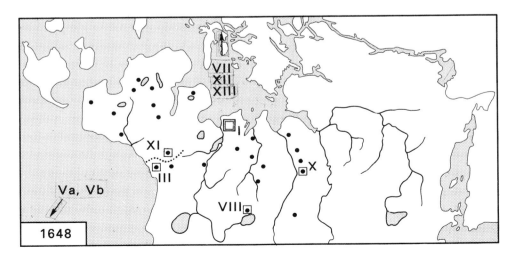

1648

gave the Jesuits permission to remain in the country until Souharissen returned. Once this permission had been granted the French laymen returned to the Huron country with their skins. The Jesuits travelled with them as far as Kandoucho and then began to move systematically from one Neutral village to another, doing what they could to instruct people. In the course of their journey they passed through eighteen villages, possibly reaching Onguiaahra near the Niagara River (21:207–11).[12]

As soon as the Huron realized that the Jesuits were intending to winter among the Neutral, they sought to have the priests withdrawn. The Huron charged that Brébeuf had travelled south to make an alliance with the Seneca and that he was urging the Seneca to destroy those Huron whom the Jesuits had been unable to kill with their witchcraft. The Jesuits in the Huron country were warned that similar journeyings and rumours had been responsible for Brûlé's death eight years before. The Huron, however, aimed their most persuasive propaganda at the Neutral. They told the Neutral that the Jesuits had first plotted to destroy the Huron by witchcraft and were now plotting to kill them in a similar manner. As these stories spread through the Neutral country the Jesuits became ever greater objects of fear and hostility. It was also rumoured that Brébeuf had come south to bewitch the Seneca and cause them to die in retaliation for the Seneca having slain Chihwatenha (21:209–11). This story must have frightened the Neutral not only because of what it implied about Brébeuf's power, but also because if the Seneca blamed the epidemic that was raging in their country on the Jesuits, they might hold the Neutral responsible for letting the latter approach their borders.

Awenhokwi, the nephew of a Huron headman, visited many of the Neutral villages seeking to persuade their headmen that in self-defence they should kill Brébeuf and Chaumonot. He presented a valuable gift of nine iron hatchets to the confederacy council and told the Neutral that if they had not already slain the Jesuits, the Huron were prepared to do so as soon as they returned to the Huron country. At the same time he was making these proposals Awenhokwi befriended the Jesuits and urged them to travel with him, no doubt hoping to lead them into a trap (21:213; 34:173). Although the Huron were too frightened of losing their trade with the French to kill the Jesuits themselves, many would have been pleased to see someone else kill them. The Huron also must have hoped that if the Neutral could be persuaded to murder Brébeuf and Chaumonot, all hope of a trading alliance between the Neutral and the French would be eliminated. The same trading relations that protected the Jesuits in the Huron country exposed them to the murderous machinations of Huron politicians when they visited other tribes. Fortunately for the Jesuits the Neutral saw through these plots and were unwilling to oblige the Huron.

A Huron named Oëntara visited the Neutral settlements and repeated all of the accusations of sorcery that the Huron had made against the Jesuits in previous years. He denounced their religious observances and use of writing as proof of sorcery and stated that the Jesuits' aim was to kill all the Indians they could. Oëntara advised the Neutral that unless they wished to see themselves destroyed, they should close their longhouses against the priests and refuse to listen to them. He also confronted Brébeuf in a council and while Brébeuf believed he had cleared himself of the accusations that were made against him, many other Huron arrived at that time who reaffirmed Oëntara's charges. These accusations so frightened the Neutral headmen and elders that they held a meeting at which they decided that even in Souharissen's absence, the Jesuits' presents should be returned to them. In this way the headmen withdrew their sanction for the Jesuits to remain in their country. They also told Brébeuf that if the Jesuits had any consideration for preserving good relations between the Huron and the Neutral, they should leave immediately (21:213–17).

In spite of this warning Brébeuf and Chaumonot refused to leave. For a month and a half they continued to wander from one village to another. They were met with open hostility on every hand, often being forbidden to enter a single house. They were unable to write or even to wash their clothes without being accused of practising witchcraft and when they were given food their hosts were too frightened to eat from the same pots that they did. The Jesuits were forced to pay dearly in trade goods for any hospitality they received, while the Neutral would not accept freely given presents from them for fear they were bewitched (21:219–21).

The Neutral headmen kept warning the Jesuits that Seneca visitors might slay them and pointed out that since the last council meeting no one was under any obligation to protect them. Individual Neutral attempted to intimidate the priests and in their presence there was much banter about killing and eating them. In spite of such intimidation, which was no doubt meant to frighten the Jesuits into leaving, no real harm was done to them (21:221–23).

An exception to this ill treatment was found in the village of Khioetoa, which was inhabited by a considerable number of Wenroronon refugees. These people knew about the good treatment that the Jesuits had given to the Wenroronon when they had arrived in the Huron country, and for this reason they treated the Jesuits well and listened to them. Among them the Jesuits managed to baptize a few elderly persons and some sick children

(21:231–33). Eventually, however, as the hostility of most Neutral continued to grow, the Jesuits deemed it expedient to return to Kandoucho where they believed themselves to be the least unwelcome. They were halted by a snowstorm in Teotongniaton and there they were given shelter by an old woman who proved to be well disposed towards them. They stayed with her for almost a month, during which she helped them to draw up a dictionary and syntax comparing the Huron and Neutral languages (21:229–31). In spite of arguments and threats from the other villagers and even from people living in the same house, this woman refused to drive the Jesuits away. Because of this she and her father, who approved of her action, were accused of being sorcerers although nothing came of this (21:227). Nevertheless, she was unable to prevent other members of her household from attacking Chaumonot or other Neutral from robbing the two missionaries of their possessions (21:229). The individualism that was so highly prized by Iroquoians is exemplified by this woman's steadfast friendship for the Jesuits.

Throughout the winter the Jesuits in the Huron country received little news from Brébeuf or Chaumonot, since the Huron entrusted with their letters frequently threw them away either from malice or more often from fear of witchcraft. Rumours circulated, however, that they were in great danger and on the basis of these reports it was decided that a rescue party should be sent to fetch them home. Robert Le Coq, Teondechoren, another Huron from Ossossané, and an unidentified Frenchman made up this party which had the two Jesuits back to Sainte-Marie by 19 March 1641.

The Huron were furious that Brébeuf and Chaumonot had spent the winter among the Neutral. Many may have believed that Brébeuf had gone there in order to conspire with the Seneca; but the popularity of this rumour is best interpreted as a measure of the widespread resentment towards the Jesuits that remained from previous years. For the average Huron few actions could have been more threatening than the Jesuits having dealings with the Huron's most dangerous adversaries. Among Huron traders, however, a more immediate fear must have been that if the Jesuits succeeded in establishing a mission among the Neutral, the Jesuits would attempt to conclude a separate trading alliance with them that would undercut the Huron as middlemen.

The effect of this resentment was quickly felt by the Jesuits. Soon after Chaumonot returned he was assigned to assist Father Daniel. When they reached Scanonaenrat a Huron youth hit Chaumonot on the head with a rock and grabbed a hatchet to kill him (21:235–37). While Lalemant states that the Huron was prepared to attack either priest, the fact that he assaulted Chaumonot may be evidence of the resentment that some Huron felt against him for his part in the Neutral mission. Other Huron, however, helped to rescue Chaumonot.

The anger that was directed against Brébeuf was far stronger and can be documented more certainly. It was clearly because of this anger that Brébeuf returned to Quebec early in the summer of 1641 and remained there until 1644. For reasons of discretion, the real reason for Brébeuf's departure is nowhere stated in the *Jesuit Relations*; Lalemant merely notes that in the course of his affairs he was compelled to send Brébeuf to Quebec (23:35). Brébeuf had broken his left clavicle in a fall on the ice while crossing Lake Simcoe on his return from the Neutral country and some writers have attributed his departure to this injury (Latourelle 1966:123; Talbot 1956:241–42; Jones 1908:324). It is very difficult to believe, however, that a man with a disabled arm would have left the relative comfort of Sainte-Marie and undertaken an excruciating journey to Quebec to seek help for such an injury. More significantly, it was two years before he disclosed the nature of his injury to a surgeon there. When Lalemant writes of sending Brébeuf to Quebec it is within the context of Huron rumours about him being bribed by the Iroquois. Brébeuf travelled in a convoy of two canoes manned by four French and six Huron, all of whom were Christians or converts undergoing intensive instruction (Thwaites 1896–1901, 23:35). One of the latter was Charles Tsondatsaa. The composition of the convoy and the haste with which it travelled to Three Rivers ahead of the other Huron traders suggests a concern for Brébeuf's safety at the hands of the Huron.

That care was needed is evident from a rumour that arose on the way down the Ottawa River. Brébeuf's canoes reached Three Rivers safely but some others that followed them were attacked by the Iroquois. This caused the Huron traders to speculate that Brébeuf was not attacked because he had a secret agreement with the Iroquois. A Huron who had escaped from the Iroquois said that the Iroquois confirmed that Brébeuf had talked with the Seneca the previous winter. He also claimed that the Mohawk had recently met Brébeuf at night and that he had given them presents and told them where they might ambush the Huron who were following him (21:75–77; 23:35–37). According to this Huron Brébeuf aided the Iroquois because he wished to exterminate the Huron. This improbable rumour indicates how deeply the Huron hated and feared Brébeuf and explains why a series of excuses were found to keep him at Quebec and Three Rivers until Huron anger had cooled. Even after Brébeuf returned to the Huron country he was attached to the Sainte-Marie mission until his death, rather than working farther afield (34:169–71).

The miscalculation of the Neutral mission affected more than the lives of Brébeuf and Chaumonot. Although certain Neutral headmen invited the Jesuits to return to their country (23:183), the Jesuits feared Huron displeasure to the point where they felt obliged to abandon this mission (23:179–81). To help compensate for this, a number of Huron Christians visited the Neutral in 1642 and 1643 and instructed them. One of these native preachers was Etienne Totiri from Teanaostaiaé. He visited one of the northern Neutral villages in the company of his brother. Another was Barnabé Otsinonannhont from Scanonaenrat, who went to the heart of the country and made a longer stay there. His work was of particular importance as he was one of the leading headmen of his tribe and had numerous trading partners among the Neutral. All of these men probably did their preaching in the course of regular trading activities. Yet their influence among the Neutral was no doubt greater because of this, and in the spring of 1643 about 100 Neutral came to visit the Jesuits in the Huron country (27:21–25). In spite of this, the Jesuits' mission to the Neutral was never re-established and there is no evidence that these indirect mission efforts had any more substantial results.

It is even more indicative of the depth of Huron feeling that their resentment also brought an end, albeit a temporary one, to the Tionnontaté mission. In the winter of 1640–41 Fathers Garnier and Pierre Pijart spent several months among the Tionnontaté. They found themselves better treated than they had been the year before (20:97), although their presents were rejected by the Tionnontaté council as they had been by the Neutral one (21:179). Nevertheless, Huron accusations of sorcery continued to generate fear and resentment of the Jesuits (21:177). On one occasion, while they were travelling from one village to another they were knocked down and their assailants shouted that they were dead men, but in spite of this nothing happened to them. While some headmen were convinced that the Jesuits wished to destroy the Tionnontaté and one of them ordered the priests to leave the country, the missionaries generally found themselves favourably received in the villages and were able to baptize a few children (21:179–85).

Despite this substantial progress, in 1641 it was decided that the Tionnontaté mission would be abandoned. One reason that was given was that more attention needed to be paid to the Huron missions (21:283), but Huron opposition was probably the key consideration. In 1641–42 the work of the Jesuits among the Tionnontaté was confined to a few brief journeys, which did not arouse the antagonism of the Huron; hereafter the Tionnontaté were left alone until 1646. A few Tionnontaté Christians are reported to have left their country and settled near Sainte-Marie so as not to lose contact with the Jesuits and others visited the Jesuits from time to time (21:283; 23:179–81).

The Huron Church

THE JESUITS ADOPT A HARD LINE

Although the missions to the Neutral and Tionnontaté had suffered a severe setback, from 1640 onwards the Jesuits began to enjoy success in their efforts to convert the Huron. After most of their former converts had abandoned their profession of Christianity during the smallpox epidemic, the Jesuits acknowledged that in their haste to convert the Huron they had adopted too lax a standard for baptism. It was therefore decided that converts would have to be instructed and tested more thoroughly than they had been in recent years before they could be baptized (Thwaites 1896–1901, 26:213; 30:115). By this time the developing linguistic skills of the Jesuits made it possible for them not only to explain the details of their dogmas (28:65) but also to understand the intricacies of Huron religion as explained to them by their converts. This new knowledge convinced the Jesuits that they had erred in believing that there was little to native religious beliefs and that all that was required to convert the Huron was to convince them of the truth of Christian teachings. It was recognized for the first time that the Huron had a complex set of beliefs which had to be understood and counteracted before a genuine conversion was possible (23:151–53). To prevent backsliding and to encourage conversion the Jesuits continued to emphasize the torments that they believed would be inflicted on a non-Roman Catholic or an apostate after death. These threats were vividly impressed on the imagination of the Huron by explicitly drawing parallels between the sufferings of the damned and the torments that the Huron inflicted on prisoners of war.

Few Huron desires were so selfish or materialistic that the Jesuits disdained to make use of them in order to induce Huron to want to become Christians. Tangible rewards of many kinds were lavished on converts, which exploited their acquisitiveness or sense of need. One old man named Atiessa was accused by his fellow villagers of having converted only in order to obtain a blanket from the Jesuits (23:51). In times of famine and other difficulties the Christians were the first, and sometimes the only, Huron to receive charity from the Jesuits; indeed, the Jesuits described the food that was distributed in the famine of 1643 as a public testimonial to the close union that existed between them and the Huron Christians (27:65).

The advantages Christians enjoyed when they traded at Quebec and Three Rivers had long been an inducement for Huron traders to convert. More psychological pressure was brought to bear on these traders in 1641 when Montmagny gave his annual presents to the Huron. On this occasion he stated that these presents were given not solely on account of the French-Huron alliance, but also as a pledge of the truth of what the Jesuits were saying. This affirmation was widely discussed in Huron councils after the traders returned home. Many headmen believed that the French traders would soon insist on at least a nominal adherence to Christianity as a prerequisite for their continued friendship. As a result of this belief the Jesuits in the Huron country claimed to have considerably larger audiences when they preached to the Huron (22:311). There can be no doubt that trade played an important role in encouraging Huron men to become Christians at this time. By 1648 when less than fifteen per cent of the Huron population was Christian, over half of the 250 traders who came to Three Rivers either had been baptized or were receiving instruction (32:179).

The sale and distribution of muskets only to Christians became another strong inducement for young and middle-aged men to seek baptism after Charles Tsondatsaa became the first Huron to own a gun in 1641. By 1643 twenty-two men in a single war party were Christians and the Jesuits were informing their readers that God seemed to intend selling guns only to Christians to be a legitimate way to render Christianity acceptable among the Huron (25:27). It may be that it was specifically in order to be able to buy guns that young men were willing to spend a winter in the Jesuit school at Quebec or Three Rivers. This may also explain why men who were actively engaged in warfare began to express a desire for baptism and to learn about Christianity from their fellow warriors (23:199–203; 28:89–91). In dangerous situations Huron Christians sometimes granted preliminary baptisms to fellow warriors who might not live to return to the Huron country. Because of the abhorrence that the Huron felt about being separated from their kinsmen after death, the conversion of a warrior often led to the conversion of his whole family. In this way the Jesuits were able to start a snowballing process which they had good reason to believe would eventually lead to the conversion of whole villages and tribes (29:277–79).

Had the Jesuits been willing to baptize every Huron who expressed the desire to become a Christian, they might quickly have acquired a series of congregations made up of nominal Christians. The Jesuits were aware of this and were determined to use the materialistic desires of the Huron only as a means of bringing pressure to bear on potential converts to undergo prolonged instruction. By requiring such people to offer proof of their ability to live as Christians prior to baptizing them, the Jesuits were, in effect, compelling them to make radical changes in their behaviour and to acquire a working knowledge of basic Christian doctrines insofar as the Jesuits could make these intelligible. It was the Jesuits' hope that this would lead to understanding and eventually produce genuine Christians. Such methods would have seemed not unusual to most seventeenth-century Europeans, who viewed censorship, enforced church attendance, fines, public penances, brutal tortures, and public executions as efficacious means of promoting and safeguarding religious values. Except in cases of serious illness, probationary periods of one to two years were now required prior to baptism (30:115). Once an individual was deemed worthy of baptism he was sent to Sainte-Marie, where he was carefully examined before the ceremony was performed. Most baptisms were at Christmas, Easter, and Pentecost, when large numbers of Christians assembled at mission headquarters (23:21–23).

The new Jesuit policy was facilitated by the cessation of the epidemics and the abundant harvest that was collected in the autumn of 1640 (21:131). The return of prosperous conditions led to a reduction in overt hostility towards the Jesuits, although many Huron continued to fear them. Some became alarmed when they saw a Jesuit because they feared that he would bring sickness to their village; others demanded assurances of longevity before they would consent to have dealings with any of them. Many Huron professed to be interested in what the Jesuits said, no doubt hoping that in this way they could avoid becoming victims of sorcery without having to live as Christians (21:133–35). Gradually, however, baptism began to lose its odious connotations of sorcery and came again to be viewed as a means by which initiates were able to join relatives in heaven rather than in the traditional villages of the dead. These conditions provided a milieu in which the Jesuits, under the protection of the French-Huron trading alliance, were able to carry out an effective program of instruction.

In spite of the more than 1000 Huron who were baptized during the smallpox epidemic, by the spring of 1640 only a few Huron professed to be Christians. Between the summers of 1640 and 1641, 100 Huron were baptized (20:99), of whom about sixty survived illnesses and other misfortunes to become professing Christians (20:103). The following year 120 persons were baptized (23:23), and in 1642–43 about 100 more (23:267; 26:213). Many were baptized in 1643–44 (27:69); over 170 in 1644–45 (28:61); and 164 in 1645–46 (29:261). This suggests an average of about 100 baptisms a year until 1643, and over 150 a year thereafter. Some baptisms were undoubtedly of people who were dying and a considerable number of Christian warriors were probably killed in encounters with the Iroquois. The figures suggest, however, that by 1646 there were probably about 500 professing Huron Christians.

CONVERTS

The Jesuits had their greatest success in the larger towns. This happened, in part, because the Huron headmen and traders who had the closest ritual and economic ties with the French lived in these communities. They were also the settlements that the Jesuits had chosen as their mission centres and where they spent the most time. It is no accident that after 1640 the majority of conversions were made in Ossossané and Teanaostaiaé, where the Jesuits had lived prior to the founding of Sainte-Marie (Thwaites 1896–1901, 23:151; 25:85).

The most flourishing of the Christian missions was at Ossossané (23:43). By 1643 there were already so many professing Christians in this town that the Jesuits and their converts were looking forward to it becoming entirely Christian and the first indigenous centre of Christianity in the Huron country (26:255). When the Huron were fearing an Iroquois attack in the winter of 1641, they asked the Jesuits to baptize the whole community so that all of its inhabitants might go to heaven together (23:107).

The nucleus of this church was the family of Chihwatenha, whose members were model Christians. In particular, Chihwatenha's brother Teondechoren was zealous in his support of the Jesuits. The village headmen began to seek his assistance in matters in which his friendship with the Jesuits and the French was thought to be of value (21:147–57). After he escaped from the Iroquois in 1643 his stories of Jogues's fortitude and his attribution of his survival to his faith in Christianity did much to enhance the prestige of the missionaries (26:233–43). Neither Teondechoren nor Chihwatenha's widow, Aonetta, expressed any doubts about

Christianity, although both lost young daughters through illness and this was widely interpreted as the result of their being Christians and refusing to allow curing rituals to be performed for them (23:59–61). Devotion to Chihwatenha's memory was undoubtedly an important factor inspiring his relatives to remain, as well as to become, Christians.

The most influential single member of the Ossossané church, after Chihwatenha's death, was René Tsondihwané (21:159–65). Tsondihwané was about sixty years old and was the head of one of the most important families in the town (19:239). He appears to have been baptized early in 1639 and although eleven people in his longhouse died of smallpox in the months that followed (19:211), he continued to profess to be a Christian; although at one point he yielded to his wife's demands and permitted Huron curing rituals to be performed for one of his daughters, who subsequently died (19:243–45). By 1640 Tsondihwané was recognized as the leader of the Ossossané congregation. In the absence of the missionaries, he kept the key to their chapel and conducted the prayers that were said there (21:159). In the autumn of 1642 he went hunting with his eldest son and while they were away he persuaded him to become a Christian (26:249–51). Tsondihwané was noted for his zeal in visiting the sick, instructing Christians, preaching to non-Christians, and saying long private prayers (23:77–81; 29:287–91).

Another convert was Charles Tsondatsaa, a relative of Chihwatenha and the son of Anenkhiondic, the principal headman of the Attignawantan (20:215). Although he was the leader of an important curing society, before the smallpox epidemic he had expressed a desire to become a Christian and during the epidemic he had permitted his relatives and even his own children to be baptized (20:215). In the spring of 1641 Tsondatsaa burned his hunting charms and publicly renounced the customs of his ancestors, but the Jesuits preferred to test his faith further before baptizing him (20:215–17). When he accompanied Father Brébeuf to Quebec in 1641, Montmagny publicly interceded on his behalf (no doubt following prior arrangement with the Jesuits) and he was baptized at Sillery on 26 June (20:217–31). After returning home Tsondatsaa insisted that his wife should allow herself to be baptized (20:225) and by 1642 there were twelve Christians living in his longhouse (23:93). Tsondatsaa appears to have gone each year to trade with the French. In 1642 he was attacked by the Mohawk and lost not only all of his trade goods but also a brother and son who were travelling with him (26:219). It must have been to avenge them that Tsondatsaa joined the Huron war party that went to the St. Lawrence Valley in 1644 (26:65).

About 1643 an important headman named Hotiaouitaentonk became a Christian (30:75). He too appears to have been a fur trader. The conversion of some of the principal inhabitants of Ossossané disposed many Huron to follow their example and eventually a number of whole families were converted. One man who was ill persuaded first his daughter and then a son to be converted. This, in turn, induced their mother to be baptized. Soon after, an entire family requested to be baptized at one time (26:223–25). These examples indicate the strong role that family loyalty played in the spread of Christianity.

Prior to 1642 Christianity made little progress in Teanaostaiaé (21:175). One of the few Huron who had been baptized before or during the smallpox epidemic and who continued to profess to be a Christian was an old woman Marie Outenen (23:121–23). Of greater importance was the family of Etienne Totiri. In the winter of 1641–42 they invited the Jesuits to construct a chapel at one end of their longhouse even though this deprived the dwelling of much of its storage space (21:285; 23:135). Totiri was related to some of the most important families in Teanaostaiaé. His mother, Christine Tsorihia, had been baptized in 1639 (26:289), and the rest of the family before 1642. These included Totiri's wife, Madeleine, his daughter Catherine, and his younger brother Paul Okatakwan. Totiri became the guardian of the chapel in Teanaostaiaé and also a catechist and prayer leader (29:275). This encouraged both Totiri and his wife to be zealous proselytizers. As we have already noted, it was Totiri and his brother who carried Christian instruction to the Neutral in the spring or summer of 1643.

The previous summer Totiri had been travelling with Isaac Jogues when the latter was captured by the Iroquois. Totiri escaped, but lost all of his trade goods and did not return to the Huron country until the following spring (26:259–61). In September 1643 he visited the Jesuits before leaving to avenge the attack of the previous year (26:291). Saouenhati was another individual who prior to the smallpox epidemic had professed the desire to become a Christian; however, during the epidemic he renounced such interests in order to avoid persecution. By 1642 he began to live like a Christian and claimed that he had never lost his faith in Christianity (23:139). In 1642 Saouenhati spent about a month in the hospital at Sainte-Marie and soon after this he was slain by the Iroquois while gathering hemp with other people from Teanaostaiaé (26:203–5; 23:241).

In 1642 the Jesuits greatly strengthened their position in Teanaostaiaé by baptizing a number of important residents. The most important was the forty-year-old warrior Ahatsistari (23:25). Ahatsistari had requested baptism in the spring of 1639, but at that time he had refused to give up certain practices of which the Jesuits disapproved (23:27). It is possible that his greater willingness to meet Jesuit demands by 1642 was the result of his desire to obtain a gun. Whatever his motives, he convinced the Jesuits of his sincerity and was baptized at Sainte-Marie on the Saturday preceding Easter. After Easter, Ahatsistari went to war against the Iroquois; he then travelled to Quebec with Totiri, Teondechoren, Tsondatsaa, and a number of other companions. On the way home he was captured by the Mohawk and tortured to death.

Ahatsistari's brief career as a Christian was important for the development of the Huron mission. Because he was a famous warrior, many young men were encouraged to become Christians. His conversion thus accorded social respectability to a trend that was already nurtured by the desire of these men to obtain guns. After he was slain, many of his companions were inspired to convert so that they would not be separated from him after death. Among these was his close friend Tehoachiakwan, who also lived in Teanaostaiaé. He was a famous warrior and one of the principal headmen of the Wenroronon who were living among the Huron. Tehoachiakwan had promised Ahatsistari that eventually he would become a Christian and rather than turning against the Jesuits when Ahatsistari was killed, his desire to be reunited with his friend after death led him to seek baptism immediately (26:293). Tehoachiakwan's baptism encouraged many Wenroronon to follow his example.

Of no less importance were the conversions of an important headman named Tsondakwa and his sister Andiora.[13] Since 1639 the Jesuits had stayed in Tsondakwa's longhouse when they visited Teanaostaiaé; although they would have preferred to live with Etienne Totiri in order to be near their chapel, they believed Tsondakwa's support to be of such importance that they dared not reject his hospitality (23:241). Tsondakwa had always professed friendship for the French, but being a headman he had refused to give up the responsibility for directing the traditional rituals for which his office made him responsible. He also refused to become a Christian because he did not want to be cut off after death from friends and relatives who were not Christians (26:265–269). In the autumn of 1642 he was with Thomas Saouenhati when the latter was killed by the Iroquois. Tsondakwa's desire not to be separated from Saouenhati after death finally led him to become a Christian and adopt his dead friend's Christian name (26:203–5, 265–67). After his conversion, the Jesuits were able to leave his longhouse and go to live with Totiri (23:241).

A clear example of the moral dilemma that faced converts to Christianity can be seen in the case of Assiskwa, a young headman from Teanaostaiaé. Assiskwa had demonstrated his sincerity to the Jesuits and was invited to Sainte-Marie to be baptized at Easter 1642. As he was about to enter the church, he felt himself seized by a supernatural force. He cried out that a spirit had entered his body and had ordered him to kill all the French since they were ruining the Huron people. He set off for home, but as he travelled through the villages of St. Jean and Taenhatentaron he burst into long-houses and went about smashing their contents. Since he was possessed by a spirit no one attempted to restrain him. When he returned to Teanao-staiaé he struck people and, when seized and questioned about his soul desires, he demanded that all the French should be killed. This statement released a wave of anti-Jesuit feeling throughout the community. Assiskwa then began to attack the Huron Christians and tried to break into their chapel.

When the Jesuits returned to Teanaostaiaé from their Easter assembly, they found that he had gone for almost a week without food or rest. Seeing them Assiskwa became calm, but for several days he continued to abuse them. Following this he reverted to his old self. He announced that the spirit that had been controlling him had departed and visited the Jesuits at Sainte-Marie to ask their pardon and to request that they proceed with his baptism (23:141–49). This was done several months later and he remained an ardent Christian (23:243). Assiskwa's crisis was probably only a more dramatic and public display of the doubts and social and moral confusion typical of most conversions at this time. In spite of such doubts, the baptism of several leading men in Teanaostaiaé within a short time played an important role in persuading other people, there and in surrounding villages, to follow their example (26:275–77). In particular, the Jesuits valued the moral example set by their lives and actions, which seemed in every way to live up to the Jesuits' expectations.

The work of conversion went on more slowly in Scanonaenrat. There were no Christians in the community prior to 1642 except Andehoua, who claimed to believe the Jesuits' teachings but does not seem to have professed his faith publicly. The Jesuits visited Scanonaenrat in the winter of 1641–42, but although they were listened to, no one expressed willing-ness to become a Christian (23:169–71). The first converts were the head-man, Paul Atondo, and his friend Okhukwandoron who had spent the winter of 1641–42 at the Jesuit school at Quebec. Following their return home, Atondo made a public profession of his new faith at a feast that he gave in his capacity as a headman. At this feast he renounced his former claims that the Jesuits had practised sorcery against the Huron. He gave further proof of his unwavering loyalty to the Jesuits after his niece died of illness and his sister was slain by Iroquois raiders. It was through his efforts and those of Okhukwandoron that a chapel was erected at Scanonaenrat in the autumn of 1642 and the village was made the centre of a new mission (26:293–99). These activities rekindled Andehoua's interest in Christianity and led to the conversion of Barnabé Otsinonannhont, who was one of the principal headmen of the town (26:307–9).

The Jesuits' work tended to progress more slowly in the eastern part of the Huron confederacy (33:141). At first considerable attention was paid to Contarea, which was not only the principal town of the Arendarhonon, but also the residence of the senior Huron ally and trading partner of the French. No doubt because of this alliance, both Atironta and his brother Aëotahon had requested baptism as early as 1641, although the Jesuits said they were not yet ready for it. Soon after, Atironta was slain and his brother was baptized prior to being installed as the new tribal headman of the Arendarhonon. The new Atironta was the first adult of this mission to be baptized in good health (23:159–61). His conversion induced many other Arendarhonon to ask for baptism, although the Jesuits selected carefully in order to maintain their standards (23:169). They erred seriously, however, when they agreed to baptize a shaman who had been frightened by their teachings about hell and had publicly thrown his charms into the fire. Before he was baptized he changed his mind and soon became one of their most dangerous opponents (27:33–35). In spite of their early successes, in the long run the Jesuits made little progress in Contarea and later the town was notorious for its aversion to Christianity (42:73). On the basis of existing evidence, it would appear that converting Taenhatentaron got started even more slowly than at Contarea (27:29). Eventually, however, a chapel and residence were established in the longhouse of Ignace Onaconchiaronk who was one of the richest men in the village and whose family appears to have been largely Christian (33:167).

Most Huron seem to have become Christians in order to obtain guns, more favourable trading relations, or other tangible benefits from the French, or to be able to join dead relatives in heaven; some, however, had other motives. A few converted to be able to refuse to participate in traditional rituals which required them to redistribute their possessions. Many Huron noted that Christianity made fewer material demands on a convert than did their own religion (23:129, 173), but very few consciously became Christians in order to escape from such responsibilities. Converts who did not find ways to compensate their fellow villagers for withdrawing from their traditional obligations found themselves in serious trouble.

After Onakonchiaronk was baptized in 1645–46, he soon found that the whole village had turned against him. Opportunities were sought to attack him and he was accused of being a sorcerer whom anyone had the right to slay as a public enemy (30:19–21). While the origin of this hostility is not explained, it undoubtedly arose because Onakonchiaronk was violating Huron rules of generosity.

When the Huron learned about Jogues's conduct after he had been captured by the Iroquois, many of them admired his courage and began to treat the Jesuits with more respect. All of the Christians who escaped from the battle were loud in their praise of Jogues and attributed their own safety to the Christian god (26:259). Those who escaped from the Mohawk country related additional tales of Jogues's courage. In the midst of battle Jogues had baptized the pilot of his canoe. This man named Atieronhonk later escaped from the Mohawk and, when he reached home, reported his experiences to everyone (26:187–89). After Bressani returned to the Huron country in 1645, the Huron examined his hands with admiration, noting where the Iroquois had cut off his fingers. The sufferings of Jogues and Bressani proved to them that the Jesuits were willing to suffer in order to live with them and that the Iroquois were, indeed, their common enemy. This, as Ragueneau noted, was a more persuasive preacher than all the words the Jesuits had uttered (30:69).

Although the Jesuits remained convinced that the consistency of their doctrine and the supernatural powers the Huron attributed to writing played major roles in the acceptance of their teachings, considerations of self-interest and of an emotional sort were probably considerably more important. As the general concern about the epidemics subsided, it again became possible for the missionaries to contact and influence Huron on an individual basis. At least a few converts regarded learning prayers and catechisms as an intellectual challenge and, in some families, this became a group activity (23:103). No doubt, these converts equated the learning of catechisms with mastering the myths and rituals of their own healing societies. Some Huron were genuinely interested in the theological content of the Jesuits' teachings, although these were couched in a cultural idiom that made it very difficult for the Huron to comprehend them. The Jesuits noted that the most intelligent Huron were often the hardest to convince of the validity of Christian beliefs (23:129). They also observed that the greatest difficulty that the Huron had was in understanding the notions of judgement after death and of the resurrection of the body (30:73). Explaining the former had been a longstanding problem.

THE SOCIAL IMPACT OF CHRISTIANITY

By 1640–41 the Jesuits had launched an ambitious scheme to counteract instability in Huron marriages in which one or both partners were Christians. It was noted that one of the main causes of divorce was a man's inability to provide the things that his wife and her family expected of him. Therefore, readers of the *Jesuit Relations* were requested to donate money that could be used to provide assistance to such families (Thwaites 1896–1901, 21:135–39). In some cases, perpetual annuities of ten or twelve écus were established with the understanding that Huron who were supported by these stipends should be given the Christian names of their benefactors. Although it is unclear how this money was spent, it was probably used to provide the heads of selected families with the trade goods they required. It was hoped that this charity would give the Jesuits sufficient influence to regulate the lives of the recipients and their families much as they wished. While this technique must have been effective only for controlling less productive families, according to Lalemant it resulted in the conversion of a goodly number of Huron (23:187–89; 27:69–71). Although this may be a pious exaggeration, we have here an early example of a later world-wide technique for enticing converts: "rice Christians."

The decision to live as the Jesuits required of a Christian must have been a very difficult one for any Huron to make, especially since the rationale for most of the rules that converts were asked to observe was not understood by them. The Jesuits now appreciated the important role that the traditional religion played in everyday Huron life and observed that it was more difficult to keep a Huron Christian than it was to convert him in the first place (28:55). The Jesuits also realized that the Huron depended on religious practices to cure the sick, ripen crops, and bring almost every kind of activity to a successful conclusion. In spite of this, to become a Christian the Jesuits still required a man or woman to renounce all of the charms and rituals that had hitherto provided them with a sense of security (23:185–87; 28:53). On a more general level, the Jesuits observed that the Huron had no concept of hierarchical authority nor did their laws permit the personal punishment of those who had committed crimes. It was concluded that this spirit of liberty was contrary to that of Roman Catholicism, which required men to submit their will and judgement to a law that was "not of this earth and is entirely opposed to the laws and sentiments of corrupt nature" (28:49–51).

The Jesuit missionaries recognized the degree to which Christianity was the expression of a coercive, state-organized society. They were, however, unable to transcend this limitation and search for a way to adapt Christianity to the needs of a tribal organization. Instead, while admitting that Huron society functioned well enough, they justified their own beliefs by concluding that Huron society was institutionally, as well as theologically, primitive. In order to provide the church with the authority required to enforce its decrees and to establish the punitive justice that Christian morality required, the Jesuits now foresaw that the Huron must be made to evolve some rudimentary state institutions. The implementation of such a scheme was impossible, however, until the Christians were in a majority in at least one large community. Until then, the Jesuits could only hope to restrain traditional practices among their followers.

When it came to providing moral support for their converts, the Jesuits were also not very successful. They vigorously attacked any reliance on dreams as guides to action without providing any other guide except an ill-defined and amorphous recourse to prayer (21:161–63; 30:43–45), which was also advocated as a general substitute for all charms and shamanistic practices. Because they still did not replace these time-honoured sources of moral support with more specific and more easily recognizable Christian substitutes, the Jesuits continued to undermine their converts' self-confidence. The temptation to have recourse to traditional aids was consequently very strong, and even long-standing converts required careful supervision to prevent backsliding. The situation was made worse by the converts' uncertainty concerning which aspects of their traditional culture were contrary to Jesuit teachings and which were not. Christian families would rehearse their weekly confessions before going to the priest, in the hope of sorting out such problems ahead of time. Most Huron seem to have been totally unable to distinguish between major and minor offences or even between permissible and impermissible behaviour (23:107–15). The result was uncertainty about even the most trivial actions. It seems certain that few if any Huron understood what Christianity as a whole meant to the Jesuits. They were attempting to satisfy the Jesuits by doing in a piecemeal fashion what was required of them.

THE DEVELOPMENT OF A CHRISTIAN FACTION

In order to protect converts from traditional influences, the Jesuits encouraged them to avoid contact with non-Christians as much as possible. As more Huron were converted, Sainte-Marie became the centre where, at the main Christian festivals and once every fortnight during the summer, large numbers of converts gathered for religious observances. At these assemblies converts would encourage one another and, under Jesuit guidance, would hold meetings to plan for the advancement of Christianity and for the eventual elimination of what they were taught to view as the paganism of their fellow tribesmen (26:211). A strong sense of Christian identity was also built up by the prayer meetings and church services that were held with some frequency in the larger settlements. In the absence of the priests converts acted as native preachers, instructing potential converts and leading public prayers (27:67–69). These meetings developed a sense of common identity among Christians and distinguished them from non-Christians (30:43). In an effort to maintain the ritual purity that was demanded of them by the Jesuits, Huron Christians broke many of their links with the rest of Huron society.

An example of this can be given in terms of its effect on a particular relationship. A non-Christian woman of high status wished to contract a ritual friendship with a Christian woman. This was an accepted thing to do, and as the friendship was greatly to the advantage of the Christian the latter readily agreed to it. The non-Christian sent her a dog, a blanket, and a load of firewood as presents and gave a feast to proclaim their new relationship. Later, however, the Christian woman and her husband learned that the non-Christian woman had sought this friendship after a spirit had ordered her to do so in a dream. As soon as this was known the husband returned the presents and repudiated the friendship on behalf of his wife. The Jesuits rejoiced that there was "no bond of friendship that Faith will not sever rather than see a Christian separated from God" (23:125).

As early as 1642 while they were gathered at Sainte-Marie a group of Huron Christians resolved, probably under Jesuit direction, that they did not wish to be buried alongside non-Christians in their village cemeteries, nor did they wish their bodies reburied at the Feast of the Dead (23:31). This resolution formally realized a desire to provide separate burials for Christians that the Jesuits had first tried to implement in 1637. By refusing to participate in what was the most sacred of Huron rituals and the supreme expression of community solidarity, these Christians were striking at the heart of Huron unity. They were also severing ties with their families and with other Huron on which their own sense of identity depended. In addition, they resolved that when travelling they would lodge, whenever possible, with other Christians rather than with their clansmen as they had been accustomed to do. They agreed to reveal their problems and difficulties only to one another and not to non-Christians. In this way it was hoped that the bonds of friendship uniting Christians could be made to exceed in importance all other bonds (23:31).

As early as 1641 groups of Christians were tending to travel together to Quebec, often in the company of the Jesuits or their lay assistants. By 1643 the Huron who came to trade at Three Rivers were publicly separated into Christian and non-Christian (traditionalist) groups. As might be expected the Christians played a prominent role in dealing with the French, while the traditionalists were reported to be decreasing both in numbers and boldness (23:267). Because of the shamanistic divinations associated with traditional warfare, Christians were also refusing to fight alongside non-Christians. When in the summer of 1642 a shaman predicted that Iroquois warriors would be located and defeated to the south, the Christians decided on principle that they could not seek the enemy in that direction. They set off by themselves towards the west. The Huron who went south encountered the Iroquois, but, lacking sufficient manpower, were defeated (26:175–79).

The Jesuits continued to forbid Christians to participate in any traditional religious rituals, which were a part of almost every public gathering or celebration. This resulted in physical as well as psychological hardships, since it deprived converts of most opportunities to eat meat and other delicacies (23:65, 187). When the Ononharoia was celebrated at Ossossané during the winter of 1641–42, the Christians met separately, not to guess each other's dreams but to state desires of a religious nature, such as to go to heaven or to live better. As everyone celebrating the Ononharoia had to pass through their longhouse, this was believed to be an effective means of disseminating Christian propaganda (23:103–5). Similarly, at the installation of an important headman an old man who was responsible for reciting the Huron creation myth, but who had become a Christian, insisted on reciting the Christian one instead. When the headman who was in charge of the investiture heard this, he requested the old man to stop and began to recite the traditional myth himself. After listening for a while the old man told the headman to be silent and denounced the traditional myth as a lie (30:61–63). Such attacks on cherished beliefs, combined with a refusal to participate in celebrations and curing rituals, emphasized the growing rift between Huron Christians and those who remained faithful to Huron traditions.

The increasingly frequent conversions of high ranking Huron posed crucial political problems. The Jesuits observed that to be a headman and a Christian was a contradiction in terms, since the principal duties of a

headman consisted of "obeying the Devil, presiding over hellish ceremonies, and exhorting young people to dances, feasts, and most infamous
lewdness" (23:185). Most headmen who became Christians seem to have
tried to avoid such duties (23:109), which must have made the management of the country more difficult; however, when Assiskwa became a
Christian he insisted on resigning his public office so as to break all of his
connections with curing rituals (23:243). Yet, from all appearances, he
continued to wield considerable influence in his village. Another headman,
who is described as being one of the highest rank in the whole country, also
renounced his office rather than participate in a non-Christian ritual. This
led to a political crisis which it was feared might split his community apart.
Finally an agreement was worked out, whereby the Christian continued to
be a headman and to administer public affairs, while a deputy was appointed
to take charge of traditional religious matters (28:87–89). This must have
seemed a great victory to the Jesuits, as it set a precedent for separating
political power from traditional religious beliefs. For the still small
Christian community it represented further isolation from the majority of
their people, while to the Huron as a whole it signified the erosion of their
traditional culture and increasing social disintegration.

Until 1645 the zeal of Christian converts had largely confined itself to
the longhouses of Christians and to separate assemblies. The Jesuits had
persuaded converts to wear rosaries around their necks as a sign of their
faith (26:287), but, in general, the Christians had avoided antagonizing
their neighbours by a too public display of their new beliefs and practices.
By 1645, however, the Christians felt sufficiently numerous and influential
to abandon this façade. Since the 1630s most Huron had opposed the
baptism of Iroquois prisoners, either because they believed that their souls
should not be allowed to go to heaven or because they objected to the
Jesuits showing any friendship for the Iroquois. Hence the Jesuits often
found themselves objects of public abuse when they persisted in such
endeavours and the Huron expressed their resentment by torturing the
prisoners more cruelly (21:169–71; 23:33–35; 26:179–81). Converts
sometimes attempted to help the Jesuits, as Anne Outennen did when she
secretly went to a family that had adopted a prisoner and offered them an
iron axe if they would permit him to be baptized (29:269–71). In general,
however, converts were frightened to aid the Jesuits publicly, lest they be
thought traitors.

In 1645–46 Totiri broke with this attitude when he attended the torture
of a prisoner at Taenhatentaron. After the prisoner had been tortured for
some time, he began to proclaim publicly that here one could see a

demonstration of the eternal fate of non-Christians and in spite of pushing and many insults, he succeeded in giving summary instruction to the prisoner and then baptized him. Many traditionalists who were present regarded Totiri's behaviour as evidence of madness or spirit possession and it was greatly admired by the other Christians (29:263–69). It is significant, however, that neither Totiri nor any of the other Christians dared to offend public opinion to the point of seeking to prevent a prisoner from being tortured; nor did the Jesuits regard this as a feasible goal.

The Christians also began to organize public processions, such as one held in Teanaostaiaé in which a large cross was carried from the chapel and erected in the Christian cemetery outside the town (29:275). Christians now began to make a point of praying aloud and in public in order to bear witness to their affiliations. They did this especially when they believed that it was likely to annoy non-Christians (30:53–57). While rationalized as a kind of martyrdom, the Jesuits must have hoped that such witness would help to undermine the self-confidence of the traditionalists. Christians also began to carve crosses on trees near the town (30:47) and to expiate their sins gave feasts to which traditionalists were invited. At these the penitent would testify to his belief in Christianity and announce that henceforth he would do nothing contrary to Jesuit teachings (30:77–79). The Christians simultaneously intensified their efforts to persuade their relatives to become Christians (29:277–79).

All of these activities strengthened a growing feeling among the Christians that they constituted a group set apart from other Huron. Seeing their numbers increase, many Christians became confident that the whole confederacy would eventually be converted and they no longer feared the ability of traditionalists to reverse this trend (26:255). Often they treated traditionalists who complained about the abandonment of the customs of their forefathers with contempt (27:69). Totiri summed up the factional spirit of many Christians when he stated that he was more attached to the Jesuits than to his country or to his relatives and vowed that he was willing to follow the Jesuits wherever they might go (23:137).

THE TRADITIONALIST REACTION

The majority of Huron were deeply troubled by the growing success of the Jesuits and the breakdown of their traditional way of life. They noted that since the arrival of the Jesuits, one disaster after another had befallen the confederacy, while the Iroquois who had no contact with the Jesuits and had not forsaken the ways of their ancestors were prospering (Thwaites 1896–1901, 25:35–37). In spite of this the traditionalists did not seriously consider killing the Jesuits or expelling them from the country. Individual Huron chased the Jesuits out of their houses (23:39), and in the winter of 1645–46 a priest in Teanaostaiaé was threatened with an axe during the celebration of the Ononharoia (30:101); however, the only priests who seem to have been in any real danger were Brébeuf and Chaumonot and this was because of their visit to the Neutral and their suspected dealings with the Iroquois. In the Huron country traditionalists, as well as Christians, took pains to protect the Jesuits from every possible danger. The reason for this was clearly their desire to continue trading with the French. This relationship had saved the Jesuits' lives during the epidemics, hence there was no question of it not being effective when conditions were easier and the Huron's dependence on the French was greater than before. However much the traditionalists may have resented what the Jesuits were doing, there seemed to be no practical way of getting rid of them. This allowed the Jesuits to undermine the traditional Huron way of life with little fear that the Huron would or could do anything to stop them.

If, however, the traditionalists were unable to express their strong disapproval of what the Jesuits were doing, the same was not true of their feelings towards their countrymen who had become Christians. The principal charge that was levelled against converts was that of witchcraft. This resulted from them refusing to perform various traditional functions that the Huron believed were necessary to assure the welfare of their community and of its individual members. We have already noted that wealthy converts were not only accused of sorcery but also threatened with death for refusing to participate in redistributive rituals (30:19–21). Christians were accused of endangering their communities by failing to join in rituals to avert the threat of crop failures. For example, in 1641 two women in Ossossané refused to obey a public order to burn tobacco in their fields and to stop gathering wild hemp in order to prevent a bad harvest. This resulted in a further proclamation by the town council stating that the Christians were causing a famine and in a general denunciation of these women (23:55–57). It was also said that rosaries and medals could be used to do evil, since they stole away the souls of those who looked at them as well as caused blood to pour forth (23:135).

The majority of witchcraft complaints were about the refusal of Christians to join in healing rites, including dream guessing. Frequently, these accusations arose within a convert's own household. A man from Ossossané, who is described as of no particular importance and the only remaining Christian in his household, was driven out by his relatives after the death of his niece who had also been baptized. These relatives urged him to renounce Christianity and when he refused they would not give him anything to eat. Lacking other relatives to whom he could turn, he was forced to beg for food and to do his own cooking, which made him an object of ridicule throughout the community. Men amused themselves picking quarrels with him and if he attended a feast, people would cry out that because he was a Christian he ought not to be there. He was said to bring misfortune wherever he went and people warned him that since he was a sorcerer, he must be prepared to die at any moment (23:67).

In Teanaostaiaé a husband and wife who had lived together in the wife's longhouse for fifteen or sixteen years and who had five children were both baptized. As soon as the wife's mother learned about this, she flew into a rage and persuaded her daughter to renounce her baptism. When the husband refused to follow his wife's example, the older woman ordered him out of the house and forced her daughter to divorce him. A young man who refused to renounce Christianity in spite of repeated promises and threats admonished his grandmother that even if he were burned, he would not give in to her. He clearly expected that his stubbornness would result in charges of witchcraft (23:127).

Shortly after Charles Tsondatsaa announced to his family that he had been baptized, one of his nephews fell ill, a niece became frenzied as a result of spirit possession, and another nephew was reported drowned. Some of his nearest relatives accused him of being responsible for these misfortunes and a quarrel broke out that nearly led to bloodshed. Tsondatsaa refused to renounce his conversion and, ultimately, all three relatives were found to be out of danger. Sometime later another niece fell ill, and her sickness was diagnosed as being curable by means of the dance of which Tsondatsaa had formerly been the leader; however, Tsondatsaa refused to perform this dance or to permit it to be performed for her. She too recovered (23:85–89). After Tsondatsaa refused to fulfil a dream wish for a friend, the friend invited him to join him and some other Huron in a steam bath. There, the traditionalists promised not to tell the Christians if Tsondatsaa would fulfil his friend's wish. At the same time they threatened to suffocate him if he did not. In spite of increasingly violent threats, Tsondatsaa refused to grant this man's request. Finally, he passed unconscious and the Indians who were with him rescued him from the steam bath (26:243–49).

Tsondatsaa was not the only prominent Huron who was persecuted by friends and relatives for becoming a Christian. When the new Atironta refused to allow shamans to attend his ailing son, his wife left him, took the boy with her, and soon remarried (23:165). This left Atironta unable to remarry according to the laws of the Roman Catholic church. We do not know whether this first wife died or returned to him, or whether some special dispensation allowed him to remarry, but when Atironta visited Quebec several years later he was accompanied by a wife and two-year old son (27:113). This quarrel demonstrates the bitterness that was generated by conversions even within the most important lineages of the confederacy.

Christians were also blamed for not taking part in healing rituals that were prescribed by their village councils. Sometimes the organizers of these rituals would tell Christians that the Jesuits had secretly agreed that they might join in them or would argue that by confessing afterwards, converts could obtain forgiveness for their participation. On other occasions, the traditionalists stated that the country was being ruined because the sick were no longer being cared for, and would plead with Christians to join in the ceremonies one more time. When such pleas were unsuccessful, the traditionalist headmen frequently became angry and denounced the Christians for conspiring to kill their fellow countrymen. Sometimes hatchets were wielded over the heads of Christians to frighten them into joining in traditional celebrations (23:43–53).

The leaders of the curing societies came to play an active role in persuading converts to renounce the new religion and sometimes were successful in doing so. Threats, promises, and bribes were all used for this purpose. The most strenuous efforts of these societies were directed towards recovering members who had become Christians. One of these was a woman named Andotraaon who lived in Taenhatentaron and was probably a member of the Awataerohi society. A headman who was one of the principal officers of this society informed her that at a secret meeting its leaders had resolved that if she did not rejoin their group, they would murder her the following summer. By scalping her while she was working in her fields, the killing would be made to look as if the Iroquois had done it (as Chihwatenha's had been done) (30:23). While the curing societies obviously had a special corporate interest in resisting the spread of Christianity, the members of this one were primarily objecting to Andotraaon's unwillingness to help her fellow Huron, which they interpreted as evidence of sorcery.

The shamans also had a vested interest in opposing the spread of Christianity, and were among the harshest critics of those who converted (23:117–19; 27:33). They were able to use their expert knowledge of

Huron religion to indicate how Christians were endangering people's lives by refusing to participate in the religious life of their communities. In this way they managed to stir up much hatred of the Christians (23:55). Sometimes, however, the Jesuits were able to undermine the resistance of these shamans by converting relatives, thus bringing pressure to bear on them to convert also (23:117–21).

The relationship between Christians and traditionalists was much affected by Jesuit demands that Christians should abstain from all forms of extra-marital sexual intercourse. The Jesuits strove to inculcate in their converts what in their opinion was an appropriate sense of shame about sex and although their teachings ran counter to Huron culture, they appear to have succeeded somewhat in this endeavour. As early as 1642 a fifteen or sixteen-year-old Christian girl rebuked her traditionalist companions for talking about sexual matters (23:99). The Jesuits believed that some Christian girls tried to appear melancholy in public in the hope that men would not be tempted to approach them (23:71–73). A Christian adolescent was approvingly reported to have gone into the forest and rolled unclad in the snow for a long time in order to stifle his sexual urges (30:39).

The refusal of young Christians to respond in what the Huron regarded as a normal way to sexual advances astonished other Huron. It was regarded as yet another example of antisocial behaviour with sinister connotations of sorcery. This was particularly so when young people met in the woods or in other remote places where their sexual intercourse would not become public knowledge and thus be brought to the Jesuits' attention. Christian men were reported to have fled from one village to another to make certain that they would not succumb to a woman's advances (23:63), while a girl told her traditionalist admirer that she would prefer to be slain rather than submit to him (26:229). Most traditionalists regarded such behaviour as folly and told the Christians that they were making a mistake to deny themselves the pleasures of youth through their fear of an imaginary hell. Those who were rejected sometimes became angry with the Jesuits because of it (26:229).

Sexual temptation was, however, clearly one of the weak points of converts, especially young ones. By 1645 the traditionalists were deliberately exploiting such weaknesses in order to undermine commitments to Christianity. Headmen publicly incited girls to seduce Christian men. The Jesuits viewed this as a serious threat and took comfort in the steadfastness of those who resisted such advances. They reported that one woman who had no success in seducing Christian men concluded that Christianity must indeed confer special powers on the believer and expressed the wish to become a Christian (30:33–37). Gradually, the prudery of converts seemed to undermine the traditional patterns by which young Huron met and came to know one another. One young Christian is reported to have asked his uncle to provide a wife for him, sight unseen (30:37–39).

The traditionalists collectively opposed the spread of Christianity in many ways. Christians were taunted and ridiculed as a group in an effort to persuade them to give up their religion. In Teanaostaiaé they were nicknamed Marians, because they were frequently heard invoking the Virgin Mary in their prayers (23:135). Children and adults were mocked that they had become Christians because they were cowards and were afraid of the fires of hell (23:97; 26:229). Among the children, such taunts sometimes led to fights and vigorous exchanges of insults between Christians and traditionalists.

Organized resistance to Christianity varied considerably from one community to another. In Ossossané, which was the oldest of the missions, there was little organized opposition. When the Ononharoia was celebrated in the winter of 1641–42, the leading men of the town approached every Christian separately and attempted to bribe or frighten them into joining in the celebration (23:43–55). When the Christians stood firm efforts at intimidation ceased. At the opposite extreme was Teanaostaiaé, where the communal persecution of Christians was violent and prolonged. The first outburst was in spring 1642, when French workmen arrived to construct a chapel in Etienne Totiri's longhouse. People began to say that the progress of Christianity would ruin the village and that converts should be made to renounce it or be expelled from the community. Even Totiri's kinsmen joined in the demand that he and his Christian relatives should leave Teanaostaiaé. One of the council chiefs warned Totiri's nephew that if they did not cease to practise Christianity, they would be torn out of the earth like a poisonous root; this was a stock expression that the Huron used to intimidate suspected sorcerers (23:133–35). Hostility against the Christians continued and rose to a fever pitch when Assiskwa returned from Sainte-Marie and demanded that all Frenchmen should be slain (23:145).

This hostility was renewed the following winter when the Christians, who were somewhat more numerous, again refused to join in Huron religious ceremonies. They were accused of practising witchcraft and thereby exposing their countrymen to dangers of war, starvation, and disease. The growing strength of the Iroquois was also attributed to the

Christians' public condemnation of the customs of their forefathers. Suggestions were made that a general council should be called that would require all Christians to renounce Christianity or to practise it secretly and without criticising Huron customs. If Christians would not do this, they should be expelled from the country; meanwhile, all contact should be broken off with them and they should not be allowed to attend any Huron feasts or councils. Public antagonism against the Christians became so fierce in Teanaostaiaé that the Christians were forced to consider ways of conciliating public opinion (26:279–81). When the Ononharoia was celebrated in 1645–46, a serious commotion broke out in the course of which several Christians were beaten and an old man named Laurent Tandoutsont was wounded with a blow from a hatchet. He had raced into the crowd, which was milling about the chapel, shouting "Today I shall go to heaven" (30:101–3). The same year the Christians were mocked when they formally erected a large cross in their cemetery. Later the children of Teanaostaiaé pelted the cross with rocks and filth (29:275).

The public opposition in other villages appears to have been less persistent and less well organized than it was in Teanaostaiaé. In 1643–44 a Kichesipirini headman named Agwachimagan wintered at Scanonaenrat and began to denounce the Jesuits and the French. At a secret meeting with the headmen of the village, he compared the teachings of the French with what he had seen at Quebec and Three Rivers. On this basis he found their teachings to be lies. Agwachimagan said that the real aim of the French was to destroy the Huron as they had already destroyed the Montagnais and the Algonkin. As proof he described a house at Quebec that was kept full of fleshless skeletons and lame, crippled, and blind people who had resolved to be Christians. This was his understanding of the hospital. He told the Huron that if they converted to Christianity, not one of them would be alive within three years. News of this warning spread terror through the town. Christianity was denounced and many who had requested baptism now decided to postpone it a while longer (26:301–7).

In Taenhatentaron the first persecutions of Christians are recorded for 1645–46, but they may have started earlier. Although they were as violent as elsewhere, they appear to have consisted mainly of individuals being threatened with death rather than of public expressions of opposition to Christianity. Headmen and leaders of curing societies played a prominent role in opposing Christianity (30:19–25). The late dissemination of

Christianity to this town, and possibly a lack of headmen among the converts, may explain the form that this opposition took. It may also explain why in autumn 1645, some of the Christians decided to offer a gift to the traditionalist headmen of the village, to induce them not to try to persuade Christians to join in customary Huron rites. When the Jesuits learned about this they reproved these converts, because they feared that this example might encourage traditionalists to attempt to extract similar presents elsewhere (29:271).

There can be no doubt that the development of Christian factions in various Huron villages gave rise to new tensions that cut across the segmentary structure of lineages, clan segments, and tribes. The traditional religion had helped to unite these disparate groupings and to assure the unity of the Huron confederacy. Moreover, until the coming of the Europeans, new rituals had supplemented rather than conflicted with existing ones. The exclusive nature of Christianity prevented it from fitting into this traditional pattern and its gradual spread created a rift in Huron society between Christians and traditionalists that threatened to cut across all existing social groupings. The unity of Huron society had never before been threatened in this manner and the traditionalists were faced for the first time with an organized threat to the Huron way of life.

Yet, in spite of these efforts to intimidate the Christians, there is no evidence that any Christian was killed or expelled from his village and very few of them were injured. One may conclude that the aim of these attacks was to coerce Christians into conforming with traditional norms of behaviour. What the traditionalists did not appreciate was that under Jesuit guidance the Christians were no longer sufficiently tied to the values of their society for coercion of this sort to be effective. Often the traditionalists found their own norms being used against them. For example, when the cross in the Christian cemetery at Teanaostaiaé was attacked, Totiri summoned a general meeting of all the people in the town and accused the traditionalists of one of the most heinous of all Huron crimes: violating a cemetery. This charge so troubled the traditionalist headmen that they ordered that hereafter the children should leave the cemetery alone (29:275–77).

While the majority of non-Christians remained attached to the old ways and believed that Christianity was responsible for most of the troubles that were afflicting them, the Jesuits noted, with considerable satisfaction, that a growing number of them seemed to feel that there was no longer any hope of resisting the spread of the new religion. The Jesuits believed that such a spirit of despondency and resignation would facilitate the dissemination of Christianity. A certain amount of evidence appeared to justify this opinion. Some headmen, when going through villages to invite people to join in curing ceremonies, publicly declared that Christians need not attend or even encouraged them to remain in their houses (26:255–57). In a similar vein a non-Christian woman, who became the guardian of a little girl after her parents died, refused to have traditional curing ceremonies performed for her. She argued that since the child's parents had been Christians, she must not be separated from them after death. When the child died she buried her body in a separate place away from the non-Christians (26:227).

By 1645 the headmen in one of the larger villages complained that the traditional rituals lacked the fervour of former years and attributed this to the growing number of conversions. Yet, instead of attacking the Christians, they went through the community asking that the converts cease to be Christians for twenty-four hours and join in the traditional rites so that they might be performed properly (29:273). One result of this growing lack of confidence was the tendency for some Huron to convert in order to emulate those who had already done so. An aged man at Teanaostaiaé sought to become Christian so as not to be excluded when his friends went to the chapel to pray (30:99–101). Another, named Saentarendi, was one of the greatest opponents of Christianity in Taenhatentaron. Nevertheless, when he was near death he inexplicably requested baptism and urged the traditionalists, who had come to drive the priests away, to recommend to everyone that they should become Christians (30:105–7).

NATIVIST MOVEMENTS

What the Jesuits paid less attention to, but which seem to have been important in the light of what happened later, were movements that aimed at organizing some sort of ideological resistance to Christianity. These appear to have begun to gather strength about 1645. Although little was recorded about them, their goal seems to have been to refute the teachings of the Jesuits and to reinforce the oral traditions of the Huron. One group of reports stated that Iouskeha had appeared to various people in the forest in the form of a giant holding ears of corn in one hand and fish in the other. He announced that it was he who had created the world and taught the Huron how to earn a living and promised that if the Huron honoured him he would bring them good fortune. He also said that to believe that anyone was destined to be burned and tortured after death was a false idea that the Jesuits had propagated in order to frighten people. He assured the souls of all Huron who were faithful to their traditions a happy life in the villages of the dead (30:27).

Two other stories attempted to counteract the Jesuits' teachings even more specifically. One stated that some Algonkin had recently returned from a distant journey, in the course of which they had come across the villages of the dead. There, they had learned that the stories the Jesuits told about heaven and hell were untrue; instead, after death all souls find new bodies and a more comfortable environment, but continue to live much as they did on earth (30:27). The second story was specifically anti-Jesuit. It claimed that a Huron woman who was buried at Sainte-Marie had returned from the dead to warn her people that the French were false friends whose aim was to capture and torture the souls of Indians. According to this story, as soon as this woman died her soul went to heaven, but when she arrived there she found that the French were waiting for her at the gate armed with firebrands and burning torches which they used to torture her. She learned that the souls of all Indians who converted to Christianity were treated in heaven as prisoners of war. After the woman had been severely tortured, she was tied down for the night, but someone who felt sorry for her had broken her bonds and shown her a deep valley through which she could descend to the earth. On her way she saw from afar the villages inhabited by the souls of Huron who were not Christians. There she heard singing and dancing in a true paradise from which all unpleasantness had been banished. Rather than go there, however, she felt obliged to return to the living to warn her people what the Jesuits were doing (30:29–31).

The Jesuits were unable to discover in what part of the Huron country this story had originated and it was unclear whether it was the report of someone's dream or a deliberate fabrication. It is easy to understand why the story became so popular, was believed in all parts of the Huron country, and was remembered years afterwards. It not only served to discredit the Jesuits and to justify a longstanding belief that they were hostile to the Huron but provided traditionalists with a highly plausible explanation of why the Jesuits had come to the Huron country. The story was also convincing, since the geographical proximity of the Christian heaven to the sun suggested to the Huron that it might be a place of fire (30:31–33). The Jesuits were thus compelled to face a popular rumour that equated them with enemy warriors lurking in the Huron country to snatch victims for their fires.

Conclusion

It is difficult to believe that the Jesuits did not perceive in these stories evidence of growing opposition to their work among what was still a majority of the Huron people. It must be assumed, therefore, that they felt sufficiently sure of their own safety (as guaranteed by the French-Huron alliance) and of the ultimate success of their plans to convert an increasing number of Huron that they no longer saw the need for caution in their dealings with non-Christians.

It is also difficult to believe that the Jesuits were unaware of the divisive effects that their mission was having on Huron society. Christians now observed Huron customs only when they did not conflict with their religion and this meant a growing rift between Christians and traditionalists about many vital issues. The mutual distrust of these two groups made political decisions more complicated and the refusal of Christians to fight alongside traditionalists lessened the military effectiveness of the confederacy at the same time that the growing hostility of the Iroquois made more fighting necessary. While the new factions that were developing among the Huron were not yet openly antagonistic, it must have been clear to the Jesuits that their work was not conducive to the well-being of the confederacy at such a critical period. They may have believed that their goal of converting the Huron was soon to be achieved and that a Christian people would once more be a united people; however, it seems unlikely that they could have believed that this process would outstrip the growing power of the Iroquois. The Jesuits must have known that their efforts to convert the Huron would multiply loyalties and viewpoints precisely when as much unity as possible was required. Their actions therefore make sense only if we assume that the Jesuits placed the conversion of the Huron ahead of all other considerations. The Jesuits may have known that it was impossible, under the circumstances, to be both a good Christian and a good Huron. Nevertheless, in accordance with their own values, they placed the salvation of souls ahead of preventing divisions in Huron society.

Chapter 11  The End of the Confederacy

The Growing Power of the Iroquois

NEW COOPERATION AMONG THE IROQUOIS

No later than the autumn of 1646 the Iroquois tribes began to coordinate a series of military campaigns that were soon to fulfil the Jesuits' earlier, and then unfounded, predictions that they would destroy the Huron. Prior to the death of Isaac Jogues, the Mohawk sent valuable presents to confirm their alliances with the other Iroquois tribes and to invite them to join in an attack on the French and their allies (Thwaites 1896–1901, 30:227). One of their aims was to harass, and if possible to destroy, the French settlements at Montreal and Three Rivers so that these might no longer hinder their raids against the Algonkin. They probably also hoped that by cutting off trade at these posts, they would cripple the economy of New France sufficiently to force the French to adopt a genuinely neutral policy in their dealings with the Indians (45:191). At the same time, the Mohawk, with help from the Oneida and Onondaga, intensified their raids against the Indians living to the north and east. Roving bands of Mohawk warriors took advantage of what they had learned about the distribution of Algonkin hunting bands during the two years of peace to attack and plunder these bands more effectively. There were numerous raids both north and south of the St. Lawrence River, one of which culminated in the capture of over 100 Algonkin south of Three Rivers in March 1647 (30:161, 227–53). Another successful raid was launched against the Algonkin, from the upper part of the St. Lawrence Valley, who had gathered on Morrison Island while waiting to travel down-river with the Huron. Forty prisoners, as well as a vast quantity of beaver pelts that had been collected for trading with the French, were taken in this raid (30:281–95). Hereafter, Mohawk predation in the north increased steadily in range and intensity for several decades. The Mohawk were also encouraged to attack the Susquehannock by the Dutch, who saw this as a way of harming their Swedish trade rivals (F. Jennings 1968:24–25).

By 1646 the western tribes of the Iroquois confederacy were better armed and more self-confident than they had been previously, although they probably still did not have nearly as many guns in relationship to their numbers as the Mohawk had. The Onondaga, who had formerly been the dominant tribe in the confederacy, became increasingly jealous of the growing power and arrogance of the Mohawk, but they, like the Seneca and Cayuga, were in need of furs. Thus they were willing to join in schemes that were likely to increase the volume of furs that were available to them. As has already been noted, the western tribes of the confederacy were surrounded by agricultural peoples. These other tribes engaged in the fur trade and therefore any attacks that were launched against them were likely to yield furs. Because of their sedentary way of life, however, such tribes were far more dangerous to attack than were the hunter-gatherers and semi-horticulturalists who were being attacked by the Mohawk. It was only to the north and west of the Huron country that the Seneca and their neighbours could hope to find hunters and hunting territories that they might prey upon as the Mohawk were preying upon the Algonkian-speaking peoples of Quebec and northern New England.

Possibly after discussions with the Mohawk in the summer of 1646, the Seneca adopted what seems to have been a radically new policy towards the Huron. Hitherto, they had been content to raid them for furs. These raids had steadily become more violent and had resulted in the destruction of a Huron village in 1642. They had, however, grown out of the blood feuds of an earlier period and, no doubt, had continued to be viewed as such by the Seneca. Now the Seneca decided to destroy the Huron confederacy and disperse the Huron people (map 29). Ordinary Seneca may have viewed the dispersal of the Huron as an act of blood revenge, but the scale and planning that went into it far exceeded any military efforts reported for earlier times among the four western tribes of the Iroquois confederacy. The success of this campaign depended on the Seneca securing the active assistance of the other Iroquois tribes and, in particular, of the Mohawk, who had the most muskets. Mutual self-interest therefore compelled the Mohawk and the Seneca to coordinate their activities against the Huron and the French.

It is not known precisely how the Seneca formulated this policy; however, their efforts to secure more furs resemble the methods that the Mohawk had adopted prior to 1609 to steal European goods. The annihilation or dispersal of groups that interfered with such activities was nothing new for the Mohawk. It is possible that by 1646 the Mohawk, in an effort to enlist more support from the rest of the Iroquois confederacy, drew on their own experience to suggest this policy to the Seneca. It is also possible that the Mohawk had been urged to do this by Dutch traders, who were anxious that the number of furs falling into the hands of the Iroquois should increase as rapidly as possible. It seems likely, however, that as the

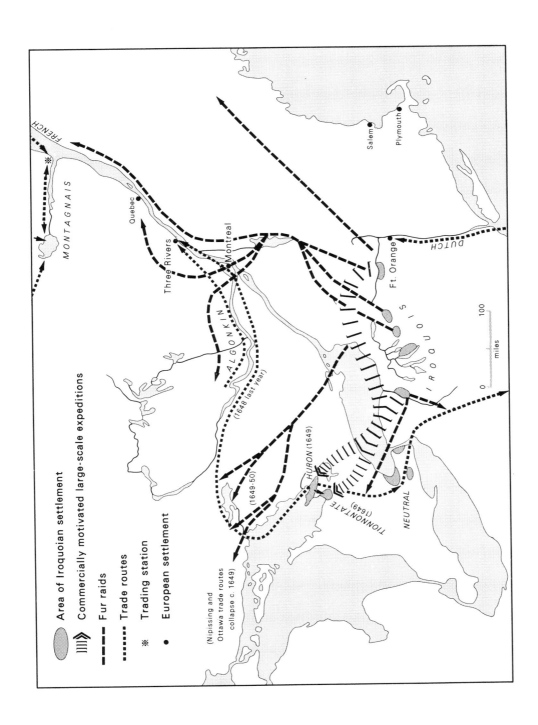

MAP 29. *Intertribal relations, 1648 to 1650.*

Seneca's need for furs increased, they would have sought these furs in the regions to the north and west of them. Therefore, any strategy for dealing more effectively with the inhabitants of those regions would have been carefully considered.

The crucial question is what the Seneca hoped to gain by dispersing or destroying the Huron. In keeping with his obsession with middlemen, Hunt (1940:91) has suggested that the Iroquois sought to divert the trade of the Huron into their own hands. As he put it, "It became evident that so long as the Hurons held the Georgian Bay–Lake Simcoe region they would control the northern fur trade. Repeated attempts to get the trade by treaty had failed, but there remained one way of obtaining it. If the Hurons were gone, nothing would stand in the path of Iroquois prosperity and ambition. The Hurons must go."

This explanation leaves vital questions unanswered. Why did the Iroquois believe it necessary to disperse the Huron, rather than try to force them to barter their furs with the Iroquois instead of with the French? Had the Iroquois been able to do the latter, they would have had at their disposal all of the Huron's entrepreneurial skills and been able to benefit from existing trading relations between the Huron and the northern Algonkians. Hunt claims that having already negotiated trading agreements that the Huron had failed to honour, the Seneca and Mohawk were unwilling to trust them any longer. This, he says, explains why these tribes refused to listen to any offers of trade that the Huron made after 1646.

This is not a plausible explanation, if we consider the broader context of what happened after 1649. It does not explain why the Iroquois attacked the Nipissing and Ottawa as soon as the Huron had been dispersed. These were the major trading partners of the Huron and if the Iroquois had been anxious to secure the Huron's trade for themselves, they should at least have tried to establish a stable trading relationship with them. Hunt implies that this is what the Iroquois intended to do, using force, if necessary, to compel these groups to cease having dealings with the French. They were foiled, however, when the Ottawa, encouraged by the French, began to play a role in the fur trade of the upper Great Lakes region similar to that played by the Huron. This does not explain, however, why the Iroquois dispersed the Nipissing and Ottawa without making any effort to negotiate with them or even to intimidate them. This dispersal destroyed the trading patterns of the Georgian Bay area, which Hunt saw the Iroquois attempting to control for their own benefit. Hunt implies that the Iroquois miscalculated.

But did they? None of the Iroquois tribes were located in an advantageous, or even a suitable, location to continue the Huron's trade with the north. Either the Algonkians or the Iroquois would have had to travel an additional 300 miles to trade with one another and this would have involved carrying heavy loads of furs and corn overland for half that distance. There is no evidence that the Iroquois planned to resettle in the Huron country; indeed, none lived anywhere in Ontario until some of the Cayuga settled along the north shore of Lake Ontario to escape the attacks of the Susquehannock in the late 1660s (Hunt 1940:140). This meant that if the Iroquois wished to trade, they had to have agents in Ontario who would barter with the north and re-sell the furs to them. Yet the Iroquois systematically eliminated not only the Huron but all the groups that might have played such a role.

The evidence thus supports the conclusion that the aim of the Iroquois was not to replace the Huron as middlemen in their trade with the north, but to intensify the warfare that they were waging against the Huron and their neighbours to the point of dispersing them. In the short run, both the Mohawk and the Seneca stood to gain by uniting their forces to attack the Huron and plunder their villages of all the furs and European trade goods that could be found inside them. In the long run, the Seneca stood to gain from the dispersal of the Huron, who hitherto had prevented their hunting and raiding parties from safely penetrating into the fur rich territories to the north (A. Saunders 1963:8–10). With the Huron out of the way, the Seneca could hunt in central Ontario and raid the Algonkian-speaking peoples around the shores of Lake Huron in the same manner that the Mohawk raided the Algonkin, Montagnais, and Abenaki. Because these northern hunting peoples were more dispersed than the Huron, they were easier to attack and thus seemed to be a stable prey that the Seneca could continue plundering for a long time. The violent attacks that the Iroquois launched against the northern hunting peoples, as soon as the Huron were dispersed, thus were not a mistake, but an integral part of Iroquois strategy. This strategy aimed to provide the Seneca and the other western Iroquois tribes with a northern hinterland in which they could hunt and rob furs, as the Mohawk were already accustomed to do farther east.

The substantial plunder that the Mohawk hoped to seize while helping to disperse the Huron no doubt was viewed by them as adequate compensation for helping the Seneca. To secure this plunder the Mohawk temporarily diverted their raiding away from the St. Lawrence Valley to the Huron country. In 1648 and 1649 the French enjoyed a respite from Iroquois attacks while the Mohawk mustered their forces to attack the Huron (Thwaites 1896–1901, 34:85).

The Iroquois's strategy was to concentrate their attack in its early stages against the Arendarhonon settlements, which lay on the eastern borders of the confederacy. Having destroyed these villages, they planned to press westward and attack the Attigneenongnahac and Tahontaenrat towns. Only after these had been destroyed were the Iroquois prepared to attack the Attignawantan, who remained the largest of the Huron tribes. In this way, they hoped to be able to devastate one or two Huron communities at a time while holding out promises of peace to the others, in the hope that the Huron tribes would not band together to oppose them (Perrot 1911:148). Even before the Mohawk joined in the attack, the deteriorating ability of the Huron to resist the Iroquois had produced a growing feeling of insecurity throughout the confederacy. By 1645 a number of Huron families had retreated to a remote place called Tangouaen, which was surrounded on all sides by lakes and rivers. There, on the Canadian Shield, they lived among the Algonkians hoping to be safe from Iroquois incursions (30:87).

NEGOTIATIONS WITH THE ONONDAGA

The Huron were anxious to find ways to counteract or turn aside the (to them) inexplicably growing menace of the Iroquois. Two events, which occurred early in 1647, gave the Huron some hope of doing this and led to a flurry of diplomatic activity that continued for over a year (Desrosiers 1948). The first event was the arrival in the Huron country of a delegation of Susquehannock who offered to help the Huron make peace with the western Iroquois tribes or, failing this, to help fight them (Thwaites 1896–1901, 30:253). The Susquehannock wanted to renew their alliance with the Huron because of the growing danger of war between themselves and the Mohawk. Just as the Mohawk and Seneca were coordinating their efforts for aggressive purposes, the Susquehannock were proposing to the Huron that they coordinate theirs in order to defend themselves better.

The second event was the capture by the Huron of an important Onondaga headman named Annenraes. He was one of a band of Onondaga raiders who were sighted on the frontiers of the Huron country early in 1647, and who were pursued and defeated by a Huron war party. The Iroquois who led this band was killed on the spot and the rest of the prisoners were tortured to death, but because of his importance Annenraes's life was spared. He continued to live among the Huron as their prisoner, probably in Taenhatentaron, which was either an Arendarhonon or an Attigneenongnahac town.

The arrival of the Susquehannock and the capture of Annenraes stimulated a fierce debate among the Huron concerning the policy to follow with
regard to the Iroquois. The Jesuits reported that the Attignawantan, who
had as yet suffered relatively little from Iroquois attacks, were strongly
opposed to making peace with them, while the Arendarhonon wanted
peace in the hope that their people who were being held prisoners by the
Iroquois might be released as a result of it (33:119–21). This difference in
the attitude of Huron tribes towards peace may also have been a difference
between Huron Christians and traditionalists. It is probably no accident
that the Attignawantan had the largest number of converts of any of the
Huron tribes, while the people of Contarea, the main Arendarhonon
village, were later described as having a strong aversion to Christianity
(42:73). The diplomacy that followed suggests that by 1647 a self-conscious
traditionalist faction had developed within the confederacy and that many
of its more active supporters had come to oppose not only the Jesuits and
their Huron followers, but also the trading alliance with the French from
which the Jesuits derived their protection and influence. The composition
of delegations and the political activities described by the Jesuits also testify
that the split between those who were for and against Christianity had
become the dominant factor in Huron politics by this time.

It is not unlikely that in their efforts to support the French-Huron
alliance, the Jesuits encouraged their converts to oppose any discussion of
peace with the Iroquois. On the other hand, the more active traditionalists
favoured such negotiations and also appear to have wished to discuss the
possibility of developing trading relations with the Iroquois. In this way,
they hoped to win the goodwill of the Iroquois. Moreover, so long as European goods could be obtained only from the French, the Huron Christians
enjoyed a great advantage and used this advantage to bolster their own
prestige and power within the confederacy. Trade was carried on only with
the French because the Huron, as a whole, feared the Iroquois and had
wanted an alliance with the French for military and economic reasons.
Now, a growing number of traditionalists came to view the Iroquois as less
of a threat to their way of life than were the French. The leaders of this
group sought to obtain European goods from the Iroquois in order to
eliminate the Huron's total dependence on the French and to counteract
the growing claims to power that were being made by the leaders of the
Christian faction.

In the spring of 1647 some Huron who were angry that Annenraes had
been allowed to live talked about killing him. Learning of this, Annenraes
had discussions with certain important council chiefs who decided to help

him return to his own country. These headmen secretly gave Annenraes a series of presents to convey to the Onondaga headmen and escorted him safely from their village in the dead of night (33:117–19).

Unfortunately, we are not told who these headmen were or what their motive was, except that they hoped that Annenraes might do them a good service. Council chiefs generally favoured peace and often acted in a circumspect manner when they believed public welfare to be involved, but did not wish to antagonize popular feeling. It is also possible that these headmen were traditionalists seeking to advance a factional cause. In any case, it is evident that afterwards Christians and traditionalists were still able to agree on a policy that was flexible enough that for a short period it offered both sides the hope of ultimately achieving their particular objectives.

The basis of this policy was a decision to begin, if possible, to negotiate a peace with the Onondaga, in the course of which the Huron would present gifts of furs to the Onondaga headmen and perhaps offer to trade with them. It would also be implied that if conditions were right the Huron were willing to extend this treaty to embrace the other tribes of the Iroquois confederacy. Those who wished for peace, to offset the growing power of the Jesuits, undoubtedly hoped for the success of these negotiations, while the Christians supported them in the hope that they might secure the neutrality of the Onondaga or at least their temporary withdrawal from the war. This compromise solution meant that it was unnecessary for the Huron to resolve among themselves the question of whether they wished for peace or merely to divide the enemy. The answer to this question could be postponed until the intentions of the Iroquois became clearer.

On 13 April the Huron dispatched their envoys to the Susquehannock. It is indicative of the power of the Christians that this mission was led by a devout Christian, Charles Ondaaiondiont, and that he was accompanied by four other Christians and four traditionalists. The Huron carried large numbers of presents with them and arrived at the Susquehannock town of Andastoé early in June. There, a number of meetings were held at which Ondaaiondiont outlined the problems that the Huron were facing. It was arranged that the Susquehannock should send envoys to the Iroquois who would urge them to conclude a peace treaty with the Huron that "would not hinder the trade of all these countries with one another" (33:131). The Onondaga were, however, the only tribe who were approached about this matter, the Susquehannock leaving their gifts with them prior to 20 August. While Ondaaiondiont was waiting for these envoys to return, he visited New Sweden, which was only three days' journey from Andastoé.

He was well treated by the colonists, but was surprised to learn that they were not Roman Catholics and were uninterested in missionary work. At the same time, he learned of the death of Isaac Jogues from a European vessel whose crew had recently visited New Amsterdam.

When the Susquehannock envoys had not returned from the Onondaga by 15 August, Ondaaiondiont decided to leave for home before the winter set in, so that he might tell the Huron what the Susquehannock were doing. He left one of his companions at Andastoé to bring later reports and with the remainder of his men reached the Huron country on 5 October, after making a long detour to avoid the Seneca. The latter had learned about his mission and were seeking to intercept him on his way home (33:129–37, 183–85). In addition to whatever official presents Ondaaiondiont carried from the Susquehannock to the headmen of the Huron confederacy, he brought 14,000 wampum beads that he had obtained in trade from either the Susquehannock or the Swedes. Thus for him it proved to be a very profitable journey. He decided, however, to give half of these beads to the Jesuits as a grateful offering for his safe return (33:185–87).

In the meanwhile, when the freed Annenraes reached the south shore of Lake Ontario, he met 300 Onondaga warriors who were making canoes in order to cross the lake and join a large number of Seneca and Cayuga to attack the Huron. The immediate purpose of the Onondaga was to avenge the death of Annenraes and his companions. Annenraes persuaded them not to embark on the raid, but to return with him to the main Onondaga town. There he conveyed the Huron's proposals to the Onondaga headmen and persuaded the tribal council to begin negotiating with them. The Onondaga agreed to do this because they were pleased that Annenraes's life had been spared and because they resented the growing power of the Mohawk and the dominant role that they were trying to play in the affairs of the confederacy. The Onondaga also saw a peace treaty with the Huron as a means of avoiding trouble with the Susquehannock and of assuring that if the latter went to war with the Mohawk, the Onondaga might keep clear of this struggle and force the Mohawk to defend themselves. In this way, the Onondaga had reason to hope that without destroying the confederacy, they might see the Mohawk cut down to size (33:123).

In June the Onondaga dispatched their envoys to negotiate with the Huron. They were led by a famous warrior named Soionés who was a Huron by birth, but had lived among the Onondaga for so long that he regarded himself as one of them and had led many raiding parties against his former homeland. The Onondaga brought with them three recently captured Huron and released them after they arrived at Taenhatentaron on 9 July (33:119). The Onondaga presented a number of wampum collars to the Huron headmen, signifying that they were interested in making peace. Their positive response gave rise to a new and more heated debate between those Huron tribes and religious factions who really wanted to make peace with the Onondaga and those who opposed it.

Ultimately, the opinion seems to have prevailed that it was best to make peace with the Onondaga, if only to divide the Iroquois confederacy. It was therefore decided to send envoys to the Onondaga. Under the leadership of Atironta, five Huron set out on 1 August, carrying valuable presents of furs in return for the wampum that Soionés had brought them. It was perhaps because of the reluctance of the Attignawantan to join in these discussions that the leader of the delegation was an Arendarhonon; nevertheless it seems indicative of the power of the Jesuits and of their Christian supporters that this man was their convert Atironta. Although Atironta was the principal headman of the Arendarhonon, his close ties with the French and the Jesuits made him a poor choice to represent the interests of the vast majority of his tribesmen who were not Christians. On the other hand, the Huron may have considered a Christian who was also an Arendarhonon to be an ideal choice to lead a delegation on a mission about which Huron opinion was so divided. Atironta may have been one of the few headmen acceptable to both the pro-French and pro-peace factions that were emerging among the Huron. Unfortunately, we are not informed who the four other members of Atironta's party were.

Atironta travelled to the Onondaga country in the company of Soionés and arrived there after a journey of twenty days. This was followed by a month of councils and celebrations, during which both sides proclaimed their desire for peace and the adjacent Iroquois tribes were sounded for their opinions. The Cayuga announced that they too were ready for peace and released a Huron captive with two wampum collars as evidence of their benevolent intentions. The Oneida also proclaimed their interest in making peace, in spite of strong opposition from the Mohawk and Seneca, who were bent on waging war. This division within the Iroquois confederacy suggests that in addition to rivalries over tribal rankings, the central tribes may have felt that in the long run they had less to gain from the expansion of hunting and raiding territories than did the Mohawk and Seneca. Under these circumstances, the prospect of getting Huron furs through trade or ritual exchange, even for a short time, may have seemed more promising to them than did joining at once in an attempt to annihilate the Huron.

After these meetings, the Onondaga decided to make peace with the Huron and resolved to send a second embassy to the Huron country with

Atironta. This delegation was led by an aged headman named Scandouati, and contained two other prominent Onondaga. To guarantee their safety, one of Atironta's companions agreed to remain with the Onondaga. The Onondaga took with them as gifts seven splendid wampum collars, each consisting of 3000 or 4000 beads, and fifteen Huron captives, whom they granted freedom. They also carried a promise that if the peace endured, 400 more Huron would be released. These envoys arrived at Taenhaten-taron on 23 October, having taken thirty days to cover the route because of bad weather. When the other envoys returned home, Scandouati and two other Onondaga remained with the Huron as a pledge of their people's good faith (33:117–25). From the point of view of all of the Huron, the main benefit derived from this round of negotiations was that the Onondaga had remained out of the war for the summer and there was hope that they and their neighbours would stay out of the conflict longer still.

In spite of these diplomatic gains, the Huron decided not to trade with the French in 1647. As a result of two years of successful commerce, the Huron had large quantities of French goods and were less inclined to expose themselves to danger than they had been in previous years. The Huron knew that the Mohawk had resumed their blockade of the Ottawa and Saint Lawrence Rivers and feared that if they attempted to visit Three Rivers, they would be attacked (30:221; 32:179; 33:69). This did not, however, prevent about fifty Huron from travelling through central Quebec to trade with the Attikamegue. This made it possible for letters to be conveyed between Quebec and Sainte-Marie by means of these inter-mediaries (30:189; 31:219).

The main reason that Huron men had decided to stay home was a rumour that the Iroquois were planning to launch a major attack against the Huron country that year (33:69). In the middle of the summer, a report that the Iroquois were only a short distance from Teanaostaiaé caused much dismay in that community before it was realized that it was a false alarm (33:99). A war party, reported to number over 1000 men, had, in fact, been raised among the Seneca, Cayuga, and Onondaga in the spring of 1647, but the expedition had been called off after the Onondaga and Cayuga withdrew their support. Later in the summer, the Seneca fell upon the Aondironnon Neutral. The Seneca stated that this was an act of blood revenge, although some additional motive seems necessary to explain the ferocity of this attack upon former friends. We have already discussed the possibility that it was an effort to secure much needed hunting territories, although Hunt (1940:90) and Desrosiers (1948:243–44) regarded it as a foolish act resulting from the Seneca's fear of isolation and encirclement.

Whatever the explanation for the timing of the attack, the Seneca probably viewed it as the first phase in a projected dispersal of the Neutral, which would give them free access to the rich beaver grounds around Lake St. Clair. When the massive raid against the Huron failed to materialize, the Seneca may have selected this single Neutral village as an easy prize, which would yield considerable quantities of furs and trade goods. That the Seneca decided so easily to rupture the longstanding peace between themselves and the Neutral suggests that rather than being terrified or desperate, they were supremely self-confident, as they well might be against a group that had neither muskets nor any direct source of European goods.

Events were to justify their confidence. The Huron hoped that the Neutral would go to war against the Seneca and for a time both sides were on the alert for fear of further attacks. War was not declared, however, and while the Huron continued to speculate that the Neutral were hoping to secure the release of some of their own people before they declared war, it is more likely that the Neutral feared to attack the Seneca (Thwaites 1896–1901, 33:81–83).

While the threat of a concerted Iroquois attack was averted for 1647, harassment of the Huron continued and seems to have been intensified. The effectiveness of Mohawk and Seneca raids increased as more Huron prisoners could be pressed into serving as guides for these expeditions. More Iroquois marauders began to be sighted around Sainte-Marie as the military situation in the eastern part of the confederacy continued to decline (33:75). In late summer 1647 a band of Iroquois attacked a Huron fishing cabin on an island in Lake Simcoe, killing four or five Huron on the spot and taking seven others prisoners. The latter included a Christian woman named Marthe Andionra. A man who escaped from this attack carried the news of it to Contarea. There, a rescue party was organized, which cut the Iroquois off some twenty to twenty-five miles to the south. In a swift encounter, the leader of the Iroquois war party was captured and all the Huron prisoners were rescued unharmed (33:91–93).

Minor victories of this sort were all too rare, however, and after the harvest was in, the Arendarhonon living near Lake Simcoe decided that their position was no longer tenable and abandoned their villages. Some seem to have sought refuge in Taenhatentaron, although the dispirited state of this town soon afterwards suggests that this community was also doubtful about its future. Antoine Daniel, who had been the resident missionary at Contarea prior to this time, was sent to replace Charles Garnier at Teanaostaiaé (Jones 1908:369); this suggests that the majority of people from Contarea and adjacent villages may have found refuge there.

Each family probably carried its own food reserves along with it and thus they did not constitute the same burden to their hosts that refugees from farther away would have done. Nevertheless, houses had to be built for them and it is unlikely that enough fields could have been cleared by spring to permit them to plant all of the crops they required. Since their hosts would be obliged by Huron custom to share their fields with them, this move must have threatened some Huron towns with food shortages in the coming year. As a result of the retreat of the Arendarhonon, the Huron gave up their control of the rich fishing resources of Lakes Simcoe and Couchiching and the Sturgeon Valley became *de facto* the eastern frontier of the Huron country.

THE GROWING POWER OF THE JESUITS

As the Huron grew increasingly uncertain about their ability to defend themselves, ever greater numbers turned to the Jesuits for aid and protection. When nearby villages were believed to be in danger, women and children often sought temporary refuge in the Indian Compound at Sainte-Marie (Thwaites 1896–1901, 33:101). Ragueneau estimated that between April 1647 and 1648, over 3000 people had sought protection and sustenance at Sainte-Marie, each being given an average of three meals (33:77). By March of the following year, an additional 6000 had done so (33:257; 34:199). Huron Christians naturally sought aid with more confidence than did non-Christians (33:77) and it is reasonable to assume that the Jesuits tried to convert any non-Christians who visited them. The growing danger also encouraged non-Christians who wanted to join Christian relatives after death to seek baptism. When Teanaostaiaé was thought about to be attacked in the summer of 1647, many Huron who had been indifferent to Christianity hastened to the village church and asked to become Christians (33:99). Under these circumstances, Father Daniel felt obliged to grant their requests. Yet, even though the report turned out to be a false alarm, the majority of those who had been baptized remained practising Christians.

In 1647–48 the Jesuits relaxed many of their more stringent requirements for baptism and adopted a more tolerant attitude towards numerous traditional practices. Their aim in so doing was to increase the number of converts and to realize their goal of converting whole communities. Unlike their early laxity, however, this action was a measure of the Jesuits' success among the Huron. It also reflected an improved understanding of Huron thinking. The superior of the mission, Father Paul Ragueneau, played a leading role in the Jesuits' reassessment of Huron customs. Unlike his predecessors, he was sceptical that witchcraft was practised by the Huron. He stated that after careful examination, he found no reason to believe that those who were accused of practising witchcraft actually did so any more than shamans were able to extract charms from people's bodies (33:217-21). He likewise doubted that the devil used the Huron's beliefs in dreams to lead them astray. He regarded their dreams as a natural phenomenon whose truth or falsehood tended to be largely a matter of chance (33:197).

On the basis of such observations, Ragueneau concluded that the Jesuits had required exemplary behaviour from their early converts that went far beyond the limits of what was required of born Christians. They had forbidden, as contrary to Christianity, many practices that were "foolish" rather than diabolical and anti-Christian, thereby depriving their converts of many harmless amusements. This prevented these converts from having everyday contact with other Huron and bearing a full witness of their faith. Ragueneau stressed the need to re-examine Huron customs and not to confuse what was offensive to the Jesuits as Europeans with what was offensive to them as Christians. Many traditional customs could best be dealt with, not by forbidding them, but by slowly encouraging the Huron to see their folly and hence to abandon them of their own volition (33:145-47).

While Ragueneau did not doubt the superiority of French customs over Huron ones, his policy marked a significant step forward in the Jesuits' understanding of Huron ways and in their taking account of these ways in their work. Yet this new toleration of Huron customs did not evolve as an end in itself; it was adopted as a policy to hasten the conversion of the Huron, at a time when the Jesuits felt that the groundwork for such an accelerated program had been laid.[1] Having worked until then to segregate Christians from traditionalists in order to protect their converts' faith, the Jesuits now judged Christianity to be well-enough established that their converts could be trusted again to participate in community activities, and even to assume a leading role in them.

Unfortunately, the Huron *Relations* are preoccupied with describing the rapidly developing political crisis and lack the detailed descriptions of the behaviour of individual converts that formerly were an important part of these accounts. Therefore, little is known about how these policies affected the lives of individuals. It is clear, however, that the Jesuits now heartily approved of efforts to reinterpret traditional practices in keeping with Christian concepts. For example, Christians who were dying were encouraged to celebrate an athataion, or death feast, at which they publicly proclaimed their steadfast belief in Christianity. The changing attitude towards the athataion is evident in the performance of this rite for a young Christian boy in the Scanonaenrat mission. When he learned that his mother was preparing such a feast, he asked her to stop, because he understood the custom to be among those that were forbidden by the Jesuits. Finally the boy's mother, who was judged to be an excellent Christian, had the priest in charge of the mission explain to her son that in its revised form, this rite was no sin (34:113). The child was later carried to the hospital at Sainte-Marie, where he died and apparently was buried in the mission cemetery.

These new regulations and the growing sense of dependence on the Jesuits as the Iroquois became more menacing, resulted in many more conversions. We have estimated that by the spring of 1646, about 500 Huron considered themselves to be Christians. The following year over 500 were baptized (30:223) and in 1647–48, another 800.[2] There were approximately 1700 baptisms in 1648–49, not counting the many that took place during the destruction of Teanaostaiaé (33:257). From July 1648 to March 1649, about 1300 people were baptized.[3] These figures indicate the degree to which the Huron turned to the Jesuits for leadership in the final crisis that overwhelmed them. By the summer of 1648 about one Huron in five was a Christian and as the crisis deepened, this figure rose to almost one in two. By 1648 the number of Christians in Ossossané, Teanaostaiaé, Scanonaenrat, and Taenhatentaron had increased to the point where people had to stand outside the village chapels during Sunday services, even though successive masses were said (33:141).

Another indication of the growing influence of the Jesuits was that in 1646 they were able to renew their work among the Tionnontaté, which Huron opposition had forced them to abandon after 1641. The Jesuits claimed that the Tionnontaté urged them to return (33:143) and the latter may have done so to develop closer relations with the French. The Jesuits were undoubtedly eager to continue this mission, which suited their desire both to work farther afield and to extend French influence among other tribes, who might be useful trading partners for the French should the Huron be dispersed or break off their alliance.

To make a new beginning among the Tionnontaté, Fathers Charles Garnier and Léonard Garreau were dispatched to Ekarenniondi, the chief settlement of the Deer group, in October 1646 (Jones 1908:361). There they began the Mission of St. Mathias. The following year, Father Garreau remained at Ekarenniondi, while Garnier opened the Mission of St. Jean at

Etharita, which was the principal village of the Wolf group and also the largest of the Tionnontaté settlements (ibid. 370; Thwaites 1896–1901, 33:143; map 30). In February 1649 Noël Chabanel became a missionary to the Tionnontaté at Ekarenniondi (St. Matthieu) (Jones 1908:380). The work among the Tionnontaté was considered sufficiently important that in 1648 a member of the royal family was persuaded to become its patroness. This no doubt involved extending considerable financial support to these missions (Thwaites 1896–1901, 32:137).

THE END OF THE TRUCE

Early in January 1648 the Huron dispatched another embassy to the Onondaga to reaffirm the peace between them and to present beaver pelts to the Onondaga headmen to counteract gifts from the Mohawk and Seneca urging them to resume their attacks on the Huron. Six Huron were chosen to make this trip and they set out with one of the three Onondaga who had remained behind as hostages after the rest of the Onondaga had returned home the previous autumn. The other two hostages remained behind, one of whom was Scandouati, the chief ambassador. Not far from Taenhatentaron 100 Mohawk warriors killed all but two of the Huron envoys; those who escaped are reported to have continued on their way. They also spared the life of the Onondaga hostage, planning to return him to his own country (Thwaites 1896–1901, 33:125). It is likely that these Mohawk warriors had been sent to intercept the Huron envoys and thereby to break off communications between the Huron and Onondaga, just as the Seneca were trying to disrupt contact between the Huron and Susquehannock.

It is uncertain how quickly the Huron learned about the fate of their mission; however, Scandouati disappeared from Taenhatentaron about 1 April and it was generally believed that he had fled to save his life. A few days later, his corpse was found in the nearby forest and it was publicly stated that he had cut his own throat. His companion who remained with the Huron stated that Scandouati had killed himself because of the affront that the Mohawk and the Seneca were committing against his honour by continuing to attack the Huron. He told the Huron that Scandouati had instructed the Onondaga who returned home the previous autumn to remind their allies that he was an important man for whom they should cease their attacks so long as his life was in any danger. While the refusal of the Mohawk and Seneca to do this might have affronted Scandouati's

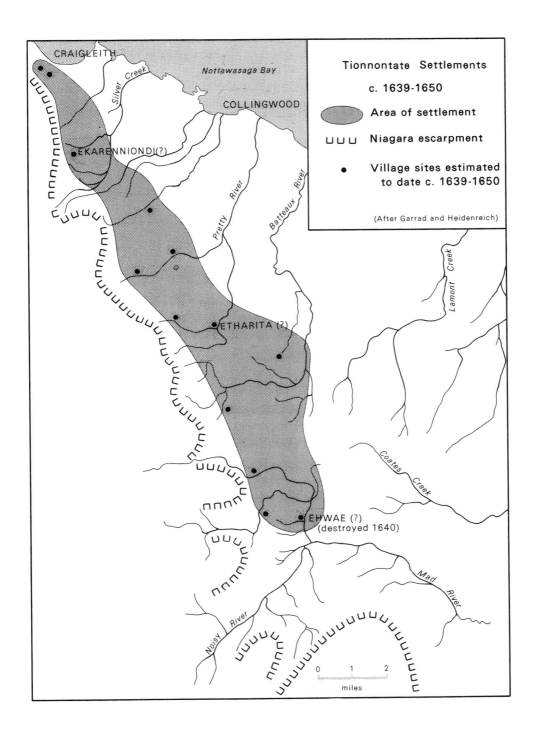

MAP 30. *Tionnontaté settlements, c. 1639 to 1650.*

honour to the point of driving him to commit suicide, his death (if it were suicide) more likely resulted from his conviction that as a result of what the Mohawk had done, the truce between the Huron and his own people was bound to collapse. Yet, even after he was dead, some Huron continued to hope that their negotiations with the Onondaga might continue (33:127) and they asked Scandouati's companion to absolve them of any responsibility for his death. Soon after, the Onondaga were once again raiding the Huron.

Scandouati thus appears to have judged correctly the effect that the slaughter of the Huron embassy would have. When the Onondaga saw that their two most powerful allies were not interested in obtaining Huron furs through the ritual exchange associated with a peace treaty and were determined to have them join in an attack on the Huron, they must have decided that the best way to satisfy their requirements for furs was by joining these allies.

Towards the end of the winter of 1647–48, a band of Seneca attacked an isolated cabin of Huron men and women who were part of a larger group of some 300 Huron who were hunting deer two days south of Taenhatentaron. Seven Huron were killed on the spot and twenty-four more were taken prisoner. Most of the inhabitants of this cabin were Christians and among those who were killed was a young man named Ignace Saonaretsi whom the Jesuits regarded as a model convert. The Seneca also captured the Onondaga who had remained behind with Scandouati as a hostage. He had been invited to accompany the Huron on their hunting expedition. When the Seneca recognized him, they treated him as an ally, but compelled him to join them as a member of their band (33:83–89, 165–67).

A few days later the rest of the hunting party from Taenhatentaron visited the site of this cabin to collect the bodies of the dead and to retrieve the deer meat that remained there. Being convinced that the Seneca had retired with their booty, they returned home in small groups. They did not know that the Mohawk warriors who had attacked the Huron envoys in January were still roaming in the vicinity of Taenhatentaron in the hope of intercepting any further messages to the Onondaga. These Mohawk had been in contact with the Seneca and thus knew what had happened a few days before. They therefore lay in wait for the Huron as they retired to Taenhatentaron and killed, or took prisoner, some forty more of them (33:89). The most important of those who were taken prisoner was Nicolas Annenharisonk, the only son of Ignace Onaconchiaronk, in whose cabin the Jesuits lived. In addition, Onaconchiaronk lost five nephews and a niece in these raids (33:167). One woman was captured by the Onondaga hostage who had joined the Mohawk. As the Iroquois made ready to return to their own country, he announced that he could not follow them, as his honour constrained him to remain with the Huron and his own people would not forgive him if he were to return to them under the present circumstances. The Iroquois allowed him to return to Taenhatentaron and to take with him the Huron woman he had captured. It was from her that the Huron learned the details of what had happened.

These attacks convinced the inhabitants of Taenhatentaron that the Mohawk and Seneca were planning to launch a major assault on their town. Because of this they began to disperse. Many sought shelter in villages that were located closer to Sainte-Marie and the Jesuits dismantled the chapel that they had established in one of the longhouses (33:89, 167). By the middle of April, the village was nearly deserted. Felix Martin and later writers have assumed that following the advice of the Jesuits, the inhabitants of Taenhatentaron founded a new village located closer to Sainte-Marie, where the French could more easily come to their aid. Father Brébeuf is said to have helped the Huron to fortify this settlement in the French manner. The site of the new community has been hypothetically fixed on the west bank of the Sturgeon River, near where it enters Matchedash Bay (Jones 1908:366). According to this theory, the new town bore the same name, or at least the same Christian name, as had the previous one.

The major objection to this theory is that the Taenhatentaron (St. Ignace) that was attacked by the Iroquois in 1649 was no nearer to Sainte-Marie than the original village had been; both were about two leagues distant and appear to have been located on the east bank of the Sturgeon River.[4] Thus the strategic advantage of the proposed move seems highly problematical. Bressani states that St. Ignace was impregnable in 1649, both because of its natural location and because of the defences that the French had constructed there (Thwaites 1896–1901, 39:247). This suggests that after an initial panic, when the inhabitants of Taenhatentaron fled towards Sainte-Marie, they were persuaded to return to their settlement by the Jesuits, who agreed to protect them against the Iroquois.[5] Presumably the strengthening of the defences of the town did not involve rebuilding the sixteen-foot-high stockade of pine trunks that already surrounded it, but rather meant the addition of towers from which French musketeers could defend these stockades. It may even be that when Taenhatentaron was originally constructed, its walls were laid out with such defences in mind, as had happened considerably earlier at Ossossané. Whatever aid the French provided, it seems that at least some of the inhabitants of Taenhatentaron returned to their town and planted crops there; however, by the beginning of the winter of 1648–49, many of the inhabitants again grew fearful of Iroquois attack and withdrew to other villages, leaving only about 400 people to spend the winter there.

The Defeat of the Traditionalists

It might have been anticipated that as the Iroquois pressed their attack against the Huron, the more radical anti-Jesuit faction would have become discouraged and cease to fight for their cause. On the contrary, by the spring of 1648 the wrath of a goodly number of the more traditionally oriented Huron had increased to the point where they were prepared for the first time to act decisively to put an end to the influence of the Jesuits, even if this meant breaking off trading relations with the French. The Jesuits do not identify the leaders of this movement by name, but it is clear that important headmen from various parts of the Huron country were involved in it (Thwaites 1896–1901, 33:229–31) and that they counted on support from many Huron in an open confrontation with the Jesuits and their Christian supporters. It also appears that the refugees from Contarea, who were now dispersed in other Huron villages, were among those who most zealously supported this movement. They had formerly been the most vocal in support of the peace treaty with the Onondaga and their behaviour at this time may explain why the Jesuits later felt such an aversion to them (42:73). The Jesuits mention that one individual who was very hostile to Christianity lived in Scanonaenrat (34:115). Doubtlessly men of this sort could be found in most Huron communities.

These ardent traditionalists felt strongly enough to challenge the basic pillar of the French-Huron alliance: the French demand that the Jesuits be permitted to live and teach in the Huron country. That they were prepared to do this suggests they were convinced that an alternative to the alliance with the French existed. This meant that they believed they could find an alternative source of European goods. While the Jesuits, not unexpectedly, have little to say about the activities or motivations of these people, it seems clear that they thought that peace with the Iroquois was possible if the Huron agreed to stop trading with the French and diverted their surplus furs to them. They must have convinced themselves that the Mohawk and Seneca had refused to consider earlier peace proposals because they believed that the Christian Huron who were negotiating with the Onondaga were seeking to sow dissension among the Iroquois rather than to make peace. Even the Onondaga might have sensed this duplicity and consequently rejected Huron peace proposals. The logical outcome of this line of reasoning was a conviction that the Huron had to make a dramatic gesture of good faith before their proposal would become credible to the Iroquois and be accepted by them. The most dramatic gesture would be the renunciation by the Huron of their alliance with the French.

The termination of this alliance was, of course, fraught with danger. It would deepen the existing cleavages between Huron who were Christians and those who were not and the expulsion of the Jesuits from the Huron country might induce many Huron Christians to follow them, thus reducing the numerical strength of the confederacy. There was also no assurance that the Iroquois would not take advantage of any weakness that would result from the rupture of the French-Huron alliance and attack the Huron more violently than before. Finally, the traditionalists must have known that even if they succeeded in making peace with the Iroquois, they would henceforth be dependent on their former enemies for all types of European goods. This was tantamount to accepting a position of permanent subordination to the Iroquois.

Yet, in spite of the warfare that had gone on between the two groups for many generations, the Huron and Iroquois shared a common cultural pattern; therefore domination by the Iroquois posed no cultural threat to the traditionalists. Indeed, an alliance with the Iroquois could be expected to strengthen precisely those aspects of the Huron way of life that were being undermined by the Jesuits. It is a measure of how threatened those Huron who were committed to maintaining traditional ways had become that now, for the first time, a respectable body of opinion had emerged which viewed an alliance with longstanding enemies who shared similar beliefs to be preferable to one with European allies who were seeking to change the Huron way of life. To be rid of the Jesuits, many Huron were now willing to gamble their very survival in an effort to secure the goodwill of the Iroquois.

It is unknown whether the leaders of this emerging anti-Jesuit faction had any contact with the Iroquois. It is not unlikely, however, that such contacts did take place, possibly through the Onondaga hostage, who was living with the Huron as late as April 1648. It is possible that the Seneca and Mohawk sought to divide their intended victims by encouraging the more extreme Huron traditionalists to believe that peace was still possible.

In April 1648 six leading headmen from three different (unnamed) communities decided to precipitate a crisis by murdering a Frenchman and then demanding that the Jesuits be expelled from the Huron country. To appreciate the significance of this act, it must be remembered that only one Frenchman had ever before been slain by the Huron. That was Etienne Brûlé, who was killed because he was suspected of having dealings with the Iroquois and then only after it was clear that the French had disowned him. Even in the midst of epidemics, for which most Huron blamed the Jesuits, none of the Huron dared to carry out the threats that they had made against the Jesuits' lives.

The six headmen persuaded two brothers to go to Sainte-Marie and kill the first Frenchman whom they met alone there. The brothers left their village on the morning of 28 April and journeyed over twelve miles to Sainte-Marie. Towards evening they encountered a twenty-two-year-old donné named Jacques Douart who was wandering near the settlement. They killed him with a hatchet and left his body to be found by the French. He was almost certainly buried in the cemetery at Sainte-Marie and his grave plausibly has been identified as that containing a skeleton of European type found there by Wilfrid Jury. This skeleton was of a man five feet, two inches tall and around its neck was a brass religious medal and a rosary of blue porcelain beads (Jury and Jury 1954:94–95). Douart had come to Sainte-Marie as a boy helper in 1642 and had become a donné four years later.

As news of the murder spread, Christians came from neighbouring villages to warn the Jesuits that a conspiracy against them was afoot and to offer to help protect them. The French put Sainte-Marie on a defensive footing and took out of service the ferry that ran between their settlement and the west bank of the Wye River (Thwaites 1896–1901, 33:247). Meanwhile, the whole of the Huron country was reported to be in a state of great excitement and headmen were summoned to attend a general meeting of the confederacy council which lasted for two or three days. It is not recorded where this meeting was held and because the Jesuits were not invited to attend, little is known about what happened at it. It is known, however, that the headmen who had instigated Douart's murder demanded that the Jesuits be refused entry to all Huron villages and that they should be made to leave the Huron country as soon as possible. They further demanded that Huron who had become Christians should either agree to abandon their religion or be made to leave the country also. The *Jesuit Relations* do not reveal whether these headmen proposed that the Huron should break off trade with the French and henceforth ally themselves with the Iroquois. Yet it seems inconceivable that they could have proposed the expulsion of the Jesuits without also advocating a realignment of trade and a solution to the deteriorating military situation. The Christians accused these traditionalists of secretly receiving rewards from the Iroquois for betraying the Huron to the enemy.

The contest between the Christian headmen and those who had instigated this crisis, or who espoused their views, was also a personal contest for power. Hitherto, Christian headmen had derived additional prestige from the importance that the Huron attributed to maintaining good relations with the French. If Christianity were to flourish in the Huron country and the French were to continue to discriminate markedly in favour of Christian traders and headmen, it was inevitable that Huron leaders who chose not to become Christians would suffer a continuing loss of influence among their own people. An alliance with the Iroquois offered headmen who did not wish to become Christians an opportunity to regain their influence and to undercut that of the Christian headmen.

Unfortunately for these traditionalists, the very nature of Huron society, with its emphasis on individual freedom and lack of any concept of religious exclusiveness, made the development of an anti-Christian faction impossible until Christianity had become a force among a sizable portion of the population. In the late 1630s, when the Jesuits were widely believed to be sorcerers seeking to destroy the Huron, it might have been possible for a determined group of traditionalists to persuade the Huron to expel them, had they been able to propose an alternative trading arrangement. At that time, however, there was no clear awareness of the threat that the Jesuits posed to the Huron way of life and an alliance that made the Huron dependent on the Iroquois was inconceivable. By 1648 it was a feeling of total desperation that drove a minority of the traditionalists to propose such a relationship as being preferable to tolerating the continued presence of the Jesuits. As it turned out, a majority of the non-Christians still feared the Iroquois to the point that they were unwilling to break off their trade with the French, even though not doing so meant accepting the continued presence of the Jesuits and the growth of Christianity. Many of the moderate traditionalists probably resented the missionaries as much as did the more radical ones. For them, however, there was no alternative to the alliance with the French. In the end, these traditionalists sided with the Christians to oppose the termination of the alliance. It was therefore concluded that public reparations should be made to the Jesuits in the name of the whole confederacy (33:229–33).

Once this decision had been made, the Jesuits were invited to the council. A spokesman informed Ragueneau that the Huron regarded the alliance with the French as essential to their survival and condemned the murder of Douart as a heinous crime. Only the Iroquois, he said, could derive satisfaction from seeing their enemies fighting among themselves. The Jesuits were asked not to withdraw from the Huron country and thereby abandon it to its enemies, but rather to state what compensation they required to re-establish normal relations with the Huron.

The Jesuits understood the operation of the Huron legal system and realized that only by conforming with local practice was it possible for them to re-establish a good working relationship with the Huron and ensure their own safety. The Huron Christians advised them that in order to protect Christians generally they must demand a large amount of compensation. The Jesuits therefore asked for approximately 100 presents, each worth ten beaver skins. This was the largest reparations payment ever recorded among the Huron. The Jesuits presented a bundle of sticks to the council, indicating the number of presents that were required. These were divided among the representatives of the tribes and clan segments of the confederacy and the representatives returned to their villages to collect what was required. As usual, the Huron vied with one another in contributing to the public good (33:233–41).

Towards evening on 10 May, a large number of Huron gathered outside Sainte-Marie and four headmen (two Christians and two traditionalists) approached the settlement to speak with Father Ragueneau. At the entrance, they presented their first reparations that the gate might be opened and they might be permitted to enter. Three presents were then given to Ragueneau to placate his anger and nine more which were meant symbolically to erect a sepulchre for the deceased. Following this, eight headmen representing each of the Huron clans presented gifts that symbolized the bringing together of the principal bones in Douart's body. In accordance with Huron custom, Ragueneau reciprocated by offering them 3000 wampum beads to indicate that his anger was abating (33:241–43).

The following day the Jesuits erected a platform outside Sainte-Marie, on which fifty presents were exhibited. It is possible that each of these presents was given by one of the fifty clan segments that were represented on the Huron confederacy council, as the first round of presents had been given on behalf of the four Huron tribes and the second on behalf of the eight clans. The Jesuits had the right to examine these presents and to reject any that did not satisfy them. Finally, a series of presents were given that were meant symbolically to clothe the deceased, erase the memory of his murder, and restore normal relations between the French and the Huron. The latter presents included one asking that Sainte-Marie be re-opened to Huron visitors, who seem on principle to have been excluded from the settlement since the crisis began. The last three presents were given by the three principal Huron headmen, either the tribal chiefs of the Attignawantan, Attigneenongnahac, and Arendarhonon, or, more likely, the heads of three Huron phratries. These presents urged the Jesuits always to love the Huron.

In return, the Jesuits gave presents to the representatives of each of the eight Huron clans. These presents were designed to assure the Huron of the Jesuits' friendship and to refute the rumours that the Jesuits were responsible for all the wars, famines, and disease from which the Huron suffered. They also exhorted the Huron to remain united and assured them that the French at Montreal, Three Rivers, and Quebec would forget this murder and treat them kindly since they had made reparations for it (33:243–49).

The defeat of the anti-Jesuit faction put an end to organized resistance to the missionaries in the Huron country and averted any danger that the Huron would renounce their trading relationship with the French. In the short term, the Jesuits had every reason to be pleased with the outcome of this crisis. A well-organized attempt to expel them from the country had been unsuccessful and a majority of the Huron had once again been forced to acknowledge their dependence on the French, and now more specifically on the Jesuits. Any danger that the Huron confederacy would break their alliance with the French and conclude an alternative one with the Iroquois could now be ruled out.

Fears of such a treaty, which would have diverted the Huron fur trade from the St. Lawrence into the Hudson Valley, had haunted the French for a long time. Although such an alliance might have assured the survival of the Huron confederacy, it would almost certainly have undermined the prosperity of New France to the point where the survival of the colony, and of the French presence in North America, would have been very doubtful. While the destruction of the Huron confederacy was to be a serious set-back for the French, within a short time they were able to put together the rudiments of a new trading network in the upper Great Lakes area. Whether or not the Jesuits realized it at the time, the destruction of the confederacy was less of a threat to French interests than its survival as an economic satellite of the Iroquois and the Dutch would have been.

In spite of this, the Jesuits' victory was not achieved without cost to the Huron people, as the Jesuits themselves must have realized. They urged the Huron to remain united so that they might better resist their enemies. Yet, the factionalism that they deplored was mainly of their own creation and the bitterness of those Huron who resented the spread of Christianity was no less because most of them also believed that their trading alliance with the French was indispensable since it protected them against the Iroquois. The rejection of the proposal that they expel the Jesuits at the cost of breaking the alliance revealed to many Huron into what a weakened and dependent state they had fallen. The majority of Christians already looked to the Jesuits for leadership and had staked their future on the Jesuits providing them with the guidance and protection that they required for their survival. This, however, was leadership that still had to be put to the test.

Following the crisis, overt opposition to the Jesuits' teachings declined sharply and many Huron who had formerly been outspoken in their opposition ceased to speak against the Jesuits and even began to pay attention to them (34:101–3). While the Jesuits rejoiced that the progress of Roman Catholicism was surpassing their fondest hopes, it is possible to detect in this reaction a growing feeling of apathy and resignation among the traditionalists, who no longer felt able to control their own destiny. Far from being animated by a new faith, many Huron apparently ceased to try to influence events and looked towards the future with a sense of bitter resignation. Numerous Huron who had supported the expulsion of the Jesuits were probably as prepared to see an Iroquois victory as to see the creation of a Christian Huron nation. Those who had relatives living as captives among the Iroquois were lured by hopes of being reunited with these relatives and, by becoming Iroquois, to remain part of a traditional Iroquoian society.

As the Iroquois menace increased, the Huron traditionalists split internally between those who were willing to throw themselves on the mercy of the Iroquois, or to find refuge among some other traditional Iroquoian group, and those who sought the protection of the French. Later, when the Jesuits revealed their inability to offer adequate leadership or protection against the Iroquois, many who had relied on their protection also sought a home for themselves among the Iroquois. As the Jesuits outflanked the opposition to their activities amongst the Huron, they found themselves responsible for a situation in which a growing number of Huron lacked the will to provide leadership or to continue to assume responsibility for the destiny of their own society.

The Destruction of the Huron Confederacy

THE END OF THE ATTIGNEENONGNAHAC

Because of their fear of the Iroquois, the Huron did not go to trade with the French in 1647. This resulted in considerable financial loss for the French traders and made them uncertain about the future. Their fears were doubtlessly compounded by new ones for the safety of the Jesuits, since rumours about the Huron's negotiations with the Iroquois were reaching Quebec. Early in 1648 it was decided that an envoy should bear the French governor's voice to the Huron councils to acquaint the Huron with the state of affairs in Quebec and to encourage them to come to trade. Conditions were so uncertain, however, that the messenger was given further orders that when he arrived in the Huron country, he should obtain Father Ragueneau's permission before saying or doing anything. The man chosen for this job, a soldier surnamed Chastillon, left Three Rivers in the company of two Huron Christians, René Oheraenti and Michel, on 24 April. A pinnace escorted them as far as the Rivière des Prairies and they presumably arrived safely in the Huron country (Thwaites 1896–1901, 32:69, 85). While this gesture may have helped to reassure the Huron, the necessity of obtaining hatchets, gunpowder, and other French products that were in short supply had already convinced them that in spite of the dangers involved, they had to trade with the French that year (32:179). By the beginning of July, many Huron men had left their communities and were preparing to carry their furs to the St. Lawrence or to engage in trade elsewhere. Still others appear to have gone in search of the enemy, no doubt in the hope that they might give warning of any impending attack. Because of the need to trade, the Huron were compelled to abandon their careful defensive posture of the previous year.

It was just as these traders were preparing to leave that a force of several hundred Iroquois managed to penetrate the Huron country undetected and to destroy Teanaostaiaé, one of the largest and best-fortified Huron settlements. They also sacked a small neighbouring community, probably the one variously known as Ekhiondastsaan, Tiondatsae, or La Chaudière (Heidenreich 1971:44). Both communities were Attigneenongnahac and Teanaostaiaé had been singled out for possible attack because it was located in the upper part of the Sturgeon Valley, which was now the southeastern frontier of the Huron country. The destruction of Teanaostaiaé spread terror throughout the Huron confederacy.

The raiders, who were well-armed with muskets, approached Teanaostaiaé on the night of 3 July. From some prisoners they had captured, they learned that many young men were absent and on the basis of this information they resolved to attack the town. Teanaostaiaé was located above the fork of a steeply banked stream flowing into the Sturgeon River; the Iroquois were therefore only able to approach it from the north (39:239; map 31). At sunrise, the Christians of Teanaostaiaé had gathered in the local church to hear mass. Scarcely was the mass over, when the Iroquois burst into the town and began to loot, kill, and set fire to the longhouses. In spite of the confusion, many Huron took up arms and, for a time, they seem to have contained the enemy. Father Daniel encouraged this resistance and, by sprinkling water into the crowd, baptized large numbers of Huron who sought this additional form of supernatural protection as they hurled themselves into the battle. At the same time, many women and children took advantage of this respite to flee through the various gates of the town and to try to make their way to safety.

Eventually, however, the defenders began to disperse and it became evident that the Iroquois would soon control the town. At this point, Father Daniel went through the remaining longhouses to baptize certain sick and aged people he had been instructing and finally made his way back to the church, which was full of Christians who had gathered there to receive baptism and absolution. When the Iroquois learned that a large number of Huron had gathered in the church and that much booty could be obtained there, they hastened to attack it. Father Daniel advised the Christians to flee, but he himself advanced to the front door of the church to meet the enemy. His appearance surprised the Iroquois, who stared at him for a time before they killed him with arrows and gunfire. They stripped him of his robes in anger because they had not taken him alive, and began to hack up his body. After the flames from the longhouses had set fire to the church they tossed his body into the burning building (33:259–65; 34:87–93; 39:239–43).

This diversion gave the Huron more time to escape. Although the Iroquois later searched for these refugees in the nearby forests, many managed to reach other villages and no small number made their way to Sainte-Marie, where the Jesuits provided them with food and clothing. On their way home, the Iroquois compelled their captives to carry the furs and trade goods that they had pillaged from the two communities and killed those who were unable to keep up with them. Of a normal population of about 2000, which was doubtlessly swollen by Arendarhonon refugees, 700 people are estimated to have been killed or taken prisoner by the Iroquois. Most of these were women and children (34:99). While more Huron

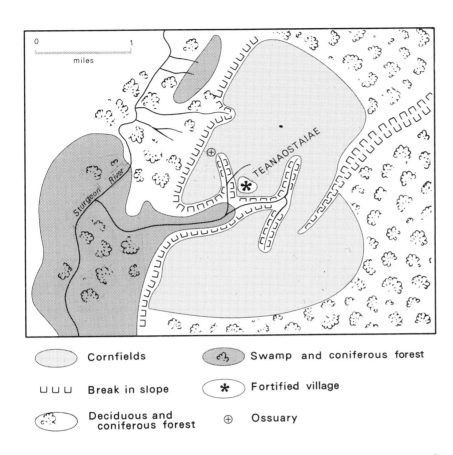

Cornfields

Break in slope

Deciduous and coniferous forest

Swamp and coniferous forest

* Fortified village

⊕ Ossuary

MAP 31. *Reconstruction of the field pattern and natural setting of Teanaostaiaé c. 1648 (Lot 12, Conc. IV, Medonte Twp.)(after C. E. Heidenreich).*

escaped from Teanaostaiaé than were lost there, the destruction of this one community cost the Huron about one-tenth of their remaining population. It was thus a very serious blow to the confederacy. Moreover, while Father Daniel's death again demonstrated that the Jesuits were willing not only to live with the Huron but also to die alongside them (39:243), it did little to reassure the Huron that the French were able to protect them.

After this attack, Teanaostaiaé remained abandoned. The dislocation of over 1000 Huron in mid-summer, when it was impossible to clear and plant new fields, combined with the general panic that seems to have seized the Huron elsewhere, probably accounts for the famine of the following winter. Since the Jesuits had no problem with their crops (33:259), drought or natural crop damage had little to do with this famine. The likely destruction of the crops at Teanaostaiaé and the fear that women had of going to work in their fields elsewhere would have used up the surpluses and cut into the essential supplies of the remaining Huron villages. Hunt (1940:94) has correctly noted the important role that starvation played at this time in weakening the Huron, but he was wrong about the reason for it. He argued that in the years prior to their destruction, the Huron had engaged so exclusively in trade that they neglected farming and obtained most of their corn from the Neutral and Tionnontaté. According to Hunt, the Iroquois raids of this period were sufficient to destroy the finely spun trading networks on which the Huron were totally dependent for their subsistence. The inadequacies of Hunt's theories about the decline of Huron agriculture have been discussed in chapter 6 and they do not explain the famine at this time.

THE TRADE OF 1648

In spite of the disaster at Teanaostaiaé, about 250 Huron accompanied by Father Bressani and two other Frenchmen journeyed to Three Rivers in order to trade with the French. They departed under the leadership of five headmen and, unlike most years, kept their canoes close together over the entire route in order to be able to defend themselves better. No Iroquois were encountered along the Ottawa River, no doubt because the Mohawk and Oneida bands who habitually waited to attack the traders as they came down-river were inadequate to challenge so many Huron at one time.

When the Huron came within sight of Three Rivers, they anchored their canoes in the reeds along the north shore of the St. Lawrence to paint their faces and grease their hair so as to be suitably attired to meet the French. Some Huron who were acting as scouts were sighted by Iroquois lurking on the opposite bank of the St. Lawrence. The latter crossed the river in force to attack the Huron. The Huron's forward guard observed what was happening and before the Iroquois arrived, the Huron had time to seize their weapons and form a semi-circle in the woods around the spot where the Iroquois were landing. The Iroquois charged the Huron line, firing their muskets. The Huron escaped injury by dropping to the ground; then, as the Iroquois charged, the Huron rose and fired their guns at them. The Iroquois broke up in confusion, some fighting their way through the Huron line. The more agile Huron pursued these refugees, killing and scalping some and taking others prisoners (Thwaites 1896–1901, 32:179–83). The desire to reach Three Rivers prevented the Huron from pursuing the

Iroquois as relentlessly as they might have done, but the extent of their victory is indicated by the fact that in addition to the ten or fifteen Iroquois who were killed (32:97), eighteen to twenty more were taken prisoner (32:179). One Iroquois was so frightened that he made his way to Montreal, where he voluntarily surrendered himself to a French woman in the court-yard of the hospital (32:183). Another, however, when he saw his brother taken prisoner, made his way to Three Rivers and surrendered to the Huron. He did this because he had promised never to abandon this brother (33:43–45).

After the battle was over, the Huron took their prisoners into their canoes and ordered them to sing as they approached Three Rivers. When they landed, the Christians, who made up about half of the expedition, forced the prisoners to kneel with them before a cross that had been erected at the gate of the fort. This was done to make them apologize for having broken down a cross that the French had set up near the mouth of the Richelieu River (33:45). The prisoners were then made to ascend a scaffold and one of them was given to the Algonkin, who killed him, but without torture, so as not to anger the French. A Huron who had become naturalized among the Iroquois was tortured to death; to mollify the French, it was pointed out that he was a heretic who had been baptized but had abandoned the Christian religion after he had been adopted by the Iroquois (32:185). The other prisoners apparently were kept by the Huron and eventually were taken home with them.

The Huron reached Three Rivers between 17 and 22 July (32:97, 173–75), and, soon after, Montmagny arrived to attend the annual re-affirmation of the French-Huron alliance. The Huron offered their tradi-tional presents to salute him and request that the price of trade goods be reduced. Then, two extra presents were given to thank the Jesuits for exposing themselves to so many dangers to carry out their mission work and to urge them to persevere in the propagation of Christianity among the Huron (32:185–87). While these presents undoubtedly reflect the growing influence of the Christian faction, they were also an elliptical request for protection against the Iroquois. So long as the Jesuits continued to live among the Huron, the latter felt assured that the French would do all in their power to protect the Huron. Montmagny gave the Huron presents to assure them that the French at Quebec no longer sought revenge for the murder of Douart, since the Huron had atoned for this murder according to the laws of their country (32:187). For the Huron, these presents marked the formal end of the Douart affair. Montmagny also required the Huron to keep their promise to listen to the Jesuits. The Huron traders were given an escort of eight soldiers, who were to remain at Sainte-Marie over the winter. They were to defend the settlement and possibly to help with the fortifications that were being constructed there. The soldiers were to return to Quebec the following summer with the Huron traders (33:253).

The French also dispatched to the Huron country four missionaries newly arrived from France, Gabriel Lalemant (nephew of Jérôme), Jacques Bonin, Adrien Greslon, and Adrien Daran; one lay brother, Nicolas Noircler; nine workmen; and three boys (32:99). Four more soldiers were to be picked up at Montreal, although these do not appear to have reached the Huron country (33:253). The French also took with them large quantities of supplies to replenish Sainte-Marie. These included a heifer and a small cannon. They left Three Rivers on 6 August. After reaching Montreal Island, some proceeded up the Rivière des Prairies, while others visited Ville-Marie seeking the four soldiers that had been promised them. The French feared that this splitting of the Huron convoy would expose them to attack by the Iroquois (32:189–91), but all of the Huron reached their homes safely in early September (34:101). They were jubilant about their victory over the Iroquois and their successful trade.

NEW TROUBLE ON THE ST. LAWRENCE

What must have pleased the returning Huron far less was their discovery that the French had again been discussing peace with the Mohawk. These discussions had begun on 18 May, when two Iroquois canoes arrived at Montreal. Their occupants had reiterated the longstanding Mohawk offer to make peace with the French, provided the latter would let them wage war on the Algonkians, whom they described as their sole enemies. Their main aim seems to have been to secure the release of a Mohawk who had been taken prisoner by the French the previous autumn. This man, who was believed to have slain Jogues, had remained behind to aid his wounded brother. What the Mohawk did not know was that this prisoner had been taken to Sillery, where Montmagny had turned him over to the resident Indians. The latter had slain him shortly after he was baptized in October 1647 (Thwaites 1896–1901, 32:19–27).

The French were anxious to recover two of their own men, but finally they had to admit that their Mohawk prisoner was dead. The Mohawk claimed not to be upset by this news and announced that soon some of the oldest and most prominent of their headmen would be coming to Montreal to confer with the French. Yet, at the same time a Frenchman who had gone hunting near Montreal was attacked by an Iroquois and the nets that the French had set in the river near the fort were carried off by the departing "peace mission" (32:143–49).

On 30 May a Mohawk and a Huron who had been adopted by the Mohawk voluntarily surrendered to a party of Frenchmen who were fishing opposite Three Rivers. The three other Iroquois who accompanied these men feared to approach the French when they saw that the latter were accompanied by their Huron and Algonkin allies. They tried to flee, but one was overtaken by an Algonkin, who killed him and tore off his scalp. The Iroquois who had turned himself over to the French announced that he was one of the prisoners whose lives Montmagny had saved in 1644. He claimed to have been wounded trying to save Father Jogues and that his intention was to promote better relations between his people and the French. The French did not trust either him or his companion and put both of them in iron leg-fetters.

On 20 June twenty-nine Iroquois entrenched themselves on the south shore of the St. Lawrence and began to communicate with Three Rivers. At first they claimed to number about 400 and to have with them headmen who wished to discuss peace, but later they admitted that these claims were untrue. After conferring with the Iroquois who was held prisoner, two more Iroquois agreed to remain as hostages with the French. In return, the French temporarily released their prisoner and sent him and the younger of the hostages back to their own people to urge them to negotiate in good faith (32:149–57). They returned soon after.

On 3 July the Huron who had surrendered to the French was given permission to go to Montreal in order to collect some beaver skins that he claimed to have left there. His aim, however, was to meet a band of over eighty Mohawk, who he knew would be lurking in the vicinity of Lake St. Peter. He told these Iroquois that the Mohawk who were held prisoner at Three Rivers were being treated badly by the French and were certain to be killed by them. This report incited the Mohawk to conduct a raid near Three Rivers, in the course of which a number of French and Huron were killed and taken prisoner. Not long after, the French learned that 100 Mohawk commanded both sides of the St. Lawrence near Three Rivers. They also learned that these warriors were confused by the conflicting stories they had heard from the envoys who were seeking peace and the former Huron who was spreading rumours that the French were ill-treating their prisoners.

The French therefore gave the oldest of the prisoners permission to visit his people, after which he returned to the French. The Mohawk warriors asked for food at this time, claiming to be hard pressed, although eighty sacks of corn were later found in their fort. While the Mohawk were negotiating an exchange of prisoners, they continued to harass the Indians around Three Rivers. Further negotiations were cut short, however, when the Iroquois, as mentioned above, were defeated and scattered by the Huron traders who were coming to Three Rivers (32:157–85). The Iroquois who had originally surrendered to the French was sent to France, where he remained in the care of the Jesuits. In 1650 he died of a lung infection in Paris (36:21–45).

The motive for these tortuous negotiations is far from certain. Possibly, the Mohawk were interested in trying once more to persuade the French to abandon their allies and assume a more neutral role in their dealings with the various Indian tribes. By now, however, the Mohawk must have been fully aware of the unlikelihood of this happening. The prisoners had likely been seeking to reconnoitre the defences at Three Rivers prior to an attack and were surprised when the French kept them in such close confinement that their intended escape became impossible. This compelled the Mohawk to negotiate for their release before an attack could be launched. Rumours had reached the Huron country prior to the departure of the Huron traders that the Mohawk were intent on attacking Three Rivers and were directing their war songs against both the French and the Algonkin (32:169). A Huron captive, who was part of the Mohawk band in the vicinity of Three Rivers, also warned a Huron who was living with the French that the Iroquois would soon invite the French to a conference where they planned to kill the lot of them (32:175). Not long afterwards, about a dozen Iroquois ambushed some Frenchmen who were working near Montreal and killed one of them (32:169).

The Huron did not comment on the negotiations between the French and the Mohawk while they were at Three Rivers. They must, however, have viewed the actions of the Mohawk as an attempt to separate the French from their Algonkin and Huron allies so that they might attack each of the latter more easily. The Huron had always been mistrustful of negotiations between French and Mohawk, for fear they would undermine their own relationship with the French. It was undoubtedly from Huron who had returned from Quebec that the Tionnontaté heard that in order to prevent an Iroquois attack on the French settlements, Montmagny had sent presents to the Iroquois urging them to attack the Huron instead. According to these rumours, which were probably spread by Huron traditionalists,

Montmagny had ordered the French to aid their Huron and Algonkin allies in appearance only, but to load their guns with powder but no shot so they would do no harm to the Iroquois (35:165).

A POSSIBLE REPRIEVE FOR THE TRADITIONALISTS

After 1645 important changes took place in the organization of trade in New France. It is unlikely, however, that the Huron were sufficiently aware of the nature of these changes to be able to assess the impact they would have on the ability of the Jesuits to impose their will upon them. In March 1645 the French government approved an arrangement whereby the Compagnie des Cent-Associés granted an absolute monopoly of the fur trade to a new association made up of French settlers who were resident in the colony. This Communauté des Habitants undertook to meet the colony's public expenses and to promote settlement as previous monopoly holders had done.

The decree announcing these changes was posted at Quebec in August 1645. Soon after, the new directors reversed the former policy of the Compagnie des Cent-Associés by forbidding anyone to have individual dealings with the Indians in beaver or other furs, under penalty of fines and confiscation. The Jesuits who had helped to promote the new trading association were, however, secretly excluded from this order, provided that they conducted their business discreetly (Lanctot 1963:183–87; Thwaites 1896–1901, 27:99). In 1647 a new regulation granted settlers in New France the right to purchase furs directly from the Indians, but only in exchange for produce originating in New France. The settlers were required to sell all such furs to the community stores at prices set by a council that was established to manage the affairs of the colony (Lanctot 1963:190). This regulation gave the Jesuits considerably more bargaining power, since they could threaten to allow private trade at Sillery. This would divert skins from direct exchange at the official warehouse at Quebec and reduce the profit made by the community (Thwaites 1896–1901, 30:187).

After the death of Cardinal Richelieu, the Jesuit missionaries lost the support of the Duchesse d'Aiguillon at the French court (Lanctot 1963:183) and in the later half of the decade the influence of the Société de Notre-Dame de Montréal increased rapidly. In 1648 the Jesuits suffered a further setback when their protégé Montmagny was replaced as governor of New France, after he had held that office for twelve years. He was succeeded by the thirty-six-year-old Louis d'Ailleboust, who had settled in Canada in 1643 and had served as Maisonneuve's lieutenant at Montreal. As soon as he returned from France, d'Ailleboust published a new decree authorizing the settlers to import their own trade goods and granting them the legal right to barter furs among the Indian tribes of the interior (ibid. 192–94). While primarily designed to stimulate the dwindling and imperilled fur trade of New France, the right of laymen to visit distant tribes on their own initiative eliminated the de facto control over contact between French and Huron on which the Jesuit mission program had been based. If large numbers of traders began to frequent the Huron country, the Huron would soon realize that being a Christian was no longer a vital part of their trading relationship with the French and an indifferent attitude towards Christianity might reassert itself. The Jesuits also must have feared that these traders would undermine the high moral standards they had striven to set for their converts. Commercial interests were threatening the Jesuits' monopoly of souls in the Huron country.

While the last regulation was announced too late to allow French settlers to visit the Huron country in 1648, the soldiers who went there for the winter took advantage of their new rights to trade with the Indians without restriction. When two of these soldiers, the brothers Desfosses, returned to the St. Lawrence in 1649, they brought with them 747 pounds of beaver skins that they had obtained from the Huron (Thwaites 1896–1901, 34:59–61). While it is safe to assume that these soldiers lived under Jesuit supervision, the furs indicated what enterprising traders might hope to achieve there. Privately financed expeditions, whose members were independent of Jesuit control, were now only a matter of time.

CHRISTIAN SUPREMACY IN OSSOSSANÉ

The famine and dislocation resulting from the dispersal of the Attigneenongnahac led increasing numbers of Huron to turn to the Jesuits for relief and protection. Throughout the summer of 1648 and the following winter, thousands of Huron visited Sainte-Marie for varying periods in search of food and shelter. Thus, for a while, the influence of the Jesuits increased still more as the Huron looked to them for leadership. One result of this was particularly evident in Ossossané, which was the oldest of the surviving Jesuit missions. As late as the summer of 1648, the traditionalists were a majority there, although three of the principal headmen of the town were Christians and they were able to enforce respect for Christianity (Thwaites 1896–1901, 33:141).

By the beginning of the winter, however, the Christians had become a majority. At that point, they assembled and conferred about their future course of action. It is not clear that any Jesuits were present at this meeting, but it is likely that beforehand the Jesuits had coached their leading converts what to say so that their policy would appear to be the Indians' own ideas. At this council it was decided that the priest who had charge of the Ossossané mission would henceforth be regarded as the principal headman of the community. He was also empowered to forbid any public practice that was contrary to Roman Catholic teaching and, more generally, to reform the ritual and moral life of the community.

Throughout the winter the Christian headmen conferred with Father Chaumonot and carried out his orders. Because the Christians occupied a majority of seats on the village council, they were able to prevent public approval from being given for the performance of all non-Christian rituals, thus effectively putting a stop to them. No public assistance was extended to anyone to help him to fulfil dream wishes. A traditionalist of some renown attempted to challenge the hold that the Christians had acquired over life in Ossossané. When the villagers assembled to perform a war dance, he announced that a dream had ordered him to break open the door of the church and to cut down the pole from which the Jesuits' bell was suspended. Normally, he could have relied on public opinion to support him in fulfilling his wishes, in either a literal or symbolic fashion. As he advanced towards the church, an old Christian, probably René Tsondihwané, announced that this man would have to kill him before he could attack these symbols of Christianity. Seeing that the majority of those who were present supported the old man, rather than himself, the traditionalist stopped singing and desisted from further action (34:105–9).

The traditionalists now found themselves in an unanticipated, and hitherto inconceivable, situation. It would never have occurred to a Huron to refuse to lend assistance to anyone to perform the ceremonies that he believed were necessary for his health and well-being, although the extent of this support would have varied according to the status of the individual and of his lineage. Refusal to perform such rites would have been regarded as evidence of public enmity bordering on witchcraft. Now, however, under Jesuit supervision, such behaviour had become the public policy of Ossossané, which embodied the moral requirements of the new religion.

In March the traditionalist minority decided to appeal for support to neighbouring villages. A sick man requested that a traditional dance be performed to cure him and that this be followed by an andacwander. The latter ritual, involving public sexual intercourse, was, of all Huron practices, the one most certain to anger the Jesuits. When the Christians learned about this request, they opposed it so strongly that no local headman dared to announce the ceremony. A shaman from a neighbouring village was invited to Ossossané to perform the ceremony and with him came some headmen who had promised to support the traditionalists; however, these visitors were compelled to leave the town when they found themselves unable to influence the local council (34:107, 217). Traditionalists now had the option of either conforming with Christian rules and regulations or moving elsewhere. Ossossané was called "the village of Christians" by the rest of the confederacy (34:217).

It may have been in Ossossané that a number of incidents took place about this time that reflect the growing influence of Christianity over the daily lives of the Huron. Husbands and wives are described as resorting to prayer to settle domestic quarrels, which they were taught were caused by the devil (33:163). A "very good Christian woman" is also reported to have beaten her four-year-old son (33:177–79), an action which the Huron regarded as unnatural and reprehensible. The Jesuits considered the traditional Huron attitude to be scandalously indulgent and as nurturing low moral standards; hence they viewed this innovation with great satisfaction.

ST. IGNACE AND ST. LOUIS

In the autumn of 1648 the Iroquois assembled an army of over 1000 men, mainly Seneca and Mohawk, who were well supplied with firearms and ammunition. These men spent the winter in the forests north of Lake Ontario so that they might surprise the Huron early in the spring. The dispersal of the Arendarhonon and Attigneenongnahac seems effectively to have deterred the Huron from attempting to use their hunting territories east of Lake Simcoe that winter and, as a result, this large Iroquois war party was able to advance as far as the Sturgeon Valley without being detected (Thwaites 1896–1901, 34:123–25).

On the night of 16 March the Iroquois reconnoitred Taenhatentaron, which, like Teanaostaiaé, was protected on three sides by ravines. In spite of the fortifications having been strengthened by the French to the point where they were believed to be impregnable, the Iroquois soon learned that

the Huron had largely abandoned the town the previous autumn. Moreover, none of its remaining inhabitants was expecting the Iroquois so
early in the year; hence the watchtowers were unguarded. During the
night, the Iroquois made a breach in the palisade and quietly entered the
town while the Huron were still asleep. Some Huron were killed on
the spot; the others were taken captive. The settlement was not burned, but
its palisades and houses, along with their provisions, were turned into an
armed camp by the Iroquois. Of the 400 people who remained in Taenhatentaron, only three men are reported to have escaped. Ten Iroquois lost
their lives in this operation.

Still before dawn, part of the Iroquois force set out to attack the fortified
village of St. Louis, which was located midway between Taenhatentaron
and Sainte-Marie. Before they reached the village, however, the refugees
from Taenhatentaron warned what was happening. The headmen ordered
the women and children to flee and more than 500 of the inhabitants of St.
Louis departed for Sainte-Marie, carrying their more valuable possessions
with them. Eighty warriors remained to fight the Iroquois and with them
stayed Father Jean de Brébeuf and the newly arrived Father Gabriel
Lalemant. These priests had charge of the five villages making up the
Mission of St. Ignace. The Huron repulsed the first two assaults of the
Iroquois, killing about thirty and wounding others. Finally, however,
the Iroquois were able to break down the palisades in several places and
entered the village. They killed the sick and aged, who had been unable to flee,
and either slew or took captive all but two of the warriors, both Christians. The
latter, in spite of serious wounds, carried news of the battle to Sainte-Marie.
Brébeuf and Lalemant had been urged to escape at the first alarm, but had
stayed behind to baptize those who wished it and to give absolution to the
Christians, who appear to have made up the larger part of the defenders.
When the situation appeared desperate, one of the traditionalists advised
making a run for it, but he was overruled by Etienne Annaotaha, a famous
Christian warrior who refused to abandon the Jesuits. The Jesuits, as well
as the warriors who had been taken prisoner, were led back to Taenhatentaron, while the houses at St. Louis were plundered and set on fire
(34:25–27, 125–31; 39:247–51). This fire was visible from Sainte-Marie
about nine o'clock in the morning.

As soon as Brébeuf and Lalemant were captured, they were stripped and
some of their fingernails were torn out. On entering Taenhatentaron, they
were made to walk between rows of Iroquois warriors and were beaten by
them. The Iroquois then proceeded to torture them and the other prisoners

in the usual manner (plate 47). Because of his stoicism, Brébeuf became the object of intensive torture and died the same afternoon, whereas Lalemant suffered more lingering torments until the following morning (34:139–49). Many Huron were present who in the past had been taken prisoner by the Iroquois and been adopted by them. These Huron played a leading role in torturing the Jesuits, whom they regarded as sorcerers responsible for the ruin of their homeland. Their animosity against Brébeuf was particularly evident in their taunting of him. In addition to the usual torments, the Huron amused themselves by repeatedly pouring boiling water over the priests in mockery of baptism (34:27–29, 145). Their attitude probably was typical of the Huron who had been captured by the Iroquois up to that time. These prisoners all must have had relatives still living in the Huron country, whom they were anxious to rescue as the Huron confederacy collapsed. Their hatred of the Jesuits was probably shared by most traditionalists still living in the Huron country. Those who tortured Brébeuf were nevertheless impressed by his fortitude and, once he was dead, they roasted and ate his heart and drank his blood in order to acquire his courage (34:31).

On the evening of 16 March the Iroquois sent scouts to reconnoitre Sainte-Marie and, on their return, a war council was held and it was decided to attack the Jesuit settlement the next morning. The destruction of Sainte-Marie not only would eliminate the strongest defensive position in the Huron country, but would provide the Iroquois with many furs and the Mohawk with valuable prisoners to use in their bargaining with the French. At the same time, after learning of the destruction of Taenhatentaron and St. Louis, about 300 Attignawantan armed themselves and gathered near Sainte-Marie to oppose any further advances by the Iroquois. Most of these warriors were Christians and the majority of them came from Ossossané, although more northerly villages were also represented.

The next morning, the Iroquois left a small force behind to garrison Taenhatentaron, while their main body of men moved westward across the snow-covered hills to attack Sainte-Marie. An advance party of about 200 encountered some of the Huron warriors and forced them to retreat to within sight of the French settlement. Many Huron were killed, but, finally, the Huron mustered their strength and drove this advance party inside the palisade at St. Louis, which, unlike the cabins, had not been destroyed by the fire. About 150 Huron assaulted and took possession of the village, capturing some thirty Iroquois (34:131–33).

Soon, however, the main body of the Iroquois arrived. Rather than proceeding to Sainte-Marie, they tried to regain St. Louis. The Huron who

PLATE 47. *The martyrdom of Brébeuf and Lalemant from the* Novae
Franciae Accurata Delineatio, *1657. This engraving is probably the earliest
on this theme in existence and if Bressani was the author of the map it is
based on first-hand information about Iroquois torture. As in the vignette
on the left half of the map (see plate 37) captives are shown bound facing a
stake rather than as modern artists show them with their backs to it. Huron
captives played an active and willing role in killing these two Jesuits.
Courtesy Public Archives of Canada.*

were occupying the village fought long and hard against the Iroquois, re-pelling numerous attacks. An important Iroquois headman was seriously wounded and nearly 100 of their men were slain in the course of the battle. St. Louis was not recaptured until late in the night and, by the time the Iroquois had entered the village, not more than twenty Huron remained alive and most of these had been wounded. The ferocity of this contest is indicated by the fact that contrary to custom, it continued after sunset (34:133–35). Among those killed were a large number of leading Christians from Ossossané. According to reports emanating from the battlefield, these included René Tsondihwané's son-in-law Tsoendiai, while Charles Ondaaiondiont, who had been the Huron envoy to the Susquehannock, and René Tsondihwané's son, Ihanneusa, were taken prisoner (34:217–19). It is clear, however, from later reports that the Iroquois released at least some of their prisoners probably hoping that they would persuade friends and kinsmen to join the Iroquois.

Their losses at St. Louis discouraged the Iroquois from attacking Sainte-Marie. After they had re-captured St. Louis, the Iroquois withdrew to Taenhatentaron, where they spent the following day recuperating. By 19 March the Iroquois were reported to be frightened and some were with-drawing from the Huron country on their own initiative. To prevent the premature breakup of their army, its leaders ordered a retreat. Those prisoners who were unable to follow the Iroquois were tied down inside various tinder-dry longhouses, which the Iroquois set on fire as they left the village. The rest were loaded, often beyond their strength, with vast quantities of spoils and made to march south. Those who could not keep up were hatcheted or burned along the way. An old woman who escaped from Taenhatentaron carried news of the Iroquois retreat to Scanonaenrat. Several hundred warriors from that town pursued the Iroquois for two days, but, because they had few guns, they were careful not to confront the enemy. Finally, lacking provisions, they returned home (34:135–37).

On 25 April 1649 Charles Garnier (1930:40) wrote that the Iroquois had destroyed four Huron villages at the end of the previous winter in addition to the two villages they had burned in 1648. None of the more detailed accounts of the Iroquois attack in the spring of 1649 mentions the destruc-tion of villages other than Taenhatentaron and St. Louis, hence the "four" in Garnier's letter may be a scribal error or his own confusion. On the other hand, it is possible that while the Iroquois were bivouaced in the ruins of Taenhatentaron they destroyed the neighbouring hamlets of St. Jean and St. Joachim, as well as St. Louis. This would have eliminated the last Huron settlements in the Sturgeon Valley (cf. Heidenreich 1971:53).

The Winter at Gahoendoe

THE DIASPORA

Although the Huron, particularly those who were Christians and had guns, had put up a creditable resistance to the Iroquois, the confederacy had lost at least another 700 people and everyone had been thrown into a state of terror. The Huron were already gripped by famine and the presence of the Iroquois so early in the season indicated that women would be unable to tend their crops in peace in 1649, any more than they had been able to do the year before. The remaining Huron, whether Christians or traditionalists, quickly became convinced that their position was untenable. Within less than two weeks, all of the Huron villages had been deserted and burned by their inhabitants, lest they should be used by the Iroquois as Taenhatentaron had been (Thwaites 1896–1901, 34:197) (map 32). Thus the Huron abandoned not only their houses and villages but also their fields, on which they had formerly depended for their subsistence (35:79). Because of the dislocation of the previous year, these refugees had little in the way of food reserves to take with them and it was probably the prospect of prolonged famine that led them to divide into smaller groups, once they had abandoned their villages. The exception were the people of Scanonaenrat, who had been the last tribal grouping to join the confederacy and seemingly the least integrated members of it. They stayed together both as a tribe and as a community. Accompanied by some Arendarhonon refugees who had adhered to them in 1647, the Tahontaenrat moved south and joined the Neutral (36:119).

Ossossané was one of the first towns to be abandoned. News of the defeat of its war party did not reach there until the night of 19 March. When it did, the cry went up that the Iroquois were about to attack. The old men, women, and children made their way through the snow along the trail that led to the Tionnontaté country, where many of them remained for several months. They were followed in their flight by Father Chaumonot (Jones 1908:382). Like Ossossané, the other Huron villages split up and clan segments, lineages, and individual families scattered in search of new homes. Many Huron sought refuge among the Tionnontaté. Some probably went to live with their trading partners, on whom, as adoptive relatives, they had the right to call for support (Thwaites 1896–1901, 34:223, 203; 35:79–81). This influx of refugees, combined with a drought in the summer of 1649, led to a shortage of food among the Tionnontaté, which, by the following winter, had become a serious famine (35:147, 127). Other

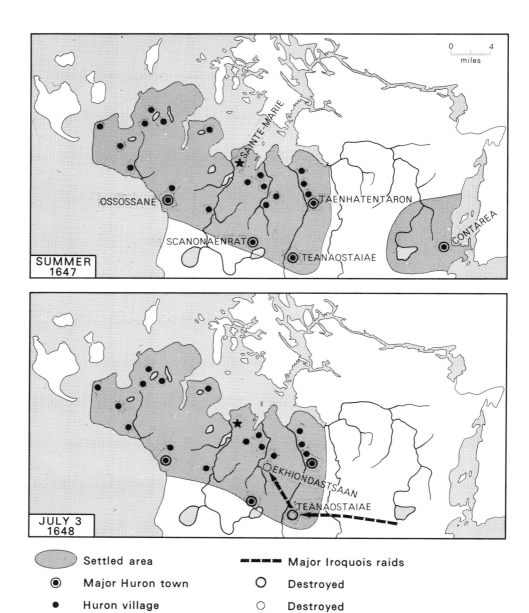

MAP 32. *Disintegration of the Huron confederacy, 1647 to 1650.*

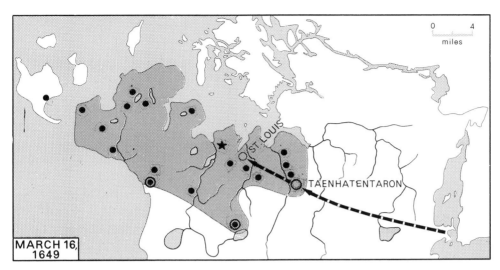

MARCH 16, 1649

ST LOUIS

TAENHATENTARON

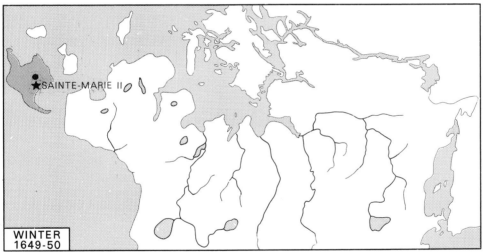

WINTER 1649-50

SAINTE-MARIE II

Huron besides the Tahontaenrat sought refuge with the Neutral (35:79), among whom many of them probably had trading partners. There is no warrant for Hunt's (1940:94) claim that the Neutral fell upon these refugees, killing some and enslaving the rest, since his only source attributes this behaviour to the Iroquois rather than to the Neutral.[6] Many other Huron fled north, seeking refuge either on the small islands in the northern part of Georgian Bay or along the shores of remote lakes and rivers (Thwaites 1896–1901, 35:79, 173). There they hoped to open small clearings and plant crops and if these failed, to live off the fish and wild vegetable foods that could be collected in the adjacent forests.

Other Huron remained in their own country for a time, but sought refuge by moving closer to Sainte-Marie. Some of these Huron proposed to move to Quebec and sent a headman there to find out if the French governor would approve this plan and be prepared to assist them (34:223). It may have been this Huron who arrived at Quebec on 20 July and first informed the colony of the dispersal of the Huron and of the deaths of Brébeuf and Lalemant (34:57). Other Huron fled to Gahoendoe, or Christian Island, which lies within sight of the Ontario mainland off the western tip of the Penetanguishene Peninsula. Some Huron had settled on this island a year or more before, since Ragueneau states that Jesuit missionaries had begun to visit the island in 1648 (34:203). Father Chaumonot and some of the refugees from Ossossané arrived on Gahoendoe by 1 May 1649. Most of his followers were reduced to eating acorns and wild roots, and the work of clearing new fields and erecting cabins was impeded by the lack of adult males in his party, which was made up mainly of the widows and children of men who had fought the Iroquois at St. Louis (34:215–17). It is questionable, however, whether Chaumonot's widows and children were significantly worse off than most Huron who were attempting to live on their own by the summer of 1649 (34:197).

THE MOVE TO GAHOENDOE

In spite of the dispersal of the Huron, Ragueneau continued the Tionnontaté missions and sent missionaries to visit different parts of Georgian Bay in order to instruct the Algonkians and Huron refugees who were living there (Thwaites 1896–1901, 35:81). As no Huron dared to continue living in their homeland, it became clear that Sainte-Marie was no longer either a suitable mission centre or a safe place to reside. It was exposed to Iroquois attack and the Jesuits feared that without Huron villages to draw their fire, the next time the Iroquois returned they would focus their whole attack against this settlement. Even if they were unable to capture Sainte-Marie, they could destroy the Jesuits' crops and cut off movement to and from the settlement. The Jesuits therefore decided to abandon Sainte-Marie and establish a new mission centre elsewhere, where they hoped to draw some of the Huron refugees together and ensure that trade with the French and their own mission work would continue (34:203). At first the Jesuits thought of moving to Manitoulin Island, where they had begun an Algonkian-speaking mission the previous autumn. The island was more remote from the Iroquois and was convenient for maintaining contact with the Neutral and Tionnontaté, as well as with Indians living to the west. The Jesuits had noted that the island was fertile and the fishing good. They anticipated that once the Huron were settled there, they would recover and soon be able to resume the fur trade (34:203–9).

This idea did not appeal to the Huron with whom the Jesuits remained in contact, and for good reason. In spite of its many natural advantages, Manitoulin Island had a shorter frost-free season than the Huron country and was very close to the line beyond which it was impractical to depend upon maize for subsistence (Yarnell 1964:129). If the Huron had moved to Manitoulin Island, they might have continued to plant corn, but they could not have depended on it for their own subsistence, let alone for trade.

On 12 May twelve headmen held a formal council with the Jesuits. They presented the missionaries with ten large wampum collars and told them that many Huron intended to settle on Gahoendoe Island. They invited the Jesuits to join the Huron there in order to minister to them and to protect them from the Iroquois. To attract the Jesuits they stated that even the traditionalists who planned to settle on Gahoendoe had resolved to become Christians and that the presence of the missionaries would make Gahoendoe an island of Christians. The headmen spoke for over three hours and after they had finished, the Jesuits agreed to abandon their plan to move to Manitoulin Island and to follow this remnant of the Huron people to Gahoendoe (Thwaites 1896–1901, 34:209–11). Many historians have criticized the Jesuits' decision to do this on the grounds that the new mission was almost as exposed to attack as the old one had been; however, so long as the Huron were unwilling to change their mode of life, the Jesuits had no alternative but to act as they did.

The Jesuits stripped Sainte-Marie and built a large raft. On 14 May their workmen loaded the raft with their livestock, food supply, and all the portable objects from their settlement, including the cannon. Sainte-Marie was then put to the torch to prevent it from falling into the hands of the

Iroquois or the Dutch, who might use it as a trading post. The Jesuits then journeyed about thirty miles to a site on the northern side of the great bay that indents the southeastern shore of Gahoendoe where the Huron refugees were founding a new settlement, named Sainte-Marie by the Jesuits. As the Jesuits travelled along the shores of the Penetanguishene Peninsula, bands of Iroquois were roaming the countryside, capturing and slaying Huron stragglers (34:223–25; 35:81–83).

When the Jesuits arrived on Gahoendoe, they found that approximately 300 families had taken refuge there (34:223). Most of them were Christians who were continuing to count on the Jesuits for leadership. Some fields had been cleared but the crops that had been planted were threatened by a serious drought (35:85). The Huron had been able to clear too little land to supply their needs and in spite of a temporary improvement in the weather, 1649 was a year of desperately poor crops. As soon as they arrived the Jesuits set their men to work cutting trees, so that they and the Huron might at least hope to harvest enough corn the following year (34:225). Because so many Huron families lacked adult male members, the French had to help them clear their fields (35:27).

Shortly after they arrived, the Jesuits began to build fortifications both for themselves and for the Huron. The main unit was a fort about 120 feet square with bastions at the four corners. It was located over 100 feet from the lake shore. To prevent the Iroquois from setting fire to this fort, or undermining it, both the bastions and the curtain walls were solidly built of stone and the rules of military architecture were carefully observed (35:85). Ragueneau contrasted the stone wall surrounding this fort with the wooden palisades that had surrounded much of the European compound at Sainte-Marie on the Wye up to the time the latter was abandoned (35:27). In the centre of the fort was a stone-lined cistern, about nine feet square, to provide water for the defenders (Jones 1908:6–8; plates 48 and 49). While the interior arrangements of this building are unknown, it evidently enclosed the Jesuits' living quarters. The masonry was finished by the end of the summer (Thwaites 1896–1901, 40:47).

The Jesuits also fortified the Huron village which was adjacent to their residence. Palisades were erected and strengthened with bastions guarding the approaches, which armed Frenchmen were to man (35:85). During the summer the population of the Huron village grew, as various groups of refugees learned of its existence and flocked there in search of protection and succour. Eventually there were said to be over 100 cabins in the village. Although Ragueneau's statement that its population rose to between 6000 and 8000 people must be an exaggeration (35:87), even a few thousand

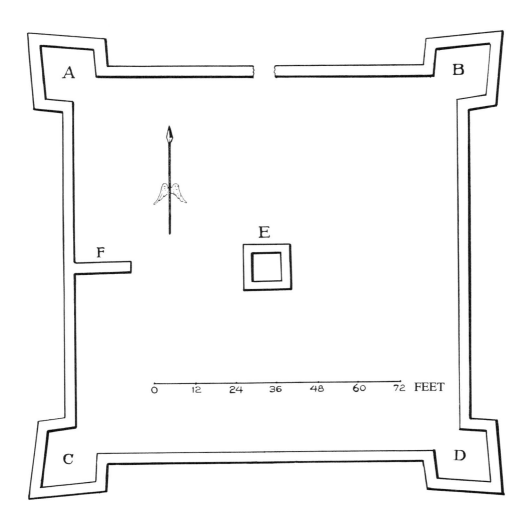

PLATE 48. *Plan of the remains of Sainte-Marie II on Christian Island.*
Prepared by Félix Martin in 1855. Courtesy Archives of Ontario.

PLATE 49. *Sketch of the ruins of Sainte-Marie II. By Félix Martin, 1855. Courtesy Archives of Ontario and Archives de la Compagnie de Jésus, Province du Canada-français.*

would have created unprecedented difficulties. Most of these people were dependent on fish, wild fruit, and vegetables and, large as Gahoendoe was, it was unable to supply the needs of so large a population from natural resources. The Huron were thus forced to visit the mainland to search for food, even though roving bands of Iroquois made these visits extremely dangerous. To attend to the spiritual needs of their converts, priests sometimes accompanied the Huron on these expeditions, although none were attacked by the Iroquois while doing so (34:225–27).

When the Jesuits arrived at Gahoendoe, they brought with them the surplus corn that they had accumulated at Sainte-Marie. Enough remained to feed themselves and their workmen for over a year, as well as 400 bags that were earmarked for the Huron (40:49); however, the latter were kept in reserve for the difficult winter ahead. In the autumn, the Jesuits dispatched canoes to buy food from the Algonkian peoples who lived around the shores of Georgian Bay. This netted 500 to 600 bushels of acorns, as well as a supply of dried fish (35:99–101).

TRADE IN 1649

On 6 June 1649 thirty-four Frenchmen and two Huron left the St. Lawrence Valley for the Huron country (34:53). The French in Quebec did not yet know about the dispersal of the Huron and the purpose of this expedition is not stated. In a letter that he wrote in September 1649, Jérôme Lalemant implies that d'Ailleboust had sent this "expedition" to the Huron country to carry ammunition there and to help to resist the Iroquois (34:83). He also stated, however, that the expedition was to return in the autumn. Possibly the French feared that the Huron would not come to Three Rivers in 1649, as they had not come in 1647; hence some traders may have decided to take advantage of their right to visit the interior to trade for furs. On 7 August about twenty Huron arrived at Three Rivers and five days later a number of French soldiers and domestics left for the Huron country to spend the winter there (34:59, 83). Lalemant states that altogether about sixty Frenchmen travelled to the Huron country in 1649 (34:83). In mid-August Father Bressani was ordered to journey from Gahoendoe to Quebec. It is unclear how many Huron accompanied him on what, in normal years, would have been the annual journey to Three Rivers. Indirect evidence suggests, however, that his expedition was made up largely of Frenchmen who either like the brothers Desfosses had spent the winter in the Huron country, or had gone into the interior in June. One of the members of the expedition was Robert Le Coq, who spent the following winter at Sillery (34:65). Bressani left Gahoendoe 12 August and arrived at Quebec September 19. In spite of the disruptions of the previous year, the French brought 5000 pounds of beaver skins with them that they had obtained from the Huron (34:59–61). On 28 September Bressani started to return to the Huron country with four canoes, but after reaching the Rivière des Prairies, this group turned back and Bressani and his companions spent the winter on the St. Lawrence.

The ownership and disposition of the 5000 skins that were brought to Quebec is a mystery, which serves to reveal how little we know about the fur trade at this time and of the role that the Jesuits played in it. The following year Ragueneau stated that he planned to use 20,000 livres worth of furs that had been brought for the Huron from their own country in order to help cover the expenses incurred in caring for Huron refugees at Quebec (36:250). The value of these skins suggests that they amounted to most, if not all, of the 5000 brought to Quebec in 1649, which would have sold for four or five livres per pound. Elsewhere, however, it is implied that the profits from these furs belonged to individual Frenchmen (34:59–61). These two statements are not irreconcilable since if most of the French were donnés, their earnings would have belonged to the Jesuit order (*see also* Jaenen 1970:68).

THE DISPERSAL OF THE TIONNONTATÉ

Although the Jesuits were in control at Gahoendoe where the Huron were mainly Christians who acknowledged their leadership and looked to them for support, the situation elsewhere was different. Many Huron Christians had sought refuge among the Tionnontaté, but others who joined them were traditionalists who blamed the Jesuits for the destruction of their country and spread rumours about a secret understanding between the French and the Iroquois. These stories led a group of Tionnontaté headmen to hold a meeting in St. Matthieu (Ekarenniondi) to discuss how the spread of Christianity might be halted and the Tionnontaté might thereby escape the fate of the Huron. It was reported that a Huron who had recently escaped from the Mohawk had seen wampum belts that the French governor had sent to the Mohawk inviting them to attack the Huron rather than the French. Some of the headmen urged that the French missionaries ought to be killed and it was finally agreed that the Tionnontaté should murder the first Frenchman that they met, just as Douart had been slain. When the two resident priests returned to the village a few days later, they were treated as if they were prisoners of war. The headmen were, however, unable to agree who should kill them and they were soon allowed to continue their rounds (Thwaites 1896–1901, 35:165–67). In another village the chapel and bell pole that the Jesuits had erected were torn down and the furniture from the chapel carried about as if it were the spoils of war, while it was proclaimed that the Jesuits ought to be slain (35:169).

Throughout the summer small bands of Iroquois continued to harass the Huron country; however, towards the end of November two Huron Christians reported that they had escaped from a band of 300 Iroquois who were undecided whether to attack Gahoendoe or to proceed against the Tionnontaté (35:91, 107). Although there is no proof of serious hostility between the Iroquois and the Tionnontaté prior to the late 1640s, the Iroquois evidently feared the Tionnontaté, both as a nucleus around whom the Huron might attempt to stage a revival and as a group that could be drawn into a trading partnership with the French. Either development might strengthen them to the point where they could menace Iroquois raiders attempting to penetrate the north and thereby protect the northern hunters as the Huron had done. For these reasons it is likely that the Iroquois were intending to attack the Tionnontaté, but had designated Gahoendoe as an alternative objective in case such an attack proved impossible.

When the Jesuits learned that a large Iroquois force was advancing northward, they persuaded the Huron at Gahoendoe not to set out after them and sent news of their approach to the Tionnontaté. Far from dismaying the latter, this news delighted them, since they anticipated that they would be able to surprise and defeat the Iroquois. When the latter were slow in arriving, the warriors from Etharita grew impatient and decided to go and meet them. They set out 5 December and made their way along the route they expected the Iroquois to follow. The Iroquois advanced towards Etharita along another route and, learning that the men of the town were away, they entered and plundered it. Some of the inhabitants fled to nearby villages, but many were slain or taken prisoner. Among the dead was Charles Garnier, the resident missionary. When the men of Etharita returned on 9 December, they were stunned to find the town in ashes and spent a day sitting motionless in grief. The Iroquois, in the meanwhile, retreated southward with their prisoners and booty (35:107–19).

When Father Ragueneau warned the Tionnontaté that the Iroquois were approaching, he ordered Father Garnier's missionary companion, Noël Chabanel, to return to Gahoendoe. He did this because of the famine and because he thought it unwise to expose two missionaries to the enemy unnecessarily by having them remain in the same community. On 5 December Chabanel left Etharita in the company of seven or eight Huron Christians and travelled northward through Ekarenniondi. On the night of 7–8 December he and his companions slept in the forest. About midnight they heard the victorious Iroquois, who were journeying homeward with their prisoners. The Huron scattered in the dark and made their way to the nearest Tionnontaté village, inadvertently leaving Chabanel alone in the forest.

The next day Chabanel made his way towards Gahoendoe, but was robbed of his possessions and murdered soon after he had crossed the Nottawasaga River. At first it was thought that he might have been killed by the Iroquois. A Huron named Honareenhac, who had renounced Christianity, was in possession of his hat, blanket, and book bag but claimed that Chabanel had given these things to him after he had ferried him across the Nottawasaga River, in order to be less encumbered on his journey. The Jesuits soon learned, however, that among the Huron Honareenhac was boasting that he had killed Chabanel to avenge himself for the extraordinary misfortunes that had afflicted him and his family after they had been baptized. Honareenhac was living in Ekarenniondi, which suggests that there was substance to Ragueneau's claim that Chabanel's murder was related to the outbreak of hostility against the Jesuits that had centred in this village only a short time before (35:147–51, 169; Jones 1908:394–96). Ragueneau was convinced that Honareenhac could be proved guilty of the murder, but felt that under the circumstances it was best for the Jesuits to close their eyes to what had happened (Thwaites 1896–1901, 35:151). A quarrel with Honareenhac's friends and kinsmen about whether or not he had killed Chabanel was more than the Jesuits wished to enter into at this time.

After Chabanel's death Fathers Léonard Garreau and Adrien Greslon, who were stationed at Ekarenniondi, were made responsible for the whole Tionnontaté mission. Because of illness Greslon had to be recalled to Sainte-Marie by January 1650 and Garreau was recalled the following spring. This ended the Tionnontaté mission.

THE HUNGRY WINTER

Evidence concerning the fate of some of the Huron who sought refuge by fleeing north is provided in the Jesuit account of the Mission of St. Charles.

In the summer of 1649 two Jesuits, who were visiting the shores of Georgian Bay to minister to indigenous Algonkians and Huron refugees, found a considerable number of Huron living in a single location and recommended that a priest spend the winter with them. One was dispatched on 1 October. He was received into the homes of some Christian Huron who encouraged him to erect a small chapel. Some other Huron, who were not Christians, came to receive instruction but still others, and in particular those who had the most provisions, refused to do so. The latter attributed the Huron's misfortunes entirely to abandoning their old ways. In the course of the winter provisions ran out and fishing through the ice proved unproductive. As the famine grew worse the traditionalists ceased to denounce the Jesuits and the whole village began to turn to the resident priest for suggestions. Towards spring the inhabitants of the village were forced to disperse in different directions in search of food. Some followed the priest on a six-day journey across the ice of Georgian Bay in the hope of finding relief on Gahoendoe. While the Jesuits claimed that these Huron were not courting the priest's favour for material gain, their behaviour seems to belie this conclusion (Thwaites 1896–1901, 35:173–77).

For many of the Huron who had fled north, the winter of 1649–50 was one of terror, as well as of hunger and starvation. No longer having to fear being cut off by the Huron, the Iroquois launched a series of raids into central Ontario, attacking and robbing the Indians and probably trapping beaver there as well (35:181). These raids were directed against the indigenous Algonkians as well as Huron refugees. The Nipissing, who were wintering around the shores of their lake, were attacked and dispersed. The following spring two Iroquois forts were found to have been erected to the east of that lake (35:201). At the same time, smaller bands of Iroquois roamed the shores of Georgian Bay, looting and killing (35:181, 199). These raids continued the following year (36:189), by which time most of the indigenous inhabitants of central Ontario had fled to the north and west. The area then became a hunting territory for the Iroquois.

As more Huron made their way to Gahoendoe in the autumn and winter of 1649, a situation that had been desperate gradually became hopeless. Only the Jesuits had any reserves of food but, in spite of their intrepid efforts to accumulate as many fish and sacks of acorns as possible, these were inadequate to support more than a few hundred people over the winter.[7] To make matters worse, fishing through the ice proved exceptionally unproductive on Georgian Bay that winter (35:175), thus limiting the Huron's capacity to provide for themselves. Moss, bark, and fungus were eaten, but these were totally inadequate to support the large numbers of people who crowded onto Gahoendoe. As the winter progressed, the death rate began to rise sharply as a result of malnutrition and illness and all of the Huron on Gahoendoe turned to the Jesuits for whatever help they could provide. The Jesuits, who were now called the "fathers of the Huron people" (35:25), spent their days tending, as best they could, to what they perceived as being the essential physical and spiritual needs of the Huron. They passed many hours each day visiting the Huron village in order to assist the hungry and the dying and to try to convert any remaining traditionalists to Christianity.

In order to regulate the distribution of food, the Jesuits made small copper tokens, which each missionary distributed, as he judged best, among the Indians who were in his charge. This was done once a day, usually in the morning. The Indians who received these tokens assembled at the door of the Jesuits' residence about noon and exchanged their tokens for acorns, smoked fish, or, in the case of the most favoured, corn meal boiled in water (35:99). While it was necessary to control the distribution of food, this particular system was susceptible to various abuses, although the Jesuits probably did not view them as such. It encouraged starving Huron to make a display of Christian piety in the hope of receiving preferential treatment. Inducements such as this, and the lack of anything else to do, may explain the displays of intense religious fanaticism that were a feature of life at Gahoendoe that winter. The church was filled to overflowing with Huron ten or twelve times each morning and again in the late afternoon. Those wishing to be baptized were assiduous in attending instruction, while confession was also popular.

The Jesuits spent the middle part of the day making their rounds of the Huron longhouses and, following the afternoon church services, they encouraged neophytes to give an account of what they had thought each day: how often they had remembered God, how they had served him; whether they had offered him their labour, their hunger, and their misery (35:101–105). The Jesuits perceived that material wants played an important role in encouraging these displays of piety, but instead of regarding them as insincere, they thanked God that by thus afflicting the Huron and giving the Jesuits the means of aiding some of them, he had made their hearts so tractable that they could now quickly be persuaded to become Christians (35:91, 97). Convinced that the Huron were near to extinction, the Jesuits viewed the inadequate supplies of food that they had to distribute less as a means of keeping them alive than of preparing them for heaven (35:97, 105). The Huron were said by the Jesuits to be greatly pleased by the charity that was extended to them (35:95–99); yet few would have dared to appear otherwise. It could not have gone unnoticed among the Huron that while they died by the hundreds, the Jesuits, who reserved a special allotment of supplies for their own use, neither became ill nor went hungry. The Jesuits were able to satisfy their own consciences by viewing such efforts to keep fit as essential so that they, as priests, could attend to the needs of the dying (35:27, 97).

In terms of baptisms, the Jesuits' program was a success. Between the middle of March 1649 and the following August, more than 1400 Huron were baptized (34:227), and between then and March 1650 about 1600 more (34:227; 35:23, 75). Some of these baptisms undoubtedly took place among the Tionnontaté and others at the old Jesuit settlement of Sainte-Marie prior to its abandonment. Yet, the vast majority of baptisms after 14 May took place on Gahoendoe and must have numbered more than 2000. The majority of Huron who went to Gahoendoe were either Christians or Huron who were inclined to accept Jesuit leadership. One may conclude, therefore, that many of the Indians who were baptized at Gahoendoe had indicated a willingness to become Christians prior to their decision to settle there. It is clear, however, that some others were traditionalists who had gone to Gahoendoe either because they were desperate for food or wished to live with Christian relatives.

As the winter progressed increasing numbers of Huron died from hunger and contagious diseases, which became more lethal as poor nutrition robbed progressively more people, particularly children, of their ability to resist infection (35:91). In a desperate effort to survive, Huron began to eat the excrement of men and animals and to disinter the bodies of the dead in order to devour them. The latter was done in secret since the Huron regarded eating kinsmen and fellow countrymen with even greater abhorrence than did the French. In spite of this, necessity was driving people to feed upon their deceased parents, siblings, and children (35:21, 89).

The mortality rate was made worse by a lack of clothing. Some Huron are reported to have sold the few items of fur that remained in their possession for a single meal of acorns (35:93). This might suggest that Huron who had food were using it to accumulate skins to trade with the French. Yet such behaviour was contrary to the customary rules of sharing that were observed by the Huron and would have done the small number who had extra food little good, since they too would have gone hungry unless at some point they had been able to trade the furs they were accumulating for still more food.

It seems likely that the Huron had been largely depleted of their furs during the summer when the French traders had visited them. Possibly at that time many Huron had been willing to exchange their furs for European trade goods, in the expectation that they could later exchange these goods for corn or fish with neighbouring tribes. By the winter the lack of furs became sufficiently serious that the living had begun robbing the dead of clothing in order to keep warm (35:95). That furs continued to be sold for acorns suggests that the soldiers or other laymen who were working for the Jesuits may have been carrying on a clandestine trade with the Indians. A few Huron may have been recruited to work as agents for these Frenchmen in return for enough food to trade and to survive the winter. While the priests probably knew little or nothing about such activities and almost certainly would have disapproved of them, the resulting perversion of Huron social values compounded the outrage to Huron consciences that was embodied in the Jesuits' well-meaning efforts to save the souls of what they saw to be a dying nation. The Huron grew so weak that towards spring they were unable to dispose of the bodies of their own dead. Some of the priests and French laymen then charged themselves with laying out and burying the corpses that were accumulating in the long-houses. They described this as an act of charity that they extended to fellow Christians "however barbarous and lowly they may have been" (35:95).

The Move to Quebec

SPRINGTIME AT GAHOENDOE

At the beginning of March a considerable number of Huron left Gahoendoe in bands of fifty or more, or even as single families. Their aim was to search for acorns in places where the snow was beginning to melt or to try their luck at favourite fishing spots. Before leaving, they confessed and received holy communion, since many of them did not expect to survive the journey. They hoped, however, that by splitting into small groups, at least some of them might avoid the Iroquois. The ice was still frozen between Gahoendoe and the mainland, but as they crossed it began to break up and many Huron, especially children and old people, were drowned or froze to death. It was hoped that the dispersal of so many from the island would relieve the pressure on those who remained behind. Unfortunately, on 25 March an Iroquois war party, whose aim was to ensure that the Huron did not resettle in their own country, reached the Penetanguishene Peninsula. Within two days they killed or captured every band of Huron that had returned to the mainland (35:183–89).

The Huron who remained on Gahoendoe were thoroughly terrified when they learned what had happened, but the Jesuits' supplies of food ran out and disease, starvation, and cannibalism grew worse than before. More Huron felt obliged to leave the village. On Easter day, 17 April, a general communion was celebrated and the following day another band departed for the mainland, leaving what possessions they had in the care of the Jesuits. Most of them publicly made the Jesuits their heirs, as they had no hope of surviving. A few days later a few members of this band returned to Gahoendoe to report that the rest had either been slain or taken prisoner by the Iroquois. Some of the latter, including women and children, had been burned on the spot. In spite of this, hunger overcame many Huron's fear of death or being taken prisoner by the Iroquois and within a week still more of them crossed to the mainland to meet a similar fate. It was then that the Huron learned that two more Iroquois armies were on their way north-ward to relieve, or reinforce, the one that was already at work. The aim of these expeditions was to see that no Huron resettled or planted crops on the sites of their former villages and to kill, or capture, any who attempted to do so (35:189–91).

LEAVING GAHOENDOE

Most Huron were now convinced that they had to abandon Gahoendoe and find permanent places of refuge elsewhere. The majority intended either to scatter in small groups in the forests of central Ontario or to seek refuge in the vicinity of Lakes Michigan and Superior. The former were probably not yet aware of the extent of Iroquois raids into central Ontario or of the latter's determination to use this area to obtain furs. Others spoke of mak-ing their way south to join the Susquehannock or of voluntarily joining the Iroquois. Many of the latter were in contact with relatives who had been taken prisoner and who were counselling them to leave Gahoendoe as soon as possible, rather than perish there (Thwaites 1896–1901, 35:193). It is unclear how these contacts were made, but messages may have been carried by Huron who "escaped" from the Iroquois, and Huron allied with the Iroquois may have visited Gahoendoe without the French knowing about it.

While the French not unexpectedly have little to report about Huron voluntarily joining the Iroquois at this time, many Huron clearly did this. It is likely that as soon as the Huron dispersed in 1649, many who had relatives already living among the Iroquois went to join them. This probably involved more Arendarhonon than other Huron, since more Arendarhonon were prisoners among the Iroquois than were members of any other tribe. Moreover, a larger percentage of Arendarhonon were traditionalists than were members of other tribes and integration with the Iroquois must have seemed more acceptable to them than it did to even nominal Christians. By 1650, however, even many Christians had come to believe that throwing themselves on the mercy of the Iroquois offered them the best chance of survival, particularly when this meant rejoining relatives.

In late May or early June the leaders of the various groups who remained on Gahoendoe held a council in the dead of night, without the French being present. They discussed plans to leave the island and scatter in various directions. The next day two headmen, representing some 600 people drawn from all the Huron tribes, approached Father Ragueneau. After informing him that the Huron had decided to abandon Gahoendoe, they asked the Jesuits to lead them to Quebec. The Huron argued that if the French would support them there until they could harvest their own crops in the summer of 1651, they would be able to stay together as a group and remain practising Christians. As it was, the Jesuits were too few in number to accompany all of the tiny bands into which the Christians of Gahoendoe were being forced to split up (35:191–95).

At first, the Jesuits were uncertain what course of action they should follow, but after numerous conferences and forty hours of prayer, they decided that neither Gahoendoe nor the Huron country was defensible. While the French felt unable to provide for large numbers of Huron at Quebec, the relatively few Christians who were seeking refuge seemed manageable. Allowing them to settle at Quebec would permit them to remain under Jesuit guidance and would also supply men who were experienced in guerilla warfare to help defend the colony.

To prevent the Iroquois from learning about their plans, the Jesuits decided to leave for Quebec as quickly as possible. About half of the 600 Huron chose to remain at Gahoendoe until the corn ripened, but promised that afterwards they would come to Quebec (36:179–81). These Huron took possession of the French fort as soon as the French left. On 10 June the remaining 300 set off with the Jesuits for Quebec. They followed the usual route past Lake Nipissing and down the Ottawa Valley. In order to defend themselves, the Huron and French travelled in a tight formation.

As far as Lake Nipissing they found evidence of successful Iroquois raids during the previous winter.

The Kichesipirini derived no little satisfaction from seeing the Jesuits in full retreat, since they held them responsible for encouraging the Huron to ignore the Algonkin's role as middlemen. When Ragueneau gave orders that the Huron should pass Morrison Island without paying their usual tolls, and justified this by claiming that the French exerted sovereignty over the Algonkin, Tessouat had him seized and suspended from a tree by his armpits (Perrot 1911:176–78). While the French deeply resented this indignity, they and the hungry Huron who accompanied them were no match for Tessouat's men and the tolls were paid.[8] This was probably the last occasion on which the hard-pressed Kichesipirini were able to humble the French and assert their claim to control the upper part of the Ottawa River.

News of the abandonment of the Huron country came as a great surprise to a mixed party of Frenchmen and Huron who had left Three Rivers on 7 June in order to visit the Huron country. The party was made up of Father Bressani, a lay brother, and three domestics, who were carrying supplies to the Jesuits on Gahoendoe, as well as of twenty-five to thirty French traders and an equal number of Huron who had spent the winter at Quebec (Thwaites 1896–1901, 35:45, 201–3). The traders must have been well aware of the disasters that had befallen the Huron the previous summer, although they did not know about the even worse winter that had followed on Gahoendoe. It is difficult to understand how they could have expected the Huron to have many furs to trade, but their cupidity probably led them to hope that either the Huron or some of their former trading partners would be able to provide them with skins. On the way up the Ottawa River, seven Huron belonging to this group were killed by the Iroquois. All of them were described as good Christians and one was Atironta, who had wintered at Quebec after he had accompanied Bressani there the previous autumn. It is of interest that the paramount headman of the Arendarhonon should have left the Christian remnant of his own tribe in a time of major crisis. It would seem that as a result of cultivating his roles as a Christian and as the principal ally of the French, Atironta had forfeited much of his traditional importance as a tribal leader.

When Bressani's group encountered that of Father Ragueneau, all of the French decided to return to Quebec; however, at least some of the Huron who were heading up the Ottawa River continued on their way, hoping to join the 300 others who were spending the summer on Gahoendoe. When they were on Georgian Bay, about thirty miles from Gahoendoe, they were attacked by 300 Iroquois who lay in wait as they passed (36:181). All of the members of this band, which included two Huron named Andotitak and Thawenda, were reported to have been taken prisoner (36:119).

A smaller group of Huron warriors, led by Ohenhen, returned to the Huron country in the autumn of 1650. Three of his men were slain when they were attacked by Iroquois, but Ohenhen withstood the attack and eventually he and the rest of his men forced the Iroquois to take flight (36:121). Ohenhen's mission was to carry two wampum collars from the French governor to either the Tahontaenrat or the Neutral, urging them to trade with the French and form an alliance with them against the Iroquois (36:133). A band of fifty Tionnontaté who attempted to travel to Quebec in order to trade or get guns were attacked and wiped out by the Iroquois who were lying in wait for anyone using the Lake Nipissing trade route.

Throughout the summer of 1650 the Iroquois continued to roam through the Georgian Bay area, killing many of the Huron who had sought refuge there (36:181). Late in the summer a Huron named Atendera and his six companions were captured on Beckwith or Hope Island, near Gahoendoe. One of the members of this party was Ondaaiondiont, who was reported to have been killed at St. Louis, but who seems to have escaped from that battle.[9] The following summer he was forced to accompany eleven Iroquois in a raid against Quebec, but he escaped from them and carried a warning of their plans to the French (36:119).

In the summer of 1650 some thirty Iroquois landed on Gahoendoe and built a fortified camp from which they sallied forth to kill and capture some of the Huron who remained on the island. An attempt was made by the Huron to drive these Iroquois away, but they defended themselves bravely and killed a leading Huron warrior. For a time, the Iroquois besieged the Huron, who remained inside the French fort (36:181). These attacks, which prevented the Huron women from tending their fields no doubt did more to ruin the harvest than did a late frost that was reported to have injured the crop. The famine continued and when the autumn came the Huron neither had enough food nor did they feel safe enough to undertake their intended journey to Quebec. Some corn appears to have matured, however, and a population of only 300 probably had a reasonable chance of surviving on Gahoendoe by foraging there and on the adjacent mainland.

In late autumn, Onondaga warriors erected a fort on the mainland, opposite Gahoendoe, in order to capture any Huron who were compelled to venture in that direction in search of food. Although over 100 Huron were reported to have been taken prisoner (36:123), the Onondaga's main objective appears to have been to persuade the rest of the Huron to live with them. When they captured the warrior Etienne Annaotaha, they sent him back to the Huron to tell them that the Onondaga had brought rich presents inviting them to join them and become a single people. Three Iroquois accompanied him to the island as envoys. Although Annaotaha and the Huron headmen mistrusted the Onondaga and had no intention of going with them, they pretended to accept their proposal. The Huron women were urged to be ready within three days to leave for the Onondaga country. When this was reported to the Onondaga, the latter were confident that the Huron would return home with them and many visits were exchanged on both sides until the Huron had attracted over thirty Iroquois into their fort. At this point, the Huron fell on these Onondaga and killed all but three of them in order to avenge former injuries. The three who escaped did so because Annaotaha warned them what was about to happen. He did this because these were the men who had released him and also because the Iroquois had spared his life when they had captured him at St. Louis, no doubt as part of a general policy to encourage the Huron to desert to them. When the rest of the Iroquois learned that so many of their comrades had been killed, they gave up the siege of Gahoendoe and returned home as quickly as possible (36:181–87).

Because the Huron were certain that the Onondaga would return to avenge those who had been slain, they hastened to abandon the island as early as possible in the spring of 1651. Some left before the ice had broken up on Georgian Bay, others as soon as it was possible to launch their canoes. The latter did not leave too soon, as a few families and some children and old people who had no one to care for them were slain by the Iroquois before they could get away. These Huron fled north to Manitoulin Island (36:187–89). Both Manitoulin Island and the Lake Nipissing area were found to be exposed to the Iroquois (37:111); therefore, after a short time, the Huron left Manitoulin and in some forty canoes made their way to Quebec, where they joined the Huron who had arrived there the year before. They brought no provisions with them. All of those who arrived at Quebec were said to be Christians (36:189–91).

After the summer of 1651 few Huron remained in the Huron country or anywhere in the vicinity of Georgian Bay or central Ontario. In the summer of 1652 it was learned in Quebec that the Onondaga had defeated a small group of Huron who visited Gahoendoe towards the end of the previous summer to gather Jerusalem artichokes (37:105). Prior to July 1651 fifty Iroquois attacked and defeated the people of Tangouaen, somewhere along the shores of Lake Nipissing (36:131). These included, if they did not consist entirely of, Huron who as early as 1646 had retreated north to elude the Iroquois. From this time onwards, the Huron country and much of the region to the north remained desolate and uninhabited, while the Huron were scattered in every direction.

Chapter 12   Betrayal and Salvation

Temporary Havens

The Huron confederacy ceased to exist in 1649 and only one of its tribes, the Tahontaenrat, outlived it as a coherent group. Individuals, families, and clan segments scattered in every direction in search of new homes. Many Huron joined other Iroquoian-speaking groups, hoping to be absorbed by them. Others banded together in various places, seeking to survive and to preserve their identity. This chapter is an account of the early years of this struggle for individual and collective survival by the remnants of the Huron confederacy.[1]

THE DISPERSAL OF THE NEUTRAL

The Huron who fled to the Tionnontaté, Neutral, and Erie found only temporary refuge among these groups. A famine that broke out among the Tionnontaté, partly as a result of the influx of so many Huron, soon forced many of the latter to move to Gahoendoe or to join other tribes. Many women and children were killed when Etharita was destroyed in December 1649. After Father Garreau was recalled to Gahoendoe in the spring of 1650, the Tionnontaté abandoned their tribal lands and retreated to the northwest. Some Huron travelled with them although we do not know how many. The number of Tionnontaté-Huron refugees who survived the decade was no more than 500.

As soon as the Tionnontaté had been coerced into leaving southern Ontario, the Iroquois mustered their forces to attack the Neutral. While in the long run this campaign was primarily of interest to the Seneca as the Huron one had been, the relative lull in Iroquois attacks on the St. Lawrence indicates that many Mohawk and Oneida participated in it (Thwaites 1896–1901, 36:177). Until 1647, the Neutral had been friendly with both the Huron and the Iroquois and probably had obtained European goods from both groups. Consequently, after the Huron had been dispersed, the Seneca might have maintained good relations with the Neutral and sought to become the sole suppliers of European goods to them. Yet, although the Neutral were reputed to lack skill in handling canoes, the Tahontaenrat who had taken refuge among them were no doubt seeking to continue their role as middlemen between the Neutral and the French. Furthermore, the French had attempted to conclude a trading alliance with the Neutral in 1626 and again perhaps in 1640; therefore they might try once more, now that the combined power of the Huron tribes did not stand in their way. As a result of this, the Neutral themselves might fill the commercial vacuum that had been created by the dispersal of the Huron. The Tahontaenrat may also have been encouraging the Neutral to seek alternative sources of European goods among the Erie and the Susquehannock in order to curtail the influence of the Seneca.

Such considerations persuaded the Seneca that it was necessary to attack and disperse the Neutral, rather than to nourish an insecure trading relationship with them. It was also recognized that by attacking the Neutral, all the Iroquois might secure other benefits that were important to them at this time. First, they could seize the beaver skins that must have been accumulating in many of the Neutral villages since the Huron trading network had collapsed. Secondly, they might open an alternative route by which Iroquois warriors could travel north through Michigan, as well as through Ontario, to raid the tribes of the upper Great Lakes. Thirdly, they could gain possession of the rich beaver grounds around Lake St. Clair and along the Thames and Sydenham Rivers, for control of which the Neutral themselves recently had been fighting. For geographical reasons, the latter objective was of more interest to the Seneca than to the other Iroquois tribes. The desire to secure these goals no doubt contributed to the growing enmity between the Iroquois and the Neutral in the late 1640s. Fear that the Neutral would seek revenge for the attack of 1647 must have encouraged the Seneca to seek their dispersal as quickly as possible.

The Iroquois seem to have resumed raiding the Neutral in the spring of 1650; by that summer a large-scale war was in progress. Six hundred Indians who were living in the Neutral country (very likely the Tahontaenrat) sent word to Quebec that the following summer they were coming to solicit arms and other support from the French (35:215). It was probably in reply to this message that Ohenhen was sent on his perilous mission to carry two wampum belts from the governor of New France to the Neutral country (36:133). Ohenhen accomplished this mission, in spite of his encounter with the Iroquois on Georgian Bay. There were also reports that the Neutral and Susquehannock had formed an alliance against the

Iroquois (37:97). If so, this was probably an alliance that Huron refugees had helped to promote.

The Iroquois struck too soon and too hard, however, for any of these new contacts to be of use to the Neutral. The Neutral had no guns, except for a few that were owned by Christian Tahontaenrat who were short of ammunition. In the autumn of 1650 an Iroquois force, variously estimated to be of between 600 (36:121) and 1500 (36:119) men, destroyed a major Neutral village. Later, however, the Neutral, led by the Tahontaenrat, fell upon this army, killing or capturing some 200 of the enemy (36:119). It may have been this victory that gave rise to the report told to the French eighteen months later by the Mohawk that, at one point in the war, the women of the principal Seneca town had been terrified by rumours of a Neutral victory and had fled to the Cayuga (37:97).

In the winter of 1650–51, 1200 Iroquois returned to the Neutral country to avenge the losses of the previous autumn (36:119). This force destroyed the principal town, Teotongniaton (36:141–43). Many prisoners were taken and this raid effectively spelled the end of the Neutral confederacy. The inhabitants of the remaining Neutral villages decided that they were unable to resist the Iroquois and abandoned their houses and fields to the enemy (36:177). Some 800 Neutral are reported to have spent the winter of 1652–53 at Skenchioe, which seventeenth-century maps locate on the large peninsula between Saginaw Bay and Lake Huron (38:181). Although these Neutral planned to join the Tionnontaté, there is no evidence that this happened and nothing more is known about this group.[2] The Sanson map of 1656 suggests that a sizable number of Neutral (Attiouandaron) may have found refuge in the Ohio Valley. Some Huron may have accompanied these and other Neutral groups. Wherever the Neutral went, however, they dispersed and lost their identity so that none were later recorded as an identifiable ethnic unit.

Other Huron who had been living with the Neutral sought refuge among the Erie and Susquehannock. On 27 May 1651 messengers arrived at Three Rivers to say that some of these Huron were coming to join the ones already at Quebec (36:179). There is, however, no record that these refugees ever arrived. When the resourceful Tahontaenrat saw what was happening, they and the Arendarhonon who had joined them proposed to go and live among the Seneca. The Seneca, as we shall see, had their own reasons for being lenient at this time and allowed them to establish a village on Seneca tribal territory, where they might retain their own customs and special usages. Hereafter, the Tahontaenrat and the Seneca lived side-by-side in the greatest amicability (36:179; 44:21; 45:243). By the autumn of 1651 rumours were reaching Quebec that the Tahontaenrat were encouraging the Seneca to make peace with the French and begin trading with them. It was also rumoured that four Tahontaenrat and two Seneca envoys were coming to confer with the French (36:141–43).

THE ERIE WAR

In the winter of 1651–52, with Dutch encouragement the Mohawk had attacked the Susquehannock, hoping to disperse them as the Iroquois had already dispersed the Huron, Tionnontaté, and Neutral. The Susquehannock were, however, well armed by their Swedish trading partners and the Mohawk seem to have suffered the worst of this engagement. It was not until after the Dutch had seized New Sweden in 1655 that they were able to coerce the Susquehannock into making peace with the Mohawk (F. Jennings 1968:23–26; Thwaites 1896–1901, 37:97). In spite of the later success of a combined force of Iroquois against the Scahentarronon (37:111), this failure to deal with the Susquehannock was complicated for the Mohawk by the growing hostility of the Mahican and Sokoki, who once again were allied with the Abenaki and the Canadian Algonkians. Both the Mahican and Sokoki had supported the Mohawk in the 1640s, but they resented the lack of respect that the Mohawk had shown for them, as well as the Mohawk's heavy demands for wampum as the price of continued friendship (36:103–5). Now, the Mohawk were forced to penetrate into increasingly remote areas in search of furs (map 33). In the early 1650s their raiding parties entered the territory of the Attikamegue for the first time and they also made their first appearance in the Lake St. John area (36:147; 37:67, 69). By the end of the decade, raids were taking the Mohawk as far east as Tadoussac and deep into the Hudson Bay watershed of Quebec (46:173, 205, 287, 289).

Under these increasingly difficult circumstances, it is not surprising that the Mohawk called upon the western Iroquois tribes to repay the assistance they had given them, by helping them to attack the French (38:61–63). The Mohawk hoped that by destroying Montreal and Three Rivers, their raiders would be able to penetrate into the northeast more easily and satisfy their need for furs. Even after the Neutral had been dispersed, however, the Seneca refused to help the Mohawk, claiming that they still had dangerous enemies on their borders whom they had to eliminate. These were the Erie, who appear to have been trading partners of the Susquehannock.

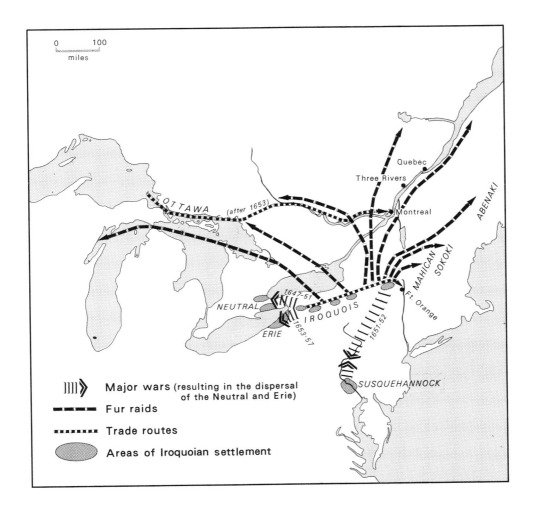

MAP 33. *Intertribal relations, 1650 to 1657.*

Just as the Huron had blocked Seneca raiding in the north and diverted the northern furs to the French, so the Erie prevented the Seneca from hunting and raiding in the Ohio Valley and carried the furs from this region to the Susquehannock and New Sweden. While this does not appear to have been as lucrative a trade as that of the Huron, the Ohio Valley was a worthwhile prize for Iroquois who sought to secure more furs by raiding and hunting. The Seneca and Onondaga had more important reasons, however, for refusing to repay the help that the Mohawk had given them. They resented the arrogance of the Mohawk, which resulted from their larger supply of guns and trade goods and also from their right to grant or withhold permission for the western tribes to travel across their territory to trade at Fort Orange.

Huron and Neutral refugees were encouraging anti-Iroquois feeling among the Erie and eventually provided the Seneca with an excuse to declare war on their hosts (41:83). When thirty Erie envoys visited the Seneca to reconfirm the peace between them, a Seneca was accidentally slain by an Erie. The Seneca were so angered by this killing that rather than accepting reparations, they slew all of the Erie envoys they could lay their hands on, thus challenging the Erie to fight. A band of Erie probably led by Huron refugees penetrated southern Ontario and cut to pieces the rear guard of a victorious force of Onondaga, who were on their way home from Georgian Bay. One of the men they captured was Annenraes, whose release by the Huron in 1647 had led to the final short-lived truce between the Huron and the Onondaga. Although the woman who adopted Annenraes was expected to release him, she demanded that he be slain and eventually the Erie gave in to her demands. His death by torture greatly angered the Onondaga and led the four western Iroquois tribes to join in the war against the Erie (41:81; 42:177–79). The Erie were reported to have attacked and set fire to a Seneca town, although this may have been a false rumour reflecting the current mood of crisis. The Seneca and Onondaga followed traditional Iroquois policy by offering to make peace with the French and their allies in order to fight the Erie more effectively (41:217).

The four western tribes began to negotiate with the French in the spring of 1653. Their aim was to conclude a peace treaty that would allow them to trade with the French. The Onondaga also wanted to persuade the French to settle in their midst to trade and to offer them military aid as they had formerly offered such help to the Huron. This would have involved repairing their guns and helping to defend their towns against enemy attack (44:151). The Mohawk were appalled by these negotiations since they threatened to divide the confederacy and to ally most of its members with the French, whom the Mohawk regarded as their most dangerous adversaries. Rather than risk such a split, the Mohawk decided to conclude a temporary peace with the French themselves (37:109–11).

Although the French were aware that the Mohawk had no intention of stopping their raids on the Algonkin and Montagnais, their military position was so precarious that they made no effort to dictate terms to the Mohawk envoys. The Jesuits strongly supported making peace. They no longer had the Huron mission to protect and therefore saw little reason to continue fighting the Iroquois. They also reasoned that peace would allow them to re-establish contact with many Huron who had been baptized and were now living among the Iroquois. It would additionally open up a new mission field to replace the one that they had lost among the Huron. Thus, by the autumn of 1653 the French were in fact, if not yet by treaty, at peace with all the Iroquois tribes.

In spite of this, the rift that became apparent between the Mohawk and the other Iroquois tribes was to last for a long time. In their efforts to end the friendship between the upper Iroquois and the French, the Mohawk appear to have murdered three important Seneca who visited Quebec over the winter of 1656–57 to have talks with the French. This led to an armed confrontation between the Seneca and the Mohawk (43:99–103; 44:149–151). Even after the peace with the French had collapsed, the Mohawk remained angry and showed little interest in helping their neighbours. They tended to remain aloof from the conflict that dragged on from 1659 to 1675 between the Susquehannock and the three western Iroquois tribes, and which resulted in frequent and serious setbacks for these tribes (map 34).

All of this, however, was some time in the future. In the summer of 1654 the western Iroquois tribes raised an army of 1200 to 1800 men, and attacked the Erie (31:83, 121; 42:179). The Erie did not possess firearms (41:83) and the few Huron refugees among them who did were short of ammunition (42:181). Two of the Iroquois who led the expedition dressed in French clothes in order to intimidate the Erie by making them believe that Europeans were fighting alongside the Iroquois (42:181). After the fall of important towns such as Gentaienton (61:195) and Rigué, the Erie rallied in a fortified location where they defended themselves bravely for a time with their poisoned arrows.[3] Among those who died in Rigué was René Tsondihwané, the elderly Huron from Ossossané who had been baptized as early as 1639. Tsondihwané had led his family to Rigué by unknown stages and had continued to pray and to maintain other Christian

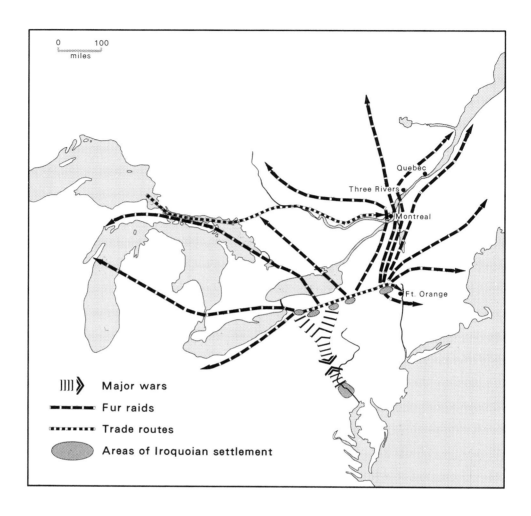

MAP 34. *Intertribal relations, 1659 to 1663.*

observances. His daughter, Gohatio, was taken prisoner by the Iroquois but after seeing her twin children killed, she too was slain by her captor because of an ailment from which she suffered. Her son, Tehannonrakouan, was killed by the Susquehannock. It is unclear whether this happened before or after he was captured by the Iroquois (42:75, 187–89).

Desultory fighting continued until at least 1657, with Iroquois warriors returning home from time to time with small numbers of captives and loot from the Erie country (42:191–99; Adams 1961:63). Many Erie were taken prisoner, but others drifted southeastward and established themselves near Chesapeake Bay,[4] possibly under the protection of the Susquehannock (plate 50). About 1680 some 600 men, women, and children of this group surrendered themselves to the Iroquois, fearing that otherwise the Iroquois would attack them (Thwaites 1896–1901, 62:71). Others may have survived for a time as the "Black Minquas," but as a recognizable ethnic group the Erie, like the Neutral, disappeared. The Seneca and their neighbours were now free to raid into the Ohio Valley, where they are said to have encountered tribes that still had no knowledge of European goods (44:49). These raids eventually brought the Iroquois into conflict with the Shawnee, Illinois, and other tribes living to the south and west of them (47:145; Perrot 1911:154–57).

THE HURON ON THE ST. LAWRENCE: 1647–1650

During the three last years of the Huron confederacy, many Huron had spent considerable periods of time in the St. Lawrence Valley. As before, some were prisoners who had escaped from the Iroquois and made their way to the French settlements. One of these was Jean-Armand Andehoua, who was captured by the Iroquois in 1647 and severely tortured. The following year he was forced to accompany a Mohawk raiding party that was investing the St. Lawrence River near Three Rivers. Knowing he was near a French settlement, he managed to escape from the Iroquois and made his way there, where he was recognized and warmly welcomed (Thwaites 1896–1901, 32:161–63).

Other Huron had come either to trade or to help the Algonkin and Montagnais wage war on the Mohawk and were prevented, either by the winter or by Iroquois blockades, from returning home. Some spent the onset of winter living under Jesuit supervision at Sillery or joined the Montagnais in their winter hunts south of the St. Lawrence River. Others appear to have hunted by themselves in the same area (30:165). Still other

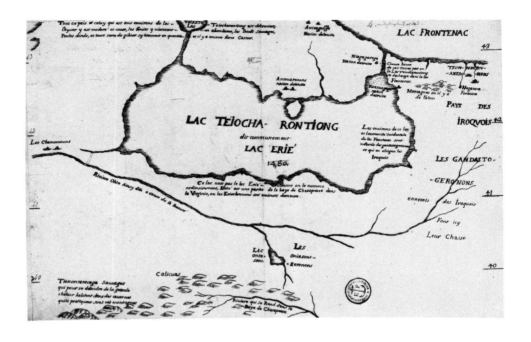

PLATE 50. *Anonymous map of Lake Erie, probably by Abbé Claude Bernou, c. 1680. The inscriptions indicate that at this period the Susquehannock were hunting in the upper part of the Ohio Valley. The claim that the Erie had always lived around Chesapeake Bay refers to Erie who sought refuge there after their defeat by the Iroquois. Courtesy Public Archives of Canada.*

Huron wintered among the French at Quebec (34:63) or Montreal (30:229), or with the Algonkian-speaking Indians who lived under French protection at Three Rivers (30:173). In 1649 many Huron who came to the St. Lawrence on business were unable to return home before winter set in. Because of this, approximately twenty Huron spent the following winter at Three Rivers and twenty more at Quebec. Half of the latter were lodged at the hospital and, to maintain them over the winter, the Jesuits had to supply them with a cask of eels, a barrel of corn, six blankets, two pairs of snowshoes, and other goods (34:63).

In spite of the informal nature of these groups, they made decisions that formerly would have required ratification by tribal councils in the Huron country. When in the spring of 1650 a Huron named Skandahietsi was discovered to have surrendered to the Iroquois and to be acting as a spy for them, the Huron who were wintering at Quebec condemned him to death and executed him. One of these Huron, Outarahon, made a long speech justifying the execution. In it, he assured the French that the Huron headmen would approve what had been done (35:47–49, 217–23). While the Huron executed traitors, it is likely that the men who were wintering at Quebec, all of whom were Christians, were influenced to act on their own initiative by the French. Formerly such a decision would have been discussed by Huron headmen very carefully, and in full council, before steps were taken to implement it.

In 1646–47 the various groups of Indians who were wintering at Three Rivers appointed the Algonkin headman, Simon Pieskaret, to be responsible for good relations between them and the French, and also between the Huron and Algonkin (31:287). The Huron who were wintering at Quebec and Three Rivers remained in close contact with one another and travelled back and forth between these two settlements at frequent intervals. These trips made it easier for the French to relay letters and verbal messages from one community to the other during the winter (32:69, 77, 107).

The mortality rate among these Huron was high, since many were killed or captured in encounters with the Iroquois. In the spring of 1647 some Indians from Sillery accompanied three French pinnaces up the St. Lawrence River, seeking to discover and flush out Iroquois raiders. On their return from Montreal a Huron canoe that was in the vanguard of this expedition was captured by the Iroquois on Lake St. Peter, while a Huron who was reconnoitring an Iroquois fort was shot and eaten by the enemy (31:171–75). Other Huron were captured by the Iroquois when they went into the forests to hunt (30:229–31). More than a dozen were killed or captured in 1647 alone. Another Huron was killed accidentally. This was

Aonchiarre, who came from the village of Caldaria (Tiondatsae or Ekhiondastsaan), near Teanaostaiaé. He was shot in the leg by a companion on the last day of December 1647, carried to the hospital at Quebec, and baptized the same day. His leg had to be amputated and he died from complications about two weeks later. At the request of his companions, he was interred in the cemetery at Quebec as an expression of solidarity between the Christian Huron and the French (32:71, 243).

The number of Huron requesting baptism at Quebec or Three Rivers appears to have been less than it had been previously and there is no evidence that young men were still coming to these places specifically to receive instruction. This suggests the greater ease with which baptism could now be obtained in the Huron country. Aside from Aonchiarre, only two Huron baptisms were recorded. One was that of Saondionrhens, who was from Ossossané. He was baptized on Easter evening 1648 (32:81).

In spite of this, examples of Huron piety were not lacking. In 1646 Michel Exouaendaen (Ekouaendaé) brought a young girl to Quebec to join the Ursulines in their nunnery. He was an Assistaronon, who had been taken prisoner as a child and adopted by a Huron family in Scanonaenrat. In his adolescence, he suffered from a lingering ailment that left him partially paralysed. It is reported that when his relatives ignored him, he turned to the Jesuits for help. Being told about the miraculous cures resulting from pilgrimages to Roman Catholic shrines in Europe, he decided to make a similar pilgrimage to Sainte-Marie. Although he had not attempted a long journey for a number of years, he covered the distance from Scanonaenrat to Sainte-Marie in fifteen hours and upon arriving there, was instantly cured (30:89–97). It appears to have been in return for this cure that he volunteered to transport this young girl to Quebec. She was the next Huron after Thérèse Oionhaton to be instructed by the Ursulines.

When Exouaendaen was ready to return to the Huron country, it was already too late in the year for him to do so safely. He therefore spent the winter living in the house of the Ursulines' chaplain and doing odd jobs for them. Although most of the Huron staying at Quebec were Christians, it is indicative of their more independent attitude that they ridiculed Exouaendaen for taking orders from women and performing tasks such as hauling water, which the Huron believed women should do for themselves. He was especially ridiculed when he refused to join an expedition against the Iroquois without permission from the Ursulines (31:175–79). Because of Iroquois raids, the girl that he brought with him was unable to return to the Huron country until 1648. When she left, the Ursulines gave her a complete set of French clothes and sent presents to her parents to express the joy they had experienced from having her live with them (32:215). Exouaendaen returned to Quebec after the dispersal of the Huron and died in the care of the Hospital nuns sometime prior to October 1651 (36:205).

Another indication of the growing involvement of some Huron in the mission work of the Jesuits was the entry into their service on 9 August 1648 of Pierre Onaatichiae. Since he turned over twenty-one pounds of beaver skins to the Jesuits, and they remained accountable to him for them if he should leave their service, it would appear that he became a donné (32:99). He had been baptized, apparently at Quebec, on 17 July (32:95).

What is unclear is whether any Huron families were settled in New France at this time. Etienne Girault de Villeneuve, writing in 1762, suggests that in the decade prior to 1650, a considerable number of Huron had settled at Sillery in order to live a peaceful life there (70:207). There are, however, no contemporary references to entire Huron families having settled at Sillery or elsewhere in the St. Lawrence Valley and it seems likely that Girault de Villeneuve misinterpreted references to individual Huron wintering at these places. To be sure, Atironta and his family spent the winter of 1645–46 at Sillery, but they do not count as settlers any more than do the various groups of warriors and traders.

The Huron Refugees at Quebec

THE SETTLEMENT ON THE ILE D'ORLEANS

Prior to the Jesuits moving to Gahoendoe in 1649, a Huron headman was sent to determine whether the French authorities would approve of Huron refugees settling at Quebec (Thwaites 1896–1901, 34:223). Caring for such refugees depended upon charity, which, according to the ideas of the day, was a concern of the religious orders and of interested individuals rather than of the government of New France. The Jesuits at Quebec discussed this problem at Easter 1650, so that Father Bressani could convey their answer to the Huron when he returned to Gahoendoe. At this meeting the Jesuits decided that it was their duty to permit Huron families to settle on their lands at Beauport, near Quebec, but that these families must be few in number and carefully selected for their Christian piety. The Jesuits estimated that initially they would have to spend 3000 livres a year in order to establish these Huron (35:39). Cold as this decision may seem, it was economically realistic. The few French settlers at Quebec did not produce enough food to support a large number of refugees, nor could the trading company have imported what was needed on short notice, even if its directors had been inclined to do so.

Father Ragueneau's decision to lead 300 Huron from Gahoendoe to Quebec was taken independently of discussions at Quebec and brought more Huron refugees to the St. Lawrence than the Jesuits at Quebec had planned to support. When Ragueneau's Huron arrived at Montreal, they rested for two days and were cared for by the French settlers. The latter tried to persuade some Huron to settle there, hoping that they would help to re-establish trade with the interior; however, the Huron were too frightened to remain in a place that was as exposed to attack as Montreal was and they soon hurried down-river. Some stayed at the Indian settlement at Three Rivers (37:181), while the rest continued on to Quebec, arriving there 28 July. Three or four leading Frenchmen at Quebec each agreed to care for one (extended?) Huron family. The Hospital nuns took charge of the sick and of several more families, while Madame de La Peltrie and the Ursulines undertook to feed and clothe the numerous family, or clan segment, of Pierre Ondakion, who was one of the leading headmen of Ossossané and an early convert to Christianity (35:209). They also enrolled a number of little girls in their school, including Ondakion's daughter, Geneviève-Agnès Skanudharoua, who, with the financial support of a god-mother in France, was able to remain with the Ursulines. She took her final vows as a nun shortly before she died in 1657 (44:259–75). The Ursulines also took in a twenty-three-year-old widow named Cecile Arenhatsi, who agreed to work for them as a servant (36:213). When the Ursulines' dwelling burned to the ground at the end of 1650, the Huron had their headman, Louis Taiaeronk, present two large wampum belts to the Ursulines as a token of their sympathy (36:215–21).

This charity left 200 other Huron in need of food, clothing, and shelter and caring for them became the responsibility of the Jesuits. Most Huron erected their longhouses in the Upper Town between the Ursulines' residence and the hospital, whose chapels served them as parish churches (35:211; 36:55, 59). There, the Huron were under the protection of near-by Fort St. Louis. The Jesuits and the nuns distributed corn and pea soup to the Huron, who came each day to their residences to collect it (35:211; 36:59–61). During the first year, it cost the Jesuits about 8000 livres to feed the Huron and additional funds had to be obtained in order to supply them with iron hatchets, kettles, clothing, and other necessities (36:203; 41:139). In the course of the winter, only three men and two women died, which indicates that the Huron were being well looked after (36:203–5).

Knowing that more Huron were on their way to Quebec, the Jesuits were anxious to secure a suitable location for permanent Huron settlement. On 19 March 1651, they obtained possession of some cleared land that belonged to Eléonore de Grandmaison. This land was located on the west end of the Ile d'Orléans, within sight of Quebec (36:117). Some thirty Huron families, who had wintered either at Quebec or among the Algonkians at Sillery, moved to the island in March 1651. Each family was assigned a plot of land, none of which was larger than half an arpent (36:117). Although these could not produce enough to feed the Huron over the following winter, crops were planted soon after they arrived and French workmen helped the Huron to clear more land. Wood from these clearings was used by the Huron to construct their longhouses. These were located under the shelter of a fort that the Jesuits constructed and which was said to be about the same size as the one on Gahoendoe. The Jesuits also constructed a chapel for the Huron and a house where Father Garreau, another priest, and four donnés were to live. Although the Huron had a good harvest in 1651, not enough land had been brought under cultivation to feed them; moreover, the population of the settlement was increased that autumn by the arrival of forty canoes bearing the starving and impoverished Huron who had made their way from Gahoendoe to Manitoulin Island (36:143, 189). By 1653 the two groups had cleared about 300 arpents and were able to feed themselves.

The Jesuits were anxious that the Huron who settled at Quebec should become fully self-supporting as soon as possible. Yet, until the Huron produced surplus corn, they were not in a position to resume trading for furs. The hard-pressed Montagnais of the Quebec City area, who had joined the Jesuits' settlement at Sillery as supplies of game declined in their hunting territories, had been encouraged by the Jesuits to trade European goods with Indian groups who lived farther down the St. Lawrence. By purchasing European goods at the cheaper prices available to Christians and reselling them at a higher price to Indians who were not converts, these Montagnais were able to make a small profit in furs, which covered the cost of food and other necessities that they needed to obtain from the French. By reselling French trade goods to non-Christians at just under the price that the latter were charged for them at Quebec, the Indians at Sillery were assured of a long-term source of income.

There is some evidence that the Jesuits encouraged the Huron to engage in an analogous form of trade. In November 1651, three Frenchmen who worked for the fur trader Robert Giffard de Moncel were drowned while crossing the St. Lawrence at night, in order to trade for beaver skins on the

Ile d'Orléans (36:147). On 6 June 1652, six Huron men and three children were drowned in a storm while returning from Tadoussac, where they had gone to trade cornmeal for skins in order to make robes "for their own use." All of these Huron were from Ossossané and the dead included Joseph Teondechoren (37:169). Since the Huron were not able to feed themselves at this time, the cornmeal that they were trading must have come either from the Jesuits or from French traders. Since the best quality furs were worn for some time before being traded with the French, the Huron's making robes "for their own use" does not rule out the likelihood that they later sold these furs to the French. Radisson states that the Huron on the Ile d'Orléans made robes of greased beaver skins from which the Jesuits derived a "profit" of 10,000 livres tournois annually (Adams 1961:50); possibly this figure represents the total value of the furs that the Huron supplied to the trading company. Since skins exchanged for from three to five livres each, this suggests that the Huron were supplying more than 2000 skins a year. While the volume of this trade is surprising, it is not unexpected that the Jesuits would encourage extensive commercial activities to reduce the expenses they incurred in running the Huron settlement. The development of trading along the lower St. Lawrence would also explain why, when Jean Bourdon made his journey around the coast of Labrador in the summer of 1657, he took two Huron guides with him (Thwaites 1896–1901, 44:189). Some time before he turned back, these Huron were killed by Indians or Eskimo, who also wounded one Frenchman.[5] In spite of the volume of this trade, it was only of marginal significance to the French traders, since it tapped fur resources that were already available to them.

IROQUOIS HARASSMENT CONTINUES

From 1650 to the summer of 1653 the Mohawk sent raiding parties into the St. Lawrence Valley with increasing frequency. During this period a minimum of forty Huron were killed or carried off by Iroquois, not counting those who were captured but later escaped. Although this was not a large number of individuals, it represented the loss of between five and ten percent of the Huron population along the St. Lawrence. Most of these Huron were taken in the vicinity of Montreal and Three Rivers. In the autumn of 1650 seven Huron, led by Hondakont, were captured close to Montreal even though there were ten canoes in their party, while the Mohawk had only three (Thwaites 1896–1901, 35:59). In the spring of

1651 Jacques Ondhwarak and his uncle Aontrati were captured while hunting, although the younger man later managed to escape (36:133). In July another group of Iroquois killed one Huron and captured another, who were gathering hay for the French opposite Three Rivers (36:133–35) and in the autumn of 1651 another Huron was captured at Montreal (36:149).

Early in 1652 three Huron were captured after they had set out from Montreal on a raid against the Mohawk (37:95–97). In March ten more Huron were captured, at least three of whom were killed. These Huron were accompanying a party of Algonkin men and women from Three Rivers to Montreal. Their leader, Toratati, was among those who were tortured to death (37:93; 38:49). A Huron named Ahoskwentak, who was taken prisoner, later managed to escape (37:101). On 15 May a Huron woman, her daughter, and the latter's four-year old son were seized near Montreal when they went to flesh a moose that had been shot nearby (37:101). In spite of their former avoidance of Montreal, at least a few Huron were now living or wintering there.

The rest of the incidents recorded for 1652 took place around Three Rivers. On 10 May Thomas Tsondoutannen, who was accompanying Father Jacques Buteux up the St. Maurice River, was captured by the Iroquois in an engagement in which the priest and his French companion were slain; however, Tsondoutannen soon managed to escape and returned to Three Rivers. On 8 June two Huron were killed while fishing opposite Three Rivers (37:105; 38:53). On 7 August one Huron of a group of eighty Huron and Algonkians who were returning from Montreal was slain (37:111) and ten days later Saouenhati and his wife were killed while working in their fields at Three Rivers (37:115). This Saouenhati was the namesake of an early Christian convert from Teanaostaiaé. In November another Huron woman was killed (37:117) and in December two more men were captured a few miles from Three Rivers (38:169). In the spring of 1653 four more Huron were seized while hunting or travelling between Three Rivers and Quebec (38:171). Another Huron was taken prisoner on 30 May but was later rescued (38:177). Two others, who were captured three weeks later, were not so fortunate (38:179).

The majority of Huron were killed or captured as a result of the general warfare that was going on between the Mohawk and the French; however, the emphasis that the Mohawk placed on capturing Huron prisoners reflected their long-term ambition to incorporate all of the Huron who had come to Quebec into their own society or, failing this, to kill them. This would rob the French of allies who were skilled in guerilla warfare and would neutralize the desire of Huron prisoners among the Iroquois to join relatives who were living with the French. It also provided a means by which the Mohawk, who were hard-pressed by spiralling losses from disease and warfare, could augment their numbers.

When the Mohawk harassed Three Rivers in July 1652, the French and Algonkin were displeased to note that sundry negotiations went on between the Huron and the Iroquois. The Huron were anxious for news about their relatives who were living among the Mohawk and who made up part of the Mohawk force, while the Mohawk were equally interested in persuading the Huron to desert the French (38:55). The French believed that it was only in order to encourage defections that the Mohawk headman, Aontarisati, pretended to wish to discuss peace with them. The French persuaded a number of Huron to seize him when he landed for these talks, and he and a companion were burned at Three Rivers the next day (37:107–111). The French hoped that this would rule out any further friendly relations between Huron and Iroquois.

Although the Mohawk swore to avenge the death of Aontarisati by henceforth killing every Huron they captured (40:97), their main resentment appears to have been directed against the French at Three Rivers. In August 1653 the Mohawk besieged the settlement, after failing to take it by surprise. As the siege was prolonged, it provided another opportunity for the Huron to renew their contacts with the Mohawk. Soon the meetings between these two groups became more important than the warfare that was going on. Some Huron who were fighting with the Mohawk joined their kinsmen who were living with the French, but another carried off his daughter who had been staying at Three Rivers (40:113–15).

THE RAPE OF THE QUEBEC HURON

When the Mohawk who were besieging Three Rivers learned that peace talks were progressing well between the Onondaga and the French and about the defeat of another Mohawk band on Montreal Island, the leaders of this war party decided that, rather than be left out, the time had come for them to negotiate for peace also. They delegated several Mohawk, led by the headman Andioura, to accompany the Onondaga to Quebec. Andioura met secretly with the Huron headmen from the Ile d'Orléans and offered them presents to induce their followers to leave the island and settle among the Mohawk. Later, Atsina, a Huron headman living at Three Rivers, gave the Mohawk three presents to signify that the Huron accepted this proposal (Thwaites 1896–1901, 41:19).

The Onondaga delegates also visited the Huron settlement on the Ile d'Orléans. Although they claimed that they had come only to make peace with the Huron (40:165–69), the Onondaga were as interested as were the Mohawk in persuading these Huron to live with them. It is therefore not surprising that the Huron also gave the Onondaga presents as tokens of their willingness to join them (41:21). These presents explain why, when the Montagnais denounced the idea of making peace with the Iroquois, the Huron remained unmoved, while their headmen unexpectedly announced that in the past the Montagnais and Algonkin had behaved as badly as the Iroquois (40:189).

The Huron at Quebec and Three Rivers doubted that the French could defend them against a concerted Iroquois attack and therefore were anxious to encourage at least the appearance of cordial relations with their formerly avowed enemies. It is clear, however, that these Huron had no desire to surrender themselves to the Iroquois. They rightly feared that the Onondaga would avenge former injuries should they get them in their power and that rivalry between the Mohawk and Onondaga would result in whichever tribe these Huron decided not to live with seeking to harm them (41:59).

Such fears are evident in the Huron's dealings with the four Onondaga who arrived at Montreal on their way to Quebec in January 1654. When the French learned that they came to have dealings with the Huron on the Ile d'Orléans, they were at first reluctant to let them continue on their journey. At a secret night session Tsiraenie, the leader of this group, informed the Huron that the following spring, 400 Onondaga men and 100 women were coming as far as the St. Francis River to help the Huron transport their possessions to the Onondaga country. He instructed the Huron headmen that they were to tell their people that since peace now prevailed, they were going to re-settle at Montreal; only the Huron headmen should know the actual destination of this move until they had contacted the Onondaga. Terrified by the implications of this suggestion, the Huron headmen replied that their promise of the previous year had been misunderstood; they had merely meant to assure the Onondaga that if war broke out again between the French and the Iroquois, the Huron and Onondaga would remain on sufficiently good terms that any Onondaga the Huron captured would not be slain (41:21).

Desperate for the safety of their own people, the Huron headmen decided to inform the Jesuits and French officials about their secret dealings with the Iroquois. The French temporarily suspected a conspiracy between the Huron and the Onondaga; then they feared that it would endanger the fragile truce between the Iroquois and the French if the Onondaga were to believe that there was no hope of the Huron at Quebec ever joining them voluntarily. The Jesuits and Governor d'Ailleboust told the Huron to inform Tsiraenie that the French knew about their discussions and that he would have to apply to the French for permission before the latter would allow the Huron to join the Onondaga. It was agreed that d'Ailleboust would delay approving such a move by saying that he would discuss it only once the peace between the French and the Onondaga was well established (41:21–23). The Huron were also instructed to tell the Onondaga that the Jesuits wished to found a settlement in their country and to imply that the Huron would only be allowed to go there after this had been accomplished (41:61–63). A desire to escape further pressure from the Mohawk may explain why most of the Huron who were at Three Rivers joined the settlement on the Ile d'Orléans in April 1654 (70:205–7).

While serving to placate the Onondaga and to advance certain French interests, the advice that the French gave to the Huron did little to make the latter feel secure about their future or about the long-term willingness of the French to protect them. Indeed, these negotiations indicated the increasing expendability of the Christian Huron at Quebec in the eyes of French officials and the Jesuit clergy. The peace of 1653 seemed miraculous to the French, who did not understand why the various Iroquois tribes needed to disengage themselves from fighting with them. While the French might be rueful about a peace that had been dictated by the Iroquois rather than imposed on the latter by force, they had a desperate interest in seeing that it continued.

Both the Mohawk (40:185) and the Onondaga (42:53) were anxious that the French should conclude an alliance with them that would involve having Frenchmen settle in their midst, as they had formerly done among the Huron. This would provide them with hostages to ensure that the French would not aid their enemies and a garrison for their protection, as well as facilitating trade. With a French settlement in their midst, the Mohawk could play French and Dutch traders off against one another and dominate the western Iroquois. Conversely, the Onondaga hoped for a French settlement so that they might have an alternative source of European goods and no longer be dependent on the goodwill of the Mohawk. They also hoped for French assistance against the Erie and other enemies (42:53).

The Jesuits were delighted at the prospect of undertaking mission work among one or more of the Iroquois tribes and believed that if the Quebec Huron were resettled among the Iroquois under Jesuit protection, the move would not harm the Huron and would help to promote the spread of Christianity. The hitherto inexplicable dispersal of the Huron was now seen by the Jesuits as an act of divine providence that was about to open promising new mission fields. The Jesuits' enthusiasm to placate the Iroquois and to exploit these mission fields supports Radisson's claim that it was mainly at their insistence that most of the Huron ultimately left Quebec to join the Iroquois (Adams 1961:50).

The Onondaga visited Quebec in September 1655 to reaffirm their treaty with the French and the latter's Indian allies. This was done in the name of all the Iroquois tribes except the Mohawk. While there, the Onondaga formally invited the French to live in their country as they had formerly lived among the Huron (42:53). The Jesuits enthusiastically accepted this invitation and Fathers Pierre Chaumonot and Claude Dablon were dispatched to the Onondaga as an advance guard of the seven priests and approximately fifty workmen who were to establish the Jesuit residence of Sainte-Marie-de-Ganentaa the following summer (42:57–59). The Onondaga interpreted the acceptance of their invitation as ensuring that the Huron at Quebec would join them rather than the Mohawk, and the Jesuits recognized the resettlement of the Huron as being one of the conditions for establishing a mission there.

The Huron correctly perceived that further dealings with the Onondaga would arouse the bitter enmity of the Mohawk. When the latter saw themselves being out-manoeuvred by the Onondaga, they became more determined than ever that they would compel the Huron to live with them. No course seemed open but to coerce the Huron, while at the same time offering to maintain peace with the French (42:49). On 25 April 1656 two Mohawk raiders killed one Huron and wounded another along the shore of the St. Lawrence below Quebec. The Huron set out in pursuit of the raiders and captured one of them some fifty miles up-river. The French urged the Huron to spare the prisoner's life so they might use him to turn away a large band of Mohawk who were reported to be on their way to harass the Huron settlement; however, the relatives of the murdered man were influential and they demanded that the prisoner be tortured to death, which was done after he was baptized (43:105–7).

The Mohawk warriors continued down the St. Lawrence River, camping at Three Rivers and cordially conferring with the Jesuits and French officials there. The French gave the Mohawk presents and attempted to dissuade them from attacking the Huron, but at no time did they threaten to use force to stop them for fear this would endanger the security they derived from their own tenuous peace treaty. When the Mohawk finally disbanded to go hunting and raiding in different directions, the French believed they had been successful (43:107–13). On 18 May, however, the Mohawk reassembled and two days later, without being sighted from Quebec, they landed on the Ile d'Orléans near the Huron village. In the morning, after mass had been said, the Huron set out to work in their fields and the Mohawk, who meanwhile had secreted themselves between the church and the fort, fell upon them. Some Huron found refuge in the Jesuits' fortified house but approximately seventy, including many young women, were killed or taken prisoner. All the while, the Mohawk were careful not to harm the French who were living on the island (43:115–19). They forced their prisoners to embark in forty canoes and travelled up-river past Quebec in broad daylight. As they passed the French settlement they compelled the prisoners to sing, in order to mock both the Huron and the French. When the Mohawk reached Three Rivers, one of the Jesuits visited their camp to console the Huron captives, but no attempt was made to rescue them (43:123).

Many French settlers were surprised that the governor accepted what had happened passively. It was later explained that nothing was done to save the Huron because the lives of the missionaries who were already working among the Iroquois would have been endangered if war broke out (Perrot 1911:192–93). In fact, the military and economic situation in the colony was so precarious that few traders or officials were willing to risk another war with the Iroquois in order to protect these refugees. Among the prisoners was Jacques Oachonk, who was judged to be the most fervent Christian in the settlement, and Joachim Ondakont, a famous warrior (43:119–23). Both men were tortured to death by the Mohawk, but many others were allowed to live. Perrot (1911:158, 193) later observed that none of the Huron, whether living among the Iroquois, at Quebec, or with the Tionnontaté, ever forgave this act of treachery by which the French abandoned so many of their people to the mercy of their enemies. The Huron who remained at Quebec realized that they could not count on the French to protect them so long as they lived on the Ile d'Orléans and on 4 June they returned uninvited to Quebec (70:207). Some of the French, appalled by what had happened, offered plots of land to these Huron to compensate them for the fields they had abandoned. One of the Huron who was offered the most land was the popular Ignace Tsaouenhohoui, who was later recognized as the principal headman of the Huron colony.[6] Although he was given this land for his own use, he distributed it, in Huron fashion, to the families who had the greatest need of it (53:121). Many Huron seem to have gone to live at Sillery, which was fortified and at that time was partially abandoned by its Algonkian inhabitants (43:35; 45:115).

In spite of moving to Quebec, the Huron could not feel secure until they had settled their differences with the Mohawk. An agreement was concluded the following autumn, but only after all of the remaining Huron had again promised to join their enemies. This agreement was formally ratified by three Huron who visited the Mohawk villages to confer with the Mohawk headmen. The latter stated that their people would come to fetch the remaining Huron in the spring of 1657 and warned the Huron not to attempt further delays or evasions (43:187). Four Mohawk returned to Quebec with these envoys, to remain with the Huron and observe their good behaviour (42:261). Both the Huron and the French knew that this promise conflicted with the Huron's previous undertaking to join the Onondaga. To complicate matters, in November 1656 the Oneida publicly offered presents to the Huron inviting them to resettle among them. This was apparently a proposal that the Oneida had made twice before (42:253–55). Father Ragueneau saved the Huron from having to reply to the Oneida by giving the latter to understand that further negotiations would have to be conducted through Father Le Mercier once the French and Huron were established among the Onondaga (42:257).

The Onondaga became extremely angry when they learned about the latest agreement between the Mohawk and the Huron. In April 1657 fifty of them arrived at Quebec publicly vowing to wage war on the Huron and Montagnais. The Onondaga had already wounded a Huron woman while crossing Lake St. Peter (43:35). At Quebec they killed another Huron, and the young men vented their anger against the French by killing their domestic animals. The French did nothing to hinder them and breathed a sigh of relief when it became evident that the aim of these warriors was to force the Huron to honour their earlier promise to join the Onondaga. While a protracted series of conferences during the month of May accomplished little, the Huron lost hope that the French would do anything to defend them and eventually the Arendarhonon at Quebec agreed to join the Onondaga. The large number of Arendarhonon already living among the Onondaga explains this choice. By contrast, the Attignawantan preferred to join the Mohawk rather than the western Iroquois tribes who were their traditional enemies. In spite of the small number of Huron who came to Quebec, tribal affiliation remained crucial in determining foreign policy (43:35–43, 199–207).

The Arendarhonon publicly agreed that they would join the Onondaga when the French went to live there in the summer and several days later the Onondaga departed, accompanied by three Huron envoys. Although the Mohawk who had spent the winter at Quebec were present throughout these negotiations and had joined in them in an apparent spirit of goodwill, the Mohawk at Three Rivers and Montreal prevented the Huron envoys from journeying any farther. These Mohawk included about 100 armed men, who had come to transport the Huron to their villages (43:45–47, 187). Their main force bivouaced up-river, while twenty-five or thirty Mohawk travelled to Quebec to summon the Huron to depart. They arrived there 28 May (43:45, 187). The Huron did not want to leave Quebec, but, with the French unwilling to defend their right to stay, they believed they had to go or die at the hands of the Mohawk (43:191).

A whole night was spent in urgent consultation. The Attigneenongnahac refused to leave Quebec, while the Arendarhonon reluctantly reaffirmed their pledge to join the Onondaga. The Attignawantan promised to join the Mohawk. The next morning Atsina, the headman of the Attignawantan, announced his people's willingness to follow the Mohawk, regardless of the consequences. Pathetically, he intimated that if the Attigneenongnahac and the Arendarhonon saw that the Attignawantan were well treated by the Mohawk, they might be willing to join them at a later date. The Mohawk promised to treat the Attignawantan as relatives and, appreciating the crucial role that the Jesuits had played in encouraging the Huron to join the Iroquois, they formally invited the Jesuits to visit them so the Attignawantan might remain Christians. Although the Mohawk asked the French to provide pinnaces to transport the Huron up-river, the French refused to do this. Thus, the Indians worked for several days to make extra canoes and spent the nights giving farewell feasts. The most splendid of these was given by Atsina to take leave of the French and of the Indians who remained at Quebec (43:187–95); however, when the time came to leave, all but fourteen women and children deferred their departure (43:49). If those who remained behind hoped that rivalry between the Mohawk and Onondaga over their custody would save them from having to join either tribe, they were mistaken. In August 100 Mohawk returned to Montreal, of whom twenty travelled down-river to Quebec. On 21 August some more Attignawantan left Quebec with these Mohawk, while the final group, led by Father Le Moyne, followed them a few days later (43:53–55; 44:189).

The fifty Arendarhonon who had opted to join the Onondaga left Quebec on 16 June. The French conveyed them to Montreal in pinnaces and there they awaited the arrival of a group of Seneca and Onondaga who were to

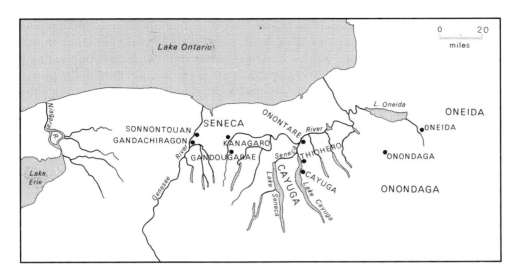

MAP 37. *Settlements of the four western Iroquois tribes, showing the location of Gandougarae.*

particular lineage. On the other hand, whole extended families who voluntarily joined the Iroquois seem to have been adopted by a clan segment, rather than by families, and were allowed to live in separate longhouses. The heads of such households were not granted any voice in public councils, which conservatism and deliberate policy seem to have restricted to old Iroquois families (43:293). In time, however, even these Huron families became united with Iroquois ones through intermarriage, which no doubt promoted cultural assimilation.

The distinction between Huron who joined the Iroquois voluntarily and those who had been taken prisoner was not always a clear one or carefully observed by the Iroquois. This is illustrated by the treatment of the Quebec Huron who joined the Onondaga under duress and by the preliminary torture of the Huron who surrendered at the Long Sault. An Iroquois who felt especially obliged to avenge a dead kinsman, or who identified a particular Huron as an enemy who had inflicted specific injuries on members of his family, might demand that this Huron be treated as a prisoner of war, even if he had surrendered voluntarily. Prisoners of war almost always were treated roughly. Men or women who were ill or seriously injured and hence unable to keep up with a war party were killed immediately and almost all the men were tortured to some degree as soon as they were captured. When the Iroquois returned home, families were broken up and individual prisoners were assigned to different Iroquois longhouses for adoption (42:75). These extended families had the right to kill such prisoners and often exercised this right if the prisoner was old or weak, or a member of their own family had been slain. One important headman is reported to have adopted some eighty prisoners and had them tortured to death to avenge his brother who had been killed in war (48:169). A prisoner who was allowed to live could be killed any time that his or her behaviour displeased their adoptive relatives (42:137), while other Iroquois, anxious to avenge old scores, might seek to kill or injure a Huron even though he had been formally adopted.

As the number of prisoners increased out of all proportion to what the Iroquois were accustomed to deal with, the Iroquois became insecure and more anxious to intimidate these prisoners. Prisoners were known to be slain if they became seriously ill (43:295, 303), if their behaviour displeased any of their adoptive kinsmen (49:107), or for quite capricious reasons. A warrior killed two female captives and their children rather than permit the village council to assign them for adoption. Likewise, the Iroquois did not question the propriety of children being slain if they hindered their mothers from working (Adams 1961:69). Prisoners were made to perform much of the hardest and least pleasant work, such as hauling food and trade goods over long distances (ibid. 28). Some headmen were now accompanied by a number of prisoners wherever they went (Thwaites 1896–1901, 48:171). The French called such prisoners slaves, in reference to the brutal manner in which they were treated. The term failed, however, to take account of the kinship basis of Iroquois society and of the fact that the ultimate aim of this brutality was the assimilation of these aliens as full members of Iroquois society.

Yet, in spite of the harsh treatment of prisoners, the Jesuits exaggerated the loss of life that resulted from it. Pierre Esprit Radisson, who lived as a prisoner among the Iroquois, describes Huron captives as generally living in a state of freedom. Many men may have been killed because particular Iroquois bore personal grudges against them or feared them. Yet, because of the similarity in their cultural patterns, Huron men had many skills which made them an asset to Iroquois society. Because of this, the Iroquois did not kill them on principle as they did Algonkian men (27:287). A male or female prisoner who was capable, and showed signs of wanting to please and identify with their adoptive parents, appears to have had a tolerably good chance of surviving. Some Huron men were forbidden to accompany war parties against their own people for a long time after they were captured for fear they would attempt to escape (Adams 1961:25–27); others were soon made to accompany such expeditions to test their reactions.

Forced involvement in wars was believed to strengthen a prisoner's loyalty to his adoptive relatives, since he was made to experience hardship and danger alongside them.

For those who survived the first few years of captivity, life appears to have become increasingly secure and normal by Iroquoian standards. At least one Huron headman who was taken prisoner became an Iroquois headman soon after he was adopted into a lineage that had a vacant office (Thwaites 1896–1901, 42:57). He participated, along with other Onondaga headmen in confirming the peace that was made at Quebec in September 1655. Iroquois men are reported to have preferred to marry Huron women because these marriages did not oblige them to serve their wives' kinsmen. Radisson's adoptive parents lived together for over forty years and his Huron mother was reported to be well-loved by her Mohawk husband (Adams 1961:26). In the 1680s the Jesuits drew attention to a leading headman of the Onondaga who, in their opinion, was much abused by two former prisoners whom he had adopted to replace his deceased sisters. Yet, because public opinion did not support him, he was unable to do anything to make them behave better (Thwaites 1896–1901, 62:61–63). These stories illustrate the fate of prisoners who survived the early years of assimilation, as well as later wars and epidemics, to become Iroquois. The large numbers of aliens who were successfully incorporated into the Iroquois tribes at this time and the thoroughness with which their natal allegiances were eliminated are evidence of the outstanding success of the emergency measures that the Iroquois were forced to adopt at this time.

THE HURON REFUGEES AND THE FRENCH

How did the Huron who joined the Iroquois feel about the French and the Jesuits and what were the feelings of the 1000 or more refugees who had been baptized in the Huron country? Because our data come almost entirely from French accounts, only partial answers can be given. In general, most Huron who were taken prisoner prior to 1649 and the traditionalists who joined the confederacy afterwards appear to have been vocal in their denunciation of the French. They accused the Jesuits of being sorcerers and warned that if they were permitted to visit the Iroquois, they would use their spells to ruin crops and slay the Iroquois, as they had done to the Huron (Thwaites 1896–1901, 31:121). They also repeated the more specific accusations against the Jesuits that had circulated in the Huron country. These included charges that the Jesuits bewitched the names they recorded in their baptismal records in order to make the bearers of these names die (42:135) and that they sought to convert Iroquois so they could torture their souls in heaven (42:151). Many Huron who had been baptized renounced their Christian affiliations and hastened to confirm the accusations of the traditionalists (43:291). Most of these were probably Huron who had favoured their own traditions, but had been led by opportunism or affection for relatives to become Christians.

When the Jesuits began to visit the Iroquois villages in the 1650s, many Huron traditionalists and former Christians became still more vocal in their opposition. They praised the Dutch for allowing the Iroquois to live in their own fashion and said that by doing this they had preserved the Iroquois, whereas the Jesuits had ruined the Huron by trying to convert them (43:291). They clearly perceived the difference between the secular approach of the Dutch traders and the intertwined economic and religious goals that had dominated the policies of New France since 1625. When the Jesuits first visited the Cayuga in 1656, they were received very coolly on account of the fears that the Huron had instilled (43:307). Over a decade later, when the Jesuits tried to baptize the daughter of a Huron convert, her father pointed out that in former times Brébeuf had made people die in just such a manner (52:187). Brébeuf's reputation as a malevolent sorcerer had outlived him among the Huron for over two decades. When the Jesuits were constructing boats to escape from the Onondaga in the spring of 1658, a Huron named "Jaluck" saw what was going on and reported that the Jesuits were planning to flood the world and had built an ark in which they hoped to survive (Adams 1961:71–72). Such accusations indicate the deep hatred that many Huron continued to feel towards the Jesuits. These feelings were reinforced as the Huron who had joined the Iroquois saw Huron forced to come from Quebec to the Iroquois villages, and as Huron and Tionnontaté traders were carried off in peacetime with the apparent acquiescence of the French. Accusations by these people that the French had betrayed them (ibid. 70) must have helped to convince many Huron captives that their only hope of survival lay in pleasing the Iroquois.

On the other hand, when the Jesuits visited the Iroquois, numerous Huron, including some who had once fulminated against the Jesuits, welcomed them as old friends and courted their favour. In particular, Huron women who had been baptized sought out the Jesuits so that they might perform their devotions. Some did this secretly, alleging to their Iroquois kinsmen that they were going to fish or trade (Thwaites 1896–1901, 47: 197). Others presented their children for baptism, assembled in cabins to receive instruction to renew their faith, and, where the Jesuits were allowed to construct chapels, began regularly to attend services as they had formerly done in the Huron country (51:187, 191, 209–11). The Jesuits were told that before they had arrived among the Mohawk, Huron women gathered in the forests and in remote cabins to hold prayer meetings, even though by doing so they were laying themselves open to charges of witchcraft (47:57; 49:107; 50:115). Huron were reported to have professed their faith openly elsewhere among the Iroquois, in spite of similar dangers.

The Jesuits credited much of their influence among the Iroquois to help they received from Huron captives (52:163). As early as 1653, the Onondaga were reported to have been well disposed to the French because of favourable statements that certain captive women had made concerning the missionaries (41:119). Even many Huron from Contarea, which had been notoriously hostile towards the Jesuits in the later years of the Huron mission, welcomed the Jesuits to the Onondaga country in 1656 and feigned to listen to their teachings (42:73). In 1670 the Jesuits reported that the vast majority of Christians were either of Huron descent or other aliens (54:41–43).

It cannot be doubted that some Huron who were living as prisoners or refugees were well disposed towards the French. Those who had been hosts to the Jesuits in the Huron country or who had been the recipients of special benefits or acts of kindness from them almost certainly felt such an attachment, which they expressed by being receptive to the Jesuits' teachings. Many of these Huron were among the "Iroquois" who later went to join the Huron at Quebec or to the other mission settlements along the St. Lawrence River (55:35; 57:75; 60:295). A far larger number of Huron, however, including traditionalists as well as professing Christians, seem to have resumed their old policy of being outwardly friendly to the French, whatever they personally felt about them. In dealing with the Jesuits, this took the form of listening politely and not contradicting them. The Jesuits often interpreted this more as approval of what they had to say than, in fact, it was. Real or imaginary former relationships were also appealed to, in an effort to forge bonds of friendship and reciprocity with the Jesuits. Nor was this practice limited to the Huron. A dying Cayuga whom the Jesuits encountered in 1656 claimed to have offered two wampum belts to the Mohawk in exchange for Fathers Brébeuf and Lalemant. He said that he had intended to return them to the French, but the Mohawk had later reclaimed and burned the two men (43:311–13). His motive for telling this story was obviously his hope that the Jesuits would cure him.

This policy no doubt seemed a prudent one to the Huron, most of whom continued to regard the Jesuits as possessing dangerous supernatural powers that could be turned against them; however, the traditionalists were also aware of the strong mistrust that the Iroquois had of the French and knew that so long as the Iroquois traded with the Dutch or the English, the Jesuits would never acquire the same influence among the Iroquois that they formerly had among the Huron. Thus they could relax and deal with the Jesuits with some of the same assurance they had prior to the development of Christian and traditionalist factions in the Huron country. When the various Iroquois tribes sought good relations with the French, the Huron were able to serve Iroquois interests as well as their own by befriending the French who visited their villages. Conversely, when the Iroquois ceased to be on good terms with the French, the Huron would compromise their own good relations with the Iroquois if they continued to be friendly with the French. At such times, all but the staunchly believing Christians seem to have become cool to the Jesuits, while anti-Jesuit feeling which was generally covert in peacetime was again expressed openly.

This pattern is clearly exemplified by the Jesuits' relations with the people of Gandougarae. When Father Chaumonot first visited them in 1656, he was received as an old friend. Christians asked for absolution for themselves and baptism for their children and many adult Huron who had formerly despised Christianity asked to be baptized (44:25). The Tahontaenrat also invited the Jesuits to establish a mission in their settlement (46:73). Although this was not accomplished until after the peace of 1667, the Jesuits entertained high hopes for Gandougarae and described it as already inhabited entirely by Christians (47:113) or at least by a goodly number (52:55). A chapel was erected there in September 1669. In addition to about forty adults whom the Jesuits judged to be practising Christians, there seemed to be a great eagerness for baptism among the rest of the Huron (54:81–83). A few years later, some converts discussed the possibility that they might join the Huron settlement at Quebec (56:67).

While a small number of the inhabitants of Gandougarae lived up to the Jesuits' expectations, the missionaries soon realized that their success was to be limited. Father Jacques Frémin found it necessary to live with one of the leading traditionalists in the town, so that this man might protect him against ill treatment by his enemies (54:121) and, with few exceptions, the villagers refused to give up any of their traditional rituals (58:229). When Gandougarae caught fire and burned to the ground, its inhabitants were persuaded that this might be supernatural retribution for their resistance to the Jesuits' teachings. Yet this is an indication of the degree to which fear rather than affection coloured their attitude towards the Jesuits. While they asked Father Julien Garnier to remain with them and promised to build a better chapel for him than the one that had been destroyed, the superior of the Canadian missions doubted their sincerity (55:79). In fact, for a year Father Garnier does not appear to have been missed when he did not bother to return to the town (57:191).

The Jesuits soon learned that the apparent desire of any Seneca community to be converted depended on temporal considerations and particularly on the Seneca's attitude towards peace with the French (56:59). As the Iroquois once again drifted towards conflict with the French in the 1670s, the Seneca's receptiveness to Christian teachings declined markedly (55:89–91). The Jesuits reluctantly concluded that the Seneca were particularly hard to convert because of their remoteness from the French and that the Tahontaenrat were no more promising than the rest (58:229, 237). The missionaries who remained among the Seneca were reduced to baptizing children without their parents' knowledge and received many rebuffs as they tried to instruct the sick (62:227). In later years, neither Gandougarae nor the other Seneca villages were to testify to anything but the failure of these missions.

The Huron who lived among the Cayuga showed a similar shift in sentiment as the Iroquois' policies towards the French changed. When the Jesuits first visited them, the Cayuga were reported to have shown them more goodwill than did any of the other Iroquois tribes and the missionaries were received with joy by the Huron who lived there (47:185–87). By 1671, however, the missionary to the Cayuga was experiencing difficulty as the result of an aversion to Christianity that was attributed to certain "renegade Huron" (56:51). A decade later, the Cayuga were ranked alongside the Seneca as being particularly unreceptive to Christianity (62:227).

The kinds of choices that were made, even by Huron favourably disposed towards the French, are exemplified by the fate of Chihwatenha's niece, Thérèse Oionhaton. The French had failed to secure her release in the peace negotiations of 1645, about which time she was given in marriage to an Onondaga. In 1655 she was still living among the Onondaga and came with a baby in arms to greet Fathers Chaumonot and Dablon when they visited that tribe. Although she was happy to see the Jesuits and stated that she had baptized her own child, there is no evidence that Oionhaton ever again visited Quebec or attempted to settle there. One of her sisters was living as a prisoner among the Onondaga (42:81) and it would appear that Oionhaton's loyalty to blood kin, her child (or children), and possibly to her husband were sufficient to fill her life. If this was so for a woman who had lived with the Ursulines and who had learned to speak and write French, it must have been even more so for the average Huron who found himself gradually becoming a respectable member of Iroquois society.

THE HURON AS IROQUOIS

It appears that the overwhelming majority of Huron prisoners and refugees, whatever their personal attitude towards the French may have been, were convinced that it was in their interest to behave in accordance with Iroquois policy. When the Iroquois were anxious to convince the French of their goodwill, the Huron were encouraged to emphasize their former friendship with the Jesuits, but when the French and the Iroquois were at odds, the Huron were free to express any hostility they felt towards the French for what the latter had done to them.

At first a considerable number of Huron may have been motivated to act in this way by their fear of the Iroquois; but to attribute all their behaviour to this motive is grossly misleading. The relatively small number of Huron who took advantage of opportunities to move to the special missions that the Jesuits established for their Iroquois converts indicates that the majority must eventually have found it rewarding to continue living among the Iroquois. This feeling was reinforced by intermarriage, as well as by daily contact, which forged personal bonds between former enemies. The development of such bonds eventually led the descendants of these refugees to forget that they were of non-Iroquois origin. The Huron language totally disappeared, and an ethnic identity emerged based on membership in the five Iroquois tribes that was as strong as it had been among the Iroquois prior to the incorporation of these other Iroquoian peoples.

It is almost impossible, on the basis of historical evidence, to trace the contributions that the Huron made to Iroquois culture in the course of becoming Iroquois. The high degree of similarity between the Huron and Iroquois ways of life precluded a wide range of influence at the same time that it facilitated the assimilation of the Huron. The popularity of Tahontaenrat curing rituals suggests that in this sphere, the incorporation of the Huron helped to diversify and enrich at least one aspect of Iroquois life. Harold Blau (1966:577–78) has also suggested that the False Face curing society was introduced by Huron refugees. Further evidence would be required to substantiate this.

In 1668 François Le Mercier distinguished the Seneca from the other Iroquois tribes by saying that they were more inclined to be farmers (*laboureurs*) and traders than warriors (Thwaites 1896–1901, 52:53). Assuming that there is some truth to this statement, it might be asked whether this distinction was an aboriginal one or reflects the influence of Huron who, because of the Tahontaenrat, probably joined the Seneca in larger numbers than they joined any other Iroquois tribe. Again, we are posing a question that it is impossible to answer. Differences in the natural resources of the tribal territories may account for minor variations in the subsistence patterns of the various Iroquois tribes. It may be no accident that the Seneca, who were the most numerous tribe, were apparently also the most dependent on horticulture (Fenton 1940:224, 230; Trigger 1963b:96).

What does seem fairly plain is that whatever talents as traders the Huron brought with them, were squandered by the Iroquois. It was not until 1659 that there is an explicit reference to the Mohawk inviting the Algonkin and Quebec Huron to come to their villages to trade (45:103) (plate 51). More than a decade was to pass before the Iroquois tribes began to develop trading relations with the Ottawa and Tionnontaté and even then they did this very tentatively. This appears to have been a development that would have taken place whether or not large numbers of Huron had been incorporated into Iroquois society.

It must be concluded that because of the geographical difficulties involved in trading with northern peoples and the success of Iroquois hunting and raiding expeditions at the time of the Huron's dispersal, the Iroquois were not interested in making use of their captives' special talents. Many of the leading traders may have been killed in battle or murdered by the Iroquois because they considered them to be dangerous and wished to deprive the Huron refugees of leadership. Other Huron men appear to have been quickly drafted into Iroquois raiding parties to satisfy a pressing need for manpower. By the time that the Iroquois war machine had begun to falter and an alternative means of acquiring furs was recognized as desirable, the special skills and, what is more important, the personal contacts that the Huron could have used to develop this trade were irretrievably lost. Whether certain basic skills were transmitted from one Huron generation to the next that would have been useful to the Iroquois in their later entrepreneurial ventures is another question.

The dispersal of the Huron thus presents a curious irony. The handful of Huron who survived their betrayal by the French and stayed at Quebec remained Huron in name, but were subject to continuing acculturative pressure by Europeans. Those who joined the Tionnontaté eventually gave their name to the larger group, but this group regressed because of its small

PLATE 51. *Anonymous map of southeastern Ontario, probably by Abbé Claude Bernou, c. 1680. The inscriptions identify central Ontario as a major beaver hunting area for the Iroquois and Mahican and also refer to*

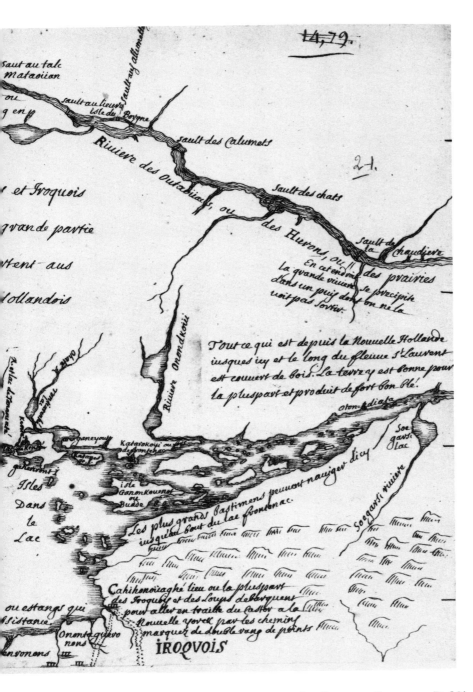

*trade relations between the Iroquois and the Ottawa. Courtesy Public
Archives of Canada.*

size and a growing emphasis on trapping, until their economy and way of life resembled those of northern hunting peoples more than they did those of the historic Huron.

Many times the number of Huron who found refuge in these two groups ended up living with their traditional enemies, the Iroquois. Although their initial sufferings at the hands of the Iroquois should not be underestimated, within a generation the descendants of these Huron had fully merged with the Iroquois and the two groups had assumed a common Iroquois identity. After a continuing struggle to avoid, and then to cope with, white domination, these Iroquois remain one of a small number of native peoples of eastern North America who continue to reside in the heartland of their ancestral territories and who have kept their sense of identity and many of their traditions alive to the present day.

As a result of the conflicts engendered by the fur trade, the Iroquois must have killed, either directly or indirectly, several thousand Huron, although not nearly so many as died of European diseases. Ironically, however, they also provided homes and an acceptable life for more Huron than were to survive anywhere else. Having been pitted against one another in the earliest phases of European activity in eastern North America, the aboriginal Iroquois and these assimilated Huron were henceforth to confront as one people the growing power of Europeans to direct their lives. Conquerors and conquered were to share a single destiny.

Chapter 13  Conclusions

The Huron were only one of hundreds of Indian groups that were dispersed or lost their independence as a result of European activities. It is appropriate, therefore, to conclude this study by summarizing certain aspects of the Huron experience that may be useful for interpreting the early phases of interaction between Europeans and other Indian groups, or between complex and small-scale societies generally.

Archaeological data demonstrate the fallacy of the notion that prior to European contact the northern Iroquoian-speaking peoples were in a state of cultural equilibrium. Changes went on in the Indian cultures of eastern North America at all periods, but beginning before A.D. 1000 the way of life of the Iroquoians started to change more rapidly as they adopted a horticultural subsistence economy. Large, multi-clan communities came into existence, whose social organization grew more complex as bonds of kinship were supplemented by increasingly important ties of reciprocity. Gift giving, curing societies, and ritualized forms of competition came to have growing regulatory importance in Iroquoian life. Village councils on which clan segments had representation provided a model for political integration that could be expanded to embrace tribes and ultimately whole confederacies.

Far from being unchanging in prehistoric times as many ethnologists formerly imagined, almost every facet of Iroquoian culture appears to have undergone significant change in the centuries preceding European contact. By expanding and altering existing institutions to meet the requirements of rapid change, the prehistoric Iroquoians show themselves to have been the very opposite of conservative. At the same time they appear to have forged a set of cultural values that have permitted the survival to the present day of a distinctively Iroquoian identity and style. While a similar degree of change cannot be attributed automatically to other Indian groups, archaeological work indicates that such changes were not unusual in late pre-Columbian times. If historians are to interpret correctly the impact that Europeans had on other groups, it is necessary that they pay adequate attention to archaeological and other types of evidence that bears on the nature of change among these groups prior to the time of contact.

It can also be ascertained from the archaeological record that both the Huron and the Iroquois had been obtaining European goods from Indians living nearer the coast for some time prior to any direct encounter with Europeans. These goods were prized for their novelty from the beginning and the superiority of iron tools and weapons was quickly recognized. As rival groups began to obtain iron tools on a regular basis, the economic and military advantage that this conferred on them made it essential for tribes living farther from the trading places to find ways of obtaining these goods in larger quantities.

The manner in which different Indian groups went about this strongly supports Nancy Lurie's (1959:37) observation that Indians made their first adjustments to the problems posed by Europeans in terms of existing institutions. Among the Iroquoians, the early years of the fur trade were a period of broadening alliances and increasing warfare with more remote groups. For the Huron at least, major changes were brought about even at the stage when trade goods were regarded principally as a novelty. Both the Huron and the Iroquois confederacies appear to have expanded to include more tribes, if they did not come into being at this time. While the forging and maintaining of these confederacies are evidence of great political skill, the confederacies themselves were extensions of political institutions already existing at the tribal level and did not require the formulation of new principles of political organization. These developments encouraged more emphasis on ritualism to promote political and social integration. This can be seen in the elaboration of the Huron Feast of the Dead and in the increasing emphasis that was placed on grave goods among the Iroquois.

It is also apparent that pre-existing differences between Iroquoian societies helped to mold the different responses that these societies made to the challenge of securing European goods. The Iroquois, who in the sixteenth century were surrounded on all sides by groups that had a horticultural subsistence economy similar to their own, first attempted to secure European goods by waging war against the inhabitants of the St. Lawrence Valley who had easier access to these items. For many decades the Iroquois were to rely almost exclusively on warfare as a means of obtaining the pelts and additional hunting territory that they required if they were to continue bartering with their Dutch and English trading partners.

By contrast, archaeological and ethnographic evidence indicates that, for at least several centuries, the Huron who lived in Simcoe County had systematically traded with the semi-horticultural hunting and fishing bands living to the north of them. When confronted first by the desire and then by the need to obtain more European goods, the Huron expanded their trade with these northern groups and, in this manner, secured the furs that they needed to trade with the French. The Huron likewise became suppliers of trade goods to the other Iroquoian tribes of southern Ontario and seem to have begun trading with the Susquehannock at this time. These developments, which reflect the Huron's skill as traders, probably were responsible for the suppression of blood feuds among all the tribes of southern Ontario.

The contrasting responses of the Huron and the Iroquois reflect not only their different geographical locations, but also longstanding cultural differences that had arisen as a result of cultural adaptation to these locations. The persistence of these respective responses throughout the first half of the seventeenth century suggests grave limitations to Hunt's (1940:5) thesis that "old institutions and economies had profoundly altered or disappeared completely at the electrifying touch of the white man's trade, which...wrought social revolution a thousand miles beyond the white man's habitations, and years before he himself appeared on the scene."

While the overall impact of European contact upon Iroquoians can scarcely be minimized, it can be demonstrated that the response that each Iroquoian group made to the challenge of the fur trade was determined by that group's interpretation of what was happening and by their experience in dealing with analogous situations. There was no single overriding "logic of the fur trade" that existed independently of prevailing customs and intertribal relationships and which could supplant these relationships instantaneously. Instead, the fur trade developed largely in terms of responses by Indians who were guided by their former experiences and who extrapolated from these experiences to adapt to novel and ever-changing situations. This does not mean that, in due course, Iroquoian and other tribes did not find themselves being used against their will as instruments of policy by rival fur traders or colonial administrations. Nor does it mean that even in the early period Indian history can be understood independently of European colonial history, any more than the latter can be understood without the Indians. It does mean, however, that in dealing with the early historic period, the specific cultures of the Indian groups involved, as distinguished from their general mode of adaptation, must be taken into account, as well as the history of intertribal relations preceding the rise of the fur trade.

Although the officials who came to New France in the early days lacked power to coerce the Indians, they considered it their natural right to do so. Unlike the Dutch, the French did not bother to purchase land from the

Indians prior to settlement nor did they recognize them as sovereign peoples. Instead they sought to have the Indians formally pledge their allegiance to the representatives of the French crown. Most of these officials resented having to deal with Indians from other than a position of strength and in terms of other than their own conceptions about law and government.

The Huron, however, lived too far from the areas of French settlement to be affected by these ambitions. The kind of alliance that was concluded between the French and the Huron and the rules that governed their trade conformed wholly to the traditional practices by which the Huron regulated their relations with other tribes. French merchants quickly discovered that conforming with such practices was the most effective way to promote trade with the Indians. Until 1634 almost all of the French who visited the Huron were sent there by trading companies to maintain the friendship of the Huron and to encourage them to come to the St. Lawrence Valley to trade. These agents were few and because their aim was to win the trust and friendship of the Huron, they did not criticize or openly challenge the latter's ways of doing things. On the contrary, traders such as Brûlé were happy to adopt many outward trappings of Huron behaviour. Their attempts to change Huron culture were limited to encouraging the Huron to want more trade goods.

Because of their lack of basic language skills, the Recollet and Jesuit missionaries who visited the Huron country prior to 1634 were unable to work there effectively. The principal changes that occurred at this time came about as a result of the Huron responding to an influx of trade goods into their villages, rather than to the presence of the French. The influx of European goods tended to emphasize existing status differences but there is no evidence that this did more than magnify properties that were inherent in Iroquoian society. Trade appears to have been controlled by the traditional headmen, who enhanced their status by distributing the European goods they acquired as they previously had distributed other wealth. There is nothing to indicate that these developments were compromising the tribal basis of Iroquoian society, or that social classes were emerging that were based on the retention rather than the redistribution of wealth. The increasing involvement of men in warfare, trade, hunting, and other activities that kept them away from their villages for longer periods seems to have reinforced the matrilineal tendencies in Iroquoian society. These developments were pushing Iroquoian social organization along the same trajectory that it had been following in prehistoric times.

There is no evidence that any fundamental restructuring of Iroquoian society was about to take place.

The period from 1610 to 1634 can thus be classified as one of "non-directed contact" between the Huron and the French (Spicer 1961:521). This implies that the French who traded with the Huron neither were able to bring regular sanctions to bear against the Huron nor were they interested in doing so in order to effect changes in their behaviour. The French and Huron had to treat one another as equals, since each alone was able to supply what the other wanted. It was also characteristic of this period that both sides remained convinced of their cultural superiority. Because of their greater numbers, and because it was they who visited the French settlements to trade and who determined what Frenchmen might live in their midst, the Huron viewed the French as they did their other northern trading partners. While they interpreted the trade goods supplied by the French as evidence of superior achievements in the technological sphere, they regarded the difficulties that the French experienced in learning to speak Huron and to live and travel with the Indians as proof of innate physical and intellectual inferiority.

From 1634 onwards, relations between the French and the Huron were controlled by the Jesuits. By that time the Jesuits had acquired sufficient influence, both at the French court and over the Company of New France, that they were able to exclude from the Huron country all Frenchmen who were not subject to their authority. Armed with this power, they began a determined campaign to convert the Huron to Roman Catholicism. Unlike the Recollets, who believed that it was impossible to convert the Huron or any other group of Indians before they had first Europeanized them, the Jesuits sought to convert the Huron while changing their way of life as little as possible. They did not believe that converts needed to learn to speak French; on the contrary, they were convinced that by preventing them from having verbal as well as physical contact with other Frenchmen, they were protecting them from corrupting influences. Although it has been suggested that the Jesuits wished to introduce European methods of farming among the Huron, there is no good evidence that they contemplated doing so, or altering any other aspect of Huron culture that was not in conflict with Christian beliefs and moral practice. On the contrary, when they arrived in the Huron country, the Jesuits were convinced that by eliminating a small number of Huron customs and catechizing them, the Huron could be converted to Christianity.

There can be no question that in undertaking this work, the Jesuit missionaries were acting altruistically. While the Jesuits were well aware that the Huron mission was dependent on the prosperity of the fur trade in New France and therefore were anxious to support this trade, suggestions that they went among the Huron primarily to trade with them or to promote French colonial interests cannot be substantiated. Their work was dominated by their conviction that every Huron they converted was a soul saved from certain damnation and eternal suffering. To save these souls most, if not all, of the Jesuits were willing to risk their own lives. Their fanaticism also meant that the Jesuits did not feel obliged to restrict themselves to reasoning with the Huron in their efforts to convert them. On the contrary, the Jesuits found it all too easy to believe that their religious ends justified the means they used to pursue them. They did not hesitate to use their influence over the Company of New France to have its traders insist that the Huron allow missionaries to live in their country as part of the French-Huron trading alliance, or even to force the Huron headmen to let them remain there when most of the Huron wanted them to leave. By ensuring that Christians could buy French trade goods more cheaply than non-Christians could, and that only Christians were permitted to obtain guns, the Jesuits created strong incentives for many Huron men to become at least nominally Christian. This, in turn, permitted them to exploit the Huron's dread of being separated from friends and kinsmen after death in order to convert still more Huron.

While the French colonists in Quebec remained few in number, under the guidance of the Jesuits their officials began to bring pressure to bear that was designed to compel the Huron to change their behaviour along lines that the Jesuits, rather than they themselves, judged to be desirable. Because of this, relations between the Huron and the French entered into a phase of what anthropologists have termed "directed contact" (Spicer 1961), but which might better be called "coercive contact." This is because the Jesuits erred when they believed that they were able to bring about the changes they desired while leaving most facets of Huron life unaffected. They lacked sufficient understanding of the Huron way of life to predict what impact their activities would have upon it. While the Jesuits had the power to coerce the Huron to change, they lacked the skills to refashion Huron society along predetermined lines.

The problems involved in the attempt by persons reared in a seventeenth-century European monarchy and an Amerindian tribal society to interact understandingly with one another are illustrated by the difficulties that the Huron and the French experienced when they attempted to communicate on the subject of religion. Because the Jesuits were accustomed to think about religion in terms of formal institutions, at first they believed that the Huron had few religious beliefs and concluded that it would be easy to fill this void with their own teachings. Later, when they realized the extent of Huron beliefs and practices, they interpreted these as the means by which satanic powers were corrupting and misleading the Huron. Hence, they dramatically visualized their missionary work as a struggle with the devil, who was using the Huron as his pawns.

The Jesuits were even slower to recognize the degree to which Huron religious beliefs permeated every facet of their lives. They were misled by the European view that religious beliefs and practices could be clearly defined and treated separately from other aspects of a person's life. The Jesuits regarded this particular feature of Roman Catholicism and of other international religions as being a characteristic of all religions. Yet, while the Huron had no explicitly formulated creed or corpus of ritual that could be renounced in favour of any other, they possessed a network of beliefs and practices that embued them with confidence in all of their everyday activities, provided the occasions for their most important public celebrations, and armed the individual with potent powers to deal with social pressures and psychic disturbances. This far-reaching interpenetration of religion and everyday life meant that whether the Jesuits wished it or not, if the conversion of the Huron was to be effective, it required major alterations in aspects of their culture that the Jesuits, on the basis of previous experience, had no reason to suspect had anything to do with religion.

In his own doctrinaire way, Jérôme Lalemant may have had in mind a major restructuring of Huron life when he advocated withdrawing Christian Huron from their villages and having them found a new settlement, or *reduction*, at Sainte-Marie. The Huron attachment to their kin, as well as the Jesuits' desire to exploit this attachment to promote the conversion of whole villages, meant that this policy was not carried out. Instead, the Jesuits attempted to eradicate non-Christian practices among their converts without offering them effective substitutes. The result was to undermine their converts' supernatural sources of self-confidence and peace of mind at the same time they cut them off from normal social contact with other Huron. This systematic effort to destroy many of the most cherished and significant features of Huron life eventually forced a considerable number of Huron to oppose the Jesuits openly, thus fragmenting Huron society into factions based on varying degrees of sentiment for and against both the French and the Jesuits. The multiplication of social cleavages, at the same time that many individuals were disorientated either by the Jesuits' teachings or by the erosion of important landmarks in Huron culture, was a serious handicap to a people already threatened by increasingly powerful enemies. These problems were undoubtedly made worse by the death of many knowledgeable Huron leaders and ritualists during the epidemics of 1634 to 1640.

The Huron were unable to muster an effective resistance to the Jesuits' efforts to convert them because at first they were unable to understand the nature of the demands that the Jesuits were making on them. Nothing in Huron religious experience prepared them to cope with the requirements of an exclusive and intolerant religion, the very concept of which was alien to them. The Huron readily borrowed rituals of all kinds from each other and from neighbouring peoples and incorporated these rituals into their society alongside existing ones. Drawing on their own experience, they initially viewed Christianity as a ritual society and the Jesuits as its adepts. Although they were puzzled by the lifelong celibacy of the Jesuits, even this could be interpreted as an extension of their own practice of seeking supernatural power through sexual abstinence. This view of Christianity accounts for the initial willingness of many Huron to become Christians, which elated the Jesuits, and for their apparent apostasy soon after. Even after it was apparent to the Huron that the Jesuits were intolerant of other religious beliefs and practices, it would have been impossible for Huron to understand the uncompromising theological basis for this attitude.

As frequently happens in such situations, both the Huron and the Jesuits interpreted those portions of each other's beliefs that they could not understand, or that they believed threatened their own interests, as manifestations of evil as each conceived of it. Most Huron became convinced that the Jesuits were malevolent sorcerers who sought to destroy the Huron people. Motives were established why the Jesuits should do this and as the Huron learned more about what the Jesuits believed and did, their actions and possessions were interpreted as proof that they practised witchcraft. This reinterpretation of Jesuit behaviour in terms of Huron stereotypes about witchcraft became so pervasive during the period of the epidemics that the Jesuits felt it necessary to refrain from explaining the more intimate details of their rituals to all but their most promising converts. The Jesuits, for their part, were only too willing to interpet all Huron religious practices as being satanic inventions or perversions of Christian rituals that the devil had foisted upon the Huron. Some Jesuits viewed any opposition to their teachings as the devil's efforts to protect his kingdom. Only in the final years of the Huron mission, when the Jesuits were anxious to baptize as many Huron as possible, did they adopt a more tolerant attitude towards many aspects of traditional Huron culture.

Both the French and the Huron used their own concepts of evil as a means of structuring their respective lack of understanding of each other's ways. It is not surprising that the Huron, who knew little about Europeans and had limited opportunities to observe their culture, should have fallen back upon such explanations. Indeed, this tendency was reinforced by the Jesuits' own policy of keeping the Huron isolated from other Frenchmen. The Jesuits, however, had deliberately set out to study Huron religious beliefs to conduct their mission work more effectively. Their failure to understand Huron beliefs, or to work effectively to change these beliefs from within, must therefore be attributed to the limited and pragmatic nature of their research and to their inability even for strategic purposes to transcend intellectually the values to which they were so fiercely committed. The Jesuits' desire to destroy Huron religion outstripped their search to understand it.

As early as 1640 the Jesuits had become concerned about the threat that was posed to the Huron and to their own missionary work by Iroquois attacks. Yet they remained paternalistic in their efforts to deal with the growing menace of the Iroquois, even after the latter had begun to obtain large numbers of guns. Partly to encourage Huron to convert and partly to assure their own safety, the Jesuits insisted that guns be supplied only to Christian Huron, and even to them in small numbers. At the same time, they advocated that the French should either expel the Dutch from the Hudson Valley or crush the Iroquois. These initiatives proved ineffectual and the scarcity of guns, combined with the larger number of men that were needed to carry on trade with the French by comparison with the number that the Iroquois needed to trade with the Dutch, put the Huron at a serious disadvantage. By the time that the Iroquois launched their final series of attacks on the Huron, Jesuit policy had deprived the latter of the weapons that they needed for their own defence and seriously weakened their will to resist the enemy.

Although the Jesuits had thwarted all efforts to expel them from the Huron country, many traditionalists were too alienated, both from the Jesuits and from the society that they now dominated, to rally to its defence. While some of the Christian Huron fought bravely against the Iroquois, as a group they looked to the Jesuits for a degree of leadership and protection that the latter were unable to provide. It is impossible to demonstrate that the Huron would not have succumbed to Iroquois attack if the Jesuits had never worked among them. It is nevertheless certain that however cunningly and apparently successfully the Jesuits pursued their goal of converting the Huron, the result of their activities was to divide and dishearten the Huron at the very time they needed to pull together for their own defence. The Jesuits therefore unwittingly played a major role in ensuring the Iroquois victory over the Huron.

The Jesuits who undertook to convert the Huron were intelligent men who were prepared to forego comfort and safety in order to save mankind from eternal damnation. The suffering that their policies brought about was an unintentional consequence of their efforts to convert the Huron, even though the Jesuits later seemed to regard these sufferings as worthwhile, or at least far from being in vain. There are, however, more general reasons why attempts such as this to effect coercive change frequently turn out badly. It is recognized as a truism that the consequences of people's actions often end up escaping them, since every undertaking has repercussions upon a vast number of unsuspected relationships within a society (Sartre 1963 : 47–48). Because of this, actions may have the opposite effect from what was intended. When those who are involved come from different cultural traditions, the dangers of misunderstanding and miscalculation are multiplied, and well-intentioned actions frequently prove disadvantageous, if not disastrous, for all concerned. As a mixture of creativity and destructiveness, all men, no less than the Huron and Jesuits, show themselves to be Aataentsic's children.

Notes

CHAPTER SEVEN

1. Trudel (1966*a*: 526) suggests Manet, Nicollet, or Richer; however, only Richer worked exclusively among the Algonkin in the late 1620s (ibid. 496–500).

2. However, see n. 4, chapter 6.

3. For another version of this incident, see Biggar 1922–36, 5: 229–31.

4. See, for example Le Jeune to Richelieu, Thwaites 1896–1901, 7: 241–45 and 9: 171.

5. Cranston 1949: 137–44. For other ideas, see Jurgens 1966: 133.

6. For an instance of a household moving from one village to another, see Thwaites 1896–1901, 10: 285.

7. Grant 1952: 8, based on Laverdière. Campeau (1951–52) vigorously denies this claim.

8. For the latest account of this trip, see Hamelin 1966*b*: 517. Lurie (1960: 800–801) provides an effective critique of the more extravagant interpretations of his mission.

9. The *Jesuit Relation* of 1642–43 states specifically that this peace was between the Huron and the Winnebago (Thwaites 1896–1901, 23: 277); however, in 1636 Le Jeune mentions the Winnebago breaking their truce with the Algonkian-speaking Amikou people (10: 83). This suggests that the truce was, in fact, between the Winnebago and the Ottawa or other Algonkian-speaking groups. For a discussion of this point, see Lurie 1960: 794.

10. The two other Frenchmen who embarked are said to have gone with the Algonkians. They were probably Nicollet and a companion.

11. Talbot (1956: 128) implies that the Jesuits' old cabin was still standing in Toanché. The cabin Brébeuf refers to was clearly a Huron dwelling.

CHAPTER EIGHT

1. If Ihonatiria had 300 inhabitants, about eight deaths per year would have been normal and most of these would have occurred during the winter. Yet in the winter of 1634–35, five people died in one longhouse (of 30 inhabitants?). It is impossible to know if the number for this house was higher than the average for the village as a whole or the average for the village was higher than that for the Huron as a whole.

2. For an exception, see Thwaites 1896–1901, 8: 139.

3. In later times, the French *collier* meant a wampum belt and it probably did at this time as well; however, because we have no description of Huron *colliers* for this early period, I have chosen to use the more neutral "collar" to translate this term. For a discussion of the use of these belts in Indian diplomacy, see Vachon 1970 and 1971.

4. Nicolas Rehault, Marquis de Gamache provided the funds for this school (Thwaites 1896–1901, 8: 227). This gift, amounting to 16,000 écus of

gold and an annuity of 3000 livres as long as he should live, was given to the Jesuits in support of the Canadian mission after his eldest son joined the order (6:327 n. 9).

5. Le Jeune erroneously describes him as *Ouanda Koca*'s (= Endahiaconc's) son (Thwaites 1896–1901, 12:57). This is another illustration of the trouble the French experienced in discerning genealogical relationships through Huron kinship vocabulary.

6. At first identified only as a town about one league from Ossossané (Thwaites 1896–1901, 14:253). For positive identification as Scanonaenrat, see 15:171.

7. Some seventy of these Indians died (Thwaites 1896–1901, 14:99), which is the same number of dead that the Nipissing took away with them in the spring of 1637.

8. This identification is suggested as Aouandoïé previously had been faced with accusations of witchcraft on several occasions (Thwaites 1896–1901, 8:95).

9. As far as I can determine, E. Jury (1966*f*:610) errs in stating that Ondakion and his family were the first Huron to embrace Christianity.

10. For a discussion of the probable archaeological evidence of Wenroronon in the Huron country, see Ridley 1973. Most of the pottery from the small Edwards site, near Ossossané, may be Wenroronon as well as 22 percent of the pottery at Ossossané.

11. Cf. letter of J. Lalemant to Richelieu, 28 March 1640 (Thwaites 1896–1901, 17:219–25) and that of C. Lalemant to E. Charlet, 28 February 1642 (21:269–73).

12. For an assessment of this aspect of his personality by a modern Jesuit, see Talbot 1956:208–9.

13. This interpretation was first advanced by me in 1966*b*. I did not know

at that time that Talbot (1956:221–22) had implied the same interpretation.

CHAPTER NINE

1. In an article published since this book was written, W. Smith (1973) argues that by the 1640s the Huron were being by-passed by the fur trade as a result of the French establishing trading links with tribes living farther into the interior. His main evidence (p. 31) is that by 1633 "the first trading fleet of Ottawa Indians arrived at Quebec." This is based on Hunt 1940:48. Had Smith examined Hunt's references he would have found them (like so many other references of that author) to be in error. There is no evidence of the Ottawa visiting the St. Lawrence prior to the dispersal of the Huron. Here is an example of a clever theory nullified by inadequate standards of historiography.

2. The reference to Indians in the Huron country wanting to settle at Montreal (Thwaites 1896–1901, 24:221) undoubtedly refers to these refugee Algonkin and not to Huron.

3. For further proof, see ibid. 32:289. Note that at Quebec knowledge of the reaction of Huron traders meeting Christian Indians in northern Quebec was based entirely upon reports from missionaries in the Huron country.

4. Grassmann 1966*b*. Du Creux calls her Chihwatenha's daughter (i.e., brother's daughter?).

5. It is clear that *petit fils* should be translated " small (i.e. young) son " and not " grandson " as Thwaites (27:91) has done. Elsewhere, this boy is identified as Mathieu, aged two years. He is explicitly stated to be the son of Atironta's wife Caterine (27:113).

6. Estimated at half the total number of skins exported from the colony (Trelease 1960:43).

7. Note, however, that the Huron presented the Iroquois with wampum as well as beaver, while the Algonkians gave only skins.

8. Lom d'Arce de Lahontan (1905, 1:227) comments on the necessity of the Iroquois obtaining furs to purchase armaments and other trade goods.

9. White (1971a:31) suggests that these latter enemies from the west may have been the Neutral.

10. White (1972) identifies the Aondironnon (Ahondihronon) with the Ondieronii of Du Creux's map and on this basis proposes to locate them between the Niagara and Genesee Rivers (pp. 69–70). She interprets the phrase *"les plus voisins de nos Hurons"* as referring to the Neutral as a whole, rather than to the Aondironnon specifically. While seventeenth-century grammar is ambiguous enough to make this interpretation a possibility, the fact that Huron warriors pursued an Iroquois raider from the Tionnontaté country to the gates of the Aondironnon village suggests that the conventional interpretation of this passage, which would have the Aondironnon as the closest Neutral group to the Huron, is correct. It may be noted that Desrosiers (1948:243) located them in the Niagara Peninsula.

11. For the tribal distributions in southern Michigan prior to *c.* 1650, see Goddard 1972. Archaeologists note a lack of historic sites in this region and on this basis some have concluded that the area was not settled at this time (Fitting 1965).

12. On the map attributed to Bernou of *c.* 1680, central Ontario bears the inscription: "From here the Mahican and Iroquois draw most of the beaver skins

that they carry to the English and the Dutch" (see our plate 51).

13. The Gendron letters were published by Jean-Baptiste de Rocoles in 1660, during Gendron's lifetime. It is curious, however, that much of his first letter describing the tribes who were neighbours of the Huron is copied from the Huron *Relation* of 1648. This raises the question of whether Gendron and Ragueneau both made use of the same document, already in existence at Sainte-Marie. Alternatively, Ragueneau could have transcribed and abridged a copy of Gendron's letter or the letter was composed after the date ascribed to it and was largely based on the published relation of 1648. While much of the information in the Gendron letters seems authentic, his implication that the Huron country was rich in beaver (as distinct from beaver pelts) (p. 13) runs counter to much other evidence.

14. This was also Jogues's opinion (Thwaites 1896–1901, 25:47).

15. Hunt 1940:78. For the major critique of Hunt's interpretation of this treaty, see Desrosiers 1952.

16. Desrosiers 1947a:336; based on Tessouat's gift so that "the landmarks and the boundaries of all those countries be removed and that everyone should find himself everywhere in his own country."

17. For a more detailed examination of this problem, see Garrad 1973.

CHAPTER TEN

1. Jones 1908:376–79. Forty-six is the number given in Ragueneau's letter to the general of the Jesuit order; however, Jones's *Catalogus Personarum* gives the names of more donnés than the twenty-three that Ragueneau states were there and, even so, omits the name of Gendron.

2. Campeau (1966: 551) makes no mention of Poncet de La Rivière's return to the Huron country after he went to Quebec in 1640; however, Jones (1908: 346–47) lists him as being in the Huron country from 1645 to 1650.

3. Although attached to the Huron mission, Claude Pijart worked mainly among the Algonkians. Jones (1908: 319–98) has him with the Huron mission every year from 1640 to 1650. Monet (1966b: 549) implies interruptions during this period.

4. Jones's (1908) *Catalogi* note special skills such as *sutor, pharm., faber lign.* Most donnés are described as *ad omnia* (handymen).

5. Jury and Jury (1954: 88) state that Tourmente was a donné. Jones (1908: 358, 365) lists him among the *domestici et alii*, not the donnés.

6. Oliveau appears to have been sent to Quebec as a miller, but was sent on to the Huron country when he proved not to be qualified. It seems less likely that he was sent from France with the intention that he should go directly to the Huron country. If, however, Russell (1965) is right in conjecturing that the Jesuits were planning to install a grist mill at Sainte-Marie, this conclusion may require revision.

7. For some of these arguments, see also Russell 1965: 16.

8. Frank Ridley formulated this interpretation many years ago, although he has not published on this subject (Heidenreich and Ridley, personal communications, 1970).

9. Ragueneau's 1649 statement that the bulk of the Jesuits' food was furnished by the Huron (Thwaites 1896–1901, 34: 207) is almost certainly in error (cf. 34: 225).

10. For a discussion of the first introduction of European plants and animals into Canada, see R. Saunders 1935.

11. Note, however, that Hamaleinan (1973) suggests that hybrid pottery found at Sainte-Marie was made by the French for their own use.

12. The Neutral settlements used to be believed to extend as far west as Windsor. A clay nodule bearing the date 1640 that was found in Middlesex County has been claimed as a possible relic of the Brébeuf-Chaumonot journey (Thomas 1936). This find now seems more likely to have been a hoax. Thomas mentions that another "Jesuit stone" inscribed "1641" was found in Vaughn township near Toronto about 1895.

13. Thwaites 1896–1901, 23: 147 implies that Tsondakwa was the principal headman of the town, suggesting that he might be the same as, or a replacement for, Endahiaconc.

CHAPTER ELEVEN

1. Note, however, that a similar change seems to have been made in mission policy at Sillery at the same time (Thwaites 1896–1901, 32: 211). Thus effectively the new policy in the Huron country may have resulted from a general directive from Quebec, issued following or not following prior discussion with Father Ragueneau.

2. 1300 baptisms for 1646?–48 (Thwaites 1896–1901, 33: 69) minus 500 for 1646–47 (30: 223) gives 800 for 1647–48. These figures probably include Tionnontaté but baptisms of the latter were few in number before 1648.

3. The figures are: 1700 recorded baptisms in the year preceding 1 March 1649 (Thwaites 1896–1901, 33: 257); 1300 between 4 July 1648 and 17 March

1649 (34:227); 1400 between 17 March 1649 and August 1649 (34:227); and 1800 in the year preceding May 1649 (34:103). These figures suggest approximately 400 conversions between March and July 1648; 1300 between July 1648 and March 1649; 300 in March and April 1649; and 1100 between May and August 1649.

4. "St. Ignace I" was located in the Sturgeon Valley and was no more than three leagues from Sainte-Marie even by a roundabout route (Thwaites 1896–1901, 23:143). Heidenreich (1966:123) estimates the direct distance to have been two leagues. "St. Ignace II" was two leagues from Sainte-Marie (Thwaites 1896–1901, 34:125–27) and must also have been in the Sturgeon Valley.

5. Heidenreich (1971:46) notes that in a personal communication dated 1967 Frank Ridley has argued that St. Ignace II never existed, but Heidenreich reserves judgement on this theory. In my opinion, Ridley has interpreted the evidence correctly.

6. Hunt has misread Thwaites 1896–1901, 45:243, which states that the Iroquois, rather than the Neutral, carried the Huron who had sought refuge among the Neutral into a harsh captivity.

7. Bressani (Thwaites 1896–1901, 40:49) says there were 400 bags of corn and 400 bags of acorns to feed the Indians, which seems to amount to between 500 and 600 bushels of each food (35:99–101). If we generously assume that acorns and corn are of equivalent nutrient value this would mean the equivalent of 1200 bushels of corn. If 10 bushels are needed to carry a person over the winter (see chapter 2, n. 16), this suggests that the Jesuits had enough to feed only about 120 people.

8. Perrot errs in saying that Jérôme Lalemant was the leader of this party;

evidently he confused Ragueneau with his predecessor.

9. Under the circumstances, it seems unlikely that this was someone who had inherited Ondaaiondiont's name.

CHAPTER TWELVE

1. In this chapter I am not attempting to trace Huron history in as great detail as in the preceding ones. My chief aim is to account for the dispersal of the Huron after 1650. For a detailed analysis of French-Iroquois relations during the latter half of the seventeenth century, see the following papers by Desrosiers (these papers are cited in approximately chronological order): 1953; 1959; 1960; 1961; 1966; 1962; 1955; 1964; 1957; 1958; 1954; 1963; 1956; and 1965. See also Desrosiers 1947b.

2. Hunt (1940:98) interprets Perrot (1911:149–50) to mean that they were later compelled to join the Iroquois, but there is no clear proof of this, since by Detroit Perrot may having been referring to the old Neutral country. Hunt (1940:97) suggests that some joined the Catawba, although the evidence is admitted to be weak. He also suggests (p. 98) that the Negawichi may have been a remnant of the Neutral.

3. Thwaites 1896–1901, 42:179–83. The *Jesuit Relation* of 1655–56 describes this fortified location as a hastily constructed wooden fort.

4. See the note on the Bernou map of 1680 (?) (our plate 50) concerning Lake Erie: "This lake is not Lake Erie as people regularly call it. Erie is part of Chesapeake Bay in Virginia, where the Erie have always lived." Evidently the author of this map mistook the location of these refugees for the original homeland of the Erie.

5. Cf. Hamelin 1966*a*:112. Hamelin has the death of these Huron as the cause of Bourdon turning back.

6. He seems to have come from the village of Arethsi ("Tsawenhohi from Arhetsi," Thwaites 1896–1901, 36:141).

7. For a study of Jesuit power in early New France, see Trudel 1973:230–45.

8. Thwaites 1896–1901, 45:115. For a discussion of Thwaites's translation of this passage, see Donnelly 1967:166.

9. Is this the Aotonatendia mentioned as their destination for the autumn of 1653 (Thwaites 1896–1901, 38:181)? It was located three days journey southwest of Sault Sainte Marie. For a discussion of the archaeology of the Huron-Tionnontaté after 1650, see Quimby 1966:114–16; 130; 134–36.

10. On the identity of Groseilliers's companion, see Nute 1966:224.

11. Reported by D. Lenig according to J. V. Wright, personal communication 1973. I have been unable to confirm this with Mr. Lenig.

References

The following are works cited in the text and notes or consulted in their preparation. In general, works of an ephemeral nature or preliminary reports later superseded by more definitive studies have been omitted.

ABBREVIATIONS

AA	*American Anthropologist*
AARO	*Annual Archaeological Report, Appendix to the Report of the Minister of Education, Ontario*
Am. Ant.	*American Antiquity*
BAE	*Bureau of American Ethnology*
CdD	*Les Cahiers des Dix*
CHR	*The Canadian Historical Review*
DAUTRR	Toronto: *Department of Anthropology, University of Toronto, Research Report*
DCB	*Dictionary of Canadian Biography*
NMC	*National Museum of Canada*
Ont. Arch.	*Ontario Archaeology*
Ont. Hist.	*Ontario History*
Penn. Arch.	*Pennsylvania Archaeologist*
PAPS	*Proceedings of the American Philosophical Society*
RHAF	*Revue d'histoire de l'Amérique française*
ROM-OP	*Royal Ontario Museum, Art and Archaeology, Occasional Paper*
SWJA	*Southwestern Journal of Anthropology*
TRSC	*Transactions of the Royal Society of Canada*
UMAP	*University of Michigan, Anthropological Papers*

ABLER, THOMAS S.

1970   "Longhouse and Palisade: Northeastern Iroquoian Villages of the Seventeenth Century." *Ont. Hist.* 62:17–40.

ADAIR, E. R.

1944   "France and the Beginnings of New France." *CHR* 25:246–78.

ADAMS, A. T.

1961   *The Explorations of Pierre Esprit Radisson.* Minneapolis: Ross and Haines, Inc.

ANDERSON, JAMES E.

1964   "The People of Fairty: An Osteological Analysis of an Iroquois Ossuary." *NMC, Bulletin* 193:28–129.

1968   *The Serpent Mounds Site Physical Anthropology. ROM–OP*, no. 11.

Atlas of Canada

1957   Ottawa: Department of Mines and Technical Surveys, Geographical Branch.

AVERKIEVA, J.

1971   "The Tlingit Indians." *North American Indians in Historical Perspective.* Ed. E. B. Leacock and N. O. Lurie. New York: Random House, pp. 317–42.

BACQUEVILLE DE LA POTHERIE, CLAUDE CHARLES LE ROY, SIEUR DE

1753   *Histoire de l'Amerique septentrionale.* 4 vols. Paris: Nyon fils.

1911–12   "History of the Savage Peoples Who Are Allies of New France." *The Indian Tribes of the Upper Mississippi Valley and Region of the Great Lakes.* 2 vols. Ed. E. H. Blair. Cleveland: Arthur H. Clark Company, 1:273–372; 2:13–136.

BAILEY, ALFRED G.

1933   "The Significance of the Identity and Disappearance of the Laurentian Iroquois." *TRSC*, 3rd Series, 27, ii:97–108.

1937   *The Conflict of European and Eastern Algonkian Cultures, 1504–1700: A Study in Canadian Civilization.* Saint John: New Brunswick Museum. (A second edition of this work with the same pagination was published by the University of Toronto Press in 1969.)

1938   "Social Revolution in Early Eastern Canada." *CHR* 19:264–76.

1972   "Vanished Iroquoians." *Culture and Nationality: Essays by A. G. Bailey.* Toronto: McClelland and Stewart Ltd., pp. 14–28.

BAKER, D.

1972   "Color, Culture and Power: Indian-White Relations in Canada and America." *Canadian Review of American Studies* 3:3–20.

BARBEAU, MARIUS

1914   "Supernatural Beings of the Huron and Wyandot." *AA* 16:288–313.

1915   *Huron and Wyandot Mythology.* Ottawa: *Department of Mines, Geological Survey, Memoir* 80.

1917   "Iroquoian Clans and Phratries." *AA* 19:392–402.

1949   "How the Huron-Wyandot Language was Saved from Oblivion." *PAPS* 93:226–32.

1960   *Huron-Wyandot Traditional Narratives in Translations and Native Texts. NMC, Bulletin* 165.

1961   "The Language of Canada in the Voyages of Jacques Cartier (1534–1538)." *NMC, Bulletin* 173:108–229.

BAWTREE, E. W.

1848   "A Brief Description of Some Sepulchral Pits, of Indian Origin, Lately Discovered near Penetanqueshene." *The Edinburgh New Philosophical Journal* 45:86–101.

BEAUCHAMP, WILLIAM A.

1898   "Wampum Used in Council and as Currency." *American Antiquarian* 20 (1):1–13.

1901   "Wampum and Shell Articles Used by the New York Indians." *New York State Museum, Bulletin*, no. 41:319–480.

1905   "Aboriginal Use of Wood in New York." *New York State Museum, Bulletin*, no. 89:87–272.

BEAUGRAND-CHAMPAGNE, A.

1936   "Les anciens Iroquois du Québec." *CdD* 1:171–99.

1948   "Les origines de Montréal." *CdD* 13:39–62.

BIGGAR, H. P.

1901   *The Early Trading Companies of New France.* Toronto: *University of Toronto Studies in History.*

——, ed.

1911   *The Precursors of Jacques Cartier, 1497–1534.* Ottawa: *Publications of the Canadian Archives*, no. 5.

1922–36   *The Works of Samuel de Champlain.* 6 vols. Toronto: The Champlain Society.

1924   *The Voyages of Jacques Cartier: Published from the Originals with Translations, Notes, and Appendices.* Ottawa: *Publications of the Public Archives of Canada*, no. 11.

1930   *A Collection of Documents Relating to Jacques Cartier and the Sieur de Roberval.* Ottawa: *Publications of the Public Archives of Canada*, no. 14.

BISHOP, M.

1948   *Champlain: The Life of Fortitude.* New York: Alfred A. Knopf.

BLAU, H.

1966   "Function and the False Faces: A Classification of Onondaga Masked Rituals and Themes." *Journal of American Folklore* 79:564–80.

BOUCHER, PIERRE

1664   *Histoire véritable et naturelle des moeurs et productions du pays de la Nouvelle-France, vulgairement dite le Canada.* Paris: F. Lambert (the most recent photographic reprint is by the Société historique de Boucherville, 1964).

BRASSER, T. J. C.

1971   "Group Identification Along a Moving Frontier." *Verhandlungen des XXXVIII Internationalen Amerikanistenkongresses.* Munich, Band II, pp. 261–65.

BROSE, DAVID S.

1970   *The Summer Island Site: A Study of Prehistoric Cultural Ecology and Social Organization in the Northern Lake Michigan Area.* Cleveland: *Case Western Reserve University Studies in Anthropology*, no. 1.

BUTTERFIELD, C. W.

1898   *History of Brulé's Discoveries and Explorations.* Cleveland: Helman-Taylor Company.

CALDWELL, J. R.

1958   *Trend and Tradition in the Prehistory of the Eastern United States.* Washington: *American Anthropological Association, Memoir* 88.

CAMPEAU, LUCIEN

1951–52   "Les Jésuites ont-ils rétouché les écrits de Champlain?" *RHAF* 5:340–61.

1966   "Joseph-Antoine Poncet de La Rivière." *DCB* 1:551–52.

CARMACK, R. M.

1972   "Ethnohistory: A Review of its Development, Definitions, Methods, and Aims." *Annual Review of Anthropology.* Ed. B. J. Siegel. Palo Alto: Annual Reviews, 1:227–46.

CARPENTER, EDMUND

1942   "Iroquoian Figurines." *Am. Ant.* 8:105–13.

CARR, E. H.

1967   *What is History?* New York: Vintage Books.

CARRUTHERS, P. J.

1965   "Preliminary Excavations at the Supposed Site of Ste. Marie II." Ms. in Dept. of Public Records and Archives, Toronto.

CHAFE, W. L.

1964   "Linguistic Evidence for the Relative Age of Iroquois Religious Practices." *SWJA* 20:278–85.

CHANNEN, E. R. and N. D. CLARKE

1965   *The Copeland Site: A Precontact Huron Site in Simcoe County, Ontario. NMC, Anthropology Papers*, no. 8.

CHAPMAN, L. J. and D. F. PUTNAM

1966   *The Physiography of Southern Ontario.* 2nd ed. Toronto: University of Toronto Press.

CHARLEVOIX, PIERRE F. X.

1866–72   *History and General Description of New France.* 6 vols. New York: J. G. Shea.

1923   *Journal of a Voyage to North America.* 2 vols. Ed. L. P. Kellogg. Chicago: The Caxton Club (originally published in French, 1744).

CHARLTON, THOMAS H.

1968   "On Iroquois Incest." *Anthropologica* 10:29–43.

CHAUMONOT, PIERRE J. M.

1869   *Le Père Pierre Chaumonot de la Compagnie de Jésus: autobiographie et pièces inédites.* Ed. A. Carayon. Poitiers: H. Oudin.

1920 (Author uncertain) "Grammar of the Huron Language...translated from the Latin by Mr. John Wilkie." *Fifteenth Report of the Bureau of Archives for the Province of Ontario*. Toronto: Clarkson W. James, pp. 725–77. (Also published in *Transactions of the Literary and Historical Society of Quebec* 2 [1831]:94–198.)

CHURCHER, C. S. and W. A. KENYON
1960 "The Tabor Hill Ossuaries: A Study in Iroquois Demography." *Human Biology* 32:249–73.

CLARK, GRAHAME
1945 "Farmers and Forests in Neolithic Europe." *Antiquity* 19:57–71.

CLARKE, P. D.
1870 *Origin and Traditional History of the Wyandotts*. Toronto: Hunter, Rose and Company.

COLE, D.
1973 "The Origins of Canadian Anthropology, 1850–1910." *Journal of Canadian Studies* 8:33–45.

CONNELLY, WILLIAM E.
1900 "The Wyandots." *AARO*, 1899:92–123.

CÔTÉ, JEAN
1956–57 "Domestique séculier d'habit, mais religieux de coeur." *RHAF* 10:183–90; 448–53.
1961–62 "L'institution des donnés." *RHAF* 15:344–78.

CRANSTON, J. H.
1949 *Etienne Brûlé: Immortal Scoundrel*. Toronto: The Ryerson Press.

CRANSTONE, B. A. L.
1971 "The Tifalmin: A 'Neolithic' People in New Guinea." *World Archaeology* 3:132–42.

CROUSE, N. M.
1924 *Contributions of the Canadian Jesuits to the Geographical Knowledge of New France, 1632–1675*. Ithaca: Cornell Publications.

CRUICKSHANK, J. G. and C. E. HEIDENREICH
1969 "Pedological Investigations at the Huron Indian Village of Cahiagué." *The Canadian Geographer* 13:34–46.

DAY, GORDON M.
1971 "The Eastern Boundary of Iroquoia: Abenaki Evidence." *Man in the Northeast* 1:7–13.

DEETZ, JAMES
1965 *The Dynamics of Stylistic Change in Arikara Ceramics*. Urbana: *Illinois Studies in Anthropology*, no. 4.

DELANGLEZ, J.
1939 *Frontenac and the Jesuits*. Chicago: Institute of Jesuit History.

DENYS, NICOLAS

1908   *The Description and Natural History of the Coasts of North America.*
Ed. W. F. Ganong. Toronto: The Champlain Society (first printed
1672).

DESJARDINS, P.

1966   *La Résidence de Sainte-Marie-aux-Hurons.* Sudbury: *La Société
Historique du Nouvel-Ontario, Documents Historiques*, no. 48.

DESROSIERS, LÉO-PAUL

1947a   *Iroquoisie.* Montreal: Institut d'Histoire de l'Amérique française.
1947b   "Premières missions Iroquoises." *RHAF* 1:21–38.
1948   "L'année 1647 en Huronie." *RHAF* 2:238–49.
1952   "La rupture de la paix de 1645." *CdD* 17:169–81.
1953   "Les Onnontagués." *CdD* 18:45–66.
1954   "Préliminaires du massacre de Lachine." *CdD* 19:47–66.
1955   "Iroquoisie, terre française." *CdD* 20:33–59.
1956   "Négociations de paix (1693–1696)." *CdD* 21:55–87.
1957   "L'expédition de M. de la Barre." *CdD* 22:105–35.
1958   "Denonville." *CdD* 23:107–38.
1959   "La paix-miracle (1653–1660)." *CdD* 24:85–112.
1960   "Il y a trois cents ans." *CdD* 25:85–101.
1961   "Les années terribles." *CdD* 26:55–90.
1962   "Revers et succès (1662–1663)." *CdD* 27:77–95.
1963   "Frontenac, l'artisan de la victoire." *CdD* 28:93–145.
1964   "La paix de 1667." *CdD* 29:25–45.
1965   "Fort Orange (Albany) à l'époque des guerres indiennes." *CdD*
30:19–33.
1966   "Guérillas dans l'île de Montréal." *CdD* 31:79–95.

Dictionary of Canadian Biography

1966, 1969   Vols. 1 and 2. Toronto: University of Toronto Press.

DIONNE, NARCISSE-E.

1891, 1906   *Samuel Champlain.* 2 vols. Quebec: A. Côté et Cie.

DOBYNS, H. F.

1966   "Estimating Aboriginal American Population: An Appraisal of
Techniques with a New Hemispheric Estimate." *Current Anthropology*
7:395–449.

DONNELLY, JOSEPH P.

1967   *Thwaites' Jesuit Relations, Errata and Addenda.* Chicago: Loyola
University Press.

DOUGLAS, MARY, ed.

1970   *Witchcraft Confessions and Accusations.* London: Tavistock Publications.

DRIVER, HAROLD E.

1961   *Indians of North America.* Chicago: University of Chicago Press.

DU CREUX, FRANÇOIS (CREUXIUS)

1951–52   *The History of Canada.* 2 vols. Toronto: The Champlain Society.

DUFF, WILSON

1964   *The Indian History of British Columbia.* Vol. 1, *The Impact of the White Man.* Victoria: *Anthropology in British Columbia, Memoir* 5.

DUIGNAN, P.

1958   "Early Jesuit Missionaries: A Suggestion for Further Study." *AA* 60:725–32.

DUMAS, G.-M.

1966   "Georges Le Baillif." *DCB* 1:433.

DUNNING, R. W.

1959   *Social and Economic Change Among the Northern Ojibwa.* Toronto: University of Toronto Press.

DYK, W.

1938   *Son of Old Man Hat: A Navaho Autobiography.* New York: Harcourt, Brace and Company.

EGGAN, FRED R.

1952   "The Ethnological Cultures and Their Archeological Backgrounds." *Archeology of Eastern United States.* Ed. J. B. Griffin. Chicago: University of Chicago Press, pp. 35–45.

1966   *The American Indian: Perspectives for the Study of Social Change.* London: Weidenfeld and Nicolson.

ELTON, G. R.

1969   *The Practice of History.* London: Collins.

EMERSON, J. N.

1954   *The Archaeology of the Ontario Iroquois.* Ph.D. Dissertation, University of Chicago.

1959   "A Rejoinder Upon the MacNeish-Emerson Theory." *Penn. Arch.* 29 (2):98–107.

1961a   ed. *Cahiague, 1961.* Orillia: University of Toronto Archaeological Field School. Mimeographed.

1961b   "Problems of Huron Origins." *Anthropologica* 3:181–201.

1967   "The Payne Site: An Iroquoian Manifestation in Prince Edward County, Ontario." *NMC, Bulletin* 206:126–257.

1968   *Understanding Iroquois Pottery in Ontario: A Rethinking.* Toronto: Ontario Archaeological Society, special publication.

EMERSON, J. N. and R. E. POPHAM

1952   "Comments on 'The Huron and Lalonde Occupations of Ontario'." *Am. Ant.* 18:162–64.

FENTON, WILLIAM N.

1940   "Problems Arising from the Historic Northeastern Position of the Iroquois." *Smithsonian Miscellaneous Collections,* vol. 100:159–252.

1941   "Iroquois Suicide: A Study in the Stability of a Culture Pattern." *BAE, Bulletin* 128:70–138.

1951   "Locality as a Basic Factor in the Development of Iroquois Social Structure." *BAE, Bulletin* 149:35–54.

1957   *Indian and White Relations in Eastern North America.* Chapel Hill: University of North Carolina Press.

1966   "Field Work, Museum Studies, and Ethnohistorical Research." *Ethnohistory* 13:71–85.

1971   "The Iroquois in History." *North American Indians in Historical Perspective.* Ed. E. B. Leacock and N. O. Lurie. New York: Random House, pp. 129–68.

FENTON, WILLIAM N. and E. S. DODGE

1949   "An Elmbark Canoe in the Peabody Museum of Salem." *American Neptune* 9:185–206.

FIEDLER, L. A.

1968   *The Return of the Vanishing American.* New York: Stein and Day.

FISCHER, D. H.

1971   *Historians' Fallacies: Towards a Logic of Historical Thought.* London: Routledge and Kegan Paul.

FITTING, JAMES E.

1965   *Late Woodland Cultures of Southeastern Michigan. UMAP,* 24.

1968   "Environment Potential and the Postglacial Readaptation in Eastern North America." *Am. Ant.* 33:441–45.

1970   *The Archaeology of Michigan.* New York: The Natural History Press.

1972   "The Huron as an Ecotype: The Limits of Maximization in a Western Great Lakes Society." *Anthropologica* 14:3–18.

FITTING, JAMES E. and C. E. CLELAND

1969   "Late Prehistoric Settlement Patterns in the Upper Great Lakes." *Ethnohistory* 16:289–302.

FLORES SALINAS, BERTA

1964   *México visto por algunos de sus viajeros (siglos XVI y XVII).* Mexico: Universidad Nacional Autónoma de México.

FORBES, A.

1970   "Two and a Half Centuries of Conflict: The Iroquois and the Laurentian Wars." *Penn. Arch.* 40 (3–4):1–20.

FORBES, J. D., ed.

1964   *The Indian in America's Past.* Englewood Cliffs: Prentice-Hall.

FORD, C. S.

1941   *Smoke from their Fires.* New Haven: Yale University Press.

FOX, W. A.

1971   "The Maurice Site (BeHa-2): Lithic Analysis." *Palaeoecology and Ontario Prehistory. DAUTRR,* no. 2:137–65.

FOX, WILLIAM S. (and W. JURY)

1949   *St. Ignace, Canadian Altar of Martyrdom.* Toronto: McClelland and Stewart.

FREEMAN, J. E., comp.

1966   *A Guide to Manuscripts Relating to the American Indian in the Library*

of the American Philosophical Society. Philadelphia: American
Philosophical Society. (For Huron grammars and dictionaries,
see pp. 185–87.)

FRENCH, M. J.

1949   *Samuel de Champlain's Incursion Against the Onondaga Nation.*
Ann Arbor: Edwards Brothers.

GAMST, F. C.

1969   *The Qemant.* New York: Holt, Rinehart and Winston.

GANONG, W. F.

1964   *Crucial Maps in the Early Cartography and Place-nomenclature of the
Atlantic Coast of Canada.* With an introduction by T. E. Layng.
Toronto: University of Toronto Press.

GARNIER, CHARLES

1930   "Saint Charles Garnier" (letters). *Rapport de l'Archiviste de la
Province de Québec pour 1929–30.* Quebec: The King's Printer,
pp. 1–43.

GARRAD, CHARLES

1969   "Iron Trade Knives on Historic Petun Sites." *Ont. Arch.* 13:3–15.
1970   "Did Champlain Visit the Bruce Peninsula? An Examination of an
Ontario Myth." *Ont. Hist.* 62:235–39.
1971   "Ontario Fluted Point Survey." *Ont. Arch.* 16:3–18.
1973   "The Attack on Ehwae in 1640." *Ont. Hist.* 65:107–11.

GENDRON, FRANÇOIS

1868   *Quelques particularitez du pays des Hurons en la Nouvelle France
rémarquées par le Sieur Gendron, docteur en médecine qui a démeuré
dans ce pays-là fort longtemps.* Albany: J. G. Shea (originally published
Paris 1660).

GÉRIN, L.

1900   "The Hurons of Lorette." *Report of the British Association for the
Advancement of Science, 1900,* pp. 549–68.

GIRARD, R.

1948   *Trois Grands Hurons.* Sudbury: *La Société Historique du
Nouvel-Ontario, Documents Historiques,* no. 16.

GODBOUT, A.

1942   "Le néophyte Ahuntsic." *Bulletin des recherches historiques*
48:129–37.

GODDARD, IVES

1972   "Historical and Philological Evidence Regarding the Identification of
the Mascouten." *Ethnohistory* 19:123–34.

GODEFROY, F.

1938   *Dictionnaire de l'ancienne langue française et de tous ses dialectes.*
Paris: Librairie des Sciences et des Arts.

GOLDSTEIN, R. A.

1969   *French-Iroquois Diplomatic and Military Relations, 1609–1701.*
The Hague: Mouton.

GRANDSAIGNES D'HAUTRIVE, R.

1947   *Dictionnaire d'ancien français: moyen age et renaissance.* Paris:
Librairie Larousse.

GRANT, W. L., ed.

1952   *Voyages of Samuel de Champlain 1604–1618.* New York: Barnes and
Noble (originally published 1907).

GRASSMANN, T.

1966a   "Pastedechouan." *DCB* 1:533–34.
1966b   "Thérèse Oionhaton." *DCB* 1:523–24.
1969   *The Mohawk Indians and Their Valley.* Fonda, N.Y.: Mohawk-
Caughnawaga Museum.

GRIFFIN, JAMES B.

1952   *Archeology of Eastern United States.* Chicago: University of Chicago
Press.
1961   ed. *Lake Superior Copper and the Indians: Miscellaneous Studies of
Great Lakes Prehistory. UMAP,* 17.
1965   "Late Quaternary Prehistory in the Northeastern Woodlands."
The Quaternary of the United States. Ed. H. E. Wright, Jr. and
D. G. Frey. Princeton: Princeton University Press, pp. 655–67.

GUYART DE L'INCARNATION, MARIE

1876   *Lettres de la révérende Mère Marie de l'Incarnation (née Marie
Guyard), première supérieure du monastère des Ursulines de Québec.*
2 vols. Ed. P. F. Richaudeau. Paris: Librairie Internationale.

HAGAN, W. T.

1961   *American Indians.* Chicago: University of Chicago Press.

HAKLUYT, RICHARD

1589   *The Principall Navigations Voiages and Discoveries of the English
Nation.* Facsimile edited by D. B. Quinn and R. A. Skelton.
Cambridge: Cambridge University Press, 1965.

HALE, HORATIO, ed.

1963   *The Iroquois Book of Rites.* Reprinted with an Introduction by
William N. Fenton. Toronto: University of Toronto Press (originally
published 1883).

HALLOWELL, A. I.

1955   *Culture and Experience.* Philadelphia: University of Pennsylvania
Press.

HAMALEINAN, P.

1973   "'Home-made' Pottery from Sainte-Marie I." Ontario Archaeological
Society, *Arch Notes* 73, no. 5:10–15.

HAMELIN, J.

    1966*a*   "Jean Bourdon." *DCB* 1:111–13.

    1966*b*   "Jean Nicollet de Belleborne." *DCB* 1:516–18.

HAMMOND, J. H.

    1905   "North and South Orillia." *AARO*, 1904:77–86.

    1924   "Exploration of the Ossuary Burial of the Huron Nation, Simcoe County." *AARO*, 34:95–102.

HANZELI, VICTOR E.

    1969   *Missionary Linguistics in New France: A Study of Seventeenth- and Eighteenth-Century Descriptions of American Indian Languages.* The Hague: Mouton.

HARPER, J. R.

    1952   "The Webb Site: A Stage in Early Iroquoian Development." *Penn. Arch.* 22 (2):49–64.

    1971   *Paul Kane's Frontier.* Toronto: University of Toronto Press.

HARRIS, MARVIN

    1968   *The Rise of Anthropological Theory.* New York: Thomas Y. Crowell.

HAYES, CHARLES F., III

    1967   "The Longhouse at the Cornish Site." *Iroquois Culture, History, and Prehistory.* Ed. E. Tooker. Albany: The University of the State of New York, pp. 91–97.

HEIDENREICH, CONRAD E.

    1966   "Maps Relating to the First Half of the 17th Century and Their Use in Determining the Location of Jesuit Missions in Huronia." *The Cartographer* 3:103–26.

    1967   "The Indian Occupance of Huronia, 1600–1650." *Canada's Changing Geography.* Ed. R. L. Gentilcore. Scarborough: Prentice-Hall, pp. 15–29.

    1968   "A New Location for Carhagouha, Récollet Mission in Huronia." *Ont. Arch.* 11:39–46.

    1970   "Review of *The Huron: Farmers of the North*." *CHR* 51:451–53.

    1971   *Huronia: A History and Geography of the Huron Indians, 1600–1650.* Toronto: McClelland and Stewart Limited.

    1972   *The Huron: A Brief Ethnography.* Toronto: *York University, Department of Geography, Discussion Paper* no. 6.

HEIDENREICH, C. E. et al.

    1969   "Maurice and Robitaille Sites: Environmental Analysis." *Palaeoecology and Ontario Prehistory. DAUTRR*, no. 1:112–54.

HELMS, MARY

    1970   "Matrilocality, Social Solidarity, and Culture Contact: Three Case Histories." *SWJA* 26:197–212.

HERMAN, MARY W.

    1956   "The Social Aspect of Huron Property." *AA* 58:1044–58.

HÉROUVILLE, P. D'

1929   *Les Missions des Jésuites au Canada, XVIIe et XVIIIe siècles;*
        avec Leymaire, A.-L., *Analyse des documents exposés par la*
        Compagnie de Jésus et sur les Jésuites. Paris: G. Enault.

HEWITT, J. N. B.

1894   "Era of the Formation of the Historic League of the Iroquois."
        AA, O.S. 6:61–67.
1907   "Huron." *BAE, Bulletin* 30, vol. 1, pp. 584–91.
1910a   "Seneca." *BAE, Bulletin* 30, vol. 2, pp. 502–8.
1910b   "Susquehanna." *BAE, Bulletin* 30, vol. 2, pp. 653–59.
1910c   "Wenrohronon." *BAE, Bulletin* 30, vol. 2, pp. 932–34.

HICKERSON, HAROLD

1960   "The Feast of the Dead Among the Seventeenth Century Algonkians
        of the Upper Great Lakes." *AA* 62:81–107.
1962   *The Southwestern Chippewa: An Ethnohistorical Study.* Washington:
        American Anthropological Association, Memoir 92.
1970   *The Chippewa and Their Neighbors: A Study in Ethnohistory.*
        New York: Holt, Rinehart and Winston.

HICKERSON, HAROLD, G. D. TURNER and N. P. HICKERSON

1952   "Testing Procedures for Estimating Transfer of Information among
        Iroquois Dialects and Languages." *International Journal of American*
        Linguistics 18:1–8.

HOEBEL, E. A.

1960   "William Robertson: An 18th Century Anthropologist-Historian."
        AA 62:648–55.

HOFFMAN, B. G.

1959   "Iroquois Linguistic Classification from Historical Materials."
        Ethnohistory 6:160–85.
1961   *Cabot to Cartier: Sources for a Historical Ethnography of*
        Northeastern North America, 1497–1550. Toronto: University of
        Toronto Press.

HOFFMAN, D. W. et al.

1962   *Soil Survey of Simcoe County, Ontario.* Ottawa and Guelph: *Ontario*
        Soil Survey, Report no. 29.

HOMANS, GEORGE C.

1962   *Sentiments and Activities: Essays in Social Science.* Glencoe: The Free
        Press.

HUDSON, CHARLES

1966   "Folk History and Ethnohistory." *Ethnohistory* 13:52–70.

HUNT, GEORGE T.

1940   *The Wars of the Iroquois: A Study in Intertribal Trade Relations.*
        Madison: University of Wisconsin Press.

HUNTER, ANDREW F.

1889   "French Relics from the Village Sites of the Hurons." *AARO,*
        1889:42–46.

1899   "Notes on Sites of Huron Villages in the Township of Tiny (Simcoe County) and adjacent parts." *Appendix to the Report of the Minister of Education*, 42 pp.

1900   "Notes on Sites of Huron Villages in the Township of Tay (Simcoe County). *AARO*, 1899:51–82.

1902   "Notes on Sites of Huron Villages in the Township of Medonte (Simcoe County)." *AARO*, 1901:56–100.

1903   "Notes on Sites of Huron Villages in the Township of Oro, Simcoe County, Ontario." *AARO*, 1902:153–83.

1904   "Indian Village Sites in North and South Orillia Townships." *AARO*, 1903:105–25.

1907   "Huron Village Sites" (including surveys of Flos and Vespra Townships). *AARO*, 1906:3–56.

HUNTER, WILLIAM A.

1959   "The Historic Role of the Susquehannocks." *Susquehannock Miscellany*. Ed. J. Witthoft and W. F. Kinsey III. Harrisburg: The Pennsylvania Historical and Museum Commission, pp. 8–18.

HURLEY, W. M. and C. E. HEIDENREICH, eds.

1969   *Palaeoecology and Ontario Prehistory*. *DAUTRR*, no. 1.

1971   *Palaeoecology and Ontario Prehistory II*. *DAUTRR*, no. 2.

HURLEY, WILLIAM M. and I. T. KENYON

1970   *Algonquin Park Archaeology*. *DAUTRR*, no. 3.

HURLEY, WILLIAM M. et al.

1972   *Algonquin Park Archaeology*. *DAUTRR*, no. 10.

INNIS, H. A.

1940   *The Cod Fisheries: The History of an International Economy*. New Haven: Yale University Press.

1956   *The Fur Trade in Canada*. Toronto: University of Toronto Press (revised edition; original edition published by Yale University Press, 1930).

IVERSEN, J.

1956   "Forest Clearance in the Stone Age." *Scientific American* 194 (3):36–41.

JAENEN, C. J.

1970   "The Catholic Clergy and the Fur Trade." *Canadian Historical Association, Historical Papers, 1970:* 60–80.

JAMES, C. C.

1906   "The Downfall of the Huron Nation." *TRSC*, 2nd Series, 12, ii:311–46.

JAMESON, J. F., ed.

1909   *Narratives of New Netherlands, 1609–1664*. New York: Charles Scribner's Sons.

JENNESS, DIAMOND

1960   *The Indians of Canada*. 5th ed. *NMC, Bulletin* 65.

JENNINGS, FRANCIS

    1966   "The Indian Trade of the Susquehanna Valley." *PAPS* 110:406–24.

    1968   "Glory, Death, and Transfiguration: the Susquehannock Indians in the Seventeenth Century." *PAPS* 112:15–53.

JENNINGS, J. D.

    1968   *Prehistory of North America.* New York: McGraw-Hill Book Company.

JOHNSTON, RICHARD B.

    1968a   *Archaeology of Rice Lake, Ontario. NMC, Anthropology Papers* 19.

    1968b   *The Archaeology of the Serpent Mounds Site. ROM-OP*, no. 10.

JONES, ARTHUR E.

    1908   *"8endake Ehen" or Old Huronia.* Toronto: Fifth Report of the Bureau of Archives for the Province of Ontario.

JOUVE, O.-M.

    1915   *Les Franciscains et le Canada.* Vol. 1, *Etablissement de la foi, 1615–1629.* Quebec: Couvent des ss. stigmates.

JURGENS, OLGA

    1966   "Etienne Brûlé." *DCB* 1:130–33.

JURY, E. M.

    1966a   "Anadabijou." *DCB* 1:61.

    1966b   "Atironta (Darontal, Durantal)." *DCB* 1:70.

    1966c   "Atironta (Aëoptahon), Jean-Baptiste." *DCB* 1:70–71.

    1966d   "Atironta, Pierre." *DCB* 1:71–72.

    1966e   "Auoindaon." *DCB* 1:73.

    1966f   "Skanudharoua." *DCB* 1:610–11.

JURY, W. and E. M. JURY

    1954   *Sainte-Marie Among the Hurons.* Toronto: Oxford University Press.

    1955   *Saint Louis: Huron Indian Village and Jesuit Mission Site. University of Western Ontario, Museum of Indian Archaeology, Bulletin* no. 10.

KAPLAN, L.

    1967   "Archaeological Phaseolus from Tehuacan." *The Prehistory of the Tehuacan Valley.* Vol. 1, *Environment and Subsistence.* Ed. D. S. Byers. Austin: The University of Texas Press, pp. 201–11.

KENNEDY, J. H.

    1950   *Jesuit and Savage in New France.* New Haven: Yale University Press.

KENYON, WALTER A.

    1968   *The Miller Site. ROM-OP*, no. 14.

KERRIGAN, ANTHONY, trans.

    1951   [Andrés González de] *Barcia's Chronological History of the Continent of Florida.* Gainesville: University of Florida Press.

KIDD, KENNETH E.

    1949a   *The Excavation of Ste. Marie I.* Toronto: University of Toronto Press.

    1949b   "The Identification of French Mission Sites in the Huron Country: A Study in Procedure." *Ont. Hist.* 41:89–94.

1950 "Orr Lake Pottery." *Transactions of the Royal Canadian Institute* 28 (2):165–86.

1952 "Sixty Years of Ontario Archeology." *Archeology of Eastern United States*. Ed. J. B. Griffin. Chicago: University of Chicago Press, pp. 71–82.

1953 "The Excavation and Historical Identification of a Huron Ossuary." *Am. Ant.* 18:359–79.

KIDD, K. E. and M. A.
1970 "A Classification System for Glass Beads for the Use of Field Archaeologists." *Canadian Historic Sites: Occasional Papers in Archaeology and History*, no. 1:45–89.

KINIETZ, W. V.
1940 *The Indians of the Western Great Lakes, 1615–1760*. Ann Arbor: University of Michigan Press.

KNOWLES, NATHANIEL
1940 "The Torture of Captives by the Indians of Eastern North America." *PAPS* 82:151–225.

KROEBER, A. L.
1939 *Cultural and Natural Areas of Native North America*. Berkeley: *University of California, Publications in American Archaeology and Ethnology*, vol. 38.

1952 *The Nature of Culture*. Chicago: University of Chicago Press.

LAFITAU, JOSEPH-FRANÇOIS
1724 *Moeurs des sauvages ameriquains, comparées aux moeurs des premiers temps*. 2 vols. Paris: Saugrain l'aîné.

LA MORANDIÈRE, CHARLES DE
1962–66 *Histoire de la pêche française de la morue dans l'Amérique septentrionale*. 3 vols. Paris: G. P. Maisonneuve et Larose.

LANCTOT, GUSTAVE
1930 "L'Itinéraire de Cartier à Hochelaga." *TRSC*, 3rd Series, 24, i:115–41.

1963 *A History of Canada*. Vol. 1, *From Its Origins to the Royal Régime, 1663*. Toronto: Clarke, Irwin and Company.

1964 *A History of Canada*. Vol. 2, *From the Royal Régime to the Treaty of Utrecht, 1663–1713*. Toronto: Clarke, Irwin and Company.

1967 *Canada and the American Revolution, 1774–1783*. Toronto: Clarke, Irwin and Company.

LATOURELLE, RENÉ
1952–53 *Etude sur les écrits de Saint Jean de Brébeuf*. 2 vols. Montreal: Les Editions de l'Immaculée-Conception.

1966 "Jean de Brébeuf." *DCB* 1:121–26.

LATTA, M. A.
1971 "Archaeology of the Penetang Peninsula." *Palaeoecology and Ontario Prehistory II. DAUTRR*, no. 2:116–36.

LAVERDIÈRE, C.-H., ed.
1870 *Oeuvres de Champlain*. 2nd ed.; 3 vols. Quebec: G.-E. Desbarats.

LAWRENCE, JOHN

1916   "Ekarenniondi: The Rock that Stands Out." *AARO*, 28:40–48.

LEACOCK, E. B. and N. O. LURIE, eds.

1971   *North American Indians in Historical Perspective.* New York: Random House.

LEBLANC, P. G.

1968   "Indian-Missionary Contact in Huronia, 1615–1649." *Ont. Hist.* 40:133–46.

LE BLANT, R.

1972   "Le Commerce compliqué des fourrures canadiennes au début de XVIIe siècle." *RHAF* 26:53–66.

LE BLANT, R. and R. BAUDRY

1967   *Nouveaux documents sur Champlain et son époque.* Vol. 1 *(1560–1622).* Ottawa: *Publication of the Public Archives of Canada*, no. 15.

LE CLERCQ, CHRESTIEN

1691   *Premier établissement de la foy dans la Nouvelle-France.* 2 vols. Paris: A. Auroy.

LEE, THOMAS E.

1959   "An Archaeological Survey of Southwestern Ontario and Manitoulin Island." *Penn. Arch.* 29 (2):80–92.

LEMAY, S. (FATHER HUGOLIN)

1932–33   *Notes bibliographiques pour servir à l'histoire des Récollets du Canada.* 5 vols. Montreal: Imprimerie des Franciscains.

1936   "L'Oeuvre manuscrite ou imprimée des Récollets de la Mission du Canada (1615–1629)." *TRSC*, 3rd Series, 30, i:115–26.

LESCARBOT, MARC

1907–14   *The History of New France.* 3 vols. Trans. W. L. Grant. Toronto: The Champlain Society.

LÉVI-STRAUSS, CLAUDE

1968   *Mythologiques. 3, L'origine des manières de table.* Paris: Plon.

1971   *Mythologiques. 4, L'homme nu.* Paris: Plon.

LIGHTHALL, W. D.

1899   "Hochelagans and Mohawks: A Link in Iroquois History." *TRSC*, 2nd Series, 5, ii:199–211.

LINDSAY, L. S.

1900   *Notre-Dame de la Jeune Lorette.* Montreal: La Cie de publication de la Revue Canadienne.

LLOYD, H. M. *See* MORGAN, L. H. 1904.

LOM D'ARCE, [BARON] DE LAHONTAN, LOUIS ARMAND DE

1905   *New Voyages to North America.* 2 vols. Ed. R. G. Thwaites. Chicago: A. C. McClurg and Company.

LONGLEY, WILLIAM H. and JOHN B. MOYLE

1963   *The Beaver in Minnesota. Minnesota Department of Conservation, Technical Bulletin*, no. 6.

LURIE, NANCY O.

1959 "Indian Cultural Adjustment to European Civilization." *Seventeenth-Century America.* Ed. J. M. Smith. Chapel Hill: University of North Carolina Press, pp. 33–60.

1960 "Winnebago Protohistory." *Culture in History: Essays in Honor of Paul Radin.* Ed. S. Diamond. New York: Columbia University Press, pp. 790–808.

LOUNSBURY, FLOYD G.

1961 "Iroquois-Cherokee Linguistic Relations." *BAE, Bulletin* 180:9–17.

MACDONALD, GEORGE F.

n.d. "Archaeological Survey of the Grand River Between Paris and Waterloo, Ontario, 1961." National Museum of Canada, files.

MACFARLANE, ALAN

1970 *Witchcraft in Tudor and Stuart England.* London: Routledge and Kegan Paul.

MCGUIRE, JOSEPH D.

1901 "Ethnology in the Jesuit Relations." *AA* 3:257–69.

MCILWAIN, C. H., ed.

1915 Peter Wraxall, *An Abridgment of the Indian Affairs . . . Transacted in the Colony of New York, from the Year 1678 to the Year 1751.* Cambridge: *Harvard Historical Studies*, volume 21.

MCILWRAITH, T. F.

1930 "The Progress of Anthropology in Canada." *CHR* 11:132–50.

1946 "Archaeological Work in Huronia, 1946: Excavations near Warminster." *CHR* 27:394–401.

1947 "On the Location of Cahiagué." *TRSC*, 3rd Series, 41, ii:99–102.

1949 "Anthropology." *The Royal Canadian Institute, Centennial Volume, 1849–1949.* Ed. W. S. Wallace. Toronto: Royal Canadian Institute, pp. 3–12.

MACNEISH, RICHARD S.

1952 *Iroquois Pottery Types: A Technique for the Study of Iroquois Prehistory. NMC, Bulletin* 124.

MCPHERRON, ALAN

1967 "On the Sociology of Ceramics: Pottery Style Clustering, Marital Residence, and Cultural Adaptations of an Algonkian-Iroquoian Border." *Iroquois Culture, History, and Prehistory.* Ed. E. Tooker. Albany: The University of the State of New York, pp. 101–7.

MARRIOTT, A.

1948 *Maria, the Potter of San Ildefonso.* Norman: University of Oklahoma Press.

MARTIJN, CHARLES A.

1969 "Ile aux Basques and the Prehistoric Iroquois Occupation of Southern Quebec." *Cahiers d'archéologie Québecoise* (mars), 53–114.

MARTIN, FÉLIX

1898   *Hurons et Iroquois: Le P. Jean de Brébeuf, sa vie, ses travaux, son martyre.* 3rd ed. Paris: Téqui.

MÉTRAUX, A.

1948   "Jesuit Missions in South America." *BAE, Bulletin* 143, volume 5:645–53.

MOIR, JOHN S.

1966   "Kirke, Sir David," *DCB* 1:404–7.

MONET, J.

1966a   "Philibert Noyrot." *DCB* 1:521–22.
1966b   "Claude Pijart." *DCB* 1:549.

MOONEY, JAMES

1928   *The Aboriginal Population of America North of Mexico.* Washington: *Smithsonian Miscellaneous Collections,* 80.

MORGAN, LEWIS H.

1852   "Reports on the Fabrics, Inventions, Implements and Utensils of the Iroquois." *Annual Report of the University of the State of New York,* no. 5: 67–117.
1871   *Systems of Consanguinity and Affinity of the Human Family.* Washington: *Smithsonian Contributions to Knowledge,* vol. 17.
1904   *League of the Ho-dé-no-sau-nee, or Iroquois.* Ed. H. M. Lloyd. New York: Dodd, Mead and Company (originally published 1851).

MORISON, SAMUEL E.

1971   *The European Discovery of America: the Northern Voyages.* New York: Oxford University Press.
1972   *Samuel de Champlain: Father of New France.* Boston: Little, Brown and Company.

MORISSONNEAU, C.

1970   "Développement et population de la réserve indienne du Village-Huron, Loretteville." *Cahiers de géographie de Québec,* no. 33:339–57.

MÖRNER, M.

1953   *The Political and Economic Activities of the Jesuits in the La Plata Region—The Hapsburg Era.* Stockholm: Library and Institute of Ibero-American Studies.

MORTON, W. L.

1963   *The Kingdom of Canada.* Toronto: McClelland and Stewart.
1972   "Canada and the Canadian Indians: What Went Wrong?" *Quarterly of Canadian Studies for the Secondary School* 2: 3–12.

MURDOCK, G. P.

1949   *Social Structure.* New York: The Macmillan Company.
1959   "Evolution in Social Organization." *Evolution and Anthropology: A Centennial Appraisal.* Ed. B. Meggers. Washington: The Anthropological Society of Washington, pp. 126–43.

MURRAY, J. E.
    1938   "The Early Fur Trade in New France and New Netherland." *CHR* 19: 365–77.

MURRAY, L. W., ed.
    1931   *Selected Manuscripts of General John S. Clark, Relating to the Aboriginal History of the Susquehanna.* Athens, Pennsylvania: Society for Pennsylvania Archaeology.

NAROLL, RAOUL
    1969   "The Causes of the Fourth Iroquois War." *Ethnohistory* 16: 51–81.

NEATBY, L. H.
    1966   "Henry Hudson." *DCB* 1: 374–79.

NEEDLER, G. H.
    1949   "Champlain's Route with the Huron War Party in 1615." *Ont. Hist.* 41: 201–6.

NEWELL, WILLIAM B.
    1965   *Crime and Justice Among the Iroquois Nations.* Montreal: Caughnawaga Historical Society.

NOBLE, WILLIAM C.
    1968   *Iroquois Archaeology and the Development of Iroquois Social Organization (1000–1650 A.D.).* Ph.D. Dissertation. University of Calgary.
    1969   "Some Social Implications of the Iroquois 'In Situ' Theory." *Ont. Arch.* 13: 16–28. [This work is a summary of Noble 1968.]
    1971   "The Sopher Celt: An Indicator of Early Protohistoric Trade in Huronia." *Ont. Arch.* 16: 42–47.

NOBLE, WILLIAM C. and IAN T. KENYON
    1972   "Porteous (AgHb-1): A Probable Early Glen Meyer Village in Brant County, Ontario." *Ont. Arch.* 19: 11–38.

NUTE, G. L.
    1966   "Médard Chouart des Groseilliers." *DCB* 1: 223–28.

O'CALLAGHAN, E. B. and B. FERNOW, eds.
    1856–87   *Documents Relative to the Colonial History of the State of New York.* 15 vols. Albany: Weed, Parsons and Company.

OTTERBEIN, K. F.
    1964   "Why the Iroquois Won: An Analysis of Iroquois Military Tactics." *Ethnohistory* 11: 56–63.

PARKER, A. C.
    1916   "The Origin of the Iroquois as Suggested by Their Archaeology." *AA* 18: 479–507.

PARKMAN, FRANCIS
    1867   *The Jesuits in North America in the Seventeenth Century.* Boston: Little, Brown and Company (reprinted 1927).

PATTERSON, E. P.

  1972   *The Canadian Indian: A History Since 1500.* Don Mills: Collier-
         Macmillan.

PEARCE, R. H.

  1965   *The Savages of America.* Baltimore: Johns Hopkins University Press.

PENDERGAST, JAMES F.

  1964   "The Payne Site." *NMC, Bulletin* 193: 1–27.
  1965   "Other Ideas on 'The Ontario Iroquois Controversy'." *Ont. Arch.* 8:
         39–44.

PENDERGAST, J. F. and B. G. TRIGGER

  1972   *Cartier's Hochelaga and the Dawson Site.* Montreal: McGill-Queen's
         University Press.

PERROT, NICOLAS

  1864   *Mémoire sur les moeurs, coustumes et relligion des sauvages de
         l'Amérique septentrionale.* Ed. J. Tailhan. Leipzig and Paris: A. Franck.
  1911   "Memoir on the Manners, Customs, and Religion of the Savages of
         North America." *The Indian Tribes of the Upper Mississippi Valley
         and Region of the Great Lakes.* Ed. E. H. Blair. Cleveland: A. H. Clark
         Company. Vol. 1: 23–272.

POPHAM, ROBERT E.

  1950   "Late Huron Occupations of Ontario: An Archaeological Survey of
         Innisfil Township." *Ont. Hist.* 42: 81–90.

POTIER, P.

  1920a "Elementa grammaticae huronicae, 1745." Facsimile of ms. in St.
         Mary's College, Montreal. *Fifteenth Report of the Bureau of Archives for
         the Province of Ontario.* Toronto: Clarkson W. James, pp. 1–157.
  1920b "Radices Huronicae." Facsimile of ms. in St. Mary's College, Montreal.
         Fifteenth Report of the Bureau of Archives for the Province of Ontario.
         Toronto: Clarkson W. James, pp. 159–455.

POULIOT, LÉON

  1940   *Etude sur les Relations des Jésuites de la Nouvelle France (1632–1672).*
         Paris and Montreal: Studia Collegii Maximi Immaculatae Conceptionis,
         V.
  1958   *Le premier retraitant du Canada: Joseph Chihouatenhoua.* Montreal:
         Editions Bellarmin.
  1966   "Jérôme Lalemant." *DCB* 1: 413–15.

PRATT, PETER P.

  1964   "The Question of the Location of the Champlain-Iroquois Battle of
         1615: A Study in Historic Site Archaeology." Mimeographed.

QUAIN, BUELL

  1937   "The Iroquois." *Cooperation and Competition among Primitive Peoples.*
         Ed. Margaret Mead. New York: McGraw-Hill, Inc., pp. 240–81.

QUIMBY, GEORGE I.

1960 *Indian Life in the Upper Great Lakes, 11,000 B.C. to A.D. 1800.* Chicago: University of Chicago Press.

1966 *Indian Culture and European Trade Goods.* Madison: University of Wisconsin Press.

RAGUENEAU, PAUL

1925 "Mémoires touchant la mort et les vertus des Pères Jésuites." *Rapport de l'Archiviste de la Province de Québec pour 1924–25.* Quebec: The King's Printer, pp. 1–93.

RANDS, R. L. and C. L. RILEY

1958 "Diffusion and Discontinuous Distribution." *AA* 60: 274–97.

REDFIELD, ROBERT

1956 *Peasant Society and Culture: An Anthropological Approach to Civilization.* Chicago: University of Chicago Press.

RICH, E. E.

1966 *Montreal and the Fur Trade.* Montreal: McGill University Press.

RICHARDS, CARA

1967 "Huron and Iroquois Residence Patterns 1600–1650." *Iroquois Culture, History, and Prehistory.* Ed. E. Tooker. Albany: The University of the State of New York, pp. 51–56.

RIDLEY, FRANK

1947 "A Search for Ossossané and Its Environs." *Ont. Hist.* 39: 7–14.

1952a "The Huron and Lalonde Occupations of Ontario." *Am. Ant.* 17: 197–210.

1952b "The Fallis Site, Ontario." *Am. Ant.* 18: 7–14.

1954 "The Frank Bay Site, Lake Nipissing, Ontario." *Am. Ant.* 20: 40–50.

1958 "Did the Huron Really Migrate North from the Toronto Area?" *Penn. Arch.* 28 (3–4): 143–44.

1961 *Archaeology of the Neutral Indians.* Etobicoke: Etobicoke Historical Society.

1963 "The Ontario Iroquoian Controversy." *Ont. Hist.* 55: 49–59.

1973 "The Wenro in Huronia." *Anthropological Journal of Canada* 11 (1): 10–19.

RITCHIE, WILLIAM A.

1961 "Iroquois Archeology and Settlement Patterns." *BAE, Bulletin* 180: 25–38.

1965 *The Archaeology of New York State.* New York: The Natural History Press.

RITCHIE, WILLIAM A. and ROBERT E. FUNK

1973 *Aboriginal Settlement Patterns in the Northeast.* Albany: *New York State Museum and Science Service, Memoir* 20.

ROBERTSON, WILLIAM

1812 *The History of America.* 2 vols. Philadelphia: J. Bioren and T. L. Plowman (first American, from the 10th London edition).

ROBINSON, PERCY J.

1942   "The Origin of the Name Hochelaga." *CHR* 23: 295–96.

1948   "The Huron Equivalents of Cartier's Second Vocabulary." *TRSC*, 3rd Series, 42, ii: 127–46.

ROCHEMONTEIX, CAMILLE DE

1895–96   *Les Jésuites et la Nouvelle-France au XVIIe siècle.* 3 vols. Paris: Letouzey et Ané.

ROUSSEAU, JACQUES

1954–55   "L'annedda et l'arbre de vie." *RHAF* 8: 171–212.

RUSSELL, W. A.

1965   "A Mill at Sainte Marie I." *Ont. Arch.*, Series B, 3: 11–17.

SAGARD, GABRIEL

1866   *Histoire du Canada et voyages que les Frères mineurs recollects y ont faicts pour la conversion des infidèles depuis l'an 1615 . . . avec un dictionnaire de la langue huro̧nne.* 4 vols. with consecutive pagination. Paris: Edwin Tross.

SALISBURY, RICHARD F.

1962   *From Stone to Steel.* Victoria: Melbourne University Press.

SARTRE, JEAN-PAUL

1963   *Search for a Method.* New York: Alfred A. Knopf.

SAUER, C. O.

1971   *Sixteenth Century North America.* Berkeley and Los Angeles: University of California Press.

SAUNDERS, A.

1963   *Algonquin Story.* Toronto: Ontario Department of Lands and Forests.

SAUNDERS, R. M.

1935   "The First Introduction of European Plants and Animals into Canada." *CHR* 16: 388–406.

SAVAGE, HOWARD G.

1971a   "Faunal Analysis of the Robitaille Site (BeHa-3)—Interim Report." *Palaeoecology and Ontario Prehistory. DAUTRR*, no. 2: 166–72.

1971b   "Faunal Analysis of the Maurice Site (BeHa-2)." *Palaeoecology and Ontario Prehistory. DAUTRR*, no. 2: 173–78.

SCHNEIDER, DAVID M. and K. GOUGH

1961   *Matrilineal Kinship.* Berkeley and Los Angeles: University of California Press.

SERVICE, E. R.

1962   *Primitive Social Organization: An Evolutionary Perspective.* New York: Random House.

SHEA, J. G.

1881   *The First Establishment of the Faith in New France.* 2 vols. New York: J. G. Shea.

SIMARD, ROBERT

    1970   *Le site de Métabetchouan, Lac Saint-Jean ; rapport préliminaire.*
            Chicoutimi : Société d'archéologie du Saguenay.

SIMMONS, L.

    1942   *Sun Chief.* New Haven : Yale University Press.

SMITH, ALLAN

    1970   "Metaphor and Nationality in North America." *CHR* 51 : 247–75.

SMITH, P. E. L.

    1972   "Land-use, Settlement Patterns and Subsistence Agriculture : A
            Demographic Perspective." *Man, Settlement and Urbanism.* Ed. P. J.
            Ucko, R. Tringham, and G. W. Dimbleby. London : Duckworth, pp.
            409–25.

SMITH, WALLIS M.

    1970   "A Re-appraisal of the Huron Kinship System." *Anthropologica* 12 :
            191–206.
    1973   "The Fur Trade and the Frontier : A Study of an Inter-cultural
            Alliance." *Anthropologica* 15 : 21–35.

SNYDERMAN, GEORGE S.

    1948   "Behind the Tree of Peace : A Sociological Analysis of Iroquois
            Warfare." *Penn. Arch.* 18 (3–4) : 1–93.
    1951   "Concepts of Land Ownership among the Iroquois and Their
            Neighbors." *BAE, Bulletin* 149 : 15–34.

SOROKO, O. S.

    1966   "A Soviet Critique of *The Canadian Historical Review.*" *CHR* 47 :
            50–58.

SPALDING, H. S.

    1929   "The Ethnologic Value of the *Jesuit Relations.*" *American Journal of
            Sociology* 34 : 882–89.

SPENCER, R. F., J. D. JENNINGS, et al.

    1965   *The Native Americans.* New York : Harper and Row.

SPICER, E. H.

    1961   ed. *Perspectives in American Indian Cultural Change.* Chicago :
            University of Chicago Press.
    1962   *Cycles of Conquest.* Tucson : University of Arizona Press.
    1969   *A Short History of the Indians of the United States.* New York : Van
            Nostrand.

STANLEY, GEORGE F. C.

    1949   "The Policy of 'Francisation' as Applied to the Indians during the
            Ancien Régime." *RHAF* 3 : 333–48.
    1952   "The Indian Background of Canadian History." *Canadian Historical
            Association, Annual Report, 1952,* pp. 14–21.

STEARN, E. W. and A. E.

    1945   *The Effect of Smallpox on the Destiny of the Amerindian.* Boston : Bruce
            Humphries.

STITES, S. H.
>1905   *Economics of the Iroquois.* Lancaster: New Era Printing Company.

STOTHERS, D. M.
>1970   "The Princess Point Complex and Its Relationship to the Owasco and Ontario Iroquois Traditions." Ontario Archaeological Society, *Archaeological Notes*, March, pp. 4–6.
>1974   "The Glass Site AgHb-5, Oxbow Tract, Brantford Township, Brant County, Ontario." *Ont. Arch.* 21: 37–45.

STRUEVER, STUART
>1968   "Woodland Subsistence-Settlement Systems in the Lower Illinois Valley." *New Perspectives in Archeology.* Ed. S. R. and L. R. Binford. Chicago: Aldine Publishing Company, pp. 285–312.

STRUEVER, STUART and K. D. VICKERY
>1973   "The Beginnings of Cultivation in the Midwest-Riverine Area of the United States." *AA* 75: 1197–1220.

STUIVER, M. and H. SUESS
>1966   "On the Relationship between Radiocarbon Dates and True Sample Ages." *Radiocarbon* 8: 534–40.

STURTEVANT, WILLIAM C.
>1966   "Anthropology, History, and Ethnohistory." *Ethnohistory* 13: 1–51.

SULTE, BENJAMIN
>1907   "Etienne Brûlé." *TRSC*, 3rd Series, 1, i: 97–126.

TALBOT, FRANCIS X.
>1956   *Saint Among the Hurons: the Life of Jean de Brébeuf.* Garden City: Image Books (originally published by Harper and Brothers, 1949).

THEVET, ANDRÉ
>1878   *Les singularitez de la France antarctique.* Ed. P. Gaffarel. Paris: Maisonneuve et Cie (originally published 1578).

THOMAS, H. M.
>1936   "A New Relic of the Jesuit Mission of 1640–41 in Western Ontario." *TRSC*, 3rd Series, 30, ii: 185–92.

THOMAS AQUINAS
>1852–73   *Opera Omnia.* 25 vols. Parma: Tipis P. Fiaccadori.

THWAITES, REUBEN G.
>1896–1901   *The Jesuit Relations and Allied Documents.* 73 vols. Cleveland: The Burrows Brothers Company.

TOOKER, ELISABETH
>1960   "Three Aspects of Northern Iroquoian Culture Change." *Penn. Arch.* 30 (2): 65–71.
>1963   "The Iroquois Defeat of the Huron: A Review of Causes." *Penn. Arch.* 33 (1–2): 115–23.
>1964   *An Ethnography of the Huron Indians, 1615–1649.* Washington: *BAE, Bulletin,* 190.

1970a   *The Iroquois Ceremonial of Midwinter*. Syracuse: Syracuse University Press.

1970b   "Northern Iroquoian Sociopolitical Organization." *AA* 72: 90–97.

TOWNSEND, W. H.

1969   "Stone and Steel Tool Use in a New Guinea Society." *Ethnology* 8: 199–205.

TRELEASE, ALLEN W.

1960   *Indian Affairs in Colonial New York: The Seventeenth Century*. Ithaca: Cornell University Press.

TRIGGER, BRUCE G.

1960   "The Destruction of Huronia: A Study in Economic and Cultural Change, 1609–1650." *Transactions of the Royal Canadian Institute*, 33, no. 68, pt. 1: 14–45.

1962a   "The Historic Location of the Hurons." *Ont. Hist.* 54: 137–48.

1962b   "Trade and Tribal Warfare on the St. Lawrence in the Sixteenth Century." *Ethnohistory* 9: 240–56.

1963a   "Order and Freedom in Huron Society." *Anthropologica* 5: 151–69.

1963b   "Settlement as an Aspect of Iroquoian Adaptation at the Time of Contact." *AA* 65: 86–101.

1965   "The Jesuits and the Fur Trade." *Ethnohistory* 12: 30–53.

1966a   "Amantacha." *DCB* 1: 58–59.

1966b   "Chihwatenha." *DCB* 1: 211–12.

1967   "Settlement Archaeology—Its Goals and Promise." *Am. Ant.* 32: 149–60.

1968a   "Archaeological and Other Evidence: A Fresh Look at the 'Laurentian Iroquois'." *Am. Ant.* 33: 429–40.

1968b   "The French Presence in Huronia: The Structure of Franco-Huron Relations in the First Half of the Seventeenth Century." *CHR* 49: 107–41.

1969a   *The Huron: Farmers of the North*. New York: Holt, Rinehart and Winston.

1969b   "Criteria for Identifying the Locations of Historic Indian Sites: A Case Study from Montreal." *Ethnohistory* 16: 303–16.

1970   "The Strategy of Iroquoian Prehistory." *Ont. Arch.* 14: 3–48.

1971a   "Champlain Judged by His Indian Policy: A Different View of Early Canadian History." *Anthropologica* 13: 85–114.

1971b   "Review of Bailey (1969) and Wallace (1970)." *CHR* 52: 183–87.

1971c   "The Mohawk-Mahican War (1624–28): The Establishment of a Pattern." *CHR* 52: 276–86.

TRUDEL, MARCEL

1963   *Histoire de la Nouvelle-France, Les Vaines Tentatives, 1524–1603*. Montreal: Fides.

1966a   *Histoire de la Nouvelle-France, Le Comptoir, 1604–1627*. Montreal: Fides.

1966b   "Guillaume de Caën." *DCB* 1: 159–62.

1966c   "Samuel de Champlain." *DCB* 1: 186–99.

1973   *The Beginnings of New France, 1524–1663.* Toronto: McClelland and Stewart Limited.

TUCK, JAMES A.

1971   *Onondaga Iroquois Prehistory: A Study in Settlement Archaeology.* Syracuse: Syracuse University Press.

TYYSKA, A. E.

1968   "Settlement Patterns at Cahiague." Report submitted to the Archaeological and Historic Sites Board of the Province of Ontario.

1969   "Archaeology of the Penetang Peninsula." *Palaeoecology and Ontario Prehistory. DAUTRR*, no. 1: 61–88.

TYYSKA, A. E. and W. M. HURLEY

1969   "Maurice Village and the Huron Bear." Paper presented at the second annual meeting of the Canadian Archaeological Association, Toronto.

VACHON, ANDRÉ

1966   "Thomas Godefroy de Normanville." *DCB* 1: 341.

1970   "Colliers et ceintures de porcelaine chez les Indiens de la Nouvelle-France." *CdD* 35: 251–78.

1971   "Colliers et ceintures de porcelaine dans la diplomatie indienne." *CdD* 36: 179–92.

VAN DER DONCK, A.

1841   "Description of the New Netherlands." *Collections of the New-York Historical Society*, 2nd series 1: 125–242.

VAN LAER, A. J. F., ed.

1908   *Van Rensselaer Bowier Manuscripts.* Albany: University of the State of New York.

1924   *Documents Relating to New Netherland, 1624–1626, in the Henry E. Huntington Library.* San Marino: Huntington Library.

VIGNERAS, L. A.

1953   "El viaje de Samuel Champlain a las Indias Occidentales." *Anuario de Estudios Americanos* 10: 457–500.

1957–58   "Le Voyage de Samuel Champlain aux Indes occidentales." *RHAF* 11: 163–200.

WALKER, J. W.

1971   "The Indian in Canadian Historical Writing." *The Canadian Historical Association, Historical Papers 1971*: 21–51.

WALLACE, A. F. C.

1958   "Dreams and the Wishes of the Soul: A Type of Psychoanalytic Theory Among the Seventeenth Century Iroquois." *AA* 60: 234–48.

1970   *The Death and Rebirth of the Seneca.* New York: Alfred A. Knopf.

WALLACE, P. A. W.

1966   "Dekanahwideh." *DCB* 1: 253–55.

WARWICK, J.

1972   "Humanisme chrétien et bons sauvages (Gabriel Sagard, 1623–1636)." *XVIIe Siècle* 97: 25–49.

WASHBURN, W. E., ed.

    1964   *The Indian and the White Man*. Garden City: Doubleday.

WHALLON, ROBERT, JR.

    1968   "Investigations of Late Prehistoric Social Organization in New York State." *New Perspectives in Archeology*. Ed. S. R. and L. R. Binford. Chicago: Aldine Publishing Company, pp. 223–44.

WHITE, MARIAN E.

    1961   *Iroquois Culture History in the Niagara Frontier Area of New York State. UMAP*, 16.

    1963   "Settlement Pattern Change and the Development of Horticulture in the New York-Ontario Area." *Penn. Arch.* 33 (1–2): 1–12.

    1971a "Ethnic Identification and Iroquois Groups in Western New York and Ontario." *Ethnohistory* 18: 19–38.

    1971b "Review of *The Bennett Site*." *Am. Ant.* 36: 222–23.

    1972   "On Delineating the Neutral Iroquois of the Eastern Niagara Peninsula of Ontario." *Ont. Arch.* 17: 62–74.

WILLEY, G. R.

    1966   *An Introduction to American Archaeology*. Vol. 1, *North and Middle America*. Englewood Cliffs: Prentice-Hall.

WILLEY, G. R. and P. PHILLIPS

    1958   *Method and Theory in American Archaeology*. Chicago: University of Chicago Press.

WILSON, DANIEL

    1862   *Prehistoric Man*. 2 vols. Cambridge: Macmillan and Company.

    1884   "The Huron-Iroquois of Canada, A Typical Race of American Aborigines." *TRSC*, 1st series, 2, ii: 55–106.

WILSON, H. C.

    1956   "A New Interpretation of the Wild Rice District of Wisconsin." *AA* 58: 1059–64.

WINTEMBERG, WILLIAM J.

    1926   "Foreign Aboriginal Artifacts from post-European Iroquoian Sites in Ontario." *TRSC*, 3rd series, 20, ii: 37–61.

    1931   "Distinguishing Characteristics of Algonkian and Iroquoian Cultures." *NMC, Bulletin* 67: 65–125.

    1936   "The Probable Location of Cartier's Stadacona." *TRSC*, 3rd series, 30, ii: 19–21.

    1942   "The Geographical Distribution of Aboriginal Pottery in Canada." *Am. Ant.* 8: 129–41.

    1946   "The Sidey-Mackay Village Site." *Am. Ant.* 11: 154–82.

WINTERS, HOWARD D.

    1968   "Value Systems and Trade Cycles of the Late Archaic in the Midwest." *New Perspectives in Archeology*. Ed. S. R. and L. R. Binford. Chicago: Aldine Publishing Company, pp. 175–221.

WITTHOFT, JOHN

    1951   "Iroquois Archaeology at the Mid-Century." *PAPS* 95: 311–21.

1959   "Ancestry of the Susquehannocks." *Susquehannock Miscellany*. Ed. J. Witthoft and W. F. Kinsey, III. Harrisburg: The Pennsylvania Historical and Museum Commission, pp. 19–60.

WRAY, C. F. and H. L. SCHOFF
  1953   "A Preliminary Report on the Seneca Sequence in Western New York, 1550–1687." *Penn Arch.* 23 (2): 53–63.

WRIGHT, JAMES V.
  1962   "A Distributional Study of Some Archaic Traits in Southern Ontario." *NMC, Bulletin* 180: 124–42.
  1965   "A Regional Examination of Ojibwa Culture History." *Anthropologica* 7: 189–227.
  1966   *The Ontario Iroquois Tradition. NMC, Bulletin* 210.
  1967   *The Laurel Tradition and the Middle Woodland Period. NMC, Bulletin* 217.
  1968   "Prehistory of Hudson Bay: the Boreal Forest." *Science, History and Hudson Bay*. Ed. C. S. Beals and D. A. Shenstone. Ottawa: The Queen's Printer, vol. 1, pp. 55–68.
  1969   "The Michipicoten Site." *NMC, Bulletin* 224: 1–85.
  1972   *Ontario Prehistory: An Eleven-thousand-year Archaeological Outline.* Ottawa: National Museum of Man.

WRIGHT, JAMES V. and J. E. ANDERSON
  1963   *The Donaldson Site. NMC, Bulletin* 184.
  1969   *The Bennett Site. NMC, Bulletin* 229.

WRONG, G. M., ed.
  1939   *The Long Journey to the Country of the Hurons.* Toronto: The Champlain Society.

WROTH, L.
  1954   "An Unknown Champlain Map of 1616." *Imago Mundi* 11: 85–94.

YARNELL, RICHARD A.
  1964   *Aboriginal Relationships Between Culture and Plant Life in the Upper Great Lakes Region. UMAP,* 23.

Index

NOTE Successive Indians bearing the same name by
      inheritance are distinguished by **1, 2, 3**

A

Aataentsic, 77–78, 87, 850
Abduction of Indians by Europeans,
  182–83, 186, 198–200, 458. *See also*
  Domagaya, Donnacona, Taignoagny
Abenaki, 226, 588, 604, 653
Achelacy, 190, 193, 200, 204–5, 447 *n.* 11
Achiendassé (Huron name for Jesuit
  superior), 366
Acorns. *See* Famine foods
Adirondack Mountains as hunting area,
  345, 488, 618
Adoption: of prisoners by Huron, 72, 816;
  of French by Huron, 298; of prisoners by
  Iroquois, 615, 627, 638, 640, 733, 755,
  757, 764, 766, 783–84, 816, 826–31,
  836–40. *See also* Prisoners
Aenons, **1**, 474–76, 491, 493, 509, 517–21,
  530, 540, 544–45, 549–50, 596; **2**, 821
Agojuda: possible identity, 196–97
Agona, 195–96, 198–99, 203–5
Agriculture. *See* Horticulture
Agwachimagan, 720
Ahatsistari, 638, 659, 704–5
Ailleboust de Coulange, Louis d', 760, 775,
  808, 815
Akhrakvaeronon. *See* Scahentarronon
Alcoholic beverages: Huron view of, 433;
  use by Indians, 457, 461–62, 478;
  French policy concerning sale of, 462
Alfonse, Jean, 207
Algonkians: term defined, I, xxiii;
  Jesuit missions to, 588, 594, 608–9,
  770–71, 778–79
Algonkin: traditional culture: 110, 170,
  197, 230–31, 279–81; sell furs to
Huron, 337; oppose Huron trade with
French, 342, 369, 462, 479, 484, 492,
496–97, 553; bad relations with
Montagnais, 464, 498; affected by
epidemics, 500–501; disrupted by
Iroquois attacks, 609–10, 626, 637–38;
access to firearms, 632; and truce of
1645, 648–50, 653–54. *See also*
Alliances, Arendarhonon, Converts,
Huron history, Kichesipirini,
Monopolies, Nipissing, Petite Nation,
Tolls, Trade routes, Truce, Warfare;
and for individual Algonkin,
Agwachimagan, Iroquet, Nibachis,
Oumasasikweie, Partridge, Pieskaret,
Tawiscaron, Tessouat
Algonquin Park, 170
Alliances: between Huron and
  Susquehannock, 97, 305–6, 313–14,
  624, 730, 732–33; Donnacona's search
  for alliance with French, 183, 185–90;
  between Achelacy and Cartier, 190,
  193; between French and Montagnais,
  212, 252, 256–57; between French,
  Montagnais, and latter's allies, 228–33,
  255, 482, 552–53; between Montagnais
  and Algonkin, 230–31, 257, 498, 552;
  between French and Algonkin, 236,
  257, 262, 270, 273, 523–24; between
  Algonkin and Huron, 244; between
  French and Huron, 246–48, 264,
  267–68, 273, 293, 296–97, 301, 305,
  320–21, 323–24, 327–29, 331, 337,
  363–65, 369, 382–84, 391–92, 397, 406,
  473, 476, 480–85, 492, 495–96, 513, 518,
  520–22, 524, 526, 541, 544–46, 561,
  567, 569, 594, 596, 598, 633, 644, 657,

Alliances *(continued)*
    694, 700, 701, 715, 724, 731, 814;
    attempt to terminate French–Huron
    alliance, 744–50, 755–56; between
    individual French and Huron, 298,
    364–65, 368–69, 525, 544, 547, 549,
    565, 567, 616; between French and
    Tionnontaté, 318; between Neutral and
    Ottawa, 319; between French and
    Neutral, 399–401, 689, 694, 696, 790;
    between Dutch and Mahican, 463–64;
    Mahican–Sokoki and Mohawk, 615,
    620, 634, 647, 653; between Dutch and
    Mohawk, 631, 647; between Neutral
    and Susquehannock, 790. *See also*
    Confederacy, Government, Tribe
Allumette Island I site, 108
Amantacha, 397–98, 405, 407,
    452 *n.* 19, 456–57, 460–62, 473, 476,
    478–80, 489, 504, 515, 522–23, 547–48;
    relative of, 543
Amiskou, 488
Anadabijou, 230–31, 233–34, 449 *n.* 7;
    his son, 270
Andacwander, 83, 442 *n.* 49; Jesuit
    opposition to, 530, 660, 762
Andaste. *See* Susquehannock
Andastoé, 732, 733
Andatouha, 611
Andehoua, 525, 555–57, 564, 612, 614,
    659, 706–7, 797
Andeouarahen. *See* Andehoua
Andiataé, 527, 531, 540
Andiora, 705. *See also* Tsondakwa
Anenkhiondic, 57, 440 *n.* 35, 481–82,
    492–93, 519–20, 540, 542–43, 550,
    561
Angioraste, 395, 431
Angont, 66, 589
Angoutenc, 513, 541–42
Annaotaha, 763, 787, 816
Annenraes, 730–33, 794
Anonatea, 531
Anthropology: traditional aims, 11;
    weakness of historical approach, 11–12
Antouhonoron. *See* Entouhonoron
Aondironnon, 624, 735, 853 *n.* 10

Aonetta, 551, 702
Aotonatendia, 856 *n.* 9
Aouandoïe, 475, 494, 539, 852 *n.* 8
Archaeology: value of evidence, 7, 11, 13,
    20, 335, 669–81; prehistoric, 105–76;
    on historic Iroquoian sites, 236–43,
    309–11, 318, 357, 360–61, 421, 423,
    451 *n.* 1, 828, 852 *n.* 10, 856 *n.* 9
Archaic cultures, 106–10. *See also*
    Laurentian Archaic, Maritime Archaic,
    Shield Archaic
Arendarhonon: name and location, 30,
    437 *n.* 5; join confederacy, 58, 244;
    relations with Algonkin, 63, 227,
    243–44, 248, 268, 292, 320–24, 354;
    houses, 151; origins, 156; relations with
    St. Lawrence Iroquoians, 227; relations
    with French, 246–47, 262, 288–90, 324,
    327, 490–91, 592–94, 596; dispersal,
    660, 730, 736–37, 784; seek peace with
    Iroquois, 731; many join Onondaga,
    811–13, 827–28
Arendiwane. See Shamans
Arenté, 474, 531, 539, 563, 571, 614, 688
Aretsan. See Shamans
Arhetsi, 856 *n.* 6
Armour, Iroquoian, 70, 196–97, 252, 254,
    360, 417–18
Arrowheads. *See* Stone tools
Art, European: Huron reaction to, 430,
    480, 537, 561, 592–93; Jesuit use of,
    549
Asqua, 49, 367
Assimilation. *See* Francisation,
    Prisoners
Assiskwa, 705–6, 713, 719
Assistaronon, 319, 417, 488, 624–25, 659,
    800. *See also* Central Algonkians,
    Exouaendaen
Astrolabe, 278–79, 449 *n.* 8
Ataronchronon: name and location, 30,
    437 *n.* 6, 587; sell land to Jesuits, 587;
    missions to, 590
Ateiachias, 558, 567
Athataion (death feast), 52, 72; Brébeuf's,
    544; Christianized, 739
Atirenda, 80–81

Atironta: name and office, 57, 449 *n.* 2,
594, 616–17; **1** (Darontal), 246–47,
288–89, 305, 317, 321, 324, 326–28,
593–94, 707; **2** (Aëotahon), 344, 616,
653, 660, 707, 716–17, 734–35, 785,
801; his family, 557, 852 *ch.* 9 *n.* 5
Atondo, 613–14, 706–7
Atsina, 806, 812
Attignawantan: name and location, 30,
437 *n.* 4; distinctive characteristics, 32;
internal dissension, 57, 290–92,
475–76, 518–20, 539; join Huron
confederacy, 58; dominate Huron
confederacy, 58–59, 288–90, 474;
relations with Nipissing, 63, 170, 292,
354; origins, 156; trade with French,
290–92, 344, 374–75, 491; relations
with Kichesipirini, 497–98; oppose
peace with Iroquois, 731, 734; some
join Mohawk, 811–12
Attigneenongnahac: name and location,
30, 437 *n.* 5; join Huron confederacy,
58; origins, 156–57; trade with French,
490–91; dispersal, 751–54; remain at
Quebec, 812
Attikamegue, 611, 735, 792
Aubert de La Chesnaye, Charles, 215
Auhaitsique, 366, 373, 384, 396
Authority, Huron understanding of, 312,
378–79, 393–94, 429
Auoindaon, 57, 290, 298, 391, 433;
relationship to Aenons, 57, 475;
relationship to Aouandoïé, 475
Avunculocal residence, 55, 100–12, 419
Awataerohi, 80, 509, 533, 600, 717;
Jesuit opposition to, 530
Axes, greater efficiency of iron, 412. *See
also* Stone tools

B

Bacqueville de La Potherie, Claude-
Charles, 354, 356, 645
Bailey, Alfred G., 4, 209, 216
Baouichtigouian. *See* Ojibwa
Baptism: significance for Indians, 193,
391, 505–7, 516–17, 531–32, 546–47,

550, 564, 567, 593, 699–702, 704,
707–8, 720, 737, 752; of St. Lawrence
Iroquoians in France, 200–201;
Recollet policy concerning, 379, 389,
394–95, 405, 505; of Amantacha, 398;
Jesuit policy concerning, 406, 505, 531,
569, 613, 699–701, 737–38; of Huron,
Neutral, and Tionnontaté by Jesuits,
406, 504–7, 516–17, 530–32, 540,
547–51, 558, 562–65, 568, 590–91,
593, 595, 599, 613–15, 633, 695, 698,
703–9, 716, 722, 737, 739, 752, 755,
763, 778, 780, 800–801, 832, 834;
significance for Jesuits, 503–4;
numbers, 505, 516, 532, 540, 562–65,
589, 594, 701–2, 739, 781, 854 *nn.* 2, 3;
Huron resistance to, 532; surreptitious,
532, 590; of Iroquois prisoners, 563–64,
568, 570–72, 713–14, 756, 809; by
other Indians, 700; of Iroquois, 835.
See also Converts, Susquehannock
Barbeau, Marius, 825
Barentsen, Pieter, 463
Baron, Simon, 489, 491–92, 524, 527,
529, 576
Basques, 209–10, 229, 235, 256
Batiscan, 256, 265, 457
Battles. *See* Warfare
Beads, glass, 181, 190, 193, 199, 220,
242–43, 255, 360, 394, 410–11, 427;
used as prizes by Jesuits, 507; value of
in 1630s, 529
Beads, Indian: of shell, 39, 44, 62–63, 70,
103, 111, 113, 139, 147, 169, 198, 203,
244, 353, 355, 374, 410, 416, 427,
441 *n.* 40, 545, 547, 559, 634, 671,
753; of stone, 44, 360, 410; of copper,
110, 113, 139, 169, 242; of bone, 410;
used in diplomacy, 290, 320–21, 540,
542, 619, 654, 748, 792, 853 *n.* 6; and
fur trade, 346, 471. *See also* Wampum
belts
Beans, 34, 100, 118, 120, 126, 148;
nutritional qualities of, 137
Beards, Huron opinion of, 432
Bear sacrifice, 41
Beaugrand-Champagne, A., 207

Beauport, Jesuit estate at, 801, 818
Beaver: primary interest in fur, 209, 336;
    varying quality of fur, 229, 351, 383,
    804; number of pelts supplied to French,
    286, 336–37, 462, 603–5; value of
    pelts, 336, 450 *n.* 12, 451 *n.* 3, 458, 460,
    603, 776, 804; sale of castoreum, 336,
    451 *n.* 2; weight of pelts, 337, 603,
    451 *n.* 5; depletion of, 337, 350–51, 416,
    577, 618–21, 625; number of pelts
    supplied to Dutch, 618; number of pelts
    supplied in general, 620
Beaver grounds, 350, 624–26, 735–36,
    790
Begourat, 233
Bells, for Jesuit missions, 507, 687, 761,
    777
Bennett site, 128–31, 137, 446 *n.* 27
Benson site, 242
Biard, Pierre, 218, 403
Biencourt de Poutrincourt, Jean de, 403
Biggar, H. P.: translation error, 311
Binet, Etienne, 523, 575
Biography as historiographic technique, 4,
    22–23
Bishop, Morris, 274
Black Minquas, 797
Blau, Harold, 533–34, 836
Bleeding of sick, 527, 529, 562
Blood feud, 59–61, 68, 98, 103, 144–45,
    162, 319–20; with trading partners,
    64–65, 261, 265, 317, 322, 490, 549,
    554; Recollet view of, 380; Jesuit view
    of, 512; by means of witchcraft, 536.
    See also Reparation, Warfare
Bogaert, Harmen Meyndertsen van den,
    151, 488, 602, 617–18, 630
Boivin, Charles, 667
Bone carving: tools, 44, 410; florescence
    in historic period, 425–26
Bonin, Jacques, 756
Booty, 103, 198, 221, 254, 258, 416, 640,
    642, 658, 660–61, 664, 725–26, 729,
    736, 752, 764, 766, 777, 779, 790, 797.
    See also Iroquois, as plunderers
Boucher, Pierre, 419, 439 *n.* 24, 592, 622,
    628

Bourbon, Charles de, Comte de Soissons,
    272
Bourbon, Henri de, Prince de Condé, 272,
    286, 403, 450 *n.* 13
Bourdon, Jean, 654, 804
Bouyer, ?, 269
Brasser, T. J., 14
Brébeuf, Jean de: prior to 1629, 333,
    396–97, 399, 401, 404–8, 458;
    Huron name, 336; return to Huron
    country, 479–81, 484, 489–91, 493–94;
    as superior of Huron mission, 496–97,
    501–5, 507–13, 516–20, 522, 526–27,
    528–30, 535, 539–45, 547–48, 561,
    563–64; made a Huron headman, 561;
    under J. Lalemant, 572, 575, 577, 587,
    592, 598, 672; map by, 581; visit to
    Neutral, 688–97, 715; at Quebec,
    1641–44, 613–15, 637, 644, 662,
    697–98, 703; later, 666, 743; death,
    763–64; posthumous references,
    832–33; as source, 141, 396, 420–22,
    426, 473, 500–501. *See also* La Roche
    Daillon
Bréhaut Delisle, Achille de, 545–46, 549,
    556
Bressani, François, 298, 562, 581, 615,
    617, 643, 647, 708, 743, 754, 775–76,
    785, 801
Brose, David S., 112, 115, 140
Brothers (religious), 333, 394, 471–72,
    667, 756. *See also* Brouet, Burel,
    Duplessis, Gaubert, Masson, Noircler,
    Regnault, Scot
Brouet, Ambroise, 667
Bruce Peninsula, 319
Brûlé, Etienne: with Huron, 261–62,
    265–66, 268–69, 287–88, 292, 328,
    331, 338, 340, 342–43, 367–75,
    450 *n.* 22, 488; visit to Susquehannock
    and Iroquois, 305–8; and Jesuits, 398,
    404–6, 452 *n.* 19; and English, 459–60,
    462; murder of, 396, 473–76;
    posthumous concerns with, 479–82,
    484–85, 489, 491, 494, 496–97, 509,
    518–20, 536, 595, 609, 694
Bruyas, Jacques, 826

Buade de Frontenac, Louis de, 471, 818
Burel, Gilbert, 472
Burial: Huron primary interments, 52–54;
 variant forms, 52, 440 *n.* 30, 533;
 Neutral, 96; prehistoric, 109, 111, 113,
 118, 137, 147; Algonkian, 270, 280; of
 Frenchmen, 390–91, 473, 518–20, 746;
 of Christian Huron, 506, 518, 520, 549,
 669, 671, 687, 711, 714, 720, 722, 739,
 782, 800; sanctity of, 721
Buteux, Jacques, 805
Butterfield, C. W., 372

C

Caën, Emery de, 397–98, 405, 456, 459,
 462, 466–67
Caën, Guillaume de, 358, 381, 384, 403–4,
 456, 459, 462, 467
Cahiagué, 248, 300–305, 307–8, 317,
 320–21, 324, 393, 450 *n.* 20
Calendrical rituals among Iroquoians,
 15–16, 20, 103–4
Cannibalism, 74–75, 254, 323, 488, 568,
 764, 799; prehistoric, 144–45, 158, 162;
 Jesuit opposition to, 530; non-ritual,
 781. *See also* Transubstantiation
Cannon at Sainte-Marie, 677–79, 756,
 771
Canoes: Huron, 44, 166; northern
 Algonkian, 44, 166, 821; Neutral, 96,
 401, 790; travelling in, 172, 340;
 carrying capacity, 336–37; Iroquois,
 552; Tionnontaté, 821
Capitanal, 477–78
Carantouan, 306–7
Carhagouha, 298, 300–301, 317, 319, 373,
 384–85
Carleill, C., 209
Carmaron, 300
Cartier, Jacques: first voyage, 1534,
 177–83; second voyage, 1534–35,
 183–201, 447 *n.* 10; third voyage,
 1541–42, 201–6. *See also* Alliance
Castoreum, 336, 451 *n.* 2
Catechism, 408, 507–8, 511, 515, 525,
 561, 708

Catlinite, 44, 439 *n.* 24. *See also* Red slate
Cats, domestic: as gifts to Huron, 424, 431
Cattle taken to Huron country, 685, 756
Cayuga: location, 98; settlements north of
 Lake Ontario, 729; prepared for truce
 with Huron, 734; Jesuit mission to,
 832–33, 835
Celibacy. *See* Sexual abstinence
Cemetery. *See* Burial
Census of Huron, 578
Central Algonkians: dispersal of, 625;
 historic location, 853 *n.* 11
Chabanel, Noël, 512, 600, 644, 740,
 777–78
Chafe, Wallace, 20, 103
Chamberlin site, 121
Chambly Rapids, 249, 254, 258
Champlain, Samuel de: voyage of 1603,
 224, 229, 233–34; in Maritimes, 234;
 founds Quebec, 234–36; 1609 campaign
 against the Iroquois, 247–56; voyage of
 1610, 256–63; voyage of 1611, 264–71;
 failure to visit Canada in 1612, 273;
 explores Ottawa Valley in 1613,
 275–86; visit to Huron country, 231,
 268, 296–305, 307, 315–27, 369; 1615
 expedition against Iroquois, 308–15;
 after 1616, 337–39, 345, 347; plans to
 conquer Iroquois, 207, 465–66, 628; as
 colonizer and vice-regal official, 212,
 271–75, 287, 322, 325, 327–30, 349,
 377, 452 *n.* 13, 456, 459, 473–74, 477,
 489, 628; belief in prehistoric Iroquois
 offensive, 227–28, 251, 308; attitudes
 towards and dealings with Indians, 249,
 251, 254, 271–72, 274–75, 286–87,
 300–302, 304, 309, 312–13, 315–16,
 322–23, 325, 327–30, 363, 366, 380–81,
 457–58, 477–85, 488; character,
 274–75, 329–30; relations with
 missionaries, 377, 381, 384, 403–4,
 408, 477, 480–82, 496, 519;
 posthumous references, 328, 521, 536,
 545; as source, 116, 151, 218, 222, 243,
 246–47, 288, 336, 382, 463, 528, 630
Champlain, Lake, 233, 251–52, 345
Chance culture, 150

Chapels and churches: in the Huron country, 387, 495, 537, 549, 561–62, 577, 587–88, 593, 668–69, 671–72, 687, 703–7, 719–20, 737, 739, 743, 752, 761, 779, 780; among Tionnontaté, 777; for Huron at Quebec, 803; among Iroquois, 833–34

Charioquois (name for Huron), 290

Charles I, King, 456, 461

Charlesbourg-Royal, 203–6

Charlevoix, Pierre: as source, 215; treatment of Sagard, 333

Charms: personal, 39, 63, 78–79; used in witchcraft, 66–67, 535–37, 542–43; Jesuit opposition to, 570, 703, 707, 709–10

Chaste, Aymar de, 229, 234

Chastellain, Pierre, 521, 541, 666

Chastillon, ?, 751

Chaton de La Jannaye, Etienne, 210

Chaudière Falls, 278, 639–40, 642

Chaudron, Guillaume, 372, 374, 390–92, 452 *n*. 14, 473, 518–20

Chaumonot, Pierre-Joseph-Marie, 366, 512, 560, 587–88, 592, 666, 689–98, 715, 761, 767, 770, 809, 834–35

Chauvigny de La Peltrie, Marie-Madeleine de, 632, 802

Chauvin de La Pierre, Pierre, 255

Chauvin de Tonnetuit, Pierre de, 212, 228–30

Chequamegon, Huron settlement at, 820

Cherokee, 105

Cherououny, 464

Chesapeake Bay, 97, 306, 797

Cheveux Relevés. *See* Ottawa (tribe)

Chief. *See* Headmen

Chihwatenha, 550–51, 558, 561–62, 565–67, 588, 591, 594–95, 598–601, 616, 694; his family, 702–3. *See also* Aonetta, Oionhaton, Saoekbata, Teondechoren

Children, exchange of. *See* Trading partners

Chomedey de Maisonneuve, Paul de, 613, 629, 632

Chomina, 457–58

Chouart des Groseilliers, Médard, 668, 821, 824

Chouontouaronon (Seneca), 311

Christian Island. *See* Gahoendoe

Citizenship granted to certain Indians, 366, 456, 547

Clans: Huron, 15, 54, 748–49, 820; Wyandot, 15, 825; Tionnontaté, 94; Iroquois, 98; Iroquoian, 102; development of, 154

Clan segment: defined and explained, 54–57, 60, 88, 99, 155, 268, 340, 440 *n*. 31, 442 *n*. 53, 687, 748; development of, 110, 112–13, 134, 143, 153

Clarke, Peter Dooyentate, 19, 825

Climatic change: A.D. 1600 to present, 31; prehistoric, 106–7, 120, 217–18

Clock, of Jesuits, 495

Cloth, bewitched. *See* Charms

Clothes: Huron, 37–39; skins used for, 41, 132–33, 168, 308; European, worn by Indians, 186, 359–60, 460, 617–18

Cod fisheries, westward spread of, 208

Coercive contact, 845–46

Collecting: food, 36; fibre, 39, 661, 704, 715. *See also* Famine foods

Colombage pierroté, 671, 673–74, 677

Colonization by Europeans: in sixteenth century, 201–7, 210, 212, 220; in seventeenth century, 228–30, 234–35, 265, 270–72, 280, 286–87, 325, 327, 338, 380–81, 403–4, 455–56, 489, 629, 759; projected for Huron country, 268, 325, 379; rights of colonists to trade, 359, 460, 759–60; Jesuit view of, 468, 476

Communauté des Habitants, 759

Compagnie de Caën, 403–4, 455

Compagnie de la Nouvelle France. *See* Compagnie des Cent-Associés

Compagnie des Cent-Associés, 455–56, 467, 471, 476, 613, 759

Compagnie du Canada, 286–87, 343

Company of Adventurers, 456, 461

Comparative approach: problems and objectives, 13–14; specific sources concerning Huron, 14–15; other types of comparison, 15–17

Compensation for wounding or murder. *See* Reparation

Confederacy: origins and growth, 14, 58–59, 162–63, 174–76, 224, 842; government, 58–59; aims, 59–60, 98, 162

Confession, 710

Contarea: mission to, 588, 592–94, 660–62, 688, 707, 736; aversion to Jesuits, 731, 744, 833

Converts: Huron converts to Christianity, 546–51, 555, 558, 565, 570, 590–92, 594, 598, 699–710, 737–38; separated from traditionalists, 518, 669, 672, 710–13; material rewards for, 547, 613, 699–701, 709, 747; Algonkin headmen as, 610; persecuted by Huron traditionalists, 715–21; Christian Huron among Iroquois, 832–36

Copeland site, 151

Copper: native, 63, 108–11, 113, 118–19, 139, 169, 196, 171–72, 200, 257, 375, 441 *n.* 42; trade in sixteenth century, 173, 184, 196–97, 243; mines, 254, 375. *See also* Metalworking

Copper route from Lake Superior to Saguenay River, 171, 197, 213–14, 219, 230, 271, 356–57, 376, 611

Corn (maize): description and identification, 34, 100, 438 *n.* 13; arrival in Ontario, 118–20, 122–26, 148, 444 *n.* 9; advantages over wild rice, 133–34; nutritional qualities, 137; role in northern trade, 166–68, 244; carried to Quebec, 1629, 458–59; grown by Jesuits, 684

Corporal punishment: Huron view of in respect of children, 47, 186, 263–64, 522; Jesuits oppose this view, 762

Coton, Pierre, 396, 403

Couillard, Guillemette, 349

Councils. *See* Government

Couture, Guillaume, 638, 647–49, 654, 668

Creation myths, 19, 27, 77–78; rejected

by Huron converts, 712

Cree, 283

Crosses: erected as landmarks by Europeans, 182, 199, 283; as Christian symbols in the Huron country, 407, 510, 518, 592, 687, 714, 720, 721; venerated at Three Rivers, 755

Cuisine: Huron, 37, 70, 251; Indian opinion of French cooking, 186, 431

Cultural relativism, 469–70

Curing societies, 14, 20, 80–81, 103, 154–55, 529, 533, 703; relations with Jesuits, 564, 570, 716–17, 720. *See also* Awataerohi

Curler, Arent van, 620, 631, 645

D

Dablon, Claude, 809, 835

Daillon. *See* La Roche

Dances, Huron, 85

Daniel, Antoine, 479–80, 489, 491–94, 504, 512, 521, 523–24, 535, 556, 593, 666, 696, 736–37, 752–53, 825

Daran, Adrien, 756

Davost, Ambroise, 479–80, 489, 491–92, 494, 504, 521, 523, 666

Deer. *See* Hunting

Deetz, James, 135

Deities. *See* Spirits

Des Prairies, ?, 258

Desrosiers, Léo-Paul, 1, 4, 260, 497, 735

Devils, Jesuit view of, 503, 511, 573, 738, 762

Dictionaries and Grammars: Huron, 298, 393, 398, 511, 544, 696. *See also* Jesuits, Recollets

Directed contact. *See* Coercive contact

Discipline. *See* Corporal punishment

Disease, Huron theories of, 81

Division of labour: among Huron, 32–45; among Iroquoians, 100

Divorce: traditional Huron view of, 49–50; Jesuit view of, 512, 530, 532, 539, 558, 709; problems for converts, 716–17

Dogs, 41, 82, 415, 431, 671; dog burials, 170, 446 *n.* 27
Dolbeau, Jean, 287
Dollard des Ormeaux, Adam, 5, 816–17
Domagaya, 182–200
Dominique (hired man), 489, 576
Donaldson site, 113
Donck, Adriaen van der, 620
Donnés, 575–76, 667–68, 776, 801, 803. *See also* Boivin, Boucher, Couture, Douart, Gendron, Goupil, Guiet, La Lande, Lambert, Le Coq, Levrier, Molère, Onaatichiae
Donnacona, 182–201, 203, 209. *See also* Alliance
Douart, Jacques, 746, 748, 755
Dreams and dream wishes, 76–77, 79–83, 251–52, 447 *n.* 9, 592–94, 615, 711, 723; Jesuit opposition to, 530, 710, 712, 738, 761
Drought, 36, 165, 389, 406–7, 509–10, 662, 767, 772
Du Creux, François, 419, 559, 578
Du Fay, Polycarpe, 395
Duff, Wilson, 4
Du Gua de Monts, Pierre, 228–29, 234–36, 255–57, 262, 271–74, 343
Du Peron, François, 355, 572, 666
Du Plessis, Armand-Jean, Cardinal de Richelieu, 333, 404, 455–56, 467, 628, 669, 759
Du Plessis-Bochart, Charles, 467, 490–91, 493, 498, 521, 524
Duplessis, Pacifique, 287
Dutch: on Hudson River, 260, 293; captured by Susquehannock, 305, 346; relations with Mohawk, 345–47, 464, 485–89, 497–98, 615, 617–22, 628, 631, 725–26, 792; control wampum, 346; seek trade with northern Algonkians, 346, 463; aid Mahican, 463; assist Jesuits, 615, 647, 772; sell firearms to Iroquois, 630–32; alliance with Mohawk, 631; character of traders, 632, 832, 843. *See also* Mohawk, Susquehannock, Trade with Europeans, Warfare; *and for*

individuals, Barentsen, Bogaert, Hendricksen, Rasiere, Rensselaer, Stuyvesant
Duval, Jean, 234–35, 449 *n.* 11
Du Vernay, ?, 372–73
Dwarfs: symbolism for Huron, 79, 81, 529, 534

E

East Sugar Island site, 111
"Eat-all" feasts, 83
Ecaregniondi, 87
Echon. *See* Brébeuf
Eclipses: solar, 163; lunar, 469, 516, 566
Economic determinism in Iroquoian studies, 7–8
Education. *See* Schools
Eggan, Fred, 102, 136
Ehwae, 318, 594–95, 658–59
Ekarenniondi, 739–40, 776, 778
Ekhiondastsaan, 527, 540, 554, 751, 800
Endahiaconc, 57, 524, 852 *ch.* 8 *n.* 5
English: in New France, 455–62, 466–67, 476–77; in Huron visions, 535–36; trade with Iroquois, 620, 631; sell guns to Iroquois, 631
Entouhonoron, identity of, 227, 311, 320
Epidemics: Indian susceptibility to European diseases, 200, 499; prior to 1634, 194, 208, 218, 237, 270, 499; after 1634, 95, 98, 103, 355, 491, 499–501, 526–28, 544–45, 562, 588–98, 657, 826; viewed as witchcraft, 510, 534–38, 541–44, 589–96; effects, 601–7, 618, 623. *See also* Algonkin, Neutral, Ottawa, Petite Nation, Seneca, Mortality rate
Equilibrium theories: applied to Amerindian societies, 6–7, 841
Erie, 62, 96, 148, 441 *n.* 39, 624, 792–97, 814
Erie stones, 62
Erouachy, 363, 457
Etchemin. *See* Malecite
Etharita, 740, 777–78, 789

Ethnohistory: scope, 12; contributions, 12–13; comparative approach, 13–17; need of good historical method, 17; limitations and potential of written sources, 17–19; auxiliary sources, 19–20; major studies, 20–21; levels of analysis, 21–26. *See also* Archaeology, Historiography, Oral traditions

Exouaendaen, 800–801

Exploration: French desire to explore interior, 236, 254–55, 261, 264–65, 271–72, 275–86, 297–319, 331, 369, 375, 390, 465

Extended families, 45–46, 115–17, 136. *See also* Matrilocality, evolution of

F

Factionalism in Iroquoian politics, 158, 195–96, 595–96, 645, 732, 744–50. *See also* Jesuits, separation of Christians and traditionalists

False Face Society, 81, 836

Fairty ossuary, 147

Family size, Huron, 46–47

Famine: among Montagnais, 275; among Neutral, 595; among Huron, 662, 684, 700, 715, 753–54, 760, 767, 772, 775, 779, 781–83, 786; among Tionnontaté, 767, 777, 789; among Wyandot, 821

Famine foods, 36, 662, 770, 775, 779–80, 782

Fast days, Christian, 547, 569

Feast of the Dead: among Huron, 85–90, 422, 426–29, 474, 518–20; in prehistoric times, 147; among northern Algonkians, 170–71, 442 *n*. 50, 609; rejected by Christian Huron, 711

Feasts: Huron, 79, 84–85, 269; Hochelagan, 192; Algonkian, 280; missionary opposition to, 388, 399, 530, 570, 712; Christian Huron, 714

Fenton, William N., 216, 218

Fire: burns cabins, 43, 50, 510, 543; burns villages, 51, 510, 834; origin myth, 77

Firearms: advantages and disadvantages of, 248, 252, 258, 260, 265, 312–16, 339, 430–31, 478, 513, 629, 634, 658, 736, 754, 767, 786, 790, 821; official policy concerning sale of, 273, 629–33; sale to Indians, 362, 467, 629–33, 647; number possessed by Iroquois, 617, 631, 638–39, 725–26, 794; French restrict sale only to Christians, 632–33, 700, 705; quality, 632; number possessed by Huron, 633, 766, 791, 795, 816, 849; Iroquois seek from French, 635–37. *See also* Huron, desire for armed French

Fishing: methods and importance, 31, 41, 100, 168; rituals, 75; role in prehistoric times, 109, 112–113, 132, 135; Huron fishing lodges, 116; bad year, 779

Flat Rock Point, 679

Flint, trade in, 94, 169

Food. *See* Cuisine.

Forest clearance. *See* Horticulture

Fortifications: traditional Huron, 43–44, 69, 439 *nn*. 22, 23; development of, 121–22, 128, 144, 150; Huron–Iroquois differences, 150–51, 309; Jesuit influence on, 513–15, 743

Fox. *See* Central Algonkians

France-Roy, 206

Francis I, King, 177, 182, 198–201

Francisation of Indians, 272, 287, 325, 378–80, 394, 512, 685, 818

Frank Bay site, 169–70

Free trade. *See* Monopolies, European

Frémin, Jacques, 834

French: problems understanding Huron, 15, 17–18, 40, 46–47, 61, 64, 76, 190, 312, 419, 846–49; desire to trade with Iroquois, 224, 236, 260, 267, 316, 322–23, 345, 347, 380, 644–45, 647; murdered by Indians, 338, 363, 380, 432, 457, 578, 482–84, 746, 778 (*see also* Viel); Huron names for, 366; Huron view of, 429–33, 566, 845; similarities of French and Huron culture, 504, 572; character of officials, 632, 843–44. *See also* Alliance,

French *(continued)*
Interpreter, Jesuits, Prisoners,
Recollets, Soldiers, Surgeons, Torture,
Truce, Warfare
Friendship, ritual, 711
Furs: as symbols of alliance, 225, 267–68,
270, 290, 345, 480, 482, 520, 537, 619,
651–52, 732, 734, 740, 742; in other
rituals, 427, 429

G

Gahoendoe, 679, 770–87, 789, 803, 813.
See also Sainte-Marie II
Gambling, 84, 479, 559
Games, 84, 154
Gandagaron, 638, 645, 826
Gandougarae, 828, 834–35
Garakontie, 815
"Garden of Eden" syndrome. *See*
Equilibrium theories
Garihouanne. *See* Sagard
Garnier, Charles, 513, 521, 540–41, 594,
666, 684, 698, 736, 739, 766, 777
Garnier, Julien, 835
Garoga site, 150
Garrad, Charles, 157, 318
Garreau, Léonard, 644, 739, 778, 789,
803, 824
Gaspé, Peninsula and Harbour, 178–84,
216
Gaubert, Louis, 667
Gendron, François, 62, 351, 633, 667,
853 *n.* 13
Generosity as Huron ideal, 50, 59–60,
82–84, 104, 424, 512, 535, 708, 748.
See also Reciprocity
Gentaienton, 795
Giffard de Moncel, Robert, 803
Girault de Villeneuve, Etienne, 801
Glacial Kame culture, 111
Glen Meyer culture, 126, 139–41, 148
Godbout, A., 396
Godefroy de Normanville, Thomas, 269,
278, 281–82, 321, 460, 470, 635
Godet Du Parc, Jean de, 263
Godois, Pierre, 615

"Good Iroquois" (name for Huron), 243
Gough, K., 420
Goupil, René, 638, 646, 667
Gourds, 63, 118, 441 *n.* 41
Government: principles of among Huron,
54; of villages, 56–57; of tribes, 57–58;
of confederacies, 58–59; development of,
143, 154, 162
Graham-Rogers site, 242
Grammars. *See* Dictionaries
Grandmaison, Eléonore de, 803
Grapes, wild: collected by Jesuits, 569,
684
Gravé Du Pont, François, 210, 228, 233,
236, 247–49, 255–56, 261, 263–65,
267, 290, 297, 326, 343, 347, 459
Grave offerings, 88–89, 139, 147, 169,
243–44, 427, 671, 842
Green Lake, 278–79
Grenole, ?, 372–73, 375, 399, 401
Greslon, Adrien, 756, 778
Groseilliers. *See* Chouart
Gros-Jean. *See* Richer
Guiet, Jean, 667
Guns. *See* Firearms
Guyart, Marie, 573, 599, 616
Guyot, Charles, 195

H

Hagouchonda. *See* Achelacy
Hakluyt, Richard, 210
Handsome Lake, 19, 21, 104
Headhunting. *See* Scalps and heads as
trophies
Headmen, 102–3; peace chiefs or civil
headmen, duties, 43, 51, 55–59,
67–68, 81–82, 195, 307, 376, 474–75,
537, 732; civil headmen, control of
trade, 65, 288–91, 327, 421–22, 425,
492–93; war chiefs, roles and duties,
55–56, 67, 69, 72–73, 307, 537, 541–43;
war chiefs, origin, 146–47; Huron
terms for, 289, 421–22; impact of
European trade on, 421–23, 450 *n.* 14,
844; Jesuits recognized as, 561, 761;
problems of conversion, 570, 712–13.

For individual Huron headmen, see also Aenons, Anenkhiondic, Angioraste, Assiskwa, Atironta, Atondo, Atsina, Auoindaon, Endahiaconc, Ochasteguin, Onaconchiaronk, Ondakion, Ongyata, Onorotandi, Ontitarac, Otsinonannhont, Sangwati, Saouenhati, Taratouan, Taretandé, Totiri, Tregouaroti, Tsondakwa

Hébert, Louis, 359, 404, 430

Heidenreich, C. E., 157, 298, 337, 358, 385, 509, 578, 581

Helms, Mary, 420

Hemp. *See* Indian hemp

Hendricksen, Cornelis, 346

Henri IV, King, 230, 234, 255, 403

Hewitt, J. N. B., 96–97

Hickerson, H. E., 21

Historical ethnography, 16

Historical knowledge possessed by: Huron, 19, 825; Iroquois, 19; Winnebago, 19

Historiography: historical study of Canadian Indians, 2–4; unique properties of Canadian Indian history, 3–4; weaknesses of traditional studies, 4–11; methods used in present study, 25–26. *See also* Ethnohistory

Hochelaga, 184, 186–92, 204, 447 *nn.* 10, 14; name, 226

Hochelagans: traditional culture, 178–79; and Roberval, 205–6; dispersal, 219–23, 225–27. *See also* Onontchataronon, St. Lawrence Iroquoians

Hoffman, B. G., 216–17

Homans, George C., 23

Honareenhac, 778

Hontom, Hans Jorissen, 485

Hopewell culture, 117–19

Horticulture: northern limits, 31, 119, 131, 165, 217, 299, 771; Huron, 34–36, 40–41, 136, 438 *nn.* 11, 14, 15, 16, 445 *n.* 15, 525, 770–72, 803; prehistoric development, 100, 118–20, 122, 126–28, 131–34, 137, 144, 146, 148; among northern Algonkians, 223, 231, 279, 281, 318, 448 *n.* 31; impact of

fur trade on, 351–53, 359, 413–15, 420; influence of European cultigens, 387, 415; impact of population decline, 606; crop rituals, 715

Hospital: at Quebec, 616, 720, 799, 800; in Huron country, 669, 671

Hospital nuns, 613–14, 801–2

Houel, Louis, 287, 377

Houses: Huron, 43, 45–46, 151–53, 439 *nn.* 20, 21, 444 *n.* 8; differences between Huron and Iroquois houses, 100, 113–17, 121–22, 128–31, 136, 143, 150–53, 171, 413, 444 *n.* 10; changes in historic period, 413, 421; number of occupants, 439 *n.* 26; expulsion from, 716. *See also* Fire, Fishing, Matrilocality

Huault de Montmagny, Charles, 477, 522, 556, 575, 597–98, 608, 612–13, 633, 635, 637, 639, 644, 647–50, 652, 654, 700, 703, 755–59

Hudson, Henry, 260, 283–84

Hudson Bay, 214, 255, 275, 281–85, 299, 320–21, 337

Hudson River, 220, 260, 293, 339, 346

Hunchbacks. *See* Dwarfs

Hunt, George T., 7–8, 413, 619–21, 624, 626, 629, 632, 648, 650–55, 657, 663, 728, 735, 754, 770, 843, 852 *n.* 1, 855 *nn.* 2, 6

Hunter's Home culture, 119

Hunting: among Huron, 39, 41–43, 146, 308, 317, 439 *n.* 19, 639, 742; skins required for clothing, 41, 132–33, 168; rituals, 76, 155; among Neutral, 95; affected by warfare, 103, 345; in prehistoric times, 106–7, 109, 112–13, 132–33, 148, 158; in Algonquin Park, 170; among Stadaconans, 195; impact of fur trade on, 208, 350, 415–16, 569; impact of population decline on, 606; northern Algonkians famed as hunters, 651

Hunting territories, traditional: 132–33, 145; Huron, 43, 164, 350; Neutral, 94, 350; Iroquois, 153, 220; Tionnontaté, 350. *See also* Iroquois

Huron, traditional culture: tribal
structure, 27–30, 445 *n.* 23; names, 27,
243, 290, 359–60, 436 *nn.* 2, 3;
religion, 27, 75–90, 506, 567;
population, 31–32, 437 *n.* 8, 589, 602,
642; villages and houses, 31–32, 43–44,
69, 448 *n.* 39; self-esteem, 32–34, 65,
430, 432, 433; male-female
relationships, 34, 39–40, 45, 47–50,
52–53, 55, 60, 74–75, 78, 155–56,
367–68, 410, 413–15, 440 *n.* 29, 523,
556, 565, 716, 800; subsistence
activities, 34–36, 39–43, 135–36;
cuisine, 37; clothing, 37–39;
handicrafts, 44–45; family and kinship,
45–46; life cycle, 46–54; ideal
behaviour, 48, 50, 431–32; warfare, 51,
68–73, 314; political organization,
54–59, 422; law, 59–62, 66–68; trade,
62–65, 340; treatment of prisoners,
70–75; dialects, 174; skill as traders,
175–76, 622, 837, 842–43; sense of
history and chronology, 246, 448 *n.* 28,
825. *See also* Collecting, Fishing,
Government, Horticulture, Hunting,
Trade, indigenous, Trade routes,
Trails, Warfare

Huron, history: relations with northern
Algonkians, 32–34, 63–65, 165–68, 173,
245, 292, 342, 441 *n.* 44; internal tribal
rivalries and disagreements, 58–59,
288–90, 474, 730–31; origins, 148–50,
163, 445 *nn.* 19, 20; military strength
before 1640, 164, 417–18, 489;
military strength after 1640, 608,
627–28; development of confederacy,
174–76, 244; relations with
Tionnontaté, 174–75, 244–45, 318, 417;
early references to, 197; first contact
with French, 207–8, 246–55, 258–70;
first receive European goods, 236–45;
visit Quebec, 249, 236–37, 343–44,
398–99, 785; degree of reliance on
French, 286, 545, 596–98, 601, 603,
608; formal sharing of fur trade,
287–90; defame French to other tribes,
318, 401, 594, 657, 694–95, 698, 758,

776, 813, 831–32; view of French,
325–26, 374, 388–89, 429–33, 596–98,
848–49; desire to master French
technology, 325; desire for armed
Frenchmen, 325, 338–39, 367, 373–74,
384, 406, 408, 418, 471, 484, 490–91;
relations with Algonkin, 328, 341–42,
462, 479, 490–92, 496–98, 520–21,
553; winter on St. Lawrence, 344,
612–13, 615–17, 797, 801; relations
with Neutral, 402, 417; relations with
Assistaronon, 417; dealings with
English, 462; understanding of
Christianity, 496, 530, 848; fear
French want to destroy them, 500,
535–36, 563, 593, 720; talk of colony
on St. Lawrence, 525–26, 556, 616;
punished by Montmagny, 597–98;
loss of leadership, 601; acquire
firearms, 633; oppose truce of 1645,
649, 653, 758–59; opposition of
Christian and traditionalist factions,
672, 706, 712–22, 724, 731–32, 734,
744–50, 771, 781, 784, 827, 847;
dispersal, 660–61, 725–27, 740–44,
751–54, 762–75, 782–89; help to torture
Brébeuf, 764; as refugees among
Iroquois, 750, 783–84, 826–40; as
refugees among Tionnontaté, 767–76;
as refugees on Gahoendoe, 770–88; as
refugees among Neutral, 770; as
refugees in north, 770, 778–79, 783,
787, 820–25; as refugees at Quebec,
770, 784–85, 787, 801–20; as refugees
among Erie, 791, 794; as refugees
among Susquehannock, 783, 791; lack
furs on Gahoendoe, 781–82; engage in
fur trade from Quebec, 803–4, 816;
assimilated by Iroquois, 826–31,
836–40; attitudes of refugees toward
French, 831–36; contrast French and
Dutch Indian policy, 832. *See also*
Adoption, Alcohol, Alliance, Baptism,
Converts, Epidemics, Famine, Hunting,
Iroquois, Jesuits, Mortality rate, Names,
Nativist movements, Ossuaries,
Prisoners, Shamans, Torture, Trade,

indigenous, Trade with Europeans, Trade goods, Trade routes, French traders, Truce, Village, Warfare

Huron country: geography and topography, 27–31, 299–300; climate, flora, fauna, 31, 165; ties with north, 31, 165–68, 174, 299; reason for settlement in northern Simcoe County, 163–68, 446 *n*. 25; extent in late prehistoric times, 236–42; contraction in historic times, 416; changing military significance of location, 607–8; abandonment, 767–70

Huron language. *See* Iroquoian languages, Lingua franca

Huron of Lorette, 14, 818–20

Huronia, I, xxiii. *See also* Huron country

I

Inebriation. *See* Alcohol

Iahenhouton, 531

Ihonatiria, 475–76, 491, 493–95, 504–10, 513, 516–17, 520, 523–24, 526–32, 537–41, 548–49, 563, 571, 851 *ch.* 2 *n.* 1

Illinois (tribe), 357

Incest, 49, 54, 102, 110, 136, 512

Indian hemp, 39, 661, 704, 715

Indians: taken to France, 186–87, 200–201, 212, 230, 233, 263–64, 398, 448 *n.* 24, 460–61, 758; rights to French citizenship, 366, 456, 547; as visitors in England, 456–57

Influenza, 500, 526, 529

Innis, Harold, 2, 4, 215–16

In situ theory of Iroquoian development, 105, 181

Interest groups: defined, 23–25

Interpreters: Indians used as, 183–84, 212; lack of, 190, 192, 203, 251–52, 305, 313; French as, 204, 261–62, 267, 269, 285–86, 337, 490; official title, 367, 459–60; suppression of, 404–5, 470–71. *See also* Traders

Iouskeha, 77–78, 87, 593–94, 722–23

Iron tools: salvaged by Stadaconans, 199;

advantages of, 360, 409–10, 417; reworked by Huron, 411; prized by Iroquois, 617; manufactured by French in Huron country, 685. *See also* Metalworking, Stone tools

Iroquet, 236, 247–49, 257, 261–62, 265, 268–69, 304, 309, 317, 320–21, 350, 354, 401

Iroquoian: defined, I, xxiii

Iroquoian cultural pattern, 15–16, 90–91, 99–104, 444 *n.* 68; development of, 154–56; male-female relations, 155–56

Iroquoian languages: Tionnontaté, 94; Neutral, 95; Susquehannock, 97; Iroquois, 98; Huron, 174; St. Lawrence Iroquoian, 178, 180, 447 *n.* 4; development of, 105, 141

Iroquoian periods: early, 119–39; middle, 139–47; late, 148–53

Iroquois: knowledge of, 15; traditional culture, 97–99, 147; location, 98, 122, 607, 619, 627, 726, 728–29, 734; changes resulting from European contact, 103–4, 155–56; origin of confederacy, 162–63, 224; reliance on trade goods, 220–21, 617–18; strategies for obtaining European goods, 221–23, 293, 621–27, 842; as plunderers, 221, 292–93, 339, 626–28, 634, 658, 661, 725–26, 729, 790, 792, 826; European names for, 227, 311; epidemics among, 602, 826; as traders, 622–23, 837; expansion of hunting territories, 623–26, 643, 645, 653, 663–64, 735–36, 790; claim to southern Ontario, 626; incorporation of refugees, 627, 638, 640, 750, 766, 783–84, 826–31, 836–40; acquire firearms, 632 (*see also* Mohawk); warned against Jesuits by Huron, 657; internal dissension, 726, 733–34, 794–95, 807–9, 811–12, 814–15; Jesuit missions to, 795, 808–15, 832–36; carry off Huron refugees from St. Lawrence Valley, 804–15, 817. *See also* Adoption, Alliance, Prisoners, Trade with Europeans

Isle Royale, 108, 172

J

Jamet, Denis, 214, 225–26, 287, 297, 381
Jennings, Francis, 620
Jesuits: mission policy, 206, 467–69,
    502–4, 512, 516–17, 531, 557–58,
    569–70, 574–78, 632, 665–66, 672,
    685–89, 699–701, 709–10, 724,
    737–38, 760, 818, 845–46, 854 *n.* 1;
    educate Amantacha, 398; policies in
    France, 402–3; work in New France,
    1611–13, 403; relations with traders
    and trading companies, 403–5, 455,
    460, 467–68, 470–72, 476, 496, 524,
    544, 575, 759–60, 776; work in and
    around Quebec, 1625–29, 404–5, 459;
    language learning, 405–6, 408, 469,
    504, 511–12, 689, 696, 699; residence
    at Quebec, 405; residences in Huron
    country, 406, 481, 494–95, 502, 510,
    517, 537, 540, 543, 546, 561, 564,
    574–75, 587, 668, 687 (*see also* Sainte-
    Marie among the Huron); among
    Huron, 1626–29, 406–8; feared as
    witches, 407, 502, 509–10, 526, 528,
    534–38, 541–44, 551, 554, 568, 571,
    589–96, 689, 694–95, 698, 701, 706,
    714–15, 723, 764; as rainmakers, 407,
    510, 561; views of history, 421;
    education and intellectual stance,
    469–70, 503–4; secular employees,
    470–71, 539, 573, 575–76, 665–68,
    673, 689, 694, 776 (*see also* donnés);
    return to Huron country, 1633–34,
    479–83, 490–94; official support for
    Huron missions, 480–81, 495–96;
    mission from Ihonatiria, 494–95,
    501–20, 526–40; efforts to impress
    Huron with their superiority, 495, 562,
    565–66, 668, 708; Recollet influence on,
    501–2, 504, 522, 558, 578; education of
    young people, 502, 507–8, 519, 522–26,
    554–58, 681; relations with shamans,
    502–4, 510, 529–30, 535; residence with
    Huron families, 502, 564, 591, 593,
    704–5, 707; mortification of the flesh,
    502; conversion of adult males, 508–10,

547, 558, 563–65; failure to understand
    Huron culture, 508, 517, 531, 738,
    846–50; seen as threat to Huron culture,
    508, 530, 567–68; intolerance of
    Huron culture, 508–9, 574, 782;
    summer work, 510–12; study of Huron
    culture, 512, 569–70, 738; military aid
    to Huron, 513, 515, 737, 752, 763, 770,
    772; separation of Christians and
    traditionalists, 518, 669, 672, 710–13,
    738; appreciated by Huron, 521, 708;
    care of sick, 529, 669, 671; threatened
    with expulsion from Huron country,
    538, 744–50; proposed to kill as
    sorcerers, 538, 543, 590–91, 595–96,
    599, 694; tried for witchcraft, 541–43,
    594, 596; defended by Huron fur
    traders, 544–46, 597; material rewards
    for converts, 547, 613, 699–701, 731;
    recognized as headmen, 561, 761; visit
    all of Huron country, 565, 578;
    harassed by Huron, 568–69, 592–93,
    715; harassed by Neutral, 695; harassed
    by Tionnontaté, 698, 776–78; alleged
    dealings with Iroquois, 571, 694,
    697–98; missions from Sainte-Marie,
    588, 590–95, 685–714, 737–40;
    individuals attacked by Huron, 591–92,
    598, 696–97, 715; attitude towards
    Dutch, 628; attitude towards sales of
    firearms, 632–33; slain for witchcraft by
    Iroquois, 646, 657; food reserves, 684,
    775, 779–80, 854 *n.* 9, 855 *n.* 7;
    leadership sought by Huron, 739,
    748–50, 753, 755, 760–61, 771–72, 776,
    779–81, 784–85; regime at Ossossané,
    761–62; move to Gahoendoe, 771–75,
    779–84; return to Quebec, 784–85;
    support peace with Iroquois, 795;
    Huron missions at Quebec, 801–4,
    817–18; accused of witchcraft by Huron
    refugees, 831–32. *See also* Algonkin,
    Art, Ataronchronon, Baptism, Blood
    feud, Cayuga, Charms, Contarea,
    Corporal punishment, Curing societies,
    Devils, Divorce, Dreams,
    Fortifications, Iroquois, Maps, Marriage,

Mohawk, Neutral, Onondaga, Ossossané, Recollets, Sainte-Marie, Scanonaenrat, Schools, Sexual promiscuity, Sillery, Taenhatentaron, Tahontaenrat, Teanaostaiaé, Tionnontaté, Traders; *and for individual priests*, Biard, Bonin, Bressani, Bruyas, Buteux, Chabanel, Chastellain, Chaumonot, Dablon, Daran, Davost, Du Peron, Frémin, C. Garnier, J. Garnier, Garreau, Greslon, Jogues, C. Lalemant, G. Lalemant, J. Lalemant, Le Jeune, Le Mercier, S. Le Moyne, Massé, de Noüe, Noyrot, C. Pijart, P. Pijart, Poncet de La Rivière, Ragueneau, Raymbaut

Jesuit Relations, 17, 55, 215, 246, 471–72, 544, 550, 578, 600–601, 658, 668, 697, 709, 738, 746

Jogues, Isaac, 522, 541, 594, 609, 617, 638, 640, 645–47, 654–57, 663, 666, 702, 704, 708, 725, 733, 756–57

Joutaya, 505–7

Juntunen site, 116, 171–72

Jury, Wilfrid, 151, 515, 587, 669–74, 677, 679–81, 684, 746

K

Kakouchakhi, 611

Kandoucho, 689, 694, 696

Keinouche. *See* Quenongebin

Kettles. *See* Pottery

Khinonascarant. *See* Quieunonascaran

Khioetoa, 624, 695

Kichesipirini: location and culture, 231, 279–80, 309; opposition to French–Huron contact, 248, 262, 297, 326, 341–42, 785; relations with French, 270–71, 279–85, 309, 389, 396, 483, 574, 785; relations with Nipissing, 281–82, 284, 321, 498; relations with Huron, 351, 383, 490, 492, 496–98, 520–21, 553; relations with Mohawk, 485–98; independence, 498, 610; relations with Abenaki, 588; disrupted by Iroquois, 610, 637–38; reject French claims of sovereignty over them, 785

Kidd, Kenneth E., 360, 669, 673–78, 680–81, 685

Kin terms, 20, 46, 102, 136–37, 440 *n.* 27, 445 *n.* 17

Kiotsaeton, 647–49, 651, 654

Kipp Island culture, 119

Kipp Island No. 4 site, 113

Kirke, David, 456, 459

Kirke, Gervase, 456

Kirke, Thomas, 460–61

Kleynties, ?, 346

Knives. *See* Stone tools

Krieckenbeeck, Daniel van, 463–64, 478, 630

L

La Chaudière. *See* Ekhiondastsaan

Lachine Rapids, 192, 204–5, 207, 233, 263, 265, 268, 270, 273, 275, 280–81, 283–85, 296, 326, 340, 342, 396

La Criette, 372, 452 *n.* 14

La Grenouille. *See* Oumasasikweie

La Lande, Jean de, 655

Lalemant, Charles, 358, 373, 397, 404, 469, 477, 489, 502, 572, 628–29

Lalemant, Gabriel, 756, 763–64, 833

Lalemant, Jérôme, 284, 503, 567, 572–88, 597–98, 605, 611, 628, 642, 644, 649, 660, 665–66, 668, 672, 685–89, 696–97, 709, 775, 847

La Marche, ?, 373

Lambert, Eustache, 668

La Montagne, ?, 372

Lanctot, Gustave, 10, 24

Languages. *See* Iroquoian languages

La Peltrie. *See* Chauvigny

La Roche Daillon, Joseph de, 335, 344, 373, 375, 396, 398–402; influence on Brébeuf, 405–6, 501, 509, 689

La Roche de Mesgouez, Troilus de, 212

La Rocque de Roberval, Jean-François de, 201, 206–7

Laumet de Lamothe de Cadillac, Antoine, 820

Laurel culture, 112

Laurentian Archaic, 107–10

Laurentian hypothesis, 2
Lauson, Jean de, 467, 476
Laval, François de, 817
La Vallée, ?, 372–73, 375, 399
Lay brothers. *See* Brothers
Le Baillif (of Amiens), 459
Le Baillif, Georges, 381, 393
Le Caron, Joseph, 287, 296–98, 300,
    317–19, 324–26, 333–36, 344, 364,
    373–74, 376–77, 379, 381, 384–95,
    397, 399, 424, 431, 455, 601
Le Clercq, Chrestien: as source, 297–98,
    301, 318, 335–36, 347, 349, 382, 384,
    396
Le Coq, Robert, 489, 576, 589–90, 667,
    696, 776
Ledesma catechism. *See* Catechism
Leindohy (stinking corn), 37
Le Jeune, Paul, 115, 350, 364, 373, 396,
    430, 466, 469, 470, 472–73, 480–81,
    483–84, 486, 488, 496, 500, 522–23,
    546, 575, 619, 628, 630, 648
Le Mercier, François-Joseph, 496, 511,
    527, 536, 539, 541, 543, 575, 590, 666,
    811, 836
Le Moyne, Charles, 668
Le Moyne, Simon, 573, 593, 666, 812
Lent: observance by Huron converts, 569
Le Royer de La Dauversière, Jérôme, 629
Lescarbot, Marc: as source, 214, 221, 225,
    263, 274, 431, 433, 569
Letters carried from the Huron country
    via central Quebec, 611, 735
Lévis, Henri de, Duc de Ventadour, 398,
    404, 455
Levrier, Jacob, 667
Lingua franca: Huron as, 65, 355; along
    St. Lawrence, 213, 364
Locks: Jury's theory for Sainte-Marie,
    679–81
Longhouse. *See* Houses
Long Sault Rapids, 278, 640, 655, 816,
    829
Lorette, 818–20
Lounsbury, Floyd G., 20
Louis XIII, King, 271, 375
Lurie, Nancy O., 8, 842

M

McCluskey site, 172
McKenzie site, 242
McIlwain, C. H., 7, 619, 621
McIlwraith, T. F., 2, 4
McMurchy site, 242
McPherron, Alan, 172
Madawaska River, 278
Magnan, Pierre, 464
Mahican: sale of land to Dutch, 464.
    See also Alliance, Warfare
Maisouna, 205, 447 *n.* 15
Maize. *See* Corn
Malecite, 213, 230–31
Mance, Jeanne, 613, 629
Manitoulin Island, 771, 787, 803, 820
Maouatchihitonnam. *See* Matabachouwan
Maps: Jesuits as cartographers, 469, 578;
    individual maps, 96, 99, 170, 210, 225,
    305, 309, 311, 319, 331, 578, 581, 688,
    791, 798, 838–39, 853 *n.* 11, 855 *ch.* 12
    n. 4
Marguerie, François, 635
Marie de l'Incarnation. *See* Guyart
Maritime Archaic, 107
Marriage: traditional Iroquoian pattern,
    49–50, 52, 102; between Huron and
    Algonkians, 65, 173; in prehistory, 107,
    109–10, 136–37, 444 *n.* 4; between
    French and Huron, 365, 368–69, 496,
    539, 575; Jesuit view of, 512, 557–58;
    remarriage of Christians, 551, 563. *See
    also* Divorce, Matrilocality
Marsolet, Nicolas, 404–5, 452 *n.* 19, 459,
    470
Martijn, Charles, 172
Martin, Félix, 743
Martyrdom: Jesuit view of, 503–4, 574,
    601, 714
Massawomecke, 97
Massé, Enemond, 403–4, 408, 472, 479
Masson, Pierre, 667, 684
Matrilineality: among Iroquoians in
    historic period, 47, 55, 60, 100–102, 154;
    evolution of, 134–36, 444 *n.* 14;
    alleged influences of fur trade, 420–21;

continuing importance of, 523, 536, 716, 827, 831, 844

Matrilocality: among Iroquoians in historic period, 45–46, 55, 100, 445 *n.* 22; evolution of, 107, 109–10, 112–13, 115–17, 135–36, 141, 420, 445 *n.* 16; alleged influences of fur trade, 418–21; continuing importance of, 523, 716

Matabachouwan, 171, 197, 356, 611

Matouweskarini, 278

Mattawa River, 298, 356

Maurice site, 350, 413, 415

Maxon-Derby site, 121

Meadowood culture, 111

Menstrual observances, 48

Mesoamerican influences, 100, 106, 145, 147

Metalworking by Huron: stimulated by European trade, 409, 411–12, 425–26. *See also* Copper

Miami (tribe), 375

Michel, Jacques, 456, 459, 471

Michilimackinac Island, 820, 824

Michipicoten site, 172–73

Micmac, 177–78, 183, 208–9, 213, 216, 359, 361

Middlemen. *See* Monopolies

Middleport site, 144

Middleport substage, 139, 143

Midewiwin, 14

Miller site, 128, 137–38

Missionaries. *See* Jesuits, Recollets

Mission system: established by Jérôme Lalemant, 576–78, 588, 608–9, 687–88

Mohawk: location and culture, 98, 220, 346, 607, 645, 657; villages, 150, 443 *n.* 57; as hunters, 220, 439 *n.* 19, 623; relations with other Iroquois, 224, 622, 655, 725–26, 806, 808–9, 812, 814; relations with Dutch, 260–61, 293, 345–47, 382–83, 463–64, 845–49, 617–20, 622, 631, 647, 663; relations with the French, 342–49, 383–84, 464, 635–37, 647–57, 662, 756–59, 795, 806–10, 812–13, 824; acquisition of

firearms, 630–32, 634; desire for French neutrality, 639, 644, 652, 725, 756, 758, 808; internal factionalism, 645, 647; long-term strategies, 663–64; role in dispersal of Huron, 729–30, 740, 742, 762; seek Huron refugees, 806, 809–12; Jesuit mission to, 808; absorb refugees, 826. *See also* Alliances, Kichesipirini, Monopolies, Trade with Europeans, Truce, Warfare; *and for individuals*, Kiotsaeton, Tokhrahenehiaron

Moieties. *See* Phratries

Molère, Joseph, 667

Monopolies, European, 210–12, 228–29, 234, 255, 257, 271–73, 286, 362–63, 403, 455–56, 462, 477–78, 630, 759. *See also* Trade with Europeans

Monopolies, Indian: and growth of confederacies, 163; Huron, 166, 175, 356, 374–76, 399–400, 696, 729, 790; St. Lawrence Iroquoian, 187–88, 219, 221; Montagnais, 213–14, 217, 230, 256, 264–65, 267; Algonkin, 248, 262–63, 278, 280–81, 285, 293, 321, 324, 326, 328, 341; Nipissing, 284; Ottawa, 319; Mohawk, 382–83, 464, 619, 627–28; as explanations for Iroquois wars, 621–23. *See also* Tolls, Trade, indigenous

Montagnais: location and culture, 115–16, 223, 230–31, 255, 448 *n.* 31; and fur trade, 208, 213–14, 216, 228–34, 248, 256–57, 264, 267, 342, 359, 361–64, 452 *n.* 12, 803; opposition to French trade with western tribes, 265–67, 270, 273, 326, 342; famine, 275; relations with French, 331, 338, 353, 366, 380, 456–58, 477–78, 500, 597; relations with Huron, 351, 807; relations with missionaries, 376, 405, 468, 522, 577; relations with English, 456, 458, 630; use of alcohol, 462; epidemics, 500–501; access to firearms, 630; hunting territories proposed for, 643; some killed by Sokoki, 654. *See also* Alliances, Monopolies, Sillery,

Montagnais *(continued)*
    Tadoussac, Trade routes, Truce,
    Warfare; *and for individuals,*
    Batiscan, Begourat, Capitanal,
    Cherououny, Erouachy, Pastedechouan
Montaigne, Michel de, 9
Montmorency, Henri II, Duc de, 403–4
Montreal Island: sixteenth-century
    European visits, 190–92, 204–5, 207,
    210; Algonkin claim Huron attack on,
    215, 219, 225–26; Champlain visits and
    plans to colonize, 224, 265, 280, 327,
    349; trade at, 265–71, 273, 275–78,
    284–86, 296–97, 326, 343; Ville Marie
    established on, 613, 629, 639; refuge
    for Indians, 609–10, 613; Huron visit,
    616, 756, 799; harassed by Iroquois,
    640, 658, 725, 757–58, 792; Iroquois
    visit, 654; Huron refugees at, 802. *See
    also* Onontchataronon
Moon: as spirit, 77
Monts. *See* Du Gua
Morrison Island, 231, 278–83, 285, 341,
    521, 556, 610, 638, 725, 785
Mortality rate: prehistoric, 138, 440 *n.* 28;
    differentials, 144, 527, 590, 601, 781,
    848; in epidemics, 242, 501, 527–28,
    589, 780, 851 *ch.* 2 *n.* 1; among other
    tribes, 602, 826
Morton, W. L., 10
Murder, 59–60. *See also* Blood feud
Muskrat Lake, 278

N

Names: clan property, 47; avoid use of,
    51; inheritance of, 55, 600; problems of
    recognition in texts, 247; Huron names
    for Frenchmen, 366; Huron given
    Christian names, 505, 590, 709
Naroll, Raoul, 8, 632
Nassau, Fort, 293, 346
Native preachers, 556–57, 561, 565, 594,
    703–4, 711
Nativistic movements among Huron,
    593–94, 722–23
Nets, 41, 44, 63, 76

Neutral: name and culture, 94–96, 148,
    443 *nn.* 58, 59, 60; origin, 148;
    relations with other tribes, 245, 319,
    350, 354, 402, 417, 443 *n.* 63, 561,
    595, 623–25, 695, 789; French visits
    and missions to, 319, 374–75, 393,
    399–402, 688–96, 698, 704; epidemics,
    602; dispersal, 735–36, 789–91, 828. *See
    also* Alliances, Famine, Hunting,
    Hunting territories, Seneca,
    Souharissen, Tahontaenrat, Warfare
Nekouba, 611
New Brunswick, 116, 208, 234
Newfoundland, 117, 206, 208
New Netherland. *See* Dutch
New Sweden, 725, 732–33, 792
Nibachis, 278–79
Nicollet de Belleborne, Jean, 355–56,
    452 *n.* 8, 460, 470, 478, 486–88, 608,
    851 *n.* 10
Nipissing: winter among Huron, 63, 170,
    319, 492, 528, 608–9; traditional
    culture, 116, 170, 173, 361; relations
    with Algonkin, 281–82, 284, 321, 324,
    498, 534; Champlain's dealings with,
    298–99, 320–21, 353, 526; population,
    299; visit St. Lawrence, 353, 478, 521,
    608–9; relations with missionaries, 376,
    390, 536, 608–9; dispersal, 799. *See also*
    Attignawantan, Trade routes
Noble, William C., 242
Noble Savage, 9–10
Noël, Jacques, 210
Noircler, Nicolas, 667, 756
Non-directed contact, 408–9, 845
Northern Algonkians, 32–34, 39, 44,
    63–65, 79, 165–68, 171, 173, 353, 526,
    606, 820–24
Northern Ocean. *See* Hudson Bay
Nouë, Anne de, 399, 401, 406, 472, 512
Nova Scotia, 208, 234, 403
Noyrot, Philibert, 398, 404, 455–56
Nudity, as regarded by: Huron, 37, 83;
    Ottawa, 37, 299; Neutral, 96; Jesuits,
    502
Nuns at Quebec, 523, 599, 614. *See also*
    Hospital nuns, Ursuline nuns

O

Oak Hill culture, 141

Ocata. See Shaman

Ochasteguin (ethnonym), 290

Ochasteguin (headman), 246–49, 257, 261–62, 265, 288–89, 313, 317, 326

Ohenhen, 786, 790

Ohio Valley, 357, 791, 794, 797

Oionhaton, 616, 638, 654, 835–36, 852 *n.* 4

Ojibwa, 166, 353, 609, 625

Okhukwandoron, 613, 706–7

Oki, 75–76, 79. *See also* Spirits

Old Copper culture, 108, 111

"Old Men," 56–57, 60; skills of old men, 75

Oliveau, Pierre, 668, 854 *n.* 6

Onaatichiae, 801

Onaconchiaronk, 530, 707–8, 742

Ondaaiondiont, 732–33, 766, 786

Ondakion, 802, 852 *n.* 9

Onderha, 75

Ondoutawaka, 611

Oneida: location and traditional culture, 98, 151; attacked by Champlain, 311; decimated by Huron, 560; ignore truce of 1645, 653, 655; seek and absorb Huron refugees, 811, 826. *See also* Prisoners, Trade with Europeans, Truce, Warfare

Onekagoncka, 602

Onguiaahra, 694

Ongyata, 389, 391, 395

Onnentisati, 491, 504, 527, 531, 541

Onnontioga, 828

Onondaga: location and traditional culture, 98–99, 421; prehistory, 153; origins of conflict with Huron, 293; relations with French, 488, 654–55, 794, 806, 808–9, 811–13; rivalry with Mohawk, 725, 806, 809, 812, 814; some killed at Gahoendoe, 787; seek and absorb Huron refugees, 807, 809, 811–13, 815, 826–28; Jesuit mission to, 808–9, 811–13, 832–33. *See also* Truce, Warfare; *and for individuals,*

Annenraes, Garakontie, Scandouati, Soionés, Tsiraenie

Ononharoia, 83, 423–24, 561, 715, 719–20; reinterpreted by Christian Huron, 712

Ononkwaia, 559, 571

Onontchataronon: winter among Huron, 63, 227, 248, 262, 288, 317, 320–24, 610; claim to Montreal Island, 215, 225, 610; identity, 225–26; relations with Neutral, 350, 354; attacked by Iroquois, 552, 638, 640, 655. *See also* Alliance, Algonkin, Petite Nation, Warfare

Onontio (Huron title for French Governor), 522

Onorotandi, 290, 298, 391

Ontario Point Peninsula culture, 112, 118

Ontitarac, 542–43

Oonchiarey, 365, 385

Oquiaendis, 505, 539. *See also* Sangwati

Oral traditions, value of, 19–20, 228, 825

Orange, Fort, 346–47, 383, 463–64, 618, 620, 654

Origin myths. *See* Creation myths

Orléans, Ile d', 184–85, 803–4, 807, 810, 816

Oscotarach, 87

Ossernenon, 638, 645, 655, 657

Ossossané (Tequenonquiaye), 300, 317, 360, 373–75, 384–85, 390, 392, 416, 426–27, 450 *n.* 17, 475, 481–82, 492, 494, 513, 522, 524, 527–28, 530, 532–33, 537, 540–45, 550–51, 554, 561–63, 571, 601, 668, 715, 800; Jesuit visits to, 504, 518–20, 531, 599; mission to, 540–46, 556, 561–63, 575, 577, 588, 591, 669, 687, 702–4, 719, 760–62; fights Iroquois invaders, 764–66; abandoned, 767; refugees, 770, 804. *See also* Ossuaries

Ossuaries: Huron, 88–90, 243; Neutral, 96, 148; development of, 138–39, 144, 147, 445 *n.* 18, 427; Nipissing, 170; at Juntunen site, 171; at Sopher site, 242; at Ossossané, 360

Otaguottouemin, 298, 450 *n.* 16

Otoüacha. *See* Toanché

Otsinonannhont, 698, 707

Ottawa: traditional culture, 134, 166, 318; as traders, 243, 299; Champlain's visits with, 299, 318–19; afflicted by epidemics, 536; replace Huron as traders, 820–24, 852 *n.* 1. *See also* Monopoly, Trade, indigenous, Trade routes, Truce, Warfare

Otter Society, 533

Oukhahitoüa, 491, 504

Oumasasikweie, **1**, 497–98, 552; **2**, 545, 610, 632

Ounontisastan, 399, 401–2. *See also* Teotongniaton

Outetoucos, 265, 270

Owasco culture, 119–22, 126, 131, 135, 137, 139, 143

P

PalaeoIndian period in Ontario, 106

Palisades. *See* Fortifications

Pan-Indian traits, 16, 19

Paraguay, Jesuit missions to, 468, 577–78, 685

Parker, A. C., 19

Parkman, Francis, 472, 622

Partridge (headman), 490, 496

Pastedechouan, 460–61

Patterson, E. P., 4, 21

Peace treaties. *See* Truce

Pendergast, James F., 180

Perrot, Nicolas, 215–16, **1**, 417, 810, 821

Personal chant (death song), 48, 52, 72, 571

Petite Nation: legend concerning, 215; territory, 225–26, 278; kill Frenchman, 478–83, 490; epidemics, 499. *See also* Algonkin, Onontchataronon, Trade with Europeans

Petit-Pré, François, 489, 526, 576

Petun. *See* Tionnontaté

Phratry, 52, 54, 102, 749, 825; evolution of, 110, 154; political significance of among Mohawk, 645, 657

Pickering culture, 126–31, 137–41, 147–48, 171–72

Pic River site, 172

Pieskaret, 799

Pigs: introduced to the Huron country, 685

Pijart, Claude, 608, 854 *ch.* 10 *n.* 3

Pijart, Pierre, 496, 511, 540–41, 547, 554–55, 558, 588, 666, 698

Pipes: historic Huron, 45, 425–26, 439 *nn.* 24, 25; prehistoric, 110–11, 119, 126, 141–43, 148; significance of designs, 143, 439 *n.* 25; pewter, 671

Point Peninsula culture, 112

Poisoning, 598

Poncet de La Rivière, Joseph-Antoine, 588, 666, 854 *ch.* 10 *n.* 2

Pontchartrain, Fort, 820

Population: Huron, 31–32, 437 *n.* 8; Tionnontaté, 91, 422 *n.* 56; Neutral, 94; Iroquois, 98; Nipissing, 299; density, 91, 132, 168, 444 *n.* 11; in prehistory, 107, 109, 112, 119–20, 132–34, 143, 148, 153; pressure leads to adoption of horticulture, 132–33; control, 133; decline, 578, 589, 602, 662, 753, 767; Lalemant on decline, 628

Porteous site, 122, 128

Post-natal observances, 47

Potawatomi, 625, 820

Pottery: Huron, 39, 411, 438 *n.* 17; Susquehannock, 97; prehistoric, 110–12, 116, 119–21, 126, 135, 140–41, 148, 150, 157, 159; as clue to prehistoric warfare and population movements, 159–62, 169–73, 226, 445 *n.* 24, 446 *n.* 29; compared to metal kettles, 360, 411; Montagnais, 362; Jesuit, 685. *See also* Pipes

Poulain, Guillaume, 349, 376

Pratt, Peter, 226, 309

Princess Point cultures, 122–26

Prisoners: treatment of, 70–75, 145, 309, 416–17, 766; Iroquois captured by Algonkians, 233, 254, 258, 275, 464, 466, 486, 552; Iroquois captured by French, 233, 260, 263, 267; Iroquois captured by Huron, 254, 258, 306, 309, 315, 320, 323, 416, 552, 559, 570–72,

643–44, 647, 649, 659, 662, 730–32, 736, 755–58, 764, 809; Algonkians captured by Iroquois, 269, 638, 655, 725, 830; Dutch captured by Susquehannock, 305; released or exchanged, 464–65, 486, 489, 635, 650–52, 654, 733–34, 743; Assistaronon as, 488, 624; Huron captured by Iroquois, 489, 515, 554, 559, 615–16, 637–40, 642–44, 661–63, 705, 736, 742–43, 752, 763, 783, 786–87, 799, 804–5, 810, 815–17, 826–27, 829–31; Huron escape from Iroquois, 613, 615, 637, 642–44, 708, 736, 783, 786, 797, 799, 805, 817, 824; Huron naturalized by Iroquois, 615, 640, 733, 755, 757, 816, 826–31; French captured by Iroquois, 615, 635, 638, 763–64; used as guides, 736; Tionnontaté captured by Iroquois, 777–78, 824; Iroquois captured by Erie, 794; Erie captured by Iroquois, 797; Iroquois naturalized by Huron, 816. *See also* Abductions, Baptism
Prisoner sacrifice. *See* Cannibalism, Torture, Warfare
Promiscuity. *See* Sexual promiscuity
Protestants: excluded from New France, 379, 381, 455
Prouville de Tracy, Alexandre de, 818
Psychotherapy. *See* Soul desires

Q

Quebec: Iroquois attack, 223, 349; French settlement and trading post at, 234–35, 255, 257, 263–64, 271–72, 274–75, 286, 296–97, 331, 342–43, 362–63, 376–77, 381, 395, 402–4, 408, 462, 467, 604, 630; Indians visit, 246–49, 255–56, 326–27, 345, 361, 398–99, 405, 430, 458, 476, 478–84, 495–96, 524, 599, 605, 616, 717, 785, 799, 806–7, 809–13; held by English, 455–62, 466–67; schools at, 522–26, 554–58, 613–14, 616; Huron refugees at, 801–20

Quenongebin, 278
Quieunonascaran, 290, 298, 364, 373–74, 385, 387–92, 399, 416–17, 440 *n.* 33, 475, 531

R

Racist interpretations of Indian behaviour and history, 7, 9–11
Radisson, Pierre, 804, 809, 813, 830
Ragueneau, Paul, 541, 554, 581, 591, 611, 662, 666, 708, 738, 748, 751, 770, 772, 776–78, 784–85, 802, 811, 813
Rainmakers. *See* Jesuits, Recollets, Shamans
Rasiere, Isaack de, 463
Rasles, Sébastien, 512
Raymbaut, Charles, 608–9, 666
Reciprocity: in Huron households, 36; in Huron society, 50–51, 62, 83, 90, 426–29; in foreign trade, 64; reinforcement of, 66–67, 423–25; and prestige of headmen, 421–23; effect of conversion on, 570, 707–8, 715
Recollets: arrive in Canada, 287; missionary residences, 298, 300, 373, 377, 385–89, 404, 431; and Jesuits, 333–35, 402, 404, 406; relations with Huron, 365, 387–91, 394–95; relations with French traders, 368, 374, 380, 401, 405; work in and around Quebec, 376–77; mission policy, 377–81, 385, 387, 394; relations with Champlain, 377, 379–81, 384; Huron missions, 382–402; viewed as shamans or witches, 385, 388, 394, 401, 402; viewed as rainmakers, 388–89; linguistic research, 393; grow plants in Huron country, 415; departure from New France, 458–59; excluded from New France, 467; sources, 333–35. *See also* Baptism, Schools, Traders; *and for individual Recollets*, Duplessis, Jamet, La Roche Daillon, Le Baillif, Le Caron, Le Clercq, Poulain, Sagard, Viel
Redistribution. *See* Reciprocity
Red slate, 44, 410. *See also* Catlinite

Reductions, 577, 666, 685–87, 847. *See also* Paraguay

Refugees, intertribal, 159–61, 562, 623–24, 767–70, 776–78, 789–97

Regnault, Christophe, 667

Religion, Iroquoian: 75–77, 103–4; impact of population decline on, 607

Relocation of villages, 36–37, 41, 44, 147, 158, 358, 509, 513, 517–18, 576, 602

Rémy de Courcelle, Daniel de, 620

Rensselaer, Kiliaen van, 463–64, 618, 620–21

Rensselaerswyck, 485, 620, 630–31

Reparation, 60–61, 64, 308, 432, 748–49; French refusal to accept, 380, 432, 457, 478, 482–84

Residence. *See* Matrilocality

Rice. *See* Wild rice

Rice Lake, 118, 138

Richards, Cara, 418–19

Richelieu, Cardinal de. *See* Du Plessis

Richelieu, Fort, 609, 614, 629, 639–40, 643–44, 647

Richelieu River, 198, 220, 233, 248–49, 251, 254, 257–58

Richer, Jean, 460, 851 *ch. 7 n.* 1

Rideau Lakes, 634

Ridley, Frank, 95, 169–70

Rigué, 795

Ritchie, William A., 119, 135, 139

Rivière des Prairies, 296, 340–41, 395, 640

Roberval. *See* La Rocque

Robinson, P. J., 226

Robitaille site, 350, 409–11, 413

Roquemont de Brison, Claude, 456

Rosaries, 390, 671, 713, 715, 746

Russell, W. A., 680

S

Sackett site, 121, 137

Sagard, Gabriel: visits Huron, 342–43, 349, 364–65, 384–85, 387–95, 411, 415, 430; Huron name, 366; statements of Recollet policy, 379; as source, 143, 172, 223, 225, 263–64, 280, 290, 297–98, 304, 318, 333–35, 339–41, 344,

350–51, 353, 355–56, 358, 360, 363, 366–67, 369, 373, 381, 396, 409, 416–17, 424, 431, 433, 458, 460, 473, 611

Saguenay: Kingdom of, 196–97, 207; River, 197, 207; region, 356, 376

Saint Charles, Mission of, 778–79

Saint Denys (village), 588

Sainte Anne (village), 588–90

Sainte Elizabeth (village), 588

Sainte Foy, 818

Saint Eloi Island, 248

Sainte Magdelaine (village), 688

Sainte-Marie among the Huron: location, 581–87; Jesuit residence and mission headquarters, 587, 589, 665, 668–73, 681–85, 687, 696–99, 701, 704–6, 710–11, 739, 746, 748–49; demolition and rebuilding at, 587, 674, 677, 681, 756, 772; centre for Indian devotion, 599, 800; soldiers kept at, 644; staff, 666–68; as a fort, 669, 677–79, 756; modern reconstruction, 673–81; threatened by Iroquois, 736, 764–66; refuge for Huron, 737, 752, 760, 763, 770; abandoned, 770–72

Sainte-Marie II, 679, 772

Sainte-Marie-de-Ganentaa, 809, 815

Sainte Térèse (village), 591

Saint Francis-Xavier (village), 688

Saint Ignace (Huron village). *See* Taenhatentaron

Saint Ignace (Wyandot village), 820

Saint Ignace II: site, 151; theory of, 743, 855 *ch.* 11 *n.* 4. *See also* Taenhatentaron

Saint Ignace Island, 257–58, 261, 342–43

Saint Jean (village), 588, 598, 688, 706, 766

Sainte Jean-Baptiste (village). *See* Contarea

Saint Joachim (village), 588, 766

Saint John, Lake, 171, 197, 214, 356, 611, 792

Saint Lawrence Iroquoians: identity and culture, 99, 139, 170, 178, 180–81,

187, 193, 218–19, 447 *n.* 8; dispersal, 214–24, 448 *n.* 27, 499; possible survivors, 225–27. *See also* Baptism, Hochelagans, Stadaconans, Warfare

Saint Lawrence River: as trade artery, 231, 237, 345, 349, 560, 652

Saint Louis (village), 515, 588, 590, 596, 763–66

Saint Maurice River, 256, 265, 356

Sangwati, 505, 516–17

Saoekbata, 638, 642

Saouenhati: **1**, 592, 704–5; **2**, 805

Sartre, Jean-Paul, 23

Satouta, 523–25, 554

Saugeen culture, 112

Sauk. *See* Central Algonkians

Sault-au-Récollet, 395

Sault Sainte Marie, 63, 355, 372, 375, 609, 625

Savignon, 261–69, 395, 429

Scahentarronon, 97, 443 *n.* 65, 792

Scalps and heads as trophies, 70, 145, 233, 255

Scandouati, 735, 740–41

Scanonaenrat, 516, 525, 527, 540, 557, 564, 571, 659, 687, 744, 800; mission to, 564–65, 588, 688, 696, 706–7, 720, 739; Jesuits expelled from, 592; pursue Iroquois, 766

Schneider, D. M., 420

Schoff, H. L., 220

Schools: Recollet, 379–80, 395, 430, 460–61; Jesuit, in France, 398, 460–61; Jesuit, at Quebec and Three Rivers, 496, 519, 523–26, 553–58, 613–15, 700; Ursuline, 616, 800–801; projected school in Huron country, 681, 851 *ch.* 8 *n. 4. See also* Amantacha, Andehoua, Ateiachias, Atondo, Okhukwandoron, Pastedechouan, Satouta, Tewatirhon, Tsiko

Scot, Dominique, 667

Scurvy; among Europeans, 194, 206, 248, 264, 275; Stadaconan cure for, 194

Sedentariness, preference for, 133

Sedentarization of Indians, 366, 378, 380

Seneca: location and history, 21, 98;

emphasis on horticulture, 98, 836–37; trade goods among, 221, 411; dealings with French, 306, 308, 474, 792; dealings with Neutral, 402, 624, 635–36, 694; accused of slaying Chihwatenha, 598, 694; epidemics, 602; relations with Wenroronon, 623–24; disperse Huron, 726–28, 742, 762; interrupt Huron contact with Susquehannock, 733; Jesuit mission to, 834–35. *See also* Tahontaenrat, Truce, Warfare

Serpent Mounds site, 138–39

Sexual abstinence: traditional Huron usages, 73, 79, 84, 388; view of celibacy, 388

Sexual promiscuity: among Huron, 49; French reaction to, 367–68, 388; Jesuit opposition to, 718–19; subverts Christian converts, 718–19

Shamans: Huron, 66–67, 78–79, 81–82, 317, 374, 421; Wenroronon, 97; Stadaconan, 189–90; Algonkian, 251; Tionnontaté, 318; priests viewed as, 388–89, 431, 484, 493, 495, 502–3, 508, 510, 530, 561, 565, 567; relations with French, 391, 407, 529, 535–36, 598, 738; as rainmakers, 406–7, 510, 561; in epidemics, 529, 533–34, 551; innovation by, 533–34; conversion of, 707, 718; rejected by Christian Huron, 717; oppose Christianity, 717–18. *See also* Tehorenhaegnon, Tonneraouanont, Tsondacouané

Shell, marine: prehistoric trade in, 62, 108, 113, 118, 139, 169, 198. *See also* Beads

Shield Archaic, 107

Sidey-Mackay site, 226, 350

Sillery: Montagnais encampment at, 342; Jesuit mission at, 577–78, 633, 643, 647, 703, 756, 776, 779, 803, 854 *n.* 1; Algonkin shelter at, 609–10, 637; Huron winter and shelter at, 612–16, 797, 801, 803, 810, 815; trade at, 759

Sioux, 357, 820, 824

Sitadin, 184, 199

Skanudharoua, 802

Skenchioe, 791

Sky: in Huron mythology, 52, 76–77

Smallpox, 499, 588–95, 598, 602, 826

Smith, Wallis M., 418–21

Smoking. *See* Pipes, Tobacco

Social organization. *See* Clan, Clan segment, Kin terms, Matrilineality, Matrilocality

Société de Notre-Dame de Montréal, 629, 759

Society of Jesus. *See* Jesuits

Soionés, 733–34

Sokoki, 634, 647, 653–54, 792

Soldiers, French: sent to Huron country, 524, 604–5, 644, 649, 662, 667, 677, 756, 760

Sononkhiaconc, 538–39

Sopher site, 151, 242, 439 *n*. 21

Soranhes, 392, 397–98, 460, 489, 504, 547–48

Sorbonne, 379

Souharissen, 399, 401, 689, 694–95

Soul, Huron beliefs concerning, 51–52, 87

Soul desires, 81–84, 535, 568, 592–93, 706, 716

Sources, critique of, 17–19, 331–35, 436 *n*. 1

Spanish: settlements in North America, 196, 357; in Newfoundland, 205

Spicer, Edward, 6, 21

Spirits, Huron, 75–78, 430, 537. *See also* Oki

Squash, 34, 100, 118, 120, 137, 148, 438 *n*. 12

Squawkie Hill culture, 118

Stadacona, 184–85, 188, 192–95, 447 *n*. 6

Stadaconans: traditional culture, 178–81, 193, 195; activities on lower St. Lawrence, 178–84, 205; relations with French, 181–90, 192–207; settlements, 184, 190; involvement with fur trade after 1543, 209, 213; dispersal, 210, 216, 218–19. *See also* St. Lawrence Iroquoians, Warfare

Stanley, George F., 4

Stereotypes of Indians, 3, 8–10. *See also* Noble Savage

Stone ornaments, 110–11, 126, 140, 439 *n*. 24

Stone tools: Huron, 44, 77–78; prehistoric, 106–8, 140; compared with iron ones, 360, 409–10, 417; Jesuits give iron tools to Huron, 513

Stuyvesant, Peter, 631

Suicide, 47, 84, 104, 548, 740–42

Summer Island site, 113–16, 128

Sun: as spirit, 73, 77–78, 145, 252, 559; eclipse of, 163

Sunflower, 34, 100, 118, 144

Superior, Lake, 375

Surgeons, French, 667, 697

Susquehannock: trade, 62–63, 623, 448 *n*. 30; relations with Huron, 63, 97, 244, 305–6, 313–14, 375, 390, 568, 624, 730, 732–33, 783, 791; traditional culture, 97, 443 *n*. 64; living in Huron country, 97; early contact with Europeans, 97, 220, 224; relations with Dutch and Iroquois, 260, 305, 346, 624, 725, 729, 792, 795; striken by epidemics, 528, 545, 602; baptized, 563, 568; as envoys for Huron, 732. *See also* Warfare

Sweating: ritual, 81, 367, 388, 716

Symbiosis between horticulturalists and hunters, 165–68, 216, 243

T

Tabor Hill ossuaries, 144

Tadoussac: trade at, 209–10, 212–13, 228–31, 248, 256–57, 261, 264, 286, 296, 337, 358, 363, 476–77, 612, 804; and Montagnais, 214, 233, 255, 275; as port, 234, 336, 342, 462; seized by English, 456

Taenhatentaron, 515, 525, 571, 706, 713, 740, 742; Jesuits visit, 565, 588, 733, 735; Jesuits expelled from, 592; mission to, 688, 707, 717, 720–22; dispersal and capture of, 743–44, 762–66

Tahontaenrat: name and location, 30, 437 *n*. 5; traditional culture, 57, 174, 828, 836; origins, 58, 156–57, 244; join

Neutral, 767, 786, 789–91; join Seneca, 791–92, 826, 828, 834–35; Jesuit Iroquois mission to, 834–35

Taignoagny, 182–200

Talbot, F. X., 406

Tangouaen, 730, 787–88

Taratouan, 524–25, 545, 553–55, 559

Taretandé, 530, 538–39

Tattooing, 94, 96, 299

Tawiscaron (headman), 225

Tawiscaron (spirit), 77–78

Teanaostaiaé, 554; Jesuits visit, 504, 516, 527, 540, 547–48, 571, 661–63, 689; fire at, 510; oppose Jesuits, 543; mission to, 563–64, 570, 575, 588, 591–92, 598, 687–88, 702, 704–6, 714–16, 719–22, 736–37; Jesuits expelled from, 592; destruction of, 735, 751–54

Tehorenhaegnon, 406–7, 510, 516, 533

Teondechoren, 600, 616, 638, 642–43, 696, 702, 705, 803

Tequenonday, 190

Tequenonquiaye. *See* Ossossané

Teotongniaton, 689, 696, 791. *See also* Ounontisastan

Tessouat: **1**, 231, 270, 279–84, 457, 482–85, 497–98, 521, 608; **2**, 521, 610, 632, 653–55, 785

Tewatirhon, 524–25, 554–58

Theft: Huron attitude towards, 61–62; by Indians from Europeans, 181, 194, 361, 387, 390, 555, 589, 696; by French from Indians, 374, 616

Thevet, André, 194, 201

Thomas Aquinas, 503

Three Rivers: early references, 210, 224; as trading place, 342–43, 345, 361, 431, 642; Indian settlement at, 466, 610; French settlement at, 477, 489, 614–15; trade at, 490–91, 500, 521, 523–24, 545–46, 549, 554–57, 604–5, 608, 611, 642, 667, 697, 754–55, 775, 820; Iroquois harass, 553, 635–37, 658, 725, 792, 806; Indians seek refuge at, 609; Huron winter at, 612, 799; conferences at, 647–50, 653–54; Huron refugees at, 802, 806–8

Ticonderoga, Point, 252

Tides, Huron knowledge of, 344

Tiondatsae. *See* Ekhiondastsaan

Tionnontaté: name and culture, 91–94, 442 *n.* 55, 739–40; relations with Ottawa people, 94; origins, 148, 157; not admitted to Huron confederacy, 174–75, 244, 417; relations with French, 317–18, 374–75, 758; reputation as thieves, 387, 390; relations with Jesuits, 504, 535, 537, 540, 588, 594–95, 599–600, 688, 698–99, 739–40, 770, 776–78; epidemics, 540; attacks on, 659, 777–78; famine, 767; dispersal, 777–78, 786, 789, 820–25. *See also* Hunting territory, Huron, Population, Tobacco

Tionontoguen, 638, 645

Toanché, 292, 300, 326, 340, 344, 469, 374, 384–85, 399, 406–7, 415–16, 473–76, 481–82, 484, 493

Tobacco: pouches, 39; cultivation, 41, 415, 438 *n.* 18; trade in, 62–63, 165, 245, 351, 355, 394, 426, 491; ritual use of, 76, 79, 278, 280, 663, 715; grown by Tionnontaté, 94; in prehistoric times, 119, 126, 143; used by St. Lawrence Iroquoians, 193; imported from Europe, 358; distributed by Jesuits, 507, 565

Tokhrahenehiaron, 647–48

Tolls: charged by Indians, 268, 280, 341–42, 484, 521, 785

Tonneraouanont, 529, 533–35

Tooker, Elisabeth, 13, 20, 103

Tortoise: in Huron mythology, 27, 77

Torture: techniques and significance, 70–71, 73, 75, 95, 145–46, 258, 441 *n.* 46; of witches, 67, 537; origin, 145; of Iroquois by Huron, 254, 258, 416, 474, 522, 559, 563, 568, 571, 647, 659, 662, 713–14, 730, 755, 806, 809; of Iroquois by Algonkians, 254, 258, 309, 464, 644, 647, 756; European opinion of, 254, 329, 512; of Algonkians by Iroquois, 269, 638; of French by Iroquois, 307, 615, 646–47, 708, 763–64; of Dutch by Susquehannock,

Torture (*continued*)
346; of Huron by Iroquois, 349, 489,
615, 638–39, 642, 705, 783, 797, 805,
810, 829–30; how affected by European
trade, 418; of Assistaronon by
Algonkians, 488; of Assistaronon by
Neutral, 624; of Iroquois by Erie, 794
Totiri, 698, 704–5, 713–14, 719, 721
Toudaman, 183, 218
Touaguainchain, 300
Tourmente, Pierre, 667–68, 677, 679,
854 *n.* 5
Trade, indigenous: Huron trade with
northern Algonkians, 62–63, 166–76,
243, 351–55, 605–7; intertribal
trading of furs, 62; Huron trade with
Neutral, 62, 355; Huron trade with
Tionnontaté, 62, 94, 355, 550; Huron
trade with Susquehannock, 63, 244–45;
rules, regulations, and ritual, 63–65,
214, 754; in prehistoric times, 108–9,
117–19, 139, 147, 168–76; pricing
mechanisms, 193–94, 264, 363–65,
432, 457, 465, 488, 608–12; between
Indians of Maritimes and New
England, 208–9, 220, 448 *n.* 30;
between Erie and Susquehannock, 790,
794; between Iroquois and Wyandot-
Ottawa, 824, 837
Trade, with Europeans: impact on Huron
economy and society, 175–76, 288–89,
358, 408–29, 545, 596–98, 601, 603,
605–7; early development along east
coast, 178, 181–82, 208–9, 213; early
development along upper St. Lawrence
River, 190, 200, 201, 205, 209–10; fur
trade along St. Lawrence, 1609–15,
248–49, 256–58, 261, 265–71, 273, 275,
278, 283, 285–86, 296, 326; fur trade
along St. Lawrence, 1616–29, 324,
335–43, 373, 406–7, 458; fur trade
along St. Lawrence, 1630–40, 462,
472–73, 477–79, 490, 520–22, 528,
545–46, 553, 560, 588, 600, 635; fur
trade along St. Lawrence, 1640–60,
604–5, 637–39, 642, 644, 649, 655, 703,
735, 751, 754–56, 760, 776, 820–24;

primary interest in beaver pelts, 209,
336; competition between European
monopolists and free traders, 210–12,
229, 234–36, 255–57, 262–64, 269,
271–72, 285–86, 343, 362–63;
development of professional fur traders,
210; Dutch and fur trade, 260, 293,
336, 345–47, 369, 382–83, 390, 463–65,
486, 497, 621, 630–31, 725–26, 792;
volume of trade, 286, 336–37, 462,
603–5, 618; price of furs, 336,
450 *n.* 12, 451 *n.* 3, 458, 460, 603,
776, 804; French trade with Oneida,
347, 488–89; profits from, 448 *n.* 23;
French promotion of trade in 1634,
486–88; Huron village refuses to trade
with French, 545; Christian Indians
granted preferred rates, 547, 613, 700,
803; between Abenaki and French, 604;
Huron refugees at Quebec engage in fur
trade, 803–4, 816. *See also* Beaver
Trade goods: types of goods supplied to
Indians before 1600, 178, 181–82,
189–90, 192, 199, 204, 220, 230;
received by Iroquois, 220–21, 617–18;
volume and types reaching Huron and
their neighbours, 242–43, 304,
358–62, 394, 409–11, 427, 449 *n.* 40,
545; Huron preferences for and value
of, 360–61, 409–11, 529; Huron opinion
of French material culture, 429–31, 566
Trade routes: control of, 14, 65, 168–69,
298, 376; Huron, 63, 166, 168–74,
244–45, 292, 340, 350–58, 376, 383,
610–12, 655, 735, 852 *n.* 3; Nipissing,
171, 243, 275, 281–84, 299, 320–21,
353, 355, 449 *nn.* 9, 10, 452 *n.* 11;
Montagnais, 233–34; Algonkin, 233–34,
245; Ottawa, 299, 354–56; maximum
extent of c. 1650, 357
Traders, French: scarcity of sources
concerning, 18, 331–33; along east
coast and St. Lawrence River, 208–14,
228–29; among Huron before 1629, 326,
339, 367–76, 408, 458, 844; relations
with missionaries, 368, 380, 397,
401, 404–5, 470–71; visit Iroquois, 488;

laymen barter furs in Huron country after 1634, 504, 605, 644, 689; rights of Jesuit employees to trade, 668, 776; breakdown of Jesuit control of trade, 760, 775–76, 782, 785. *See also* Donnés, Jesuits, Recollets; *and for individuals*, Du Vernay, La Criette, La Marche, La Montagne, La Vallée

Trading partners, 64, 595, 698, 767; exchange of children, 64, 173, 183, 185–86, 188–90, 193, 204, 212, 233, 261–62, 269–70, 325, 519, 524. *See also* School

Trails: in the Huron country, 32, 493; to Neutral, 32, 94, 305, 375, 399, 689; to Tionnontaté, 32, 87, 91, 317, 767

Translation, problems of into Huron, 393–94, 511–12

Transubstantiation, Huron view of, 389–90, 537

Treason, 67–69, 747, 799

Tregouaroti, 261, 265, 268–69

Trent site, 226

Trent Valley: Huron hunting territory, 43, 308, 350, 383; prehistoric occupation, 118, 147, 150, 156, 161, 226–27, 237, 243, 308; known to Algonkians c. 1603, 233

Tribe: government of, 57–58; evolution of, 110, 122, 153–54, 159; role in diplomacy, 268, 748; lasting importance of, 811–12, 820, 825

Truce: French-Algonkian with Mohawk, 1624, 342, 344–49, 383–84, 464; Huron with Iroquois, 1623 and 1624, 382, 417; Algonkians with Mohawk, 1633–35, 465, 485, 489, 497; Ottawa with Winnebago, 488, 851 *ch.* 7 *n.* 9; Huron with Seneca, 1634–38, 489, 509, 551–52, 560; general truce of 1645, 616, 647–57, 662; Huron-Mohawk discussions of, 1640–45, 634–35, 644–45, 648, 651; French-Mohawk discussions of, 635–37, 756–59; Huron with Onondaga, 1647–48, 730–36, 740–42; Cayuga and Oneida prepared for truce with Huron,

734; French with Iroquois, 1653, 795, 806, 808–10, 815; French and Iroquois, 1667, 818

Trudel, Marcel, 269, 274, 283–84, 314, 347, 349, 372, 396

Tsiko, 524–25, 554, 852 *ch.* 8 *n.* 5

Tsindacaiendoua, 506–7

Tsiouendaentaha, 529, 548–49

Tsiraenie, 807–8

Tsondacouané, 533–34, 536

Tsondakwa, 591, 705, 854 *n.* 13. *See also* Andiora

Tsondatsaa, 633, 643, 661, 697, 700, 703, 705, 716

Tsondihwané, 351, 591, 703, 761, 766, 795

Tsorihia, 669, 704; his family, 704

Tuck, James, 153, 163

Turtle. *See* Tortoise

Tuscarora, 59, 105

Tutonaguy. *See* Hochelaga

U

Uren site, 144

Uren substage, 139–41, 143–44

Ursuline nuns, 599, 613–14, 616, 800–802. *See also* Chauvigny, Skanudharoua

V

Ventadour. *See* Lévis

Verrazzano, Giovanni da, 220

Victory, Cape, 342–43

Viel, Nicolas, 373, 384–85, 390, 392–93, 395–97, 399, 405, 452 *n.* 17, 496–97

Vignau, Nicolas de, 270, 275–86, 299

Vignerot, Marie de, Duchesse d'Aiguillon, 628, 759

Village: Huron, 32, 437 *n.* 9; as unit of association, 56, 687; government, 56–57; Neutral, size of, 95; prehistoric development, 119–22, 126–32, 134, 137, 143, 155, 157–59; factors controlling size, 158. *See also* Fire, Relocation

Ville Marie. *See* Montreal
Vimont, Barthélemy, 356, 581, 639, 648
Vision quests, 48
Vitelleschi, Mutius, 576, 672
Vows administered by Jesuits to Huron,
    529–30, 569
Voyer d'Argenson, Pierre de, 816

W

Wallace, A. F. C., 21
Wampum belts, 198–200, 268, 320, 342,
    519, 535–36, 548, 647–48, 651, 663,
    689, 734–35, 771, 776, 786, 790, 802,
    833, 851 *ch.* 8 *n.* 3. *See also* Beads
War camps, 223, 233, 251–52, 254, 258,
    312–13, 553, 559, 635, 637, 642,
    662–63, 758, 763, 779, 786
War chiefs. *See* Headmen
Warfare: traditional motives, 51, 68–69,
    103, 145–47, 312–13, 416, 444 *n.* 69;
    traditional campaigns, 69–70, 249–52,
    293, 648; rituals, 76; between
    Assistaronon and Neutral, 94, 624–25;
    development in prehistoric times,
    144–47, 158–62; between Huron and
    Neutral, 159, 339, 390; between Huron
    and Tionnontaté, 159, 245; between
    Huron and Iroquois, 159, 234, 244,
    306, 339, 349, 416–17, 513, 520,
    552–53, 658–64, 704, 730, 733,
    735–36, 742–43, 751–55, 762–66,
    772, 775, 782–83, 786–88, 804–6,
    809–11, 815–17; between Huron and
    St. Lawrence Iroquoians, 161, 174, 197,
    219–20; between Huron and Seneca,
    161–62, 416, 418, 489, 560, 662;
    between Micmac and St. Lawrence
    Iroquoians, 183, 216; between French
    and St. Lawrence Iroquoians, 205–6;
    between Malecite and Micmac, 213;
    Mohawk attacks in St.Lawrence Valley
    and warfare between Algonkians and
    Iroquois before 1610, 218, 220–24,
    229–35, 247–61; Iroquois attacks in
    St. Lawrence Valley after 1610, 349,
    464, 466, 477, 552–53, 615, 617, 626,
    628, 635–44, 658, 703–5, 725, 729,
    735, 754–55, 757–58, 804–6, 809–11,
    815–17; in Ottawa Valley, 221, 260,
    292–93, 311, 315, 339, 609–10, 634,
    637–39, 642–43, 785; new economic
    motives for, 221, 223, 293, 347, 603,
    609, 634, 663–64, 725–30; French aid
    Indian allies, 229–30, 235–36, 247–60,
    268, 273–74, 281, 283, 286, 296–97,
    300–16, 323, 338–39; between French
    and Iroquois, 235–36, 247–61, 349,
    383, 478, 553, 635–37, 639–40, 643,
    658, 725, 792, 805, 815–18; major
    defeats of Iroquois, 252–54, 258–60,
    312–15, 416, 552, 559–60, 659, 754–55,
    764–65, 787, 791; between Mohawk
    and Susquehannock, 260, 725, 792;
    between Algonkians and Iroquois after
    1610, 271, 275–78, 281, 292–93,
    465–66, 497–98, 552, 609–10, 612,
    626, 635, 637, 640, 643, 655, 658, 725,
    792; between Mahican and Mohawk,
    293, 346–47, 463–67, 792; between
    Huron and Oneida-Onondaga, 293,
    338, 559–60; between western
    Iroquois and Susquehannock, 306, 729,
    795; between Assistaronon and Ottawa,
    319; facilitates exploration, 321;
    between Ottawa and Winnebago,
    354–56, 488; impact of European trade
    upon strategy and tactics of, 417–18,
    453 *n.* 22, 609, 634, 639–40, 660–61,
    725–30; between English and French,
    455–59; between Dutch and Mohawk,
    463–64, 485; major defeats of Huron,
    489, 553, 642, 660–63; impact of
    population decline on, 607–8; between
    Huron and Mohawk, 612, 638–39,
    642–44, 703–5; between Algonkians
    and Sokoki, 647, 654; between
    Abenaki and Mohawk, 653; between
    Iroquois and Tionnontaté, 659, 777–78,
    786, 824; Christian Huron refuse to
    fight alongside traditionalists, 712;
    between Iroquois and Neutral, 735–36,
    789–91; Iroquois attack in central
    Ontario and upper Great Lakes, 779,

785, 790, 797, 820; between Erie and
Iroquois, 792–97; between Mohawk
and Seneca, 795; between Sioux and
Wyandot, 820
Warminster site, 151, 242, 302–4, 421,
423, 439 *n.* 21
Webb site, 143
Weirs, 41, 308
Wendat, 27, 436 *n.* 3, 825
Wenrio, 474–75, 495, 505–6, 509,
516–17, 530–31, 540, 688
Wenroronon: original location and
culture, 96–97, 401, 443 *n.* 62,
852 *n.* 10; relations with Neutral,
443 *n.* 63, 695; dispersal, 562–63,
623–24; knowledge of Europeans, 562;
epidemics, 562, 602; conversion of,
562–63, 705
Weskarini. *See* Petite Nation
Whallon, Robert, 135, 137
White, Marian E., 95, 97, 623
White Fish People. *See* Attikamegue
Wild rice, 112, 118, 133–34, 444 *n.* 13
Wilson, Daniel, 10
Winnebago, 19, 65, 354–56, 488, 625
Wisconsin, 625
Witchcraft, 66–68, 81, 407, 424–25,
447 *n.* 9, 494, 738; and blood feud,

356; Christian converts accused of, 424,
599–601, 708, 715–19, 833; accusations
during epidemics, 500, 534–39, 541–44,
589–96; those accused threatened or
slain, 537, 596, 599, 646, 657, 696;
trials for, 541–43, 594, 596;
Christianity seen as, 761. *See also*
Charms, Jesuits
Witthoft, John, 146
Woodland cultures: Early, 110–11;
Middle, 111–19; Late, *see* Iroquoian
periods
Wounding, 61, 308
Wray, Charles F., 220
Wright, James V., 108, 113, 139–40,
156–58
Writing: Indian sign writing, 340;
Indians learn European script, 398, 461,
525, 551, 616; Indian view of, 430,
565–66, 590, 695–96, 708
Wyandot, 14–15, 19, 136–37, 820–25, 837
Wye River: water level, 679

Y

Young men: position in Huron society,
51, 58, 65, 68–69, 103, 145, 154, 187,
307, 522, 543, 557, 568, 599